Commentary on Aristotle's Nicomachean Ethics

Aristotelian Commentary Series

Commentary on Aristotle's Nicomachean Ethics

St. Thomas Aquinas

Translated by
C. I. Litzinger, O.P.

Foreword by
Ralph McInerny

DUMB OX BOOKS
Notre Dame, Indiana

Manufactured in the United States of America

ISBN: 1-883357-50-0 clothbound; 1-883357-51-9 paperbound

2   3   4   5   6   7   07   06   05   04   03   02   01   00   99   98

To the memory of

Donald J. McMahon, O.P.

CONTENTS

FOREWORD

This is the long-awaited reprinting of the Litzinger translation of Thomas Aquinas's *Commentary on the Nicomachean Ethics of Aristotle*, published in 1964 and out of print for many years. Typographical alterations have been made which make it easier to relate the comments to the text commented upon. The commentary is divided according to the ten books of the Aristotelian text, and each book is divided into *lectiones*. Each *lectio* is preceded by a portion of the text, the paragraphs of which have been numbered to facilitate matching with the commentary. Each numbered paragraph of the Aristotelian text is followed by the Bekker lines which correlate the translation with the Greek text as well as by the relevant paragraph numbers of the commentary. Father Litzinger's elaborate outline of the text and commentary has been dropped. Making the commentary available in one volume rather than two should also facilitate using the work.

In an ideal world, the Litzinger translation, which was based on the Marietti edition, would be bettered by making use of the critical Leonine text which appeared five years after this English translation.[1] If the critical edition contained massive emendations of the text, that course might even seem required. In the flawed real world of poor forked animals, with its exigencies of time and resources, and given the prolonged and widespread desire for this translation, it seemed best to bring this reprinting out now, and leave to the future the admittedly desirable task of correcting the translation with the help of the Leonine text. For over thirty years, the Litzinger translation has served scholars well, and it has many miles to go before it disappears into the black hole reserved for superseded translations.

For many years, Aristotelian scholars curiously overlooked the Thomistic commentaries; recently there have been notable exceptions to this neglect, indeed enthusiastic recommendations of Thomas's expositions. To some extent, this neglect was encouraged by confusion among Thomists as to the nature of the commentaries. The suggestion that Thomas was simply using Aristotle for his own theological purposes—"baptizing Aristotle," in the misleading phrase—would scarcely induce a scholar puzzling over the Aristotelian text to consult Thomas. But it is a libel to characterize the commentaries in this way. No one can

---

1   Sancti Thomae de Aquino, *Opera Omnia*, Tomus XLVII, Rome, 1968, edited by the Dominican Fathers and introduced by R. A. Gauthier, O.P. Annoyingly, the Leonine editions ignore the paragraph numbering which the Marietti editions had either borrowed from or modeled upon earlier Leonine editions. Since it is to those Marietti editions that the scholarship of years referred, a concordance would have been appreciated.

read the *De unitate intellectus*, written in the same brief period when some dozen commentaries on Aristotle were written by a Thomas Aquinas extremely busy with many other things, without seeing that Thomas took his first and primary task to be getting the Aristotelian text right. Far from baptizing Aristotle, Thomas as a commentator is intent on rescuing Thomas from the misreadings of Averroes and others.[2]

Thomas exhibits familiarity with Aristotle from the very beginning of his literary career, doubtless because of the nature of the instruction he received at Naples as well as his good fortune in studying under Albert the Great. Thus, although the commentaries belong to the end of Thomas's career—to a period beginning perhaps in 1268 and ending, with several of them incomplete, in 1273 when, a year before his death, Thomas put down his pen—they are the culmination rather than the commencement of his study of Aristotle. The enthusiasm of some Thomists for his originality has obscured the fact that Thomas Aquinas was the greatest Aristotelian in the history of Western philosophy. He would readily have subscribed to Dante's description of Aristotle as the master of those who know. Students of Aristotle should read this commentary as a commentary; its value must be assessed in terms of the way it does or does not cast light on the text.

More and more scholars are finding that the Thomistic commentaries, in which, as Chenu observed[3], the commentator, engaging in the same task as the author of the text, seeks to discover its *intentio* and implications, put us in touch with the mind and thinking behind the text. Perhaps it is modern Aristotelians who have been reading the text through the lens of their presuppositions—Hegelian, Heidegerrian, Analytic—seeking to make Aristotle a party to later debates rather than to enter into the sinuous rhythms of his thought, and by a sympathetic reenactment of the intellectual drama of the text find in it correctives as well as correlatives of contemporary thinking.

Those of us who glory in the title of Thomist have a particular motivation to assimilate the letter and the spirit of these commentaries. All too often Thomists have sought to separate their master from his master—with disastrous results. The reprinting of this translation is dedicated to a new generation of students of St. Thomas who will see that they must become, as he was, a close student of Aristotle.

Ralph McInerny
Notre Dame
August 1993

---

2   See *Thomas Aquinas Against the Averroists: On There Being Only One Intellect*, text and translation, with an introduction and commentary by Ralph McInerny (Lafayette, Ind.: Purdue University Press, 1993).

3   M.-D. Chenu, O.P., *Introduction à l'étude de Saint Thomas d'Aquin*, deuxième édition (Paris: Vrin, 1954, pp. 173–190).

INTRODUCTION

Many good English translations of Aristotle's *Nicomachean Ethics* are in circulation; but so far as we know, no complete translation of St. Thomas' *Commentary* on this work exists. Since all are not as gifted as St. Augustine, who read and understood the *Categories* unaided,[4] some clarification is almost imperative because of Aristotle's depth of thought and conciseness of style. To fill this need J. A. Stewart (1892) and J. Burnet (1900) have written excellent commentaries; H. H. Joachim's commentary,[5] first published in 1951, was reprinted in 1962. Frequent notes in H. Rackham's translation is further evidence of the necessity for an explanation of the text.

Our age is not alone in its inability to understand Aristotle fully without the aid of a commentator. The thirteenth century, too, looked for similar help during the revival of interest in the Greek philosophers; and St. Thomas wrote his commentary to furnish such assistance to his contemporaries. In the centuries following, this has been the classical explanation of Aristotle's *Nicomachean Ethics* for the Western World; that it can be helpful also to the student today is recognized by such scholars as Paul Shorey, who says: ". . . if I had the choice of putting into the hands of a student of Aristotle the commentary of Thomas or the book of some recent interpreter of Aristotle, I would choose the medieval schoolman as more educative in sensible methods and less likely to mislead and confuse the student."[6]

St. Thomas' unique qualifications as an interpreter of Aristotle is attested by Professor Harry V. Jaffa who maintains that the teaching of Aristotle can be discovered more readily in St. Thomas than in Aristotle himself; that St. Thomas is unequaled in his mastery of the whole of Aristotelian doctrine and in his ability to co-ordinate its parts.[7] The Professor goes on to note this significant fact about St. Thomas' interpretation of the *Ethics*: "Thomas rarely, if ever, attempts to explain any statement of Aristotle except in terms of other of his statements. Nothing extraneous to the *Ethics* itself is, apparently, permitted to serve as the basis for the interpretation of the *Ethics*."[8]

Unfortunately this font of thomistic ethical doctrine has not been available to English readers. At the present time there is keen interest in Aristotle's approach

---

4   *Confessions*, Bk. IV, 28.
5   *Aristotle: The Nicomachean Ethics*, Clarendon Press, Oxford 1962.
6   *Platonism Ancient and Modern* (p. 90), University of California Press: 1938.
7   *Thomism and Aristotelianism* by Harry V. Jaffa. University of Chicago Press: 1952, p. 6-7.
8   Ibid., p. 19.

to moral problems and in his theories on politics.[9] Some of this interest we trust extends also to St. Thomas' interpretation of that teaching. In this expectation we thought it opportune to offer an English translation of St. Thomas' *Commentary on the Nicomachean Ethics* together with a new rendition of Aristotle's text.

But why, it may be asked, add another translation of Aristotle's text when we already have such readable and scholarly translations as those of Ross and Rackham? In the beginning it was intended to use one of the existing texts in English, but as the work progressed it became evident that St. Thomas' understanding of Aristotle occasionally differs from the current translations. Since our primary purpose is to put into English St. Thomas' understanding, it was decided to attempt a translation that would be more conformable to his Commentary.

The present translation of the text of Aristotle has been made from the Latin version, generally attributed to William of Moerbeke, as found in the Cathala-Spiazzi edition. This *versio antiqua* was used because it has great authority among scholars,[10] and because it was the basis for the Commentary, although St. Thomas at times varies from this rendition. In general, Spiazzi's divisions of the text and the Commentary have been followed.

The purpose of a translator is to present the author's ideas, to convey these thoughts through the medium of another language, and to express their meaning intelligibly in that language. It goes without saying that the translator must first of all thoroughly understand the ideas. Hence an adequate knowledge of the author's language is indispensable. To this must be added a competence in the language of the translation to insure the incorporation of the author's thought into the new medium. Moreover, the translator must formulate and express that thought in words understandable to his prospective readers.

How these ends can best be achieved is a problem the translator must solve. Should he translate word for word, phrase for phrase, construction for construction? Evidently William of Moerbeke did this in translating the *Nicomachean Ethics* into Latin. Such a method has the advantage of excluding interpretation that has no place in a translation. But literalness can be self-defeating, since a simple rendering of a text may not serve to make the meaning clear. On the other hand, the translator certainly cannot ignore the author's words, phrasing, and sentence construction; to do so would be to assume the role of interpreter.

Evidently a middle course must be followed, for the translator is under obligation to present as clearly as possible the meaning of the author. When a literal translation best serves this purpose it should be used; when a freer rendition is necessary to bring out the thought, he should not hesitate to adopt this more suitable means. Thus he will make a faithful reproduction of the original, an essential quality of any translation.

St. Thomas confirms this procedure in the *Contra Errores Graecorum:*[11] ". . . There are many expressions that sound well in Greek which would perhaps be

9   *The Politics of Aristotle* by Ernest Barker. Oxford University Press, New York: 1961, p. iv sq.

10   Cf. H. Rackham, *Aristotle: The Nicomachean Ethics*, Introduction p. xxvi.

11   *Opuscula Theologica*, Vol. I, p. 315 sq., Marietti 1954.

awkward in Latin.... Consequently the skillful translator in the exercise of his work . . . will retain the meaning and fashion his manner of expression in accordance with the peculiar genius of the language into which he is translating. Obviously, if what is said literally in Latin is expressed in the vernacular, the exposition of the material will be awkward when the rendition is simply word for word. What is more, obscurity is not surprising when a slavish literal translation is made." How successfully these norms have been observed must be left to the judgment of others.

A special debt of gratitude is due Father Urban Voll, O.P., of Catholic University of America for his invaluable assistance in the production of this work. He generously devoted his free time, apart from the demands of a busy schedule, to reading the entire manuscript. His corrections eliminated imperfections that would have marred the translation. His suggestions and advice have helped to clarify the ideas expressed and make them acceptable to the reader. It is no exaggeration to say that without his aid the translation would not have been published.

Father Francis Conway, O.P., former professor of Ethics at St. John's University, Brooklyn, N.Y., and now at Emmanuel College, Boston, Massachusetts, gave unstintingly of his time and talent to make the translation accurate. His comments have been most helpful in determining the meaning of the text, especially where St. Thomas apparently differs from modern translations of Aristotle. He kindly pointed out latinisms, circumlocutions, and unevenness in expression and suggested appropriate ways to avoid these defects. His resourcefulness in recommending alternatives for monotonous repetitions has contributed to a smoother reading.

I am indebted to Father Anthony D. Lee, O.P., who, besides arranging the details of publication, read part of the manuscript and offered constructive criticisms of the contents. He has given helpful suggestions to insure agreement between the outlines and the body of the Commentary.

The students of St. Stephen's House of Studies, Dover, Massachusetts, made important contributions to these volumes. They used the first draft of the translation as a help to the Latin text studied in class, and their questions were the occasion of changes that clarified the meaning of passages difficult to render into English. They also assisted in looking up references and checking footnotes to guarantee accuracy.

It should be added that any merit the present work may possess is due in no small measure to the generous co-operation of my fellow professors at St. Stephen's. Their continued interest in the progress of the translation was a constant source of encouragement. Their patience in listening to my difficulties was matched by their promptness in proposing and finding correct solutions. Their readiness in assuming extra professorial duties made possible the leisure requisite for translation.

Finally, I should like to express my gratitude to Father Ferrer Smith, O.P., Regent of Studies for St. Joseph's Province, for his advice and good offices in promoting publication; to Father W. D. Marrin, O.P., Provincial, for his help and fatherly interest; to Father Aniceto Fernandez, O.P., Master General, with whose paternal blessing the translation is appearing.

BOOK ONE
THE GOOD FOR MAN

LECTURE I
Subject Matter and End of Moral Philosophy: Diversity of Ends

TEXT OF ARISTOTLE (1094a1–1094a18) Chapter 1

1. All arts and all teaching, and similarly every act and every choice seem to have the attainment of some good as their object.

1094a1–2; 8

2. For this reason it has correctly been proclaimed that good is what all desire.

1094a2–3; 9–11

3. Now a certain diversity of ends is apparent, for some are operations while others are works outside the operations.

1094a3–5; 12–13

4. If the ends are works then the works are better than the operations.   1094a5–6; 14

5. Since there are many operations and arts and sciences there must also be different ends for each of them. Thus the end of medical art is health; of ship-building, navigation; of strategy, victory; of domestic economy, riches.

1094a6–9; 15

6. In all such skills a subordination of one to another is found. For instance, the art of bridle-making is subordinated to the art of riding as also are the arts which make riding equipment. The art of riding in turn, and all military operations, come under strategy. In a similar way other arts are subordinated to still others.

1094a9–14; 16

7. It follows then that in all these, architectonic ends are more desirable than the ends subordinated to them. The reason is that men seek the latter for the sake of the former.

1094a14–16; 17

8. It does not matter whether the ends are operations themselves or something other than the operations as in the skills mentioned above.

1094a16–18; 18

COMMENTARY OF ST. THOMAS

1. As the Philosopher says in the beginning of the *Metaphysics* (Bk. I, Ch. 2, 982a18; St. Th. Lect. II, 41–42),[1] it is the business of the wise man to order. The reason for this is that wisdom is the most powerful perfection of reason whose characteristic is to know order. Even if the sensitive powers know some things absolutely, nevertheless to know the order of one thing to another is exclusively the work of intellect or reason. Now a twofold order is found in things. One kind is that of parts of a totality, that is, a group, among themselves, as the parts of a house are mutually ordered to each other. The second order is that of things to an end. This order is of greater importance than the first. For, as the Philosopher says in the eleventh book of the *Metaphysics* (Bk. XII, Ch. 10, 1075a15; St. Th. Bk. XII, Lect. XII, 2629–2631), the order of the parts of an army among themselves exists because of the order of the whole army to the commander. Now order is related to reason in a fourfold way. There is one order that reason does not establish but only beholds, such is the order of things in nature. There is a second order that reason

---

1   Reference to the text of Aristotle will be given according to Bekker. Reference to the Commentary of St. Thomas on the *Metaphysics* is based on *In Duodecim Libros Metaphysicorum Aristotelis Expositio.* Cathala-Spiazzi Edition, Turin: Marietti, 1950.

establishes in its own act of consideration, for example, when it arranges its
concepts among themselves, and the
signs of concepts as well, because
words express the meanings of the concepts. There is a third order that reason
in deliberating establishes in the operations of the will. There is a fourth order
that reason in planning establishes in
the external things which it causes,
such as a chest and a house.

2. Because the operation of reason is
perfected by habit, according to the different modes of order that reason considers in particular, a differentiation of
sciences arises. The function of natural
philosophy is to consider the order of
things that human reason considers
but does not establish—understand
that with natural philosophy here we
also include metaphysics. The order
that reason makes in its own act of
consideration pertains to rational philosophy (logic), which properly considers the order of the parts of verbal
expression with one another and the
order of principles to one another and
to their conclusions. The order of voluntary actions pertains to the consideration of moral philosophy. The order
that reason in planning establishes in
external things arranged by human
reason pertains to the mechanical arts.
Accordingly it is proper to moral philosophy, to which our attention is at
present directed, to consider human
operations insofar as they are ordered
to one another and to an end.

3. I am talking about human operations, those springing from man's will
following the order of reason. But if
some operations are found in man that
are not subject to the will and reason,
they are not properly called human but
natural, as clearly appears in operations of the vegetative soul. These in no
way fall under the consideration of

moral philosophy. As the subject of
natural philosophy is motion, or mo-
bile being, so the subject of moral philosophy is human action ordered to an
end, or even man, as he is an agent
voluntarily acting for an end.

4. It must be understood that, because man is by nature a social animal,
needing many things to live which he
cannot get for himself if alone, he naturally is a part of a group that furnishes
him help to live well. He needs this
help for two reasons. First, to have
what is necessary for life, without
which he cannot live the present life;
and for this, man is helped by the domestic group of which he is a part. For
every man is indebted to his parents for
his generation and his nourishment
and instruction. Likewise individuals,
who are members of the family, help
one another to procure the necessities
of life. In another way, man receives
help from the group of which he is a
part, to have a perfect sufficiency for
life; namely, that man may not only
live but live well, having everything
sufficient for living; and in this way
man is helped by the civic group, of
which he is a member, not only in regard to bodily needs—as certainly in
the state there are many crafts which a
single household cannot provide—but
also in regard to right conduct, inasmuch as public authority restrains
with fear of punishment delinquent
young men whom paternal admonition is not able to correct.

5. It must be known moreover that
the whole which the political group or
the family constitutes has only a unity
of order, for it is not something absolutely one. A part of this whole, therefore, can have an operation that is not
the operation of the whole, as a soldier
in an army has an activity that does not
belong to the whole army. However,

this whole does have an operation that is not proper to its parts but to the whole—for example, an assault of the entire army. Likewise the movement of a boat is a combined operation of the crew rowing the boat. There is also a kind of whole that has not only a unity of order but of composition, or of conjunction, or even of continuity, and according to this unity a thing is one absolutely; and therefore there is no operation of the part that does not belong to the whole. For in things all of one piece the motion of the whole and of the part is the same. Similarly in composites and in conjoined things, the operation of a part is principally that of the whole. For this reason it is necessary that such a consideration of both the whole and its parts should belong to the same science. It does not, however, pertain to the same science to consider the whole, which has solely the unity of order, and the parts of this whole.

6. Thus it is that moral philosophy is divided into three parts. The first of these, which is called individual (monastic) ethics, considers an individual's operations as ordered to an end. The second, called domestic ethics, considers the operations of the domestic group. The third, called political science, considers the operations of the civic group.

7. Thus Aristotle as he begins the treatment of moral philosophy in the first part of this book called *Ethics*, or morals, first gives an introduction in which he does three things. First [1094a1–b12] he shows what he intends to do. Second [Lect. III], at "Our study will be etc." (1094b13), he deter-

mines the manner of treatment. Third, in the same lecture, at "Now every man etc." (1094b29), he explains what manner of person the student of this science ought to be. In regard to the initial point he does two things. First he presents in advance certain things necessary to explain his intention. Second [Lect. II], at "If our actions etc." (1094a19), he manifests his intention. In regard to the first he does two things. Initially he shows how it is necessary to start with the end. Then [5], at "Since there are many etc.," he compares habits and acts with the end. On the first point he does three things. He states initially that all human beings are ordered to an end. Next [3], at "Now a certain diversity etc.," he shows that there can be a number of ends. Last [4], at "If the ends are works etc.," he makes a comparison among ends. In regard to the first point he does two things. He states his intention; and then, at "For this reason etc." [2], he explains his purpose.

8. In regard to the first we should consider that there are two principles of human acts, namely, the intellect or reason and the appetite, which are active principles as explained in the third book *De Anima* (Ch. XI, 434a5–a22; St. Th. Lect. XVI, 840–846).[2] The intellect or reason considers both the speculative and the practical. The rational appetite is concerned with choice and execution. Now all these are ordered to some good as to their end; for truth is the end of speculation. Therefore, in the speculative intellect he includes teaching by which science is conveyed from teacher to student, while in the practical intellect he locates art which

2   Sancti Thomae Aquinatis, *In Aristotelis Librum De Anima Commentarium*. Ed. Pirotta (Turin/Rome: Marietti, 1948).

is right reason applied to things to be made, as is stated in the sixth book of this work (1153).[3] He indicates that the act of the appetitive intellect is choice, and that execution is "actus." He does not mention prudence, which is in the practical reason together with art, because choice is properly directed by prudence. He says therefore that each of these faculties obviously seeks some good as an end.

9. Then [2], at "For this reason," he manifests his intention by the effect of good. In regard to this we should bear in mind that good is enumerated among the primary entities to such a degree—according to the Platonists—that good is prior to being. But, in reality, good is convertible with being. Now primary things cannot be understood by anything anterior to them, but by something consequent, as causes are understood through their proper effects. But since good properly is the moving principle of the appetite, good is described as movement of the appetite, just as motive power is usually manifested through motion. For this reason he says that the philosophers have rightly declared that good is what all desire.

10. There is no problem from the fact that some men desire evil. For they desire evil only under the aspect of good, that is, insofar as they think it good. Hence their intention primarily aims at the good and only incidentally touches on the evil.

11. The saying "... **what all desire**" is to be understood not only of those who knowingly seek good but also of beings lacking knowledge. These things by a natural desire tend to good, not as knowing the good, but because they are moved to it by something cognitive, that is, under the direction of the divine intellect in the way an arrow speeds towards a target by the aim of the archer. This very tendency to good is the desiring of good. Hence, he says, all beings desire good insofar as they tend to good. But there is not one good to which all tend; this will be explained later (58–59; 108–109). Therefore he does not single out here a particular good but rather discusses good in general. However, because nothing is good except insofar as it is a likeness and participation of the highest good, the highest good itself is in some way desired in every particular good. Thus it can be said that the true good is what all desire.

12. Then [3], at "**Now a certain diversity**," he indicates that there is a diversity of ends. In this we must keep in mind that the final good, to which the inclination of each thing tends, is its ultimate perfection. Now the first perfection is possessed after the manner of a form, but the second perfection by way of an operation. Consequently, there must be this diversity of ends: some are operations and others are the objects achieved, that is, the products which exist apart from the operations.

13. For evidence of this we must consider that activity is of two kinds, as noted in the ninth book of the *Metaphysics* (Ch. 8, 1050a23; St. Th. Lect. VIII, 1862–1865). One, which remains in the agent himself, as seeing, wishing and understanding, is an operation of the type properly called "action." The other is an operation passing over into external matter and is properly called

---

3   The Spiazzi Edition gives the reference in such cases to the Commentary and not to the text. We have done the same, since the translation is based on this edition.

"making." Sometimes a person accepts external matter only for use, as a horse for riding and a zither for playing, and at other times he takes external matter to change it into some other form, as when a carpenter constructs a house or a bed. Accordingly, the first and second of these operations do not have any product which is their term, but each of them is an end. The first, however, is more excellent than the second, inasmuch as it remains in the agent himself. But the third operation is a kind of generation whose term is a thing produced. So, in operations of the third type, the things done are the ends.

14. Then [4], at "**If the ends,**" he presents the third type, saying that whenever the products which are extrinsic to the activities are ends, the things produced necessarily are better than the operations that brought them to be, as the thing generated is better than the generative action. The end is more important than the means—in fact, the means have goodness from their relation to the end.

15. Then [5], at "**Since there are many operations,**" he compares habits and acts with the end. In this matter he does four things. First [5] he shows that different things are ordered to different ends. He says that, since there are many operations and arts and sciences, there must be different ends for each of them, for the ends and the means are proportional. This he shows by saying that the end of medical art is health; of shipbuilding, navigation; of strategy, victory; and of domestic economy or managing a household, riches. He accepts this last example on the opinion of the majority of men, for he himself

proves in the first book of the *Politics*[4] (Ch. 3–4, 1253b12–1254a; St. Th. Lect. II, 46–51; Ch. 9–11, 1256b40–1259a36; St. Th. Lect. VII–IX, 71–100) that riches are not the end of domestic economy but the instruments thereof.

16. Second [6], at "**In all such skills,**" he arranges the order of habits among themselves. It happens that one operative habit, which he calls virtue (skill), is subordinated to another, as the art of bridle-making is subordinated to the art of riding because the rider tells the bridle-maker how he should make the bridle. In this way the rider is the designer, that is, the chief producer of the thing itself. The same arguments hold for the other arts making additional equipment needed for riding, such as saddles or the like. The equestrian art is again subordinated to the military, for in ancient times the army included not only mounted soldiers but everyone who fought for victory. Hence under military science there is not only the equestrian but every art or skill ordered to the prosecution of war—archery, ballistics and everything else of this kind. In this same way other arts are subordinated to still others.

17. Third [7], at "**It follows then,**" he lays down the order of ends according to the order of habits. He says that in all arts or skills it is commonly true that the architectonic ends are absolutely more desirable to everyone than are the ends of the arts or skills that are subordinated to the chief ends. He proves this from the fact that men follow or seek the ends of the inferior arts or skills for the sake of the ends of the superior. The text, however, is suspensive, and should be read as follows: In

---

4　Sancti Thomae Aquinatis, *In Libros Politicorum Aristotelis Expositio*. Ed. Spiazzi (Turin/Rome: Marietti, 1951), pp. 13 sq; pp. 34 sq.

all such skills a subordination of one to another is found . . . in all these the architectonic ends etc.

18. Fourth [8], at "**It does not matter,**" he shows that it makes no difference in the order of ends, whether the end is a product or an activity. He says that it makes no difference in what pertains to this order that these ends be activities or some product other than the activities, as is evident from the explanation given above (16). The end of bridle-making is a finished bridle; but the end of horsemanship, which is of greater importance, is an operation, that is, riding. The contrary is true in medicine and gymnastics, for the end of medicine is something produced, namely, health. But of gymnastics which is comprised under it, the end is an activity, which is exercise.

LECTURE II
The Supreme End of Human Affairs; Political Science

TEXT OF ARISTOTLE (*1094a18–b11*) Chapter 2

1. If our actions have an end that we wish for itself and if we wish other things for that end, and not each 20 thing on account of another (for this would involve us in an infinite process making our desire useless and in vain) then obviously that will be not only a good end but a supreme end.   **1094a18–22; 19–22**

2. A knowledge of it, therefore, will be a great help in human living, for like archers keeping their eye on the target, we will more likely attain our objective.   **1094a22–24; 23**

3. This being the case, we must try to determine the general characteristics of this end and to which of the sciences or skills its study pertains.   **1094a24–26; 24**

4. It seems undoubtedly to belong to the most truly architectonic science. This, to all appearances, is political science.   **1094a26–28; 25**

5. Now such a science ordains which studies are to be followed in a state, and who are to pursue them and to what extent. Hence we see the noblest of the operative arts, for example, strategy, domestic economy, and rhetoric fall under political science.   **1094a28–1094b3; 26–28**

6. Political science in fact makes use of other practical sciences, even legislating what is to be done and what is not to be done. Its end, therefore, embraces the ends of the other practical sciences. For these reasons, then, this end will be the good of man.   **1094b4–7; 29**

7. Even though the good be the same for one man and for the whole state, it seems much better and more perfect to procure and preserve the good of the whole state. It is admirable, indeed, to preserve the good of an individual but it is better still and more divine to do this for a nation and for cities. With such a good as the object of our inquiry we may call our study political science.   **1094b7–11; 30-31**

COMMENTARY OF ST. THOMAS

19. After having stated premises on which his proposition must rest, the Philosopher now begins to manifest it, that is, to show what the principal purpose of this science is [B]. To achieve this he does three things. First [1] he shows from what he has already said, that there is some supreme end of human affairs. Second [2], at "A knowledge of it etc.," he shows that it is necessary to know this end. Third [4], at "It seems undoubtedly," he shows to which science this knowledge belongs. He gives three proofs for the first statement. The principal one is this. Whenever an end is such that we wish other things because of it, and we wish it for itself and not because of something else, then that end is not only a good end but a supreme one. This is obvious from the fact that an end for the sake of which other ends are sought is of greater importance than they, as is evident from his earlier remarks (16). But it is necessary that there be some such end of human affairs. Therefore, human life or activity has some good end which is supreme.

20. He proves the minor premise by an argument leading to an impossible conclusion. Thus, it is evident from the premises (16) that one end is desired on account of another. Now, either we arrive at some end which is not desired on account of another, or we do not. If we do, the proposition is proved. If, however, we do not find some such end, it follows that every end will be desired on account of another end. In this case we must proceed to infinity.

But it is impossible in ends to proceed to infinity. Therefore, there must be some end that is not desired on account of another.

21. That it is impossible in ends to proceed to infinity is proved also by an argument having an impossible resolution. If we should proceed to infinity in our desire for ends so that one end should always be desired on account of another to infinity, we will never arrive at the point where a man may attain the ends desired. But a man desires fruitlessly what he cannot get; consequently, the end he desires would be useless and vain. But this desire is natural, for it was said above (9) that the good is what all beings naturally desire. Hence it follows that a natural desire would be useless and vain. But this is impossible. The reason is that a natural desire is nothing else but an inclination belonging to things by the disposition of the First Mover, and this cannot be frustrated. Therefore, it is impossible that we should proceed to an infinity of ends.

22. It follows that there must be some ultimate end on account of which all other things are desired, while this end itself is not desired on account of anything else. So there must be some supreme end of human affairs.

23. Then [2], at "**A knowledge of it,**" he shows that the knowledge of this end is necessary for man. He proves this in two steps. First [2] he shows that it is necessary for man to know such an end. Second [3], at "This being the case etc.," he manifests what man should know about it. He concludes then from what has been said (19–22), that it is necessary for man to know that there is

a supreme end of human affairs because this has great importance for life, that is, it is of great help in all phases of human living. This conclusion is apparent for the following reasons. Nothing that is directed to another can be immediately attained by man unless he knows that other to which it is to be directed. An obvious indication of this is found in the example of the archer who shoots straight because he keeps his eye on the target at which he is aiming. Now man's whole life ought to be ordered to the supreme and ultimate end of human life. It is necessary, therefore, to have a knowledge of this end of human life. The explanation is that the reason for the means must always be found in the end itself, as also is proved in the second book of the *Physics* (Ch. 9, 199b34–200b10; St. Th. Lect. XV, 184–188).[5]

24. Then [3], at "**This being the case,**" he shows what ought to be known about that end. He states that inasmuch as the knowledge of the supreme end is necessary for human life, we must determine what is the supreme end, and to which speculative or practical science its study belongs. By sciences he understands the speculative sciences, and by skills the practical sciences since there are principles of some operations. According to him we must make this attempt, in order to suggest the difficulty there is in grasping the ultimate end of human life, as in considering all ultimate causes. He says then that we should understand it in its general outlines, that is, with only the evidence of probability because such a manner of understanding is largely what is available in human

---

5   Sancti Thomae Aquinatis, *In Octo Libros Physicorum Aristotelis Expositio*. Ed. Maggiolo (Turin/Rome: Marietti, 1954), pp. 132 sq.

things, as he will explain later on (131–134). Now the first of these two belongs to the treatise on this science because such a consideration is about the matter of this science. But the second belongs to the introduction, where its purpose is explained.

25. Therefore when immediately after this material he says "**It seems undoubtedly**" [4], he shows to which science the consideration of this end should belong. In regard to this he does two things. First [4] he gives a reason in proof of his statement. Second [5], at "Now such a science etc.," he proves something which he had previously presumed. First then, he states the reason for his proposal, which is this: the supreme end belongs to the most important and most truly architectonic science. This is clear from what was said above, for it was pointed out (16, 20) that the sciences or arts treating of the means to the end are contained under the science or art treating of the end. So it is necessary that the ultimate end should belong to the most important science concerned with the primary and most important end and to the truly architectonic science as directing the others in what they should do. But political science appears to be such, namely, the most important and the most truly architectonic. Therefore, it belongs to it to consider the supreme end.

26. Then [5], at "**Now such a science,**" he proves what he had taken for granted: that political science is such a science. First he proves that it is most truly architectonic, and next [7], at "For even though the good etc.," that it is most important. He handles the first statement in two ways. First he ascribes to political science or politics the things which belong to an architectonic science. Second [6] from this he draws

the conclusion he intended, at "Political science etc." There are two characteristics of architectonic knowledge. One is that it dictates what is to be done by the art or science subject to it, as the equestrian art dictates the manner of bridle-making. The other is that it uses it for its own ends. Now the first of these is applicable to politics or political science both in regard to speculative and in regard to practical sciences—in different ways, however. Political science dictates to a practical science both in the matter of its activity, that is, whether or not it should operate, and in regard to the objects to which its operation is to be directed. It dictates to the smith not only that he use his skill but also that he use it in such a fashion as to make knives of a particular kind. Both (characteristics of architectonic knowledge) are ordered to the end of human living.

27. But political science dictates to a speculative science only as to activity, but not concerning the specification of its proper activity. Political science orders that some teach or learn geometry, and actions of this kind insofar as they are voluntary belong to the matter of ethics and can be ordered to the goal of human living. But the political ruler does not dictate to geometry what conclusions it should draw about a triangle, for this is not subject to the human will nor can it be ordered to human living but it depends on the very nature of things. Therefore, he says that political science ordains which sciences, both practical and speculative, should be studied in a state, who should study them, and for how long.

28. The other characteristic of an architectonic science, the use of subordinate sciences, belongs to political science only in reference to the practical sciences. Hence he adds that we see

the most highly esteemed, the noblest skills, i.e., the operative arts, fall under political science—for example strategy, domestic economy, and rhetoric. Political science uses such skills for its own end, that is, for the common good of the state.

29. Then [6], at "**Political science in fact**," he draws a conclusion from two premises. He says that since political science uses the other practical sciences, as already noted (28), and since it legislates what is to be done and what omitted, as previously stated (27), it follows that the end of this science as architectonic embraces or contains under itself the ends of other practical sciences. Hence, he concludes, the end of political science is the good of man, that is, the supreme end of human things.

30. Then [7], at "**For even though the good be the same**," he shows that political science is the most important science from the very nature of its special end. It is evident that insofar as a cause is prior and more powerful it extends to more effects. Hence, insofar as the good, which has the nature of a final cause, is more powerful, it extends to more effects. So, even though the good be the same objective for one man and for the whole state, it seems much better and more perfect to attain, that is, to procure and preserve the good of the whole state than the good of any one

man. Certainly it is a part of that love which should exist among men that a man preserve the good even of a single human being. But it is much better and more divine that this be done for a whole people and for states. It is even sometimes desirable that this be done for one state only, but it is much more divine that it be done for a whole people that includes many states. This is said to be more divine because it shows greater likeness to God who is the ultimate cause of all good. But this good common to one or to several states is the object of our inquiry, that is, of the particular skill called political science. Hence to it, as the most important science, belongs in a most special way the consideration of the ultimate end of human life.

31. But we should note that he says political science is the most important, not simply, but in that division of practical sciences which are concerned with human things, the ultimate end of which political science considers. The ultimate end of the whole universe is considered in theology which is the most important without qualification. He says that it belongs to political science to treat the ultimate end of human life. This however he discusses here since the matter of this book covers the fundamental notions of political science.

LECTURE III
Qualities of the Student and Teacher

TEXT OF ARISTOTLE (*1094b13–1095a13*) Chapter 3

1. Our study will be adequately treated if it is investigated according to the nature of the subject matter. The same certitude should not be sought in all discussions just as the same exactness should not be expected in all the productions of art. Now good and just deeds, with which political science is concerned, are differently and mistakenly judged to such a degree that none of them seems to be good and just by nature but merely by disposition of law. Because of bad judgment, many have been harmed even by good things: some men have lost their lives by reason of riches, others by reason of physical courage. It is desirable therefore when treating of these variable subjects and when arguing from them as premises, to bring out roughly the outlines of the truth, and to conclude about those things which occur in the majority of cases.
1094b10–22; 32–35

2. In this same spirit the student ought to take whatever is taught, for it is proper to an educated man to look for as much certitude in each study as the nature of the subject admits. It approximates the same thing to allow a mathematician to use rhetorical arguments and to demand conclusive demonstrations from a rhetorician.
1094b22–27; 36

3. Now every man is a good judge of the things he knows. Accordingly, then, one educated in a particular subject judges well what belongs to that subject. But the man who is well educated in all subjects can judge well about all.
1094b27–1095a2; 37

4. In keeping with this a young man is not a good student of political science, for he is inexperienced in the ways of life that are the starting point and subject matter of this science.
1095a2–4; 38

5. Furthermore, because he is strongly influenced by his emotions, he will study political science without result and uselessly, for the end of this science is not knowledge but human action. Nor does it matter whether the student be immature in age or immature in character, for the deficiency is not due to time but to a life lived according to the passions and to the pursuit of each object of passion. Such men gain no profit from their knowledge; and the same is true of the incontinent.
1095a4–9; 39–40

6. But it will certainly be very useful to have a knowledge of moral matters for those who desire and act according to the dictates of reason. To sum up what has been treated in the introduction: we have discussed the student, the method of demonstrating and the purpose of our science.
1095a10–13; 41–42

COMMENTARY OF ST. THOMAS

32. After the Philosopher has shown what is the good principally intended in this science, he now determines the method proper to this science. He does this first on the part of the teacher [1]; and then, at "In the same spirit etc.," on the part of the student [2]. In regard to the first he lays down this reason. The method of manifesting truth in any science ought to be suitable to the subject matter of that science. He shows this from the fact that certitude cannot be found, nor should it be sought, in the same degree in all discussions where we reason about anything. Likewise, the same method is not used in all products made by art; but each workman works with the material in a way suited to that material, in one way with the soil, in another with clay, in still another with metal. Now the matter of moral study is of such a nature that

perfect certitude is not suitable to it. He shows this from two classes of things which seem to belong to the material with which moral study is concerned.

33. In the matter of morals the first and foremost place is held by virtuous works. They are called just and are the chief concern of political science. Regarding them there are no agreed opinions, but rather a decided difference is found in what men judge about them. In this matter a variety of errors occur, for certain actions, considered just and good by some, are looked upon as unjust and bad by others according to different times and places and persons. Now a deed is considered vicious at one time and in one country, but at a different time and in a different country it is not considered to be so. Because of this disagreement, it happens that some are of the opinion that no action is just or good by nature but only by disposition of law. We shall treat more fully of this opinion in the second book of this work (245–254).

34. Second, external goods that are used purposively by men have a moral consideration. In regard to them it happens that we find the mistake just mentioned inasmuch as these material goods are not always used in the same way by everyone. Some men are helped by them, while others indeed are harmed by them. Many are ruined by having riches—for instance, those who are murdered by robbers. Some by reason of their physical courage on which they rely have carelessly exposed themselves to dangers. Thus it is evident that moral matters are variable and divergent, not having the same certitude each time.

35. Because, in the art of demonstrative science, principles must conform to conclusions, it is desirable and preferable when treating subjects so variable, and when proceeding from premises likewise variable, to bring out the truth first in a rough outline by applying universal principles to singulars and by proceeding from the simple (universal) to the complex (particular) where acts are concerned. For it is necessary in every practical science to proceed in a composite (i.e., deductive) manner. On the contrary in speculative science, it is necessary to proceed in an analytical manner by breaking down the complex into elementary principles. Second, we should bring out the outlines of the truth, that is, an approximation to the truth. This is to proceed from the proper principles of this science. Moral science treats the acts of the will, and the thing moving the will is not only the good but even fictitious good. Third, we must speak of events as they happen in the majority of cases, that is, of voluntary acts that proceed from the will, inclined perhaps to one alternative rather than another but never operating under compulsion. In these, too, we must proceed in such a way that principles are conformable to conclusions.

36. Then [2], at "**In this same spirit**," he shows that the student must accept this limitation in moral matters. He says that it is proper that each one should take whatever is said to him by another in the same spirit, that is, as the matter warrants. The reason is that a learned or well-instructed man should look for as much certitude in any matter as the nature of the subject admits. There cannot be as much certainty in variable and contingent matter as in necessary matter which is always the same. Therefore, the educated man ought not to look for greater, nor be satisfied with less, certitude than is appropriate to the subject under discussion. It seems an equal fault to allow a

mathematician to use rhetorical arguments and to demand from a rhetorician conclusive demonstrations such as a mathematician should give. But mistakes happen because the method appropriate to the matter is not considered. Mathematics is concerned with matter in which perfect certitude is found. Rhetoric, however, deals with political matter where a variety of views occurs.

37. Then [3], at "**Now every man**," he shows what sort of person the student of this science ought to be. First he shows who is an incompetent student; and second [5], at "Furthermore etc.," who is an unprofitable student. Third [6], c], at "But it will certainly etc.," he explains the characteristics of the ideal student. In respect to the first he does two things. First he introduces certain things necessary to explain his proposition. He states that each man can judge well only the things he knows. Thus a man educated in one particular subject can judge well what belongs to that subject. But the man who is well educated in all subjects can judge well about all, without restriction to a particular subject.

38. Second [4], at "**In keeping with this**," he proves his statement, namely, that a young man is not a good student of political science nor of any part of moral science comprised under political science, because as was said (37) a man can judge well only the things he knows. Now every student should make good judgments about what he studies, so that he may accept what is true but not what is false. Therefore, no one can be a good student unless he has some knowledge of what he ought to study. But a young man does not have a knowledge of things belonging to moral science, which are known mostly by experience. A young man is inexperienced in the ways of life because of the very brevity of his life, while the principles of moral science proceed from what pertains to and also treats of the actions of human life. For instance, if it be said that the generous man keeps the cheaper things for himself and makes a present of the more expensive to others, a young man will perhaps judge this not to be true because of inexperience. It is the same with other social dealings. Hence it is evident that a young man is not a good student of political science.

39. Then [5], at "**Furthermore**," he shows who is an unprofitable student of this science. Here we must consider that moral science teaches men to follow reason and to refrain from the things to which the passions incline, such as concupiscence, anger, and the like. Toward these, men are inclined in two ways. In one way by choice, for instance, when a man of set purpose intends to satisfy his concupiscence. Such a one he calls a slave of his emotions. In another way, when a man resolves to abstain from harmful pleasures but is sometimes overcome by the urge of passion, so that contrary to his resolution he follows the promptings of passion. A man of this type is said to be incontinent.

40. He affirms then that the one who is ruled by the emotions will study this science in vain, that is, without any result and uselessly without attaining its proper end. The end of this science is not knowledge alone, which those enslaved to passion can perhaps gain. But the end of this science, as of all practical sciences, is human action. Now those who follow the emotions do not attain virtuous acts. So in regard to this it makes no difference whether the student of this science is immature in age or immature in character, that is,

a slave of the emotions. The reason is that, as the person immature in age fails to achieve the end of this science that is knowledge, so the immature in character fails to achieve the end that is action. His deficiency is not due to time but to the fact that he lives according to his emotions, seeking everything to which the emotions incline. Now, for such men the knowledge of this science is useless; the same may be said of the incontinent who do not act in accord with their knowledge of moral matters.

41. Then [6], at "**But it will certainly,**" he indicates the good student of this science. He says that it is very useful to have a knowledge of moral matters for those who regulate their desires and act in externals according to the dictates of reason.

42. Last, in the conclusion he sums up what has been discussed in the introduction (1–41), stating that certain things have been said in a preliminary manner about the student—this was treated last; stating also what is the method of demonstrating—this was treated in the middle of the introduction; and last what is our purpose, namely, what is the principal aim of this science—this was treated first.

LECTURE IV
Opinions About Happiness

TEXT OF ARISTOTLE (*1095a14–1095b13*) Chapter 4

1. *Since all knowledge and choice have some good for their objective, let us ask on resuming our inquiry what it is that we call the objective of political science? What is the highest good of all human actions?* **1095a14–17; 43**

2. *As to the name nearly all agree, for both the common people and the educated say it is happiness. They identify happiness with living well and acting well.* **1095a17–20; 44–45**

3. *But as to where happiness is to be found men are at variance. The multitude differs from the philosophers, for the people generally think that happiness consists in something apparent and obvious such as pleasure or riches or honors; some place it in one of these, others in another; and oftentimes even the same person shifts his position. For instance, the sick man thinks happiness is found in health, the poor man considers that it is found in riches, while men conscious of their own ignorance esteem those happy who give utterance to lofty ideas that are above their comprehension. Some philosophers were of the opinion that, over and above the many goods, there exists an absolute good which is the cause of goodness in all other things.* **1095a20–28; 46–49**

4. *It is perhaps vain to examine all these opinions, and it will be sufficient to give special attention to those appearing probable on the surface or are thought by many to have some probability.* **1095a28–30; 50**

5. *In this matter we should be aware of the difference in arguments, some of which proceed from principles and others to principles. Previously Plato had learnedly discussed the subject when he examined the question whether we proceed from or to principles like athletes in the race-course running from or toward the judges. In either case we must start from things known. Now these are of two kinds, namely, things known to us and things known absolutely. Presumably then we should begin from what is known to us.* **1095a30–1095b4; 51–52**

6. *One who is going to devote himself seriously to the study of good and just deeds and to political affairs in general ought to have been accustomed to a virtuous life. This will serve as a principle and if it be adequate he will have no need to know the reasons for virtuous conduct. A student with this upbringing will discover working principles within himself or readily acquire them from someone else. The man, however, who can do neither of these things should listen to the verdict of Hesiod. That man, the poet says, is best who understands everything by himself; and that man good who takes what is well said by another. But he who neither himself understands nor takes to heart what he hears from another is indeed a useless fellow.* **1095b4–13; 53–54**

COMMENTARY OF ST. THOMAS

43. Having finished the introduction, Aristotle here begins the treatise on the science itself. He divides the treatise into three parts. In the first part he investigates happiness, which is the supreme human good, and he comes to the conclusion from a study of the subject that happiness is activity flowing from virtue. In the second part [Lect. XIX] he discusses virtues at "If then happiness is a kind of operation according to perfect virtue etc." (1102a4). In the third part he completes his treatise on happiness, explaining which operation it is and of what nature. This he does in the tenth book (1172a19) at "After these matters we ought perhaps next to discuss pleasure." In regard to

the first he does two things. First [1] he explains his intention. Second [2], at "As to the name etc.," he carries it out. He says first, resuming what he was investigating before (9–13), that since all knowledge and choice aim at some good, that is, are ordered to some desired good as an end, we must discuss the nature of that good to which political science is ordered. Such is the highest good of all actions, that is, the highest among those attainable by human operation. Moreover, it was said above (18) that these two notions must be studied about the ultimate end of human good; what it is—this is here proposed for consideration—and to what science it belongs and this was treated above in the introduction (25–30).

44. Next [2], at "**As to the name**," he treats happiness. He proceeds here in two steps. First he investigates the opinions of others about happiness. Second [Lect. IX], at "Let us return again to a consideration etc." (1097a16), he states his own opinion. In regard to the initial point he does two things. First [2] he gives the opinions of others about happiness. Second [Lect. V], at "Let us return to the subject etc." (1095b12), he examines these opinions. He handles the first point in two ways. Initially [1] he presents opinions about the ultimate end of human actions. Then [4], at "It is perhaps vain," he points out how we should examine opinions of this kind. In regard to the first he does two things. He indicates the aspects of general agreement [2]; and then [3], at "But as to where happiness etc.," he shows in what way there is disagreement.

45. In the beginning he presents two points on which there is general agreement about the ultimate end. First [2], at "**As to the name**," he asserts that both the many, that is, the common people and the cultured or philosophers, name happiness the highest human good. Second, they have a common understanding of the term because all consider that living well and acting well are identified with being happy.

46. Then [3], at "**But as to where happiness**," he shows in what respect the opinions of men differ about happiness. He affirms that especially about the nature of happiness men are at variance, i.e., hold different opinions. This difference is threefold. First of all the multitude does not think in this matter like the philosophers. People commonly consider that happiness consists in something apparent and obvious among the objects of sense, which alone are evident to the multitude and, therefore, so obvious as not to need exhaustive search—such as pleasure, riches, honor, and the like. The views of the philosophers on this point are given later (49).

47. The second difference is found among the common people themselves. Some of them place happiness in one sensible good, others in another. The avaricious place it in riches, the self-indulgent in pleasures, the ambitious in honors.

48. The third difference arises from the end in itself. Since it is characteristic of the ultimate end that it be greatly desired, people consider that to be happiness which is desired most of all. Now, need of a good increases the desire for it, and so the sick man who lacks health judges the supreme good to be health; the beggar looks upon riches in the same way. Likewise those who are conscious of their own ignorance esteem as happy others who give utterance to lofty ideas which are above the comprehension of the igno-

rant. All this pertains to the opinion of the multitude.

49. But some among the philosophers, the Platonists, were of the opinion that, over and above the many different sensible goods, there exists one which is absolute good and which is the separated essence of goodness itself. As the separated form of man was called by them "man in himself" so the separated good was "good in itself," and this is the cause of the goodness of all other things as they partake of that highest good.

50. Then [4], at "**It is perhaps vain**," he shows how we should proceed in our investigation of the aforesaid opinions. He handles the discussion in three steps. First [4] he shows which of these opinions we ought to investigate. Second [5], at "In this matter we should etc.," he shows in what order we should do this. Third [6] he shows how the student should be disposed so that he may properly understand what is taught. He says then that to examine all opinions men hold about happiness would be useless for a good philosopher, inasmuch as some of them are altogether unreasonable. But it suffices to examine at most the opinions that on the surface are probable either because they give that appearance or at least are considered to have weight by many.

51. Then [5], at "**In this matter we should be aware**," he shows in what order we must discuss opinions of this sort and in general all moral matters. He points out a difference in the manner of reasoning. There are some argumentations proceeding from principles, that is, from causes to effects, such as demonstrations of the reasoned fact (*propter quid*). On the contrary, there are other argumentations proceeding from effects to causes or principles. These do not produce a demonstration of the reasoned fact but only of the fact (*quia*). This distinction was previously made by Plato when he inquired whether we should proceed from or to principles. Then he offers this example from the racecourse. In order to judge athletes running in a race certain *agonothetes* or judges were stationed at the beginning of the course. Sometimes the athletes started from the judges and ran to the finishing line, and sometimes they started from the end and ran toward the judges. Likewise there is a twofold order in the process of reasoning.

52. In order to know the order of procedure in any subject we should reflect that it is necessary to begin from what is better understood. Through things better known we arrive at a knowledge of things unknown. Now things are said to be better known in two ways. Some are better known in regard to us such as the composite and the sensible; others are better known absolutely and in themselves, as the simple and the intelligible. Because we acquire knowledge by reasoning, we must proceed from what is better known to us. Now if the better known absolutely are the same as the better known to us, the reason proceeds from principles as in mathematics. If, however, the better known absolutely are different from the better known to us, then we must use the effect-to-cause procedure as in the natural and moral sciences.

53. Then [6], at "**One who is going**," he shows how a student of such subjects should be disposed. He says that since in moral matters we ought to begin from what is better known to us, that is, from certain effects noted about human acts, a man who wishes to be a competent student of moral science must be well-informed and experi-

enced in the ways of human living, that is about external good and just actions or works of virtue, and in general about all civil matters like laws and political affairs and other things of this sort. The reason for this is that in moral matters we must take as a principle that a thing is so. For example, we accept from experience and custom that concupiscence is restrained by fasting.

54. If this is obvious to someone it is not so necessary for him in acting to understand the total explanation. Thus to effect a cure a physician need know only that this medicine cures a particular malady. But to know the reason, we must have a scientific knowledge that is sought chiefly in speculative sciences. Now one who is skilled in human affairs either discovers working principles for himself and sees them as self-evident, or he readily acquires them from someone else. But a man about whom neither of these things can be correctly said should listen to the verdict of the poet Hesiod. He calls that man best who can understand by himself, and that man good who takes what is said by another. But the man who is capable neither of understanding by himself nor of bearing in mind what he hears from another is useless as far as acquiring a science is concerned.

LECTURE V
Examination of the Opinions

TEXT OF ARISTOTLE (*1095b14–1096a10*) Chapter 5

1. *Let us return to the subject from which we have digressed. Some seem to think, not without reason, that the supreme good called happiness is a good belonging to this life.*
1095b14–16; 55

2. *Now, most men, including some very eminent persons, place happiness in pleasure and so logically prefer a sensual life.*
1095b16–17; 56–57

3. *There are indeed three very prominent types of life: that just mentioned, another called public life, and last the contemplative life.*
1095b17–19; 58–59

4. *The majority of men seem quite bestial in choosing to live a life of pleasure.*
1095b19–20; 60

5. *They justify their choice on the plea that many in high places share the tastes of Sardanapalus.*
1095b21–22; 61

6. *Men of superior refinement, however, and those occupied in the active life, place happiness in honor.*
1095b22–23; 62

7. *for honor seems to be nearly the whole purpose of public life.*
1095b23; 63

8. *But this seems too superficial to be the good we are looking for. Honor consists in the action of those rendering it rather than anything in the power of the person honored; while happiness certainly should be a good proper to man and a thing not easily taken from him.*
1095b23–26; 64

9. *Another reason is that men appear to seek honor to convince themselves of their own good qualities. They strive to be honored by the prudent, by those who know them best and for their virtue. Obviously then, in their opinion, virtue is a better thing than honor.*
1095b26–30; 65

10. *From this someone may conclude that virtue rather than honor is the end of public life.*
1095b30–31; 66

11. *But apparently virtue too is lacking in perfection because a man may have a habit of virtue when he is asleep or when he has no opportunity to exercise its acts for a lifetime.*
1095b31–33; 67

12. *Moreover, he may be subject to evils and very often may be ill-favored by fortune. No one would call such a man happy, unless he were merely defending an argumentative position. Enough has now been said, for we treated the subject sufficiently in the Encyclis.*
1095b33–1096a4; 68

13. *Later on we shall investigate the third type of life, the contemplative.*
1096a4–5; 69

14. *As to the accumulator of riches, he lives a life of constraint;*
1096a5–6; 70–71

15. *and riches themselves are not the good we seek, for they are merely useful and sought for the sake of something else. Rather therefore the things previously treated are considered ends, since they are desired for themselves. Yet even these are not the supreme good and happiness, although many arguments have been marshalled to prove this. But these discussions must be terminated now.*
1096a6–10; 72

COMMENTARY OF ST. THOMAS

55. After the Philosopher has recounted the different opinions about happiness, he begins to investigate the truth of these opinions. First he examines the opinion of those discussing happiness from the moral point of view who place happiness in some good of this life. Second [Lect. VI], at

"Perhaps it will be better" (1096a12), he examines the opinion of those who do not discuss happiness from the moral point of view but place it in some separated good. In regard to the first he does two things. He lays down a notion [A] that opinions on this subject have in common; and next [2], at "Now, most men," he begins to investigate the variety of opinions. Then, because the Philosopher seemed to have made a digression from his principal purpose while he was determining the mode of procedure, he returns to the point whence he had digressed, that is, to the opinions about happiness. He asserts that some seem to think, not without reason, that the final good called happiness is a good belonging to this life on the purely human level. This is the goal of all the works of life. Now, means are proportionate to that end. Hence it is probable that happiness is among the number of goods belonging to this life. But what the truth may be in this matter will be indicated later (60, 64, 65, 70–72).

56. Next [2], at "**Now, most men,**" he searches for the truth about the things on which the opinions differ. In regard to this he does two things. First he examines the opinions that seem more likely to be true. Second [14], at "As to the accumulator of riches etc.," he examines an opinion rather remote from the truth. In regard to the first he does three things. First he examines the opinion placing happiness in the things that pertain to a life of pleasure. Second [6], at "Men of superior refinement etc.," he examines the opinion placing happiness in the things pertaining to public life. Third [13], at "Later on we shall investigate etc.," he mentions the contemplative life. In regard to the first he does three things. First [2] he presents the opinion. Second

[3], at "There are indeed three etc.," he distinguishes three types of life without elaborating on them. Third [4], at "The majority of men etc.," he examines the truth of the opinion presented.

57. He says then in the first place that some men, from the goods of this life, choose pleasure and place happiness in it. They include not only the majority of the common people who by and large favor pleasure, but also persons eminent either in knowledge and teaching or in uprightness of life. Even the Epicureans, who considered pleasure the highest good, carefully cultivated the virtues. They did so, however, on account of pleasure, that is, for fear their pleasure would be hindered by means of contrary vices. The vice of gluttony, for instance, causes bodily suffering through excessive eating; because of theft a man is thrown into prison. So different vices are an impediment to pleasure in different ways. Since then the ultimate end is exceedingly delectable, they who make pleasure the highest good intensely love the life of pleasure.

58. Then [3], at "**There are indeed three,**" he distinguishes three types of life: the sensual just mentioned, the public, and the contemplative. These he calls the most prominent types. For evidence of this we must now bear in mind what will later be discussed in the ninth book (1944–1949), that every man thinks his life to be that to which he is most strongly drawn, as the philosopher to philosophizing, the hunter to hunting, and so on. Because man is most strongly drawn to the last end, it is necessary that the types of life be distinguished according to the diversity of the ultimate end. Now the end has the nature of good, and good is threefold: the useful, the pleasurable, and the virtuous or honorable. Two of

these, namely, the pleasurable and the virtuous or honorable, have the nature of end because both are desirable for their own sake. That indeed is called virtuous which is good according to reason, and this has pleasure attached to it. Hence the pleasurable, as distinguished from the virtuous, is so called in reference to the senses. Reason, we must remember, is both speculative and practical.

59. Therefore, that life is called sensual which fixes its end in the pleasures of the senses; and that public which fixes its end in the good of the practical reason, for example, in the exercise of virtuous deeds; and that contemplative which fixes its end in the good of the speculative reason or in the contemplation of truth.

60. Next [4], at "**The majority of men**," he examines the opinion cited above. In regard to this he does two things. First [4] he disproves it. Second [5], at "They justify their choice etc.," he advances a reason why some are drawn to this life. In regard to the first we must consider that the sensual life, which fixes its end in sense pleasure, necessarily has to place that end in those very intense pleasures following from the natural operations by which the individual is preserved by eating and drinking and the race by sexual intercourse. Now pleasures of this kind are found in both men and beasts. It follows then that the multitude of men who fix their end in such pleasures seem quite bestial in choosing a life which even the pigs enjoy. If the happiness of man would consist in this, dumb animals enjoying the pleasure of food and sexual intercourse would have to be called happy for the same reason. Assuming that happiness is a characteristically human good, it cannot possibly consist in these things.

61. Then [5], at "**They justify their choice**," he gives the reason why some hold this opinion. He says that the reason they offer is that many in high places, like kings and princes who are considered very happy by the common people, share the tastes of a certain Assyrian king named Sardanapalus who was much given to sensuality. On this account it is thought that pleasure is something very good since it is a thing highly esteemed by the great.

62. At "**Men of superior refinement**" [6] he investigates opinions concerning the active or public life. First [6] he does this in regard to honor; and second [10], at "From this someone etc.," in regard to virtue. This is a reasonable procedure, for the active or public life aims at the honorable good. Now it is called honorable as pertaining to the state of honor. Hence both honor itself and virtue, which is the cause of honor, appear to belong to it. In regard to the first he does three things. First [6], in presenting the opinion, he notes that persons of superior refinement, namely, the virtuous and those occupied in the active life, place happiness in honor.

63. Second [7], at "**for honor seems**," he offers a reason for this: the sole purpose of public life appears to be honor which is rendered as a reward to the politically successful. Therefore, for those engaged in public life happiness probably seems to consist in honor.

64. Third [8], at "**But this seems**," he disproves this opinion by two reasons. In the first [8] of these he says that in a way we divine the true nature of happiness, that is, we surmise happiness to be a good proper to the happy man, a thing belonging preeminently to him and taken from him with difficulty. But this is not true of honor which seems rather to consist in the action of the one

rendering the honor, and to be in his power rather than in the power of the one honored. Therefore honor is something more extrinsic and superficial than the good we are seeking, which is happiness.

65. He gives the second reason at "**Another reason**" [9]. Happiness is some very good thing which is not sought on account of another. But there is something better than honor, namely, that on account of which honor is sought. Men appear to seek honor in order to confirm the solid opinion they have formed of themselves that they are good men and that they may be assured of this by the judgment of others. They look, therefore, for honor from prudent men with correct judgment and from those who know them best and can be better judges. Hence they seek to be honored for their virtue, which is the source of man's good, as will be shown in the second book (307–308). So virtue, for whose sake honor is sought, is a better thing than honor. It follows then that happiness does not consist in honor.

66. Then [10], at "**From this some-one**," he investigates the opinion of those who place happiness in virtue. In regard to this he does two things. First [10] he states the opinion and says that perhaps someone will think, by reason of what was just said, that virtue rather than honor is the end of public life.

67. Second [11], at "**But apparently**," he rejects this for two reasons. The first is that happiness seems to be a most perfect good. But virtue is not of such a nature, for sometimes it is found without the perfection of activity, as we see in those who are asleep and yet have the habit of virtue. It is possible, too, that a man may have the habit of virtue, but for lack of opportunity not perform a single act of a particular vir-

tue during his whole life. This is particularly evident regarding magnanimity and magnificence, virtues perhaps possessed by a poverty-stricken person who is never able to perform great deeds. Therefore virtue is not the same as happiness.

68. He gives the second reason at "**Moreover he may be**" [12]. It is this. It happens that one who has the habit of virtue may be ill-favored by fortune. Who will call such a man happy except someone obstinately defending a thesis against the plain truth? Therefore happiness is not the same as virtue. This, he says, is sufficient for his purpose. Enough has been said on the subject in his *Encyclis*, that is, in certain learned verses that Aristotle composed on happiness.

69. Then [13], at "**Later on we shall investigate**," he mentions the contemplative life, saying that it will be investigated later on in the tenth book (2086–2125).

70. At "**As to the accumulator of riches**" [14], he examines another opinion, less probable, which places happiness in a thing which has the nature of a useful good, money. But this is incompatible with the nature of an ultimate end, for a thing is called useful because it is ordered to an end. However, since money has an over-all utility in respect of temporal goods, the opinion that places happiness in money has some probability.

71. But he rejects it for two reasons [14]. The first is that money is acquired under coercion and is parted with under coercion. But this is not in keeping with happiness, which is the goal of voluntary operations. Consequently happiness does not consist in money.

72. He gives the second reason [15] at "**and riches themselves**." It is this. We look for happiness as a good that is

not sought for something else. But money is sought for something beyond itself since it is by its nature a useful good, as was just said (70). Therefore happiness does not consist in money.

73. A further conclusion notes that pleasure, honor, and virtue, all of which were treated above (57–72), can be considered ultimate ends at least in the sense that they are sought for themselves, as was said (57, 61, 63, 70). However, the ultimate end is not to be found in these, as has been shown (57–72), although many arguments have been marshalled by various philosophers to prove that happiness consists in these goods. But these discussions must be terminated.

LECTURE VI
Happiness and a Separated Good

TEXT OF ARISTOTLE (1096a11–34) Chapter 6

*1. Perhaps it will be better to investigate thoroughly the existence of the universal good and
to inquire about its nature,*   1096a11–12; 74

*2. even if the investigation has become unpleasant owing to the fact that the doctrine of ideas
was introduced by good friends.*   1096a12–13; 75

*3. However, it seems indeed better, and in fact especially obligatory on philosophers, to
sacrifice even the rights of friendship for the sake of truth. While it is commendable to have love
for both, we ought to honor truth as sacred above friends.*   1096a14–17; 76–78

*4. Those who hold this opinion did not postulate ideas in which priority and posteriority
were found. On this account they made no provision for an idea of numbers. Now good is found
in the category of substance and quality and relation. But being in itself, i.e., substance, is
naturally prior to being in reference to something else, for the latter is likened to an offspring of
being and an accident of it. Therefore there will not be any common idea for these.*
1096a17–23; 79–80

*5. Furthermore, good is convertible with being. For good is predicated of substance such as
God and intellect. It is predicated of quality such as virtues, of quantity such as the mean, of
relation such as the useful, of time such as the opportune, of place such as a summerhouse, and
so on. Hence it is obvious that one common idea of good that is universal does not exist.
Otherwise good would not be found in every category but in one alone.*   1096a23–29; 81

*6. Moreover, because a single science treats things falling under one idea, there would have
to be a single science of all good things. But we have many sciences, even of things contained in
one category like time, for the opportune is studied in war by strategy, in disease by medicine,
and in exercise by gymnastics.*   1096a29–34; 82

COMMENTARY OF ST. THOMAS

74. After the Philosopher has rejected the opinion of those who place happiness in one of the obvious goods, here [1] he disproves the opinion of those placing it in a separate good. In regard to this he does two things. First [1] he shows the necessity of discussing this opinion. Second [4] he begins to disprove it. In regard to the first he does three things. First [1] he suggests the advantage of this inquiry. Second [2], at "even if the investigation etc.," he points out what may seem an unpleasant aspect of the investigation. Third [3], at "However, it seems etc.," he shows that this should not deter us from seeking the truth. In regard to the first we must consider that the separated good, in which the Platonists asserted that man's happiness consists, was called a universal good. By participation in it all things are said to be good. Hence he says that perhaps it is better to investigate thoroughly the existence of this universal good and to inquire what its nature is than to discuss the opinions mentioned before. The investigation of the good is more philosophical and more properly belongs to the discussion of the true good and the ultimate end than do the opinions considered in themselves. If, however, they be considered according to our stated intention of inquiring about the opinions mentioned above, it would seem to be more in

a

greement with our plan. On this account he uses "perhaps," an adverb indicating doubt.

75. Then [2], at **"even if the investigation,"** he states what might deter him from an investigation of this opinion. He says that the investigation is made reluctantly because the opinion was introduced by friends of his, the Platonists. He himself was a disciple of Plato, and by rejecting this opinion he might seem to disparage his teacher. He raises the point here rather than in his other works where he likewise rejects the opinion of Plato because the repudiation of the opinion of a friend is not contrary to truth, which is the principal object in speculative sciences. It is, however, contrary to good morals, the subject discussed in this book.

76. Then [3], at **"However, it seems indeed better,"** he shows that this consideration ought not to deter him. The reason is that it seems to be better, meaning more honorable and in agreement with good morals, and indeed obligatory, that a man should not hesitate to oppose his friends for the sake of truth. It is so necessary for good morals that without it virtue cannot be preserved. Unless a man prefer truth to his friends, it follows that he will make false judgment and bear false witness in their defense. This is contrary to virtue. While reason prescribes that all men should prefer truth to their friends, this holds in a special way for the philosophers whose calling is to study wisdom, which is knowledge of the truth.

77. That truth should be preferred to friends he proves in this way. He is the greater friend for whom we ought to have the greater consideration. Although we should have friendship for both truth and our fellow man, we ought rather to love truth because we should love our fellow man especially on account of truth and virtue, as will be shown in the eighth book (1575–1577). Now truth is a most excellent friend of the sort to whom the homage of honor is due. Besides, truth is a divine thing, for it is found first and chiefly in God. He concludes, therefore, that it is virtuous to honor truth above friends.

78. Andronicus, the peripatetic, says that piety makes men faithful to and observant of the things of God. Along the same line is the judgment of Plato who, in rejecting the opinion of his teacher Socrates, says a man ought to care more for truth than anything else. Somewhere else too he affirms that while Socrates is certainly his friend, truth is still more so. In yet another place he says that we should have some care for the views of Socrates but more for truth.

79. Then [4], at **"Those who hold his opinion,"** he rejects the position of Plato who maintains that the happiness of man consists in a common idea or form of good. In regard to this he does two things. First [1] he shows there is no one common idea or form of good. Second [Lect. VIII], at "But perhaps we should etc." (1096b29), he shows that even if there were, human happiness would not consist in it. In regard to the first he does two things. First [4] he shows that there cannot be one common idea of good. Second [Lect. VII], at "Someone will rightly etc." (1096a34), he examines the manner of speaking used by the Platonists when they talk about this idea. In regard to the first we must consider that Aristotle does not intend to reject the opinion insofar as Plato maintained a separated good on which all good

would depend. In the twelfth book of the *Metaphysics* (Ch. 10, 1075a11 sq.; St. Th. Lect. XII, 2627–2663), Aristotle expressly mentions a good, separated from the universe, to which the whole universe is ordered as an army is ordered to the good of the general. He does reject the opinion insofar as Plato held that the separated good is an idea common to all goods. He uses three reasons to disprove the opinion.

80. The first [4] of these is taken from the argument of the Platonists themselves who did not postulate an idea for these classes of things in which priority and posteriority are found, as is the case with numbers, for two is naturally prior to three. So the Platonists did not hold that number in general would have a separated idea. They did, though, place separated ideas for individual numbers, for example, two, three and so on. The reason for this is that the things in which priority and posteriority are found do not seem to be of one order and consequently do not partake of one idea. But among good things there is priority and posteriority. This is clear from the fact that good is found in the *quodquidest* or substance, and likewise in quality and also in other genera. Now it is evident that what is being in itself, such as substance, is naturally prior to all those things that have being only in relation to substance—as quantity, which is the measure of substance; quality, which is the disposition of substance; and relation, which is the reference of substance. The same is true in other categories that are all, as it were, the offspring of being or substance. This is being in the full sense, and from it are engendered and derived all other genera, which are called being to the extent that they are accidents of a substance.

From this he concludes that there cannot be a common idea of good.

81. He lays down the second reason [5] at "**Furthermore, good etc.**" To understand this we must know that Plato held the "idea" to be the "ratio" or nature and essence of all things that partake of the idea. It follows from this that there cannot be one idea of things not having a common nature. But the various categories do not have one common nature, for nothing is predicated of them univocally. Now good, like being with which it is convertible, is found in every category. Thus the *quodquidest* or substance, God, in whom there is no evil, is called good; the intellect, which is always true, is called good. In quality good is predicated of virtue, which makes its possessor good; in quantity, of the mean, which is the good in everything subject to measure. In relation, good is predicated of the useful which is good relative to a proper end. In time, it is predicated of the opportune; and in place, of a location suitable for walking as a summerhouse. The same may be said of other categories. It is clear, therefore, that there is not some one good that is the idea or the common "ratio" of all goods. Otherwise good would not be found in every category but in one alone.

82. He gives the third reason at "**Moreover, because etc.**" [6]. To understand this we must know the following. Things existing outside the mind, according to Plato, acquire the form of genus or species by participating in the "idea" so that the mind does not know a stone except by participating in the "idea" of stone. The mind in this way partakes of science and knowledge of those things when the "forms" or "ideas" of them are im-

ressed in it. It follows that there is a single science of all the things that partake of one "idea." If, therefore, there be one "idea" of all goods, it will belong to the study of one science. But we see that this is false even in regard to the goods belonging to a single category. He adds this for fear that someone may specify sciences according to the diversity of categories. We see, however, that strategy studies the opportune in war, medicine studies it in disease, and gymnastics in exercise. It remains then that there is not one common "idea" of all goods.

LECTURE VII
The Separated Good and an Absolute Good

TEXT OF ARISTOTLE (*1096a34–1096b29*) Chapter 6

1. Someone will rightly ask what they mean in calling anything "absolute" if in both absolute man and this particular man there exists one and the same nature, that of man. This is the truth for they differ in no way as man. On the same supposition an absolute good or a good in itself and a particular good do not differ as good.   **1096a34–1096b3; 83–84**

2. It may not be countered that the good in itself is better because eternal, since what endures a long time is not necessarily better by nature than a thing that lasts a day.   **1096b3–5; 85–86**

3. A more likely explanation seems to have been given by the Pythagoreans who place unity in their list of goods. In this apparently Speusippus followed them. But further discussion of the point will have to wait.   **1096b5–8; 87–88**

4. Contrary to what they have asserted, some doubt arises because their words are not said of every good and yet they do so apply. Now things are said to be good according to one species of good which are sought and desired for their own sake, and things productive or in some way preservative of these or prohibitive of their contraries are said to be good according to another species. It is obvious then that good is predicated in two ways, for some things are sought for their own sake and some for the sake of others.   **1096b8–14; 89–90**

5. Let us separate from the useful good things good in themselves and examine whether they can be called good according to one idea.   **1096b14–16; 91**

6. But what would you have enumerated among goods in themselves? Would you include even all the goods sought for themselves alone, as intelligence, sight, and some types of pleasure and honor? These are sometimes sought for the sake of another, but they always have an intrinsic value. Otherwise nothing else seems an absolute good except the "idea" or "form."
      1096b16–20; 92

7. Wherefore the idea will be empty.   **1096b20; 93**

8. If things in themselves are demonstrated as absolute good, then the same nature of goodness will have to appear in all of them as the nature of whiteness in snow and in white lead. But just as we find different natures in honor, prudence, and pleasure, so too we find differences in goodness. The absolute good is not, therefore, something common according to one idea.
      1096b21–26; 94

9. In what way then are they to be called good? Not as things purely equivocal. Are they at least to be compared as things referring to one principle or as all tending to one end? Or still better, should we say according to analogy? Indeed, as sight is the good of the body so intellect is the good of the soul and so of other things.   **1096b26–29; 95–96**

COMMENTARY OF ST. THOMAS

83. The Philosopher has shown above that there is no common idea of all goods. But because the separated good is called by the Platonists not only the "idea" or "form" of good but also absolute good, Aristotle here intends to inquire whether it is properly called by this name. In regard to this he does two things. First [1] he shows that the separated good is not properly named absolute good. Second [4], at "Contrary to what etc.," he shows that to postulate a separated good as absolute is inconsistent with saying that it is the common idea or form of all goods. In regard to the first he does three things. First [1] he shows that the separated good is not properly called absolute

absolute (*per se*) good. Second [2], at "It may not be countered etc.," he rules out a particular rejoinder. Third [3], at "A more likely explanation etc.," he compares this doctrine with the Pythagorean view.

84. In regard to the first we must consider that the separated good, which is the cause of all goods, ought to be placed in a higher degree of goodness than the good things about us because the separated good is the ultimate end of all. But it seems that, according to this doctrine, it is not a higher degree in goodness than other goods. This is apparent because the Platonists called each of the separated things absolute or in itself, as man in himself and even horse in itself. Now it is clear that one and the same nature belongs to man who lives among us and to man in himself, that is, ideal man. He proves this by the fact that ideal man and man clothed with matter do not differ as man, but they do differ in certain other respects—for example, this particular man has matter. Thus the notions of animal and man do not differ in animality but rather in man's rational principle that he has over and above animality. So too it seems that the ideal man does not differ from this particular man in the nature of man but because this particular man has matter in addition to being man. For the same reason the good that is called absolute will not have goodness different in nature from this particular good, although there can be a difference in other respects than the nature of good.

85. Then [2], at "It may not," he rules out a particular answer. Someone could say that the good in itself is better because eternal while the goods here are perishable. Indeed, a thing that lasts longer does seem better and

more desirable. To exclude this he points out that the good in itself is eternal does not mean that it is better. The eternal differs from the non-eternal by reason of duration, and the difference of duration of a thing is outside the nature of the species, as life that lasts only a day and life more enduring are not different by reason of life but only by duration. So then if good be understood as one species, its duration will be outside the nature of good. The longer duration of a thing then does not make that thing any better.

86. If we do not hold that there is one species or idea of good as the Platonists did, but that good, like being, is predicated in every genus, duration itself will be a good of time. It would, in that case, add something to goodness. Hence what is more lasting will be better. But this cannot be said if the good is one species in itself. It follows then that it is not better because eternal.

87. Then [3], at "**A more likely explanation,**" he compares this opinion with that of the Pythagoreans. We must consider that according to the Platonists the nature of the one and the good is the same, and so they identified one in itself and good in itself. Hence they were obliged to postulate one first good. The Pythagoreans did not do this, however, but they put one among the things contained in the list of the good under which they placed:

Light (The contrary evil of which they declared to be:). . . *Darkness*
Unity. . . . . *Multitude*
Knowledge. . . . . *Opinion*
Rest . . . . *Motion*
Straight . . . . *Curved*
Masculine . . . . *Feminine*
Right . . . . *Left*
Finite . . . . *Infinite*
Equal . . . . *Unequal*
Square . . . . *Rectangular*

88. He says, therefore, that on this point the Pythagoreans gave a more likely explanation than the Platonists because the Pythagoreans were not compelled to hold one nature for the good. Even Speusippus, who was a son of Plato's sister and his successor in the Academy, did not follow Plato but Pythagoras on this point. He adds that further discussion of the subject will be taken up in the *Metaphysics*. (Cf. Bk. I, Ch. 5, 986a13–986b9; St. Th. Lect. VIII, 124–133. Cf. Bk. XI, Ch. 9, 1066a13–17; St. Th. Lect. IX, 2303.)

89. Then [4], at "**Contrary to what**," he shows that the assertion that the separated good is an absolute good or a good in itself is inconsistent with their view that there is one idea or form of all goods. He does three things on this point. First [4] he shows that an absolute good cannot be an idea common to all goods. Second [5], at "Let us separate etc.," he shows that there cannot be a common idea of all things called good in themselves. Third [9], at "In what way etc.," he handles a pertinent query. He says then in the first place that contrary to what the Platonists assert, there seems to be a subtle hesitation here. When they speak about the good in itself, it does not seem from the obvious meaning of their words that the discussion concerns every good, but as much can be gathered from the context because there are various species or forms of goods.

90. Those things sought, pursued, chosen, or desired for themselves are good according to one species or form of goodness. Those desired insofar as they are good in some way for the sake of others, which in their turn are really good, are called good for another reason. In a third way, some things are called good because they prevent the contrary evil. It is clear, therefore, that good is predicated in two ways. Primary goods are good in themselves. As we have already remarked (9–13, 58) they are sought for themselves. Both of the other things called good—the productive or preservative of good and the restrictive of contrary evil—are called good in reference to things good in themselves. It is obvious then that the "ratio" of absolute good is not suited to all goods.

91. Then [5], at "**Let us separate**," he shows that the "ratio" of absolute good cannot belong to all goods in themselves. First [5] he declares his intention. We must consider that those things that are productive or preservative of goods in themselves, or restrictive of contraries, are called good because they are useful, and the nature of absolute good does not belong to the merely useful. Let us then separate from these useful things the things that are in themselves good and see whether they can be designated good according to one form, which is called absolute good.

92. Second [6], at "**But what would you**," he investigates this last point by proposing a question: what kinds of things should be considered goods in themselves? He presents this question in two parts. In the first he asks whether we are to call absolute whatever goods are sought for themselves alone to the exclusion of all others, so that they are not ordered to any further use. Such would be, for example, sight, and certain kinds of pleasure and honors. These things are sometimes sought for the sake of something else to which they are useful, but even if they have no use beyond themselves they are good and desirable in themselves. The

second part of the question asks whether there is any other absolute good besides the idea or form itself.

93. Third [7], at "**Wherefore the idea,**" he resolves the second part just mentioned. He concludes that if nothing else be a good in itself except the idea, then the idea will be a kind of exemplar whose likeness will be impressed on others. An exemplar is useless if it has no likeness to something else. Hence it follows that the idea is useless if there is no other good in itself.

94. Fourth [8], at "**Things in themselves,**" he resolves the first part in this way. If all the aforementioned things are good in themselves by partaking of the idea which is itself good, the same nature of goodness must appear in all of them, as we find the same nature of whiteness in snow and in white lead from the fact that they share in the one form. But this apparently is not true of the things mentioned above. Honor, prudence, and pleasure differ in their natures, that is, the nature of honor precisely as honor differs from the nature of prudence as prudence. Moreover, the nature of honor as a good differs from the nature of prudence as it is a good. There is not, then, one nature of goodness in all good things nor are they all desirable under the same aspect. Hence it remains that what is called absolute good is not something common as one idea or form common to all goods.

95. Then [9], at "**In what way,**" he handles a pertinent query. This inquiry belongs here since predication according to different reasons is made in the first of two ways according to meanings that are without any relation to any one thing. These are purely equivocal because it happens by chance that the same word has been used by one person for one thing and then by someone else for an entirely different thing, as is plainly evident in the case of different men having the same name. In another way, one word is used of several things with meanings not entirely different but having some sort of common likeness. Sometimes they agree in referring to one principle, as a thing is called military because it is a soldier's weapon (like a sword), or his clothing (like a uniform), or his transportation (like a horse). Sometimes they agree in referring to one end. Thus medicine is called healthy because it produces health, diet is called healthy because it preserves health, and urine in its turn is called healthy because it is a sign of health. Sometimes the agreement is according to a different proportion to the same subject, as quality is called being because it is a disposition of a being in itself, i.e., a substance, and quantity because it is a measure of substance, and so on. Or the agreement is according to one proportion to different subjects. For instance, sight has the same proportion to the body as intellect to the soul. Hence as sight is a power of a physical organ so also is the intellect a power of the soul without the participation of the body.

96. In this fashion, therefore, he affirms that "good" is predicated of many things not with meanings entirely different, as happens with things completely equivocal, but according to analogy or the same proportion, inasmuch as all goods depend on the first principle of goodness, that is, as they are ordered to one end. Aristotle indeed did not intend that the separated good be the idea and "ratio" of all goods but their principle and end.

Likewise, all things are called good by an analogy or the same proportion just as sight is the good of the body and intellect is the good of the soul. He prefers this third way because it is understood according to goodness inherent in things. The first two ways, however, are ascribed to a separated goodness from which a thing is not so properly denominated.

LECTURE VIII
This Matter Really Belongs to Another Science

TEXT OF ARISTOTLE (*1096b30–1097a14*) Chapter 6

1. *But perhaps we should now leave these subjects, for a precise determination of them properly belongs to another branch of philosophy. The same too may be said about the idea.*
1096b30–32; 97

2. *Even if there is some one good univocally predicated or if a separated good in itself does exist, it is obvious that it is not a thing produced or possessed by man. Now it is a good of this kind that we are looking for.*
1096b32–35; 98

3. *Perhaps some will think it better for the sake of the goods produced or possessed to obtain a knowledge of the separated good. Using this as a guide we will have a more thorough understanding of the objects that are good for us, and thus enlightened, we may acquire them.*
1096b35–1097a3; 99

4. *This reasoning certainly has some probability, although it does not seem to square with what we observed in the sciences.*

While sciences tend to some good and seek the necessary, they all neglect to use a knowledge of the separated good. But it is not reasonable to suppose that all artists and scientists would be ignorant of and would fail to seek a thing so advantageous to themselves.
1097a3–8; 100

5. *Indeed the separated good would be useless. What help does a knowledge of it afford a weaver and a carpenter in the practice of their trades? Or how is a man a better doctor or a better soldier by studying the idea itself? A doctor surely is not intent on health so understood but on the health of man in the concrete, or even better perhaps, on the health of this man. It is the individual man whom a doctor intends to cure. Enough has now been said on these topics.*
1097a8–14; 101–102

COMMENTARY OF ST. THOMAS

97. After the Philosopher has explained that there is no common idea of good, now [1] he shows that even if there were, it would not follow that happiness would have to be sought according to it. In regard to this he does three things. First [1] he presents a proof of his position. Second [3], at "Perhaps some will think etc.," he gives an apparent rejoinder. Third [4], at "This reasoning certainly etc.," he refutes it. He says first that the manner of predicating good according to one or different reasons must now be put aside because more accurate study of the matter properly belongs to another branch of philosophy, metaphysics. Likewise, the consideration of the idea of good is not pertinent to our purpose. As reason for these statements he maintains that if there were one good univocally predicated of all, or even if a separated good did exist in itself, it would obviously not be a thing produced or possessed by man. Now it is precisely such a thing we are seeking.

98. We are looking for the happiness that is the end of human acts. The end, however, of man is either some thing he does or some external thing. This can be the end of man because either it is produced, as a house is the end of building or it is possessed as a thing that is used. Now it is clear that the common or separated good cannot be the operation itself of man, nor is it something produced by man. Moreover, it does not seem to be something possessed by man as he possesses things used in this life. Obviously,

then, the common or separated good is not the good of man that is the object of our present search.

99. Then [3], at "**Perhaps,**" he gives an apparent rejoinder. Someone might say that the separated good, although not produced or possessed by man, nevertheless is the pattern of all the good produced and possessed. Now one who wishes to understand the copies ought to know the pattern. So it would seem that one should know the separated good itself for the sake of the goods produced and possessed. The reason is that, having the separated good as a guide, we will be better able to know and consequently better able to acquire the things that are good for us, as an artist looking at a model is better able to paint a likeness.

100. Then [4], at "**This reasoning certainly,**" he refutes this response by two reasons. The first [4] he takes from ordinary observation. While the reason given seems probable, he says that it does not appear to be in agreement with what we observe in other sciences. All sciences and arts tend to some good, as we said above (8), and to attain the end aimed at, each uses what is necessary for itself. None of them, though, uses the knowledge of this separated good. This would not be reasonable if some advantage could be derived from it. Therefore, the knowledge of this separated good contrib-

utes nothing to the goods produced and possessed.

101. He offers a second reason [5] at "**Indeed the separated good would be useless.**" This is taken from the very nature of the thing. He states that the good under consideration is altogether useless for the sciences and the arts, both in regard to their exercise, since a weaver or a carpenter is in no way aided in the practice of his art by a knowledge of that separated good, and in regard to the acquisition of a science or an art. No one becomes a better physician or a better soldier because he has studied the separated form of good. The reason he assigns is that an exemplar, at which it is necessary to gaze, must be in conformity with the work produced. Art, however, does not produce some good in common or an abstract good but a good that is concrete and individual. A physician does not intend health in the abstract but in the concrete, the health of this particular man. He does not give medicine to mankind in general but to this individual man. We must conclude then that the knowledge of a universal and separated good is not needed either for the acquisition or for the exercise of the sciences.

102. On this note he concludes his discussion of the opinions offered about happiness.

LECTURE IX
The Nature of Happiness

TEXT OF ARISTOTLE (*1097a15–1097b21*) Chapter 7

1. *Let us return again to a consideration of the good we are seeking in order to find out what it is. It seems that the good differs in different operations and arts. In medicine it is one good, in war it is another, and in other arts, still other goods. As the thing sought in every activity, the good is the end for the sake of which other things are done. This will be health in medicine, victory in war, a building in architecture, something else in some other art. In every activity and choice there is an end, the agent doing everything he does for the sake of that end. Therefore, if there is an end for all that we do, this will be the good intended. If there are many ends, there will be many goods, and in this case our discussion will go beyond the many until it arrives at that supreme good.*   **1097a15–24; 103–106**

2. *We must make a considerable effort to give this a fuller explanation. Apparently there are many ends, some of which we choose for the sake of something else like riches, flutes, and in general all instruments. It is obvious then that not all ends are perfect. But the ultimate end appears to be perfect. Wherefore, if there be only one of this kind, it will be what we are looking for. If there are a number of goods, then it is the most perfect of these. Now we call that object which is desired for its own sake more perfect than one that is desired for some further purpose. That which is never desired for any further utility is more perfect than the things desirable in themselves and for the sake of this further purpose. In the event that the object is perfect without qualification it will always be desirable for itself and never for anything beyond itself. Happiness in fact seems especially to be of this nature, for we choose it in every case for itself and never for something else. Honor and pleasure and knowledge and every virtue we do indeed choose for themselves, for we would choose every one of them even if no advantage accrued to us. But we choose them also on account of happiness because we hope to become happy. On the other hand, no one chooses happiness for the sake of these goods or for any other good whatsoever.*   **1097a24–1097b6; 107–111**

3. *The same seems to follow from the viewpoint of self-sufficiency, for the perfect good apparently is self-sufficient. We call it self-sufficient not only as adequate for a man living a solitary life by himself but also for his parents, children, wife, friends in general, and fellow citizens because this good naturally will include man's social life. But some limitation must be placed on the number provided for, since the extension to relatives, neighbors and friends might go on without limit. We must return to examine this question later. Now we call that self-sufficient which, taken alone, makes life desirable and lacking nothing. In our opinion happiness is of this nature.*   **1097b6–16; 112–114**

4. *Moreover, happiness without further addition will be the most desirable of all things. With any addition it will certainly be more desirable even though the addition be ever so slight. The reason is that the addition has increased the good, and a greater good is always more desirable. Therefore, happiness as the end of all human actions is the perfect self-sufficient good.*   **1097b16–21; 115–117**

COMMENTARY OF ST. THOMAS

103. After the Philosopher has thoroughly discussed the opinions of others about happiness, he now gives his own opinion on the subject. He divides this treatment into two parts. In the first [1] he shows what happiness is. In the second [Lect. XVIII; II], at "Having settled these matters etc." (1101b10), he

treats a particular property of happiness. He makes a twofold division of the first part. In the first division he shows what happiness is. In the second [Lect. XV], at "Many changes take place etc." (1100a5), he solves a particular problem. In regard to the first he does two things. First [1] he shows what happiness is. Second [Lect. XII], at "In our study of the principles etc." (1098b8), he shows that everything said about happiness is in agreement with this doctrine. In regard to the first he does two things. First [1] he proposes some general notions and conditions of happiness that are obvious to nearly everyone. Second [Lect. X], at "But to say that happiness etc." (1097b22), he inquires into the nature of happiness. In regard to the first he does two things. First [1] he states that happiness is the ultimate end. Second [2], at "We must make etc.," he lays down the conditions belonging to the ultimate end.

104. Therefore, he says first that, after completing the treatise (43–102) on the opinions of others, we must again return to a consideration of the good that is the subject of our inquiry—happiness—to find out what it is. Our first consideration about it must be that in different activities and arts the good sought differs. In the medical art the good sought is health, and in the military art victory, and in other arts some other good.

105. If it be asked what good is sought in every art and in every activity, we must know that it is the object for the sake of which all other things are done. In medicine everything is done on account of health, in war everything is done on account of victory, and in architecture everything is done for the sake of the building to be constructed. Likewise, in every other

activity the good sought is some one thing for the sake of which all other things are done. This good, the object of every activity or choice, is called the end, for the end is nothing else than that for the sake of which other things are done.

106. If, therefore, there should be some end immediately apparent to which all the products of all arts and human activities are directed, such an end will be the good unqualifiedly sought, that is, the thing intended in all human operations. But if at this point many goods arise to which the different ends of different arts are ordered, our reason will have to inquire beyond this number until it arrives at this one thing, that is, some obvious good. There must be, indeed, one ultimate end for man precisely as man because of the unity of human nature, just as there is one end for a physician as physician because of the unity of the art of medicine. This ultimate end of man is called that human good which is happiness.

107. Then [2], at "We must make," he lays down two conditions of the ultimate end. The first [2] is that it be a perfect thing; the second [3], that it be self-sufficient, at "The same seems to follow etc." The ultimate end is the ultimate term of desire's natural inclination. But in order that something be the ultimate term of natural inclination, two things are required. First that it be a thing actually having a species and not on the way to have a species. The generation of fire, for instance, is not terminated at the disposition to the form but at the form itself. Now a thing that has form is perfect, but a thing that is merely disposed to a form is imperfect. Therefore, the good that is the ultimate end must be a perfect good. Second, the term of the natural inclina-

tion must be integral since nature is not deficient in necessary things. Hence the end of human generation is not a deformed man but a perfect man. Likewise the ultimate end that is the term of desire must be self-sufficient as an integral good.

108. In regard to the perfection of a final good we must consider that, as an agent moves towards the end, so the end moves the desire of the agent. Hence the gradations of the ends must be in proportion to the gradations of the agent. Now an agent may be of three kinds. One, the most imperfect, does not operate by its own form but only insofar as moved by another, as a hammer forges a blade. Hence, the effect in the acquired form is not like this agent but like the one who moves the agent. Another, a perfect agent, operates indeed according to its form so that the effect is like it, as fire gives off heat, but nevertheless it must be moved by some prior principal agent. In this respect it partakes imperfectly of the nature of an instrument. A third agent, the most perfect, operates according to its own form and is not moved by any other.

109. The same is true in the order of ends. There we find an object desired not on account of some formal goodness existing in itself but only as useful for something else like bitter medicine. We find also an object is indeed desirable on account of what it is, but besides, it is desired for something else like sweet-tasting medicine. This is better than the first. But the most perfect good is that which is so desired for its own sake that it is never desired for the sake of anything else. Here then the Philosopher distinguishes three degrees of good. He says, as we have just stated (107–109), that we must give a more complete explanation of the ulti-

mate end by examining the conditions required for it.

110. There are also, it seems, many degrees of ends. Some of these we choose purely for the sake of something else, riches, for instance, which are sought for their utility in human living. Flutes on which music is made is another example. All such instruments are ends sought merely because of their usefulness. It is obvious that such ends are imperfect. The best end, namely the ultimate end, must be perfect. Therefore, if there is only one such end, it must be the ultimate end we are looking for. If, however, there are many perfect ends, the most perfect of these should be the best and the ultimate. What is desirable in itself is more perfect than what is desirable because of another. It clearly follows then that what is never desired for some thing beyond itself is more perfect than the things which, although sought for themselves, are also sought as a means.

111. Therefore, that is absolutely perfect which is always desirable for itself and never for another. But happiness appears to be of this nature, for we never seek it for something else but always for itself. We do choose honor, pleasure, knowledge, and virtue for themselves. We would choose them or have a desire for them even if no other good would come to us through them. In fact we choose them for happiness precisely because we think we will be happy in having them. But no one chooses happiness for them or for anything else. We conclude then that happiness is the most perfect good, and consequently the ultimate and best end.

112. Then [3], at "**The same seems,**" he treats the self-sufficiency of happiness—first [3] in regard to that which pertains to the nature of sufficiency,

and second [4], at "Moreover, happiness etc.," as regards the prefix "self." He says first that the same conclusion seems to follow from self-sufficiency as well as from perfection: happiness is the best and the ultimate end. Indeed, the latter two follow one another, for the perfect good seems to be self-sufficient. If it is not sufficient in some particular, it does not perfectly satisfy desire, and so it will not be the perfect good. It is called a self-sufficient good not because it suffices merely for one man living a solitary life but also for his parents, children, wife, friends, and fellow citizens as well, so that it will adequately provide the necessaries in temporal matters, instruction and counsel in spiritual matters for them too. Such extension is required because man is a social animal, and his desire is not satisfied in providing for himself but he wants to be in a position to take care of others. This, however, must be understood within limits.

113. If someone should want to extend such care not only to his own relatives and friends but even to the friends of his friends this would go on indefinitely so that no one could have a sufficiency and therefore no one could be happy, if happiness would require such infinite sufficiency. In this work the Philosopher speaks of happiness as it is attainable in this life, for happiness in a future life is entirely beyond the investigation of reason. To what extent a man needs a sufficiency to be happy will have to be investigated again elsewhere, namely, in domestic ethics or in political science.

114. Because he has already shown (112–113) that the perfect good called happiness ought to be sufficient not for one man alone but for all whose care is incumbent upon him, next he explains the nature of what is called self-sufficient. He says that the self-sufficient is that which, even when had by itself, makes life desirable and free from want. Happiness does this eminently, otherwise it would not terminate the inclination of desire if something that man needed remained outside it. Certainly everyone in need desires to have what he lacks. Hence it is clear that happiness is a self-sufficient good.

115. Then [4], at "**Moreover,**" he explains the nature of self-sufficiency as regards the expression "self." A thing is said to be self-sufficient when, taken apart from other things, it is sufficient. This can happen in two ways. First in such a manner that the perfect good, which is called self-sufficient, would be incapable of receiving an increase of goodness from another—a condition of the being that is totally good, God. As an additional part is not greater than the whole since the part itself is included in the whole, so too any good whatsoever added to God does not increase His goodness because the addition is good only by participating in the divine goodness. Likewise, a thing taken alone, no addition being made, is said to be sufficient in that it has everything a man absolutely needs.

116. In this sense happiness, the subject of our present discussion, has self-sufficiency because of itself it furnishes everything that is absolutely necessary, but it does not supply everything that can come to a man. Man can be made better by an additional good. But a man's desire for this does not remain unsatisfied because a desire controlled by reason, such as a truly happy man should have, is undisturbed by the things that are unnecessary even though attainable. Happiness, therefore, has this quality above everything else; it is desirable even when not augmented by other goods. However, if it

does receive an addition, be it ever so small, surely that is even more desirable. The reason is that by the accession, a superabundance or an increase of good is effected, and because something is a greater good, it is more desirable.

117. Last, he repeats in the epilogue the conclusion of what has been established (104–116), namely, that since happiness is the ultimate end of all our activities, it is the perfect good and self-sufficient.

LECTURE X
The Definition of Happiness

TEXT OF ARISTOTLE (1097b22–1098a20) Chapter 7

1. But to say that happiness is the best of goods seems merely to state something already perfectly obvious. However, since we wish to bring out more clearly what it is, we must investigate the matter further.   1097b22–24; 118

2. Perhaps this can be done by considering the activity of man. As the good of a flute player or sculptor or any artist, or of anyone who has some special activity, seems to consist in that activity and its skillful performance, so also the good of man who has an activity characteristic of himself precisely as man.   1097b24–28; 119–120

3. Have a weaver and a tanner a special work and activity while man precisely as man has none? Is he left by nature without a purpose?   1097b28–30; 121

4. If the eye, hand, foot, and each member have a proper operation, surely we will not refuse to concede an activity proper to man as man.   1097b30–33; 122

5. What therefore will it be? Life belongs even to plants and we are in search of something characteristic of man. The life of nutrition and growth must then be ruled out. Even the life of sense experience, which is a step higher, is shared with the horse, cow, and other animals. The remaining type of life belongs to the rational part of man and finds its expression in actions. This rational part either follows the dictates of reason, or it possesses and exercises the power of understanding. Of the two functions, the latter seems the more correct, for when we speak of reasoning, we signify the exercise of our rational powers.   1097b33–1098a7; 123–126

6. The function of man, therefore, is activity of the soul according to reason or at least not independent of reason. Now as a rule we classify in the same way the function of an artist and of a skillful artist, of a flute player and of a good flute player. This applies generally where skill is an addition to the function, for a flute player is one who plays the flute and a good flute player one who plays the flute well. If then we place the function of man in a certain kind of life, that is, of an activity of the soul according to reason, it will be proper to a good man to act well and to the best of his ability according to reason. In every case the good of man will consist in action conformable to virtue, and if there are a number of virtues, action conformable to the best and most perfect of them.   1098a7–18; 127–128

7. Further, it must extend to a complete life. A single swallow or one good day does not mean that spring has come. So one day (of goodness) or a short practice of virtue does not make a man blessed and happy.   1098a18–20; 129–130

COMMENTARY OF ST. THOMAS

118. After the Philosopher has laid down certain conditions of happiness, he here examines its definition. Concerning this he does three things. First [1] he shows the necessity of this inquiry. Second [2], at "Perhaps this can be done etc.," he searches for the definition of happiness. Third [Lect. XI], at "In this way, therefore etc." (1098a20), he shows that the definition given is insufficient and further inquiry must be made. He says first that all admit that happiness is the very best of things including the belief that it is the ultimate end and the perfect self-sufficient good. But it is rather obvious that some clarification must be made about happiness to give us a knowledge of its specific nature.

119. Then [2], at "**Perhaps this,**" he

investigates the definition of happiness in a twofold manner. First [2] he inquires into its genus, and second [6], at "The function of man," into its differences. The first point requires a threefold procedure. First [2] he shows that happiness consists in an activity of man. Second [3], at "Have a weaver etc.," he shows that there is an activity proper to man. Third [5], at "What therefore etc.," he shows which is man's proper activity. He says first that the nature of happiness can be made evident by consideration of human activity. When a thing has a proper operation, the good of the thing and its well-being consist in that operation. Thus the good of a flute player consists in his playing, and similarly the good of the sculptor and of every artist in their respective activity. The reason is that the final good of everything is its ultimate perfection, and the form is its first perfection while its operation is the second. If some exterior thing be called an end, this will be only because of an operation by which a man comes in contact with that thing, either by making it as a builder makes a house, or by using or enjoying it. Accordingly, the final good of everything must be found in its operation. If then man has some characteristic activity, his final good which is happiness must consist in this. Consequently, happiness is the proper operation of man.

120. But if happiness is said to consist in something else, either this will be a thing fitting man for an operation of this kind, or it will be something he attains by his operation, as God is said to be the beatitude of man.

121. Then [3], at "**Have a weaver**," he proves in two ways that there is an operation proper to man. He does this first [3] by activities that are incidental to man. It may happen that a man is a weaver, tanner, grammarian, musician, or anything else of the kind. In none of these capacities does he lack a proper operation, for otherwise he would possess them as empty and useless things. Now it is far more unfitting that a thing ordained by divine reason, as is the naturally existent, should be unprofitable and useless than a thing arranged by human reason. Since, therefore, man is a being possessing a natural existence, it is impossible that he should be by nature without a purpose, or a proper operation. There is then a proper operation of man no less than of the abilities that are incidental to him. The reason is that everything, either natural or acquired by art, exists by means of its form which is a principle of some operation. Hence as each thing has a proper existence by its form so also does it have a proper operation.

122. Second [4], at "**If the eye**," he proves the same truth by means of the human members. We must consider that the same mode of operation is found in the whole and in the parts of man, because, as the soul is the act of the whole body, so certain powers of the soul are acts of certain parts of the body, as sight is of the eye. But each part of man has a proper operation; for example, the operation of the eye is seeing; and of the hand, touching; and of the feet, walking; and so of the other parts. We conclude, therefore, that some operation proper to man as a whole exists.

123. Then [5], at "**What therefore**," he explores the nature of the operation proper to man. Now it is evident that each thing has an operation which belongs to it according to its form. But the form of man is his soul, whose act is life, not indeed life as the mere exist-

ence of a living thing, but a special vital operation, for example, understanding or feeling. Hence happiness obviously consists in some vital operation.

124. It cannot be said that man's happiness should arise from any kind of life, for even plants have life. But happiness is sought as a good characteristic of man since it is called a human good. Likewise, happiness must be different from the life of nutrition or growth, which even vegetables possess. From this we take it that happiness does not consist in health, beauty, strength, or great stature, for all these things result from activities of vegetative life.

125. On the step above the life of mere nutrition and growth is the life of sense experience. Again, this is not proper to man but is possessed by horses, oxen, and other animals. In this kind of life, then, happiness does not consist. So we conclude that human happiness is not found in any form of sense perception or pleasure.

126. Beyond the life of assimilation and of sense experience there remains only the life that functions according to reason. This life is proper to man, for he receives his specific classification from the fact that he is rational. Now the rational has two parts. One is rational by participation insofar as it is obedient to and is regulated by reason. The other is rational by nature as it can of itself reason and understand. The rational by nature is more properly called rational because a thing possessed intrinsically is always more proper than a thing received from another. Since, therefore, happiness is the most proper good of man, it more likely consists in the rational by nature than in the rational by participation. From this we can see that happiness will more properly be found in the life

of thought than in a life of activity, and in an act of reason or intellect than in an act of the appetitive power controlled by reason.

127. Then [6], at "**The function of man,**" he inquires into the specific differences of happiness. He divides the inquiry into two parts [6] according to the two specific differences investigated, and he begins the second part [7] at "Further, it must extend etc." First then we know from the premises (126) that the proper function of a man is a psychic activity in accord with reason itself or at least not independent of reason. The latter is mentioned because of the activity of the appetite controlled by reason. Now as a rule we find that the function of a thing generally and the efficient activity of that thing are of the same nature, except that allowance must be made for the part played by skill. For example, the function of a harpist is to play the harp, and the function of a good harpist is to play the harp well. The same is true of all other functions.

128. If, therefore, man's proper role consists in living a certain kind of life, namely, according to the activity of reason, it follows that it is proper to a good man to act well according to reason, and to the very good man or the happy man to do this in superlative fashion. But this belongs to the nature of virtue that everyone who has virtue should act well according to it, as a horse with good training or "virtue" should run well. If, then, the activity of the very good man or the happy man is to act well, in fact to act to the best of his ability according to reason, it follows that the good of man, which is happiness, is activity according to virtue. If there is only one virtue for man, his activity according to that virtue will be happiness. If there are a number of

such virtues for man, happiness will be the activity according to the best of them. The reason is that happiness is not only the good of man but the best good.

129. Then [7], at "**Further, it must extend,**" he inquires into the other specific difference of happiness. Continuity and perpetuity, to some extent, are also required for happiness. These qualities are naturally desired by the appetite of a person endowed with reason, who apprehends not a particular being, as our senses do, but also being in itself. Now being is of itself desirable. It follows then that, as an animal which apprehends a particular being by its senses desires that particular being, so also man apprehending being in itself desires it as always existing and not this particular being alone. So continuity and perpetuity, which are not found in the present life, belong to the nature of perfect happiness. Hence perfect happiness cannot be had in this life. However, the happiness attainable here must extend to a complete life, that is through the whole life of man. As the sight of a single swallow or one clear day does not prove that spring is here, so a single good deed is not enough to make a man happy. It arises rather from the continued performance of good deeds throughout his whole life.

130. From this discussion, therefore, it is clear that happiness is a virtue-oriented activity proper to man in a complete life.

LECTURE XI
The Task Before Us

TEXT OF ARISTOTLE (*1098a20–1098b8*) Chapter 7

1. *In this way, therefore, the good of happiness has been sketched, for the proper procedure is first to study a subject according to its general notions and afterwards to explain it more fully.*
                                                                    1098a20–22; 131

2. *It would indeed seem a reasonable mode of procedure to make a sketch of the matter and then to investigate its features one by one.*   **1098a22–23; 132**

3. *In this matter time seems to be, as it were, a good discoverer and a special assistant. Thus improvements in the arts have been due to successive artists, each making his own contribution.*
                                                                    1098a23–26; 133–134

4. *We must recall what was said before,[1094b11–27] that the same certitude is not to be expected in all sciences but in each according to the subject matter, and that the degree of certitude should be suited to the subject taught.*   **1098a26–29; 135**

5. *For a carpenter and a geometrician both study a straight line, but for different reasons. The carpenter does so to the extent that this is useful in his work; the geometrician as a student of truth wants to learn what a line is and how it differs from other figures. This distinction must be observed in other practical sciences lest they be burdened with discussions that are out of place.*   **1098a29–34; 136**

6. *Likewise, we must not seek causes equally in all matters but in some it suffices to establish a fact. This is the case with the first principles of a science since a principle is a starting point. Now, we understand some principles by induction, some by observation, some by custom and others in other ways.*   **1098a34–1098b4; 137**

7. *In all cases we must strive for a thorough knowledge of each set of principles according to their nature and must study how to define them properly.*

Principles are a great help in understanding what follows. Indeed a single principle seems to be more than half of the whole, for it furnishes answers to many of our questions. **1098b4–8; 138**

COMMENTARY OF ST. THOMAS

131. After the Philosopher has investigated the definition of happiness itself, he now shows in a twofold fashion what may still remain to be done. He indicates first [1] what remains to be done, and second [4], at "We must recall etc.," how this should be done. In regard to the initial point he does three things. First [1] he manifests what has been done and what remains to be done. He says that the final good of man which is happiness has been previously sketched (103–130). By a sketch he understands that knowledge through some common principles which indeed give a picture of the matter but not in such a way that the nature of that thing in particular is manifested. The reason for this is, as he himself says, that a thing should first be studied according to its general characteristics, i.e., by a general description which is like it and in a way extrinsic to it. Then with other matters clarified, we must take up what was previously sketched roughly and etch in the lines more sharply. For this reason he himself will take up in greater detail the treatise on happiness toward the end of this work (Bk. X, Ch. 6–8, 1176a30–1179a33; St. Th. Lect. IX–XIII, 2065–2136).

132. Second [2], at "**It would indeed seem,**" he assigns the reason for the

statement just made (131) saying that it seems natural for man to advance from the imperfect knowledge which covers a good description of things to a perfect knowledge of them by filling in the details. This he does by investigating first one part and then another, for it is according to man's nature to proceed by the steps of reason to a knowledge of the truth. Reason has this peculiar characteristic that it grasps the truth gradually, and as a consequence man properly perfects himself in knowledge little by little. On the contrary, separated or intellectual substances attain at once to the knowledge of the truth without any such investigation.

133. Third [3], at "**In this matter time**," he shows how a man may be helped in this procedure. He says that time seems to be, as it were, a discoverer of things well suited to sketch a subject and to be of special assistance in the work. The meaning is not that time itself contributes anything but that this help comes with time. If someone should busy himself investigating the truth for a period, he will be aided in the discovery of the truth by the passage of time. This is true in the case of the same person who will understand subsequently what he had not understood before, and also for different persons, as in the case of a man who learns the things discovered by his predecessors and adds something himself. In this way improvements have been made in the arts, in which a small discovery was made first and afterwards notable advances were made by the efforts of various men, each looking upon it as a duty to supply what is lacking in the knowledge of his predecessors.

134. But if, on the contrary, application to study be neglected, time is rather a cause of forgetfulness, as is said in the fourth book of the *Physics* (Ch. 12, 221a32; St. Th. Lect. XX, 604). We see indeed that the negligent individual forgets what he knows, and in human history we observe that many sciences which flourished among the ancients gradually have been lost when interest in them ceased.

135. Then [4], at "**We must recall,**" he shows how we must follow up the remainder of our task. First [4] he presents this in general by recalling to mind what was said in the introduction (32, 36), that we must not look for the same certitude in all subjects but in each according to the matter, namely, that which is proper to the subject taught.

136. Second [5], at "**For a carpenter,**" he makes specific what he has said. First [5] he takes up what must be handled differently for different subjects, and second [7], at "In all cases we must etc.," what must be observed generally in all subjects. In regard to the first he gives a threefold difference. The first of these [5] is the difference between a practical and a speculative science. He says therefore that a carpenter, who is a practical man, and a geometrician, who is a theorist, study a straight line for different reasons. A practical man—a carpenter—studies a line insofar as it is useful for his work, in sawing wood or in doing anything else of this nature. But the geometrician investigates what a line is—its qualities and its nature by considering the properties and potentialities. He is interested only in the study of truth. We must proceed in the first way to avoid many discussions that are out of place in the practical sciences. For instance, in moral matters we must steer clear of an exhaustive treatment of the intellect and the other powers of the soul to the neglect of the study of human acts

themselves. It is a serious defect in any science to squander time on matter outside the science.

137. He treats a second difference at **"Likewise, we must not"** [6]. Here he considers the difference between principles and deductions made from them. He says that the cause is not to be sought equally in all matters, otherwise we would proceed to infinity in demonstrating. But in some cases it is sufficient to show clearly that a thing is so. This is true of principles that are taken for granted in a science, since they are the beginning and cannot be reduced to anything previous. Now principles themselves are not manifested in the same way. But some are understood by induction from particular examples, for instance, that every number is even or odd. Some are taken from observation, as in nature, that every living thing needs nourishment. Some are taken from custom, as in morals, that sensual desires are diminished if we do not give in to them. Still other principles are manifested in still other ways, as in the practical arts principles are learned by a sort of experience.

138. Then [7], at **"In all cases we must,"** he sets down the procedure to be followed generally in all such matters. He says that a person ought to persist in going over thoroughly each set of principles, both speculatively and practically, in the way a knowledge of their nature demands and in studying how men understand them. Thus a man will learn how to distinguish one principle from another, and one set of principles from another set. A knowledge of principles is a great help in understanding the conclusions that flow from them. Indeed a single principle seems to be more than half of the whole, since the content of a science is contained in the principles. He adds that many answers we look for in a science are clear from one principle well understood and completely thought out.

LECTURE XII
Confirmation of the Definition

TEXT OF ARISTOTLE (1098b9–1099a7) Chapter 8

1. In our study of the principles we must carefully examine not only the conclusions and the premises from which the argument proceeds but also the considered views of others. Everything indeed will fall into agreement with what is true, and the truth will be quickly seen to be at variance with the false.   1098b9–12; 139–140

2. Goods have been classified as (a) external, (b) of the soul, and (c) of the body. Among these we hold that the goods of the soul are the best and most properly called goods. We attribute vital actions and operations to the soul. Therefore, our opinion must be sound for it is in agreement with that ancient one held by the philosophers.   1098b12–18; 141–143

3. It was stated accurately then that we identify the end with certain acts and operations. Thus happiness will be accounted one of the goods of the soul and not an external good.
                                                                    1098b18–20; 144

4. This coincides with the common notion that one who lives well and does well is a happy man. As a matter of fact, a good life appears to be nothing else but good activity.
                                                                    1098b20–22; 145

5. Everything that philosophers have looked for in happiness seems to be found in our notion of it.   1098b22–23; 146

6. Some have taught that happiness consists in virtue either generally, or specifically in prudence or in wisdom. Others say it consists in all or one of these virtues accompanied by pleasure, or at least not without pleasure. Still others would include a goodly share of external goods.   1098b23–26; 147–149

7. The rank and file together with some ancient philosophers held this last opinion, while a distinguished minority chose virtue. It is likely that no one was entirely wrong but each was right on one or more points.   1098b27–29; 150

8. Our definition of happiness is acceptable to those who hold that happiness consists in all or in one of the virtues, for virtuous activity clearly is something belonging to it.
                                                                    1098b30–31; 151

9. But besides, it makes a great difference whether the chief good be placed in possession or use, in habit or activity because a habit may exist in a person not actually performing any good, for instance, in one who is asleep or otherwise not engaged in any way whatsoever. This is not possible with an activity, for a man having it necessarily is active, and if the activity be virtuous he will act virtuously.   1098b31–1099a3; 152

10. At the Olympic games the best looking and strongest athletes do not receive the crown but the victorious competitors. So, too, among those who are good and best in virtuous living, those who perform righteous deeds become illustrious.   1099a3–7; 153

COMMENTARY OF ST. THOMAS

139. After the Philosopher has shown in general what happiness is, he proposes here to confirm the view he has just given, by what is said by others on happiness. Concerning this he does two things. First [1] he indicates his intention. Then [2], at "Goods have been etc.," he begins to carry it out. He says first that it is most important to have a principle thoroughly understood. The principle in practical matters is the ultimate end. To insure a more careful study of it, we must examine not only the conclusions and the

premises from which the discussion of the reasoner proceeds, but also the observations of others concerning the principle itself, namely, the ultimate end or happiness. He then assigns the reason for this procedure, that everything harmonizes with the truth. This is so because, as will be said in the sixth book (1143), truth is the good of the intellect. Good, as explained later (320), is achieved only in the concurrence of all the factors pertaining to the perfection of the thing.

140. Evil, on the contrary, comes about in a variety of ways by the defect of any single necessary qualification. No evil, however, can be found in which the good is completely corrupted, as will be shown in the fourth book (808). So not only all good things are in agreement with the good but even evil things in that they retain something of good. In a similar way all false things are in agreement with the truth insofar as they retain some likeness of truth. It is not possible that the mind holding a false opinion is completely deprived of the knowledge the truth, because by means of the true it immediately judges something false as lacking in the truth. This is what he understands by saying that the true is at variance with the false, somewhat like a right angle with an oblique angle.

141. Then [2], at "**Goods have been classified,**" he begins to carry out his intention, first in respect to what he has affirmed about happiness. In regard to this he does two things. First [2] he shows that what is the consensus of others is in agreement with his view (touching on the things said above by him at ". . . our opinion is in agreement"). Second [5], at "Everything that philosophers etc.," he shows that the points on which others disagree substantiate his view. In regard to the in-

itial point he does two things. First [2] he shows that what is commonly said by philosophers is in harmony with the given description of happiness. Second [4], at "This coincides with etc.," he shows that the same is true from what is generally affirmed by everyone. He proves the first observation in two ways, and

142. Initially [2] by dividing human goods into three classes. Of these some (a) are external, as riches, honors, friends, and such like. (b) Others are internal, and these again are of two kinds: (1) some concern the body, as physical strength, beauty, and health. (2) Others concern the soul, as knowledge, virtue, and the like. These are the chief goods, for external things are for the sake of the body, and the body for the sake of the soul, as matter for form and as an instrument for a principal agent. Now the common view of all philosophers is that the goods of the soul are the most important.

143. The Stoics and the Peripatetics held divergent views about some goods. The Stoics were of the opinion that some goods are not human goods because they do not make man better. The Peripatetics, that is, the followers of Aristotle, asserted indeed that external goods are the least of goods—the goods of the body being, as it were, means—but the chief goods in their judgment were the goods of the soul, by which man is made good. Other goods, however, according to them are called good insofar as they serve as means toward the principal goods. Thus happiness, since it is the chief good, must be numbered among the goods of the soul. Hence it is evident that the placing of happiness in an operation of the rational soul, as we said above (119–126), is in agreement with this ancient opinion common to all phi-

losophers, that the most important goods are those belonging to the soul.

144. Second [3], at "**It was stated accurately,**" he proves the same thing in a different way. The soul, he says, has two kinds of operations. Some of these pass into external matter, as weaving and building. Operations of this sort are not ends but things done for ends, that is, woven cloth and a completed house. Other operations of the soul, however, remain in the agent himself, as understanding and willing. Operations of this kind are ends. It was correctly stated (119–120), when we said that happiness is an operation and not a product, that acts and operations themselves are ends. Thus happiness is classified as one of the goods belonging to the soul and not an external good. Now in an immanent action the operation itself is a perfection and a good of the agent, but in a transient action the perfection and the good is found in the external effect. Hence not only is the aforesaid view in agreement with the position of the philosophers who hold that goods of the soul are the chief goods—and we said happiness was concerned with the operation of the soul—but also in this, that we place happiness in the operation itself.

145. Then [4], at "**This coincides,**" he shows that the things generally agreed on about happiness fit in with our view, for it was said above (45, 128) that everyone identifies living a good life and doing well with being happy. What we said is in agreement with this notion or understanding of happiness because a good life appears to be good activity and happiness seems to be of this nature. Those things truly are said to live which of themselves are moved to activity.

146. Then [5], at "**Everything that philosophers,**" he shows that even the

things in which others differ are in agreement with the aforesaid view. On this point he does three things. First [5] he brings forward the points on which men differ about happiness. Second [8], at "Our definition of happiness etc.," he shows that each of these is in agreement with the above view. Finally [Lect. XIV], at "Next we investigate etc." (1099b9), he asks and answers a certain question concerning the premises. In regard to the first he does three things. First [5] he states what he wishes to show, that everything that was looked for in happiness by various philosophers in various ways seems "to be found in our notion," that is, to be preserved in his view.

147. Second [6], at "**Some have taught,**" he gives different views on happiness. (1) The first [6] of these is that happiness consists in virtue. This has three variations. Some taught that (a) any virtue, but especially moral virtue which perfects the appetite under the control of the reason, constitutes happiness. To others it seemed that (b) happiness consists in prudence which perfects the practical reason. Still others think that (c) happiness is found in wisdom which is the ultimate perfection of the speculative reason.

148. (2) The second opinion [6] holds that all or any of these may constitute happiness provided that pleasure be added. This is understood in two senses. Some maintained that (a) virtue and pleasure almost in equal measure constitute happiness. Others (b), while placing happiness in virtue primarily, assign a secondary role to pleasure.

149. (3) A third opinion [6] adds to these elements of happiness a full measure of external goods, like riches and other material goods.

150. Third [7], at "**The rank and**

file," he indicates the difference in the persons holding the foregoing views. He says that the majority, that is, the common people and some men of antiquity who were not well-grounded in such matters, held some of these opinions such as pleasure and riches being necessary for happiness. But others, the minority but distinguished and famous men, held that happiness consisted rather in goods of the soul. It is likely that none of these was entirely wrong but that each of them was right on some points.

151. Then [8], at "**Our definition of happiness,**" he shows that these views are in agreement with what he previously assigned to happiness. First [8] he shows that this is true of the first opinion which held that virtue is happiness. Second [Lect. XIII], at "The life of those etc." (1099a9), he shows that it is true of the second opinion which adds pleasure. Finally [Lect. XIII], at "It seems, however etc." (1099a32), that it is true of the third opinion which adds external goods. In regard to the first assertion he does two things. First [8] he shows that the first opinion given is in agreement with his. Second [9], he shows how his opinion is better. He affirms, therefore, that the definition of happiness given above (130) as an activity according to virtue is acceptable to those who held that all virtue or one virtue constitutes happiness. It is evident that virtuous activity is something belonging to virtue.

152. Then [9], at "**But besides, it makes a great difference,**" he shows

that his own view is better: first [9], from reason; second [10], from a custom among men by the words "At the Olympic games." He says first that it makes a great deal of difference in external goods whether the most important good is in the possession of a thing or in its use—which is obviously better than possession. It is the same, too, with a habit of virtue and its operation or use which is of greater value than the habit. A habit can exist in a person who is not actually doing any good act, as in one who is asleep or not engaged in any way whatsoever. But this is not possible with an operation. It necessarily follows that that man should operate in whom there is an operation, and that he should produce a good effect if there be in him a virtuous operation. Consequently, a virtuous operation is more perfect than virtue itself.

153. Then [10] when he says "**At the Olympic games,**" he proves the same thing by a custom among men. Concerning this we must know that in Macedonia there is a very high mountain called Olympus where certain competitive sports, called Olympic games, were held. In these, not the strongest and best looking athletes but only the winning contestants received the crown, for those who did not compete were ineligible for the prize. So also, of those who are good and best in virtuous living, only those are illustrious and happy who actually perform good deeds. Hence it is better to say that happiness is a virtuous operation than virtue itself.

LECTURE XIII
Some Place Happiness in Virtue with Pleasure; Others Say External Goods Are Necessary for Happiness

TEXT OF ARISTOTLE (*1099a7–1099b8*) Chapter 8

1. *The life of those who act in accord with virtue is itself pleasurable.*   **1099a7; 154**

2. *Now pleasure is an activity proper to a living being. And everyone finds pleasure in what he is fond of, as a lover of horses finds pleasure in horses and a lover of shows in shows. In the same way a man who loves justice finds pleasure in just deeds, and in general one who loves virtue finds pleasure in virtuous activity.*   **1099a7–11; 155**

3. *Many experience pleasure in things that are in opposition to one another because the pleasure is not in accord with human nature. Men, however, who love the good find pleasure in the things which are inherently pleasurable. Of this kind are virtuous operations that therefore are pleasurable not only to virtuous men but also by their very natures.*   **1099a11–15; 156**

4. *This type of life then has no need of pleasure as an accessory but is pleasurable in itself.*
                1099a15–16; 157

5. *It should be added that every virtuous person rejoices in virtuous acts, for no one will call a man just who does not enjoy doing just deeds; no one will call a man generous who does not enjoy giving generously. Similarly we speak of men in other virtuous activities. From this it is clear that actions in accord with virtue are pleasurable in themselves.*   **1099a17–21; 158**

6. *Granting this, such actions are noble and good. In fact they have each of these qualities in the highest degree, if a good man judge truly in this matter as we have said he does. Happiness is the best, therefore, the noblest and most pleasurable of all things.*   **1099a22–25; 159–160**

7. *These qualities do not belong to different things as the inscription at Delos has it: "The best is the just thing, the most desired is health, and the sweetest to obtain is the heart's desire." But they are all found together in the most virtuous actions. In all these or in the best of these we say happiness consists.*   **1099a25–31; 161**

8. *It seems, however, that happiness stands in need of external goods, as we have said,*
                1099a31–32; 162

9. *for it is impossible, or at least difficult, for an indigent man to perform certain virtuous actions. Many good deeds become feasible, as we have pointed out, by the aid of friends and money and political influence. Then, too, the lack of other blessings, like noble birth, good children, and physical beauty spoil a man's happiness. One who is extremely ugly, lowborn, or alone in the world and without children cannot be entirely happy. Much less is he happy who is cursed with wayward children or evil associates or who has lost friends by death. In our opinion then it seems that happiness has need of external prosperity to a degree.*   **1099a32–1099b6; 163**

10. *For this reason some have identified good fortune with happiness. Others, however, prefer to place happiness in virtue.*   **1099b6–8; 164**

COMMENTARY OF ST. THOMAS

154. After the Philosopher has shown how the first opinion, which places happiness in virtue, is in agreement with the definition given above, and how it differs from it, he now does the same regarding the second opinion, which holds that happiness consists in virtue together with pleasure. On this point he does two things. First [1], he shows how this position harmonizes with his own opinion. Second [4], at "This type of life etc.," he shows how it differs. On the initial point he does two things. First [1] he states his propo-

sition; and then [2] gives evidence for his statement at "Now pleasure is etc." He says, therefore, first that the life of those who act virtuously is itself pleasurable. Happiness then which we place in an operation of virtue does not lack pleasure which, in their judgment, happiness requires.

155. Then [2], at "**Now pleasure is**," he proves his statement by showing first that virtuous actions should be pleasurable [2] and second [3], at "Many experience etc.," that this pleasure is preferable to others. He says first that pleasure is an activity proper to animals. Although we may attribute a natural appetite to inanimate things, we attribute pleasure only to a being having perception. From this we see that pleasure properly belongs to the activities of a soul, one of which is happiness. Now in activities of this kind, everyone finds pleasure in what he is fond of. As a lover desires the thing which is absent, so he takes pleasure in it when it is present. In this way a lover of horses finds pleasure in a horse; and a lover of shows, in a show. Hence it is evident that every virtuous person loves the activities of his own virtue as something agreeable to him. To the extent that the just man loves justice he will take pleasure in doing just deeds. It is universally true that virtuous operations are pleasurable to virtuous persons who love virtue.

156. Then [3], at "**Many experience**," he shows that this pleasure is preferable to others. He explains that the things pleasurable to the majority of men are contrary to one another. Prodigality, for instance, is a source of pleasure to the spendthrift, while hoarding delights the miser. This happens because these pleasures are not in accord with human nature common to all men, in other words with reason,

but rather with the corruption of an appetite departing from reason. But to men loving the good of virtue, these things are pleasurable that are inherently so, that is, that are agreeable to man according to reason, the perfection of his nature. Because of this, all virtuous men take pleasure in the same things—virtuous operations—which are naturally pleasurable to men according to right reason. These are pleasurable not only to men but also in their very nature. But evil actions give pleasure to men who get used to them by corrupt habits. Since then what is of itself and by nature such is preferable, pleasure arising from virtuous operation will be more delightful than other pleasures.

157. Then [4], at "**This type of life**," he shows in what respect this opinion may not be true. In regard to this he does two things. First [4] he states a proposition. Second [5], at "It should be added etc.," he gives evidence for his statement. We must, therefore, consider in regard to the first that those who hold that happiness consists in virtue together with pleasure seemed to intimate that virtue may have need of some extrinsic pleasure for the perfection of happiness. Aristotle disagrees here saying that the life of those who act in accord with virtue does not need pleasure as an extrinsic addition. That life is pleasurable in itself.

158. Then [5], at "**It should be added**," he gives evidence for what he has affirmed. In regard to this he does three things. First [5] he proves that virtuous life is pleasurable in itself. Second [6], at "Granting this, such actions etc.," he proves that it has nobility and goodness in a high degree. Third [7], at "These qualities do not etc.," he excludes a false opinion. He says first that to the reasons proving (154–156)

that virtuous actions are naturally pleasurable, we must add that pleasure necessarily belongs to virtue and pertains to its very nature. There is no virtuous person who does not enjoy the good deeds he does. He proves this inductively by saying that no one will call that man just who does not rejoice in doing just deeds. A similar observation may be made of the generous man and of a man practicing any virtue. The reason is that the act of a virtuous man is agreeable to him according to a proper habit, and as a consequence he derives pleasure from it. From this it is clear that virtuous actions are pleasurable in themselves and do not require pleasure external to them.

159. Then [6], at "**Granting this,**" he shows that actions in accord with virtue are not only pleasurable but also noble and good. Actions indeed are pleasurable to an agent when they are agreeable to him by reason of a proper habit. They are noble or beautiful because of a right order of circumstances as of parts, for beauty consists in a fitting arrangement of parts. They are good because ordered to the end.

160. He adds that each of these three qualities belongs to virtuous actions in a high degree. He proves this by the judgment of a good man. Such a man, since he has the right feeling for human works, judges them correctly. In another field the man with a healthy sense of taste will make correct judgment on flavors. But a good man judges that actions in accord with virtue are eminently pleasurable, noble, and good, so much so that he puts them before any other pleasures, beauties, or goods. Since, therefore, happiness consists in virtuous actions, it follows that happiness is the best, most beautiful, and most pleasant.

161. Then [7], at "**These qualities do**

not belong,**" he excludes from his doctrine a certain opinion. To understand this we must recall the inscription in Apollo's temple at Delos: "The best is what is most just. The most desired is to be healthy. The most delightful is that which one desires to enjoy." But the Philosopher says that these three qualities do not belong to different things, but all three belong to virtuous actions in all of which or in the best of which happiness consists. Therefore there is one—happiness—which is the best, most beautiful, and most desired or most delightful.

162. Then [8], at "**It seems, however,**" he comes to the third opinion which held that external goods are necessary to happiness. In regard to this he does three things. First [8] he brings out in what way this opinion may conform to the truth. Second [9], at "for it is impossible etc.," he gives evidence for his statement. Third [10], at "For this reason some etc.," he draws a conclusion from the premises. He says first that the third opinion given above (149) seems true in this that happiness has need of external goods, as was indicated previously (111).

163. Then [9], at "**for it is impossible,**" he gives evidence for his statement. In this matter we must consider that happiness needs certain external goods as instruments to perform the good deeds in which happiness consists. Touching on this he says that it is impossible or difficult for a man, who does not possess the means for gifts and expenditures, to practice certain virtuous acts. In many works of virtue we make use of friends, wealth, and political power, as in the case of someone who is a ruler or an official. There are some external goods which lend a beauty to happiness insofar as they make a man pleasing in the eyes of

others giving him a kind of splendor. At this point he adds that a lack of certain externals clouds a man's happiness making him as it were contemptible in the eyes of others, as is evident in a man who lacks noble birth, good children or even physical beauty. A man is not entirely happy when he is ugly since this makes him contemptible and despised. The same is true of one who is lowborn or who does not have good children. Much less is he happy who has wicked sons or friends, for this limits his virtuous activity. Likewise, it is incompatible with happiness to have lost good friends by death, for such a loss means grief of heart. So it seems then that happiness has some need of goods of fortune.

164. Then [10], at "**For this reason**," he comes to the conclusion that although happiness consists in virtuous actions, nevertheless it needs external goods to some extent. Such externals are called goods of fortune because they often fall into a man's lap, or, in bad luck, desert him. For this reason some have held that good fortune and happiness are identical. But others have identified happiness with virtue, as was said above (66–68).

LECTURE XIV
The Cause of Happiness

TEXT OF ARISTOTLE (1099b9–1100a5) Chapter 9

1. *Next we investigate whether happiness is something which can be learned or acquired by habit or attained in some way by training. Does it come to us by divine providence or by chance?*
1099b9–11; 165–166

2. *If anything is the gift of the gods to men it is reasonable to think that happiness, the best by far of all human goods, is the gift of God. But this subject is perhaps more properly treated in another science.*
1099b11–14; 167–168

3. *On the other hand, if happiness is not sent directly by God, but comes to men by virtue and study and exercise, it would still be judged most divine. As the reward and end of virtue it is apparently most excellent and divine and blessed.*
1099b14–18; 169

4. *It will also be common to human nature because, supposing it be the result of discipline and study, happiness can be had by all who are not impeded from virtuous action.*
1099b18–20; 170

5. *If such is the case, it is better that happiness be attained in this way than by chance, and it is reasonable to have it so. The things that are in accord with nature are as good as they can be by their very make-up. The same too can be said of what is produced by art or by any cause especially the highest.*
1099b20–23; 171

6. *Besides, to abandon the greatest and the best good to the vagaries of chance is most pernicious.*
1099b24–25; 172

7. *What we seek is evident from the definition of happiness as a certain kind of activity of the soul in accord with virtue. Of the remaining goods some are necessary to enrich happiness and others work instrumentally for its attainment.*
1099b25–28; 173

8. *This—that happiness is a virtuous activity—is apparent in the light of what was laid down in the beginning. [1094a27] There we stated that the end of political science is the best of human goods, for the principal aim of this science is the formation of men in such a way that they will become upright citizens and doers of good works.*
1099b28–32; 174

9. *That is why we do not say properly that a cow or a horse or any other animal is happy, for it is not possible for any of them to participate in moral activity.*
1099b32–1100a1; 175

10. *For the same reason children are not really happy, in that they have not yet attained sufficient age for the performance of virtuous deeds. Children are called happy because they give promise of happiness, while real happiness needs perfect virtue and a complete life as we have already pointed out.*
1100a1–5; 176

COMMENTARY OF ST. THOMAS

165. After the Philosopher has shown how different opinions are in agreement with the definition of happiness presented above, here he naturally investigates the cause of happiness. First [1] he states the question, and second [2], at "If anything etc.," he explains it. In regard to the first we must consider that happiness must proceed from either a *per se* and determined cause, or an incidental and indetermined cause, that is, chance. If from a *per se* and determined cause, this will be either human or divine. In the case of a human cause, the effect is produced in us in three ways: first by learning, as a science; second by practice, as a moral virtue; third by exercise, as a military drill and other things of this kind.

166. Accordingly he proposes the question in three parts. The first concerns a human cause. He asks whether happiness is something that can be learned as a science, or that can be acquired by habit as a moral virtue, or that can to some extent be had by training, like setting-up exercises. The second part concerns a divine cause. He asks whether happiness is something divine in us and a sharing in some way of godlike qualities which are above men. The third part concerns an incidental and indetermined cause. In other words he asks whether happiness occurs to man by chance.

167. Then [2], at "If anything," he explains the question first [2] as it were in parts by considering the individual sections of the question; and then [7], by offering a common reason taken from the definition of happiness at "What we seek is evident etc." In regard to the first he does three things. First [2] he shows it is eminently reasonable for happiness to have a divine cause. Second [3], at "On the other hand etc.," he shows that it is acceptable for it to have a human cause. Third [5], at "If such is the case etc.," he shows it is not fitting for it to be an effect of chance. He says first that if the gods (i.e., beings called gods by the ancients) make gifts to men, it is reasonable that happiness be the gift of the supreme God because it is the most excellent of human goods. It is obvious that a thing is led to a higher end by a higher virtue or power, for instance, man is led to a higher end by military art than by bridle-making. Hence it is reasonable that the ultimate end, happiness, should come to man from the highest power of all, that of the supreme God.

168. That separated substances may bestow something on men becomes evident from the fact that men and separated substances are alike in the power of intelligence. As the lower bodies are brought to perfection by the higher bodies so the lower intellectual beings by the superior intellectual beings. But there is no reason to delay any longer on this matter for it belongs rather to another science, metaphysics.

169. Then [3], at "On the other hand," he shows it is acceptable to say that happiness has a human cause. Although God is the principal cause, man does contribute something to happiness. Aristotle shows this in two ways. First [3], the fact that happiness has a human cause does not do away with its chief characteristic, that it is most excellent and divine. He says that if happiness is not a gift sent directly by God but comes to men by virtue as a thing acquired by habit, or by study as a thing to be learned, or by exercise as a thing to be had by training, nevertheless it seems to be something especially divine. The reason is that since happiness is the reward and end of virtue, it follows that it is something most excellent and divine and blessed. A thing is not called divine only because it comes from God but also because it makes us like God in goodness.

170. Second [4], at "It will also," he proves the same point in this way. Applicable to happiness is the idea that what belongs to the purpose of a nature should be something common to the things having that nature, for nature does not fail in what it intends except in the minority of cases. So if happiness is the end of human nature, it must be common to all or many having human nature. This principle remains intact if the cause be a human one. If happiness be had through discipline and study it could come to every-

one who is not impeded in the performance of virtuous works either by defect of nature as those who are naturally stupid, or by an evil habit which imitates nature. From this it is clear that the happiness spoken of by the Philosopher, does not consist in that contact with separated intelligence by which man can understand all things, as certain people have maintained. Such experience does not happen to very many, in fact, to no one in this life.

171. Then [5], at "**If such is the case,**" he rejects chance as the cause of happiness for two reasons. First [5], things that are in accord with nature are very good, since nature produces what is suitable. The same is true also of everything made by art or by any cause whatsoever. This is especially the case with the principal cause from which happiness, as the most excellent good, seems to depend. The reason is that art and all efficient causes operate for the sake of good. It follows, then, that every agent should most aptly arrange, as far as possible, what he does. This particularly applies to God who is the cause of all nature. The things which are in accord with nature seem to be better from their very make-up. But it is better that happiness springs from a *per se* cause, either divine or human, than from chance which is an incidental cause, for what is *per se* is preferable to what is incidental. Consequently, chance is not the cause of happiness.

172. He offers a second reason [6] at "**Besides, to abandon.**" Happiness is the most perfect of all human goods because all others are ordered to it as to an end. Now it would be very harmful if this good were to depend on chance, for other goods would be much more subject to chance. As a result man's zeal in pursuing these goods would vanish, a most perilous situation. Chance, therefore is not the cause of happiness.

173. Then [7], at "**What we seek,**" he settles the question we are considering. He says it is evident, from the definition already given (130), where the truth lies in our investigation of the present question. As was previously indicated (127–128), happiness is an activity of the rational soul in accord with virtue. Now what is in accord with virtue is according to reason influenced by some divine cause. But what is according to chance is contrary to reason. It follows that happiness does not spring from chance but from some human cause immediately and from a divine cause principally and ultimately. Certain other goods, however, in which chance plays a part, do conduce to happiness, but happiness does not chiefly consist in them. Some, though, are necessary for a certain enrichment of happiness, and others work instrumentally to attain it, as we have said (169). But we must not attribute happiness to chance because of these secondary goods.

174. Then [8], at "**This—that happiness,**" he shows that the previously discussed definition of happiness is in agreement not only with the opinions of others on happiness but also with observations made in keeping with his own opinion. In regard to this he does two things. First [8] he shows what concurs with his earlier remarks about happiness (19–42). Second [9], at "This is why etc.," he concludes what is the correct view in accord with this opinion. He says first "this"—that happiness is an activity in accord with virtue—"is apparent," that is, in harmony with the words of the introduction (19–42). We said there that the best

human good, happiness, is the end of political science whose goal manifestly is activity in accord with virtue. Political science is especially concerned with framing laws and apportioning rewards and punishments in order to develop good citizens and doers of good works. This is to operate in accord with virtue.

175. Then [9], at "**That is why,**" he concludes from the reason assigned that happiness cannot be attributed to certain beings according to what has been correctly laid down. First [9] he says that no dumb animal is called happy, and rightly so because none of them can share in the activity of virtue which is in accord with reason and which constitutes happiness.

176. Second [10], at "**For the same reason,**" he also excludes children from happiness saying that for a similar reason they cannot be called happy. Lacking sufficient age they have not attained that full use of reason requisite for the performance of virtuous actions. If children are sometimes called happy, this is because we see in them signs that give promise of future excellence. At present, therefore, they are not happy, for happiness as we have indicated (127–129) needs perfect virtue to be not only a good but the best operation and a life perfected by good activity which is continuous and permanent.

LECTURE XV
A Problem About Happiness

TEXT OF ARISTOTLE (*1100a5–1100b7*) Chapter 9–10

1. *Many changes take place in life and all kinds of fortune are met with in the course of a lifetime. Sometimes a very prosperous man falls into great misfortune in old age as we read of Priam in the epic poems. Certainly no one calls a man happy who has enjoyed such goods of fortune and then ends his days in misery.*   1100a5–9; 177–178

2. *Is no man then to be called happy so long as he lives, but must we consider the end of life, as Solon believed?*   1100a10–11; 179

3. *If we hold this to be so, it follows that a man will be happy only when he dies. But such an opinion is altogether unreasonable especially for us who maintain that happiness is a kind of activity.*   1100a11–14; 180

4. *We may say that a dead man is not happy and that Solon did not wish to assert that he is. We may say Solon meant that a man will safely be called happy at death because he is then beyond the reach of evils and misfortune. This meaning, though, gives rise to a problem. It seems that the dead no less than the living, even though unaware of it, are influenced by good and evil, for instance, by honors and dishonors, by the prosperity and misfortune of children and of descendants in general.*   1100a14–21; 181–182

5. *A difficulty, however, here presents itself. It may happen that a man lived happily to a ripe old age and has died a worthy death, and afterwards many changes take place in regard to his children. Some of them are good and have gained a position in life they well deserve, while others are just the opposite. Indeed, it does happen that children are quite different from their parents. Now it is incongruous that a dead man should suffer these same changes so that he at one time becomes happy and then again unhappy. On the other hand, it seems unfitting that the affairs of the children should in no way affect the parents, at least for a certain length of time.*   1100a21–30; 183–184

6. *But we must return to our first problem. Perhaps from its solution light will be shed on our present difficulty. Let us suppose that we must look at the end and then declare each man happy, not because he is happy but because he formerly was happy. How nonsensical, if when a man is happy we may not affirm it of him since we are unwilling to call the living happy on account of the changes in the present life, because we think happiness permanent and not easily changeable, and because fortune often goes in cycles for the same persons. Obviously, if we use fortune as our norm we will very often call the same person happy and again unhappy as though he were a chameleon, and declare him happy and yet insecure in his happiness.*   1100a31–1100b7; 185–186

COMMENTARY OF ST. THOMAS

177. After the Philosopher has shown what happiness is, he here raises a problem about happiness, namely, whether anyone can be called happy in this life. On this point he proceeds in three steps. First [1] he gives the reason for the problem. Second [2], at "Is no man then etc.," he presents the problem. Third [Lect. XVI], at "We ought not to make etc." (1100b7), he gives the solution. He says first that many changes take place in life; for life rarely remains the same either good or bad. It is stable in few things, changing from good fortune to bad and from bad to good. Sometimes, indeed, the changes occur in small matters and sometimes in great, and sometimes in

matters of medium importance. Changes of this sort occur at any age, in adolescence, maturity, or old age.

178. Sometimes it happens that a man has had an abundance of external goods all his life, and in old age falls into great misfortune as Priam did, according to the epic poem of Homer. No one will call that man happy who has enjoyed such goods of fortune and ends his life in misery. The fact that one has been reduced from great prosperity to extreme wretchedness seems to add to his misery.

179. Then [2], at "**Is no man then,**" he proposes the difficulty. But first [2] he asks a question. Second [3], at "If we hold this etc.," he brings up an objection. Third [4], at "We may say etc.," he rejects a particular answer. First then he asks the question about the view of Solon, one of the seven wise men, who framed the laws of the Athenians. Considering man's life as subject to the changes of fortune, Solon said that no one ought to be called happy so long as he lives, but only at the end of his life. In light of what happened to Priam, the question arises whether any man is to be called happy so long as he lives. Is it best, as Solon holds, to consider the end of life if happiness continues that long, in order that a man may be called happy? Or should this be disregarded?

180. Then [3], at "**If we hold,**" he brings up an objection to the question that was asked, and disproves the saying of Solon. If we hold as true what Solon said, it follows that man will be happy only when he dies. But this seems unreasonable on other grounds, for example, because death is the worst of evils and happiness the greatest of perfections. Besides, happiness is a kind of activity, as we indicated above (119–126). But a dead man does not seem to have an activity. The dead,

therefore, cannot be called happy. It should be noted that the Philosopher is not here speaking of happiness in a future life, but of happiness in the present life. Can we attribute happiness to man while he lives or only at death?

181. Then [4], at "**We may say,**" he rejects an answer, and this for two reasons. He gives the second reason [6] at "But we must return to our first problem etc." In regard to the first he does two things. Initially [4] he proposes an answer and rejects it. Second [5] by reason of this he brings up a problem at "A difficulty, however, here presents itself etc." In regard to the first point we must consider that the previous argument of Aristotle showed that a man is not happy in death. Now this will be granted by anyone who says that a dead man is not happy: Solon did not mean that a man is happy when he dies. But he did mean that when a man is dead, a valid argument can be made about his happiness, because the dead man is now beyond the danger of evils and misfortune so that there is no longer any doubt about it. But he rejects this answer saying it contains an uncertainty.

182. A dead man differs from a living man in the loss of consciousness. A good thing or a bad thing—such as defamation of character, the murder of his children, or the loss of riches— could conceivably happen to someone still living, and he might not feel it precisely because he does not know about it. By the same argument, it seems, some good or evil could happen to a dead man who is unaware of it. Here Aristotle is talking about good and evil in public life as his examples— "honor and dishonor"—show. Sometimes certain honors are given to the dead when they are praised and their memory celebrated. Likewise certain

dishonors are heaped upon them, for example, when their bodies are exhumed and their remains burned. Also something good or bad can happen to them by reason of the prosperity or misfortune of their children and their grandchildren. Then it would seem that not even the dead are entirely beyond evils and misfortunes. Consequently, even in death men cannot be called happy.

183. Then [5], at "**A difficulty, however,**" he interposes a difficulty arising from the premises. Such things as the prosperity and misfortunes of children and grandchildren present a problem for him. It happens sometimes that a man lives happily—in the way we have described happiness—to old age and dies a worthy death but afterwards many changes take place in regard to his children, some of whom are good after the example of a worthy father, but others just the opposite. Indeed it does happen that children are quite different from their parents: good parents have wicked children and wealthy parents, needy children. From this statement something unfitting seems to follow for both parents and children.

184. It is inappropriate that a dead man should suffer change because of misfortunes of this sort, so that he who at one time is happy now becomes unhappy. On the other hand it seems improper if, at least for a short time after death, the lot of children should in no way affect the happiness of deceased parents.

185. Then [6], at "**But we must return,**" he gives a second reason for rejecting the previous answer. He says

that, passing over the second problem, we must return to the first, the solution of which will shed light on the truth of the second. Now it seems that the answer given is not consistent. If we must look to the end of life and then call a man happy, not because he is then truly happy but because he was previously happy, there seems to be this inconsistency: that when a man is happy, we may not say of him that he is happy, since the truth of a statement in the past is founded on the statement being true at the time it actually occurred. Therefore *"fuisse"* is true of a thing because *"esse"* was true of it.

186. But some were unwilling to call a man happy because of the changes in the present life inasmuch as they were under the impression that happiness was something permanent and not easily changeable; otherwise it would not satisfy the natural desire. For everyone naturally desires to remain secure in the good he possesses. But the wheel of fortune very often turns for the same persons, so that they change from good fortune to bad and conversely. Thus it is evident that if in judging about happiness we should follow the consideration of fortune and should say of someone that he is happy in this life, very often we will say of one and the same person that he is happy and again that he is unhappy. In this way we will be saying that a person is happy after the manner of a chameleon, an animal which changes color in keeping with different surroundings. We will be declaring that the happy are insecure in their happiness which is contrary to the nature of happiness.

LECTURE XVI
Happiness and Changes of Fortune

TEXT OF ARISTOTLE (*1100b7–1101a21*) Chapter 10

1. *We ought not to make changes of fortune our norm because good and evil do not consist in these, although human living does stand in need of external goods, as we have indicated. But virtuous action is the dominant factor in human happiness just as vicious action is the dominant factor in man's unhappiness.*   1100b7–11; 187

2. *This contention is strengthened by what we have just learned, for virtuous actions are more uniformly constant than other human activities. They are more abiding apparently than the speculative sciences. Among the virtues the most noble seem to be more lasting both because the happy man is quite intent on them and because he lives according to them at all times. For this reason man does not forget about the virtues.*   1100b11–17; 188–190

3. *The happy man will have what we had inquired about, for he will be happy all his life. He will always, or nearly always, perform virtuous actions and be contemplating the life of virtue.*   1100b18–20; 191–192

4. *Because he is really good and four-square without reproach, he will bear all changes of fortune most admirably and will be eminently prudent in all matters.*   1100b20–22; 193

5. *Many events differing in importance happen by the change of fortune. A short run of good luck or of bad luck clearly does not notably affect life. But great and frequent good fortune will be an occasion of a happier life, for external goods were made to enrich human life and their use is becoming and a means of virtue. On the contrary, great and frequent evils cause the happy man external annoyance and internal affliction bringing about sadness and hindering many good works. However, even here the good of virtue shines forth when a man gracefully endures frequent and major misfortunes not because he is insensible to the sorrow but because he is courageous and magnanimous.*   1100b22–33; 194–197

6. *If virtuous actions play the dominant role in a happy life that we have indicated, a happy person will not become unhappy nor will he sometimes perform hateful and evil actions. As a truly good and wise man in the estimation of all, he will bear the changes of fortune in a becoming manner. He will always make the best of the existing circumstances like a general who employs his present forces to the best advantage in battle or like the cobbler who makes the best shoe possible from the leather at hand or like other artisans in similar circumstances. This being the case, then the unhappy man will certainly not become happy. We can say too that the happy man will not fall into the misfortunes of Priam. He will not easily be moved. He will not be changed from happiness by minor misfortunes but only by great and frequent ones. After such catastrophies he will not become happy again soon but, if indeed he does, it will take an abundance of good and noble deeds during a long period.*   1100b33–1101a13; 198–199

7. *What therefore hinders us from calling that man happy who acts in accord with perfect virtue and has sufficient external goods not for a short time but all during life? We must also add that he will live his whole life in this way and will die in a manner befitting reason because the future is not clear to us; and we understand happiness as an end altogether perfect in every respect. If this be so, we shall call those happy in this life—happy we must remember as men—who have now and will have the conditions we presented. Now we have said enough on these points.*   1101a14–21; 200–202

COMMENTARY OF ST. THOMAS

187. After explaining his problem, the Philosopher here solves it. First [1] he solves the principal problem. Second [Lect. XVII; 2], at "It seems quite

foreign etc." (1101a22), he solves the lesser one. In regard to the first he does two things. First [1] he introduces a point necessary for the solution of the problem. Second [2], at "This contention is strengthened," he applies it to the solution of the present problem. In regard to the initial point we should consider that while happiness consists essentially in the performance of virtuous actions, external goods that are subject to fortune are in a way tools of happiness. Hence he says we ought not to make changes of luck the norm for reckoning a man happy or unhappy, because man's good or evil, which is judged by reason, does not consist principally in such changes of luck. Human living however does stand in need of external goods as means, as has been indicated (163). But virtuous actions are the principal and predominant factor in a man's happiness so that he can be called happy principally because he acts virtuously. On the contrary, vicious actions are powerful and dominant in the opposite state, which is misery, so that he is truly miserable who is occupied with evil deeds.

188. Then [2], at "**This contention is strengthened,**" he applies what was said just now (187) to the solution of the problem. First [2] he shows that deeds of virtue are especially long-lasting compared to other human things. Second [3], at "The happy man will have etc.," he shows that in keeping with what was said, happiness can endure all during life. Third [6], at "If virtuous actions play etc.," he shows that all inconveniences are avoided if we follow this teaching. He says first that what we have now learned (186) about the permanence of happiness confirms our contention that virtuous actions are of foremost importance in happiness. The reason is that no human ac-

tivity is found so uniformly constant as these. It is clear that external goods, and even internal bodily goods, because material and corporeal, are subject to change by their nature. But the goods that belong to the soul are changeable only indirectly, and so less liable to change. Of the goods pertaining to a man's soul, some belong to the intellect as the sciences, and some to the activities of living as the virtues. These virtues are indeed more lasting than the disciplines, i.e., the demonstrative sciences.

189. However, this must not be understood as referring to the matter, for demonstrative sciences have as their object necessary things which cannot be otherwise. It is to be understood rather as referring to the exercise of the act. Now we do not have the same opportunity to cultivate the study of the sciences continually as we do to practice virtue, for situations are constantly arising where we must act according to virtue or contrary to virtue as in the use of food, association with women, conversations with other men, and similar actions with which human life is continuously concerned. Hence it is reasonable that the habit of virtue be more firmly fixed in man because it is used more than the habit of science.

190. Among the virtues themselves, the most noble seem to be more lasting both because they are more intense and because men work more constantly to live according to them. Such are the virtuous operations in which happiness consists, because they are most perfect as has been proved (128, 130, 150, 160, 164). This is naturally the reason why man does not forget to be virtuous because he continually has the occasion to exercise the virtues. Another reason too is that virtue consists chiefly in the inclination of the appetite

which is not destroyed by forgetfulness.

191. Then [3], at "**The happy man
will have,**" he shows that according to
this doctrine happiness can last a lifetime. He says that virtuous actions are
most lasting, as was pointed out (188–
190). If then happiness be placed principally in them as we have said
(153–190), it would follow that the
happy man will have what was inquired about in a previous question,
that is, he will be happy all his life. He
proves this first [3] from the actions
themselves at "He will always."

192. One who has a habit perfectly
can act always or almost continually
according to that habit in everything he
does. The happy man possesses perfect
virtue, as was explained above (187,
188). Consequently, he can always or
nearly always perform virtuous actions in a life of activity and can attentively consider in a life of
contemplation.

193. Second [4], at "**Because he is
really good,**" he shows the same thing
from the goods of fortune, an object of
lesser importance in happiness. He
says [4] that the happy man will bear
all changes of fortune most admirably
and will be eminently prudent in all
matters, since he is really a good man
and not superficially so. He is "four-
square" without reproach, or, as some
have explained, perfect in the four car-
dinal virtues. But this interpretation
does not seem to be according to the
mind of Aristotle who has never been
found making such an enumeration.
The tetragon does however indicate
something perfect in virtue after the
manner of a cube, which has six
squared surfaces and so lies evenly on
any surface. Similarly the virtuous person is of an even temperament in any
fortune. Since, therefore, it pertains to

virtue to bear all fortune becomingly,
obviously the happy man will not
cease to act virtuously because of any
change of fortune. He shows this then
in detail [5], as it were by way of division, when he adds "Many events."

194. He says that since many good
and bad things differing in importance
may happen by changes of fortune, it
is evident that a short run of good luck
and likewise a short run of bad luck do
not change life from happiness to misery or conversely. If, however, they are
great and frequent they will be either
good or bad. If good, they will make a
man's life happier. The reason is that,
as was indicated above (169, 173), happiness has need of external goods
either as adornments or as means of
virtuous actions. In regard to adornments he says that they were made to
enrich the life of man. As to the means
of virtuous actions, he says that the use
of external goods is becoming and virtuous insofar as virtues make use of
them to perform worthy deeds.

195. If on the contrary the evils
should be frequent and great, they will
cause the happy man external annoyance and internal affliction, because internally they bring about sadness and
externally they hinder good works.
However they do not eliminate virtuous action entirely, because virtue
makes good use even of misfortunes
themselves. In this way the good of
virtue shines forth insofar as a man
gracefully endures frequent and great
misfortunes, not because he may not
feel the sorrow or sadness as the Stoics
held but, being courageous and magnanimous, his reason does not succumb to such afflictions.

196. This, in fact, was the difference
between the Stoics and the Peripatetics, whose leader was Aristotle. The
Stoics held that sorrow in no way af-

flicts a virtuous man, because, in their view, corporeal or external things are not in any sense a good of man. The Peripatetics, on the contrary, said that a virtuous man is affected by sadness, yet this does not overwhelm reason but is moderated by it. In their opinion corporeal and external things do not constitute the greatest but the least good of man and this in the degree that they help him.

197. But it should be observed that some change could happen that would entirely take away a man's happiness by hindering virtuous action altogether. For example, some sickness could cause madness or insanity or any other mental breakdown. Since happiness may not be attained except by living humanly or in accord with reason, when the use of reason is gone, human living is not possible. Consequently, in what concerns living humanly, the condition of madness must be equated with the condition of death. So seemingly we must say the same of him who continues in virtuous action until loss of mind as if he had continued until death.

198. Then [6], at "**If virtuous actions play,**" he excludes the unsuitable things that seemed to follow from the premises. He says that if virtuous actions play the dominant role in happiness, as we have asserted (188), it will not follow that the happy man becomes unhappy on account of misfortunes, or that because of misfortune he will perform actions contrary to virtue. But by reason of his perfect virtue the happy man—it can be predicted—will bear all changes of fortune becomingly like a truly good and wise man. In other words he will act according to virtue under every condition. Even if he does not perform the same actions in every contingency, he will always

act most nobly according as the circumstances are favorable or unfavorable. He will use the material that fortune provides in the way that a good general with an awareness of the condition of his army ought to dispose his existing forces to the best advantage in battle. A commander will do one thing if he has seasoned troops and another if he has an army of raw recruits. Likewise, a cobbler ought to make the best shoes possible from the leather at hand. He will of course make better shoes from one piece of leather than from another. The same may be said of all other craftsmen.

199. If this is so, the unhappy man will not be made happy by any additional good fortune. The reason is that he will use that good fortune badly and the evildoer will always remain unhappy. Likewise the happy man will not fall into the misfortune of Priam. First because he will prudently guard against it. Second, because if he should be stricken unexpectedly, he will bear it most gracefully, as we have pointed out (198). He will not, therefore, be changed easily from happiness to unhappiness by any misfortune whatsoever except by frequent and great changes that deprive him of the use of reason. If he has been made unhappy, he will not readily become happy again but he will need an abundance of great and noble things acquired after a long time by the exercise of virtuous action and by the restoration of external fortune.

200. Then [7], when he says "**What therefore,**" he brings to an end his own thoughts on happiness. He says that nothing hinders us from calling that man happy who acts in accord with perfect virtue and has sufficient external goods for virtuous activity, not just for a short time but all during life or at

least for a long period. This is enough for a man to be called happy in this life.

201. If we wish to understand happiness in the most perfect sense possible, we must add to the definition of happiness that the happy man will live his whole life as we have indicated (129) and will complete it by dying in a manner befitting reason. It appears that this condition must be added because the future is unknown to us. Now all that is perfect and best seems to belong to the definition of happiness, since it is the ultimate end. In this second way Solon was speaking of happiness. If the case be as just de-scribed (200) we shall call those men happy in this life who have now and will have in the future the conditions we have laid down (177–186).

202. But because these things seem not to measure up in all respects to the conditions required for happiness above (104–117), he adds that those we call happy are men, subject to change in this life, who cannot attain perfect beatitude. Since a natural desire is not in vain, we can correctly judge that perfect beatitude is reserved for man after this life. He concludes with the remark that we have said enough on these points.

LECTURE XVII
The Fortune of Friends and Happiness of the Dead

TEXT OF ARISTOTLE (*1101a22–1101b9*) Chapter 11

1. *It seems quite foreign to the nature of friendship and contrary to the common opinion to say that changes in the fortunes of descendants and of friends have no influence on man's happiness.*
1101a22–24; 203

2. *Many and vastly different things happen in fortune. Since some of these touch us closely and others remotely, it would be a long, even an endless, task to determine the extent of each. It will be enough to discuss the subject in broad and general terms. Some of the fortunes affecting a man himself are of sufficient importance to better the conditions of life while others are of lesser moment. We can affirm the same of the events which happen to friends generally.*
1101a24–31; 204–205

3. *It makes much more difference that an experience should happen to the or the dead than that certain injustices and evils should be indicated as happening before the action of the drama or should be committed in the course of the drama. We must take this difference into consideration.*
1101a31–34; 206–208

4. *Perhaps we should rather inquire whether the dead share in any prosperity or adversity. It seems from what has been said that if any event either good or bad affects the dead, it will be fleeting and insignificant in itself or in its effect upon them. If this be the case, then the event will not be so great or of such a nature as to make happy those who are not happy, or to take away happiness from those who have it.*
1101a34–1101b5; 209

5. *The good actions done by friends, therefore, do have some influence on the dead. Misfortunes too seem to affect them. But all these take place in such a way and to such an extent that they do not make the happy unhappy nor produce any other like changes.*
1101b5–9; 210–212

COMMENTARY OF ST. THOMAS

203. After the Philosopher has solved the principal doubt concerning the change of fortune for the happy man, here he settles a doubt raised above (183) about the change of fortune in regard to friends. On this point he does two things. First [1] he compares the good fortunes and misfortunes happening to friends with those which happen to man himself. Second [3], at "It makes much more etc.," he compares the events that happen to the dead with what happens to the living. In regard to the first he does two things. Initially [1] he proposes that the things that happen to one's friends affect the man himself. Second [2], at "Many and vastly different etc.," he shows what the things are and what their nature is. He affirms, first, that to say that the prosperity or adversity of great grandchildren or of descendants in general and of all friends would have no effect on the happiness of a man, living or dead, seems to be incongruous for two reasons. Primarily indeed, because it would be contrary to the nature of friendship that is a union among friends to such an extent that one considers as his own what belongs to the other. Then too, because this would be contrary to the common opinion which cannot be entirely false.

204. Then [2], at "**Many vastly different things**," he shows what events may affect the happiness of a friend and the nature of these events. He says that many and vastly different things

happen in prosperity or adversity, in kind, in quantity, in time, and in other respects. Some of them touch us closely and others remotely. If then we should wish to determine in every case which of them affect the man himself and which do not, the task would be a long one, in fact almost endless, because differences happen in an infinite variety of ways.

205. With regard to the fortunes affecting a man himself it is sufficient to note in general, and so to speak, typically, by way of distinctive qualities or superficial likeness, that some acts of fortune are of sufficient importance and influence to change the condition of human life and do contribute to happiness. Others, however, are of lesser moment and help man's life but little. The same thing takes place in the events that happen to any of our friends except that things even of lesser moment happening to blood-relatives affect us more.

206. Then [3], at "It makes much more difference," he shows in what manner the changing fortunes of friends affect a person—it is rather evident how this touches a man while he lives, even how this may affect the dead. On this point he does two things. First [3] he shows in what way there is a difference in regard to this about the living and the dead. Second [4] he inquires whether the lot of friends affect the dead, since it is clear they do affect the living. This he does at "Perhaps we should rather inquire." On the first point we must consider that the dead are outside the present life, the happiness of which Aristotle here intends to inquire about, as appears from what has been previously said (180). They have contact with this life only as they remain in the memories of the living. The dead, therefore, may be compared

in this way to the living—when we consider this life—as the events actually happening now are compared to those that took place long ago and are now recounted—for example, the Trojan war or any incident of this kind.

207. He then remarks that it makes a great difference whether a particular misfortune befalls men while they are living or after they are dead—a far greater difference than it makes in a tragedy whether certain evil deeds like murder, robbery, or any other kind of misfortune be recounted by the playwrights as preceding the action of the drama or are performed in the course of it. The reason is that in the first case (the living and the dead) the same misfortunes affect them but in a different way because of their different states, for some are actually engaged in human affairs, while the others exist only in memory. But in the second case (in tragedies) the converse is true, for the "dramatis personae" are all engaged in human affairs, but some of the trials befalling them are recounted as here and now taking place, while others are simply indicated as having previously occurred. Because happiness refers rather to persons than to things happening externally, the Philosopher says that the first difference (which refers to the living and the dead)—precisely as it pertains to the point at issue, namely, a change of happiness—is of more importance than the second (which refers to actions in tragedies). And by reason of a similar inference concerning the difference of events, he says that we must consider the difference in our question.

208. Now it is clear that even though a recitation of past evils in a way influences the hearer who is in some measure affected by them, it does not do so to the extent of changing his condition.

Consequently, much less do fortunes change the condition of the dead. This is brought out by the Philosopher to clear up, as it were, the statement made above (184), which concluded that if something affects men who are not conscious, it affects also the dead.

209. Then [4], at "**Perhaps we should rather inquire,**" he inquires last whether things happening to friends affect the dead in some way. First [4] he examines the proposition; and second [5], he brings to a conclusion his chief proposal at "Therefore the good actions." He says first that we should rather inquire whether the dead in any way share in the prosperity and adversity that take place in this life. That a man is not changed from happiness to unhappiness or the other way round seems sufficiently established. The reason is that if an event taking place here, either good or bad, affects the dead, it will be fleeting and insignificant in itself or in its effect on them. But if this is the case, it will not be so great or of such a nature as to make them happy who are not happy, nor to take away happiness from them who have it. It has been said already (194) that trifling happenings do not cause a change in life. If then an insignificant event, among the things that happen, affects the dead, it follows that their condition of happiness will not be changed.

210. Then [5], at "**Therefore the good actions,**" he concludes his opinion. He says that the good actions done by friends or the evil befalling them seem to have some influence on the dead, and misfortunes too seem to affect them. But these take place in such a manner and to such an extent that they do not make the happy unhappy or the unhappy happy, nor do they change the dead in such things as wisdom or virtue or the like. However, the construction can be conditioned by the words "If this be the case." Then the statement "do have some influence" will be properly conditional, and the conjunctive particle will be superfluous.

211. It seems that Aristotle intends that the things said here are to be understood of the dead not as they are in themselves but as they live in the memory of men. In this way what happens to their friends after death seems to affect the dead so that their memory and glory become more distinct and more obscure. But this, he says, is indeed a fleeting thing because nothing is more fleeting than what exists only in the opinion of men. He says also that it is an insignificant thing especially for the dead themselves because it belongs to them only to the extent they are remembered by men.

212. The questions, however, whether the souls of men survive in some fashion after death and whether they are aware of or are changed in any way by what occurs in this life do not pertain to our purpose since the Philosopher here is treating of the happiness of the present life, as is evident from what was said above (206). Consequently inquiries of this kind, which need to be considered at some length, must be omitted at this point lest in this science which is practical many discussions outside its scope be carried on—a procedure that the Philosopher condemned (136). Elsewhere we have treated these subjects more fully.

LECTURE XVIII
Happiness, A Good Deserving Honor

TEXT OF ARISTOTLE (*1101b10–1102a4*) Chapter 12

1. *Having settled these matters we must investigate whether happiness is one of the goods to be praised or, more properly, to be honored. It is obviously not in the genus of potentiality.*
1101b10–12; 213–214

2. *Now a thing that is praiseworthy has a certain proportion in itself and some sort of relation to another.* 1101b12–14; 215

3. *Thus we generally praise the just, the brave, and the good man and even virtue itself because of the works and actions. We praise also the physically strong, the swift, and the like as possessing a certain natural ability, and as ordered in some way to a thing good in itself and desirable.* 1101b14–18; 216–217

4. *Our point is obvious too from the praises of the gods, for such praises would be ridiculous if judged by our standard. This happens because praises are given by reason of relation to another, as we have indicated.* 1101b18–21; 218

5. *If praise belongs to things of this kind, clearly something greater and better than praise is given to the best.* 1101b21–23; 219

6. *This seems to be true, for we call gods blessed and happy as we do the most godlike among men. We speak in a similar way of goods, for no one praises happiness as he praises a just man, but he ascribes to happiness something better and more divine, namely, blessedness.*
1101b23–27; 220

7. *Apparently Eudoxus put pleasure in the first place for a good reason. He thought that this is intimated from the fact that pleasure is a good not praised but is better than things praised, such as God and any good in itself. To things of this kind, other things are referred.*
1101b27–31; 221

8. *Praise surely belongs to virtue since good works are praised for activity of body and of soul in accord with virtue. But perhaps a consideration of this subject more properly belongs to those who labor over the study of laudatory statements. It is obvious now to us from our discussion that happiness is a perfect good and one to be honored.* 1101b31–1102a1; 222

9. *This appears to be true also from the nature of a principle. Now men do all that they do for the sake of happiness. But we look upon such a principle and cause of good as something divine and a thing to be honored.* 1102a2–4; 223

COMMENTARY OF ST. THOMAS

213. After the Philosopher has shown what happiness is, here he inquires about a certain property of happiness. First [1] he asks a question, and second [2], he ascertains the truth, at "Now a thing that is praiseworthy etc." He says that after determining the preceding matters, it is necessary to examine whether happiness is of the number of goods to be honored or to be praised. He proves that happiness must be contained under the one or the other kind

of good by the fact that happiness is not in the genus of potentiality. A man is not praised or honored because he has the potentiality to good but because he is somehow disposed to good.

214. To have an understanding of this question, we must consider that honor and praise differ in a twofold manner. First on the part of that in which honor or praise consists. In this respect honor is more extensive than praise. Honor signifies testimony

manifesting a person's excellence either by word or by deed, as when one genuflects to another or rises for him. But praise consists only in words. Second, praise and honor differ in regard to that for which they are given, for both are given on account of some excellence. Now there are two kinds of excellence. One is absolute and in this sense honor is due to it. But the other is an excellence in relation to some end, and in this sense praise is due.

215. Then [2], at "**Now a thing that is,**" he answers the question. First [2] he shows that happiness is of the number of goods to be honored, because it is a thing perfect and best. In the second place [9] he shows the same thing from the fact that happiness has the nature of a principle, at "This appears to be true also etc." On the first point he does two things. Initially [2] he shows to whom praise is given. Second [5] he concludes that something better than praise is given to the best, at "If praise belongs etc." In regard to the initial point he does two things. First [2] he presents his proposition. Second [3] he proves the proposition at "Thus we generally praise the just etc." He says first that everything that is praised seems to be praiseworthy for two reasons simultaneously: (1) because it has a certain kind of disposition in itself and (2) because it has a relation of some sort to another.

216. Then [3], at "**Thus we generally praise,**" he proves the proposition first [3] from human praises and second [4] from divine praises at "Our point is obvious too from the praises of the gods." In regard to the first we must consider that a man is praised both because of virtue of mind and because of power or strength of body. By reason of virtue of mind, a man (for instance, one who is just or brave or virtuous in any way) is praised for having virtue. The virtue also is praised, and this because of something else, namely, virtuous works and actions. The virtuous man and virtue itself then are praised insofar as they are ordered to do the work of virtue. Second, a man is praised by reason of power or strength of body because he is strong in fighting, swift in running, and so forth. This happens because the athlete is in a way ordered to something good in itself and desirable as worthy of achievement.

217. We must pay attention to the difference between virtues or powers of mind and body. It is sufficient in the praise of virtue of soul that a man be well disposed to the proper act of the virtue. The reason is that the good of man consists in the very act of virtue. But in the virtue or strength of body it is not sufficient that a man be well disposed to the act of virtue, for instance, for running or for wrestling. Human goodness does not consist in such things, since a man can run, wrestle, or fight for both a good and an evil purpose. Consequently, when speaking of the praises of the virtues of the soul he said they are praised because of works and actions (that flow from them). But in speaking of the powers of the body he indicated that they are praised in relation to something else.

218. Then [4], at "**Our point is obvious too,**" he explains what is meant by divine praises. If something be praiseworthy absolutely and not as related to some other thing, it follows that the thing is praiseworthy in all circumstances. But this is clearly false in the case of praises given to separated substances that he calls gods. It would seem ridiculous to praise them for things that are praised in men, for instance, because they are not overcome

by concupiscence or fear. This is so because praises are given by reason of a relation to something else, as has been pointed out (214).

219. Then [5], at "**If praise,**" he concludes his proposition from what has been said. First [5] he puts the conclusion this way. Praise is given to the things whose goodness is considered in relation to something else. But the best things are not ordered to anything else but rather other things are ordered to them. Therefore, something better than praise is given to the best. In a somewhat similar way, there is no science for the study of speculative principles, but something higher than science, understanding. Science is concerned with conclusions which are known by means of principles. Likewise, praise is concerned with things whose goodness is for the sake of others. But honor, a thing better than praise, is concerned with things to which other things are ordered.

220. Second [6], at "**This seems to be true,**" he proves the previous conclusion from what is commonly held. First [6] in regard to the things of which there is something better than praise; and second [8] in regard to the things of which there is praise at "Praise surely belongs etc." In regard to the first he does two things. To prove his proposition he first [6] presents what seems to be commonly held and second [7] what seemed so to Eudoxus at "Apparently Eudoxus." He says first that it seems commonly held that there is something better than praise for the best. This is made clear from the fact that those ascribing to the gods as it were something better than praise call them blessed and happy. They say the same, too, of the best among men who have a certain likeness to the gods by reason of excellence. As we ascribe

something better than praise to the best among men, so also to the best of goods like happiness. No one praises happiness in the way he praises a just or virtuous man. Something better is ascribed to happiness when we call it blessedness.

221. Then [7], at "**Apparently Eudoxus,**" he reduces the saying of Eudoxus to the same argument. Now Eudoxus called pleasure the first fruits of good, saying that pleasure is the supreme good. He thinks this is intimated from the following. Pleasure is a good that is not praised because in itself it is something better than the things that are praised. No one indeed is praised on account of pleasure, for instance, God and any other good in itself. The reason is that things whose goodness is praised are referred to things good in themselves. Things that are praised are praised precisely because they are somehow related to the things that are good in themselves.

222. Then [8], at "**Praise surely,**" he proves what he said in respect of the things to which praise is given. He says that praise belongs to virtue which makes us doers of good works, for a person is praised because of activity of body or soul as was just mentioned (216–217). But a consideration of the words used by men in bestowing compliments pertains more properly to rhetoricians who labor over the study of laudatory statements. It belongs to the kind of subject that deals with praise or dispraise (*demonstrativum genus*)—one of the three falling under the study of rhetoric, as is clear from the Philosopher in the first book of the *Rhetoric* (Ch. 3, 1358b21–1359a5) and from Tully (Cicero) in his *Rhetoric* (*De Oratore*, Bk. II, Ch. x, xi). So far as we are concerned it is obvious from the above (220) that happiness is of the

number of goods to be honored because it is a perfect good.

223. Then [6], at "**This appears to be true also**," he proves his proposition from the nature of a principle. We look upon the principle and the cause of goods as a thing to be honored, for it is as it were something divine, since God is the first principle of all good. But happiness is the principle of all human good because men do all that they do by reason of happiness. Now the end in things to be done and things to be desired has the nature of a principle because the nature of the means is understood from the end. Hence it follows that happiness is a good to be honored.

LECTURE XIX
Happiness and Virtue

TEXT OF ARISTOTLE (*1102a5–32*) Chapter 13

1. *If then happiness is a kind of operation according to perfect virtue, we must investigate the question of virtue. In this way we shall perhaps make a more profound study of happiness.*
                                                                1102a5–7; 224

2. *Now political science really seems to be concerned especially with the attainment of virtue. Its object is to produce good citizens obedient to the laws, as is exemplified by the lawmakers of the Cretes and the Spartans, and others like them. If this investigation belongs to political science, the study will be obviously conducted according to the disposition we made in the beginning.*   1102a7–13; 225

3. *The virtue we are investigating then will be human virtue, for we were seeking human good and human happiness. Now we call that virtue human which is proper not to the body but to the soul. Besides, we say that happiness is an activity of the soul. Since this is so, obviously the statesman must know to some extent the things pertaining to the soul, as he who is to heal the eyes or the whole body should know something about physiology. In fact the knowledge of the statesman should be greater insofar as political science is nobler and more important than medicine. But skillful physicians make it their business to know much about the body. Therefore, the statesman must study the soul.*   1102a13–23; 226–227

4. *The soul must be studied for the sake of the objects investigated and to the extent that suffices for them. To make a more exhaustive study would be a greater task than the subject requires.*   1102a23–26; 228

5. *Certain things about the soul are adequately treated in extraneous discourses. We should use these, for instance, this distinction of the soul into irrational and rational.*   1102a26–28; 229

6. *But whether the parts are distinct as particles of a body or anything physically divisible, or whether the parts are indivisible in nature and distinguishable according to reason alone, as the convex and concave of the circumference of a circle, is irrelevant to the present question.*
                                                                1102a28–32; 230

COMMENTARY OF ST. THOMAS

224. After the Philosopher has finished the treatise on happiness, he begins the consideration of virtue. First [1] he premises certain things necessary for the study of virtue. Second (1103a14) he begins to define virtue in the beginning of the second book at "Virtue is of two kinds etc." [Lect. I]. In regard to the first he does three things. First [1] he shows that it pertains to this science to study virtue. Second [3], at "The virtues we are etc.," he assumes certain things we must know about the parts of the soul. Third [Lect. XX], at "Virtue is divided etc." (1103a4), he divides virtue according to the division of the parts of the soul. He proves the initial point in two ways. First [1] by a reason taken from the doctrine on happiness. It was pointed out previously (128, 130, 150, 160, 164, 175, 187, 190) that happiness is an action according to perfect virtue. Hence we can study happiness better by means of knowledge of virtue. In keeping with this, he completes the treatise on happiness when he finishes the study of all the virtues in the tenth book (1953–2180). Since then the principal object of this science is the good of man, which

is happiness, an inquiry into virtue fittingly comes within the scope of this science.

225. Second [2], at "**Now political science**," he proves the proposition from the particular nature of this science. Political science seems really to make a special study of virtue and its attainment. Indeed the object of political science is to produce good citizens obedient to the laws (as is evident from the lawmakers of the Cretes and the Spartans who had model states, and from others framing similar laws to make men virtuous). But the study of the present science is connected with political science because its principles are given here. Obviously then a consideration of virtue will be suitable to this science. Accordingly in the introduction (25–31) we placed political science, which investigates the ultimate end of human actions, above all other sciences.

226. Then [3], at "**The virtue**," he takes up certain questions pertaining to the parts of the soul, which are necessary for the knowledge of virtues. On this point he does two things. First [3] he shows it is necessary that such things be discussed in this science. Second [5] he takes them up at "Certain things about the soul etc." In regard to the first he does two things. First [3] he shows that it is necessary in this science to consider certain questions about the parts of the soul. Second [4], at "The soul must be studied etc.," he shows how we must consider these questions. First, since it is our intention to investigate virtue, we understand that we are speaking of human virtue. We have just now noted (224) that we are looking for human good and human happiness in this science. If, therefore, we seek virtue for the sake of happiness,

we necessarily seek human virtue. But that virtue is peculiarly human which is proper to the soul, for it does not belong to the body nor is it shared in common with other beings. Pertinent here is what we said before (123–126), that happiness is an activity of the soul.

227. In the study of the soul whose virtue he seeks, the statesman is compared to the physician who studies the body seeking its health. Obviously then the statesman must know to some extent the things belonging to the soul, as the physician who treats the eyes and the whole body must study something about the eyes and the whole body. The obligation of the statesman to study the soul whose virtue he seeks is greater because political science is more important than the science of medicine—a fact we know from what was said previously (25–31). Consequently, the study of political science must be more thorough. We see that skillful physicians study many things which will give them a knowledge of the body and not merely what concerns cures. Hence a statesman gives some thought to the soul.

228. Then [4], at "**The soul must be studied**," he shows in what way the statesman ought to investigate these things. In this science, he says, the soul must be studied for the sake of the virtues and human actions that are the principal objects here investigated. Therefore, the study of the soul must be such as suffices for the things chiefly sought. If a man should wish to make a more exhaustive study, he will be imposing a greater task than the object of our investigation requires. So too in all other things sought for the sake of an end, the extent of them must be measured according to the end itself.

229. Then [5], at "**Certain things**

about the soul," he takes up the things we must consider here about the parts of the soul. First [5] he divides the parts of the soul into rational and irrational. Second [Lect. XX], at "One part of the irrational soul etc." (1102a33), he subdivides the irrational. Third [Lect. XX], at "If however we must etc." (1103a2), he subdivides the other member of the first division, that is, the rational part of the soul. In regard to the first he does two things. First [5] he gives the division. Second [6], at "But whether the parts etc.," he says that a certain question must be left unanswered. He says first that certain things about the soul have been adequately treated in the book *De Anima*, which he calls extraneous discussions because he wrote the book as an epistle to persons living at a considerable distance. The books that he was accustomed to teach his students (auditors) were called reports or notes (auditions), as the books of the *Physics* are entitled on the audition of classes about Nature; or they are called extraneous for the better reason that they are outside the scope of the imme-diate science. However, here we must use the things discussed in that book, for instance, one part of the soul is rational, another part irrational as is asserted in the third book *De Anima* (Ch. 9, 432a27; St. Th. Lect. XIV, 797).

230. Then [6], at "**But whether the parts,**" he asks a certain question which is to be left unanswered intentionally. Are the two parts of the soul, rational and irrational, distinct from one another in their subject according to location and position, as particles of a body or of some other divisible continuum? Plato located the rational part or power of the soul in the brain, the emotional part in the heart, and the assimilative part in the liver. Or perhaps these two parts are not divided according to subject but only in concept as in the circumference of a circle the convex and concave are not distinguished by subject but in concept alone. He says that so far as it concerns us at present, it does not matter which opinion is held. Hence he leaves the question unanswered because it does not pertain to our present purpose.

LECTURE XX
Subdivisions of the Irrational Soul

TEXT OF ARISTOTLE (*1102a32–1103a10*) Chapter 13

1. One part of the irrational soul is the vegetative soul common to all living things. By vegetative I understand that part which is the cause of nutrition and growth. Such a power of the soul is found in all things that assimilate food. It is found even in embryos and in the lowest forms of animal life. To these it is more reasonable to assign the vegetative part than some other.
1102a32–1102b2; 231–232

2. Because this power is common, it follows that it is not human. **1102b2–3; 233**

3. It seems that the vegetative part and potency of the soul are most active during sleep. Now good and evil persons are hardly distinguishable in their sleep. Hence the saying that the happy are no better off than the miserable for half their lives. This is a reasonable doctrine, for sleep is a cessation from the operation according to which the soul is called good and evil. Yet perhaps certain activities do penetrate the soul of the sleeper gradually. In this way the dreams of the virtuous become better than the dreams of other persons. But what we have now said on this subject will suffice. Therefore, discussion of the nutritive part must come to an end because it has no part in human virtue. **1102b3–12; 234–235**

4. Seemingly there is another part of the soul, irrational also but participating in reason to some extent. **1102b13–14; 236**

5. We praise the rational principle in the incontinent and continent man, for reason rightly induces to what is best. But something besides reason seems to be innate in them, which conflicts with reason and resists reason. As paralyzed members of the body are said to move wrongly to the left contrary to the will choosing the right, so also in the soul, for the movement of the incontinent are to things contrary to reason. While the uncontrolled movement can be seen in bodies, it is invisible in the soul. Nevertheless we must judge that there is something in the soul besides reason which is contrary and resistant to reason. But how this differs from reason does not matter at present. **1102b14–25; 237–238**

6. Now this part seems to share in reason, as we have said. Therefore, as found in the continent man, it is obedient to reason. But it is even more fully subject in the sober and courageous man whose every act harmonizes with reason. **1102b25–28; 239**

7. Apparently the irrational part is twofold. The vegetative power does not partake of reason at all. But the concupiscible power and every appetitive power participate to some extent because they heed and are obedient to reason. Therefore, we say that reason holds the place of a father and friends but not of mathematicians. **1102b28–33; 240**

8. Persuasion, reproach, and entreaty in all cases indicate that the irrational principle is somewhat influenced by reason. **1102b33–1103a1; 241**

9. If, however, we must say that this part shares in reason, then the rational will be of two kinds: one having reason principally and of itself, the other obedient to the reason as to a father. **1103a1–3; 242**

10. Virtue is divided according to this difference, for we call some virtues intellectual, others moral. Wisdom, understanding, and prudence are said to be intellectual virtues, while liberality and sobriety are called moral. When speaking of man's good morals we do not describe him as wise or intelligent but as mild-tempered or sober. We do praise a person for acquiring the habit of wisdom since praiseworthy habits are called virtues. **1103a3–10; 243–244**

COMMENTARY OF ST. THOMAS

231. After the Philosopher has divided the parts of the soul into rational and irrational, here he subdivides the irrational part. First [1] he presents one member of the subdivision; and then [4], he presents the other at "Seemingly there is another part etc." In regard to the initial point he does two things. First [1] he mentions an irrational part of the soul. Then [2] he shows that this part is not properly human, at "Because this power etc." He says first that one of the parts of the irrational soul is like the plant soul and is common to all things living here below. It is that part which is the cause of assimilation and growth. Such a part of the soul is found in every being that assimilates food not only in creatures after birth but even before birth, as in embryos that are obviously nourished and grow.

232. Likewise this part of the soul is discovered not only in the highly organized animals having all the senses and endowed with local motion but also in the lowest animals, like oysters having only the sense of touch and rooted to one place. Evidently all these creatures live and have some kind of soul. But this vegetative type of soul rather than some other part is more reasonably assigned to these lowest animals because the effects of this part are more evident in them.

233. Then [2], at "**Because this power,**" he shows that the aforementioned part of the soul is not human. First [2] he concludes this from the premises. We call human that which is distinctive of man If then a part of the soul is altogether common, it will not be human.

234. Secondly [3], at "**It seems that,**" he adds a proof from a particular evident sign. This part of the soul is found to be especially active during sleep, for when the natural heat has returned to the internal organs and the animal is asleep, digestion works better. But what is proper to man precisely as he is said to be good or evil operates only slightly during sleep. Good and evil persons are hardly distinguishable in their sleep. Hence the saying that the happy do not differ from the unhappy for half their life which is spent in sleep. The reason is that judgment of the intellect is bound during sleep, and the external senses do not function, although the imagination and the power of nutrition are active.

235. It is reasonable that the good and evil, the happy and the unhappy are indistinguishable while asleep because that part of man by which he is called good ceases to function during sleep. Good and evil men differ while asleep not on account of a difference occurring during their slumbers but because of what happened in their waking moments. Conscious activity gradually penetrates to the soul of the sleeper so that the things a man has seen or heard or thought while awake, present themselves to his imagination in sleep. In this way the virtuous who spend their wakeful hours in good works, have more edifying dreams than other persons who occupy their conscious moments with idle and evil works. What we have now said on this subject will suffice (234–235). We conclude then from the premises (233–235), that the nutritive part of the soul is not adapted by nature to participate in human virtue.

236. Then [4], at "**Seemingly there is,**" he presents the other member of the division. First [4] he indicates what he intends; and second [5] he proves

his proposition at "We praise the rational etc." He says first that besides the vegetative part of the soul, there seems to be another part, irrational like the vegetative, but participating in reason to some extent. In this it differs from the vegetative part that has nothing whatsoever to do with human virtue as was just said (235).

237. Then [5], at **"We praise the rational,"** he proves his proposition: first [5] that there is another part of the irrational soul; second [6] that this part participates in reason at "Now this part seems to share in reason." He proves the first by an argument taken from continent and incontinent men. In this matter we praise the part of the soul having reason because it rightly deliberates and induces to what is best, as if by entreaty and persuasion. Both—continent and incontinent—choose to abstain from unlawful pleasures. But seemingly in both there is something innate in them other than reason, and this something conflicts with reason and resists or hinders reason in the execution of its choice. Obviously it is something irrational, since it is contrary to reason. The sensitive appetite, which desires what is pleasant to sense and at times opposes what reason judges absolutely good, would be such a thing. This appetite in the continent man is restrained by reason, for he certainly has evil desires but his reason does not follow them. On the other hand the appetite in the incontinent man overcomes reason, which is seduced by evil desires.

238. Then he adds an illustration. The members of the body are incapacitated when they cannot be controlled by the regulative power of the soul, as happens to paralytics and the intoxicated who move to the left side when they wish to move to the right. This is true also of the souls of incontinent persons who are moved to the opposite of what the reason chooses. But the process is not so apparent in the parts of the soul as in the parts of the body. We see clearly in what way a bodily member moves unnaturally, but the movement of the parts of the soul is not so obvious to us. Despite this, we must judge there is something in man that is contrary to reason and resists it. But how this may differ from reason—whether by subject, or by concept alone does not matter at present.

239. Then [6], at **"Now this part,"** he shows that an irrational part of this kind participates in reason. His first argument [6] is based on acts taking place within man; his second [8], at "Persuasion, reproach," is based on acts external to man. With the first he does two things. First [6] he shows that this irrational part participates in reason. Second [7] he finishes the treatment of the difference of this irrational part from the part presented above, at "Apparently the irrational part." He says first that the irrational part, of which we have now spoken (233–235), seems in some way to participate in reason, as was just said (236). This is obvious in the continent man whose sensitive appetite obeys reason. Although he may have evil desires, nevertheless he does not act according to them but according to reason. In the sober or temperate man this part of the soul is even more fully subject to reason. Such a man has so subdued his sensitive appetite that evil desires in him are not vehement. We may say the same of the courageous man and of anyone endowed with the habit of moral virtue. The reason is that in these men nearly everything—both external actions and internal desires—harmonize with reason.

240. Then [7], at "**Apparently the irrational**," he concludes the difference between the two irrational parts from the premises. He says that according to the premises the irrational part is apparently twofold. Now the vegetative part, found in plants, does not partake of reason in any way, for it is not obedient to the direction of reason. But the concupiscible power and every appetitive power like the irascible emotion and the will participate in reason in some measure because they heed the movement of the reason and are obedient to its regulations. Hence we say reason holds the place of a father giving guidance and of friends offering advice. But reason here does not play the role of a mere theorist like the reason of a mathematician, for the irrational part of the soul does not partake in any way of reason understood in this sense.

241. Then [8], at "**Persuasion, reproach**," he shows through the things externally done that the irrational part participates in reason. In his opinion this is indicated from the fact that the persuasion of friends, the reproach of superiors and the entreaties of inferiors aim to keep a man from following his desires. But all these would be useless unless this part of the irrational soul could share in reason. From this too it is apparent that reason is not controlled by the movements of the passions of the sensitive appetite but quite the contrary—reason can restrain such movements. Therefore, reason is not governed by the motions of the heavenly bodies, which can effect some change in the sensitive appetite of the soul through a change in the human body. Since the intellect or reason is not a faculty of any bodily organ, it is not directly subject to the action of any bodily power. The same is true of the

will that is in the reason, as was said in the third book *De Anima* (Ch. 3, 427a21; St. Th. Lect. IV, 617–621).

242. Then [9], at "**If however**," he subdivides the other member of the first division, the rational part of the soul. According to him (if we must say that that part of the soul that participates in reason is rational in some way) the rational part will be of two kinds: one, having reason principally and in itself, is rational by nature. But the other is inherently adapted to obey reason as a father, and is called rational by participation. In accord with this, one member is contained under both rational and irrational. Now, one part of the soul, the vegetative, is irrational alone; another part is rational alone, the intellect and reason. Still another part is of itself irrational but rational by participation, like the sensitive appetite and the will.

243. Then [10], at "**Virtue is divided**," he divides virtue according to this difference in the parts of the soul. He says that virtue is designated or divided according to the above-mentioned difference in the parts of the soul. Since human virtue perfects the work of man which is done according to reason, human virtue must consist in something reasonable. Since the reasonable is of two kinds, by nature and by participation, it follows that there are two kinds of human virtue. One of these is placed in what is rational by nature and is called intellectual. The other is placed in what is rational by participation, that is, in the appetitive part of the soul, and is called moral. Therefore, he says, we call some of the virtues intellectual and some moral. Wisdom, understanding, and prudence are said to be intellectual virtues while liberality and sobriety are called moral.

244. He proves this point from human praises. When we wish to praise someone for good morals, we do not describe him as wise and intelligent, but as sober and mild-tempered. We do not praise a man for good morals alone but also for the habit of wisdom. Praiseworthy habits are called virtues. Therefore, besides the moral virtues, there are also intellectual virtues like wisdom, understanding, and some others of this kind. Thus ends the first book.

BOOK TWO
MORAL VIRTUE IN GENERAL
LECTURE I
Moral Virtue Is Caused by Habit

TEXT OF ARISTOTLE (*1103a14–1103b25*) Chapter 1

1. *Virtue is of two kinds, intellectual and moral. The intellectual is generated and fostered for the most part by teaching, and so requires time and experience. Moral virtue however is derived from customary action (mos). Hence by a slight variation of the original term we have this name "moral."*　　　　　　　　　　　　　　　　　　**1103a14–18; 245–247**

2. *From this it is clear that moral virtue is not instilled in us by nature, for nothing natural is changed by habit. Thus a stone that naturally gravitates downward will never become accustomed to moving upward, not even if someone should continue to throw it into the air ten thousand times. Neither will fire become accustomed to tend downward, nor will anything else that naturally tends one way acquire the contrary custom. Therefore, the moral virtues are not in us by nature nor are they in us contrary to nature. We do have a natural aptitude to acquire them, but we are perfected in these virtues by use.*　　　　　　　**1103a18–26; 248–249**

3. *Again in the things that come to us from nature, we first receive the potentialities and afterwards we put them into operation. This is obvious in the case of the senses, for we did not acquire our senses from seeing and hearing repeatedly but on the contrary we made use of the senses after we have them—we did not come into possession of them after we used them. Virtues however we acquire by previous activity as happens in different arts, for the things we must learn how to make, we learn by making. Thus men become builders by building and harpists by playing the harp. Likewise we become just by doing just actions, we become temperate by doing temperate actions, and we become courageous by doing courageous actions.*　　　　　　　　　　　　　　　　　**1103a26–1103b2; 250**

4. *Our contention is verified by what is done in the state, for legislators make men good in accordance with political norms. Such is the aim of every legislator. In fact he who does not succeed in this fails in lawmaking. It is precisely in this way that a good constitution differs from a bad one.*　　　　　　　　　　　　　　　　　　　　**1103b2–6; 251**

5. *Again, every virtue has both its origin and its deterioration from the same principles. A similar situation is found in any art, for it is from playing the harp that both good and bad harpists are made. Proportionately this can be said of builders and of all the rest. Men become good builders from building well, but they become poor builders from building poorly. If this were not so, there would be no need of a teacher but all would be born good or bad workmen. This is the case also with virtue. Of those who engage in transactions with their fellowmen, some become just and others unjust. Of those exposed to dangers who habitually experience fear or confidence, some become brave and some cowardly. We may say the same of men in reference to concupiscence and anger, for some become temperate and mild, others self-indulgent and irascible; some conduct themselves well in these matters, others badly. We may then universally state in one sentence: like actions produce like habits.*　　　　　　**1103b6–22; 252–253**

6. *Therefore, we must cultivate actions of the right sort because differences in actions are followed by differences in habits. It is not of small moment but it matters a great deal—more than anything else—whether one becomes promptly accustomed to good or bad habits from youth.*　　　　　　　　　　　　　　　　　　　　　　**1103b22–25; 254**

COMMENTARY OF ST. THOMAS

245. After the Philosopher has treated the questions introductory to virtue, he now begins the study of the virtues. He divides the treatise into two parts. In the first part [I] he treats the virtues themselves. In the second he examines certain things that follow or accompany the virtues. He does this in the seventh book (1145a15) at "Now, making a new start, we must say etc." [Lect. I]. The first part is subdivided into two sections. In the first he studies the moral virtues; in the second the intellectual virtues, in the sixth book (1138b18) at "But since we previously said etc." [Lect. I]. The reason for this order is that the moral virtues are more known, and through them we are prepared for a study of the intellectual virtues. In the first, which is divided into two parts, he investigates the matter of the moral virtues in general. In the second [Bk. III, Lect. XIV] he examines the moral virtues specifically, at "We stated previously . . . is a mean etc." (1115a7). This first is again subdivided into two parts. In the first of these he treats moral virtue in general. In the second he examines certain principles of moral actions. This is in the third book [Lect. I] beginning at "Since virtue is concerned with passions etc." (1109b30). This first has a threefold division. In the first part he is looking for the cause of moral virtue. In the second [Lect. V] he seeks to find out what moral virtue is, at "Now we must search out the definition of virtue" (1105b20). In the third part [Lect. XI] he shows how a man may become virtuous, at "A sufficient explanation has been given etc." (1109a19). On the initial point he does three things. First he shows that moral virtue is caused in us by actions. Second [Lect. II] he shows

by what actions it may be caused in us, at "The present study etc." (1103b27). In the third part [Lect. IV] he finds a particular problem in what was previously said, at "Someone may rightly ask etc." (1105a18). In regard to the first he does two things. Initially he shows the cause of the formation of virtue; and second [3] what the cause of its destruction is, at "Again, every virtue etc." On the initial point he does three things. First [1] he proposes that moral virtue originates in us from the habit of acting. Second [2] he shows that moral virtue is not in us by nature, at "From this it is clear etc." Third [4] he explains by a sign what he had said, at "Our contention is verified by what is done etc."

246. He says first that virtue is of two kinds, intellectual and moral, and that the intellectual is both generated and increased for the most part by teaching. The reason is that intellectual virtue is ordered to knowledge which we acquire more readily from teaching than by discovery. More people can know the truth by learning from others than by ascertaining it themselves. Everyone indeed who finds out from others will learn more than he can discover by himself. But because we cannot proceed to infinity in the process of learning, men must learn many truths by discovery. Besides, since all our knowledge is derived from the senses, and the senses in turn very often beget experience, it follows that intellectual virtue may need long experience.

247. But moral virtue is derived from customary activity. Now moral virtue, found in the appetitive part, implies a certain inclination to something desirable. This inclination is either from nature, which tends to

what is agreeable to itself, or from custom, which is transformed into nature. Hence the name "moral" differing somewhat from "custom" is taken from it. In Greek *ethos* spelled with epsilon—a short e—means habit or moral virtue, while *ithos* spelled with eta—a long e—signifies custom. With us also, the name "moral" means custom sometimes and other times it is used in relation to vice or virtue.

248. Then [2], at "**From this it is clearly,**" he proves from the premises that moral virtue is not produced by nature for two reasons. The first is that none of the things from nature are changed by use. He illustrates this point by the example of a stone that naturally tending downward will never become accustomed to moving upward, no matter how often it is thrown into the air. The reason is that the things which naturally operate either merely operate or they operate and are operated upon. If they merely operate, their principle of action is not changed. So long as the cause remains the same, the inclination to the same effect remains. If, however, they so operate as also to be operated upon—unless the passivity be such that it removes the principle of action—the natural tendency in them will not be destroyed. But if the passivity be such as to take away the principle of action, then it will not belong to the same nature. Thus what was previously natural will cease to be natural. When a thing operates naturally, therefore, no change is effected regarding its action. The same is also true if the operation is contrary to nature unless perhaps the motion be such that it destroys nature. But if the natural principle of the operation remains, there will always be the same action. Therefore, in the things that are according to nature and

in the things that are contrary to nature habit plays no part.

249. The reason for this is that moral virtue pertains to the appetite that operates according as it is moved by the good apprehended. When the appetite operates often, therefore, it must be often moved by its object. In this the appetite follows a certain tendency in accordance with the mode of nature, as many drops of water falling on a rock hollow it out. Thus it is obvious that the moral virtues are not in us by nature, nor are they in us contrary to nature. We do have a natural aptitude to acquire them inasmuch as the appetitive potency is naturally adapted to obey reason. But we are perfected in these virtues by use, for when we act repeatedly according to reason, a modification is impressed in the appetite by the power of reason. This impression is nothing else but moral virtue.

250. He presents the second reason [3] at "**Again in the things.**" In all the things with which nature has endowed us, potency is previous to operation. This is obvious in the senses. We did not receive the sense of sight and hearing from seeing and hearing repeatedly. On the contrary, from the fact that we had these senses, we began to use them. It did not happen that we came into possession of the senses from the fact that we used them. But we have acquired the virtues by acting according to virtue, as happens in the operative arts in which men learn by making the things that are to be made after they have mastered the skill. In this way men become builders by building, and harpists by playing the harp. Likewise men become just or temperate or courageous by doing just actions or temperate actions or courageous actions. Therefore, virtues of this kind are not in us by nature.

251. Then [4], at "**Our contention is verified,**" he makes known what he had said, by a sign. He says the statement just made (250) that by performing actions we become virtuous is verified by what is done in the state. Legislators make men virtuous by habituating them to virtuous works by means of statutes, rewards, and punishments. Such ought to be the aim of every legislator—in fact he who does not succeed in this fails in lawmaking. It is precisely in this way that a good constitution differs from a bad one.

252. Then [5], at "**Again, every virtue,**" he shows that virtue is produced and destroyed by identical works. First he explains his proposition, and second [6] he infers a corollary from what has been said, at "Therefore, we must etc." He says first that the production and the destruction of virtue have their source in the same principles taken in a different way. The same is true in any art. He shows this first from activities, because men become both good and bad harpists—understanding this proportionately—from the way they play the harp. A similar reason holds for builders and all other workmen. Men become good builders by building well repeatedly, they become poor builders by building poorly. If this were not so,

men would not need to learn arts of this kind from some master workman who would direct their actions, but there would be good and bad workmen in all the arts no matter how they would be practiced. As it is in the arts, so also in the virtues.

253. Those who act well in their dealings with their fellowmen become just, and those who act in an evil way become unjust. Likewise those faced with danger who accustom themselves to fear and confidence in the right way become courageous; in the wrong way, cowardly. This is true also of temperance and meekness in the matter of concupiscence and anger. We may then universally sum up in one sentence: like actions produce like habits.

254. Then [6], at "**Therefore, we must,**" he affirms that a person must give careful attention to the performance of such actions because differences in actions are followed by differences in habits. He concludes, therefore, it is not of small moment but it makes a great difference—indeed everything depends on it—that one becomes accustomed to perform either good or evil actions from earliest youth, for we retain longer the things impressed on us as children.

LECTURE II
Virtue and Action

TEXT OF ARISTOTLE (1103b26–1104b2) Chapter 2

1. *The present study is not pursued for the sake of contemplation like other studies. We seek the definition of virtue not in order to know but in order to become virtuous; otherwise it would have no utility. We must then thoroughly investigate what concerns actions and how they are to be performed, for actions control the formation of habits, as we have pointed out.*

1103b26–31; 255–256

2. *To be in accord with right reason is a quality common to these actions and should be taken for granted. Later we will discuss the question both as to the definition of right reason and as to how right reason is related to the other virtues.* **1103b31–34; 257**

3. *It must be presupposed that any discussion concerning actions to be performed ought to be given in a general way and not definitively. We remarked in the beginning that discussions must be pursued according to the nature of the subject matter. Now things pertaining to actions, and relevant considerations, do not have anything fixed about them any more than the things that concern health. If this be true in the general treatment, still more uncertainty will be found in the consideration of particular cases. Indeed this study does not fall under either art or tradition. But those who perform moral actions must always pay attention to what is appropriate to the occasion as is done in medicine and navigation. Although this is the situation, we ought to try to be of assistance to others in the present study.*

1103b34–1104a11; 258–259

4. *We must then first consider that moral matters are of such a nature as to be destroyed by defect and excess. To prove such notions that are not readily manifest we must use obvious signs and evidence such as we have in the case of bodily strength and health. An excessive amount of exercise no less than a lack of it impairs health. Likewise eating and drinking too much or too little causes damage to health. But health is produced, increased, and preserved by eating and drinking in moderation. It is the same then with temperance and fortitude and the other virtues. The man who is afraid of everything, who runs away and will endure nothing becomes a coward. On the other hand, the man who fears absolutely nothing and wades into every danger becomes reckless. Likewise a man who tastes every pleasure and passes up none, becomes intemperate while he who seeks to avoid all pleasures like a boor becomes as it were insensible. Temperance and fortitude are destroyed by excess and defect but are preserved by the golden mean.* **1104a11–27; 260–263**

5. *Not only the production, increase, and destruction of virtues have identical sources and causes but the actions themselves also have the same sources and causes. We see this in the more obvious actions like bodily strength. A man becomes strong from taking abundant nourishment and from hard work. Then when he is strong, he will be more able to do these things. We find the same thing in the virtues since we become temperate by giving up pleasures, and having become temperate we can be very easily give up pleasures. The same is true of the virtue of fortitude. We become brave by accustoming ourselves to despise and endure terrors, and having become brave we are very capable of enduring terrors.* **1104a27–1104b3; 264**

COMMENTARY OF ST. THOMAS

255. After the Philosopher has shown that virtues are caused in us by actions, he now inquires how this is done. On this point he does two things. First he shows what are the actions that cause virtue in us. Second [Lect. III], at

"We may understand etc." (1104b4), he shows what is the sign of virtue already produced in us. On the initial point he does three things. First [1] he shows the necessity of the present investigation. Second [3], at "It must be presupposed etc.," he treats the method of investigation. Third [4] he shows actions as causes of virtue. In regard to the first he does two things. Initially [1] he presents the necessity itself. Second [2], at "To be in accord with right reason etc.," he shows what we must suppose here. Regarding the first we must consider that in the speculative sciences where we seek only the knowledge of the truth, it is sufficient to know what is the cause of a determined effect. But in the practical sciences whose end is action, we must know by what activities or operations a determined effect follows from a determined cause.

256. He says [1] then that the present study, moral philosophy, is not pursued for the sake of the contemplation of truth like the other studies of the speculative sciences, but for the sake of action. In this science we seek a definition of virtue not only to know its truth but to become good by acquiring virtue. The reason he assigns is that if the investigation of this science were for the knowledge of truth alone, it would have little utility. It is not of great importance nor does it contribute much to the perfection of the intellect that a man should know the changeable truth about contingent actions with which virtue is concerned. This being the case, he concludes that we must thoroughly inquire about the actions we ought to perform because, as we have already observed (248–253), actions have influence and control over the formation of good and bad habits in us.

257. Then [2], at "To be in accord with right," he shows it should be taken for granted that actions causing virtue possess the common quality of being in accord with right reason. This happens because the good of everything consists in the fact that its operation is suited to its form. Now the distinctive form of man is that which makes him a rational animal. Hence man's action must be good precisely because it harmonizes with right reason, for perversity of reason is repugnant to its nature. Later in the sixth book (1109) we shall ascertain what is right reason, which belongs to the intellectual virtues, and how it pertains to the other virtues, which are the moral.

258. Then [3], at "**It must be,**" he explains the method of investigating matters of this kind. We must presume, he says, that any discussion concerned like this with actions to be performed ought to be given in a general way, that is, as a precedent or as likely, but not definitively. This was pointed out in the introduction to the whole work (24). The reason is that the discussions are to be carried on according to the nature of the subject matter, as was noted in the same place (32). We see that things pertaining to moral actions and materials useful to them, like external goods, do not have in themselves anything fixed by way of necessity, but everything is contingent and changeable. The same occurs in works relating to medicine, which are concerned with health, because the disposition of the body to be cured and the remedies used to effect a cure are changeable in many ways.

259. The teaching on matters of morals even in their general aspects is uncertain and variable. But still more uncertainty is found when we come

down to the solution of particular cases. This study does not fall under either art or tradition because the causes of individual actions are infinitely diversified. Hence judgment of particular cases is left to the prudence of each one. He who acts prudently must attentively consider the things to be done at the present time after all the particular circumstances have been taken into consideration. In this way a doctor must act in bringing about a cure and a captain in steering a ship. Although this doctrine is such as to be uncertain in its general aspects and incapable of precision in particular cases, we ought to study it so that in these matters we may be of some assistance to men in directing their actions.

260. Then [4], at "**We must then first,**" he shows what are the operations that may cause virtue. On this point he does two things. First [4] he shows by what actions virtue is caused. Second [5], at "Not only the production etc.," he shows that virtue already formed produces in turn like actions. He says first we must consider before anything else that virtues or operations causing virtues are of such a nature as to be destroyed by excess and defect. To prove this we must use certain more obvious signs and evidence, that is, the things happening in regard to the powers of the body that are more manifest than the capacities of the soul.

261. We see that bodily strength is impaired by immoderate games, that is, certain bodily exercises in which the contestants do battle naked, because the natural power of the body is weakened by excessive exertion. Likewise the lack of exercise destroys bodily strength because, when not exercised, the members remain flabby and incapable of work. A similar comment may be made about health. If someone takes either too much food or drink, or less than he needs, his health is impaired. But if a man uses exercise, food, and drink in moderation, he will become physically strong and his health will be improved and preserved.

262. It is the same with the virtues of the soul, for instance, fortitude, temperance, and the other virtues. A person who fears everything, takes to flight, and never faces anything terrifying becomes a coward. Likewise he who fears nothing and wades into every danger thoughtlessly becomes rash. The same is true of temperance. He who tastes every pleasure and avoids none becomes intemperate. But he who avoids all pleasures as a boor does, without any reason, becomes as it were insensible.

263. However we are not to conclude from this that virginity, which abstains from all venereal pleasure, is a vice. The reason is that virginity does not abstain from all pleasures, and that it abstains from particular pleasures according to right reason. Similarly, it is not a vice for some soldiers to refrain from all venereal pleasure in order to devote themselves more fully to fighting. Now these things have been said because temperance and fortitude are destroyed by excess and defect but are preserved by the golden mean, which is understood not according to quantity but according to right reason.

264. Then [5], at "**Not only,**" he shows that virtue produces actions similar to the actions that caused it. He says that the same kinds of activity cause the production and increase of virtue, and also its destruction if they are taken in a contrary way. Likewise the operations of the virtues already produced consist in these same works. This is obvious in bodily actions which are more manifest. As bodily strength

is caused from the fact that a man can take abundant nourishment and can work hard, and when he has become strong he will be more able to do these things, so also it is with the virtues of the soul. From the fact that we give up pleasures, we become temperate; and when we have become temperate, we can very easily give up pleasures. It is the same with the virtue of fortitude. We become brave by accustoming ourselves to despise and endure terrors, and having become brave we are very capable of enduring terrors. So also, fire once kindled from generated heat can give off intense heat.

LECTURE III
Signs of Virtue

TEXT OF ARISTOTLE (1104b3–1105a16) Chapter 3

1. We may understand pleasure or sorrow that follows activity as an indication of the habits that are present. Indeed the man who avoids bodily pleasures is temperate if he is glad about it; intemperate, if sad about it. Likewise, the man who encounters dangers is brave if he rejoices or is not sad, but cowardly if he is saddened. Moral virtue then is concerned with pleasure and sorrows.   **1104b3–9; 265–267**

2. We perform evil actions for the sake of pleasure and avoid good actions because of sadness. Therefore, as Plato says, we need some sort of training from our earliest years so that we may rejoice and be sorrowful about the right things, for proper instruction consists in this.
1104b9–13; 268

3. Besides, if virtues are concerned with activities and passions, and pleasure and sorrow follow every act and passion, then certainly virtue will deal with pleasures and sorrows.
1104b13–16; 269

4. Penalties inflicted because of pleasure and sorrow also prove our point, for penalties are, as it were, remedies. Remedies by their very nature work through contraries.   **1104b16–18; 270**

5. Furthermore, as we said previously, every habit of the soul has a natural disposition to do and to be busied with those things by which it is made better and worse. Men become wicked by pursuing the pleasures and avoiding the sorrows that are wrong, or by doing this at the wrong time or in the wrong manner or in some other way that one may deviate from reason. Consequently, some define virtues as certain quiescent and emotionless dispositions. But they err in speaking absolutely and in not qualifying the passions as to manner, time, and so forth. We must suppose therefore that virtue is such that it works what is best regarding pleasures and sorrows, and vice does the contrary.   **1104b18–28; 271–272**

6. Our contention will become evident from the following consideration. Three things fall under our choice: the good, the useful, the pleasurable; and three contrary things we avoid: the evil, the harmful, the sorrowful. In regard to all these, the virtuous man disposes himself rightly and the vicious man badly. This is especially true in the matter of pleasure that is common to animals and is found in all things obtained by choice, for the good and the useful seem also to be pleasurable.   **1104b29–1105a1; 273–275**

7. Pleasure, too, has grown up with all of us from childhood. Therefore, it is difficult to curb this passion which is acquired with life itself.   **1105a1–3; 276**

8. Some regulate their activities to a greater degree and others to a lesser degree by pleasure and sorrow. About these, then, our whole study must be concerned, for it is not a thing of small importance in human actions to take pleasure or sorrow in the right or wrong way.   **1105a3–7; 277**

9. As Heraclitus says, it is even more difficult to fight against pleasure than anger. Now the more difficult is always treated by art and virtue, which operate well and more efficiently in the face of difficulty. Hence the whole business of virtue and of political science is occupied with pleasures and sorrows. Assuredly he who uses these well will be virtuous, and he who uses them badly will be evil.   **1105a7–13; 278**

10. It has been said that (1) virtue treats of pleasures and sorrows, (2) virtue is produced and increased by the same actions that, when done in a different way, destroy virtue, (3) the same actions that produce virtue are in turn produced by virtue.   **1105a13–16; 279**

COMMENTARY OF ST. THOMAS

265. After the Philosopher has shown what kind of activity produces virtue, he now explains how we may recognize virtue already produced. On this point he does two things. First [1] he presents what he intends to do; and second [2], at "We perform evil actions etc.," he proves his proposition. Regarding the first we must consider that when virtue produces actions similar to the actions that formed it, as was just noted (264), the performance of this action differs before and after virtue. Before virtue man does a kind of violence to himself in operating this way. Such actions, therefore, have some admixture of sorrow. But after the habit of virtue has been formed, these actions are done with pleasure. The explanation is that a habit exists as a sort of nature, and that is pleasurable which agrees with a thing according to nature.

266. He says [1] that an indication that habits, good or bad, have already been formed is given by the pleasure or sorrow that follows the operations. He illustrates this by examples. The man who is glad that he has avoided bodily pleasures is temperate because he performs an action in keeping with the habit. Likewise, he who encounters dangers with pleasure, or at least without sorrow, is brave. Particularly in the act of fortitude it is enough not to have sorrow, as will be explained in the third book (584–585). One who faces dangers with sorrow is cowardly. He then assigns the reason for what he has said from the fact that every moral virtue is concerned with pleasures and sorrows.

267. From this we must not conclude that every moral virtue is concerned with pleasures and sorrows as its proper matter. The matter indeed of every moral virtue is that on which reason imposes a norm. Thus justice treats of dealing with others, fortitude treats of fears and aggressiveness, temperance of certain pleasures. But pleasure is the principal end of all the moral virtues, as will be said in the seventh book of the present work (1504–1515). In every moral virtue it is requisite that a person have joy and sorrow in the things he ought. In keeping with this, he says that moral virtue is concerned with pleasures and sorrows because the purpose of any moral virtue is that a man be rightly ordered in his pleasures and in his sorrows.

268. Then [2], at "We perform evil actions," he proves his proposition: first by reasons taken from things belonging to virtue, and second [6], at "Our contention will etc.," by reasons on the part of the virtuous man himself. He presents four reasons pertaining to the first point. The first reason [2] is taken from the inclination of men intent on virtue. It was shown previously (264–265) that virtue is produced and destroyed by deeds of the same person done in a contrary way. Indeed, we see that virtue is destroyed by pleasure and sadness; we perform evil actions out of a desire for pleasure, we avoid good or virtuous works because of the sadness we fear in honest labor. Hence, as Plato said, one who is intent on virtue should have some sort of moral training from his earliest years that he may rejoice and be sorrowful about the right things. This is proper instruction for youths so that they become accustomed to take pleasure in good works and be grieved in evil works. Therefore, teachers of youth compliment those who do good deeds and reprove those who do evil.

269. At **"Besides, if"** [3] he presents the second reason based on the matter of the moral virtue in the following way. Every moral virtue deals with actions (as justice which treats of buying, selling, and other things of this kind), or with passions (as mildness which treats of anger), and so with the other virtues. But pleasure or sorrow follows every passion that is nothing else but the motion of the appetitive power in pursuit of good or in flight from evil. When the good to which the appetite tends is forthcoming, therefore, or when the evil which it flees is avoided, pleasure follows. But when the contrary happens, sorrow follows. Thus the angered man rejoices in getting revenge and likewise the cowardly man in avoiding dangers. But when the opposite is true, these persons are sorrowful. It remains, therefore, that every moral virtue regards pleasures and sorrows as having the aspect of ends.

270. The third reason presented at **"Penalties inflicted"** [4] is taken from the idea of a remedy for the soul. As a medicine used for the restoration of health is a kind of disagreeable potion from which the sweetness has been removed, so a penalty used for the restoration of virtue is a kind of medicine, for a penalty consists in taking away certain pleasures or applying certain disagreeable things. The reason for this is that a medicine is naturally to be used as a contrary thing. Thus in the case of fever doctors apply cooling remedies. Hence moral virtue also is concerned with certain pleasures and sorrows.

271. At **"Furthermore, as"** [5] he presents the fourth reason, which is taken from what is contrary to and destructive of virtue. Every habit, he says, has a disposition to do and to be busied with the things by which it is made worse and better, that is, by which the goodness of a good habit and the evil of a bad habit is increased. This can be understood likewise of the things by which the habit naturally becomes worse or better, that is, by which it naturally is formed or increased (which is to be made better), or destroyed or diminished (which is to be made worse). We see that men become evil through the deterioration of virtue from the fact that they pursue the pleasures and steer clear of the sorrows which they ought not, or when they ought not, or in some other way by which one may deviate from right reason.

272. The Stoics took occasion of this to say that virtues are certain quiescent and passionless dispositions. The reason was that they saw men become evil through pleasures and sorrows, and consequently they thought that virtue consists in the total cessation of the changes of the passions. But in this they erred wishing to exclude entirely the passions of the soul from a virtuous man. It belongs, of course, to the good of reason to regulate the sensitive appetite—and the passions are movements of this appetite. Hence it is not the business of virtue to exclude all but only the inordinate passions, that is, those which are not as they ought to be and are not at the time they ought to be (he adds also all the other things belonging to the remaining circumstances). From this he then concludes that we must suppose that virtue should work what is best regarding pleasures and sorrows but vice, which is the habit opposed to virtue, should work what is evil.

273. Then [6], at **"Our contention will,"** he introduces to his proposition four other reasons taken on the part of

men in whom virtue, pleasure, and sorrow are found. The first reason [6] is derived from pleasures in general. He says that three things fall under human choice: the good or virtuous, the helpful or useful, and the pleasurable. Contrary to these are also three things: evil or vice as opposed to the virtuous, the harmful as opposed to the useful, the sorrowful as opposed to the pleasurable. In regard to all these, the virtuous man disposes himself rightly but the vicious man badly, especially in the matter of pleasure, which is more common among the things mentioned since it belongs to two of them.

274. First in regard to the things partaking of pleasure. Pleasure is found in all animals since it is not only in the intellectual power but also in the sensitive power. The useful and the virtuous, however, pertain to the intellectual power alone. This is so because the virtuous act is performed in accord with reason while the useful implies an order of one to another, and "to order" is proper to reason.

275. Another common feature is on the part of the things themselves in which pleasure is gained. Pleasure, in fact, follows everything that falls under choice. Now the virtuous is pleasurable to man because it is agreeable to reason, and the useful also gives pleasure by reason of the expected benefit. But, on the other hand, not every pleasurable action is useful or virtuous, as is obvious in the pleasures of sense.

276. At "**Pleasure, too**" [7] he presents the second reason, which is taken from an inherent characteristic of pleasure. Pleasure has grown up with us all alike from childhood, since a newborn child delights in his milk. Therefore, it is difficult for man to curb this passion acquired with life because it starts in man at the beginning of life. Hence moral virtue is especially concerned with pleasure.

277. He assigns the third reason at "**Some regulate**" [8]. This reason is derived from man's inclination. All men regulate their activities by pleasure and sorrow. They are intent on activities they find pleasant and they avoid activities they find distressing. Hence the whole business of a moral virtue, which is ordered to good activity, must concern pleasure and sorrow. It is quite important to note what activities one finds pleasant or painful, and whether rightly or wrongly so. The reason is that he who rejoices in good performs good actions, but he who rejoices in evil performs evil actions.

278. He assigns the fourth reason at "**As Heraclitus says**" [9]. This is taken from a comparison with anger. It is more difficult, as Heraclitus said, to fight against pleasure than against anger, even though it seems most difficult to fight against anger because of its vehemence. But the desire of pleasure is both more common and more natural, and besides, it lasts longer. Art and virtue however always treat of the more difficult, for anyone can operate well in the easier things. But it takes one skilled in virtue and art to operate well in difficult things. Thus it is obvious, from what has been said, that the whole business of virtue and of political science or of public affairs is concerned with pleasures and sorrows. If a man uses these well he will be virtuous, but if he uses them badly he will be evil.

279. Then [10], at "**It has been said that,**" he sums up in conclusion the points that have been made: virtue is concerned with pleasures and sor-

rows; virtue is produced and increased by the same actions that, when done in the opposite way, destroy virtue; the same actions producing virtue are in turn produced by virtue once formed.

LECTURE IV
Comparison between Virtue and Art

TEXT OF ARISTOTLE (*1105a17–1105b18*) Chapter 4

1. *Someone may rightly ask how we can say that man must become just by doing just actions, and temperate by doing temperate actions. If people perform just and temperate works they are already just and temperate, as those who produce grammatical or musical works are already grammarians or musicians.*   **1105a17–21; 280**

2. *But this is not true in the arts. A man may at times produce something grammatical by chance or with the help of another. He will therefore be a grammarian only if he produces a grammatical work in a grammatical way, that is, in accordance with the science of grammar that he possesses.*   **1105a21–26; 281**

3. *Another dissimilarity between the arts and virtues is that works of art have their perfection in themselves. It is enough then that these be made with certain qualities. Yet works of virtue are not justly and temperately performed if they have certain qualities; but the agent performing them must fulfill the following conditions. (1) He must know what he is doing. (2) He must choose the virtuous works for their own sakes. (3) He must possess the disposition and operate according to it resolutely and with stability. Except for knowledge, these conditions are not required in the other arts. Mere knowledge, however, has little or no importance to the virtues but what occurs from the frequent performance of just and temperate actions is all important.*   **1105a26–1105b7; 282–284**

4. *Works then are called just and temperate when they are such as a just and temperate man will do. Now a just and temperate man is not one who performs these actions but who performs them as the just and temperate perform them.*   **1105b7–9; 285–286**

5. *It has been well said, therefore, that a man becomes just by doing just actions and temperate by doing temperate actions. Anyone who does not perform these actions has not the slightest interest in becoming virtuous.*   **1105b9–12; 287**

6. *Many, however, fail to do good actions but, taking refuge in theory, think that by philosophizing they will become virtuous. They act like the sick who listen carefully to the doctor but do nothing he prescribes. Hence, just as those who take care of themselves in this way will never have a healthy body, so those who merely philosophize will not have a healthy soul.*   **1105b12–18; 288**

COMMENTARY OF ST. THOMAS

280. After the Philosopher has shown that virtues are caused by actions, he now raises a doubt about this assertion. Regarding it he does three things. First [A] he presents a problem. Second [2], at "But this is not true etc.," he solves it. Third [5], from the discussion of the question he comes to the conclusion principally intended, at "It has been well said, therefore, etc." The doubt that he first raises is this. What is true of virtue is true of art. But in art it is true that no one produces a work

of art except one who possesses the art, as no one produces anything grammatical unless he is a grammarian, nor anything musical unless he be a musician. It will be true in virtue, therefore, that whoever performs just works is already just and whoever performs temperate works is already temperate. Hence our previous contention (164) does not seem to be true, that men become just by doing just actions and temperate by doing temperate actions.

281. Then [2], at "**But this is not,**" he

solves this doubt first by rejecting what was assumed about art and second [3] by disproving the likeness said to exist between virtue and art, at "Another dissimilarity etc." He says first that it is not true in art, as was assumed, that whoever produces a grammatical work is already a grammarian. It happens sometimes that an ignoramus by chance pronounces a word correctly. Sometimes this happens with the help of another whose example is followed, for instance, a mimic imitates the correct pronunciation given by a grammarian. But a man is to be judged a grammarian only when he produces a grammatical work and in a grammatical way, that is, in accord with the science of grammar that he possesses.

282. Then [3], at "**Another dissimilarity,**" he gives the second solution, in two steps. First he eliminates the likeness between art and virtue. Second [4] he concludes the solution at "Works then are called just etc." He says first that there is no similarity in art and virtue since works of art have in themselves what belongs to the perfection of the art. The explanation is that art is the right plan of making things, as will be said in the sixth book of the present work (1153, 1160, 1166). "Making" is an operation that passes to external matter, and an operation of this kind is a perfection of the thing made. Hence in such actions the good consists in the object made. It is enough for the good of art, therefore, that the things made be good. But virtues are principles of actions that do not go out into external matter but remain in the agents. Hence actions of this kind are perfections of the agents. So the good of these actions is identical with the agents themselves.

283. He says, therefore, in order that actions be justly and temperately performed, it is not enough that the things done be good but the agent must work in a proper manner. Regarding this manner, he says we must pay attention to three things. (1) The first, pertaining to the intellect or reason, is that one who performs a virtuous action should not act in ignorance or by chance but should know what he is doing. (2) The second is taken on the part of the appetitive power. Here two things are noted. One is that the action be not done out of passion, as happens when a person performs a virtuous deed because of fear. But the action should be done by a choice that is not made for the sake of something else, as happens when a person performs a good action for money or vainglory. The actions should be done for the sake of the virtuous work itself which, as something agreeable, is inherently pleasing to him who has the habit of virtue. (3) The third, taken from the nature of a habit, is that a person should possess a virtuous choice and operate according to it resolutely—that is, consistently on his part—and with stability so as not to be moved by any external thing.

284. Only the first of these, knowledge, is required in the arts. A man can be a good artist even if he never chooses to work according to art and does not persevere in his work. But knowledge has little or no importance in a person being virtuous, but his goodness consists entirely in other things that take place within him by frequent actions, and thus he becomes stable.

285. Then [4], at "**Works then,**" he concludes the solution of the above-mentioned doubt. He states that things done are called just and temperate because they are similar to the things that a just and temperate man does. Whoever performs these actions need not necessarily be just and temperate, but

he who performs them as just and temperate men perform them according to the three conditions just laid down is said to be just and temperate. Men, therefore, first perform just and temperate actions—not in the same way as the just and temperate do—and such actions in their turn produce the habit.

286. If it should be asked how this is possible, since nothing can move itself from potency to act, we must answer that the perfection of moral virtue, which we are treating, consists in reason's control of the appetite. Now, the first principles of reason, no less in moral than in speculative matters, have been given by nature. Therefore, just as by means of previously known principles a man makes himself actually understand by personal effort of discovery, so also by acting according to the principles of practical reason a man makes himself actually virtuous.

287. Then [5], at "**It has been well said, therefore,**" he comes to the conclusion principally intended. First he brings his proposition to an end; and second [6], at "Many, however, fail etc.," he discredits a false opinion of certain persons. He concludes that it has been well said above (264, 280) that a man becomes just by doing just actions and temperate by doing temperate actions. But he who does not perform actions nor develop his disposition will never become virtuous.

288. Then [6], at "**Many, however**" he discredits the false opinion of certain persons who do not perform works of virtues but, by taking refuge in the discussion of virtues, think they can become virtuous by philosophizing. Such people, he says, are like the sick who carefully listen to what the doctor has to say but do nothing about carrying out his prescriptions. Thus philosophy is to the cure of the soul what medicine is to the cure of the body. Hence, as those who listen to the advice of doctors and disregard it will never have a well regulated body, so those who listen to the warnings of moral philosophers and do not heed them will never have a well regulated soul.

LECTURE V
The Definition of Virtue

TEXT OF ARISTOTLE (*1105b19–1106a13*) Chapter 5

1. Now we must determine the definition of virtue. Since there are three principles occurring in the soul: passions, powers, and habits, virtue will be one of these three. **1105b19–21; 289–290**

2. By passions I mean: concupiscence, anger, aggressiveness, envy, joy, love, hatred, desire, jealousy, pity, and all the movements followed by pleasure and sorrow. **1105b21–23; 291–296**

3. I call those principles powers in respect of which we are said to be capable of experiencing passions, for example, of becoming angry or being sad or having pity. **1105b23–25; 297**

4. I call those principles habits in respect of which we are well or badly disposed towards the passions. Thus we are badly disposed in becoming angry in a violent or feeble way, but we are well disposed in doing so with moderation. The same applies to all habits and passions. **1105b25–28; 298**

5. Neither virtues nor vices, therefore, are passions because: (1) We are not called good or evil by reason of the passions but by reason of virtue or vice. **1105b28–31; 299**

6. (2) We are neither praised nor reproached for the passions. Now a man is not praised or blamed for being afraid or angry simply but in a particular way. We are, though, praised or blamed for virtues or vices. **1105b31–1106a2; 300**

7. (3) We become angry and are afraid without willing it, but the virtues are certain choices or at least not without choice. **1106a2–4; 301**

8. (4) We are said to be moved by the passions. However we are not moved but disposed in a certain way by the virtues and vices. **1106a4–6; 302**

9. For this reason also the virtues are not powers, for we are not called good or evil, we are not praised or blamed because we are simply capable of being affected by the passions. **1106a6–9; 303**

10. Furthermore, the powers are in us by nature, but we are not good or evil by nature, as we said above. **1106a9–10; 304**

11. If then virtues are neither passions nor powers, it remains that they are habits. We say, therefore, that habit is the genus of virtue. **1106a10–13; 305**

COMMENTARY OF ST. THOMAS

289. After the Philosopher has treated the cause of virtue, he now begins to investigate the definition of virtue. He divides the investigation into two parts. In the first he shows what virtue is and in the second [Lect. X] he ascertains the opposition of virtue to vice at "There are three etc." (1108b11). The first part is treated under two headings. In the first [1] he determines what virtue is in general. In the second [Lect. VIII] he applies the adopted definition to particular virtues, at "We must speak of virtue not only under its universal aspect" (1107 a 28). This first section is also twofold, and in the first of these [1] he investigates the definition of virtue. In the second [Lect. VII] he concludes the definition, at "Virtue then is a habit etc." (1107). On the first point he first [1] investigates the genus of virtue and second [Lect. VI] its specific difference, at "We must consider not only etc." (1106 a 16). He investigates the genus by parts. Hence, regarding the first he does three things. First [1] he offers the division. Second [2], at "By passions I mean etc.," he

explains its parts. Third [5], at "Neither virtues nor vices," he argues from the accepted definition.

290. He says first that to establish the definition of virtue we have to take for granted three principles in the soul: passions, powers, and habits. Virtue must come under one of these, for he just said (282) that virtue is a principle of certain operations of the soul. Now no principle of operation is found in the soul outside these three. Sometimes a man seems to act from passion, for example, anger; sometimes from habit, as when he works by art; sometimes from mere potentiality, as when he begins a new activity. It is obvious that not absolutely everything in the soul is included under this division—the essence of the soul and the operation of the intellect do not belong here—but only the things that are principles of some operation are considered.

291. Then [2], at "By passions I mean," he indicates the members of the division just mentioned. First [2] he makes known those that are passions; second [3], those that are powers, at "I call those principles powers etc."; third [4], those that are habits, at "I call those principles habits etc." Regarding the first we must consider that passions are not attributed to the vegetative soul because the powers of this part of the soul are not passive, as they are in both the sensitive part and the intellective part, but active. The perceptive and appetitive powers, except the active intellect, are passive. Although feeling and understanding are in a way passions (i.e., they "suffer" change), passions are properly denominated not because of the apprehension of sense or intellect but only because of the appetite. The reason is that the op-

eration of the perceptive power takes place according as the thing perceived is in the knower according to the state of the knower. Now the object perceived is, so to speak, drawn to the knower. But the operation of the appetitive power takes place according as the one desiring is inclined to the thing desired. Because it is characteristic of the recipient (patientis) that he be drawn by the agent, and not the converse, it follows that only the operations of the appetitive powers, but not the operations of the perceptive powers, are called passions.

292. Even among the appetitive powers the operation of the intellective appetite is not properly called passion. It does not take place with a change of a bodily organ, which is necessary to the nature of a passion properly speaking. Also in the operation of the intellective appetite, which is the will, man is not the passive recipient, but rather he directs himself as the master of his action. It remains, therefore, that operations of the sensitive appetite, which are accompanied by a change of a bodily organ and which in a way draw man, should be called passions in a strict sense.

293. The sensitive appetite is divided into two powers: (1) the concupiscible, which concerns sensible good absolutely (this is pleasurable to sense) and evil contrary to it; (2) the irascible, which concerns good under the aspect of a certain eminence. For example, victory is said to be a kind of good, although it is not accompanied by pleasure of sense. Whatever passions concern good or evil absolutely, therefore, are found in the concupiscible appetite. Certain of these—three in number—regard the good: love (which implies a certain connaturality

of the appetite with the good loved), desire (which implies a movement of the appetite towards the good loved), and delight (which implies a repose of the appetite in the good loved). Opposed to these in respect to evil are: hatred to love, aversion or flight to desire, sadness to delight. But those passions that concern good or evil under the aspect of difficulty belong to the irascible, as fear and boldness in regard to evil, hope and despair in regard to good. A fifth is anger, which is a composite passion and so has no opposite.

294. In enumerating the passions, therefore, he says they are: concupiscence (which we call desire), anger, fear, boldness, envy (which is contained under sadness), and joy (which is contained under pleasure) for this is a non-corporeal pleasure that consists in an interior perception of the good, and likewise a love, hatred, and desire of the same interior kind. Desire differs from concupiscence in that concupiscence pertains to bodily pleasure while desire concerns every pleasure without distinction.

295. He adds jealousy and pity, which are species of sadness. Pity is sadness at another's misfortune, and jealousy is sadness because one lacks what others have.

296. He also adds that pleasure and sorrow universally follow the above-mentioned passions, because all others imply certain movements to good and evil, and these movements are accompanied by pleasure or sorrow. Hence all other passions are terminated at pleasure and sorrow.

297. Then [3], at "**I call those principles powers**," he identifies the powers not in general but those pertaining to moral study precisely as they differ from the passions. He affirms that

powers are said to exist according as we are considered capable of experiencing these passions, that is, the powers are said to "suffer" or to receive these passions. Thus the irascible power exists according as we are capable of becoming angry and the concupiscible power according as we are capable of becoming sad or showing pity.

298. Then [4], at "**I call those principles habits**," he identifies the habits. Likewise this is not done in general but in regard to those pertaining to moral study by comparison with the passions. Habits, he states, are said to exist according as we consistently use the passions well or badly. Now a habit is a disposition determining a power in reference to something. When the determination is made conformable to the nature of the thing, there will be a good habit which disposes that a thing be done well. Otherwise there will be a bad habit according to which a thing will be done badly. He illustrates what we do according to habit, how we may be angry either wrongly—when this is done in a violent or weak manner, that is, according to excess or defect—or well if done with moderation.

299. Then [5], at "**Therefore neither virtues**," he argues from the division previously given. First he shows that virtues are not passions. Second [9], at "For this reason also etc.," he shows that they are not powers. Third [11], at "If then virtues etc.," he concludes they are habits. For the first statement he assigns four reasons. The first is this. We are called good according to virtues and evil according to the opposite vices. But we are not called good or evil according to passions taken absolutely. Passions, therefore, are neither virtues nor vices.

300. He presents the second reason

at "**We are neither**" [6]. It is taken from praise and reproach, which are kinds of attestation of goodness and evil. He says that we are praised for virtues and reproached for the opposite vices. But we are neither praised nor reproached for the passions taken absolutely. A man is not praised or blamed because he is simply afraid or angry but only because he is afraid or angry in a particular way, that is, according to reason or contrary to reason. The same must be understood of the other passions of the soul. The passions of the soul, therefore, are neither virtues nor vices.

301. At "**We become angry**" [7] he presents the third reason, which is taken from a virtuous manner of acting. Virtues are either choices or not without choice, for the very act of virtue can be called virtue. If we consider the principal acts of virtues, which are interior, virtue is choice; but if we consider the exterior acts, virtue is not without choice because the exterior acts of virtue proceed from interior choice. If virtue be taken as the very habit of virtue, even in this sense it does not lack choice, as a cause is not without its proper effect. The passions, however, come to us without choice because they precede the deliberations of the reason necessary for choice. This is what he means saying that we are angry and are afraid without willing it, that is, not by choice of the reason. The passions, therefore, are not virtues.

302. He presents the fourth reason at "**We are said**" [8]. This is taken from the very nature of virtue. The passions are movements according to which we are said to be moved. The virtues and vices are qualities according to which we are said not to be moved but to be disposed in some way, whether well or badly that our movement may ensue. The passions, therefore, are neither virtues nor vices.

303. Then [9], at "**For this reason,**" he shows that virtues are not powers for two reasons. The first of these is taken from the nature of good and evil, as has just been proved (299–300) about the passions. The reason is this. No one is called good or evil, no one is praised or reproached, because he is capable of being affected by some passion—for instance, that he is capable of becoming angry or being afraid. But we are called good or evil and are praised or reproached because of virtues and vices. Virtues and vices, therefore, are not powers.

304. He gives the second reason at "**Furthermore, the powers**" [10]. It is taken on the part of the cause and is this. Powers are in us by nature because they are natural characteristics of the soul. But virtues and vices by which we are called good or evil are not in us by nature, as was proved above (248–251). Virtues and vices, therefore, are not powers.

305. Then [11], at "**If then,**" he concludes his proposition. If virtues are neither passions nor powers, it remains that they are habits according to the previously given division. Thus he concludes that virtue with regard to its generic definition obviously is a habit.

LECTURE VI
Virtue, a Kind of Habit

TEXT OF ARISTOTLE (*1106a14–1106b28*) Chapter 6

1. We must consider not only that virtue is a habit but also what kind of habit. **1106a14–15; 306**

2. We must explain, therefore, that virtue perfects everything of which it is the virtue, rendering both the possessor good and his work good. Thus the virtue or power of the eye makes good both the eye and its operation, for it is by the power of the eye that we see well. Likewise the virtue or excellence of a horse makes the horse good and also makes him good for running, riding and awaiting the enemy. If this be true in all other things, then human virtue will be a habit making man good and rendering his work good. **1106a15–24; 307–308**

3. How this takes place has already been described, [1104a27] **1106a24; 309**

4. but it will become still clearer if we study the nature of virtue. In all continuous and divisible matter, we can take the more, the less, and the equal amount. These are understood either in regard to the thing or in regard to us. But the equal is a mean between excess and defect. **1106a24–29; 310**

5. By the mean on the part of the thing, I understand that which is equally distant from both extremes and which is one and the same for everybody. By the mean in regard to us, I understand that which is neither in excess nor in defect. This, however, is not one and the same for everybody. **1106a29–32; 311**

6. For example, if ten be taken as many and two as few, then six will be the mean on part of the thing because six both exceeds and is exceeded by an equal amount. This mean is according to arithmetic proportion. **1106a33–36; 312**

7. But the mean in regard to us is not to be taken in this way. A trainer will not order six pounds of food for someone simply because eating ten pounds is a great deal and eating two pounds is a small amount. This may be much or little for the person eating. For Milo it would certainly be little, but it would be much for a champion in gymnastics; and the same holds true in running and wrestling. Thus everyone who is wise avoids excess and wants to find the mean, not on the part of the thing but in regard to us. **1106a36–1106b7; 313–314**

8. Every practical science then perfects its work by keeping in view the mean and executing the work according to the mean. Hence it is customary to tell a man who has done a good piece of work that nothing is to be added or taken away, meaning that excess and defect disfigure a work but the mean preserves it. As we have said, good workmen work with an eye on the mean. But virtue like nature is more certain and better than art. Virtue then will aim at the mean. **1106b8–16; 315–316**

9. I am speaking of moral virtue, for it treats of passions and operations in which we find excess, defect, and the mean. Thus aggressiveness, fear, concupiscence, aversion, anger, pity, and, in general, pleasure and sorrow take place with excess and defect. Both of these are evil; but to experience these passions at the right time, for the right objects, toward the right persons, with the right motive, and in the right way is the mean and the highest good of virtue. Similarly, excess, defect, and the mean are to be found in actions. Now moral virtue is concerned with passions and operations in which excess is vicious, defect is reproachable, and the mean receives praise and shows the right path. These two (praise and righteousness) pertain to virtue. Moral virtue, therefore, is a kind of middle course and aims at the mean. **1106b16–28; 317–318**

COMMENTARY OF ST. THOMAS

306. After the Philosopher has explained the genus of virtue, he now begins an inquiry into the specific difference of virtue. First [1] he presents his proposition. He says that in order to know what virtue is we must consider not only that it is a habit—thus the genus is understood, but what kind of habit—thus the specific difference is indicated.

307. Second [2], at "We must explain, therefore," he makes known the proposition. On this point he does

two things. First [2] he manifests a certain common quality of virtue. Second [3], from this quality of virtue he explains its specific difference, at "How this etc." He says first that every virtue makes its possessor good and his work good. Thus the virtue or power of the eye makes the eye good and gives us good sight, which is the proper function of the eye. Likewise the virtue or excellence of a horse makes a horse good and makes it perform well, that is, run fast, ride easily, and fearlessly await the enemy.

308. The reason is that the virtue or power of a thing is judged by the best it can do. For example, the power of one who can carry a hundred pounds is determined by his actual carrying of this weight, as is said in the first book *De Coelo* (Ch. 11, 281a8; St. Th. Lect. XXV, 249),[1] and not by the fact that he carries fifty pounds. Now the utmost or best to which the power of anything extends is called its excellent performance. It belongs to the virtue of every thing, therefore, to render an excellent performance. Because a perfect opera-

tion proceeds only from a perfect agent, it follows that everything is both good and operates well according to its own virtue. If this be true in all other things—and such was already apparent from our examples—human virtue must be a kind of habit, as was mentioned above (305). From this habit man becomes good formally speaking (as one becomes white by whiteness) and operates well.

309. Then [3], at "**How this,**" he investigates the specific difference of virtue according to the quality of virtue previously indicated. He does this under three headings: first [3] according to the property of the operations; second [4], according to the nature of virtue, at "but it will become still clearer etc."; third [Lect. VII] according to the special character of good or evil, at "Moreover, there are many etc." (1106b29). He says first that the way in which a man may become good and do good has been treated already (257). It was noted also (260–264) that we are made good in every virtue by operations according to the mean. Then having become good we perform good actions. It remains, therefore, that if virtue makes a man good and his work good, it will consist in the mean.

310. Then [4], at "**but it will become etc.,**" he proves the same by the nature of virtue. Regarding this he does three things. First he introduces certain preliminaries necessary to explain his proposition. Second [8], he concludes his proposition at "Every practical science then etc." Third [9], he explains an inference at "I am speaking of moral

---

1   Sancti Thomae Aquinatis *In Aristotelis Libros de Coelo et Mundo Expositio.* Ed. Spiazzi, Turin/Rome: Marietti, 1952.

virtue etc." On the first point he does two things. First he proposes the things necessary to elucidate the proposition. Second [5] he clarifies what he has said, at "By the mean on the part etc." He says first that the manner in which we become good and perform good acts will be clearer still if we consider the nature of virtue. For an understanding of this, we must take for granted beforehand that virtue treats three things: the more, the less, and the equal. Virtue treats these both in continuous, contingent matters, and even in any other divisible matter, whether it be numerically divided as all discrete things, or whether it be divided incidentally—for example, by intensity and indistinctness of a quality in a subject. These three are so arranged that the equal holds a middle place between the more, which pertains to excess, and the less, which pertains to defect. This can be understood in two ways: one according to absolute quantity in some thing and the other in relation to us.

311. Then [5], at "**By the mean on the part of the thing,**" he clarifies what he said about the difference on the part of the thing (objective) and in regard to us (relative): first by means of reason, and second [6] by way of example at "For example, if etc." He says first that the objective mean is the point equidistant from both extremes. It is the same for all because it is understood according to the absolute quantity of the thing. But the mean is relative in regard to us inasmuch as it neither exceeds nor falls short of a proportion suitable to us. Hence this mean is not the same for all. If we apply the relative mean to a shoe, it will not be more than the length of the foot nor less. It will not be the same for all because not all have the same size foot.

312. Then [6], at "**For example, if,**" he clarifies what he has said, by way of example: first regarding the objective mean which is equally distant from the extremes. Thus six is the mean between ten (which is the more) and two (which is the less) because six is less than ten and more than two by the same amount, four. The mean, which is taken in numbers from the equal distance between two extremes, is said to be according to arithmetic proportion which considers numerical quantity. But the mean, which is taken from the equality of proportion in regard to us, is said to be according to the geometric proportion as will be made clear afterwards in the fifth book (944, 949, 950, 972).

313. Second [7], at "**But the mean in regard to us,**" he gives examples of the mean. He says that the mean, which is understood in comparison with us, is not to be taken according to equal distance between extremes. This is sufficiently clear in the previous example of the shoe. If a shoe twenty fingers' breadth is long and a shoe four fingers' breadth is short it does not necessarily follow that one twelve fingers' breadth will be the right fit. Perhaps it will be large compared to the foot of one person and small compared to the foot of another. He also exemplifies this mean in food. If eating ten pounds or ten portions is much and eating two pounds is little, a trainer—whose duty it is to make out someone's diet—should not for this reason prescribe six pounds, since even this is much for one person and little for another.

314. This would indeed be little for a man called Milo who, according to Solinus, ate a whole beef in a day. But it would be much for a champion in gymnastics, for one who has to excel in sports—in which men used to contend

naked—and must eat lightly to be in better condition. The same is true of those who run at the stadium and of those who take up wrestling—a sport engaged in by the Greeks for exercise. So it is also in every operative science. The wise man avoids excess and defect, and wants to find the mean not objectively but relative to us.

315. Then [8], at "**Every practical science**," he argues from the premises in this way. Every operative science perfects its work in this: that in planning it aims for the mean, and in execution it carries out its work in accord with the mean. Indications of this can be had from the fact that men are in the habit of saying, when a work is well done, that not a thing is to be added nor taken away. Thus they give us to understand that excess and defect spoil a work which is preserved by the mean. Hence good workmen, as has been pointed out (313–314), work with an eye on the mean. But virtue like nature is more certain and even better than any art. Moral virtue operates by inclining in a determined way to one thing as nature does. Indeed custom becomes nature. But art, which operates according to reason, is indifferent to various objects. Hence like nature it is more certain than art.

316. Likewise virtue is better than art because by art a man is capable of doing a good work, but art does not cause him to do the good work. He can do a bad work because art does not incline to the good use of art; a grammarian for example can speak incorrectly. But by virtue a man not only is capable of operating but actually performs the action because virtue like

nature inclines to a good operation. Art alone gives only the knowledge of the operation. Consequently even for this secondary reason virtue, which is better than art, aims at the mean.

317. Then [9], at "**I am speaking**," he explains a further conclusion. He affirms that what has been said (256–263) ought to be understood of moral virtue that concerns passions and operations to which belong excess, defect and mean. He gives an example first from the passions saying that fear, aggressiveness, concupiscence, aversion (which is a fleeing from something), anger, pity, and any pleasure and sorrow may happen in greater and less degree than they ought. Both the excess and the defect are evil. But if a man should fear and dare (so of the other passions) what he ought, in the things he ought, in regard to the persons he ought, for the motive he ought, and in the way he ought, this will be a mean for the passions. It will be also the highest good of virtue. Similarly excess, defect, and mean are found in actions. Moral virtue treats of passions and actions as its proper matter so that in them excess is vicious and defect worthy of reproach, but the mean receives praise and shows the right path. These two pertain to virtue: righteousness (which is opposed to vicious perverseness) and praise (which is opposed to reproach). This and vicious perverseness follow from the first two (excess and defect).

318. Thus he concludes that moral virtue considered in itself is a kind of middle course and is an indicator of the mean inasmuch as it aims at the mean and accomplishes it.

LECTURE VII
Conclusion of the Definition

TEXT OF ARISTOTLE (*1106b28–1107a27*) Chapter 6

1. Moreover, there are many ways of sinning (for evil partakes of the unlimited in the opinion of the Pythagoreans, and good partakes of the limited). However, there is only one way of doing what is right. It is easy to sin, therefore, but difficult to do what is right. It is easy indeed to miss a bull's eye but difficult to hit it. For this reason then defect and excess pertain to vice but the mean to virtue. Men are good in but one way but evil in many ways.

1106b28–35; 319–321

2. Virtue then is a habit that chooses the mean in regard to us, as that mean is determined by reason and understood by a wise man. **1106b36–1107a2; 322–323**

3. Virtue is a mean between two vices: of that which is according to excess and of that which is according to defect. **1107a2–3; 324**

4. In regard to this mean, some vices fall short but others exceed what is right both in the passions and in actions. Virtue, however, discovers and chooses the mean. **1107a3–6; 325**

5. For this reason, virtue according to its essence and definition is a mean. But it is also an extreme as having the nature of what is best and right. **1107a6–8; 326–327**

6. Not every action or passion of the soul admits a mean. Certain ones imply vice by their very name: passions such as ill-will, shamelessness, envy and actions such as adultery, theft, murder. All these and their ilk are said to be evil in themselves and not only in their excess or defect. Neither do we have the option of acting well or badly in an action like adultery, as though it could be considered proper in itself, or done in a fitting manner, or at a right time, or in due circumstances, but to do any of them is sinful without any qualification.

1107a8–17; 328–329

7. To seek a mean in these matters would be like assigning a mean to excess and defect in unjust, or in cowardly or lustful actions. Thus there would be a mean of an excess and of a defect, and an excess of an excess and a defect of a defect. **1107a18–21; 330**

8. An excess and defect are not found in temperance and fortitude because a mean is in no way an extreme, so excess or defect cannot be the mean of vice but what is done is vicious. As a consequence there cannot be a mean in any excess or defect, nor can there be excess or defect in any mean. **1107a22–27; 331–332**

COMMENTARY OF ST. THOMAS

319. After giving the two previous reasons, the Philosopher now adds a third based upon the nature of good and evil. Accepting the Pythagorean view, he says that there are many ways of sinning because evil, which is included in the nature of sin, partakes of the unlimited, but good partakes of the limited. We must understand then, on the contrary, that there is only one way of doing what is right.

320. The reason for this can be found in the statement of Dionysius in the book *De Divinis Nominibus*,[2] that good results from a united and complete cause but evil from any single defect, as is evident in physical goodness and badness. Ugliness, which is a defect of

---

2   *Sancti Thomae Aquinatis In Librum Beati Dionysii De Divinis Nominibus Expositio*, C. IV, 237; Lect. XXII, 572. Ed. Pera, Turin/Rome: Marietti, 1950.

physical beauty, results from any member being unsightly. But beauty arises only when all the members are well proportioned and of a healthy hue. Likewise sickness, a defect in the constitution of the body, happens from a single disorder of any humor. But health is dependent on the proper proportion of all the humors. Likewise sin is committed in human action from any circumstance being inordinate in any way either by excess or defect. But goodness will be present only when all the circumstances are rightly ordered. As health or beauty comes about in a single way but sickness and ugliness in many, even in an unlimited number of ways, so also moral goodness results in only one way but the act of sin takes place in countless ways. Hence it is easy to sin because sin can happen in a variety of modes, but it is difficult to do what is right because rectitude happens only in one way.

321. He gives as an example that it is easy to miss the center of the target, because a miss can happen in numerous ways. But to hit the center spot is difficult because a hit happens in only one way. Now it is obvious that excess and defect take place in various ways but the mean in a single way. Hence excess and defect manifestly pertain to vice but the mean to virtue because men are good simply, that is, in one way, but evil at sundry times, i.e., in many ways as has just been stated (320).

322. Then [2], at **"Virtue then is,"** he infers the definition of virtue from the premises. First, 1] he presents the definition, and second [3] he explains it, at "Virtue is a mean between two etc." Third [6] he rejects an error, at "Not every action etc." In the definition of virtue he treats four points. The first of

these is the genus, which he touches on when he says that virtue is a habit (305). The second is the act of the moral virtue, for the habit must be defined by the act. This he mentions by the word "chooses," that is, acts according to choice, for the principal act of virtue is choice—he will discuss this later (432). Since the act must be determined by the object, he refers then, third, to the object or the term of the action when he says "the mean in regard to us." It was shown above (314) that virtue seeks out and uses the mean not of the thing but in regard to us. Similarly it has been said (257) that moral virtue is in the appetite, which participates in reason. He had to add, therefore, a fourth notion, which refers to the cause of goodness in virtue, by the words "determined by reason." It is good to seek the mean only insofar as it is determined by reason, but because reason can be right or erring, we must perform virtue according to right reason, as was ascertained previously (257).

323. To explain this he adds "as understood by a wise man." "Wise" here does not refer to one who is wise simply, knowing the ultimate causes of the whole universe, but rather to one who is prudent, that is, wise in human affairs, but this he will discuss in the sixth book (1163). Certainly the making of what is good in the art of building is determined by the judgment of one wise in that art, and the same is true in all the other arts.

324. Then [3], at **"Virtue is a mean,"** he explains the previously given definition in regard to his saying that virtue consists in the mean. On this point he does three things. First [3] he shows between what things there is a mean and, second [4], in reference to what thing this mean may be considered, at

"In regard to this etc." Third [5] he deduces a corollary at "For this reason virtue etc." He says first that virtue itself is a kind of middle course between two vices and between two vicious habits: one by way of excess and the other by way of defect. Thus liberality is the middle course between extravagance tending toward excess and miserliness tending toward avarice.

325. Then [4], at "**In regard to this,**" he shows in reference to what norm we are to judge excess, defect, and mean. He says we must further consider that some vices fall short of but others exceed, both in the passions and in actions, what is right. In regard to this some are deficient and others are in excess. But virtue, precisely as it observes what it ought, is said to discover the mean by reason and to choose it by the will. Thus it is evident that virtue itself is a middle course and, on the other hand, it employs the mean. It is indeed the middle course between two habits, but it uses the mean in actions and passions.

326. Then [5], at "**For this reason,**" he draws a further conclusion from his remarks: that virtue in its essence and definition is a mean. But precisely as it possesses the character of the best and as it acts or guides well in a determined genus it is an extreme. For an understanding of this, we must consider (as has been pointed out in 322), that the entire goodness of moral virtue depends on the rectitude of the reason. Hence good is in harmony with moral virtue according as it follows right reason, but evil has a reference to each vice, viz.: excess and defect inasmuch as both depart from right reason. Therefore, according to the nature of goodness and evil both vices are in one extreme, that is, in evil which is thus shown to be a deviation from reason. Virtue however is in the other extreme, that is, in good which is characterized as a following of reason.

327. By reason of this, virtue and the contrary vices do not follow the species indicated by the definition, because right reason is the motive and the extrinsic norm for the right appetite. But an evil appetite does not intend by vice to deviate from right reason—this is contrary to its intention—for it directly intends that object in which excess or defect is present. What is contrary to its intention is incidental. Now the incidental and the extrinsic do not constitute a species but the species of a habit is taken from the object to which the habit tends. But according to objects the mean belongs to virtue, and the extremes to vices. He says, therefore, that according to the nature of good, virtue lies in the extreme but according to the essential species, in the mean.

328. Then [6], at "**Not every action,**" he rejects an erroneous view. Because virtue can occupy the middle course and vice the extremes in actions and in passions, someone might think that this would happen in all actions and passions. But he rejects this by saying that not every action or passion of the soul admits a mean in the context of virtue.

329. He explains this first from reason [6], at "**Certain ones etc.**" Certain actions and passions by their very name imply vice: passions such as illwill, shamelessness, envy and actions such as adultery, theft, murder. All of these and their like are evil in themselves and not only in their excess or defect. Hence in such things a person cannot be virtuous no matter how he acts, but he always sins in doing them. In explaining this he adds that right or

wrong in actions like adultery does not arise from the fact that a person does the act as he ought or when he ought, so that then the act becomes good, but on the other hand evil when not done as it ought. Without qualification sin is present whenever any of these is present, for each of them implies an act opposed to what is right.

330. Second [7], he gives some examples by way of proof in the matter of vice, at "To seek a mean." He says that because such things imply evil in themselves, seeking a mean and extremes in them is like attributing a mean to excess and defect, whether it be in acting unjustly, or cowardly or lewdly—this would certainly be unfitting. Since these actions imply excess and defect, it follows that excess and defect would be a mean (which is a

contradiction) and that we would have to find the excess of the excess and the defect of the defect, which could go on forever.

331. Third [8], he explains the same thing by example in the matter of virtue at "An excess." Because temperance and fortitude imply a mean of themselves, they do not admit excess and defect in the sense that a man can be temperate or courageous in an excessive or defective manner. Likewise the mean of those things, which of themselves imply extremes, cannot be excess and defect. But no matter how any one of them is done, it is vicious.

332. Last he concludes that there cannot be a mean of any excess or defect, nor can there be an excess or defect of any mean.

LECTURE VIII
Explanation of the Definition in Detail

TEXT OF ARISTOTLE (*1107a28–1107b21*) Chapter 7

1. *We must speak of virtue not only under its universal aspect but we must apply the doctrine to individual 30 cases. In discussions which treat of actions, universals are not of much utility and particulars are more accurate, for actions are concerned with singulars. It is fitting then that discussions be in harmony with particulars. Therefore our teaching must be based on the explanation of individual virtues.* 1107a28–33; 333–334

2. *In actions concerned with fear and daring, the mean is fortitude. Here an excess in fearlessness lacks an applicable name (many things indeed are unnamed). But the man who is extreme in daring is called foolhardy, while the man who fears excessively and lacks daring is a coward.* 1107a33–1107b4; 335–341

3. *With regard to pleasures and pains—but not all of them—the mean is temperance (which is less concerned with pains). Excess in these things is called intemperance, but the defect does not often occur. Hence persons lacking a sense of pleasure are unnamed, although they may be called insensible.* 1107b4–8; 342

4. *In respect to the giving and receiving of money, the mean is liberality. The excess and defect are found in extravagance and stinginess, which in opposite ways do too much and too little. The spendthrift overdoes the giving and falls short in the acquisition, but the miser on the contrary is excessive in acquiring and deficient in giving. For the present we are content to discuss these matters in outline and as contained under headings, later we shall treat them more in detail.* 1107b8–16; 343

5. *Having to do with the use of money are other habits, the mean of which is magnificence. The magnificent or princely person, as concerned with bestowing great sums, differs from the liberal person who gives small amounts. Excess in magnificence is called apyrocalia (vulgar display) and banausia, but the defect, meanness. These extremes differ from the extremes opposed to liberality, the manner however of the difference will be treated later.* 1107b16–21; 344

COMMENTARY OF ST. THOMAS

333. After the Philosopher has explained what virtue is in a general way, he now applies the definition in a special way to each virtue. On this point he does two things. First [1] he shows the necessity of this procedure. Second [2] he carries out his proposal at "In actions concerned with fear etc." He says first that we must speak of the essence of virtue not only in its universal aspect but the general doctrine must be applied to each case in a special way. The reason he gives is that in discussions concerned with actions, universals are not of much utility and particulars are more accurate because actions pertain to singulars. Fittingly then discussions about actions should be in harmony with particulars.

334. If then our study be about actions considered only universally, it will be futile both because it does not accomplish its purpose, which is the direction of individual actions, and because a study from a universal viewpoint—where deficiencies in particulars may not occur—cannot be made in these things by reason of the changeableness of the matter, as was said before (32–36). But the study of particulars is more effective, being suitable to control actions, and also more accurate because particulars are understood to the extent that the uni-

versal is verified in them. What was said (289–332), therefore, about virtue in general must have been based upon the explanation of individual virtues.

335. Then [2], at "**In actions concerned with**," he carries out his proposal, showing by particular cases that the mean is good and praiseworthy but the extreme is evil and blameworthy. He shows this first in the virtues [2]; and second [Lect. IX], in the passions at "Also in the passions etc." (1108a31). Regarding the first point we must consider that virtues have been distinguished in two ways. Some observe the distinction of virtues according to certain general modes which are four in number. The root of virtue consists in the rectitude of reason according to which we must direct our actions and passions. Actions however are to be directed in a way different from the passions, for actions in themselves do not resist reason, as buying, selling, and so forth. Consequently, for such things reason need only establish a certain equality of rectitude. But the passions indicate a kind of inclination that can be contrary to reason in a twofold way.

336. In one way it draws reason to something else, as is evident in all passions that deal with following the appetite—for example, concupiscence, hope, anger, and others of this kind. For these passions reason must establish a rectitude in suppressing and restraining them. In another way passion shrinks from what is according to reason, as in all passions that denote flight of the appetite—for example, fear, hatred, and the like. In passions of this kind reason must establish a rectitude by stabilizing the soul in what is conformable to reason. According to this we designate four virtues, which some men call principal. Rectitude of reason

itself pertains to prudence, equality established in operations to justice, constancy of soul to fortitude, and moderation of the passions—as the words indicate—to temperance.

337. Some, therefore, have understood these virtues in a general way, thinking that all knowledge of truth belongs to prudence, the equality of all actions to justice, all constancy of soul to fortitude, and all curbing and moderation of the passions to temperance. Cicero, Seneca, and others spoke of these virtues in this way. They considered such to be general virtues and called all other virtues species of these.

338. But this distinction does not seem to be appropriate. First because the above-mentioned virtues are of such a nature that without them there can be no virtue. Hence the species of virtue cannot be differentiated by this. Second, virtues and vices are not specified by reason but by their object (322).

339. Aristotle then distinguishes virtues more fittingly according to their objects or matter. Thus the previously mentioned four virtues are not called principal because they are general but because their species are taken according to certain important notions, as prudence is not concerned with all knowledge of the truth but especially with the act of reason that is command. Justice is not concerned with equality of all actions but only of those referring to another, where the better thing is the establishment of equality. Fortitude is not concerned with every kind of constancy but only that which arises at the fear of the danger of death. Temperance is not concerned with all restraint but only with that of the desires and pleasures of touch. The other virtues, however, are as it were secondary. They can be reduced, therefore, to the previously

mentioned virtues not as species to general but as secondary to principal virtues.

340. Since then these things have been taken for granted, we must know that the Philosopher does not treat justice and prudence here but later on in the fifth book (885–1108) and the sixth book (1161–1173). He does treat here, however, temperance, fortitude, and certain other secondary virtues, all of which are concerned with some of the passions. But all passions regard some object that pertains either to the bodily life of man or external goods or human acts. Therefore, he first [2] mentions the virtues touching on the passions, the objects of which pertain to bodily life. Second [4] he mentions those pertaining to external goods at "In respect to the giving and receiving of money etc."; and third [Lect. IX] those regarding exterior acts at "There are three other means etc." (1108a9). On the first point he does two things. First [1] he speaks of fortitude, which regards dangers destructive of life. Second [3] he speaks of temperance, which regards things useful for the preservation of life, such as food by which life is preserved in the individual and sex by which life is preserved in the species, at "With regard to pleasures and pains etc."

341. He says first that fortitude is a mean concerned with fear and daring precisely as they regard the danger of death. But of those sinning by excess, the state of the man who is excessive in being fearless and also deficient in fearing is not given any special name because this rarely happens. Likewise many things are without a name because men do not advert to them ordinarily so that they would give them a name. But he who is extreme in daring is called rash. Such a one differs from the fearless man who is so-called from the lack of fear, but the rash man is so-called from an excess of daring. He who fears excessively and lacks daring is called a coward.

342. Then [3], at "**With regard to pleasures,**" he discusses temperance. He says that temperance is a mean not for all pleasures and pains but for those of touch, pertaining to food and sex. It is less concerned with pains than with pleasures, for pains of this kind are caused only from the absence of pleasures. Excess in such things is called intemperance, but the defect does not often occur because everyone naturally desires pleasure. Hence this defect is unnamed. He himself, however, invents a name and calls insensible those who do not feel pleasures of this kind. One who, contrary to right reason, avoids such pleasures is appropriately called insensible.

343. Then [4], at "**In respect to the giving,**" he introduces the virtues that regard external things. First [4] he treats those virtues concerned with the desire of external goods and second [Lect. IX] those that regard external evils, at "With respect to anger etc." (1108a3). External goods are riches and honors. First then he presents the virtues regulating riches; second [Lect. IX] those referring to honors at "The mean in regard to honor etc." (1107b23). Regarding the first he does two things. First [4] he treats liberality, which is concerned with moderate riches; then [5] magnificence, which is concerned with great riches, at "Having to do with the use of money etc." He says first that liberality is a mean between the giving and receiving of money. But extravagance and stinginess constitute, in an opposite way, excess and defect. The spendthrift overdoes the giving and falls short in

the acquisition, but the miser on the contrary is excessive in acquiring and deficient in giving. These matters are here discussed in outline or as conforming to a pattern, and as falling under headings or summarily. Later (528–594; 595–648; 658–706) he will treat more accurately both these and other matters.

344. Then [5], at "**Having to do with the use of money,**" he introduces magnificence. He says that besides the above-mentioned habits, liberality and the opposed vices, there are also other virtues concerned with money, for which even magnificence is a kind of mean. The princely or munificent person, as engaged in expending great sums, differs from the generous person who gives small amounts. Excess in respect to magnificence is called *apyrocalia*: *a* meaning "without," *pyros* meaning "practice," *kalos* meaning "good," that is, without the practice of what is good. Thus those who spend a great deal care little about how they bestow their goods. This excess is also called *banausia* from *banos* meaning "furnace" because, like a furnace, the squanderer consumes everything. The defect however is called meanness. These extremes in fact differ from those that are opposed to liberality, but the way they differ will be treated subsequently in the fourth book (707–734).

LECTURE IX
Virtues Dealing with Honors

TEXT OF ARISTOTLE (*1107b21–1108b10*) Chapter 7

1. *The mean in regard to honor and dishonor is magnanimity. But the excess is* chapnotes *(i.e., presumption); and the defect, smallness of soul.* **1107b21–23; 345**

2. *As we pointed out, liberality that bestows small amounts differs from magnificence. So also there is a virtue concerned with ordinary honors that differs from magnanimity whose province is great honors. A man can desire ordinary honors in the right way, more than he ought, and less than he ought. If he is excessive in the desire of honors, he is called ambitious; if deficient, he is said to be unambitious. But he who strikes a mean has no special name. Likewise the habits are without names except for ambition, which we call the excessive love of honors. Hence persons who are in the extremes argue about the location of the mean. Even we sometimes call the man possessing the mean ambitious, and sometimes we call him unambitious. Why we do this will be explained afterwards, but for the present we should refer to the remaining states in the way indicated.* **1107b–1108a4; 346–348**

3. *With respect to anger we find an excess, a defect, and a mean. Although these are for the most part without names, we call the man following the mean "mild" and the mean "mildness." In regard to the extremes, he who is excessive is called irascible and his vice irascibility. But he who is deficient is said to be apathetic and to have the defect of apathy.* **1108a4–9; 349**

4. *There are three other means which are alike in one respect and different in another. They are all concerned with communicating what we say and do, but they differ because one of them refers to the truth, and the others to the pleasantness found in this communication. One of these latter concerns pleasantness in the things said and done in jest, the others regard the things that belong to the usual manner of living. We must speak of these things so that we may better understand that the mean is always praiseworthy but that the extremes are neither right nor to be praised but rather to be condemned. Many of these also are without special names, but as we have done with the others, we shall try to invent names for them for the sake of the clarity and the good that results.* **1108a9–19; 350–351**

5. *In regard to truth the mean is possessed by the man who is truthful and is called truthfulness. But pretension, which is the excess, is called boasting, and the pretender is known as a braggart. The defect, however, may be named dissimulation or irony and the pretender a dissembler.* **1108a19–23; 352**

6. *In respect to pleasantness concerned with amusement, the man who observes the mean is called witty and the disposition itself wit. But the excess is designated as buffoonery and the person who is excessive a buffoon. If one falls short in this matter he is said to be boorish and to have the quality of boorishness.* **1108a23–26; 353**

7. *In the remaining kind of pleasantness, that is, in life generally, the man who is pleasant as he should be is called affable, and the mean he attains is affability. But he who carries this too far merely for the sake of pleasing is called obsequious. If however he acts for his own utility he is called a flatterer. One who falls short in this matter and is always difficult is termed contentious and perverse.* **1108a26–30; 354**

8. *Also in the passions and the things regarding the passions a mean exists. Modesty, for example, is not a virtue, but it is praised as is the modest person, for in this question a mean is attainable. The person who exceeds the mean and is embarrassed at everything is bashful. But one who falls short, that is, blushes at nothing, is shameless, while the person who strikes a happy mean is called modest.* **1108a30–35; 355**

9. Righteous indignation may be assigned as the mean between envy and epicacotharchia or rejoicing in evil. These are concerned with pleasure and sorrow over what happens to our neighbors. The righteously indignant person is saddened at the unmerited prosperity of the wicked. But the envious person goes far beyond this and eats his heart out over the success of everyone. The man called epicacotharchos is so deficient in sadness that he actually rejoices. However, there will be time to treat of these matters elsewhere. Because justice is understood in various ways, we shall later treat its parts showing how the mean is constituted in them. Likewise we shall discuss the intellectual virtues.   **1108a35–1108b10; 356–357**

COMMENTARY OF ST. THOMAS

345. Having completed the virtues that concern riches, he now [1] treats those dealing with honors. First [1] he deals with the virtue referring to great honors, and second [2] with the virtue referring to ordinary honors, at "As we pointed out etc." He says first that magnanimity is the mean between honor and dishonor. But the excess in following after the things belonging to great honors is a certain disposition that is called *chaumotes* because it blazes forth in things pertaining to the desire of honor. In Greek *cauma* is fire, and *capnos* means smoke. If the word be written *chapnotes* it can be translated "exhalation" or presumption. We are accustomed to say that they who breathe with great difficulty on climbing high altitudes are wheezing or puffing. But the defect opposed to magnanimity is faintheartedness.

346. Then [2], at "As we pointed out," he proposes another virtue referring to ordinary honors. He says, as has been indicated (344), that liberality differs from magnificence because liberality bestows small amounts while magnificence bestows great sums. So too there is a virtue concerned with ordinary honors which differs from magnanimity which is concerned with great honors. That in this question there should be some virtue consisting in a mean is made clear by his adding that ordinary honors are desired as they ought (this belongs to the mean of

virtue), more than they ought (this belongs to excess), and less than they ought (this belongs to the defect). He who excessively desires honor is ambitious or a lover of honor. He who is deficient in the desire of honor is unambitious or without the desire of honor. But he who strikes a happy mean has no special name.

347. Likewise the dispositions, i.e., the habits of vice or of the mean-virtue are unnamed. However, we can invent names: calling the habit by which a person excessively loves honor, ambition; and the habit by which a person is deficient in the love of honor, "unambitiousness." But because the mean has not been named, the persons who are in the extremes argue about the location of the mean. Both maintain that they possess the mean. He explains this by drawing a comparison with two states that are in the habit of bickering over their common border when the boundary has not been fixed. Both claim the intervening territory as their own. But this is fairly common to all the vices for each of the extremes to think they possess the mean and that the virtuous are in the other extreme, e.g., the coward considers the brave man reckless; the reckless man says the brave man is a coward. Hence Aristotle states what is proper to this matter, that not only do the vicious appropriate the name of virtue to themselves, but even the virtuous use the name of

the vice as if it were a virtue because the mean has not been named.

348. This is what he refers to when he adds that even we (speaking correctly too) sometimes call a man who possesses the mean ambitious, and other times unambitious. Also at times we praise a person because he is ambitious. We are accustomed to say in commending a person that he is solicitous about his honor, and thus we call the man who loves honor, virtuous. On the other hand we sometimes praise an unambitious man, saying in his praise that he does not care about the esteem of men, but about the truth. So we call the unambitious man virtuous. Why we do this will be explained afterwards in the fourth book (794–795). But for the present we should continue with the remaining mediums in the way designated, that is, as conforming to a pattern.

349. Then [3], at "**With respect to anger,**" he proposes the virtue concerning external evils by which man is provoked to anger. He says that in regard to anger there is an excess, a defect, and a mean. Although all these for the most part are without names, we are accustomed to call the man following the mean mild, and the mean itself mildness. But he who is excessive in this passion we call irascible and we say he has the quality of irascibility. The man however who is deficient we call apathetic and say he has the defect of apathy.

350. Then [4], at "**There are,**" he proposes the virtues that concern human actions. First he shows their variety, and second [5] he gives examples of these at "In regard to truth etc." He says first that three means are alike in one respect and different in another. They are alike in that all refer to words and deeds in which men communicate among themselves. They are different in that one of them refers to the truth of such words and deeds. The others, however, refer to pleasantness in these words and deeds, so that one of them regards pleasantness in the things that are said or done in jest, the others regard what belongs to the usual manner of living, i.e., serious matters.

351. We must speak of these things so it will become more apparent that the mean is always praiseworthy and the extremes are not to be praised but rather condemned. Many of these are without special names, but, as we have done with the others, we shall try to invent names to clarify what is said for the sake of the good that will ensue. The reason is that the purpose of this science is not the manifestation of truth but virtuous activity.

352. Then [5], at "**In regard to truth,**" he gives examples of these virtues and first of that which concerns truth. He says that in regard to truth the mean is had by the man who is called truthful, and the mean itself is called truthfulness. But pretension, which is the excess (when a person pretends greater things about himself than are true), is called boasting, and the pretender is called a braggart. But dissembling, which is the defect (when a person makes pretense of certain contemptible things about himself), is called dissimulation or irony. Such a pretender is called a dissembler.

353. Second [6], at "**In respect to,**" he gives an example of the virtue concerned with amusement. He says, regarding pleasantness in amusement, that the man who observes the mean is called witty (*eutrapelos*) giving as it were a pleasant turn to every incident. The disposition itself is called wit (*eutrapelia*). But the man who is guilty of excess is called a buffoon or *bomolo-*

chus, from *bomo* meaning "altar" and *lochos* meaning "plundering." He is said to be like the bird of prey which always flew near the sacrificial altars to snatch some food. In a similar way the man who is excessive in amusement always insists on snatching a word or action of someone to give it a comic turn. The disposition however is called buffoonery. But the man who is deficient is said to be boorish and to have the quality of boorishness.

354. Third [7], at "**In the remaining**," he exemplifies the third of these virtues saying that in the remaining pleasantness, which is in life, touching on our serious actions, the mean is struck by the friendly person—not so designated from the effect of friendship but from amicable conversation. Such a one we term affable. The mean itself is called friendliness or affability. But one who overdoes this merely for the purpose of pleasing is called obsequious. If he acts for his own utility, for example, his profit, he is called a sycophant or a flatterer. One who falls short in this matter and does not fear to sadden those he lives with is called contentious and perverse.

355. Then [8], at "**Also in the passions**," he gives an example of certain laudable passions—first [8], of modesty. He says that a mean is found even in the passions and their phases, modesty, for instance, is not a virtue, as will be explained in the fourth book (867–882). The modest person is praised because a mean can be taken in such matters. One who goes to excess so that he blushes at everything is called *cataplex*, a bashful person. But he who falls short, blushing at nothing is called shameless, while he who strikes the mean is called modest.

356. Second [9], at "**Righteous indignation**," he discusses another passion called *nemesis* or righteous indignation, which is a mean between envy and *epicacotharchia* (*tharcus* meaning "rejoicing," *kakos* meaning "evil," *epi* meaning "over") or rejoicing in evil. These are dispositions concerned with pleasure and sorrow over what happens to our neighbors. The righteously indignant person or the fair critic is saddened at the prosperity of the wicked. But the envious person goes to excess in grieving over all—both good and bad—who prosper. The person however called *epicacotharchos* is so deficient in sadness that he actually rejoices over the wicked who are successful in their wickedness. But these topics are treated elsewhere, in the second book of the *Rhetoric* (Ch. 10).

357. Last, because justice has various parts in which the mean is differently understood, justice will be treated in the fifth book (885–1108) together with the manner in which the parts consist in the mean. Likewise, the rational or intellectual virtues will be discussed later in the sixth book (1109–1291).

LECTURE X
Opposition Among the Virtues and Vices

TEXT OF ARISTOTLE (*1108b11–1109a19*) Chapter 8

1. There are three dispositions, of which two are vices: one by excess, the other by defect. The third is virtue and consists in the mean. Everyone of these is opposed in some way to every other one because not only are the extremes opposed to one another and to the mean, but the mean is opposed to the extremes.
1108b11–15; 358

2. As the average is greater compared to the less and less compared to the greater, so mean habits are in excess compared to the defect and in defect compared to excess. This is true both in the passions and in actions. The brave man seems reckless compared to the coward, and cowardly compared to the reckless. Likewise the moderate man seems self-indulgent compared to the insensible man, and insensible compared to the self-indulgent. Also the generous person is a spendthrift in comparison with the miser but a miser in comparison with the spendthrift.
1108b15–23; 359–361

3. For this reason the extremes tend to throw the mean toward one another. The coward calls the brave man reckless, and the reckless man calls him a coward. A similar tendency is found in other extremes.
1108b23–26; 362

4. These things are mutually opposed in such a way that there is a greater opposition of the extremes among themselves than to the mean. The reason is that the extremes are more removed from one another than from the mean, as great is more removed from small and small from great than either from the average.
1108b26–30; 363

5. Moreover there seems to be a similarity between some extremes and the mean, for example, between rashness and fortitude, between extravagance and generosity. But between the extremes themselves a complete dissimilarity exists. Now the things that are farthest removed from one another are said to be contraries. Therefore the things most removed from one another are more contrary.
1108b30–35; 364

6. In some cases it is the defect that is more opposed to the mean but in other cases it is the excess. Thus it is not rashness but cowardice, the defect, that is more opposed to fortitude. On the contrary, however, it is not insensibility (the defect) but self-indulgence (the excess) that is more opposed to temperance.
1108b35–1109a5; 365

7. This happens for two reasons, one of which is drawn from the very thing itself. It is not the extreme that is nearer and more like the mean but its contrary that is more opposed to the mean. Thus, since rashness seems nearer and more like fortitude, it is cowardice having less likeness that is more opposed to fortitude. Things that are more removed from the mean seem to be more opposed to it. This first reason then comes from the thing itself.
1109a5–12; 366–367

8. But the other reason arises on our part. Those vices which are somewhat innate in us seem in a way to be more opposed to the mean. For example, we more naturally follow pleasure and so we are more easily moved to self-indulgence than to temperance. Therefore, we say that the vices that more readily increase are more opposed to virtue. For this reason self-indulgence (which is an excess) is more opposed to temperance.
1109a12–19; 368

COMMENTARY OF ST. THOMAS

358. After the Philosopher has shown in general what virtue is, and has applied the definition to particular virtues, he treats the opposition of vir-

tues and vices. Regarding this question he does three things. First [1] he shows that there is a twofold opposition among these habits: one, of the vices among themselves, the other, of the vices to the virtue. Then [4] he shows that the opposition among the vices themselves is the greater, at "These things are mutually opposed etc." Last [6] he shows how one of the extremes is more opposed to virtue than the other, at "In some cases etc." On the first point he does three things. First [1] he states his proposal. Second [2] he proves the proposition, at "As the average etc." Third [3] he deduces a corollary from what has been said, at "For this reason the extremes tend to throw etc." He says first that there are three dispositions of which two are vices: one by excess, and the other by defect. The third is according to virtue which consists in a mean. Everyone of these is opposed in some way to every other one, because not only are the extremes opposed to one another but also the mean to the extremes.

359. Then [2], at "**As the average,**" he proves what he had said. It was unnecessary to prove that two vices, which are compared to one another as excess and defect, are opposed since they are far removed from one another. But it will seem doubtful that virtue is opposed to vices, as was just said (358). Since virtue holds a middle place between the vices, virtue is not very far removed from either of them, while opposition is farthest apart, as stated in the tenth book of the *Metaphysics* (Ch. 4, 1055a4-32; St. Th. Lect. V, 2023-2035). Therefore, the Philosopher here makes a special point that virtue is opposed to both extremes.

360. On this subject we must consider that the mean partakes to some extent of both extremes. Precisely as it partakes of one of them it is contrary to the other, as the average—a mean be-tween the great and small—is small compared to the great and great compared to the small. Therefore, the average is opposed both to the great by reason of the small and to the small by reason of the great. Because of this there is a motion of the contrary against the mean as against a contrary, as is explained in the fifth book of the *Physics* (Ch. 1, 224b30–35; St. Th. Lect. I, 476).

361. Therefore, the habits of the mean both in regard to passions and actions appear excessive to one who is in defect and deficient to one who is in excess. Thus a brave man compared to a coward is reckless, but compared to a reckless man, a brave man is a coward. Likewise a moderate man compared to an insensible man is self–indulgent, but compared to the self-indulgent the moderate man is insensible. The same may be said of the generous man who is a spendthrift in comparison with the miser, but a miser in comparison with the spendthrift. It is evident then that virtue is opposed to the extremes.

362. Then [3], at "**For this reason,**" he deduces a corollary from what was said. Because the mean habit is constituted by comparison of one extreme with the nature of the other, the extremes tend to throw the mean toward one another. In other words, both extremes consider the mean as it were an extreme opposed to them. Thus the coward calls the brave man reckless and the reckless man calls him a coward. This is an indication of what we just stated (359, 361), that virtue is opposed to both extremes.

363. Then [4], at "**These things are mutually opposed,**" he shows there is greater opposition of the vices among

themselves than to virtue for two rea-sons. The first reason [4] is that the more removed things are from one an-other, the more opposed they are be-cause opposition is a kind of distance. But the extremes are more removed from one another than from the mean, as great and small are more removed from one another than from the aver-age, which is a mean between them. Therefore, vices are more opposed to one another than to virtue. We must consider that Aristotle speaks here about the opposition of virtue to vices, not according to good and evil—in this way both vices come under one ex-treme—but according as virtue by rea-son of its own species is a mean between two vices.

364. He states the second reason [5] at "**Moreover there seems.**" It is this. There is some similarity between vir-tue and one extreme, for instance, be-tween fortitude and rashness, between generosity and prodigality. But there is complete dissimilarity between the two extremes or vices. Therefore, they are opposed to one another in the greatest degree because their opposi-tion denotes the greatest distance, as was indicated (359).

365. Then [6], at "**In some cases,**" he shows that one extreme is more op-posed to virtue than the other. On this point he does two things. First [6] he states his proposal. Second [7] he as-signs the reasons at "This happens for two reasons." He says first that in some cases it is the defect that is more op-posed to the mean of the virtue, but in other cases it is the excess. Thus not rashness, which certainly pertains to the excess, but cowardice, which per-tains to the defect, is most opposed to fortitude. On the contrary, however, it

is not insensibility (to which lack and defect belong) but self-indulgence (to which excess pertains) that is most op-posed to temperance.

366. Then [7], at "**This happens for two reasons,**" he assigns two reasons for what he said. One [7] is taken from the thing itself, that is, from the very nature of the virtues and vices. It was just stated (364) that one extreme has a similarity to the mean of virtue. From the very fact that one extreme is nearer and more like the mean of virtue than the other, it follows that not the one more similar to the mean but the one contrary to it is more opposed to the virtue. Thus if rashness is nearer and more like fortitude, it follows that cow-ardice is more unlike and conse-quently more opposed to fortitude. The reason is that the habits more re-moved from the mean seem to be more opposed to it. But the explanation of these things must be taken from the nature of the passions.

367. What Aristotle says here touches on the moral virtues con-cerned with the passions. To these vir-tues it belongs to preserve the good of reason against the movement of the passions. Now passion can destroy the good of reason in two ways. First, its vehemence can incite to greater activ-ity than reason prescribes, especially in the desire of pleasure and in the other passions pertaining to the following of the appetite. Hence the virtue, which touches the passions of this kind, aims principally at restraining these pas-sions. For this reason the vice referring to the defect is more like the virtue, and the vice referring to the excess is more opposed to it, as is evident in temper-ance. But other passions destroy the good by withdrawing to something

less than what is according to reason, as is evident in the case of fear and other passions having to do with flight. Hence the virtue concerned with such passions strives as much as possible to strengthen man against defect in the good of reason. On this account the vice of defect is more opposed to the virtue.

368. Then [8], at "**But the other,**" he assigns another reason on our part. Since virtue ought to restrain vices, the aim of virtue is to curb more effectively those vices to which we have a stronger inclination. For this reason those vices, which are in any way somewhat innate in us, are more opposed to virtue. As from birth we more readily follow pleasures than flee from them, we are very early moved to self-indulgence which implies an excess of pleasure. Therefore, we say that those vices, which rather naturally tend to increase in us because we are by nature inclined to them, are more opposed to virtue. For this reason self-indulgence, to which excess of pleasure pertains, is more opposed to temperance than insensibility is, as has been observed (365).

LECTURE XI
The Ways of Becoming Virtuous

TEXT OF ARISTOTLE (*1109a20–1109b26*) Chapter 9

1. *A sufficient explanation has been to show that moral virtue is a mean, how it is a mean, that it is a mean between two vices—one by excess and the other by defect—and that it aims at the mean both in the passions and operations.* 1109a20–24; 369

2. *It is not easy to be virtuous because in every case it is difficult to discover the mean. Thus, not everyone can locate the center of a circle—it takes a person who knows. Likewise it is easy for anyone to become angry, or to hand out money and waste it. But not everyone (for it is not easy) can give to the right person, the right amount, at the right time, for the right purpose, in the right manner. All this pertains to virtuous giving, which is rare, praise-worthy, and good.* 1109a24–30; 370

3. *For this reason he who aims at the mean must first avoid the extreme which is more opposed to the mean. (Circe used to give this warning: keep your ship beyond spray and rolling billow. One of the extremes indeed is a greater sin and the other a lesser sin. Therefore, since it is exceedingly difficult to reach the mean, we must choose the lesser of the evils, as they say in navigation. This will be done best in the way we are going to point out.* 1109a30–1109b1; 371–373

4. *We must take into account the things to which we are easily inclined. Some of us are more prone by nature to one thing than another. Our natural inclination will be made known from the pleasure or sorrow we experience. We must then draw ourselves to the opposite, for by leading ourselves far away from sin we shall arrive at the mean. A similar thing is done by nurserymen who straighten crooked saplings.* 1109b1–7; 374–376

5. *Everyone ought to be on guard especially against the pleasurable thing and pleasure, for we cannot judge them without being unduly influenced by them. What the elders of the people felt toward Helen, we ought to feel toward pleasure, and in all that concerns pleasure repeat their words. Rejecting pleasure in this way we will fall into sin less frequently. Those who do as we have suggested under this heading will be quite able to acquire the mean.* 1109b7–13; 377–378

6. *This is perhaps difficult in individual cases. It is not easy to determine in what manner we should be angry, in regard to what persons we should be angry, in what type of things we should be angry, and for how long a time we should be angry. Sometimes we praise those who are deficient in becoming angry and call them mild; sometimes we praise the irascible and call them manly.* 1109b14–18; 379

7. *One who deviates a little from what is virtuous is not censured whether it be in excess or defect. But one who deviates much is blameworthy, for his deviation is not hidden.* 1109b18–20; 380

8. *It cannot easily be determined, in so many words, at what point and how much a person is censurable. Neither is any other thing perceived by the senses determined in this way, for these are particular things and judgment of them is in the sensitive part of the soul. This much, then, shows that the mean habit is praise-worthy in all instances. However, sometimes we must incline towards excess and sometimes towards defect. Thus we shall easily reach the mean and what is virtuous.* 1109b20–26; 381

COMMENTARY OF ST. THOMAS

369. After the Philosopher has treated the nature of virtue, he shows here how a person can acquire virtue. He does this because, as was indicated

before (351), the purpose of this teaching is not that men may know the truth but that they may become good. On this point he does two things. First [1] he shows that it is difficult for man to become virtuous. Second [3] he shows how man may attain this, at "For this reason he who aims etc." The first notion calls for a twofold procedure. First [1] he reviews what has been said. It has been sufficiently explained before (310, 316), he states, that moral virtue is a mean, how it is a mean (not objectively but relative to us), and between what things it is the mean, i.e., between two vices—one by excess, the other by defect. It has also been explained (317–318) why virtue is a middle course, namely, because it aims at the mean; virtue searches out and chooses the mean both in the passions and actions.

370. Second [2], at "It is not easy," he concludes from the premises that it is difficult to be good or virtuous because we see that in every case it is difficult to discover the mean but easy to deviate from the mean. Thus, not everyone—only an informed person who is a geometrician—can find the center of a circle. On the other hand, anyone can easily deviate from the center. Likewise, anyone can hand out money and waste it. But not everyone (for it is not easy) can give to the right person, the right amount, at the right time, for the right purpose, in the right manner—all of which belongs to virtuous giving. Indeed, because of the difficulty it is a rare and difficult thing, but praiseworthy and virtuous precisely as conforming to reason.

371. Then [3], at "For this reason," he shows the ways in which a person may become virtuous. On this point he does two things. First [3] he shows how a person can discover the mean. Second [6] he treats the discovery of the

mean at "This is perhaps difficult etc." In regard to the first he gives three admonitions. One of these [3] is taken from the nature of the thing. He states that it is difficult to become virtuous and to discover the mean. Therefore, one who aims at the mean (i.e., he who intends to attain the mean) must strive principally to avoid the extreme more opposed to the virtue. Thus if someone wishes to arrive at the mean of fortitude he ought to direct his principal efforts to avoiding cowardice, which is more opposed to fortitude than rashness is, as has been explained (365).

372. He gives an example of a certain Circe who used to warn sailors to beware chiefly of the greatest dangers from the sea, which are waves sinking the ship and mist obscuring the vision of the sailors. This was the warning: "Clear of the smoke take care and clear of the rollers to keep her," as if to say: so guard your ship that you may escape spray and waves.

373. He gives the reason for this admonition, saying that one of the extremes—that which is more opposed to the virtue—is a greater sin; but that the extreme, which is less opposed to the virtue, is a lesser sin. Therefore, since it is exceedingly difficult to reach the mean of virtue, a man ought to try to avoid at least the greater dangers that are more opposed to virtue. Thus sailors say that after the best voyage on which a man is exposed to no dangers, the next best is to choose the least of the dangers. A similar thing happens to a man's life in the way that was explained (371), that he may chiefly avoid the vices that are opposed to virtue.

374. He gives the second admonition [4] at "We must take into account." It is understood on our part, as far as concerns the things proper to

each of us. One who wishes to be virtuous, he says, must take into account that to which his appetite is naturally inclined. Different people are by nature more inclined to one thing than another. Each one can know what he is naturally inclined to from the pleasure and sorrow he experiences, because what is agreeable to each according to his nature is pleasurable.

375. Hence, if someone takes pleasure in a particular action or passion, this is a sign that he is naturally inclined to it. But men vehemently tend to the things to which they are naturally inclined, and so, easily exceed the mean in this matter. We, therefore, must draw ourselves as much as possible to the opposite. The reason is that when we make an effort to recede from sin, to which we are prone, we will finally with difficulty arrive at the mean. He makes a comparison with nurserymen who straighten crooked saplings. These men wishing to make trees straight force them the opposite way and so bring them to the mean, an upright position.

376. Here we must consider that this way of acquiring virtues is most effective: that a man should strive for the opposite of that to which he is inclined either by nature or habit. However, the way advocated by the Stoics is easier: that a man little by little withdraw from those things to which he is inclined, as Cicero relates in his work *Questiones Tusculanae* (Bk. IV, C. 31–35, n. 65–76). The way that Aristotle lays down is suitable for those who strongly desire to withdraw from vice and to attain virtue. But the way of the Stoics is more appropriate to those who have weak and halfhearted wills.

377. He lays down the third admonition [5] at "**Everyone.**" This is also understood on our part, not in the sense that it is proper to every individual, as has been said (374–376) of the second admonition, but precisely as it is common to all. All are naturally inclined to pleasure. Therefore, he says that everyone without exception who aims at virtue ought to be on his guard especially against pleasures. Because men are very inclined to pleasure, pleasurable objects apprehended easily move their appetite. Hence, he notes that we cannot easily judge pleasure by dwelling on its consideration without the appetite accepting it and bursting forth in desire for it. What the Trojan elders felt toward Helen when they decided that she must depart, we ought to feel toward pleasure; in all that concerns pleasure we ought to reecho their words in order that we may reject bodily pleasures. Rejecting pleasures in this way, we will fall into sin less frequently since the desire of pleasure leads men to many sins.

378. He concludes then that those who do what has been suggested under this heading, i.e., summarily, will be quite able to acquire the mean of virtue.

379. Then [6], at "**This is perhaps difficult,**" he shows how the mean of virtue must be determined. On this point he does three things. First he indicates the difficulty of this. Next [7] he shows what suffices to determine the mean, at "One who deviates a little etc." Last [8] he answers a latent question at "It cannot be determined etc." He says first that it is difficult to discover the mean especially when we consider the particular circumstances in individual actions. The reason is that it is not easy to determine how a thing is to be done and in regard to what persons, and in what type of things, and how long a time one should be angry. He gives a sign of this difficulty:

that those, who are deficient in getting angry for instance, are sometimes praised by us and called mild, while those who are rather irascible in inflicting punishment or making resistance are sometimes praised by us and called manly.

380. Then [7], at "**One who,**" he indicates what suffices for the mean of virtue. He says that one who deviates a little from what is done well according to virtue is not censured, whether he inclines to excess or defect. The reason is that a slight departure from the mean of virtue is hidden on account of the difficulty with the mean. But one who deviates greatly is censured because the deviation is not hidden.

381. Then [8], at "**It cannot easily,**" he answers a latent question. Someone could ask how much departure from the mean should be censured and how much should not. He himself answers that it cannot easily be determined, in so many words, at what point and how much a person departing from the mean should be blamed. Likewise no other sensible thing, which is judged rather by sense than reason, can easily be determined. Things of this kind, belonging to the operations of the virtues, are individual cases. For this reason judgment about them exists in the sensitive part of the soul, even if not in the external, at least in the internal sense by which a person judges well about singulars, and to which belongs the judgment of prudence, as will be said in the sixth book (1215, 1249). But this much suffices here to show that the mean habit in all cases is rather praiseworthy. However, sometimes we must incline toward excess and sometimes toward defect either on account of the nature of virtue or on account of our inclination, as is clear from what was explained above (369–378). Thus the mean according to which a thing is done well will be easily discovered. So ends the second book.

BOOK THREE
THE VOLUNTARY. FORTITUDE AND TEMPERANCE.
LECTURE I
Spontaneous Action and the Involuntary

TEXT OF ARISTOTLE (*B.1109b30–1110a19*) Chapter 1

1. *Since virtue is concerned with passions and actions, and since praise and censures are apportioned for what is voluntary, but pardon—or at times even pity—for what is involuntary, the study of the voluntary and the involuntary is required of those who intend to treat of virtue.*

1109a30–34; 382–384

2. *It is useful also for legislators in decreeing honors and punishments.*   1109a34–35; 385

3. *Involuntary actions seem to be those that arise either from violence or from ignorance.*

1109a35–1110a1; 386

4. *The "compulsory action" (violentum) is one whose principle is from outside and to which the person involved or the recipient contributes nothing, for example, if he is driven somewhere by the wind, or if he is in the power of other men.*   1110a1–4; 387

5. *Some things are done because of the fear of greater evils or because of the hope of some good. Thus a tyrant, having in his power the parents or children of a certain man, commands him to do a disgraceful deed on condition that they will be spared if he does it but killed if he does not do it. Here a doubt arises whether his actions are voluntary or involuntary. A similar case is found in the decision to throw goods overboard during storms at sea. Absolutely speaking, no man would do so voluntarily, but if it means that his life and that of others are saved as a result, a sensible man will do it.*   1110a4–11; 388–389

6. *Operations of this kind are mixed. However, they approach more closely to voluntary actions for they are voluntary at the time they are done, and the end of the action conforms to this particular time. An action then must be called voluntary or involuntary by reference to the time at which it was done. In our case he acts voluntarily because the principle moving his bodily members in these operations is within the man himself. Actions whose source is within man are in his power to do or not to do, and this belongs to the nature of the voluntary. But the actions may be called involuntary in the abstract (simpliciter), for no one would choose to do such a thing in itself.*   1110a11–19; 390–391

COMMENTARY OF ST. THOMAS

382. After the Philosopher has treated virtue in general, he treats here certain principles of virtuous acts. In defining virtue, he said (305) that virtue is a habit of correct choosing because virtue works by means of choice. Now he logically discusses choice together with the voluntary and "willing." The voluntary is common to these three: for the voluntary is anything that is freely done, choice however concerns the things that are for the end, and willing considers the end it- self. Hence this section falls into two parts. In the first part he deals with the three previously mentioned principles of virtuous actions. In the second part, at "Since willing regards the end etc." (1113b3), he compares these principles with the acts of the virtues [Lect. XI]. His initial point calls for a threefold procedure. First [1] he determines the voluntary and the involuntary. Next [Lect. V], at "After the treatise etc." (B.1111b4), he deals with choice. Last [Lect. X], at "As was stated before etc."

(1113a15), he treats the act of willing. In regard to the first of these he does two things. Initially [1] he shows that it pertains to the present discussion to consider the voluntary and the involuntary. Then [3], at "Involuntary actions seem etc.," he actually treats them. Two reasons are advanced in proof of the first point.

383. The first of these reasons [1] is taken from what is peculiar to our present study which concerns the virtues. He concludes from his previous remarks that moral virtue, our present concern, deals with passions and actions in such a way that in the things which are voluntary in regard to actions and passions, praise is due anyone acting virtuously and blame for anyone acting viciously. But when someone involuntarily performs an action in accordance with virtue, he does not merit praise. On the other hand, if his action is contrary to virtue he deserves pardon because he acted involuntarily, and so is less blameworthy. Sometimes he even deserves pity, and should be entirely freed from blame.

384. Pardon can also be distinguished from pity in this way: we speak of pardon when censure, i.e., a penalty is lessened or entirely absolved as a consequence of the judgment of reason. Pity, on the other hand, arises as a consequence of an emotion. But praise and blame are peculiarly due to virtue and vice. Therefore, the voluntary and the involuntary, according to which the reason for praise and blame is diversified, ought to be treated by those who intend to study virtue.

385. At "It is useful" [2] he gives the second reason. This is taken from the viewpoint of political science to which the present study is ordered. It is useful for legislators, he says, to consider the voluntary and the involuntary that they may decree honors for the law-abiding and punishments for the law-breakers, for in regard to these the distinction of voluntary and involuntary is of importance.

386. Then [3], at "**Involuntary actions seem,**" he deals with the voluntary and the involuntary. First [3] he treats the involuntary, and second [Lect. IV], at "Since the involuntary etc." (1111a22), he treats the voluntary. The reason for this order is that the involuntary proceeds from a simple cause, as ignorance alone, or violence alone, but the voluntary has to take place by the concurrence of many factors. The explanation of the involuntary is achieved in three stages. First [3] he divides the involuntary. Second [4], at "The 'compulsory action' is etc.," he treats one member of the division. Third [Lect. III], at "Every action done etc." (1110b18), he treats the other member. He says first that some involuntary actions seem to be of two kinds: those arising from violence, or those arising from ignorance. This division is made in order to indicate that the involuntary is a privation of the voluntary. But the voluntary implies a movement of the appetitive power presupposing a knowledge via sense or reason because a good perceived moves the appetitive power. A thing is involuntary on two accounts: one, because the movement of the appetitive power is excluded—this is the involuntary resulting from violence—the other, because a mental awareness is excluded—this is the involuntary resulting from ignorance.

387. Next [4], at "**The 'compulsory action,'**" he deals with the involuntary resulting from violence. Here he proceeds in two ways: first he discloses what the "compulsory action" (*violen-*

tum) is. Next [Lect. II], at "If someone should say etc." (1110b9), he rejects an error about this. His initial point requires a triple consideration. First [4] he makes known what the "physically forced action" (*simpliciter violentum*) is, and second [5], at "Some things are done because of the fear," what the "morally forced action" (*violentum secundum quid*) is. Third [Lect. II], at "What sort of actions etc." (B.1110 b), he concludes with a summary. He says first that the forced action is one whose principle is from outside. It was just noted (385) that violence excludes the appetitive movement. Hence, since the appetitive faculty is an intrinsic principle, it is appropriate that the forced action arise from an extrinsic principle. However, not every action whose principle is from the outside is a forced action but only that action which is derived from an extrinsic principle in such a way that the interior appetitive faculty does not concur in it. This is what he means by his statement that a forced action must be such that a man contributes nothing to it by means of his own appetitive faculty. A man is here said to be an agent (*operans*) inasmuch as he does something because of violence and a patient inasmuch as he suffers something because of violence. Aristotle gives an example: if the air or wind drives a thing to some place by its violence, or if rulers having dominion and power exile someone against his will.

388. At "**Some things**" [5], he explains what a morally forced action is. Three steps clarify this conclusion. First [5] he raises a doubt. Next [6], at "Operations of this kind etc.," he solves the doubt. Third [Lect. II], at "People doing such actions etc." (1110a19), he clarifies the solution. He says first that a man sometimes performs an action because he fears to incur greater evils or because he is afraid to lose some good. A tyrant, for instance, has under his dominion and power the parents or children of a certain man. This tyrant commands the man to do a disgraceful deed on condition that if he does it his relatives will be spared; if he refuses they will be killed.

389. There is then a doubt whether things done because of such fear should be called voluntary or involuntary. He gives another example of sailors who during storms at sea throw merchandise overboard. Absolutely speaking, no man does this voluntarily but what he and his shipmates do in order to save their lives, any sensible man in a similar situation does.

390. Then [6], at "**Operations of this kind,**" he solves this doubt by concluding from his previous remarks (387) that the afore-mentioned actions done out of fear are mixed, i.e., have something both of the involuntary (inasmuch as no one absolutely wishes to throw his goods overboard) and of the voluntary (inasmuch as a sensible man wishes this for the safety of himself and others). However, these actions approach more closely to the voluntary than to the involuntary. The reason is that throwing merchandise overboard, or any action of this kind, can be considered in two ways: one, absolutely and in general (involuntary); the other, in the particular circumstances occurring at the time the action is to be done (voluntary). But, since actions are concerned with particulars, the nature of the action must be judged rather according to the considerations of particulars than according to the consideration of what is general. This is what he means in his statement that these actions were done

voluntarily at the time they were performed (i.e., after having considered all the particular circumstances then occurring), and the end and completion of the action conform to this particular time.

391. Therefore, an action must be properly called voluntary or involuntary in view of the time at which the agent performed it. It is obvious that he acts voluntarily at the time. This is evident because in these actions the principle moving the bodily members to act is within the man himself. It would be different, however, if his members were not moved by himself but by a more powerful agent. The things done by an intrinsic principle are in the power of man to do or not to do, and this belongs to the nature of the voluntary. Obviously then actions of this kind are properly and truly voluntary. They are, however, involuntary simply, that is considering them in general, because no one as far as in him lies would choose to do a thing of this kind except out of fear, as was just stated (390).

LECTURE II
What Voluntary Actions Merit

TEXT OF ARISTOTLE (*B.1110a19–1110b17*) Chapter 1

1. *People doing such actions are at times praised for enduring something dishonorable or painful to achieve great and good results. But when they do the opposite of this they are blamed, for only a perverse man suffers very dishonorable things in exchange for little or no good.*
1110a19–23; 392–393

2. *Some actions do not deserve praise but only pardon, for example, if a person does things that are wrong because he fears evils beyond human endurance which no one would undergo in any case.*
1110a23–26; 394

3. *Yet it is probable that there are some actions that a man cannot be forced to do and he ought to undergo death of the cruelest kind rather than do them. (The reasons that constrained Euripides' Alcmaeon to kill his mother seem to be ridiculous.)*
1110a26–29; 395

4. *Sometimes it is difficult to judge what is to be chosen for the price and what is to be endured for the gain.*
1110a29–30; 396

5. *It is still more difficult to abide by our decisions. As often happens, the expected results are painful but the compulsory acts are disgraceful. Hence we receive praise and blame according as we yield or stand firm against the constraint.*
1110a30–1110b1; 397

6. *What sort of actions then are to be called compulsory? Those actions are entirely (simpliciter) compulsory that have their cause from the outside, the person involved contributing nothing. Some actions that in themselves are involuntary become voluntary in particular circumstances. Although of themselves involuntary, if their principle is in the agent who seeks them at this time and in these circumstances, they are voluntary. They are then more like the voluntary because actions take place in particular cases that are voluntary. It is not easy to assign the sort of things we must choose in such circumstances, for particular cases admit of many differences.*
1110b1–9; 398–399

7. *If someone should say that pleasurable and good things are the cause of violence (they are external to us and influence us), all our actions will then be compulsory because men perform all their actions for the sake of something pleasing and good.*
1110b9–11; 400–401

8. *Those who act by violence act involuntarily and with sadness, but those who act to attain something enjoyable act with pleasure.*
1110b11–13; 402

9. *It is ridiculous that a man blame external goods, and not accuse himself for being snared by such pleasures;*
1110b13–14; 403

10. *while he takes to himself the credit for virtuous deeds, and lays the blame for his shameful deeds upon pleasure.*
1110b14–15; 404

11. *It seems that the compulsory action is one whose origin is external in such a way that one who suffers violence contributes nothing to the action.*
1110b15–17; 405

COMMENTARY OF ST. THOMAS

392. After the Philosopher has solved the doubt raised about the actions done because of fear, showing that such actions are voluntary, he now clarifies the solution by explaining that praise and blame, honor and punishment are due to voluntary actions of this kind. On this point he does two things. First [1] he discloses in what way these actions merit praise and blame, honor and punishment. Next [4], at "Sometimes it is difficult etc.," he makes known the pending difficulties about this. In regard to the first he

distinguishes three grades of these actions performed by reason of fear, as far as they merit praise or blame.

393. Considering now the first grade [1], he shows that regarding such actions, which he says are a mixture of the voluntary and the involuntary, some persons are praised for suffering something dishonorable—not indeed of a sinful nature but a kind of ignominy—or even saddening or grievous in order to persevere in certain great and good things, for example, virtuous actions. When the opposite happens they are blamed since it seems that only a perverse man suffers very dishonorable things, i.e., great disorders in exchange for little or no good. No one suffers any evil to preserve a good unless that good is of greater value in his estimation than the other goods to which the evil he suffers are opposed. It belongs to a disordered desire to prefer small goods to great ones that are destroyed by greater evils. Therefore, he says this pertains to a perverse man, i.e., one who has a disordered desire.

394. At "**Some actions**" [2], he sets down the second grade, stating that some actions performed because of fear do not deserve praise but only pardon. A person should not be blamed very much for doing certain things he ought not do, such as actions unbefitting his state. These actions should not be considered seriously binding on account of the fear of evils beyond human endurance. No one would undergo such evils especially for the reason alleged, for example, if someone is threatened with punishment by fire unless he tells a jocose lie, or unless he performs some lowly menial tasks unbecoming his dignity.

395. At "**Yet it is probable**" [3], he treats the third grade. He states that

other actions are so evil that no amount of force can compel them to be done but a man ought to undergo death of the cruelest kind rather than do such things, as St. Lawrence endured the roasting on the gridiron to avoid sacrificing to idols. The Philosopher affirms this either because glory remains after death for one dying for the sake of virtue or because courageous perseverance in virtue is so great a good that continuance of life—which a man loses by death—cannot equal it. He says, therefore, that *Alcmaeona* or the poems about Alcmaeon written by Euripides seem to be satirical. These poems narrate the story of Alcmaeon who was forced to kill his mother by the command of his father. The father had ordered this when dying in the Theban war to which he had gone by the advice of his wife.

396. Then [4], at "**Sometimes it is**," he brings forward two difficulties which threaten the above-mentioned activities. The first of these pertains to the judgment of reason [4]. Sometimes it is difficult, he says, to judge what is to be chosen so that one may avoid evil and what evil is to be endured so that one may not be lacking in some good.

397. The second difficulty [5], which he gives at "**It is still more**," pertains to the stability of the affection. He says that it is even more difficult to be steadfast in a reasonable decision that has been made than to make a right judgment. He assigns the reason for the difficulty saying that—as often happens—the things that are expected are painful, i.e., afflicting or sorrowful, but those to which men are forced because of fear are disgraceful. It is difficult, however, for a man's affections not to be moved by fear of pain. Since those actions to which one is forced by a motive of this kind are disgraceful, it is

fitting that for those who are forced to do such things by fear of painful effects, blame should be forthcoming. But those who cannot be forced to do them are worthy of praise.

398. Next [6], at "**What sort of actions then,**" he sums up in conclusion the things that have been said and assigns a reason for them. First he reviews the principal question, what sort of actions are to be called compulsory (*violenta*). Then, he sums up the answer so far as concerns the entirely (*absolute*) compulsory actions, the cause of which is from the outside so that the person involved contributes nothing because of violence. Third he gives a resume of mixed actions. He says that those actions that in themselves, i.e., abstractly (*absolute*) and universally considered, are involuntary become voluntary at a definite time and by reason of certain events. Although they are involuntary in themselves, their principle is in the agent.[1] Therefore, they should be called voluntary at this time and for these reasons. Thus it is evident that these actions are more like the voluntary than the involuntary because they are voluntary when we consider the particular circumstances in which the actions are performed.

399. Last, he recapitulates what he had stated about the difficulty occurring in things of this kind. He says that it is not easy to assign the sort of thing we must choose in such circumstances. He assigns as the reason that many differences are found in singulars. Hence the judgment of them cannot be comprised under an exact rule but they are to be left to the evaluation of a prudent man.

400. At "**If someone**" [7], he rejects an error of certain philosophers concerning actions done as a result of violence. Because man is what he is by reason, it seemed to some that man of himself, and as it were voluntarily, does only that which he performs according to reason. But when it happens that man acts contrary to reason either on account of the desire of some pleasure or greed for some external good, he acts in a violent manner. They say, therefore, that pleasurable and external goods like riches cause forced actions inasmuch as being external things they force man to act against his reason. But Aristotle shows this to be false for five reasons.

401. The first reason is this [7]. If external things, precisely as they are pleasurable and seemingly good, cause violence, it would follow that all actions we perform in human affairs are forced actions and none is voluntary. (All men do what they do for the sake of these things, i.e., for something that is pleasurable or good under a certain aspect.) But this is unreasonable. Therefore, the first (that these external things cause violence) is also untenable.

402. He sets down the second reason at "**Those who act**" [8]. All who act as a result of violence, act involuntarily and with sadness. Hence in the fifth book of the *Metaphysics* (Ch. 5, 1015a26 sq.; St. Th. Lect. VI, 829–831), it is well said that necessitation is saddening because it is opposed to the will. But those who act to acquire something enjoyable act with pleasure. They do not then act by violence and involuntarily.

403. He gives the third reason at "**It is ridiculous**" [9]. He says it is ridicu-

---

1   *Operatione* in the Commentary should be *operante*.

lous that a man plead as an excuse or blame external goods and not accuse himself that he was snared, i.e., permitted himself to be overcome by such pleasures. Our will is not of necessity moved by these desirable things but it can cling to them or desert them. None possesses the nature of a universal and perfect good, as happiness (which everyone necessarily wishes) does.

404. He assigns the fourth reason at **"while he takes"** [10]. It is ridiculous, he says, that a person should call himself the cause of his good and virtuous works, and pleasurable things the cause of his shameful deeds inasmuch as they induce desire. Aristotle says it is ridiculous because directly opposed operations are referred back to the same power as a cause. Consequently it is necessary that as reason operating according to itself is the cause of virtu-

ous action so also in following the passions it should be the cause of vicious action.

405. He gives the fifth reason at **"It seems that"** [11], saying that the forced action is one whose source is from the outside in such a way that he who suffers by reason of it contributes nothing to the action. But the man who acts on account of external goods does contribute something to the action. Accordingly, although the principle inclining his will is from outside, his action is forced neither wholly (*simpliciter*) because he contributes something to the action, nor by some mixture because in mixed actions a thing is not rendered simply voluntary, as happens here. Therefore, a man acts in that case with sadness but here with pleasure, as has been stated (402).

LECTURE III
The Involuntary Resulting from Ignorance

TEXT OF ARISTOTLE (*1110b18–1111a21*) Chapter 1

1. *Every action done because of ignorance is not voluntary; it is involuntary if sorrow and repentance follow. One who does something on account of ignorance and is not sorry about what he did, cannot be said to have acted voluntarily, for he was unaware of his action. But neither can he be said to have acted involuntarily if he is not sorry. A man who has acted from ignorance and regrets his action seems to have acted involuntarily. But if he does not regret it, his case is different; let us call him non-voluntary. Because of his differing, it is better that he have a distinctive name.* **1110b18–24; 406–408**

2. *There seems to be a difference between acting on account of ignorance and acting in ignorance. A drunken or angry person does not act because of ignorance but because of one of the things mentioned (drunkenness or anger). Such a one however does not act knowingly but in ignorance. Therefore, every wicked person acts in ignorance of the things he ought to do and avoid. Men acting on account of an error of this kind become unjust and wicked generally.* **1110b24–30; 409–410**

3. *When we speak of an action as involuntary we do not mean that a man is ignorant of what he ought to do. The ignorance that accompanies choice is not the cause of an involuntary but of sin. The same may be said of ignorance that is of a general nature because a person is blamed for such ignorance. But a person who is ignorant of particular conditions about which and on which human activity is exercised deserves mercy and pardon because he who is ignorant of any of these circumstances acts involuntarily.* **1110b30–1111a2; 411–413**

4. *Perhaps it is not out of place to determine the nature and number of these circumstances: who, what, concerning what or in what one operates; sometimes, too, by what, for example, a tool; for the sake of which, for instance, safety; and in what manner, for example, quietly or violently.* **1111a3–6; 414–416**

5. *No one but a madman will be ignorant of all these circumstances. It is obvious that no one can be ignorant of the agent. How can he be ignorant about himself? But someone can be ignorant of what he does, for instance, those speaking out of turn say it escaped them unawares or they did not know that certain things were not to be disclosed, like Aeschylus when he revealed the sacred mysteries; or someone wishing to show the working of a weapon discharges an arrow; or a man mistakes his son for an assailant, as Merope did; or he thinks a piked lance blunted, or a rock merely pumice; or he may kill someone by a blow meant to save him; or a trainer sparring with a boxer to teach him takes his life.* **1111a6–15; 417–421**

6. *Since ignorance can be concerned with every one of the circumstances occurring with the action, that man seems to act involuntarily who is ignorant of one of them. This applies especially to ignorance of the most important circumstances.* **1111a15–18; 422**

7. *These seem to be the circumstances of the action and its motives.* **1111a18–19; 423**

8. *For an action to be called involuntary in respect of such ignorance it must be painful to the agent and cause repentance.* **1111a19–21; 424**

COMMENTARY OF ST. THOMAS

406. After the Philosopher has determined the involuntary resulting from violence, he now turns his attention to the involuntary resulting from ignorance. Concerning it he does two things. First [1] he shows how there is an involuntary resulting from ignorance. Second [4], at "Perhaps it is etc.,"

he explains some of his statements. In regard to the initial point he sets down three differences concerning ignorance. The first of these [1] is considered insofar as what is done on account of ignorance is related to the will in different ways. Sometimes it is opposed to the will, and then it is properly called an involuntary. But other times it is not opposed to the will but is over and above the will precisely as it is unknown. In this sense it is not called involuntary but non-voluntary.

407. He says then that what is done on account of ignorance in such a way that ignorance is the cause, is not voluntary in any case because the act of the will is not moved to it. The act of the will cannot be moved to what is entirely unknown since the will's object is the known good. But only then is that which is done out of ignorance called involuntary—as it were opposed to the will—when on becoming known, sorrow and repentance (which is sorrow over one's past actions) follow. A thing is sorrowful because it is opposed to the will, as is stated in the fifth book of the *Metaphysics* (Ch. 5, 1015a26 sq.; St. Th. Lect. VI, 829-831).

408. One who does something on account of ignorance and is not sorry about what he did after he knows it, for instance, if he takes silver thinking he took tin, cannot be said to have voluntarily (willingly) taken silver since he did not know that it was silver. It cannot be said that he involuntarily (unwillingly), i.e., against his will, took silver since he is not sorry that he did take silver by reason of ignorance. He seems to have acted involuntarily who has sorrow or repents for the fact that he took silver by reason of ignorance, just as if someone had, on the contrary, taken tin thinking he has taken silver. But because he who does not repent is

different from the man who does repent (he is said to be unwilling) let the first be called non-willing. Since he really differs from the one who is unwilling, it is better that he have a proper and separate name.

409. He sets down the second difference at "There seems to be" [2]. This is taken according to the difference of what is done in ignorance; for ignorance sometimes is the cause of an action, but sometimes the act proceeds from another cause. He says that a person acting on account of ignorance seems to be different from a person acting in ignorance. Sometimes one acts in ignorance but not on account of ignorance. A drunken or angry person does not act on account of ignorance but on account of drunkenness or anger. Neither of these, however, acts knowingly because ignorance is caused at the same time as the action by drunkenness and anger. Thus ignorance is concomitant with the action and is not its cause.

410. From this he concludes that as an angry person acts in ignorance and not on account of ignorance but on account of anger, so every wicked person acts not indeed on account of ignorance but partly in ignorance of the good he ought to do and of the evil he ought to avoid, inasmuch as he thinks that at this moment he should do this evil and refrain from this good. For this reason he sins because he does what he ought not to do. Men who act in ignorance universally become unjust with respect to others and wicked with respect to themselves. From this it is evident that when someone acts in ignorance, and not on account of ignorance, he does not cause an involuntary. The reason is that no one, by reason of what he does involuntarily, is unjust or wicked.

411. He assigns the third difference at "When we speak" [3]. This is taken from the object of the person's ignorance. Here we must consider that ignorance can be of two kinds. According to one, a person is ignorant of what he ought to do or avoid. He says this is ignorance of what is fitting—of what he ought to be doing. This ignorance does not cause an involuntary because ignorance of this kind cannot happen to a man with the use of reason except from negligence. The reason is that everyone is bound to be solicitous about knowing what he is obliged to do and to avoid. Hence if a man does not wish to avoid (as he is bound) ignorance that is considered voluntary, it follows that what is done through this ignorance should not be judged involuntary. This is the meaning of the saying that one does not wish an involuntary (i.e., what is by nature an involuntary) if he is ignorant of what he does, that is, of what is suitable under the circumstances. Of this someone can be ignorant in two ways:

412. One is in a particular choice. For instance, because of sensual desire a person thinks he should commit fornication at this time. The other way is in general, as is evident in one who is of the opinion that fornication is always lawful. Both kinds of ignorance concern what is done. Hence neither causes an involuntary. This is what is meant by saying that that ignorance accompanying choice (by which a person thinks he should do this evil at this time) is not the cause of an involuntary but is rather the cause of vice or sin. Neither is the ignorance that is of a general nature the cause of an involuntary since a person is blamed on account of ignorance of this kind. But no one is censured because of an involuntary, as was said previously (410).

413. The other ignorance (the first is in 411) is of singular conditions, for instance, that this woman is married, that this man is a parent, that this place is holy. It is about these conditions and on them that human activity is exercised; by reason of a justifiable ignorance of such conditions that a person deserves mercy and pardon because he who is ignorant of one of these conditions acts involuntarily. Therefore, it is obvious that ignorance of particular circumstances of this kind—not however ignorance of what one should do—is the cause of an involuntary.

414. Then [4], at "**Perhaps it is not**," he explains what he had referred to: those circumstances the ignorance of which is a cause of an involuntary. In regard to this he does three things. First [4] he points out what these circumstances are. Next [5], at "No one but etc.," he shows in what way ignorance of them may be present. Last [6], at "Since ignorance can be etc.," he explains how ignorance of these circumstances is the cause of an involuntary. On the first point we must consider that circumstances are nothing else but certain particular conditions of a human act. These can be taken either on the part of the causes of the act or on the part of the act itself. The cause of the act is efficient or final. The efficient cause is either the principal or the instrumental agent. On the part of the act three things can be understood: the genus of the act, the matter or the object itself, and the mode of acting. In agreement with this the Philosopher here places six circumstances. He says that it is not out of place—indeed it is very appropriate—to determine what and how many are these particular circumstances, the ignorance of which is the cause of an involuntary. He uses an adverb (*forsi-*

tan) indicating doubt, as in many other places of this book because of the uncertainty in moral matters.

415. Enumerating then these particular things he names "who," which refers to the person of the principal agent; "what is done," which refers to the genus of the act; and "concerning what," which refers to the matter or the object. But he adds also "concerning this"—which refers to the measure of the act—as belonging to the agent, i.e., place or time, since he says "or in what he operates." The reason is that all external things seem to have relation to the human act. Cicero includes what we call "concerning what" under "what." What is here called "in what" he divides into two circumstances: time and place.

416. So far as concerns the instrumental agent Aristotle adds: sometimes also "by what" (*quo*), for instance an instrument, since not every action is performed through an instrument, for example, understanding and willing. In place of this some put "by what means" (helps), for one to whom help is given uses help as an instrument. Referring to the end he says "for the sake of which," for instance, a doctor cuts for the sake of health. Referring to the mode of acting he says "and in what manner," for example, quietly, or violently, that is, strongly.

417. Next [5], at "**No one but,**" he shows in what way there may be ignorance about the preceding circumstances. He says that only a totally insane person is ignorant of all these circumstances. Among the other circumstances it is obvious that a man cannot be ignorant of what is meant by the one acting, because in this case he would be ignorant about himself (which is impossible). But someone can be ignorant of what he does, as

those who disclose things that should not be disclosed say in excusing themselves that it slipped their mind or they never knew that such things were secret, i.e., were not to be spoken. Thus were revealed the sacred mysteries or secrets by Aeschylus, a certain poet. He who speaks such things is ignorant of what he does because he does not know this is a revelation of secrets.

418. He gives another example so far as concerns what is done, for instance, an archer wishing to teach a pupil how archery is practised shoots an arrow into something. Such a one does not know what he does because he does not know he is shooting an arrow. Then he exemplifies ignorance "concerning what" (*circa quid*), thus if a man should mistake his son for an enemy besieging his home, and kill him, just as a certain woman named Merope killed her son. So it is obvious that in a case of this kind a man knows what he does because he knows he kills, but he does not know the "concerning what" of his act because he does not know he kills his son.

419. Then he gives an example of ignorance of the instrument, thus if a lancer should use a piked lance that he thought was blunted or if a thrower of rocks thinks what he throws are pumice stones.

420. Farther on he gives an example of ignorance of the end. He says that a doctor or a blood-letter lancing a patient to make him better, or a teacher striking a pupil to correct him, may take a life. These have ignorance of the end, not indeed of what they intended but of what followed from their action. They were ignorant that their action would lead to such an end.

421. Last, he illustrates ignorance of the manner of the action, for instance, a man thinks he is tapping with his fist

to show how to hit like boxers do but he strikes with force. Such a man strikes with force in ignorance or unknowingly.

422. At **"Since ignorance can be"** [6], he shows how ignorance of the previously named things is a cause of the voluntary. First [6] he says that since ignorance can be concerned with any one of the five afore-mentioned that concur with the action, that man seems to act unwillingly or involuntarily who is ignorant of one of the preceding. This does not apply in equal measure to all but it does apply especially if the ignorance concerns the most important circumstances.

423. Next [7], at **"These seem to be,"** he shows what he considers the most important circumstances. He says that the principal circumstances seem to be those on which the act takes place, i.e., the object or the matter of the act, and that "for the sake of which" or the end, because acts are specified by their objects. Just as the matter is the object of the external act so the end is the object of the internal act of the will.

424. Last [8], at **"For an action,"** he says that ignorance of these very things is not enough for an involuntary. He states that although an action may be called involuntary according to the preceding ignorance, a further requirement is that the action be connected with sadness and repentance, as was pointed out before (408).

LECTURE IV
Definition of the Voluntary

TEXT OF ARISTOTLE (*B.1111a22–1111b3*) Chapter 1

1. Since the involuntary comes about on account of force and ignorance, the voluntary seems to originate within the agent who has knowledge of the circumstances of the action.

1111a22–24; 425

2. Perhaps it is not accurate to call involuntary the things that are done on account of anger or sensual desire.

1111a24–25; 426

3. *(1)* The main reason is that neither animals nor children would then act voluntarily.

1111a25–26; 427

4. *2)* Are none of the things done by reason of sensual desire or anger done voluntarily? Are the noble actions done voluntarily but the evil involuntarily? The latter views seems ridiculous since there is one cause of all our actions. Likewise it seems unreasonable to call involuntary the things we ought to seek. We ought to be angry under certain circumstances, and we ought to desire certain things, for example, health and learning.

1111a28–31; 428

5. *(3)* Involuntary things seemingly are accompanied by sadness. But what is done in agreement with sensual desire seems to be done with pleasure.

1111a32–33; 429

6. *(4)* Further what difference is there from the viewpoint of involuntariness between sins committed after reflection and sins committed on account of anger? It is our duty to avoid both.

1111a33–34; 430

7. *(5)* The irrational passions seem to be truly human. So too then are the actions of man proceeding from anger and sensual desire. It is unreasonable, therefore, to regard these as involuntary.

1111b1–3; 431

COMMENTARY OF ST. THOMAS

425. After the Philosopher has considered the involuntary, he next turns his attention to the voluntary. First [1] he shows what the voluntary is. Then [2], at "Perhaps it is not accurate etc.," he dismisses an erroneous view of it. On the first point we must consider that although the term involuntary seems to indicate the removal of the voluntary, nevertheless the causes lead us to understand that a thing is called voluntary by reason of the removal of the things causing an involuntary, such as violence and ignorance. Because every single thing is known through its cause, he gives the definition of the voluntary by taking away the cause of the involuntary. He says that since the involuntary comes about through physical compulsion and ignorance, as has been de-termined previously (386), the voluntary seems to be: that which the agent himself originates (thus violence is excluded) in such a way that the agent knows the individual circumstances that concur with the action. Thus ignorance as the cause of the involuntary is excluded.

426. Then [2], at "**Perhaps it is**," he rejects an error. First [2] he explains it. Certain people were of the opinion that not everything, which the agent originates through a knowledge of circumstances, is a voluntary. It can happen that that principle which is from within is not the rational appetitive faculty called the will (*voluntas*), whence the voluntary receives its name, but a passion of the sensitive appetitive faculty, for instance, anger, sensual desire, or something else of

this kind. This, the Philosopher says, is not an accurate statement. It should be noted that because the passions of the sensitive appetitive faculty are aroused by external things grasped by means of an external sense, this error seems to be of the same nature as the one he discarded previously (400–405), according to which it was indicated that external things bring about violence. It was imperative to state that in that context it was a question of violence, whose origin is external. But this must be treated here where it is a question of the voluntary, the principle of which is intrinsic, for the passions are within us.

427. Second [3], at "**The main reason is,**" he rejects this opinion for five reasons. Here is his primary reason. Whatever irrational animals and children do, they do in conformity with the affections of the sensitive faculty, and not in conformity with the rational faculty because they lack the use of reason. If then the things that are done through anger, sensual desire, and the other affections of the sensitive faculty were involuntary it would follow that neither animals nor children would act voluntarily. But agents are said to act voluntarily, not because they operate under the impulse of the will, but because they operate of their own accord by their proper movement in such a way that they are not moved by any external thing. It follows then that things done by reason of anger or sensual desire are voluntary.

428. He gives the second reason at "**Are none**" [4]. If the things that are done because of anger or sensual desire are not voluntary, either this is universally true or it is true of evil actions, not of good actions, so that the good actions that a person does by reason of passion he does voluntarily but

the evil actions involuntarily. The proponents of this view were probably influenced by the fact that good actions conform to and evil actions are opposed to reason. But this second supposition seems unacceptable since the one cause of all human actions, both good and bad, is the will. A man does not rush to do whatsoever is rendered desirable by anger or sensual desire without the consent of the rational appetitive faculty. Likewise, the first supposition seems unreasonable, namely, that someone should call not-voluntary the good things that he ought to seek even according to passion, for the reason by means of the will incites to the things we ought to seek. We ought to be angry under certain conditions, for instance, to curb sin. Likewise we ought to desire certain things, for example, health and learning. It remains false then to hold that the things done on account of passion are not voluntary.

429. He assigns the third reason at "**Involuntary things**" [5]. It is this. Actions resulting from violence are accompanied by sadness, but those which are done in agreement with sensual desire are done with pleasure. Consequently they are not involuntary.

430. The fourth reason, given at "**Further, what**" [6], is this. As has been pointed out before (383, 393), voluntary faults are to be censured and avoided. This cannot be said of the involuntary because a man is neither able to avoid these nor is he censured on account of them. But as sins that are committed after reflection, that is, with deliberation, are to be avoided and are blameworthy so also sins that are committed on account of anger or another passion. A man can, by means of his will, resist passion. Hence if he does a

disgraceful act because of passion he is blamed. Therefore, they do not differ from things done by deliberation so far as they are voluntary.

431. He assigns the fifth reason at "**The irrational passions**" [7]. Irrational passions, i.e., of the sensitive appetitive faculty, seem to be human insofar as the sensitive appetitive faculty can obey reason, as was stated before (272). Therefore, the actions proceeding from anger, sensual desire, and the other passions are human. But no involuntary operation is human, for neither praise nor blame are imputed to a man who acts involuntarily. Therefore, it is unreasonable to say that things done out of passion are involuntary.

LECTURE V
Choice

TEXT OF ARISTOTLE (B.1111b4–1111b30) Chapter 2

1. After the treatise on the voluntary and the involuntary, we naturally proceed to a consideration of choice. Such a study is especially proper to virtue, for moral practices are judged by choice rather than by actions.   1111b4–6; 432–433

2. Choice certainly is something voluntary, but choice and voluntary are not identical, for the voluntary is more extensive in range. Children and all the brutes participate in voluntariety but not in choice. Then too the things done on the spur of the moment are called voluntary but they are not said to be done by choice.   1111b6–10; 434–436

3. Those who say that choice is sensual desire, or anger, or wish, or opinion of some sort do not speak accurately.   1111b10–12; 437

4. Choice does not belong to the brutes while sensual desire and anger are common both to men and brutes.   1111b12–13; 438

5. The incontinent man acts in conformity with sensual desire but not in conformity with choice. But the continent man on the contrary acts from choice and not from sensual desire.
1111b13–15; 439

6. Sensual desire is opposed to choice, but one desire is not contrary to another.
1111b15–16; 440

7. Sensual desire is accompanied by pleasure or sorrow, but choice is not necessarily associated with sorrow or pleasure.   1111b16–18; 441

8. There is less argument in favor of choice being anger, for the things done on account of anger do not seem to be done by choice.   1111b18–19; 442

9. Choice is not identical with wishing although it is closely connected with it.
1111b19–20; 443

10. Choice is not concerned with impossibles, and if a person should say that he does choose the impossible, he will appear foolish. Wishing on the other hand can be directed to the impossible, for instance, to live forever.   1111b20–23; 444

11. Wishing can be concerned with things not done by oneself, for instance, that a man pretending to be an athlete may win, or even that a man who is really an athlete may win. No one, however, chooses these things but only those that he thinks he can do himself.
1111b23–26; 445

12. Moreover, wishing is directed rather to the end, and choice to the means. Thus we wish health but we choose the remedies that restore us to health. Likewise, we wish to be happy and we do say this. Yet it is not suitable to say that we elect or choose to be happy. 1111b26–29; 446

13. In general, choice seems to be directed to the things which are within our power.
1111b29–30; 447

COMMENTARY OF ST. THOMAS

432. After the Philosopher has treated the voluntary and the involuntary, he here makes a study of choice. First he gives an explanation of choice itself, and then [Lect. VII] of counsel (which is placed in the definition of choice) at "Should men take counsel about all things etc." (1112a19). Regarding the initial point he does two things. First [1] he shows that it belongs to our present study to consider choice. Next [2], at "Choice certainly is something," he investigates the nature of choice. He says first that, after the

treatise (382–431) on the voluntary and the involuntary, he will undertake a passing consideration of choice. Here then he proposes briefly the things necessary to study choice. He proves here that it belongs to our science to consider choice because choice seems especially proper to virtue, which is our principal concern at present.

433. Its appropriateness is clearly shown by the fact that although both inner choice and outward action flow from the habit of virtue, virtuous or vicious practices are judged rather by choice than by outward works. Every virtuous man chooses good but sometimes he does not do it because of some external hindrances. On the other hand the vicious man sometimes performs a virtuous deed not out of virtuous choice but out of fear or for some unbecoming motive, for instance, vainglory or something else of this kind. Hence it obviously pertains to our present purpose to consider choice.

434. Then [2], at "**Choice certainly,**" he shows what choice is. First [2] he investigates its genus, and next [3] its different aspects, at "Those who say that choice etc." Last [Lect. VI], at "What, then, is its genus etc." (1112a13), he concludes the definition. The voluntary is the genus of choice because it is universally predicated of choice and of other things besides. Hence first he says that every choice is voluntary, but choice and the voluntary are not identical, for the voluntary is more extensive. He proves this in twofold fashion:

435. The first proof he gives by the words "... **participate in voluntariety etc.**" It is this. Children and the various brutes participate in voluntariety inasmuch as of their own accord they do things by their own movement, as has been noted above (427). But they do not communicate in choice because they do not act with deliberation, which is required for choice. Therefore, the voluntary is more extensive than choice.

436. He assigns a second reason by the words "**Then too the things done on the spur of the moment etc.**" It is this. The things we do on the spur of the moment are called voluntary because their origin is within us. However, they are not said to be according to choice because they are not done with deliberation. Therefore, the voluntary is more extensive than choice.

437. Next [3], at "**Those who say,**" he investigates the different aspects of choice, proving that choice differs from things with which it appears to agree. On this question he does two things. First [3] he explains his intent. Then [4], at "Choice does not belong etc.," he proves it. He says first that some philosophers have held that choice is sensual desire because both imply a movement of the appetitive faculty toward good. Others maintained that choice is anger, perhaps because in both there is a certain use of reason. The angry person uses reason inasmuch as he judges that an injury received deserves punishment. Still others who consider that choice is without passion ascribe choice to the rational part, either so far as concerns the appetitive faculty (saying it is wishing) or so far as it concerns perception (saying it is opinion). In these four states all the principles of human actions are included in a simple way: reason to which opinion belongs; the rational appetitive faculty that is the will; the sensitive appetitive faculty divided into irascible to which belong

anger, and concupiscible to which belong sensual desire. The Philosopher says, however, that those who hold that choice is one of these do not speak accurately.

438. At "**Choice does not**" [4], he proves his proposition. He shows first [4] that choice is not sensual desire; next [8], at "There is less argument etc.," that it is not anger; third [9], at "Choice is not identical etc.," that it is not wishing; last [Lect. VI], that it is not opinion, at "Choice is not opinion etc." (1111b31). Regarding the first he gives four reasons. The first of these [4], common to sensual desire and anger, is this. Sensual desire and anger are found both among men and brutes. But choice is not met with among the brutes as has been said (435). Therefore, choice is neither sensual desire nor anger.

439. He gives the second reason at "**The incontinent man**" [5]. It is this. If choice were sensual desire, whoever acts with choice would act with sensual desire. This, however, is false because the incontinent man acts in conformity with sensual desire but not in conformity with choice, for he does not reasonably direct his choice because of his sensual desire. But the continent man on the contrary acts from choice and not from sensual desire, which he resists by choice, as will be made evident in the seventh book (1143). Therefore, choice is not the same as sensual desire.

440. He assigns the third reason at "**Sensual desire is opposed**" [6]. It is this. Sensual desire is opposed to choice in one who is continent or incontinent. One chooses according to reason the opposite of that which the other desires according to the sensitive appetitive faculty. But the sensual desire in the one is not opposed to the sensual desire in the other, because the whole sensual desire of each one tends to the same thing, the pleasure of the senses. But this must not be understood in the sense that one desire may not be opposed to another. We do find desires of contraries, for instance, one man desires to move and another to remain in repose. Therefore it is evident that choice is not identical with sensual desire.

441. The fourth reason, given at "**Sensual desire is accompanied**" [7], is this. Sensual desire is always accompanied by pleasure because of the presence of the thing desired, or by sorrow because of the absence of that thing. Every passion is followed by pleasure or sorrow, as has been pointed out in the second book (296). But choice is not necessarily associated with pleasure or sorrow, for it can occur without any passion by the judgment of reason alone. Therefore, choice is not sensual desire.

442. Then [8], at "**There is less argument,**" he shows that choice is not the same as anger. As to this, he says that there is less argument in favor of choice being anger than sensual desire. The reason is that even according to appearances the things done from anger do not seem to be done by choice because, by reason of the swiftness of the movement of wrath, the actions done through anger are very sudden. Although in anger there is some use of reason, insofar as the angry person begins to attend to his reason as it judges that an injury ought to be avenged, nevertheless he does not perfectly heed reason in determining the manner and the order of the vengeance. Hence anger especially excludes deliberation, which is necessary for choice.

But sensual desire does not act so suddenly. Hence things done in conformity with sensual desire do not seem to be remote from choice as the things done out of anger.

443. Next [9], at "**Choice is not identical**," he explains the difference between choice and wish. First [9] he sets forth his proposition. Then [10], at "Choice is not concerned etc.," he proves it. Last [13], at "In general, choice," he deduces the origin of the difference between choice and wishing. He says first that choice is not even wishing although it seems to be closely connected with wishing. Both belong to the one power, the rational appetitive faculty or the will. Wishing designates an act of this power related to good absolutely. But choice designates an act of the same power related to good according as it belongs to an act by which we are ordered to some good.

444. At "**Choice is not concerned**" [10], he proves the statement by three reasons, of which the first is this. Because choice refers to our activity, it is said that choice is not concerned with impossible things. If a person should say that he chooses something impossible he will appear foolish. But wishing can be directed to any good even the impossible because it regards good absolutely. Thus a man can wish to be immortal, an impossible thing according to the condition of this perishable life. Therefore, choice and wish are not the same.

445. He gives the second reason at "**Wishing can be**" [11]. The wishing of someone can be concerned with things not done by himself. Thus he who is a spectator at a duel can wish that a pretender playing an assumed role may win (for example, a man who comes into the ring as a boxer when he is not a boxer) or even that one who is really an athlete may win. No one, however, chooses these things that are done by another but only those that he thinks he can do himself. Therefore, choice differs from wishing.

446. He assigns the third reason at "**Moreover, wishing**."[12] He says that wishing is directed rather to the end than to the means because we wish the means on account of the end. But that for the sake of which something exists is itself greater. But choice concerns only the means and not the end itself because the end as already predetermined is presupposed. The means, however, are sought by us as things to be ordered to the end. Thus we wish health principally since it is the end of healing. But we choose the remedies by which we are restored to health. Likewise we wish to be happy—happiness is our ultimate end—and we say we wish this. Yet it is not suitable to say that we elect or choose to be happy. Therefore, choice is not the same as wish.

447. Then [13], at "**In general, choice**," he gives the root of the whole difference to which all the previous differences in general are referred. He says that choice seems to be directed to the things that are within our power. This is the reason why it does not concern impossibles, things done by others, nor the end that, for the most part, is prearranged for us by nature.

LECTURE VI
Choice and Opinion

TEXT OF ARISTOTLE (*B.1111b30–1112a17*) Chapter 2

1. *Choice is not opinion, for opinion can concern everything—no less eternal and impossible things than things lying within our power. Then, too, opinion is divided into false and true but not into good and bad, as is the case with choice. Perhaps there is no one who maintains that choice is generally identical with opinion.*   **1111b30–1112a1; 448–449**

2. *Nor is choice identical with a particular opinion. In choosing good or bad things we are said to be good or bad but this is not the case in forming opinions about them.*
1112a1–3; 450–451

3. *We choose to accept or reject this or anything pertaining to our actions. But we have an opinion as to what a thing is or what effect it has or how it is to be used. However, accepting or rejecting something is hardly a matter of opinion.*   **1112a3–5; 452**

4. *Choice is rather praised because it chooses what it ought—as it were—in the right way, while opinion is praised because it has the truth about something.*   **1112a5–7; 453**

5. *We choose those things that we especially know are good. But we have an opinion about things we are not sure of.*   **1112a7–8; 454**

6. *And it is not necessarily the same people who make the best choices and form true opinions. Some men form a true opinion of what is better but on account of bad will they do not make the right choice.*   **1112a8–11; 455**

7. *Whether opinion should be said to precede choice or follow it, does not matter, for we do not intend to determine this but whether choice is identical with a particular opinion.*
1112a11–13; 456

8. *What then is its genus, what its specific difference, since it is none of the things previously mentioned? Seemingly it is a voluntary. However, not every voluntary—but certainly the deliberately intentional voluntary—is a thing chosen, for choice must be accompanied by reason and intellect. Even the name seems to imply that one thing be preferred to others.*   **1112a13–17; 457**

COMMENTARY OF ST. THOMAS

448. After the Philosopher has shown that choice is not the same as sensual desire; nor anger, which belongs to the sensitive appetitive faculty; nor wishing, which belongs to the rational appetitive faculty, he here shows that choice is not the same as opinion, which pertains to reason itself. He illustrates this point by a threefold consideration. First [1] he shows that choice is not the same as opinion in general. Next [2], at "Nor is choice etc.," he shows that choice is not the same as that particular opinion that concerns itself with the things we do. Last [7], at "Whether opinion should

be," he raises a doubt (which he leaves unsolved). He says first—this is apparent from the premises—that choice is not the same as opinion in general. He proves the statement by two reasons, the first of which is this [1]. Opinion can concern everything—no less eternal and impossible things than things lying within our power. But choice concerns these things only within our capacity, as was just noted (447). Therefore, choice is not the same as opinion.

449. He gives the second reason at "Then, too, opinion is divided etc." [6]. It is this. The things that are distin-

guished by various reasons are said to differ and not to be the same. Opinion, however, is divided into true and false since it pertains to the faculty of knowledge, the object of which is the truth. Opinion is not divided into good and bad as is the case with choice which belongs to the appetitive faculty, the object of which is the good. He concludes from this that choice is not the same as opinion in general. This is so obvious that no one affirms the contrary.

450. Then [2], at "**Nor is choice,**" he shows that choice is not identical with that opinion which deals with the things we do. He proves this by (five) reasons, the first of which is this [2]. From the fact that we choose good or bad things we are said to be such, that is, good or bad. But from the fact that we have an opinion about good or bad things, or about true or false things, we are not said to be good or bad. Therefore choice is not identical with opinion, which refers to eligible things.

451. The reason for this difference is that a man is not called good or bad on account of his capabilities but on account of his actions (as noted in the ninth book of the *Metaphysics*: Ch. 9, 1051a4–15; St. Th. Lect. X, 1883–1885), that is, not because he is able to act well but because he does in fact act well. When a man understands perfectly he becomes able to act well but he does not yet act well. Thus one who has the habit of grammar is able by that very fact to speak correctly, but that he actually speak correctly he must will it. The reason is that a habit is that quality by which a person acts when he wishes, as the Commentator says on the third book *De Anima*. It is obvious then that good will makes a man act well according to every capability or habit obedient to reason. Therefore a

man is called good simply because he has a good will. However, from the fact that he has a good intellect he is not called good simply but relatively good, for example, a good grammarian or a good musician. Therefore, since choice pertains to the will but opinion to the intellect, we are called good or bad by reason of choice but not by reason of opinion.

452. He gives the second reason at "**We choose to accept**" [3]. Choice has to do especially with our actions. We choose to accept or reject this thing, or whatever else there is that pertains to our actions. But opinion principally refers to things. We have an opinion as to what this thing is (for instance, what bread is) or what effect it has or how one must use it. Opinion, however, does not principally concern our actions, for example, that we are of an opinion about accepting or rejecting something. The reason is that our actions are particular contingent things and quickly passing. Hence a knowledge or opinion of them is not often sought for the sake of the truth in them but only because of something done. Therefore choice is not identical with opinion.

453. He assigns a third reason at "**Choice is**" [4]. It is this. The good of choice consists in a kind of rectitude, that is, the appetitive faculty rightly orders something to an end. This is what he means saying that choice is rather praised because it chooses what it ought, as it were in the right way, while opinion is praised because it has the truth about something. Thus the good and perfection of choice is rectitude but the perfection of opinion consists in truth. Things which have different perfections are themselves different. Therefore choice is not opinion.

454. The fourth reason, given at "**We choose those things**" [5], is this. Choice is accompanied by certitude, for we choose those things which we especially know are good. But opinion lacks certitude, for we have an opinion about the things we are not sure are true. Therefore choice and opinion are not identical.

455. He assigns the fifth reason at "**And it is not necessarily**" [6]. If opinion and choice were identical, those who make the best choices and those who have true opinions about them would necessarily be identified. This is obviously false, however, for some men form a true opinion in general of what is better but on account of bad will they do not choose what is better but what is worse. Therefore choice and opinion are not identical.

456. At "**Whether opinion**" [7] he raises a doubt whether opinion should be said to precede choice or follow it. He states that it does not matter for the present because we do not intend to determine the order of these things but only whether choice is identical with a particular opinion. Nevertheless, we must know that opinion, since it per-tains to the faculty of knowledge, strictly speaking, precedes choice pertaining to the appetitive faculty, which is moved by the cognoscitive power. However, it sometimes happens accidentally that opinion follows choice, for instance, when a person on account of the affection for things he loves changes the opinion he formerly held.

457. Then [8], at "**What then,**" he shows what choice is. He says that, since it is none of the four things previously mentioned, we must consider what it is according to its genus and what according to its specific difference. As to its genus, seemingly it is a voluntary. However, not every voluntary is a thing chosen (as has been pointed out before, 434–436), but only the deliberately intentional voluntary. That this difference should be given attention is clear from the fact that counsel is an act of the reason, and choice itself must be accompanied by an act of reason and intellect. The very name—meaning that one be accepted rather than another—seems to imply or signify this in a hidden way. It per-tains to deliberative reason to prefer one to others.

LECTURE VII
Counsel

TEXT OF ARISTOTLE (*B.1112a19–1112b9*) Chapter 3

1. *Do men take counsel about all things in such a way that everything is worthy of deliberation, or are some things not objects of counsel?*   **1112a18–19; 458**

2. *A thing must not be called worthy of deliberation because some foolish or insane person takes counsel about it but because men of good sense do so.*   **1112a19–21; 459**

3. *No one takes counsel about: (1) eternal things, for instance, about the whole universe or the incommensurability of the diagonal and the side of a square;*   **1112a21–23; 460**

4. *(2) things that are in motion provided their motion is always uniform either by necessity or from nature or on account of some other cause, for instance, the solstices and the risings of the sun;*   **1112a23–26; 461**

5. *(3) things that sometimes happen otherwise, for instance, droughts and rains;*   **1112a26–27; 462**

6. *(4) things that happen by chance, for example, the finding of a treasure;*   **1112a27; 463**

7. *(5) all human things, for instance, the Spartans do not take counsel about how the Scythians ought best to live their lives. None of these things will take place by our efforts.*   **1112a28–30; 464**

8. *We do take counsel about practicable things within our power.*   **1112a30–31; 465**

9. *There is actually no other class of things left. Seemingly the causes are nature, necessity, and chance, to which must be added the intellect and anything else causing what is done by man. Each man takes counsel about those practicable matters which can be done by him.*   **1112a31–34; 466**

10. *About certain self-sufficient branches of instruction counsel is not taken, for instance, about writing the letters of the alphabet, for there is no doubt about how the letters must be formed. But counsel is taken about whatever is determined by us.*   **1112a34–37; 467**

11. *In these matters counsel is not always taken in the same way, for instance, in regard to things pertaining to the art of medicine, to business and to navigation. In all these—inasmuch as they are less certain—we take more counsel than in gymnastics. The same is to be understood of other arts.*   **1112a37–1112b6; 468**

12. *It is more necessary to take counsel in the arts than in the sciences, for more doubts arise in the arts.*   **1112b6–7; 469**

13. *Counsel has to concern things occurring more frequently.*   **1112b7–8; 470**

14. *It must concern uncertain things where it has not been determined in what way they will come to pass.*   **1112b–9; 471**

15. *We invite counsellors in matters of importance not trusting ourselves as capable of coming to a decision.*   **1112b10–11; 472**

COMMENTARY OF ST. THOMAS

458. After the Philosopher has finished the treatise on choice, he here takes up the question of counsel. First he treats counsel in itself; and then [Lect. IX], at "The objects of counsel etc." (1113a3), he treats it in comparison with choice. On the initial point he does two things. First he shows the things about which counsel ought to be taken. Next [Lect. VIII], at "We do not take counsel about ends etc." (1112b13), he treats the method and order of taking counsel. He handles the first consideration in two steps. First

[1] he puts forward his proposition; and then [3], he executes it at ". . . about: (1) eternal things etc." In regard to this first he also does two things. Initially [1] he proposes the question he intends to treat. The question is: should men take counsel about all things in such a way that everything is worthy of deliberation, or are some things not objects of counsel?

459. Next [2], at "A thing must not," he explains the proposed question with the observation that a thing is not said to be worthy of deliberation from the fact that sometimes counsel is taken in the matter by some foolish person who perversely uses his reason, or by an insane person entirely lacking the use of reason. But something is deemed worthy of deliberation inasmuch as men with good sense do deliberate about it. Men of this type take counsel only about things that of their nature require careful consideration and that are properly said to be worthy of deliberation. Foolish people sometimes deliberate even about things wherein no counsel is required.

460. Then [3], at ". . . about: (1) eternal things," he shows where counsel should function, first [3] by distinguishing things according to their own causes; next [10], at "About certain etc.," by distinguishing things according to every cause; and last [13], at "Counsel has to concern etc.," by distinguishing things according to the qualities of the things themselves. On the first point he does (three) things. First [3] he shows where counsel is unnecessary. Then [8], at "But we do take counsel etc.," he infers the areas with which counsel does deal. Last [9], at "There is actually etc.," he shows that the conclusion follows from the premises. In regard to the first, five considerations require his attention.

First [3] he says that no one takes counsel about eternal things, that is, about things existing always and without motion. Examples of this sort are either those, the substances of which are not subject to motion (as separated substances and the whole universe itself), or those which, even though they exist in movable matter, nevertheless according to reason are separated from such matter, as mathematical entities. Hence he gives the example of the diagonal of a square and its rib or side— no one takes counsel about the commensurability of such things.

461. Next [4], at "**things that are in motion,**" he says that no one takes counsel even about things that are in action provided their motion is always uniform. This uniformity of motion may be either of necessity and not by reason of any other cause (as are those things which are of themselves necessary) or from the nature of movable bodies or through the agency of some separated cause as immaterial substances, movers of the heavenly bodies, about which he speaks here. Hence he takes an example from the revolutions or circular motions of the sun and its risings, and so forth.

462. Third [5], at "**things that sometimes,**" he says that deliberation is unnecessary about things in motion and usually following the same pattern, even though sometimes in a minor number of cases they happen otherwise. Such are the droughts that generally occur in summer and the rains that commonly fall in winter; although this may at times vary.

463. Fourth [6], at "**things that happen,**" he says that counsel is not taken about things that happen by chance as the finding of a treasure. Just as the things spoken of above (461–462) do not depend on our action, so things

happening by chance cannot depend upon our forethought because they are unforeseen and beyond our control.

464. Fifth [7], at "**all human things,**" he says, as men do not take counsel about necessary, natural, and fortuitous things, so neither do they take counsel about all human things. Thus the Spartans do not take counsel about how the Scythians—who dwell a long way from them—ought best to live their lives. He then subjoins a common reason valid in all the afore-mentioned cases when he says "None of these things will take place etc.," because none of these things that are necessary or natural or fortuitous or done by other men take place by reason of our efforts.

465. Then [8], at "**But we do take counsel,**" he concludes as it were from the premises about the proper field for counsel. He says that we take counsel about practicable things within us, that is, in our power. Counsel is ordered to action.

466. Next [9], at "**There is actually,**" he shows that this follows from the premises because, besides the things just mentioned about which it has been indicated that counsel does not apply, there remain these situations within us on whose behalf counsel is required. He proves his contention by separating the causes. Seemingly there are four causes of things: nature, which is the principle of motion either in the case of things always moved in the same way or of things for the most part preserving uniform motion; necessity, which is the cause of things existing always in the same way without motion; fortune, an accidental cause outside the intention of the agent, under which is also included chance. Besides these causes there is the intellect and whatever else is man's agent, as the

will, the senses, and other principles of this kind. This cause is different in different men so that each takes counsel about those practicable matters which can be done by him. From this it follows that counsel is not taken about things done by other causes, as already noted (464).

467. At "**About certain**" [10] he shows about what subjects counsel can be taken in the creative arts according to which we do what is within our power. On this point he does (three) things. First [10] he shows in the arts where counsel is taken and where it is unnecessary. He says that those creative arts which have a fixed mode of procedure and are self-sufficient to the extent that what is done rests on nothing extrinsic do not require counsel, as writing the letters of the alphabet. The reason for this is that we deliberate only about doubtful matters. And there is no doubt about how a letter should be formed because there is a fixed method of writing which is not doubtful and the written work depends only on the art and hand of the scribe. But counsel is taken about those situations in which we must fix for ourselves in advance how to proceed since they are not certain and determined in themselves.

468. Next [11], at "**In these matters,**" he shows that in these matters counsel is not taken in the same way but that some cases require more deliberation and others less. First he explains this difference among the creative arts themselves. He states that in those cases in which we have the final say, we do not always take counsel in the same way, that is, with equal deliberation. We deliberate more about some things which are less certain and in which we must take into consideration more external things: in the art of

medicine we must be mindful of the natural strength of the sick person; in business we must assess the needs of men and the supply of goods; and in navigation we must take into account the winds. In all these, we take more counsel than in gymnastics, i.e., the arts of wrestling and exercising that have more fixed and determined methods. According as the previously mentioned arts are less settled, by so much must we take more counsel in them. The same must be understood of other arts.

469. Last [12], at "**It is more necessary,**" he shows the difference relative to the necessity of counsel in the creative arts and in the speculative sciences. He indicates that counsel is more necessary in the arts (the practicable) than in the sciences (the speculative). In the latter, deliberation occurs not in regard to their subject matter, for these exist necessarily or by nature, but as regards the use of these things, for example, how and in what order we are to proceed in the sciences. In this, however, counsel is less mandatory than in the practical sciences about which we have more doubts because of the great variety occurring in these skills.

470. Then [13], at "**Counsel has to,**" he shows about which things counsel ought to be taken, by considering the qualities of the things themselves. On this point he puts forward three qualities of things with which counsel deals. First [13] he says that counsel has to do with things which occur more frequently. However, because they can happen otherwise it is uncertain in what way they may take place. If a man should wish to deliberate about things that rarely happen, for instance, about the possible collapse of a stone bridge over which he must pass, he will never get anything done.

471. Second [14], at "**It must concern,**" he says that counsel must attend to those situations in which no determination has yet been made of their outcome. A judge does not take counsel about how he ought to pass sentence on the cases stated in the law but rather about cases in which something is not determined in the law.

472. Third [15], at "**We invite counsellors,**" he says that we take others into our confidence for advice in things of importance, as if we did not acknowledge our own capability of deciding what we ought to do. Thus it is obvious that counsel ought not to be taken about trifling things of every kind but only about things of importance.

LECTURE VIII
Method and Order of Taking Counsel

TEXT OF ARISTOTLE (*B.1112b11–1113a2*) Chapter 3

1. *We do not take counsel about ends, only about means. A doctor does not deliberate whether he will cure a patient; an orator does not deliberate whether he will persuade people; a statesman does not deliberate whether he will achieve peace. Neither does any other agent take counsel about his end.* **1112b11–15; 473–474**

2. *But having taken the end for granted, they will deliberate how and by what means it may be achieved; when the end is attainable in several ways, by which of these it can be most effectively and most easily attained; when the end is attainable by one means only, how it will be attained through this means; and how this means itself will be attained until they arrive at the first cause, which will be the last in the order of discovery.* **1112b15–20; 475**

3. *One who takes counsel seems to inquire and to resolve by the method mentioned, as by a diagram. It seems that not every inquiry is a taking of counsel, for instance, a mathematical (in the text: "metaphysicae") inquiry, but every taking of counsel is a kind of inquiry. What is last in resolution or analysis is first in the order of production.* **1112b20–24; 476**

4. *If those taking counsel find the thing to be done is impossible, they give up the project, for instance, if they need money which cannot be provided. But if the thing to be done seems practicable, they begin to act. Things are called possible that can be done by us; what our friends do is done in some way by us, for the origin of their action lies in ourselves.* **1112b24–28; 477**

5. *At times we inquire about what instruments may be used, and at times about the way we ought to use them. It is the same in the other cases, for sometimes we investigate the means of doing a thing, sometimes we inquire how or why it is to be done.* **1112b28–31; 478**

6. *As has been previously stated, it would seem that man originates his own actions, and counsel is taken about the things which can be done by him.* **1112b31–31; 479**

7. *Actions are performed for the sake of other things. Counsel, therefore, is not taken about the end but the means to the end.* **1112b32–33; 480**

8. *We do not deliberate about particular things, for instance, whether this thing is bread, or whether the bread is properly prepared or properly baked. This belongs to sense perception. If a man goes on deliberating forever he will never come to an end.* **1112b32–1113a2; 481–482**

COMMENTARY OF ST. THOMAS

473. After the Philosopher has shown about what things counsel is taken, he here treats the method and order of taking counsel. Because counsel is a kind of inquiry, he does three things concerning it. First [1] he shows the method of deliberative inquiry; next [4], at "If those taking counsel etc.," he shows its effect; last [6], at "As has been previously stated etc.," he determines the limit of this inquiry. On the initial point he does two things. First [1] he proposes a method of deliberation. Second [3], at "One who takes counsel etc.," he explains his statement. Counsel is a practical deliberation about things to be done. Hence as in a speculative inquiry, where principles are necessarily taken for granted and certain other things are sought, so also should it be with counsel. Therefore, he shows first [1] what is taken for granted regarding counsel. Second [2], at "But having taken etc.," he shows what is the objective in taking counsel.

474. We must consider that in practicable things the end holds the place of the principle because the necessity

of practicable things depends on the end, as has been mentioned in the second book of the *Physics* (Ch. 9, 200a15 sq.; St. Th. Lect. XV, 273–274). On this account we must take the end for granted. This is what he means when he says that we do not take counsel about ends but about the means to the end. Thus in speculative matters we do not inquire about the principles but about the conclusions. He clarifies what he has said by examples: a doctor does not deliberate whether he ought to cure a patient but this is taken for granted as an end; an orator does not deliberate whether he ought to persuade people, for he intends this as an end; a statesman or a ruler of the state does not deliberate whether he ought to achieve peace which is compared to the state as health to the human body (health consists in the harmony of the humors as peace consists in the harmony of wills). Neither does any other agent take counsel about the end in this way.

475. Then [2], at "But having taken the end for granted," he shows about what and how deliberative inquiry should be made. He introduces three things concerning this. The first of these is that, having taken the end for granted, the primary intention of the one taking counsel is how (i.e., by what motion or action) he can attain that end, and by what means he must move or work toward the end, as by horse or ship. His next intention is—when he can attain some end by several things, either instruments or actions—to know by which of these he can better and more easily achieve his goal. This pertains to judgment in finding ways to the end in which some men are at times deficient. His last intention is—if it should happen that the end can be attained by one means or motion

alone, or most aptly by a particular means—that the end be procured in such a way that it is reached through this means. For this, perseverance and care are necessary. If the means for attaining the end should not be at hand, we must inquire how it can be gained and so on until we arrive at a cause which holds first place in operating (this will be last in the order of discovery).

476. Next [3], at "One who," he further clarifies his statement by its likeness to speculative inquiry. He says that the cause that is first in operation is the last in the order of discovery because one who deliberates seems to inquire (as was just pointed out in 473) by some analytic method, just as he who wishes to prove a conclusion by a diagram or a geometrical explanation must resolve the conclusion into principles until he reaches the first indemonstrable principles. All counsel is an investigation, i.e., a kind of inquiry, although not every investigation or inquiry is counsel, for example, an inquiry in mathematics. Only an inquiry about practicable things is counsel. Because the man who takes counsel inquires in an analytic manner, his inquiry must lead to that which is the principle in operation. The reason is that what is last in analysis is first in production or activity.

477. At "If those taking counsel" [4] he shows the effect of counsel. First [4] he exposes his proposition. Second [5] he explains certain things that were said by the words "At times we inquire etc." He says first that if those taking counsel, on reaching the point in the deliberative inquiry where the first operation must be done, find this impossible they give up, i.e., dismiss the whole matter as if without hope of success. For example, if in order to carry

out a business venture, a man needs money to pay certain persons and he cannot pay it, he must abandon the project. But if it is apparent that what was discovered by means of counsel is possible, operation begins immediately because, as was just mentioned (476), the point at which the analytic inquiry of counsel ends must be the beginning of operation. A thing is said to be possible to an agent not only through his own power but also through the power of others. Hence things done by friends are enumerated by him among possibles because what our friends do is done in some way by us, inasmuch as the principle of the work is found in us, for they themselves do this in consideration of us.

478. Then [5], when he says "**At times we inquire,**" he explains his previous statement, namely, the kinds of things that upon investigation we sometimes find possible and sometimes impossible. At times, he says, by counsel we inquire about instruments, for instance, a horse or a sword, and at times we inquire about the need or suitability of the instruments, that is, how we ought to use them. It is the same in the other arts: sometimes we seek the means of doing a thing, sometimes we inquire how or why (these belong to the end just mentioned).

479. Next [6], at "**As has been previously stated,**" he determines the limit or status of the deliberative inquiry. He does this under three headings. First [6] on the part of the agent himself. Hence he says, as has been previously stated (292), that man is the

principle of his activity. Every individual takes counsel about the things which can be done by him. For this reason when he arrives, in the deliberative inquiry, at what he himself can achieve, at that point counsel ceases.

480. Second [7], at "**Actions are,**" he shows that counsel has a limit or condition on the part of the end. All operations, he says, are performed for the sake of other things, that is, ends. Hence counsel is not taken about the end but about the means to the end. Evidently then there is a limit in deliberative inquiry (both on the part of the end and on the part of the agent) as in demonstrations (both from above and below) as it were on the part of either extreme.

481. Third [8], at "**We do not,**" he shows the status of deliberative inquiry on the part of particular instruments which we use in our operations as available means for arriving at the end. He says that we do not deliberate about particular things, such as whether what is set before us is bread, whether it is properly prepared, i.e., baked or made as it should be. This belongs to sense perception.

482. That the status of counsel—as also of demonstration—is according to these three considerations is proved by an argument leading to an impossible conclusion. If a man would always be taking counsel, he would be reaching to infinity, which does not fall under the consideration of the reason and consequently not under counsel, which is a kind of inquiry belonging to reason, as has been pointed out (476).

LECTURE IX
A Comparison Between Counsel and Choice
TEXT OF ARISTOTLE (*B.1113a2–1113a14*) Chapter 3

1. The objects of counsel and of choice are the same, but the object of choice has already been determined by counsel.   1113a2–4; 483

2. What was previously judged by means of counsel is an object of choice. Every individual inquiring how he is going to act ceases from counsel when he reduces the principle back to himself and this into what is to be done first. It is this which is chosen.   1113a4–7; 484

3. Our point is also brought out by the ancient political procedure delineated by Homer who presents the Greek kings as proclaiming their decisions to the people.   1113a7–9; 485

4. Since the object of choice is one of the things considered by counsel as desirable and within our power, choice will be a desire (arising by reason of counsel) for the things which are in our power. When we have formed a judgment by taking counsel we desire a thing in accordance with our deliberation.   1113a9–12; 486

5. Choice has now been defined according to type and in a general way and not as is customary according to a full explanation. It has been stated of what nature the things are with which choice deals and that choice is concerned with things which are ordered to ends.

1113a12–14; 487

COMMENTARY OF ST. THOMAS

483. After the Philosopher has considered counsel in itself, he now treats counsel in comparison with choice. A twofold procedure clarifies this point. First [1] he compares counsel with choice. Second [4], at "Since the object of choice" [2], he concludes from this what choice is. In regard to the initial point he does two things. First [1] he introduces his proposition; second [2], at "What was previously judged etc.," he proves it. First he compares counsel with choice in two ways. In one way relative to the object or matter of each where they are in agreement. Touching on this he says that an object of counsel and an object of choice are the same because both counsel and choice deal with things that act for an end. The other way is relative to the order of each. Touching on this he says that when something has already been decided by means of counsel then it is first chosen, counsel preceding choice as it were.

484. Then [2], at "What was," he

explains what he has said, by a reason [2] taken from his previous observations (473–484) about counsel. The decision of counsel, he says, precedes choice because after the inquiry of counsel a judgment concerning the things discovered must follow. Then what was previously judged is first chosen. He shows clearly that the judgment of the reason should follow the investigation of counsel, by the fact that every individual who inquires by taking counsel how he ought to act ceases from deliberation when, by analysing his investigation, he is led to what he himself can do. If he can do several things, then, when he reduces them to the preceding, that is, to what he considers should be done first, this is what is chosen, namely, what presents itself to be done first. Hence it remains that choice presupposes the decision of counsel.

485. Second [3], at "Our point is also brought out," he proves his view by an example. That choice ought to follow

the decision of counsel is brought out by the regal procedure of old, i.e., by the custom of ancient states according to which kings did not possess dictatorial power over the multitude so that they could do whatever they wished but were guides of the citizens to whom it belonged to choose the things decided by the kings in counsel. For that reason he says that the kings of old declared to the people the things they themselves had chosen by the decision of their counsel so that the people might choose what had been determined. Homer followed this by presenting the Greek rulers as proclaiming to the people what they had decided in counsel.

486. Next [4], at "**Since the object**," he shows from the premises what choice is. He says that, since an object of choice is simply one of the number of the things within our power and which is considered by means of counsel, it follows that choice is only a desire (arising by reason of counsel) for things in our power. Choice is an act of the rational appetitive faculty called the will. On this account he said that choice is a deliberating desire inasmuch as, via counsel, a man arrives at a judgment regarding the things which were discovered by means of counsel. This desire is choice.

487. Last [5], at "**Choice has now**," he shows of what nature this definition of choice is. He says that choice has now been defined by type, that is, in outline, and not as he customarily determines a thing through a full explanation, i.e., giving a definition and then investigating each element of it. But the definition of choice has been given in a general way. It has been stated (486) of what nature the things are with which choice deals, i.e., things in our power. Also it has been said that choice is concerned with things that are ordered to ends—about these, too, counsel treats.

LECTURE X
The Object of Willing

TEXT OF ARISTOTLE (B.1113a15–1113b2) Chapter 4

1. As was stated before, willing is concerned with the end.   1113a15–16; 488

2. To some it seems that willing has for its object what is of itself good, but to others what is apparently good.   1113a16; 489

3. For those who say the object of willing is what is good of itself, it follows that that thing is not an object of willing which a person does not rightly will. If something were an object of willing, it would be good but what is to prevent a man from wishing something evil.
1113a17–19; 490

4. On the other hand, for those who say the object of willing is apparent good, there is no such thing as a natural object of willing but only what appears so to each man. But different and sometimes contrary things seem to be objects of willing for different men. 1113a20–22; 491

5. If these conclusions are not acceptable, it must be said, therefore, that in an absolute or true sense it is the good that is the object of willing, but for each man it is the apparent good.
1113a22–24; 492

6. For the good man that thing is an object of willing which is truly good; for the vicious man that thing is an object of willing which seems pleasing to him. Thus when men are in good bodily health those things are healthful which are such in reality, but for men who are ill, it is otherwise. The same applies to bitter, sweet, warm, and heavy things and to others of this kind.
1113a25–29; 493

7. The virtuous person correctly passes judgment on each individual thing and in each case what appears to him is truly good. Those things which are proper to each habit seem pleasurable to it. The good man perhaps is much different in his capacity to see what is truly good in individual matters, being as it were a norm and measure of these things.   1113a29–33; 494

8. Many men are apparently deceived because of pleasure. What is not good seems good, so they desire as good the pleasurable and seek to avoid the painful as evil.   1113a33–1113b2; 495

COMMENTARY OF ST. THOMAS

488. After the Philosopher has finished the treatise on the voluntary and on choice, he here begins the study of willing. He initiates his discussion by three stages. First [1] he takes notes of what is obvious about willing. Next [2], at "To some it seems etc.," he raises a doubt. Last [5], at "If these conclusions etc.," he solves the doubt. First he restates what he has previously insisted on (466) that willing is concerned with the end itself. He speaks here of willing (voluntas) as it denotes the act of the faculty of the will. The act of any faculty is named from the faculty itself and regards that to which the faculty primarily and of itself tends.

Thus the act of the visive faculty is called vision in relation to visible things. In this manner understanding (intellectus) is named in relation to first principles that of themselves are referred primarily to the intellective faculty. Hence also willing is properly said to concern ends themselves which, as certain principles, the faculty of the will primarily and of itself regards.

489. Then [2], at "To some it seems," he raises a doubt. Regarding it he does three things. First he sets forth contrary opinions about willing. He says that to some it seems that willing has for its

object what is of itself good, but to others what is apparently good.

490. Next [3], at "For those who say," he disproves the first opinion stating that for those who say that only the good in itself is the object of willing (i.e., to which the will tends), it follows that that thing which a person does not rightly will is not an object of willing. The reason is that, according to their opinion, it would follow that if something were an object of willing, it would be good, but it happens sometimes that it is evil. Therefore willing does not always have real good as its object.

491. Last [4], at "On the other hand," he disproves the second opinion, stating that for those who say the object of willing is apparent good, it follows that there is no natural object of willing but for each one the object of willing is what seems so to him. But for different men different and sometimes contrary things seem to be the object of willing. Thus if color were not visible but only what seemed to be color were visible, it would follow that nothing would be by nature visible. This, however, would not be fitting for every natural faculty has some object determined by its nature. Therefore it is not true that the object of willing is apparent good.

492. At "If these conclusions" [5], he solves the afore-mentioned doubt. First he gives a solution according to a certain distinction. He says that if these disagreeable conclusions following from both these opinions are unacceptable, we must answer with a distinction that what seems good to a man is desirable either without qualification or under some aspect, i.e., in relation to this or that.

493. Second [6], at "For the good man," he shows with whom both parts of this distinction agree. He says that for the good man that thing is an object of willing which is truly worthy of being willed, i.e., good in itself. But for the wicked or vicious man that thing is the object of willing which attracts him, i.e., whatever seems pleasing to himself. He exemplifies this in things of the body. We see that for men whose bodies are in good health those things are healthful that are really so. But for the sick, certain other things are healthful, namely, those that moderate their diseased condition. Likewise things really bitter and sweet seem bitter and sweet to those who have a healthy taste, things really warm seem warm to those who have a normal sense of touch. Those who have normal bodily strength properly estimate the weight of objects; those who are weak think light objects heavy.

494. Third [7], at "The virtuous person," he explains what he said, first as it affects virtuous men. He says that the virtuous person correctly passes judgment on individual things that pertain to human activity. In each case that which is really good seems to him to be good. This happens because things seem naturally pleasurable to each habit that are proper to it, that is, agree with it. Those things are agreeable to the habit of virtue that are in fact good because the habit of moral virtue is defined by what is in accord with right reason. Thus the things in accord with right reason, things of themselves good, seem good to it. Here the good man differs very much indeed from others, for he sees what is truly good in individual practicable matters, being as it were the norm and measure of all that is to be done because in these cases a thing must be judged good or bad according as it seems to him.

495. Next [8], at "Many men," he

explains what he said as it affects vicious men. He says that for many, the vicious, deception in the distinction between good and evil occurs especially because of pleasure. As a consequence of this it happens that they desire as good the pleasurable, which is not good, and seek to avoid as evil what is for them painful but in itself good. The explanation is that they do not follow reason but the senses.

LECTURE XI
Virtue and Vice Are Within Our Power

TEXT OF ARISTOTLE (*B.1113b3–1114a3*) Chapter 5

1. *Since willing regards the end but counsel and choice the means to the end, the actions concerning these means will be in accordance with choice and voluntary. But virtuous actions deal with the means. Virtue then is within our power.* **1113b3–6; 496**

2. *For a similar reason vice is voluntary. If it is in our power to act, it is also in our power not to act; and contrariwise. Therefore if to do good is in our power, then not to do evil will also be in our power. If not to do good is in our power, then to do evil will also be in our power.* **1113b6–11; 497–498**

3. *If it is in our power to do and 10 likewise not to do good or evil actions (by reason of this men become good or evil), it will be within our power to be virtuous or vicious.* **1113b11–14; 499**

4. *It is said that no one is voluntarily evil and that no one is unwillingly happy. The first statement is really false and the second true. In fact no person will be happy unwillingly. Vice, on the other hand, is a voluntary thing.* **1113b14–17; 500**

5. *Must we dispute even about what has now been said and hold that man is not the principle and begetter of his actions as he is father of his children?* **1113b17–19; 501**

6. *If these things (counsel, choice and willing) seem to be principles of our actions and we cannot reduce them into principles other than those within our power, then also our actions the principles of which are under our control will themselves be in our power and voluntary.* **1113b19–21; 502**

7. *This view seems to be supported by the testimony of private individuals and of legislators themselves for legislators punish and chastise evildoers, unless these do evil by compulsion or on account of ignorance of which they themselves were not the cause. Likewise legislators decree honors for those who do good, thus encouraging them as it were but restraining the others. No one persuades a man to do whatever things are not in his power and not voluntary because before it takes place it is of no use to persuade a man not to become hot, or afflicted, or hungry, or anything whatsoever of this kind. We will suffer these things nonetheless.* **1113b21—30; 503–504**

8. *A man who is ignorant will be punished if he is the cause of his ignorance. A drunken man, for instance, is worthy of double punishment. The beginning is within him because he has it in his power not to get drunk. And his intoxication is the cause of his ignorance. Legislators punish those who are ignorant of things stated in the law that they should have known, but not those who are ignorant of the difficult things. Likewise in other cases we punish people whenever it seems that their ignorance was due to negligence because it is in their power not to be ignorant. They have it in their power to inform themselves.* **1113b30–1114a3; 505–506**

COMMENTARY OF ST. THOMAS

496. After the Philosopher has treated the voluntary, choice, counsel, and willing that are principles of human acts, he here applies what has been said to vices and virtues. Concerning this question he does three things. First [1] he determines the truth. Then [4], at "It is said that no one etc.," he rejects an error. Last [Lect. XIII], at "We have discussed virtues etc." (1114b26), he concludes with a summary of what has been said about virtue. On the first point he does three things. First [1], on the basis of his previous discussion, he shows that virtue is within us, i.e., in our power. Next [2],

at "For a similar reason etc.," he shows the same about vice. Last [3], at "If it is in our power etc.," he shows the reason for this necessary consequence. He says first that since willing regards the end but counsel and choice the means to the end, it follows that actions concerning this (i.e., the means to the end) are in accordance with choice and are consequently voluntary. The reason is that choice is a voluntary as was indicated before (434–436, 457). But virtuous actions deal with the afore-mentioned (means) and are voluntary. Consequently, virtue itself must be voluntary and within us, that is, in our power.

497. Then [2], at "For a similar reason," he shows the same thing about badness, i.e., about vice as opposed to virtue. He says that badness is likewise voluntary and within us because its operations are of this kind. He proves this in the following way: if the capacity to act is within us, the capacity not to act must also be in our power. If the capacity not to act were not in our power, it would be impossible that we would not act. Therefore, it would be necessary that we act, and so the capacity to act would not come from us but from necessity.

498. As a consequence we must conclude that wherever affirmation is within our power, negation is also; and conversely. Virtuous and vicious actions differ according to affirmation and negation. For instance, if honoring parents is good and an act of virtue, then not to honor one's parents is evil and pertains to vice. If not to steal pertains to virtue, to steal pertains to vice. Hence it follows that if the operation of virtue is within us, as has been proved (496), then the operation of vice also is within us. So consequently vice itself is within us, that is, in our power.

499. Next [3], at "If it is," he assigns the reason for this necessary inference: if the operations are within us, the habits too are within us. He says that if it is in our power to do or not to do good or evil actions, as has now been shown (497–498), while by reason of the fact that man works or does not work good or evil he becomes good or evil as was pointed out in the second book (250–253), it follows that it is within our power to be virtuous, i.e., good in conformity with the habit of virtue, and vicious in conformity with the habit of vice.

500. At "It is said" [4], he rejects an error about the afore-mentioned teaching. First he removes the error itself. Second [Lect. XII], at "Perhaps such a person etc." (1114a3], he removes its roots. On the first point his division is threefold. First [4] he explains his rejection of the error. Next [5], at "Must we dispute even about what etc.," he raises a doubt over this. Last [6], at "If these things etc.," he determines the truth. In regard to the first we must consider that some have held that no one is voluntarily evil, nor is anyone unwillingly happy or good. They say this because the will of itself tends to good. Good is what all desire and consequently the will of itself seeks to avoid evil. He says, therefore, that one of these statements is in all likelihood false, namely, that no one is willingly evil since vice is something voluntary. The other seems to be true, that no one is unwillingly good and happy.

501. Then [5], at "**Must we dispute**," he raises a doubt about things said before. If it is true that virtuous and vicious actions (and consequently virtue and vice) are voluntary, obviously what has presently been said is true. But is there anyone who believes there should be a doubt about what has been

said, so that he might say that a man is not the principle and begetter of his actions as a father is the principle of his children? He as much as says: that anyone would say this, is to be wondered at.

502. Next [6], at "**If these things,**" he confirms the truth first by reason; and then [7], at "This view seems etc.," by signs. He says first that if counsel, choice, and willing—which are in our power—are seen as principles of our actions and we cannot reduce our actions to principles other than those that are in our power (i.e., counsel and choice) it follows that our good and bad actions are within our power. Because their principles are in our power, they themselves are in our power and hence are voluntary.

503. At "**This view seems**" [7], he explains his proposition by means of signs: first [7] in the things that are clearly voluntary; and then [8], at "A man who is ignorant etc.," in the things that seem to have something of the involuntary. He says first that the particular things that are done by individual private persons seem to bear witness to what has been said, i.e., that virtuous and vicious actions are within our power. Any father of a family punishes a child or a servant who does wrong. Likewise the things that are done by legislators, who care for the welfare of the state, bear witness. They give sometimes a light, other times a heavy sentence to criminals, provided however the wrongdoers do not act under coercion or through ignorance (of which they are not the cause); if they acted by compulsion or ignorance, their acts would not be voluntary, as is evident from what was said before (400–405). Hence it is clear that they were punished as acting voluntarily.

504. Likewise legislators decree honors for those who voluntarily do good: as it were encouraging the virtuous to good deeds by means of honors, and restraining the vicious from evil by means of punishments. No one encourages a man to do the things that are not in his power and not voluntary because in such matters encouragement before the act is entirely useless. It is useless, for instance, to urge a man in summer not to be hot, or in sickness not to be afflicted or not to be hungry when there is no food, or to do anything beyond his power. The reason is that he would suffer these things notwithstanding encouragement. If, therefore, we are not urged to do the things that are not within our power, but are urged to do good and avoid evil, such things are in our power.

505. Then [8], at "**A man who is,**" he manifests the same truth in those things which seem to have something of the involuntary. Ignorance causes an involuntary, as was explained before (406–424). If, however, we are the cause of the ignorance, the ignorance will be voluntary and we will be punished for it. A man can be the cause of his own ignorance in two ways. In one way directly, by doing something, as is evident in those who get drunk and for this reason are rendered ignorant. These should be doubly blamed. First because they drank too much, and next because they committed a sinful deed in their drunkenness. The principle of drunkenness is in the man himself because he has the power to remain sober and his drunkenness is the cause of his ignorance. Accordingly in this way a man is the cause of ignorance.

506. In the other way a man is the cause of ignorance indirectly by reason of the fact that he does not do what he ought to do. On account of this, igno-

rance of the things a man can and is bound to know is considered voluntary and therefore he is punished for it. This is why he says that legislators punish those who are ignorant of laws everyone ought to know (as that which forbids stealing), but not those who are ignorant of laws which are difficult to know and which not all are bound to know (because it is not possible). The same is true of those things which men do not know apparently by reason of negligence, because they could have learned. They are masters of themselves and they can be diligent and not negligent.

LECTURE XII
Refutation of the Opinion: No One Is Voluntarily Evil

TEXT OF ARISTOTLE (*B.1114a3–31*) Chapter 5

1. *Perhaps such a person is naturally not diligent.*   **1114a3–4; 507**

2. *But men make themselves negligent by living carelessly, and unjust and incontinent by doing evil to others and spending their time in drinking and such things.*   **1114a4–6; 508–510**

3. *A man's outlook depends on the way he exercises his powers. This is clearly manifest in the case of those who devote their attention to some exercise or activity. They perfect themselves by constant practice. It seems then that only a man lacking understanding would be ignorant that habits are produced by individual actions.*   **1114a7–10; 511**

4. *Moreover, it is unreasonable to assert that a man who does unjust actions does not wish to be unjust, or who perpetrates seductions does not wish to be incontinent. If one knowingly does those things from which it follows that he is unjust, he will be voluntarily unjust.*
1114a11–14; 512

5. *Because a person becomes unjust voluntarily, it does not follow that he will cease to be unjust and become just whenever he wishes. One who is sick does not become well in this way. So too it is with a man who voluntarily becomes sick by living immoderately and disregarding the doctor's advice. Before, it was within his power not to become sick, but having placed the cause the effect is no longer within his power, just as one who throws a stone has not the power to take back the throwing. Nevertheless it is within a man's power to cast or throw a stone because the original act was under his control. So it is also with the unjust and the incontinent who in the beginning had the power not to become like this. For this reason they are voluntarily unjust and incontinent although after they have become such it is no longer within their power not to be such.*   **1114a14–21; 513**

6. *Not only vices of the soul are voluntary but also defects of the body in certain men whom we justly reproach. No one reproaches those who are born ugly but only those who are so because of slothfulness and carelessness. The same is true with weakness, disgrace, and blindness. No one justly taunts a man who is blind from birth or disease or a wound but he is rather shown sympathy. But everyone does reproach a man blind because of excessive drinking of wine or other incontinence. Men are reproached for those vices and bodily defects that are within our power; but not for those beyond our control. This being so, in other things (pertaining to the soul) the vices we are blamed for must be within our power.* **1114a21–31; 514**

COMMENTARY OF ST. THOMAS

507. After the Philosopher has rejected the error of those who hold that no one is voluntarily evil, he now removes the roots of this error: first in regard to the internal disposition by reason of which (contrary to his own will) someone can tend to evil. Then [Lect. XIII], at "Someone may say" (1114a31), in the matter of the faculty of knowledge by which a thing is judged good or bad. He handles the first point in two steps. First [1] he

proposes that which one can depend on in support of the preceding error. Then [2], at "But men make themselves," he disproves this. The Philosopher has stated (506) that it is in the power of man to be diligent or negligent about something. But someone could deny this, saying that some person is naturally not diligent. Thus we see that men with phlegmatic temperaments are naturally lazy, men with choleric temperaments are naturally irascible, men with melancholic temperaments are naturally sad and men with sanguine temperaments are naturally joyful. According to this, it is not within man's power to be diligent.

508. Then [2], at "**But men make,**" he rules out what was just said. To understand this we must consider that a man can be said to be of a particular bent in two ways. In one way according to bodily disposition following either the temperament of the body or the influence of the heavenly bodies. By reason of this disposition there can be no direct change of the intellect or will, which are faculties altogether incorporeal not using a bodily organ, as is made clear by the Philosopher in the third book *De Anima* (Ch. 4, 429a29–429b4; St. Th. Lect. VII, 687–699). But by this type of disposition some change can follow in the sensitive appetitive faculty, which does use a bodily organ, the movements of which are the passions of the soul. Accordingly, from such a disposition there is no more movement of the reason and will (which are principles of human acts) than is had from the passions of the soul, and concerning these it was likewise pointed out in the first book (241) that they are susceptible of persuasion by the reason. The other disposition is on the part of the soul. This is a habit by means of which the will or reason is inclined in operation.

509. On this account the Philosopher, having passed over the dispositions or qualities of the body, treats only the disposition of habits. On this point he does two things. First [2] he shows that habits of the soul according to which a man is negligent or unjust are voluntary from the fact that he is censured on account of them. Second [6], at "Not only vices of the soul etc.," he indicates that even bodily defects

which are blameworthy are voluntary. Regarding the first he does two things. First [2] he indicates that habits of the soul are voluntary with respect to their formation. Then [5] he shows that they are not voluntary after their formation has already been completed. Touching on the first he does two things. First [2] he brings forward his proposition; and next [3], at "A man's outlook etc.," he proves it.

510. We must consider that evil habits differ as evil acts do. Some habits are evil from the fact that they withdraw a man from doing good. With respect to habits of this kind he says that men are the cause of their own evil lives for they are not diligent in doing good; they live carelessly without attempting good works. Other habits are evil because through them a man is inclined to do evil, whether this brings about the injury of others or one's own disordered condition. With respect to these he says men by their own volition are the reason why they are unjust inasmuch as they do evil to others, and incontinent inasmuch as they live their lives in unnecessary drinking and in other things of this kind which pertain to the pleasures of touch.

511. Next [3], at "**A man's outlook,**" he proves the proposition first by means of a likeness in other things. We see that things done in individual actions make men of that particular stamp, i.e., disposed to do similar things. This is clearly manifest in the case of those who are diligent in and take pains with an exercise (like wrestling or soldiering) or any activity whatsoever. Everyone, from the fact that he does the action many times, becomes so adept that he can do similar things perfectly. Since then we see this happen in all cases, it seems that only a man lacking understanding

would be ignorant that habits are produced by operations.

512. Then [4], at **"Moreover, it is,"** he shows the same thing by a reason taken from the relation of an act to a habit. If a man wills some cause from which he knows a particular effect results, it follows that he wills that effect. Although perhaps he does not intend that effect in itself, nevertheless he rather wishes that the effect exist than that the cause not exist. Thus if someone wishes to walk when it is hot, knowing beforehand he will work up a sweat, it follows that he wishes to perspire. Although he does not wish this in itself, nevertheless he wishes rather to perspire than to forego the walk. Nothing hinders a thing from being non-voluntary in itself, although it may be voluntary on account of something else, as a bitter potion taken for health. It would be otherwise if a man were ignorant that such an effect would follow from such a cause, e.g., a voluntary is not effected when a man who walks along the road falls among robbers because he did not know this beforehand. Obviously then men who do unjust actions become unjust and those committing seduction become incontinent. Therefore, it is unreasonable for a man to will to do unjust actions and nevertheless not intend to be unjust or to will to perpetrate seductions and not will to be incontinent. Thus obviously if a man who is aware of his action does voluntarily those things which make him unjust, he will be voluntarily unjust.

513. At **"Because a person becomes unjust"** [5], he shows that evil habits are not subject to the will after they have been formed. He says that because a person becomes unjust voluntarily, it does not follow that he ceases to be unjust and becomes just when-

ever he may will. He proves this by means of a likeness in the dispositions of the body. A man who in good health willingly falls into sickness by living incontinently i.e., by eating and drinking to excess and not following the doctor's advice, had it in his power in the beginning not to become sick. But after he has performed the act, having eaten unnecessary or harmful food, it is no longer in his power not to be sick. Thus he who throws a stone is able not to throw it; however once he has thrown the stone he has not the power to take back the throwing. Nevertheless we do say that it is within a man's power to cast or throw a stone because it was from a principle under his control. So it is also with the habits of vice; that a man not become unjust or incontinent arises from a principle under his control.

Hence we say that men are voluntarily unjust and incontinent, although, after they have become such, it is no longer within their power to cease being unjust or incontinent immediately, but great effort and practice are required.

514. Then [6], at **"Not only,"** he shows by means of a likeness to bodily defects that vicious habits are voluntary. He says that not only vices of the soul are voluntary but also defects of the body in certain men. Such men we justly reproach. No one reproaches those who are born ugly but only those who are ugly by reason of some negligence in proper care. The same is true with weaknesses and blindness. No one justly taunts a man who is blind from birth or disease or a wound which is not voluntary. But on account of those things sympathy rather is shown to the victim. Thus it is evident that we are reproached for those vices and bodily defects which are within

our power. Hence obviously in other things, i.e., those things which pertain to the soul, the vices or vicious habits are in our power.

LECTURE XIII
Refutation of the Opinion: We Have No Faculty Cognoscitive of Good

TEXT OF ARISTOTLE (*B.1114a32–1115a6*) Chapter 5

1. *Someone may say that every man desires what appears good to him for we are not in command of our imagination, but according to the character of each man, so does the end seem to him.* **1114a32–1114b1; 515–516**

2. *Since, therefore, everyone is in some measure the cause of his habits, he is to some extent the cause of the manner in which his imagination reacts.* **1114b1–3; 517–520**

3. *Perhaps no one is himself the cause of the evil he does, but each acts because of ignorance of the end under the impression that something very good will follow by means of his action. It ensues then that the end is not an object desired by a man's free will but must be innate as though a man had some (moral) sight to judge correctly and to desire what is really good. He is well-born who has this good judgment from birth. For he will possess the greatest and best of gifts, one which can never be received or learned from others, but kept just as nature gave it, and to be well and nobly endowed with this will be a perfect and true and propitious heritage.* **1114b3–12; 521–523**

4. *If this is true how is virtue more voluntary than vice? For both alike, i.e., the good and the wicked, the end appears and is fixed by nature or howsoever it may be. In referring everything else to this end, men do whatever they do. Whether the end then, whatever it may be, does not so present itself by nature, but also depends on him, or whether the end is natural, and the good man using the means is voluntarily virtuous, in either case virtue as well as vice will be voluntary. For voluntariety exists in the evil man also since it influences him both in his actions and in his view of the end. If then, as is affirmed, virtues are voluntary (for indeed we ourselves are partly responsible for the way our habits dispose us and by living in a certain way we fix our end accordingly) it follows that vices also are voluntary because a similar reason is present.* **1114b12–25; 524–525**

5. *We have discussed virtues in general and the outline of their genus. We have shown that each is a mean and a habit. We have explained that habits produce the same actions by which the habits themselves are caused. We have said that habits are in our power and voluntary, that they follow right reason and that voluntary operations are otherwise than habits because we have control over our operations from the beginning to the end when we know the particular circumstances. We are masters only of the beginning of our habits, but the individual steps by which they grow are not known to us, as in sicknesses. But because it was in our power to act or not to act in this way, the habits are called voluntary.* **1114b26–1115a3; 526**

6. *Taking up again the consideration of virtues, we will discuss what each virtue is, with what matter it deals and in what way it operates. At the same time we will clearly see also how many virtues there are. First we will treat the virtue of fortitude.* **1115a4–6; 527**

COMMENTARY OF ST. THOMAS

515. After the Philosopher has overthrown the fundamental principle of those who hold that vice is not voluntary on the part of the disposition inclining the appetitive faculty, he here excludes another fundamental principle on the part of the cognoscitive power. On this point he does two things. First [1] he explains this fundamental principle; and second [2], at "Since, therefore, etc.," he rejects it. In regard to the first we must consider that good precisely as it is perceived moves the desire. As the natural desire

or inclination follows the form naturally inherent, so the animal desire follows the perceived form. In order then that a thing be desired, it is first required that it be perceived as good. Hence everyone desires what appears good to him.

516. Therefore someone can say it is not in our power that this thing should seem or appear good to us. The reason is that we are not in command of our imagination, i.e., over the way things appear or seem to us. But in accord with the disposition of a man, so does his end seem to him, that is, such as a thing seems to a person, it must be desired as good and an end. A thing is agreeable to each according to its proper form: as fire tends upward, and things of earth tend to the center. So also we see that among the animals each one strives after something as good and an end according to its own natural disposition. Hence different animals have different activities and operations, although all animals of one species have similar movements and operations. But in the human species individuals are found having different movements and operations. Hence some were of the opinion that this arose from a natural disposition on account of which this thing seems good to one person and that to another in such a way that the procedure was not subject to a man's control.

517. Then [2], at **"Since, therefore,"** he excludes the afore-mentioned principle, and concerning it he does three things. First [2] he gives the reason repudiating these allegations (516). Next [3], at "Perhaps no one etc.," he adds an answer which seems to counter this. Last [4], at "If this is true," he disproves the counterargument. On the first point we must consider that a thing can appear good to someone in two ways.

518. In one way in general, it is so by a kind of speculative consideration. Such a judgment about good follows not any particular disposition but the universal power of reason syllogizing about actions, as it does in the case of natural things. Since practicable things are contingent, reason is not forced to assent to this or that as it does when demonstration occurs. But man has the power to give assent to one or the other part of a contradiction, as happens in all practicable things especially when we have under consideration many objects, any one of which can be judged good.

519. In the other way a thing can appear good to someone, as it were by a practical knowledge, by reason of a comparison with what is to be done. The Philosopher here speaks of this type of judgment that can be made in two ways about some good. In one way, a thing may appear good to someone absolutely and in itself. This seems to be a good in conformity with the nature of the end. In the other way, a thing may appear to someone not absolutely in itself but judged by present considerations.

520. The appetitive faculty is inclined to an object on two accounts: one, by reason of a passion of the soul, the other by reason of habit. Under the impulse of passion it happens that a thing is judged good as it is at present. Thus to one who is afraid of drowning it appears good at the moment to throw his merchandise overboard; as does fornication to one filled with lust. But the judgment, by which a man accounts a thing good in itself and absolutely, arises from the inclination of habit. This we will discuss now. He, therefore, says that since a man in

some measure is the cause of his own evil habit by reason of his continual sinning—as has been pointed out (509-512)—it follows that he himself is also the cause of the imaginative reaction that follows such a habit, i.e., of the appearance by which this thing seems to be good in itself.

521. Next [3], at "**Perhaps no one,**" he gives the counterargument of the adversary against the point that has just been made (518–520). He says that perhaps someone will maintain that nobody is himself the cause of his own evil acts but each individual does evil because of ignorance of the end, inasmuch as he thinks that something very good is to follow from what he does wrongly. That a person desires a proper end does not arise from his own free will but must belong to him from birth. As from birth a man has external sight by which he correctly distinguishes colors, so also from birth he should have a well-disposed internal vision by which he may judge well and desire what is really good. Thus he must be said to be of good birth in whom the previously mentioned judgment has been implanted from birth. When a man innately has in good and perfect fashion what is greatest and best for him, this is a perfect and truly good birth. For man cannot gain this through the help or guidance of another; rather it is proper for him to possess it in the manner that nature has endowed him with it. Therefore, that a man should have this from birth renders his birth doubly praiseworthy: in one way through the excellence of the good, in the other because of the impossibility of otherwise acquiring it.

522. We must consider that this seems to be the opinion of certain mathematicians who hold that man is disposed at his birth by the power of the heavenly bodies to do this or that. This opinion is attributed by Aristotle in his work *De Anima* (Bk. III, Ch. 3, 426a21 sq.; St. Th. Lect. IV, 616–623) to those who did not hold the distinction between sense and intellect. If anyone should say, as in fact it is said in that place), that the human will is impelled by the father of men and gods, i.e., the heavens or the sun, it will follow that the will (and the reason in which the will resides) is something corporeal as the senses are. It is not possible that what is in itself incorporeal should be moved by a body. Thus the will and intellect will contain a bodily organ and they will differ in no way from the senses and the sensitive appetitive faculty. Wherefore he draws a comparison between the sense of sight and intellectual vision by which we judge a thing.

523. It must be said then that the heavenly bodies can cause in the human body a disposition inclining the sensitive appetitive faculty, the motion of which is a passion of the soul. Hence by reason of the influence of the heavenly bodies, a man does not have the inclination to judge that a thing is good absolutely and in itself (as through the habit of choice in virtue and vice) but to judge that a thing is good as it is at the moment, for example, in accordance with passion. The same observation must be made about the inclination that occurs from bodily temperament. In the present context, however, there is no question of a judgment by which we judge something good in accordance with passion, for the will is able to reject this—as was stated in (516)—but of a judgment by which we judge that something is good by means of habit. Therefore, this answer does not destroy the reason of Aristotle.

524. At "**If this is**" [4] he rejects this answer on the basis of the presuppositions of the adversary who took for granted that virtue is a voluntary but denied this of vice. Then returning to his earlier discussion (516)—which he had interrupted—he says that if this is true, namely, that the desire of the end exists in man by nature, there is no greater reason why virtue more than vice is voluntary. Reasoning in a similar fashion we say that, for both the virtuous and the vicious man, the goal must be innate no matter in what way it may seem to be perceived and actually desired. Although virtuous and vicious operation is concerned not only with the end but also with the means to the end, nevertheless men act by referring the remaining things (i.e., means to the end) to an end not from nature but howsoever it seems to them.

525. Therefore either it should be said that the end for every man does not seem to be such by nature but that it is relative to each man as it is in his power to cling to such or such an end, or even that the end is natural and by working on the means, man becomes voluntarily virtuous. Then virtue nonetheless will be voluntary. The same is true about vice because what is for the sake of the end in operations is attributable to the vicious man not less than to the virtuous, just as they are alike in regard to the end—as has been pointed out before (358-362). Therefore, if virtues are voluntary because of the fact that we are the causes of the habits by which we are disposed to fix an end of such a kind, it follows that vices also are voluntary because a similar reason holds for one as well as the other.

526. Then [5], at "**We have dis-**cussed,**" he sums up in conclusion the material previously discussed (224–525). First [5] he shows what has already been said about virtues, and then [6] what remains to be treated. He states first that virtues in general have been treated (*ibid.*) and their genus has been clearly manifested in type, i.e., according to their general characteristics. Then it has been said (324–331) what the mean is (this belongs to the proximate genus) and what the habits are (this belongs to the remote genus under which the vices are also contained). It has been affirmed also (255–279) that habits produce the same actions by which the habits themselves were caused. It has been stated too (496–525) that habits are in our power, that they follow right reason and that voluntary operations are otherwise than habits because we have control over operations from the beginning to the end, provided we know the particular circumstances. Although we do have control of habits from the beginning, afterwards, when we are inattentive, something is added in the generation of habits by means of particular operations. Thus it happens in sicknesses brought on by voluntary actions, as has been noted (513). But because it was in our power from the beginning to act or not to act in this way, the habits themselves are called voluntary.

527. Next [6], at "**Taking up again,**" he shows what remains to be treated. He says we must take up again the consideration of the virtues in order to determine what each virtue is, its subject matter, and its mode of operation. Thus we will clearly see also how many virtues there are. First we will treat the virtue of fortitude.

LECTURE XIV
Fortitude

TEXT OF ARISTOTLE (B.1115a6–1115b6) Chapter 6

1. We stated previously that fortitude is a mean dealing with fear and rashness.

1115a6–7; 528–529

2. Terrifying things are what we fear. They are the things which we universally call evil. For this reason philosophers define fear as the expectation of evil. We all fear certain evils, e.g., a bad reputation, poverty, sickness, enmity, and death.   1115a7–11; 530–531

3. But fortitude does not seem to deal with all evils.   1115a11–12; 532

4. For, to fear some things is both proper and good, and not to fear others is base. For instance, in the matter of a bad reputation, he who fears this is said to be decent and modest; one who does not have this fear is called shameless. Such a person is said by some to be brave in a metaphorical sense, because he is like a brave man inasmuch as he is without fear.

1115a12–16; 533

5. Poverty is not to be feared; neither is sickness, nor any of those things which are not caused by wickedness or man himself. But one who has no fear of these things is not called brave, except perhaps by way of similarity. Some are cowardly in the dangers of war, but generous, and courageous in the face of the loss of their fortune.   1115a17–22; 534

6. No one is called cowardly because he fears injury to his children or his wife, or because he fears envy or any other thing of this kind. No one is called brave because he does not fear a flogging.   1115a22–24; 535

7. About what kind of terrifying things is a brave man concerned? Is he concerned with the most terrifying? No one can sustain such perils more than he. Now the most frightening of all is death, for it is the end, and nothing either good or bad seems to exist any longer for the dead.

1115a24–27; 536

8. It does not seem that fortitude is concerned with death, which occurs in every case, for instance, at sea or in sickness. In what circumstances then? In the most suitable, as when men die fighting for their country.   1115a28–30; 537

9. Such men lose their lives in the greatest and noblest dangers.   1115a30–31; 538

10. Honors are given to them both in the city-states and in the monarchies. 1115a31–32; 539

11. A man is called brave principally because he is not afraid of death for a good cause nor of all emergencies that involve death. Such emergencies are to be met with most often in battle.

1115a32–35; 540

12. Moreover, brave men are unafraid both in shipwreck and in sickness. They differ from sailors, for these brave men despise this sort of death when there is no hope of rescue, while sailors may well hope to be saved by reason of their experience.   1115a35–1115b4; 541

13. Likewise, brave men act manfully in danger where it is praiseworthy to be courageous and to give one's life. But neither of these conditions exist in these other forms of death.

1115b4–6; 542

COMMENTARY OF ST. THOMAS

528. After Aristotle has finished the treatise on virtues in general, he begins here a particularized study of the individual virtues. First he treats the virtues concerned with the interior passions. Next, he treats justice and injustice (concerned with external actions) in the fifth book (Lect. I) at "We must give our attention to justice and injustice etc." (1129). The first section

falls into two parts. In the first part he treats the moral virtues dealing with the principal passions touching the very life of man. Next, he treats the moral virtues that are concerned with the secondary passions touching the external goods of man, in the fourth book (Lect. I) at "Let us next discuss etc." (1119b21). Concerning the first part he does two things. First [A] he studies fortitude, which deals with the passions touching things destructive of human life. Then [Lect. XIX] he studies temperance, which deals with the passions touching things preservative of human life, i.e., food and sex, at "Following this treatise (on fortitude) we must etc." (1117b22). On the first point he does three things. First [1] he investigates the matter of fortitude. Next, "The same thing is not terrifying etc." [Lect. XV], he treats the method of its operation (1115b7). Last, at "Although fortitude is concerned etc." [Lect. XVIII], he determines certain properties of the virtue (1117a29). In regard to the first he does two things. First [1] he reviews what was clearly evident from the premises about the matter of fortitude, i.e., with what passions it deals. Next [2], at "Terrifying things are what etc.," he investigates the objects of these passions as fortitude is concerned with them.

529. He says, as has already been explained in the second book (267, 341), that fortitude is a kind of mean dealing with fear and rashness. Fortitude denotes a firmness of soul by which it remains unmoved by the fear of dangers.

530. Then [2], at "**Terrifying things,**" he investigates the objects of the previously mentioned passions according as fortitude treats them, especially on the part of fear about which fortitude is principally concerned, as

will be pointed out later (536). The objects of fear and rashness are identical, for what one man flees because of fear, another attacks in his rashness. On this point three considerations demand his attention. First 12, a] he shows what the objects of fear are. Next [3], at "But fortitude does not etc.," he explains with what class of these objects fortitude deals, since it is concerned with fear of death. Finally [8], at "It does not seem etc.," he shows in particular what kind of death fortitude envisages.

531. He says first that terrifying things are those we are afraid of, objects of fear so to speak. All evil things are universally of this kind. Hence philosophers in giving a definition of fear say that it is the expectation of evil. Expectation is here taken generally for any movement of the appetitive faculty toward some future things, although expectation properly speaking is directed only to good, as is hope. It is evident then that we all fear some evils, like a bad reputation and disgrace (which are contrary to respectability), destitution and poverty (which are contrary to the goods of external fortune), sickness, enmity, and death (which are contrary to personal goods).

532. Next [3], at "**But fortitude does not,**" he shows that fortitude deals with the fear of some particular evils. First [3] he shows about what evils it is not concerned. Second [7], at "About what kind of terrifying things etc.," he concludes about what evils it is concerned. On the first point he does two things. First [3] he sets forth his proposition that fortitude does not seem to deal with the fear of all evils.

533. Second [4], at "**For, to fear some things,**" he proves his proposition, the first part of which is that fortitude does not deal with the fear of a bad reputa-

tion [4]. The brave man is praised because he does not fear. But there are certain things which we ought to fear in order to live a good life. It is good to fear these things inasmuch as fear is not only necessary for the preservation of respectability, but even fear itself is something honorable. There is a kind of disgrace attached to the person who does not fear evils of this sort. This is obvious from the fact that one who fears a bad reputation is praised as decent, i.e., morally good and modest. But one who does not fear evil of this kind is blamed as shameless. It is evident, therefore, that fortitude is not concerned with fear of these evils. Sometimes, it is true, a man who does not fear a bad reputation is called by some brave, in a metaphorical sense, because he has a likeness to a brave man inasmuch as he is without fear.

534. In the second part (of his proposition) at "**Poverty is not to be feared**" [5], he shows that fortitude does not deal with the fear of poverty. He says that poverty is not to be feared in the way that a bad reputation is to be feared (533). Neither is sickness to be feared, nor indeed any of those things that do not pertain to wickedness of which man himself is the cause. It is useless for man to fear what he is unable to avoid. In regard to such things, therefore, a man ought to fear lest he fall into any of them by his own wickedness. The reason is that fear is useful to avoid these very things, but not otherwise. Although it is not necessary to fear things of this sort, nevertheless one who has no fear of them is not called brave except perhaps in a metaphorical sense. The reason is that not to fear poverty seems to belong to another virtue, liberality. Some are praised for the act of this virtue, inasmuch as they spend money freely. Yet

they are called complete cowards in the greater dangers of war. Therefore, fortitude is not concerned with the fear of poverty.

535. In the third part, at "**No one is**" [6], he shows that fortitude does not deal with any fear whatsoever of personal evils. He says that a man is not called cowardly because he fears injury or envy of himself, his children or his wife, or any other thing of this kind. A person is not said to be brave because he does not fear the lash but boldly endures it, since these things are not especially terrifying. But a person is brave without qualification from the fact that he is brave in the face of the most terrifying dangers. One who is undaunted in some other circumstances is not called absolutely brave, but brave in that particular category.

536. At "**About what kind of**" [7] he shows that fortitude is concerned with the fear of certain evils, saying that man is called absolutely brave from the fact that he is fearless in the face of dangers which are most terrifying. Virtue is determined according to the maximum of the faculty, as is pointed out in the first book of De Coelo (Ch. 11, 281a8; St. Th. Lect. XXV, 249). Therefore, the virtue of fortitude must deal with the things that are most terrifying, so that no one endures greater dangers than the brave man. Among all dangers the most frightening is death. The reason is that death is the end of all present life, and after death there does not seem to be any good or evil equal to those things of this life that inflict death on us. Things belonging to the state of the soul after death are not visible to us, but that by which a man loses all his goods is appallingly frightening. Hence it seems that fortitude is properly concerned with fear of the dangers of death.

537. Then [8], at "**It does not seem,**" he shows that fortitude is concerned with the fear of a particular kind of death. On this point he does two things. First [8] he shows with what kind of death fortitude deals. Next [11], at "A man is called brave etc.," he explains the relation of fortitude to all the kinds of death. In regard to the first he does two things. First [8] he sets forth his proposition. Then [9], at "Such men lose their lives etc.," he proves his proposition. He says first that fortitude is not even concerned with death that a man suffers in some kind of accident or employment, as at sea or in sickness, but with death that he suffers from the best of causes, as happens when a man dies fighting in defense of his country. The same reason holds in the case of any other death that a person undergoes for the good of virtue. But he makes a special mention of death in battle because in that undertaking men more frequently suffer death for the sake of good.

538. Then [9], at "**Such men lose,**" he proves his proposition by two reasons. The first [9] is that death in battle happens in the greatest danger since a man easily loses his life there. It happens also in the most noble of dangers since a man undergoes the danger in that case on account of the common good that is the greatest good, as has been noted in the beginning (30). But virtue is concerned with what is greatest and best. Therefore, the virtue of fortitude especially deals with death that takes place in battle.

539. Next [10], at "**Honors are given,**" he proves the same thing from the fact that honors are given to those who die such a death or bravely expose themselves to the danger of a death of this kind. (This is the practice both in city-states that exist by association and in monarchies where kings alone rule.) The reason is that those who fight bravely in battle are honored both while they live and after death. But honor is the reward of virtue. Therefore, the virtue of fortitude is considered as dealing with death of this kind.

540. At "**A man is called brave**" [11] he shows how fortitude has a relation to all the kinds of death. First [11] he shows the way fortitude is related to the fear of death. Next [13], at "Likewise, brave men etc.," he shows its relation to boldness which is a reaction to dangers of this kind. On the first point he does two things. First [11] he explains the death about which fortitude is principally concerned. A man is called brave, he says, mainly because he is not afraid of death for a good cause, nor is he afraid of the threats—especially sudden threats—of death. The reason is that every virtue is ordered to good. Actions that must be done on the spur of the moment show in a special way that a person acts from habit. In other situations a man after careful deliberations can perform actions like those that proceed from the habit. Actions pertaining to good and the unexpected dangers in battle are especially of this kind. Hence the brave man who is not afraid is concerned principally with these actions.

541. Next [12], at "**Moreover, brave men,**" he shows how the brave man himself is without fear of other kinds of death. He says that as a consequence brave men are unafraid both in storms at sea and in sickness because they do not lose their heads and become upset because of fear of such dangers. In storms, however, they differ from sailors. Even if the brave have no hope of rescue, they nevertheless despise death and are without fear. But sailors are unafraid of dangers from the sea by

reason of their experience, for they have hope of being easily able to escape them.

542. Then [13], at "**Likewise, brave men,**" he shows that fortitude is principally concerned not only with fear of death but also with boldness in dangers of this kind. He says that brave men likewise act manfully by meeting dangers in those circumstances where fortitude is praiseworthy and where it is noble to die, as in battle. It is good that a man endanger his life for the common welfare. But in the aforesaid modes of death, by shipwreck or by sickness, fortitude is not honorable nor does any good follow from death. Hence it does not belong to the virtue of fortitude to meet such dangers boldly.

LECTURE XV
The Act of Fortitude

TEXT OF ARISTOTLE (*B.1115b7–1116a16*) Chapter 7

1. The same thing is not terrifying to all, but we do call that terrifying which is above the power of man to resist. The superhuman is frightening to every sensible person. However, what is within the power of man differs according to magnitude and degree. It is the same with daring undertakings. **1115b7–10; 543–544**

2. The brave man does not lose his head but acts like a man. He will, therefore, fear such things, and he will undergo them as he ought, and as reason will judge, for the sake of good which is the end of virtue. But man sometimes fears dangers more or less; he fears things that are not terrifying as if they were terrifying. Man is at fault because he fears at times the wrong things, at other times in the wrong way or at the wrong time and so forth. The same observation may be made about what inspires confidence. **1115b10–17; 545–546**

3. One who endures and fears the right things, for the right motive, in the right manner, and at the right time is brave. Likewise the brave man acts daringly, for he endures and acts in conformity with what is worthy and according to reason. **1115b17–20; 547–548**

4. The end of every action is conformity with its own habit. The good intended by the brave man is fortitude and this is also an end since every means is determined by its end. The brave man endures and works, for the sake of good, the things which are in conformity with fortitude. **1115b20–24; 549–550**

5. Of those who go to excess, that man who fears nothing is unnamed. We mentioned before that many vices are unnamed but a person is a madman or insensible who fears nothing, neither earthquakes nor floods, as it is said of the Celts. **1115b24–28; 551**

6. He who is excessive in daring when dealing with frightening things is called reckless. The reckless man is thought to be vain but only feigns courage. As the brave man really is in face of danger, so the vain man wishes to appear (even imitating the actions of the brave man). Hence many who seem brave, are in fact cowards. They are daring in these circumstances (of little danger) but do not stand up when fearful things occur. **1115b28–33; 552**

7. One who is excessive in fearing is a coward; he fears the things he ought not to fear, as he ought not (and similarly in the other circumstances). He is also deficient in daring but he is more conspicuous from the fact that he fears painful situations too much. **1115b33–1116a2; 553**

8. The coward is a despairing man inasmuch as he fears everything. The brave man, on the contrary, has great hope inasmuch as he is courageous. **1116a2–4; 554**

9. The cowardly, the reckless, and the brave are all concerned with these passions but are disposed towards them in a different way. The reckless and the cowardly have excess and defect but the brave man holds a middle course as he ought. **1116a4–7; 555**

10. The reckless are precipitate and rush to meet danger, but, when actually in it, they fall down. The brave however are vigorous while in action and calm beforehand. **1116a7–9; 556**

11. As has been pointed out, fortitude is a mean concerned with situations that inspire confidence or terror about which we have spoken; it desires or endures things because it is good to do so, or because it is base not to do so. But to suffer death in order to avoid poverty or a disappointed love or something painful is not characteristic of a brave man but rather of a coward. It is a kind of effeminacy not to endure these misfortunes, and besides, such a one suffers a death not for an honorable good but to escape evil. Such then is the nature of fortitude. **1116a10–16; 557–558**

COMMENTARY OF ST. THOMAS

543. After the Philosopher has investigated the matter of fortitude, he now treats its act. First he distinguishes the act of fortitude from the acts of the opposite vices. Next [Lect. XVI], at "Other kinds of fortitude are enumerated etc.," he treats certain things that have an act similar to fortitude (1116a16). He discusses the first point under two aspects. First [1] he determines how acts can be differentiated in the matter presently investigated. Then [3], at "One who endures etc.," he shows what the proper act of fortitude is by comparison with the acts of the opposite vices. He handles the first point in a twofold manner. First [1] he assigns the reason for differentiating acts in this matter. Second [2], at "The brave man does not lose etc.," he shows how they are differentiated. He observes first that the same thing is not terrifying to all.

544. Since fear is in the irascible part—the object of which is the difficult—fear is concerned only with an evil which is in some way above the power of the one fearing. Hence a thing is terrifying to a child which is not terrifying to a mature man. There are evils that exceed human power to overcome, such as earthquakes, tidal waves, and other disasters of this sort. Hence evils of this kind are terrifying to every sensible man endowed with good judgment. But that terrifying thing which does not seem to exceed man's power to resist may be viewed in a twofold way. One, according to the different magnitude of the thing, for example, it is more terrifying to have many enemies come together than to have only a few. The other, according to degree, for instance, that enemies have greater or less hatred, or that they

are closer or farther away. What has been said about terrifying things must be said likewise about things inspiring courage because fear and boldness have the same object, as has been said previously (530).

545. Then [2], at "The brave man," he shows by the reason just given how acts are differentiated in this matter. When it is affirmed that the brave man does not lose his head because of fear, this must be understood as referring to a man of sound judgment. Such a one will fear the things which are above man. Hence the brave man too will fear them. However, in case of necessity or utility, he will undergo such things as he ought and as right reason, which is proper to man, will judge. In this way he will not forsake the judgment of reason on account of the fear of such things, but will endure terrifying things of this kind, no matter how great, on account of the good which is the end of virtue.

546. It happens at times that a man fears terrifying things that are above his power, or within his power more or less than reason judges. What is more, it happens that he fears the things which are not terrifying as if they were terrifying. Man's sin consists principally in what is contrary to right reason. As sickness takes place in the body by reason of a disorder of some humor, so too sin against reason takes place in the soul by reason of a disorder of some circumstance. Hence sometimes a person sins in the matter of fear from the fact that he fears what he ought not to fear, but other times from the fact that he fears when he ought not to fear. The same must be said about the other circumstances enumerated above (544). What has been affirmed about

terrifying things is to be understood about things inspiring boldness where a similar reason is found, as has been said (544).

547. Next [3], at "**One who,**" he shows what the act of fortitude is by means of a comparison with the opposite vices. He treats this under two headings. First [3] he explains the act of the virtue and of the vices. Next [10], at "The reckless are etc.," he compares the virtue with certain things that seem similar to it. He discusses the first point in a threefold manner. First [3] he defines the acts of the virtue and the vices relating to fear and rashness; and then [8], at "The coward is etc.," those relating to hope and despair. Finally [9], at "The coward, the reckless etc.," he concludes with a summary. He handles the first point from two aspects. First [3] he defines the act of the virtuous man; and then [5], at "Of those who go etc.," the acts of the vicious man. He considers the first point in a twofold way. First [3] he expounds his proposition. Next [4], at "The end etc.," he makes clear something he had said.

548. He says first that one who endures the things he ought to endure and flees through fear the things he ought to avoid with the right motivation, in the right manner, and at the right time is called brave. Likewise, he who dares in the things he ought for the right motive and so forth is also brave. He assigns the reason for this when he says that a brave and virtuous man endures on account of fear and he acts by means of daring in conformity with what is fitting and as right reason indicates. Every moral virtue is in ac-

cord with right reason, as was stated previously (323, 326).

549. At "**The end**" [4] he makes clear something he had said, namely, the right motive for operating. He remarks that the end of every virtuous operation is in conformity with the nature of its own habit. A habit—caused by custom—operates after the manner of a nature because custom is a kind of nature, as is noted in the book *De Memoria et Reminiscentia* (Ch. 2, 452a28; St. Th. Lect. VI, 383).[2] The ultimate end of an agent naturally operating is the good of the universe, a perfect good; but the proximate end is to imprint its likeness in another. Thus the end of a warm object is to make things warm by means of its activity. Likewise the ultimate end of operative virtue is happiness, a perfect good, as was said in the first book (45, 111, 112, 117, 118, 201, 222). But the proximate and proper end is to impress a likeness of the habit on the act.

550. This is what he means in his statement that the good, which the brave man intends, is fortitude—not the habit of fortitude, for this already exists, but the likeness of it in the act. This also is the end since every means is determined by its proper end because the character of means to the end is derived from the end. For this reason the end of fortitude is something pertaining to the nature of fortitude. In this way the brave man endures and works for the sake of good, that is, inasmuch as he intends to perform the actions which are in conformity with fortitude.

551. Then [5], at "**Of those who go**

2   Sancti Thomae Aquinatis, *In Aristotelis Libros de Sensu et Sensato, de Memoria et Reminiscentia Commentarium*. Ed. Pirotta, Turin/Rome: Marietti, 1928.

to excess," he defines the acts of vicious men: first [5] of the man deficient in fear; next [6], of the man excessive in daring, at "He who is excessive in daring etc." Last [7], at "One who is excessive in fearing etc.," he defines the acts of the man excessive in fearing. He says first that there is no special term for the man who abounds—speaking of the vices pertaining to excess—in fearlessness, i.e. who fears nothing. It was said before (341) that many vices have no names. This particularly happens in things that rarely occur. And fearlessness of this sort rarely happens. It occurs only in the case of madmen and insensible persons who fear nothing—not even earthquakes, floods, or anything of this kind. This is said to happen among certain people called Celts (the name of a race). He speaks here of one who is insensible or without a sense of pain because the future things we fear and the things that cause us pain when present are the same.

552. Next [6], at "**He who,**" he treats those who are excessive in daring. He says that the man who, dealing with terrifying things, abounds in daring by boldly attacking them beyond what reason suggests is called reckless. But there is also one who is apparently but not really reckless, the vain man who pretends to be brave. Hence as the brave or reckless man really is in regard to terrifying things, so the vain man seeks to appear. Because of this the vain man imitates the works of the brave or reckless man when he can do so without danger. Hence many of those who seem brave or reckless are cowardly. Many of those who are reckless in circumstances having little danger do not endure when truly frightening things occur.

553. At "**One who**" [7], he treats of one who is excessive in fearing. The Philosopher says a man is a coward when he fears what he should not fear, in the way he should not fear, and so on. The man inordinate in fear is lacking in daring. The only reason why a person does not attack to destroy frightening things is fear. But the lack of fear can exist without the recklessness of attack. It does not follow then that everyone, who does not flee as he ought, attacks more than he ought. But whoever is deficient in attacking the right things is motivated only by fear. For this reason Aristotle separates the defect of fear from the excess of recklessness, but joins the excess of fear with the defect of recklessness. Although the coward is extreme in fearing and deficient in daring, nevertheless he is more conspicuous from the fact that he abounds in the fear of painful situations than from the fact that he is lacking in daring, because the defect is not so easily seen as the excess.

554. Then [8], at "**The coward is,**" he shows how the previously named things are related to hope and despair. For an understanding of this we must consider that the object of recklessness and fear is evil. But the object of hope and despair is good. The appetitive faculty of itself tends towards the good, but incidentally flees the good by reason of some evil attached. Likewise, the appetitive faculty of itself flees the evil. But what is essential causes that which is incidental. For this reason, hope—whose characteristic is to tend towards good—causes recklessness that tends towards the evil it attacks. For the same reason fear, which flees evil, is the cause of despair, which withdraws from good. He says, therefore, that the coward is a despairing man inasmuch as he fears his defi-

ciency in everything. On the contrary the brave man has great hope because he is courageous.

555. Next [9], at "**The cowardly, the reckless,**" he sums up what has been said, concluding from the premises that the cowardly, the reckless, and the brave man all are concerned with these passions but related to them in a different way. The reckless man exceeds in daring and is lacking in fear; the cowardly man exceeds in fear and is lacking in daring. But the brave man follows a middle course in these matters as he ought according to right reason.

556. At "**The reckless**" [10] he compares fortitude with things similar to it. First [10] he shows the difference between the brave and the reckless man. Next [11], at "As has been pointed out etc.," he shows the difference between the brave man and the man who undergoes death to escape misfortunes. The coward seems to have nothing in common with the brave man, and for this reason Aristotle does not care to assign the difference between them. He remarks that the reckless are impetuous, rushing into danger, i.e., swiftly and spiritedly going out to meet it, because they are moved by a surge of passion beyond reason. When they are actually in the danger they are checked, for the movement of the preceding passion is overcome by the threatening danger. But when the brave are in the very midst of the dangers, they are vigorous because the

judgment according to which they act is not overcome by any danger. But before they meet the difficulties, they are calm because they do not act from violence of passion but from deliberate reason.

557. Then [11], at "**As has been pointed out,**" he shows the difference between a brave man and the man who undergoes death to escape misfortune. He says, as has been noted (535–540), that fortitude is a mean in terrifying things, which are evils concerned with the dangers of death spoken of before (535–540); that fortitude tends to operate virtuously and sustains sufferings of this kind in order to bring about something good and honorable, or in order to flee something disgraceful and dishonorable. However, that one should die by laying hands on himself or by voluntarily suffering death inflicted by another (in order to escape poverty or a longing for a thing which he cannot possess or whatever else there is that causes sorrow) does not belong to a brave man but rather to a coward. This happens for two reasons. First, because a certain effeminacy of soul, contrary to fortitude, seems to exist when a person is unable to undergo hardships and sorrows. Second, because such a one does not suffer death for an honorable good, as the brave man does, but to escape a painful evil.

558. Finally, he concludes that we can know, from what was said, the nature of fortitude.

LECTURE XVI
Acts of Civic and Military Fortitude

TEXT OF ARISTOTLE (B.1116a16–1116b23) Chapter 8

1. *Other kinds of fortitude are enumerated according to five types. Among these, fortitude of the citizen holds first place, for it is most like real fortitude. Citizens apparently undergo dangers because of legal penalties and the disgrace of cowardice, and also for the sake of honor. For this reason men are found to be very brave in those states where the cowardly are censured and the brave accorded honors.*   **1116a16–21; 561–562**

2. *Homer mentions men of this kind, Diomede and Hector, for instance. Polydamas (says Hector) would be the first to reproach me. And Diomede: "Hector at some time or other when boasting to the Trojans will say: Tydides has fled from me."*   **1116a21–26; 563**

3. *This fortitude is most like that we just discussed as being exercised on account of virtue. It is indeed practiced on account of shame and the desire of the honorable, for fortitude of this sort is for the sake of honor and the avoidance of the disgrace of opprobrium.*   **1116a27–29; 564**

4. *Those who are under compulsion from their rulers will be included in the same type of fortitude. They are less worthy of the title, however, insofar as they do not act bravely because of shame but rather out of fear, for they flee not what is disgraceful, but what is painful. Masters coerce their subjects by threats as Hector did: "Anyone I find giving way to fear and not doing battle will not have a chance to escape the dogs."*   **1116a29–35; 565**

5. *Rulers do the same thing when they command their subjects not to give ground, and beat those who do. A similar judgment is to be passed on those who before battle construct walls, trenches, and other such obstacles to retreat. All such have coerced their subjects. But the virtuous man must be brave not because of constraint but because of the good of virtue.*
1116a36–1116b3; 566

6. *In particular cases experience seems to be a kind of fortitude. For this reason Socrates thought that fortitude was knowledge. As others are brave in other things from experience, so soldiers are brave in warfare. In war there are many operations without danger which soldiers know very well. Those engaged in these exercises seem brave to others who are ignorant of the nature of such things. Hence professional soldiers are especially able by reason of experience to attack their adversaries without harm to themselves: skilled in the use of arms, they are able to guard themselves from blows and to strike back. They possess other skills like those that enable them to inflict injury while they themselves are not injured. They fight against others like the armed against the unarmed, like well-trained athletes against inexperienced rustics. In athletic contests of this kind it is not the brave who can fight the most but rather those who are physically powerful and well-conditioned.*   **1116b3–15; 567–569**

7. *Soldiers turn cowards when they see that the danger exceeds their skill and that they are inferior in numbers and military preparations. They are the first to run away, while those possessing the fortitude of the citizen, refusing to leave, give up their lives. This actually happened in the battle at the temple of Hermes. Citizens think it disgraceful to flee, and choose to die rather than to be saved under such circumstances. But soldiers expose themselves to danger because from the beginning they think themselves more powerful. When the truth dawns on them they take flight fearing death more than disgrace. Not so the brave man.*
1116b15–23; 570

COMMENTARY OF ST. THOMAS

559. After the Philosopher has ascertained how the act of real fortitude and of the opposite vices is constituted, he treats here certain dispositions having

an act similar to but lacking real fortitude. This happens in five ways. Since real fortitude is a moral virtue (for which knowledge is required and because of this, choice), a person exercising an act of fortitude can fall short of real virtue in three ways. In one way because he does not operate with knowledge. This is the fifth type of counterfeit fortitude, according to which a person is said to be brave through ignorance. In another way because a person does not operate by choice but by passion (whether it is a passion urging one to undergo dangers as anger does, or a passion quieting fear of the mind as hope does). According to this consideration, there are two kinds of counterfeit fortitude.

560. The third way a person falls short of real fortitude is that he operates by choice, but he does not choose what the brave man chooses. In undergoing dangers he does not think it hazardous, because of his skill, to fight in battle, as is evident among soldiers; or he chooses to undergo the dangers not on account of the end that a brave man chooses but on account of honors or punishments decreed by rulers of states.

561. Accordingly, this portion falls into five parts. In the first part [1] he treats civic fortitude or fortitude of the citizen; in the second [6], the fortitude of the soldier at "In particular cases etc."; in the third part [Lect. XVII], fortitude that operates through anger, at "People confuse rage etc." (1116b23); in the fourth part [Lect. XVII], fortitude that operates through hope, at "Likewise the confident etc." (1117a11); in the fifth part [Lect. XVII], fortitude that operates through ignorance, at "Those

who operate in ignorance etc." (1117a23). In regard to the first he indicates three kinds of civic fortitude. The first kind [1] belongs to those who undergo dangers for the sake of honor. The second [4], to those who undergo dangers because of the fear of punishments, at "Those who are under compulsion etc." The third [5], at "Rulers do the same etc.," to those who attack and expose themselves to dangerous situations because of pressing compulsion. He discusses the first point under three headings.

562. First [1] he brings out this kind of fortitude. He says that over and above real fortitude, certain other kinds of fortitude are enumerated according to five types. Among these, civic fortitude or fortitude of the citizen holds first place because this type is very similar to real fortitude. Citizens undergo dangers to avoid penalties and disgrace which, according to the civil laws, are inflicted on the cowardly, and to acquire honors which by the same laws are bestowed on the brave. So in those states where blame is heaped on the cowardly and honors on the brave, men are found most brave according to this type of fortitude, and perhaps even according to the real virtue by reason of habit.

563. Second [2], at "**Homer mentions**," he gives examples taken from Homer who, describing the Trojan War, introduces men brave for honor or fear of blame: Diomede among the Greeks and Hector for the Trojan side. He represents Hector as saying these words: "Polydamas, the Trojan leader, will be the first to reproach me (i.e., he will find fault first of all with me) if I do not fight manfully."[3] And Diomede

_____

3   Cf. *Iliad* xxii. 100.

exhorting himself to act bravely said: "Hector haranguing the Trojans will say in praise of himself and in vituperation of me that Tydides (a name given him from his father's), alias Diomede, has fled from me and has been beaten."[4]

564. Third [3], at "**This fortitude,**" he clarifies what he has said: that this kind of fortitude is very similar to the genuine virtue. He says that the citizen's fortitude is much like the one of which we have spoken (562), since it is for the sake of virtue. This fortitude of the citizen is practiced through shame or fear of the disgraceful, inasmuch as someone flees disgrace, and through a desire of the good or honorable insofar as this fortitude seeks honor, which is the testimony of goodness. For this reason he adds in explanation that fortitude of this sort is motivated by honor and avoidance of opprobrium, which is the disgraceful. Since then honor is a thing near to an honorable good, and blame to the disgraceful, it follows that this fortitude is close to real fortitude, which seeks what is honorable and flees from what is shameful.

565. Then [4], at "**Those who,**" he indicates the second kind of civic fortitude that is practiced on account of punishment. He says that those who are brave, because compelled by the fear of punishments inflicted by rulers of the state, can be assigned the same type of civic fortitude. They are, however, inferior to the previously mentioned insofar as they do not act bravely on account of the shame of disgrace but on account of fear of punishment. This is why he adds that they do not flee what is disgraceful or dis-

honorable but what is sorrowful, i.e., painful or injurious, from the fact that someone is made sad. In this way the masters compel their subjects to fight bravely. According to Homer, Hector threatened the Trojans in these words: "Anyone running away and not doing battle, i.e., without fighting bravely, I will handle so roughly that he will not have a chance to escape the dogs."[5]

566. Next [5], at "**Rulers do the same,**" he presents the third kind of civic fortitude according as some are compelled by their rulers then and there and not only by fear of future punishment. This is why he says that rulers do the same thing by their actions when they command their subjects not to run away from battle, and beat those who do. A similar judgment is to be passed on those who, before battle, construct walls and trenches and other such obstacles to retreat so that their subjects cannot take to flight. All rulers who do things of this kind coerce their subjects to fight. And those who act under compulsion in this way are not really brave, because the virtuous man must be brave not on account of the constraint he suffers but because of the good of virtue.

567. At "**In particular cases**" [6] he treats the fortitude of the soldier. He explains this question in a twofold manner. First [6] he shows what leads soldiers to fight bravely. Next [7] he compares the fortitude of the soldier and the citizen, at "Soldiers turn cowards." He says first that in individual cases experience seems to be a kind of fortitude. In any undertaking one who has knowledge from experience works boldly and without fear, as Vegetius

---

4   Cf. *Iliad* viii. 148.
5   Cf. *Iliad* ii. 391.

says in his book on military affairs: "No one fears to do what he believes he has learned to do well."[6] For this reason Socrates thought fortitude was knowledge which is acquired by experience. He even thought all the virtues are kinds of knowledge. But this question will be studied later in the sixth book (1286). Therefore, since certain others are brave by experience in particular affairs, so soldiers are brave in warfare by reason of experience.

568. Two things follow from this. The first is that in war there are many great things like the clash of arms, the charge of the cavalry, and so on that strike the inexperienced with terror, although there is little or no danger in them. These things, as the professional soldiers know, are not really to be dreaded. Hence men seem brave when engaging, without fear, in exercises that appear dangerous to others who are inexperienced and ignorant of the nature of what is taking place. Second, it follows that by reason of experience professional soldiers in fighting can do hurt to their adversaries, and not suffer or be harmed in turn. They can guard themselves from blows and can strike back, for they are clever in the use of weapons, and they possess other skills effective in enabling them to inflict injury while they themselves are not injured. Hence it is obvious they fight against others as the armed against the unarmed. A man is in effect unarmed if he does not know how or is unable to use arms.

569. The same can be said of athletes, i.e., strong and well-trained boxers compared to simple and inexperienced farm boys. In such athletic contests it is not the brave who can fight the most but those who are physically powerful and well-conditioned.

570. Then [7] at "**Soldiers turn,**" he compares the fortitude of the soldier and the citizen. He says that soldiers fight bravely so long as they do not see danger threatening. But when the danger exceeds the skill they have in arms and when they lack numbers and adequate military preparations, they become cowardly. Then they are the first to run away; they were daring for no other reason than that they thought the danger was not imminent. Therefore, when they first see the danger, they take to their heels. But those who possess the fortitude of the citizen—refusing to leave the danger—lose their lives, as happened in a certain place where the citizens remained after the soldiers had fled. The reason is that citizens think it disgraceful to run away, and choose to die rather than save themselves by flight. But soldiers expose themselves to dangers because, from the beginning, they think themselves more powerful. But after they have recognized that the enemy is more powerful, they take to flight fearing death more than ignominious escape. It is not so with the brave man who fears disgrace more than death.

---

6   *Epitoma Rei Militaris*, Liber 1, I, 6, ll. 4–5.

LECTURE XVII
Counterfeit Fortitude

TEXT OF ARISTOTLE (B.1116b23–1117a28) Chapter 8

1. *People confuse rage or wrath with fortitude. Indeed the enraged appear brave in the way that wild animals turn on those who have wounded them. The brave man does give the appearance of rage which acts most impetuously against danger. Hence Homer warns: "Put strength into thy wrath," and "arouse thy might and wrath"; nd (in reference to a certain man) "he panted harsh courage through both nostrils," and "his blood boiled." All such expressions seem to signify the stirring up and the impulse of rage.* **1116b23–30; 571–572**

2. *The brave are incited to valorous deeds by reason of honor with rage co-operating.*
1116b30–31; 573

3. *Wild animals attack danger because of pain from a wound or from fear; undisturbed in the woods and swamps they do not come out to attack. They are not truly brave because, aroused against danger by pain and rage, they do not foresee the risks involved. Otherwise hungry jackasses would be brave since they do not stop eating when beaten. (Adulterers too undertake many risks for their sensual desire.) Animals, therefore, who are incited against danger by pain and rage are not truly brave. That reaction which is prompted by passion seems to be a most natural one, and, if to it be added choice and a proper end it is fortitude.*
111b31–1117a5; 574–575

4. *Angry men are grieved (because of injury suffered) but delighted when taking vengeance. Those who act in this way perhaps are fighters, but hardly brave men, for they do not do what is honorable, nor are they led by reason but rather by passion. They do though possess something similar to real fortitude.* **1117a5–9; 576**

5. *Likewise the confident are not truly brave; they are hopeful because they have often conquered many enemies in the midst of dangers.* **1117a9–11; 577**

6. *However, such confident people are like the truly brave because both are daring. But the truly brave are daring in the fashion already indicated, [Ch. 7, 1115b11–24.] while the confident dare because they think themselves better fighters and expect to suffer nothing. The intoxicated too act in this way, becoming abundantly hopeful, but when they fail to get what was expected, they give up. The brave man though will suffer evils that seem, and really are, terrifying to men—and this for the sake of what is honorable and to avoid disgrace.*
1117a11–17; 578

7. *Therefore, that man seems to be braver who does not fear more, and is not more disturbed by unexpected terrors than by those that were foreseen. He seems to act more by habit since he acts less from preparation. Someone can choose by reason and deliberation things that are foreseen, but in unexpected events habit asserts itself.* **1117a17–22; 579**

8. *Those who operate in ignorance of dangers seem to be brave. They do not differ greatly from people who are brave by reason of great hope. They are, however, inferior since they have no self-reliance unlike the confident who remain in the fight for some time. Those who are bold through ignorance take flight as soon as they know the situation is different from what they suspect. This happened to the Argives when they fell on the Spartans whom they thought Sicyonians. We have now discussed both the brave and those thought to be brave.*
1117a22–28; 580–582

COMMENTARY OF ST. THOMAS

571. After having disposed of two types of counterfeit fortitude, he pro- poses here to treat a third kind operat- ing by means of rage which urges to

the act of fortitude. He treats this point in a twofold manner. First [1] he shows how rage inclines to the act of fortitude. Next [2], at "The brave are etc.," he shows how this fortitude differs from real fortitude. He observes first that men in common usage of speech confuse rage with fortitude when they attribute to fortitude things that enraged or angry people do. Indeed the enraged and angry do seem to be brave. So too do beasts who, when aroused to rage, attack men beating them. Fortitude has some likeness to rage inasmuch as rage incites against danger with a very strong impulse. But the brave man strives against danger with great strength of soul.

572. As an example he quotes the verses of Homer who warned someone in these words: "Put strength into your wrath"[7] so that wrath may be directed by the virtue of the soul; "Arouse your might and wrath"[8] that the virtue of your soul may be rendered more prompt by anger. Elsewhere he remarks that certain people "pant harsh courage through both nostrils";[9] in other words, wrath, because of the beating of the heart, makes breathing so heavy that sometimes "the blood boils up"[10] through the nostrils from the force of rage. And the Philosopher observes that Homer's statements here seem to indicate that anger is aroused and gives impetus to fortitude's act.

573. Then [2], at "**The brave,**" he explains the difference between this and genuine fortitude. He discusses this point from three aspects. First [2] he shows what pertains to true fortitude; next [3], at "Wild animals attack etc.," what pertains to the rage of beasts; and finally [4], at "Angry men," what pertains to human rage. He says that the brave are not incited to perform works of fortitude by the impulse of rage but by the intention of good. Rage, however, does operate secondarily in these acts in the manner of a co-operator.

574. Next [3], at "**Wild animals,**" he shows how the anger of beasts compares with the act of fortitude. He remarks that wild animals attack dangers out of pain from harmful things—which they are actually suffering when wounded, for instance—or because of the dread of the things they fear they are about to suffer, e.g., when incited to anger by fear of being wounded, they attack men. The reason is that if they were in the woods or swamps they would not be wounded nor fear to be wounded, so would not come out to attack men. Hence it is clear that real fortitude is not found in these animals because they are aroused against the dangers only by pain and rage, since they do not foresee dangers, as those who act bravely by choice. If beasts who act by passion were brave, then by the same argument hungry jackasses (who, because of the desire for food do not stop eating even when beaten) would be brave. Adulterers too undertake many risks for the sake of lust, but real fortitude is not found in them because they do not

---

7   Cf. *Iliad* xiv. 151.
8   Cf. *Iliad* v. 470.
9   Cf. *Odyssey* xxiv. 318.
10   This occurs in Theocritus xx. 15.

act by choice of good, but by reason of passion. So it is clear that animals who are incited against danger on account of pain do not have true fortitude.

575. However much is the likeness between desire and rage, nevertheless among all the passions fortitude out of rage seems to be more connatural to genuine fortitude, so that if rage be antecedently directed by choice and the motivation of a fitting end, real fortitude will be present. He expressly says "antecedently directed" because in true fortitude rage ought to follow rather than precede choice.

576. At "**Angry men**" [4] he shows what belongs to fortitude that operates by the anger of men who seem to act by choice and to intend some purpose—the punishment of the person with whom they are angry. For this reason he says that angry men are grieved over an injury received and as yet unavenged. But when they are taking vengeance they are delighted in the satisfaction of their desire. Those who work vigorously at this may perhaps be called pugnacious but hardly brave because they are not doing the right thing, nor are they led by reason but rather by passion for the sake of which they desire vengeance. However, they do possess something similar to genuine fortitude as is evident from the premises (571–572).

577. Then [5], at "**Likewise the confident**," he mentions a fourth kind of fortitude according to which some are called brave by reason of hope. He develops this idea in a threefold fashion. First [5] he explains this type of fortitude. Next [6], he compares this type with true fortitude at "However, such confident people etc." Finally [7], he deduces a corollary from what has been said, at "Therefore, that man etc." He says first that, as those who act

bravely on account of anger are not truly brave, so neither are they who act bravely for the sole reason of their hope for victory. But they have a certain preeminence by which they differ from others. From the fact that they have very often conquered in the midst of danger, they are now confident of obtaining victory not by reason of any skill acquired through experience— this belongs to the second type of fortitude—but solely by reason of a confidence derived from their frequent victories in the past.

578. Next [6], at "**However, such confident people**," he compares this fortitude to real fortitude. He notes that those who have abundant confidence in this manner are like the truly brave because both are daring—resolute in meeting dangers—but not in the way that a reckless person is at fault. They differ however since the brave boldly attack in the fashion already indicated, i.e., by choice and on account of good. But those who have high hopes attack boldly because they think themselves more able fighters and are not going to suffer any reverse from others. They resemble drunkards who also become confident when their spirits are reinforced by wine. But when such persons fail to get what they expect, they do not persist; they run away. It is a mark of the brave man, however, to suffer—for the sake of what is honorable and to avoid disgrace evils that are terrifying to men, real evils and not merely apparent ones.

579. At "**Therefore, that man**" [7] he deduces a corollary from what has been said. Because the brave man characteristically endures terrifying things according to the inclination of a proper habit, that person seems to be braver who is not more afraid or disturbed by

unexpected terrors than by those which were apparent beforehand. Such a one seems to act more from habit inasmuch as he apparently has had less opportunity to prepare himself to endure these evils. A man can choose by reason and deliberation (even contrary to the inclination of habit and passion) the things that are foreseen. In no case is the inclination of habit or passion so vehement that reason is unable to resist provided that the use of reason—which of itself has a relation to contraries—remains with man. But in unexpected events a man cannot deliberate. Hence he seems to operate by an interior inclination according to habit.

580. Then [8], at "**Those who operate**," he introduces the fifth kind of counterfeit fortitude. He says that those who are ignorant of dangers seem to be brave when they resolutely attack things equally dangerous, but which do not seem so dangerous to them. They do not differ much from people who are brave by reason of great confidence. Each thinks that dangers do not threaten him.

581. They differ, however, in that the ignorant do not consider the evils they attack to be dangers in themselves and without qualification. On the other hand those who have high hopes know the nature of the evils they assail but do not think that these constitute dangers for them. Those who are ignorant are the more inferior to those who have high hopes inasmuch as the ignorant have no self-reliance at all, but go out to meet dangers only because of the lack of knowledge. But those who have great hopes remain for some time—even after they recognize the dangers—until the greatness of the danger overwhelms their hope. Those who are brave through ignorance, however, take flight as soon as they know the situation is different from what they suspected. The Argives, Greek citizens, reacted in this way when thinking they were fighting against Sicyonians—citizens weaker than themselves—they in fact fell upon other stronger soldiers.

582. He concludes that those we have discussed (571–581) are called brave inasmuch as they are considered brave by a similitude and not because they are truly brave.

LECTURE XVIII
The Properties of Fortitude

TEXT OF ARISTOTLE (*B.1117a29–1117b22*) Chapter 9

1. *Although fortitude is concerned with both daring and fear, it is not concerned with each in the same way. Its task rather is to manage terrifying things, for one who is not disturbed by these things, but conducts himself as he ought in regard to them, is braver than the man who behaves well in regard to daring.*   **1117a29–32; 583**

2. *As has been said, men are called brave because they endure distressing things. Consequently, fortitude is justly praised because it does not withdraw on account of pain. It is more difficult to endure afflictions, as we have indicated, than to abstain from what is pleasant.*   **1117a32–35; 584–585**

3. *Still the brave man seems to take pleasure in attaining the end for the sake of fortitude but this pleasure vanishes on account of the accompanying discomforts, as we see happen in athletic contests. Boxers take pleasure in the end they strive for, the laurel wreath and the honors. But being flesh and blood they suffer pain from blows, and all the labor they undergo is disagreeable. Because these distressing things are many and the end insignificant, they do not seem to feel any pleasure. Such also is it with the act of fortitude, for death and wounds are painful to the brave man who endures them to attain the good of virtue and to avoid disgrace.*   **1117a35–1117b9; 586–587**

4. *As a man is more perfect in virtue and happier, so much the more is he saddened by death. The virtuous man most of all deserves to live and he is knowingly deprived of the most excellent goods.*   **1117b9–13; 588–590**

5. *This is saddening but it does not lessen the virtue of the brave man. Rather a man is said to be brave because he prefers the good of fortitude in battle to those goods.*   **1117b13–15; 591**

6. *The pleasurable operation is not found in all virtues except as it attains to the end.*   **1117b15–16; 592**

7. *Nothing hinders men, who are not such as we have described, from being very good soldiers. But perhaps even those who are less brave and have no other good in view are good soldiers. They are prepared for dangers and barter their life for trifling gains.*   **1117b17–20; 593**

8. *So much then have we discussed the question of fortitude. From what has been said we can, without difficulty, understand the outline of the definition of fortitude.*   **1117b20–22; 594**

COMMENTARY OF ST. THOMAS

583. After the Philosopher has treated the matter and the act of fortitude, he considers here certain properties according as it is related to pleasure and pain. On this point he does two things. First [1] he details the properties of fortitude. Then [7] he excludes them from fortitude of the soldier, at "Nothing hinders etc." He develops the first consideration in three ways. First [1] he shows how fortitude is related to fear and daring; next [2], how fortitude is related to

pain, at "As has been said etc."; last [3], how fortitude is related to pleasure, at "Still the brave man seems etc." He says first that although fortitude is concerned with both daring and fear, it is not concerned with each in the same manner. But praise of this virtue consists rather in this, that a person behaves well with respect to terrifying things. One who is not disturbed by frightening evils but conducts himself as he ought in regard to them is more commended for bravery than one who conducts himself well in regard to daring. The reason is that fear is a threat to a man from someone stronger rising up against him. But daring originates from the fact that a man thinks that the one he attacks is not too powerful to overcome. It is more difficult to stand against a stronger man than to rise up against an equal or weaker one.

584. Then [2], at "**As has been said**," he shows in what manner fortitude is concerned with pain. To understand this we must consider that the object of fear and pain is the same, evil. But they differ according to past and future. Future evil is something terrifying while evil threatening in the present is something afflicting. It pertains to the brave man not only to stand against the fear of future dangers but also to continue steadfastly in the midst of these very dangers, as was noted previously (548). For this reason he says that men are called brave particularly because they stout-heartedly endure distressing things, i.e., immediately threatening things like blows and wounds. So it is that fortitude has pain connected with it.

585. Consequently, fortitude is justly praised because it does not withdraw from the good of virtue to escape pain. On this account it is reasonable that fortitude is most praiseworthy, since the praise of virtue consists especially in the fact that a person deals courageously with troublesome matters. It is more difficult to endure distressing things (which pertains to fortitude) than to abstain from pleasurable things (which pertains to temperance). Therefore fortitude is more praiseworthy than temperance.

586. Next [3], at "**Still the brave man**," he shows in what manner fortitude is related to pleasure. He discusses this point from three aspects.

First [3] he submits his proposition. Next [4], he rejects an error, at "As a man is more perfect etc." Last [6], he deduces a corollary from what has been said, at "The pleasurable operation etc." He says first that since fortitude consists in enduring distressing things, the brave man seems to take some pleasure in attaining the end for which he bravely struggles. But this pleasure is vapid, i.e., feebly felt on account of the accompanying griefs, as happens in athletic contests in which boxers fight with no protection.

587. Boxers take pleasure in the end they strive for, i.e., that they may receive the crown and be honored. But to take a beating is painful to them. To deny this is to deny that they have flesh and blood, because if they have sensitive flesh, hurtful things must cause them pain. Likewise, all the drudgery they suffer in fighting is disagreeable to them. Since there are many disagreeable and painful experiences they undergo, and since the good they possess as an end is something insignificant, they do not seem to be sensible of any pleasure because the pleasure is absorbed by the stronger pain. So it occurs too in the act of fortitude, for death and wounds are painful to the brave man, although he endures them to attain the good of virtue and to avoid disgrace—an end more important than that of boxers. Hence some pleasure abides rather by reason of the end.

588. At "**As a man is more**" [4] he rejects the error of the Stoics who held that virtuous men feel no pain. He considers this point in a twofold manner. First [4] he proves that very intense pain befalls the brave man; and next [5] that, because of this, his fortitude is not lessened but increased, at "This is saddening etc." He argues in the first part

from what the Stoics took for granted, that there was no human good except virtue. Therefore, they said that the virtuous man is not subject to grief because, by reason of his own good, he suffers no harm. On the contrary, the Philosopher says that as a man is more perfect in virtue and happier according to the happiness of the present life, so much more he is saddened (according to the consideration of the goods of this life) by the imminence of death.

589. A man's sadness at the loss of any good can be increased by two circumstances. First if the loss is of a deserved good, and second if the loss is of something great. Both things are present in our case because the virtuous man most of all deserves to live. Likewise he is knowingly deprived of the most excellent good, i.e., the best life and the virtues which he loses so far as the use in the present life is concerned. This causes him distress, even granted that sorrow does not befall him in respect of any other evils whatsoever that are suffered without the loss of life.

590. We must consider, however, that to some virtuous men death is desirable on account of the hope of a future life. But the Stoics did not discuss this, nor did it pertain to the Philosopher in this work to speak of those things that belong to the condition of another life.

591. Then [5], at "This is saddening," he says that this sorrow, of which we were speaking, does not lessen fortitude. Rather someone is said to be brave from the fact that he chooses the good of fortitude—which is sought in battle—in preference to those goods that he loses by death, desiring more to do one great good than to preserve many lesser goods, as will be explained later in the ninth book of this work (1879–1880).

592. Next [6], at "The pleasurable operation," he concludes from the premises that, although it was stated in the first and second books (154–160, 267, 275–279) that virtuous operations are pleasurable, the pleasurable operation is not found in all virtues, except as it attains to the end. This is noted on account of fortitude, as is evident from what was just said (586–587).

593. At "Nothing hinders" [7] he excludes the previously mentioned properties from the fortitude of the soldier. He says that nothing hinders some men from being very good soldiers, who are not such as we have described the brave man to be. But perhaps those who are less brave and attend to no other good, not even the good of fortitude, are better soldiers. They are prepared for danger not by reason of any good of virtue, but in a measure they barter their life, which they expose to risk, for trifling gains of money and booty for instance.

594. Then [8], at "So much then," he sums up in conclusion what has been said. He states that the definition of fortitude can be understood according to its general outlines, so that we may say that it is a virtue consisting in a mean according to right reason dealing with fear and daring on account of the good.

LECTURE XIX
Temperance

TEXT OF ARISTOTLE (*B.1117b23–1118a26*) Chapter 10

1. *Following this treatise (on fortitude) we must discuss temperance, for these virtues seem to pertain to the irrational parts of the soul.* **1117b23–24; 595–597**

2. *Temperance is a mean dealing with pleasures, as we have said before. It is less concerned, and not in the same way, with sorrows. Intemperance too seems to deal with these things.* **1117b24–27; 598**

3. *We must now determine with what kind of pleasures temperance has to do.* **1117b27–28; 599**

4. *There are pleasures of the body and pleasures of the soul, such as the love of honor and learning. The lovers of each of these latter (i.e., of honor 30 and learning) rejoice not as a result of any bodily passion but more as a result of mental activity.* **1117b28–31; 600**

5. *Men are not called temperate or intemperate on account of pleasures of the soul.* **1117b31–32; 601**

6. *Likewise, temperance is not concerned with any other pleasures that are not of the body. Those who love to listen to and tell stories, and who waste the day making small talk are not called intemperate but garrulous.* **1117b32–1118a1; 602**

7. *Those who are inordinately saddened by the loss of friends and money are not called intemperate. Therefore, temperance will be concerned with the pleasures of the body,* **1118a1–2; 603**

8. *but not with all of them. Those who take delight in things seen: colors, figures and writing for instance, are not called temperate or intemperate, although it happens that men take pleasure in such things as they ought, and according to excess and defect.* **1118a2–6; 604–606**

9. *Temperance is related in a similar way to pleasures concerned with hearing. No one, who delights excessively or as he ought in songs or instrumental music will be called intemperate or temperate on this account.* **1118a6–9; 607**

10. *The same is to be said in respect to those who take pleasures, except incidentally, in odors. We do not call intemperate people who delight in the fragrance of apples or roses or incense, but rather those who take pleasure in the perfume of cosmetics or the aroma of tasty dishes. The intemperate enjoy these pleasures because in this way things they desire are recalled. One may see others too taking delight in the aroma of food when hungry. But it pertains to the intemperate man to rejoice in this aroma as representing what is desirable.* **1118a9–16; 608–609**

11. *Other animals do not take pleasure according to these senses except incidentally. Hounds do not delight in the scent of rabbits for itself but in the prospect of food, the sense of which they get through smell. The lion does not rejoice in the lowing of the ox, but in the meal that he senses is at hand because of the sound he apparently enjoys. Likewise, he does not take pleasure in the sight of the stag or the wild she-goat which he discovers, but in the hope of possessing food.* **1118a16–23; 610–611**

12. *Temperance and intemperance then have to do with such pleasures as the other animals have in common with man. Hence gratifications of touch and taste seem to be servile and brutish.* **1118a23–26; 612**

COMMENTARY OF ST. THOMAS

595. After the Philosopher has treated fortitude concerned with terri- fying things which are destructive of man's life, he now takes up the ques-

tion of temperance concerned with pleasurable things which preserve human life, i.e., food and sex. On this point he does two things. First [1] he indicates what he intends to do. Next [2] he carries out his intention, at "Temperance is a mean etc." He says first that, after the treatise on fortitude, we must speak about temperance. He finds the reason for this succession in the fact that these two virtues agree in subject. Both pertain to the irrational part, according as that part of the soul is called irrational which is designed by nature both to conform to, and to obey reason, as was stated in the beginning (239). Such is the sensitive appetite to which the passions of the soul belong.

596. Hence all the virtues dealing with the passions must be placed in the sensitive appetite. Fortitude is concerned with the passions of fear and daring, which reside in the irascible part, but temperance is concerned with pleasures and pains, which reside in the concupiscible part. Consequently, fortitude is placed in the irascible part, but temperance in the concupiscible part.

597. We must consider that the pleasures of food and sex, with which temperance deals, are common to us and the brutes. Likewise, the fear of death, with which fortitude is concerned, is common to us and them. For this reason he notes particularly that these two virtues are of the irrational parts, because they belong to the irrational parts of the soul not only on account of the passions themselves but also because of the objects of the passions. There are some passions whose objects do not concern the brutes, like riches, honors and so on.

598. Then [2], at "**Temperance is a mean**," he begins to define temper-

ance. First he inquires what the matter of temperance is. Second [Lect. XX], at "Some desires are," he defines the act of temperance and of the opposite vices (1118b8). He considers the first point under two aspects. First [2] he proposes the matter of temperance in general. Next [3], at "We must now determine etc.," he inquires about its special matter. In regard to the first point he reviews three considerations which were discussed in the second book (342). The first is that temperance keeps a mean concerning pleasures. The second is that temperance deals also with sorrows that arise from the absence of pleasures. Temperance is less concerned, however, with sorrows than with pleasures because a thing acts more efficaciously by its presence than by its absence. The third is that intemperance likewise deals with pleasures and sorrows because contraries are concerned about the same thing.

599. Next [3], at "**We must now determine**," he inquires about the special matter of temperance. Three aspects claim his attention. First [3] he says what he intends to do. Then [4], at "There are," he distinguishes the kinds of pleasures. Last [5], at "Men are not called etc.," he shows with what kind of pleasures temperance deals. He says first that, since temperance deals with pleasures, we must now determine with what kind of pleasures it deals, so that the nature of temperance in particular may be known.

600. At "**There are**" [4] he distinguishes the kinds of pleasure. He says that some of them are of the soul, others of the body. Pleasures of the body are those that are completed in some bodily affection of an external sense. Pleasures of the soul are those that are completed by interior apprehension

alone. He gives an example of pleasures of the soul, beginning with the cause of pleasure—which is love. Every one takes pleasure from the fact that he possesses what he loves. In some men we find the love of honor; in others, the love of learning. This love is not perceived by an external sense but by an apprehension of the soul, which is interior. Therefore each of these, i.e., the man who loves honor or learning, rejoices on account of what he loves while he has it. This joy does not arise as the result of any bodily passion, but as a result of the mind's awareness alone.

601. Then [5], at "**Men are not called,**" he shows that temperance is not concerned with pleasures of the soul. He indicates three classes of these pleasures. Some [5] that have an appearance of propriety like honor and learning, as we have just noted (600), are pleasurable to the soul. For this reason he says that men are not called temperate or intemperate on account of such pleasures, since temperance seems to refer to pleasures which have something of shame about them. Concerned with the pleasures of honor and learning there are, however, certain other means and extremes pertaining to other virtues, as will be clearly shown in the fourth book (792–799).

602. Second [6], at "**Likewise, temperance,**" he now recalls other pleasures of the soul which consist in the sayings and deeds of men. He says that, as temperance is not concerned with pleasures of honor or learning, so also it is not concerned with other pleasures which are not of the body. Those who love to listen to and tell stories, and who waste the whole day talking about all kinds of contingent remarks and deeds (unnecessary and useless affairs) are said to be garrulous

but we do not call them intemperate. The reason is that intemperance has not only a futility about it, but also a certain baseness.

603. Third [7], at "**Those who are,**" he introduces a third class of pleasures of the soul which refer to external things, as money and friends. Hence he says that those, who are inordinately saddened by the loss of money and friends, are not called intemperate. But they can be called vicious from one aspect, because such sorrows do not show turpitude but only a disordered condition of the appetite. From this, that temperance is not concerned with any class of pleasures of the soul, he concludes that it does concern pleasures of the body.

604. Then [8], at "**but not with all,**" he shows that temperance is not concerned with all but with some bodily pleasures. First [8] he discloses that temperance does not regard the pleasures of the three senses which perceive through a separate (from the sense organ) medium. Next [Lect. XX], at "Any use of taste etc.," he explains in what manner temperance regards the pleasures of the other two senses which perceive through a contiguous (with the sense organ) medium (1118a26). He develops the first point [8] in three steps. First [8] he shows that temperance does not deal with the pleasures of the three previously mentioned senses. Next [11], at "Other animals do not etc.," he shows that such pleasures do not belong to brutes. Last [12], at "Temperance and intemperance etc.," he draws a conclusion from what has been said. Regarding the first he excludes the three senses. First [8] he proves that temperance does not concern pleasures of sight.

605. He says that temperance is not concerned with all bodily pleasures

which arise by means of the external senses. Those who take delight in things seen are not on that account called temperate or intemperate. He gives examples of three classes of visible objects. Some are the proper sensibles of sight, as colors. Others are common sensibles, which however are known most particularly through sight, as figures. Still others are sensible incidentally, as writing, by reason of what is signified through the writing.

606. This does not mean that virtue and vice are not to be encountered here. It happens in such matters that a person may take pleasure as he ought—this is the mean, or according to excess and defect, but this pertains to curiosity and not to intemperance which regards the more vehement pleasures.

607. Next [9], at "**Temperance is related,**" he proves that temperance does not have to do with the pleasures proper to hearing. He says that temperance is related in a similar way to the pleasures concerned with hearing; neither it nor intemperance is involved. If someone delights too much, or as he ought, in melodies (i.e., harmonies of human voices) and symphony (that is, the imitation of the human voice achieved through instruments) he will not be called temperate or intemperate on this account because these are not very vehement pleasures either. But this matter can belong to another virtue or vice.

608. Third [10], at "**The same is to be said,**" he proves that temperance does not have to do with the pleasures of smell. Regarding this we must consider that, as stated in the work *De Sensu et Sensato* (Ch. 5, 443b17 sq.; St. Th. Lect. XIII, 177–186), the kinds of scents are distinguished in two ways.

In one way in themselves. In the other way by a comparison with the species of savors. He says then that they are not called temperate and intemperate who take reasonable or excessive pleasure in odors considered in themselves but only when they take pleasure in odors incidentally, i.e., according as these odors coincide with the pleasures of taste and touch.

609. We do not call intemperate those who take pleasure in the fragrance of apples or roses or incense, which are species of odor in itself, but those who take pleasure in the aroma of foods or the perfume of cosmetics used by women. The intemperate delight in these pleasures on account of memory of certain things they long for. He clearly shows this by the example of the hungry who take pleasure in odors that do not interest them when they have eaten. So it is evident that these men do not take pleasure in odors as such but incidentally. In this way it pertains to the intemperate man—to whom the things represented by the odors are desirable—to take pleasure in those odors.

610. At "**Other animals do not take**" [11] he proves that pleasures arising from these senses belong only indirectly to other animals. He says that the brutes find pleasure via these three senses indirectly, i.e., by reference to taste and touch. He clearly shows this first in regard to the sense of smell. Hounds do not take pleasure in the scent of rabbits on account of the scent itself but on account of the expected food, the sensation of which they receive through smell. Second, he makes the same point in regard to the sense of hearing. He says that the lion takes pleasure in the lowing of an ox because the lion knows from the sound that a meal is near. Hence he seems to delight

in the bellow of the bull, but this is incidental. Third, Aristotle manifests the same thing in regard to seeing. He says that the lion does not take pleasure even at the sight of the stag or roe (which he calls a wild she-goat) when he finds something of this kind, but he is delighted by the hope of getting a meal.

611. The reason for these things is that the appetite of the other animals is moved by the instinct of nature alone. On this account animals take pleasure only in the things referring to the preservation of nature; that is why senses of this kind were given them. But senses have been given to men for the perception of sensible things leading in turn to a knowledge of reason which moves the appetite of man. So it is that man takes pleasure in the very appropriateness of sensible things considered in themselves, even if they are not ordered to the conservation of nature.

612. Then [12], at "**Temperance and intemperance**," he concludes from the premises that temperance has to do with such operations or pleasures as the other animals have in common with man. The same is true of intemperance. Hence pleasures of this kind seem to be servile and brutish because what we have in common with irrational animals is slavish and naturally subject to reason in us. Such are the pleasures of touch and taste which are the two senses besides the three mentioned before.

LECTURE XX
Temperance in Relation to Touch and Taste

TEXT OF ARISTOTLE (B.1118a26–1118b28) Chapter 10

1. Any use of taste made by temperance, or intemperance for that matter, is small or even non-existent. Taste here means the discernment of flavors, the occupation of wine-tasters and cooks sampling their own food. The intemperate do not take delight in these things or at least not much, but in the enjoyment by touch in the taking of food and drink and in the gratification of sex.   1118a26–32; 613–614

2. On this account a certain man by the name of Philoxenus Erichius—a voracious eater—prayed for a gullet longer than a crane's, so he could take more pleasure in the contact with his food.   1118a32–1118b1; 615

3. Touch, with which intemperance deals, is the most widely shared of all the senses. Rightly then intemperance seems worthy of reproach, since it does not exist in man as belonging to what is proper to him, but to what he has in common with the animals. To take pleasure in things of this sort and to love them above everything else is brutish. We exclude those pleasures of touch which are especially liberal, for instance, those taken in gymnasia by massages and heat-treatment. But the pleasure of touch, which the intemperate man seeks, is not that of the whole body but of certain parts of the body.   1118b1–8; 616–617

Chapter 11

4. Some desires are common, and others are proper and acquired.   1118b8–9; 618–619

5. The desire for food is natural, for everyone—when he is without it—desires food and drink (and sometimes both) just as, according to Homer, the young and growing man longs for a bed.
                                                                          1118b9–11; 620

6. Not all men, however, do want such and such a bed, or the same kinds of food. For this reason such desires seem to be peculiar to each of us, although they still have something of the natural. Different people enjoy different pleasures, and some persons take more pleasure in certain kinds of things than in chance objects.   1118b12–15; 621

7. In natural desires few men go astray and then only in one way, by excess. This happens when men eat or drink even to an immoderate fullness, which is an excess in the quantity of food nature requires. (Nature desires that its need be supplied.) These people are called "belly-mad" because they stuff their stomachs beyond need. Such persons become very brutish.
                                                                          1118b15–21; 622–623

8. But in regard to proper desires, many sin in numerous ways. Those who love such pleasures sin in delighting in things they ought not, or more than they ought, or as many of the foolish do, or not according to measure. The intemperate are excessive in all these ways because they enjoy certain odious things they ought not to enjoy. If pleasure may be taken, they delight in such things (as many do) more than they ought. Therefore, since intemperance is excess in regard to pleasures, it is despicable.   1118b21–28; 624–625

COMMENTARY OF ST. THOMAS

613. After the Philosopher has proved that temperance and intemperance do not deal with the pleasures of three senses but with the pleasures of two, i.e., taste and touch, he shows now what concerns the pleasures of taste and touch. He treats this from three aspects. First [1] he shows that temperance does not deal directly with the pleasures of taste but with pleasures of touch. Next [2], at "On this account etc.," he clarifies by an exam-

ple what he has affirmed. Finally [3], at "Touch, with which etc.," he draws a conclusion from what has been said. He says first that temperance and intemperance seem to make little or no use of what is proper to taste, namely, the discernment of flavors. Those who test wine use taste in this way; likewise, those who season food and sample to see whether their dishes have a delicious taste.

614. The intemperate do not take much delight in this, and they are not deprived of much pleasure when they do not perfectly discern the flavors of food. But all their delight consists in the enjoyment of certain pleasurable things, for instance, in eating, drinking, and sex—all of which occur through touch. It is obvious, therefore, that the pleasure of the intemperate has to do directly with the sense of touch, and with taste only because flavors make the enjoyment of food delectable. For this reason he previously said (608–611, 613) that intemperance has little use for taste, i.e., as it is ordered to touch, or no use, i.e., in respect to what belongs to taste in itself.

615. Then [2], at "On this account," he clarifies by an example what he had said. A certain man named Philoxenus Erichius who, since he ate his meals greedily, desired to have a throat longer than a crane's so the food would remain a long while in his throat. From this it is evident that he did not take pleasure in taste (which is active in the tongue and not in the throat) but in touch alone.

616. Next [3], at "Touch, with which," he draws a corollary from what has been said. The sense of touch, which temperance deals with, is the most common of all the senses because all the animals share in it. On this account intemperance seems to be really

despicable since it does not exist in man as belonging to what is proper to him, but to what he has in common with other animals. But to take pleasure in things of this sort and to love them as the highest goods seems to be especially animal-like. So it is that vices of intemperance possess the most disgusting shamefulness because they make man like the brutes. Therefore, by reason of such vices, man is rendered notoriously evil and blameworthy.

617. Someone might say that even in things pertaining to touch there is some properly human good that is not bestial. In order to answer this objection, he adds that we exclude from temperance those pleasures of touch that are especially liberal—appropriate for humans—and used according to reason. Such pleasures are found in gymnasia by massage and heat-treatment in view of the games (since some are going to wrestle or indulge in other sports). These pleasures of touch are not ordered to the desire of food or sex. The pleasure of touch which the intemperate man seeks is not that of the whole body but of certain parts of the body.

618. At "Some desires" [4] he shows how the act of temperance (in the previously mentioned matter) and of the opposite vices is constituted. Here he proceeds in twofold fashion. First [4] he explains his proposition. Next [Lect. XXII], at "Intemperance is more etc." (1119a21), he compares the vices of intemperance with certain other vices. Regarding the first he has three considerations. First [4] he treats intemperance, showing in what manner it operates in the previously investigated matter. Next [Lect. XXI], at "It does not happen etc.," he treats insensibility (1119a5). Last [Lect. XXI], at "The tem-

perate man etc.," he treats temperance (1119a12). In regard to the first he does two things. First [4] he shows how temperance is related to pleasures. Then [Lect. XXI], at "With regard to sorrows etc.," how it is related to sorrow (1118b29). Fear and sorrow are ordered to the same thing—we noted this before (584)—because sorrow has to do with present evils, as fear with future ones. So also desire (which concerns future goods) and pleasure (which concerns present goods) are ordered to the same thing. Temperance is in the reason concerned with sensual desires and pleasures. First [4] he makes a certain division of desires. Next [5], at "The desire for food etc.," he explains the division. Last [7], at "In natural desires etc.," he shows in what manner intemperance deals with both desires.

619. He says first that some desires are common and others are proper, being in addition to the common.

620. Then [5], at "**The desire for food**," he explains this division. First [5] he points out what the common desires are, saying that the desire for food in general is natural, as following the whole nature of the species and genus. Hence every man desires dry nourishment called food or moist nourishment called drink—and sometimes both—in order to succor a natural need, just as according to Homer[11] every man (the young as well as the growing, i.e., the adolescent) longs for a bed to rest in.

621. Next [6], at "**Not all men however,**" he points out what the proper desires are, saying that not all men want this particular bed—say a couch strewn with feathers and costly cover-

ing. Likewise, not everyone craves such and such a food, an expensive dish for example, or one daintily prepared. All do not yearn for the same gratification, but in such matters some desire one thing, others another. Hence desires of this kind seem to be our very own because we are not inclined to them by nature but by our own devising. Here nothing hinders a thing from being natural as belonging to the nature of the individual, although it may not belong to the nature of the genus or species. We see that different people enjoy different pleasures according to their different temperaments. And, because of natural temperament, some persons take more pleasure in certain kinds of things than in other commonplace objects.

622. At "**In natural desires**" [7] he explains in what manner intemperance has to do with the desires just mentioned. He says that in the natural desires that are common [7] few men go astray. Here transgression occurs only in one way, according as someone takes more than nature requires. This happens when someone eats or drinks what is given him in an immoderate amount, in which there is an excess in regard to the quantity of food nature needs. Nature desires only that the need be supplied. Therefore, that someone should take more than he needs is an excess above nature.

623. People of this type are called "belly-mad" (*gastrimargoi*: from *gastir* meaning belly and *marges* meaning a raving or madness) as if they had a raving or mad stomach, because they stuff nature beyond requirement. Such persons are very brutish because their

---

11   Cf. *Iliad* xxiv. 130.

only concern is to fill their bellies without discrimination like animals.

624. Next [8], at "**But in regard to proper desires,**" he explains in what manner intemperance has to do with proper desires or pleasures. He says that in regard to them, many sin in numerous ways, i.e., according to all the circumstances. Those who love such pleasures sin because they enjoy things they should not (like eating food which does not agree with them) or they sin by taking more enjoyment than they should (for instance, someone takes too much pleasure in eating agreeable dishes). Others sin by taking pleasure in foods without discernment—like most fools do—or finally they do not observe due measure in enjoyment, as they should. The intemperate are excessive in all these ways because they enjoy objects highly indecorous and blameworthy by nature, which they ought not to enjoy. Even when pleasure in certain things may be lawful, they commonly take more enjoyment than they ought without discrimination.

625. So he concludes that, since intemperance is excess in regard to pleasures of this kind, it is blameworthy like other excesses, as was explained in the second book (333–334).

LECTURE XXI

How Sorrows, Pleasures, and Desires Affect the Temperate Man

TEXT OF ARISTOTLE (*B.1118b28*) Chapter 11

1. *With regard to sorrows, one is not—as in fortitude—called temperate because he faces them, nor intemperate because he does not undergo them. But the intemperate man grieves more than he ought because he does not attain the pleasures he desires. But his pleasure is what causes him grief. On the contrary, the temperate man does not grieve for absent things, and in abstention from pleasure.*   **1118b28–33; 626–627**

2. *The intemperate man then desires all pleasures and he especially desires exquisite pleasures. He is led by sensual desire to choose pleasurable things in preference to all others. For this reason the intemperate man is saddened when he does not get the pleasure he wants; his desire in fact brings sorrow. He is like the incontinent person who is also saddened by pleasure.*   **1119a1–5; 628–629**

3. *It does not happen too often that men become deficient in pleasure, taking less enjoyment than they ought. Insensibility of this kind is not in keeping with human nature because the other animals differentiate foods in this, that they take pleasure in some things, and in others they do not. If someone finds no joy in anything and does not prefer one thing to another, he is a long way from being human. As this rarely happens, there is no special name for it.*   **1119a5–11; 630–631**

4. *The temperate man follows the golden mean in these matters. He does not delight in those shameful things in which the intemperate man takes the keenest pleasure, but rather he is saddened if they occur. In no way does he rejoice in things more ardently than he ought. He is not unnecessarily saddened by the absence of pleasurable things. If he desires them, he does so in the right measure. He does not crave pleasures more than he ought, nor when he ought not, nor according to any other unreasonable circumstance.*   **1119a11–15; 632**

5. *The temperate man desires whatever pleasures are useful to the health and well-being of the body, and he wants them according to right measure and as he ought. He desires other pleasures only if they are not a hindrance to health, nor opposed to what is honorable, nor beyond his means. One who is otherwise disposed takes more enjoyment than is reasonable. The temperate man is not of this nature but he acts according to right reason.* **1119a16–20; 633–634**

COMMENTARY OF ST. THOMAS

626. After the Philosopher has defined in what way temperance is concerned with pleasures, he now explains how it is concerned with sorrows. On this point he does two things. First [1] he shows that the brave, the temperate, and the intemperate are affected in different ways by sorrow. Then [2], at "The intemperate man then etc.," he makes clear his assertion. He says first that the brave, the temperate, and the intemperate are not disposed toward sorrow in the same way. The brave man indeed suffers many sorrows, but he is praised for this very endurance which is done nobly. This has already been remarked (584, 596). The temperate man however is not praised because he undergoes sorrows. Nor is the intemperate man blamed for not undergoing them, although the cowardly man is blamed. But the intemperate man is censured for the fact that he grieves more than he should. His sorrow does not arise from any harmful thing threatening him—which is the cause of the coward's sorrow—but he is sorry because

he does not get the pleasures he wants. Thus it is by its very absence that pleasure causes him grief. On the contrary the temperate man is praised for not grieving and for undertaking to abstain from pleasures that he does not desire very much. An effect that follows from the presence of a cause is more important than an effect that follows from its absence.

627. For this very reason fortitude is primarily concerned with sorrows which follow from the presence of harmful things. Temperance, however, is secondarily concerned with sorrows that follow from the absence of pleasures but primarily with pleasures following from the presence of pleasurable things.

628. Then [2], at "**The intemperate man then,**" he makes evident his assertion, that pleasure is the occasion of sorrow for the intemperate man. This happens because the intemperate man desires all pleasurable things. He strives after pleasure itself. On this account he strives after everything giving pleasure and he strives after the thing pleasurable in the highest degree in comparison with which he cares less for other delightful things. Therefore his pleasure is not guided by reason, but led by sensual desire to choose pleasurable things—especially those which are most abundantly so—in preference to all other useful and honorable goods. The intemperate put aside what is useful and decent in order that they may obtain pleasure. For this reason the intemperate man is saddened when he does not get the pleasure he wants. Sensual desire brings sorrow when it does not gain the thing coveted.

629. Although, according to a superficial likelihood, it seems incongruous that anyone should be saddened by reason of pleasure, nevertheless it is true that the intemperate man is distressed by pleasure. He is saddened only by its absence, like a ship lost by the absence of its pilot.

630. Next [3], at "**It does not happen,**" he considers the vice opposite to temperance which falls short in regard to pleasures. He says it does not happen very often that men become deficient in pleasures (so that they take less enjoyment than they ought, i.e., than is required for the health and well-being of the body and for decent living with others) in which this vice consists and which we have called insensibility in the second book (262, 342). This defect is not in keeping with human nature because the other animals differentiate foods in this, that they take pleasure in some, and in others not. So it seems to belong to the common nature of the genus to take some pleasure.

631. Therefore, if there is anyone, who does not take pleasure in anything, he seems to be a long way from being human. Because this rarely happens, he who falls short in this manner does not have a special name, except that before (262, 342) we called him insensible. When men abstain from pleasures for a useful or honorable reason, as merchants for gain and soldiers for victory, we do not have instances of insensibility. This is not beyond what is reasonable, as is the case with the vice.

632. At "**The temperate man follows**" [4], he explains in what way the temperate man should conduct himself in regard to the matter previously mentioned. He clarifies this point in two stages. First [4] he shows from what things the temperate man should abstain. Next [5], at "The temperate man desires etc.," he shows what things the temperate man should enjoy

and in what manner. He says first that the temperate man follows the golden mean regarding the preceding, i.e., pleasure, sorrow, and desire. First in regard to pleasure, he does not delight in those shameful things in which the intemperate take pleasure but rather is saddened if any such thing should occur. In general he does not rejoice in things he ought not, nor does he rejoice more ardently than he ought. Likewise he is not excessive according to any other circumstance. Next, in respect to sorrow he is not saddened beyond measure by the absence of pleasurable things. Third, in respect to desire he does not long for absent pleasures, because he cares little for them, or he longs for them in the right measure which is not excessive; he does not crave pleasure more than he ought, nor when he ought not, nor according to any other circumstance exceeding the norm of reason.

633. Then [5], at "**The temperate man desires,**" he shows which pleasures the temperate man enjoys and in what way. He says that the temperate man desires whatever pleasures are useful to the health of the body or its well-being so that he may be prompt and unimpeded for the things of this kind which he has to do. He desires these pleasures, however, according to the right measure and as he ought. If there are other pleasures not necessary for the two reasons previously named, the temperate man desires them under the three following conditions.

634. First, that they are not hindrances to health and well-being, like superfluous food or drink. Second, that they are not contrary to good, i.e., opposed to decency, like the pleasure of fornication. Third, that they are not beyond his means, i.e., they do not exceed a man's power to possess, as would be the case if a poor man desired to enjoy foods which are too costly. One who is so disposed that he longs for pleasures harmful to health and well-being, and contrary to decency, or exceeding his means takes more enjoyment than is reasonable. This does not pertain to the temperate man who loves these pleasures in conformity with right reason.

LECTURE XXII
Intemperance Compared with Cowardice and the Sins of Children

TEXT OF ARISTOTLE (B.1119a21–1119b18) Chapter 12

1. *Intemperance is more like the voluntary than fear is, because the former is motivated by pleasure, and the latter by pain. One of these (pleasure) is to be chosen, the other (pain) is to be avoided.*   1119a21–23; 635–636

2. *Pain stupefies and corrupts the nature of its possessor but pleasure does no such thing, and so is more voluntary.*   1119a23–25; 637

3. *For this reason intemperance is also more despicable; it is easy to become accustomed to the objects of temperance, for many occasions occur in a man's life and the habits can be practiced without danger. With terrifying objects, however, the reverse is the case.*   1119a25–27; 638–639

4. *There does not appear to be a likeness in voluntariety between fear itself and individual cases of it. Fear itself seems to be painless, but particular cases stupefy men by reason of pain, so that they throw away their arms and do other disgraceful actions. On this account these things seem to be done under compulsion.*   1119a27–31; 640

5. *In regard to intemperance the order is reversed. Particulars are voluntary because they are in accord with what a man strives for and desires, but the condition (intemperance) as a whole is less voluntary, for no one wants to be intemperate.*   1119a31–33; 641–642

6. *We transfer the name intemperance to the sins of children, for they do have a certain resemblance. But which one is named from the other does not concern us now. It is clear, however, that the later is derived from the earlier.*   1119a33–1119b3; 643

7. *This transference does not seem to be unsuitable. He who strives after what is base and increases greatly in evil must be punished. In this, sensual desire and the child are alike. Children live in accord with sensual desire and they strive most of all after pleasure. Therefore, if it will not be properly obedient, sensual desire will come to rule and increase considerably. To a stupid person the desire for pleasure is insatiable and omnipresent; and the exercise of desire increases its natural power. For the appetites are strong and violent, going even to the extent of interrupting the act of reasoning.*   1119b3–10; 644–646

8. *For this reason sensual desire and pleasure must be oderated, that is, sense pleasures must be few in number and in no way contrary to reason. Such a state is what we call obedient and disciplined. As a child must live according to the instructions of his tutor, so the concupiscent part must conform to reason; each, i.e., the tutor and reason aspires to the good. And the temperate man desires the right things at the right time as reason disposes. These then are the things we have to say about temperance.*   1119b11–18; 647–648

COMMENTARY OF ST. THOMAS

635. After the Philosopher has treated the act of temperance and the opposite vices, he now compares the sin of intemperance with other sins. He makes two points here. First [1] he compares intemperance with the vice of cowardice; and then, with the sins of children, at "We transfer the name" [6]. He clarifies the first point by a twofold distinction. First [1] he shows that intemperance has more of the voluntary than cowardice has. Next [4], at "There does not appear etc.," he shows that the voluntary in each vice is found in a different order. In regard to the first he does two things. First [1] he explains that intemperance has more of the voluntary than cowardice has. Next [3], at

"For this reason intemperance etc.," he infers a corollary from his discussion. He says first that intemperance is more like the voluntary than fear is, because intemperance has more of the voluntary. He proves this by two reasons.

636. The first of these is taken from what follows the voluntary and the involuntary as a property [1]. Everyone delights in what he does voluntarily, but is sad over what is contrary to his will. It is obvious that the intemperate man acts for the pleasure he desires. The coward, on the other hand, acts because of the pain which he flees. (Of course the operation of both is pleasing because not only is actual pleasure a matter for joy but even the hope of future pleasure.) But pain is a thing to be avoided and consequently is contrary to the will. So it is evident that intemperance is caused by what is of itself voluntary. Cowardice, however, is caused by something involuntary and repugnant. Therefore intemperance comes closer to the voluntary than cowardice.

637. He gives the second reason at "**Pain stupefies**" [2]. This is taken from the fact that ignorance causes an involuntary. Because pain follows from the presence of some contrary and harmful principle, it stupefies and corrupts the nature of its possessor. So it is that the mind of man is impeded by pain from proper knowledge. But pleasure is caused by the presence of an agreeable object that does not corrupt the nature. Hence pleasure does not stupefy nor corrupt the mind of the one who takes pleasure. From this it follows that intemperance, which operates on account of pleasure, has more of the voluntary than fear does—which is caused by pain.

638. Then [3], at "**For this reason intemperance**," he concludes that,

since in voluntary acts praise is due to the good and blame to the evil, the vice of intemperance is more disgraceful than the vice of cowardice which has less of the voluntary. To this he adds also another reason taken from the fact that a vice is more worthy of reproach insofar as it is more easily avoidable.

639. Each vice can be avoided by the contrary habit. For two reasons it is easy to become accustomed to good actions in matters of temperance. First, because pleasures in food, drink, and so forth take place very often in man's life. Hence there is no lack of opportunity to get used to virtuous actions in such matters. Second, becoming accustomed to good deeds of temperance does not constitute a danger. A person does not run any great risk in abstaining at times from some pleasure of touch. But quite the reverse is true in the vice of cowardice because the dangers from war happen rarely. Besides it is dangerous to get mixed up in wars. It follows then that the vice of intemperance is more worthy of reproach than the vice of cowardice.

640. Next [4], at "**There does not appear**," he shows that the voluntary in each vice is not found in the same order. First [4] he shows in what order the voluntary is found in cowardice; and second in intemperance, at "In regard to intemperance etc." [5]. He says first that fear does not seem to be voluntary in the same way for the universal and for particular cases. Universals seem to be without pain, for example, anyone may go into battle and attack the enemy. But particular happenings, for instance, that a man is wounded or routed or suffers other misfortune, bring such great pain that men are stupefied on account of these things—so much so that they throw away their arms and do other disgraceful actions.

Hence, since in reference to the universal these acts are voluntary, and in reference to the particular they become involuntary, they seem to be done under compulsion (inasmuch as a man is induced by an external principle to give up what he had previously wished).

641. At "**In regard to intemperance**" [5], he shows what the order is in regard to intemperance. He says that in this case the order is reversed, for singular things are voluntary in the highest degree because they occur in accordance with what a man strives for and desires. But the whole, considered in the abstract, is less voluntary—for instance, that anyone should commit adultery. No one desires to be intemperate in general. However particular things, by which a man becomes intemperate, are delightful.

642. The reason for this difference is taken from this: pain that causes fear pertains to the involuntary, as pleasure that causes intemperance pertains to the voluntary. Every inclination of the soul towards particular things is rather vehement. For this reason cowardice regarding particular things has more of the involuntary but intemperance more of the voluntary. Therefore in sins of intemperance it is exceedingly harmful to dwell upon the thought by which a man comes down to the particular that entices the will.

643. Then [6], at "**We transfer the name**," he compares the vice of intemperance with the sins of children. First [6] he states the agreement as to the name. Next [7], at "This transference etc.," he assigns the reason for the agreement. He says first that the name intemperance is transferred to the sins of children. This is more apparent in our language on the part of the virtue than on the part of the vice. We call

chastity a species of temperance, as we say that disciplined children are chastened. And those who are not disciplined can be called unchastised. So too one who is not chaste is said to be "incestuosus" (*in-castus*). The reason for this transference is that sins of this kind have a certain likeness, as will be shown later (647). But which of these is named from the other does not concern us now. It is clear, however, that the thing given the name later was called after that which had the name earlier.

644. Next [7], at "**This transference**," he assigns the reason for the previous transference in accordance with the likeness of the sin of intemperance to the sins of children. First [7] in respect to the necessity of chastising or restraining; and second [8] in respect to the manner of chastising and restraining, at "For this reason sensual desire etc." He says first that the transference of this name from one sin to another does not seem to be unsuitable because of the likeness according to which the transferences are made. It is necessary to punish, i.e., chastise and discipline, one who strives after improper things and whose evil inclination is greatly increased—points on which sensual desire and the child are in agreement.

645. This agreement seems to be reasonable because children live especially in accord with sensual desire, since they strive most of all after pleasure, which belongs to the nature of sensual desire. The reason why they strive after pleasure will be given in the seventh book (1531). Therefore, if the child and sensual desire are not rightly restrained by reason, they come to rule and increase so that the appetite for pleasure, i.e., sensual desire, will be lord and master.

646. The reason for this is that the

desire of pleasure is insatiable; indeed the more pleasure is enjoyed, the more it is desired in that pleasure itself is desirable. Hence, just as with a child and a simpleton so with sensual desire—the proper operation increases what is innate, i.e., that which is like them. If a child and a simpleton should be allowed to work according to their folly, the folly increases more in them. When a man satisfies sensual desire, it increases more in him and becomes master. This is especially true if sensual desire or pleasure is great by reason of the object, that is, things very delightful and also vehement for the man who desires and takes pleasure. This man is so influenced by pleasures that they may impede his knowledge or reasoning. The power of thought remains more efficient, the less sensual desire can dominate.

647. Then [8], at "**For this reason sensual desire,**" he shows the likeness between the two sins in respect to the manner of chastising or restraining. He

says that, since sensual desire and pleasure are vehement, they grow by themselves. For this reason they must be moderated, i.e., not excessive in extent or in vehemence of inclination or in number. They must not be contrary to reason in any way, especially in regard to the species of sensual desire or pleasure taken on the part of the object. That which is so disposed in the matter of sensual desires and pleasures is said to be readily obedient and chastised, i.e., corrected by reason. As a child must live according to the instructions of his tutor, so the faculty of sensual desire must be in conformity with reason. Each, i.e., reason and the tutor, aspires to the good. The concupiscent part in the temperate man is so disposed that he desires the right things, in the right way, and at the right time—as reason directs.

648. He says in conclusion that these are the things we have discussed about temperance. With this the third book ends.

BOOK FOUR
OTHER MORAL VIRTUES
LECTURE I
Liberality

TEXT OF ARISTOTLE (1119b22–1120a23) Chapter 1

1. Let us next discuss liberality,   1119b22; 649–650

2. which seems to be a mean in regard to wealth. No one is praised as liberal for exploits in war, or for conduct in matters with which the temperate man is concerned, or again for pronouncing judgments. But a man is praised as liberal for his giving and taking of wealth. (Wealth here means whatever can be evaluated in terms of money.)   1119b22–27; 651–653

3. Extravagance is the excess and miserliness, the defect in the use of wealth.
                                                                                      1119b27–28; 654

4. Miserliness is always attributed to people who are more careful about money than they should be.   1119b28–31; 655

5. But the intemperate are sometimes accused of extravagance by inference, for the incontinent and the intemperate are notorious as extravagant wasters. For this reason, too, they seem to be very depraved; indeed they have many vices. However, they are not properly called prodigal, for a spendthrift is a man who has acquired one vice, that of wasting his substance (he is ruined by his own fault). The dissipation of one's substance seems to be a kind of ruin of one's being, since a man lives by means of riches. It is in this sense that extravagance is treated here.
                                                                                      1119b31–1120a4; 656–657

6. Things that have utility—among which are riches—can be used well or badly. And the man who possesses the virtue concerned with particular objects uses each one best. Therefore he who has the virtue dealing with wealth will use riches to the best advantage. This man is the liberal man.   1120a4–8; 658

7. The spending and distribution of wealth seem to be the use of it; the acceptance and saving of wealth more properly are the possession.   1120a8–9; 659

8. For this reason liberality is rather the bestowal of wealth on the right persons than the acceptance of wealth from proper sources or the refusal from improper sources.   1120a9–11; 660

9. Virtue consists more in bestowing than in receiving benefits, more in performing good actions than in refraining from disgraceful ones. But it is obvious that the conferring of benefits and the performance of good deeds accompany disbursements.   1120a11–15; 661

10. Thanks and, in a special way, praise are due the giver and not the recipient.
                                                                                      1120a15–16; 662

11. Likewise, it is easier (not) to take from another than to give, for people prefer not to accept what belongs to others rather than give what is theirs.   1120a17–18; 663

12. People who give donations are called liberal, but not so those who receive gifts even honorably—such persons are praised for justice rather than liberality; those who simply accept gifts, however, are praised very little.   1120a18–21; 664

13. Of all virtuous men the liberal person is particularly loved, since he is useful because of his benefactions.   1120a21–23; 665

COMMENTARY OF ST. THOMAS

649. Having completed the study of fortitude and temperance which deals with means preservative of human life itself, he now begins to examine other mediums which concern certain subsidiary goods and evils. First he de-

fines the laudable mediums which are the virtues. Then [Lect. XVII], at "Shame is not properly spoken of etc." (1128b10), he defines the mediums that are not virtues but passions. On the first point he does two things. Initially, he considers the virtues that regard external things. Next [Lect. XIV], at "Some men seem to be etc." (1126b10), he considers the virtues pertaining to human actions. In regard to the first point he considers the virtues relating to riches. Second [Lect. VIII], at "Judging by the name etc." (1123a33), he considers the virtues having to do with honors. He handles the initial point in two ways. First he considers liberality. Then [Lect. VI], at "It seems logical etc." (1122a18), he investigates magnificence.

The first point he subdivides in a twofold manner. Initially he examines the matter of liberality and the opposite vices. Next [6], at "Things that have utility etc.," he defines their acts concerned with the proper matter. He discusses the initial point from two aspects. First [1] he shows that liberality has to do with wealth. Then [3], at "Extravagance is the excess etc.," he shows that there are opposite vices dealing with this matter. The first point is developed in three ways. Initially [1] he says what his intention is. Next [2], at "which seems to be a mean etc.," he shows the matter of liberality. Last [2], at "Wealth here etc.," he explains what he had said.

650. After the treatise on temperance, he says first that we must take up the study of liberality because of the likeness between liberality and temperance. As temperance moderates the desires of tactile pleasures, so liberality moderates the desire of acquiring or possessing external goods.

651. At "**which seems**" [2] he de-

fines the matter of liberality, saying that it is a certain mean in regard to wealth. This is obvious from the fact that a man is praised as liberal not in military affairs (with which fortitude is concerned), nor in tactile pleasures (temperance has to do with these), nor in judgments (which are matters for justice). But he is praised for the giving and taking, i.e., the acceptance of wealth—more in giving than in taking, as will be shown afterwards (660, 661, 665, 666, 683).

652. We must consider that something can be called the matter of moral virtue in two ways: in one way as the proximate matter (thus the passions are the matter of many moral virtues); in the other way, as the remote matter (thus the objects of the passions are called their matter). Accordingly the proximate matter of fortitude is fear and recklessness; the remote matter, the fear of death; the proximate matter of temperance is desires and pleasures but the remote matter is food, drink, and sexual acts. Hence we find that the proximate matter of liberality is desire or love of wealth, and the remote matter is wealth itself.

653. Then [2], at "**Wealth here**," he explains what is understood by the name "wealth," saying that the term signifies everything the value of which can be computed in dollars and cents, like a horse, a coat, a house, or whatever can be evaluated in cash. The reason is that to give or take these objects is the same as to give or take wealth.

654. At "**Extravagance is**" [3] he shows in what manner there are vices contrary to liberality. Here he makes the following points. First [3] he states his general intention, saying that extravagance and miserliness in the use of wealth are denominated such by excess and defect.

655. Next [4], at "**Miserliness is al-**vays," he mentions particularly that we always connect or charge with miserliness people who are more diligent, i.e., solicitous, about making or keeping wealth than they ought to be.

656. Finally [5], at "**But the intemperate**," he explains in what manner extravagance may be concerned with wealth. By extension the term "extravagance" is applied occasionally to the intemperate, for men who live riotously and dissipate their riches by overindulgence in food and sex are sometimes called spendthrifts. Hence they seem very depraved in the sense that they also possess many vices, like intemperance and extravagance. Although such men at times may be called extravagant, nevertheless they do not strictly deserve the name that is used to signify a vice consisting in inordinate waste or consumption of one's substance or riches. He proves the statement by the name "extravagance." The extravagant person is spoken of as ruined inasmuch as dissipation of his own riches, by which he ought to live, seems to destroy his existence—a thing sustained by riches.

657. This name should be predicated of a man in relation to himself because each thing receives its species and name from what pertains to it essentially. Therefore a man is truly called extravagant who dissipates his riches precisely because he does not have proper care of them. On the other hand, he who wastes his substance for some other reason, for example, intemperance, is not essentially a spendthrift but an intemperate person. It happens now and then that even the covetous and grasping waste their goods because of the influence of concupiscence. For the present then we are treating extravagance according as

some squander riches themselves and do not waste them in some other way.

658. Then [6], at "**Things that have**," he explains in what way liberality and the opposite vices function in this matter. Here he takes up two (three) points, considering first [6] the liberal man; next [Lect. III] the spendthrift, at "But the spendthrift etc." (1120b25); and finally [Lect. V], the miser, at "Illiberality etc." (1121b13). He treats the first point from two aspects. First [6] he examines the act of liberality; then [Lect. II], he states certain characteristics of it at "The liberal person however" (1120b5). He discusses the first point in a twofold manner. First [6] he shows what the principal act of liberality is; and next [Lect. II], what qualities this act should have, at "Since virtuous actions" (1120a23). He handles the initial point under two headings. First [6] he makes clear that the act of liberality is the proper use of wealth, by the following argument. Whatever has any utility can be used well or badly. But riches are sought because they have some utility. Therefore they can be used well or badly. Now the proper use of things pertains to that virtue which deals with those things. Consequently, the proper use of wealth belongs to liberality, which is concerned with wealth, as we proved before (651–653).

659. Next [7], at "**The spending**," he explains what the use of wealth is, indicating that it consists in spending which takes place by disbursements and gifts. To accept or save wealth is not to use it, for acceptance brings about possession, and saving is the preservation of wealth; acceptance is a kind of production, and saving is an habitual retention. Use, however, does not signify production or habit but act.

660. Finally [8], at "**For this reason**,"

he draws a conclusion from what has been said. First [8] he states it, inferring from the premises that it is more characteristic of a liberal man to distribute wealth to the right persons than to accept wealth from the proper sources (this pertains to a lawful increase of wealth), and to refuse wealth from improper sources (this pertains to removal of the contrary).

661. Then [9], at "**Virtue consists**," he substantiates the conclusion by five reasons. The first reason [9] is that it is more characteristic of virtue to bestow than to receive benefits because the act of benefitting is better and more difficult. Likewise, it is more characteristic of virtue to perform a good action than to refrain from an evil one, because departure from a terminus is the principle of motion to which the avoidance of an evil action is likened. But the performance of a good action is likened to the arrival at the goal which perfects motion. It is obvious when someone gives gifts that he bestows a benefit and performs a good action. On the other hand, it pertains to taking or acceptance to receive benefits worthily (inasmuch as a man acquires them from proper sources), and not to act unworthily (inasmuch as a man refuses them from improper sources). Consequently, it belongs to the virtue of liberality to give well rather than to receive worthily or refrain from reprehensible acceptance of gifts.

662. The second reason [10], at "**Thanks and**," follows. Praise and thanks are due in return for a good act. But each one of these is ascribed with better reason to the giver than the receiver, worthy or unworthy. Therefore, the virtue of liberality consists rather in giving than receiving.

663. The third reason is presented at "**Likewise it is easier**" [11]. Virtue is concerned with the difficult. But it is easier not to receive what belongs to others than to give what is one's own because a person giving what is his cuts himself away, so to speak, from what was a part of him. Therefore, the virtue of liberality more properly has to do with giving than receiving.

664. The fourth reason, beginning at "**People who**" [12], is taken from common usage. Men who give gifts are said to be liberal in a marked degree; those who do not accept dishonest gifts are commended not so much for liberality as justice, and those who simply accept presents are praised very little. Therefore, the virtue of liberality seems to be concerned in a special way with giving gifts.

665. The fifth reason is given at "**Of all virtuous men**" [13]. Among all virtuous men the liberal person is especially loved not by an honorable friendship—as if liberality was a most excellent virtue—but by a friendship of utility precisely as he is useful to others. The liberal are indeed useful in this that they make disbursements. Therefore, liberality deals especially with giving gifts.

LECTURE II
The Act of Liberality

TEXT OF ARISTOTLE (1120a23–1120b24) Chapter 1

1. *Since virtuous actions are good both in themselves and in their intent, the man will give with a good intention and in the right circumstances. He will make gifts to the proper persons, at the opportune time, of whatever gifts are fitting and with all the requisites of reasonable giving.*   **1120a23–26; 666**

2. *Besides, he will give with pleasure and without sadness, for a virtuous action is pleasurable and either not sad at all or in a very slight degree.*   **1120a26–27; 667**

3. *The man, however, who gives to the wrong persons, or not with the right intention, but for some other cause will be called not liberal but by some other name.*   **1120a27–29; 668**

4. *Nor will anyone be called liberal who gives with sadness, for he would choose money rather than the generous deed. Such a one surely is not liberal.*   **1120a29–31; 669**

5. *Nor will a liberal man accept a gift from an improper source, since an accepting of this sort is not characteristic of one who does not pay homage to wealth. And certainly he will not be inclined to seek favors, for it is not the usual thing that a man who bestows benefactions readily accepts them.*   **1120a31–34; 670**

6. *He will take from the proper sources, i.e., from his own possessions, for money is not good itself but necessary that he may have something to give. He will not give to everyone so that he can give to the right persons when and where it is fitting.*   **1120a34–1120b4; 671**

7. *The liberal person, however, is characteristically eager to be generous, keeping things of lesser value for his own use, for he is not solicitous about himself.*   **1120b4–6; 672**

8. *Liberality makes allowance for the amount of one's wealth, since the liberal deed does not lie in the number of gifts but in the condition of the giver who gives according to his means. Nothing hinders the smaller donor from being more liberal, if he contributes from more limited resources.*   **1120b7–11; 673**

9. *People who inherit wealth—not having any experience of need—are more liberal than those who earn their money. All men esteem more highly what they themselves have produced, like parents and poets.*   **1120b11–14; 674**

10. *It is not easy to increase the wealth of the liberal man who is inclined neither to accept nor keep riches but rather to distribute them, placing value not on riches themselves but on the bestowal of them.*   **1120b14–17; 675**

11. *Men bring the accusation against fortune that those who deserve wealth most do not become rich—a fact that has a reasonable explanation. Here (and the same is true in other matters) it is not possible for a person to possess money who does not trouble himself about it.*   **1120b17–20; 676**

12. *The liberal man, however, will not give to the wrong persons, nor at the wrong time, nor in any other wrong manner, for he would not be directed to these things according to liberality. Besides, by this squandering he would be without the resources on which to draw. As has been explained, the liberal man then spends according to his means and in the way he ought.*   **1120b20–24; 677**

COMMENTARY OF ST. THOMAS

666. After the Philosopher has made clear what the principal act of liberality is, he now shows what its qualities should be. First [1] he explains the quality of the principal act; and next [5] the qualities of the secondary acts, at

"Nor will a liberal man accept." In regard to the initial point he does two things. First [1] he shows what should be the quality of giving which is the principal act of liberality. Then [3] he shows that other kinds of donations do not pertain to liberality, at "The man, however, etc." He treats the first point in a twofold manner. First [1] he explains that the giving of the liberal man should be endowed with circumstances because all virtuous operations ought to be good, directed by reason according to the required circumstances and ordered to a good end. Since, then, giving is the principal act of liberality, it follows that the liberal man should give with rectitude of intention and of deed, i.e., in conformity with the norm of reason. This means that he bestows on the proper person, in a fitting manner and according to all other requisite circumstances called for by right reason.

667. Next [2], at "Besides, he will give with pleasure," he shows that the giving of a liberal person should be enjoyable. This is what he means saying that the liberal man gives cheerfully, or at least without sadness. It is true of any virtue, as evident in previous discussions (265–279, 371–378), that virtuous action is either pleasurable or at least without sadness. If the virtuous man has some sadness mingled with his activity, it will be very slight compared with what other men suffer. This was said before in regard to the brave man who, even if he does not take much pleasure in his operation, nevertheless is not made sad or at least has less sadness than anyone who undergoes trials of this kind in his activities.

668. Then [3], at "The man, however," he brings out that other donations do not pertain to the liberal man.

First [3] he says—speaking of disbursements that lack the proper circumstances—that one who gives to the wrong persons, or not for an honorable motive but for some other reason, good or bad, is not called liberal. But he is given a different name according to the difference of the end for which he gives, since moral matters take their species and name from the end.

669. Second [4], at "Nor will anyone," he affirms that a man who gives with sadness is not liberal. The reason is that the cheerless giver seems to prefer wealth to the virtuous action of honorable giving—which is not the case with a liberal person.

670. Next [5], at "Nor will a liberal man accept," he explains the nature of the secondary acts of liberality like receiving and so on. Here he makes two points, showing first [5] what the liberal person avoids in accepting; and then [6] what he should observe, at "He will take etc." On the first point he makes two comments. The first is that the liberal man does not take from improper sources, for to take in this way does not seem becoming to a man who does not highly prize wealth. The second is that the liberal man is not quick to make requests. As in the natural order, what is greatly active has little receptivity, for example, fire, so in the moral order the liberal person, who is prompt in making benefactions, is not eager to accept benefits from others, i.e., to be easily receptive.

671. Then [6], at "He will take," Aristotle shows what the liberal man should observe in taking and retaining. He makes three observations, of which the first is that the liberal man takes from the proper sources, i.e., from his own possessions and not from others, since he seeks wealth not as a good itself but as something necessary

for making gifts. The second is that he does not neglect the care of his own goods because he wants to have enough to bestow on others. The third is that he does not give to everyone but holds back so he can give to the right persons at a fitting place and time.

672. Then [7], at "**The liberal person**," he states four properties of liberality. The first [7] is that it pertains to the liberal person to give eagerly and generously, not however without right reason but in such a way that what he gives is more than what he retains, because he keeps less for himself than he gives to others. He is indeed content with a few things for himself but if he wants to care for many people, he must distribute much more. It is not a mark of the generous man to have himself alone in mind.

673. At "**Liberality makes allowance**," he gives the second property [8], saying that liberality is attributed according to the relative quantity of a man's substance or riches. Hence there is no reason why someone who bestows smaller gifts may not be judged more liberal, if he gives from more moderate means.

674. He presents the third property at "**People who inherit**" [9], affirming that persons who inherit riches from their parents are more liberal than those who acquire them by their own labor. He assigns two reasons for this. The first is that people who are given wealth by their parents have never felt the pinch of need. Consequently, they are not afraid to spend, as those are who have experienced poverty at one time. The second reason is that all men naturally love their own works; parents love their children, and poets, their poems. Likewise, those who acquire riches by their labor look upon them as their own works and rather desire to keep them.

675. He presents the fourth property at "**It is not easy**" [10]. He considers this point under three aspects. First [10] he indicates the property, saying that the liberal man is not easily made rich, since he is not disposed to accept or keep riches but rather to distribute them in gifts and disbursements. Nor does he value riches for themselves but for their distribution.

676. Next [11], at "**Men bring the accusation**," he makes clear by a certain sign what he had said. Since the liberal do not readily become wealthy, the common people blame fortune—to which they attribute riches—because those who would be especially deserving (i.e., the liberal who give generously to others) are not rich. But Aristotle says that this is not an unreasonable occurrence, for it is not possible that a person should possess wealth who troubles himself very little about it, just as it is not possible that anything else which a man does not care for should be retained.

677. Finally [12] he excludes a false opinion at "**The liberal man, however, will not.**" It was not said that the liberal man does not care about riches because he gives to the wrong person, or at the wrong time, or in the wrong manner according to some other circumstance. The reason is both that such an operation would not be liberal and that the liberal person would be hindered in this way from truly generous action, for by reason of useless waste he would lack the means to make the most worthy disbursements. As has been explained (658–659), he is called liberal, then, who gives donations in the proper manner and according to the condition of his own resources.

LECTURE III
Extravagance

TEXT OF ARISTOTLE (1120b24–1121a15) Chapter 1

1. *But the spendthrift is a man who squanders. Hence we do not call tyrants spendthrifts, for it is not easy to be excessive in gifts and expenditures with a vast sum of money in their possession.*   **1120b24–27; 678**

2. *Since liberality is the mean concerned with the giving and taking of wealth, the liberal man will both give and expend whatever he ought and in the way he ought, whether the sum be large or small. He will also do this gladly.*   **1120b27–30; 679**

3. *Likewise he will accept both large and small amounts from the proper sources and under the proper conditions. Since virtue consists in the mean regarding both (taking and giving), he will do both as he ought because virtuous taking goes hand in hand with virtuous giving, while improper taking is contrary to virtuous giving. Accordingly, the operations that go hand in hand exist at the same time in the liberal man, but contrary operations obviously cannot.*   **1120b30–1121a1; 680**

4. *If it should happen that he spends inopportunely and unsuccessfully, he will be sad but in a moderate and fitting manner, for it is characteristic of virtue to be pleased and saddened at the proper things and in the proper circumstances.*   **1121a1–4; 681**

5. *But the liberal man is disposed to share his wealth with others. He is even willing to suffer loss by not valuing money highly.*   **1121a4–5; 682**

6. *He is more grieved over failure to make an appropriate outlay than over an inopportune expenditure—a thing displeasing to Simonides.*   **1121a5–7; 683**

7. *The spendthrift, however, sins in these matters too. Besides, he neither takes pleasure in the right things, nor is saddened when he should be. This will be clarified by what follows.*   **1121a8–10; 684**

8. *We have seen that extravagance and miserliness pertain to excess and defect, and occur in two actions, namely, giving and taking. Extravagance then abounds in giving and falls short in taking. On the other hand, miserliness falls short in giving and abounds in taking, except in trifling things.*   **1121a10–15; 685**

COMMENTARY OF ST. THOMAS

678. After the Philosopher has finished the study of the liberal man, he now begins the consideration of the spendthrift. First he treats the person who is altogether extravagant; and next [Lect. IV] the person who is partly extravagant and partly liberal at "But, as we have noted etc." (1121a30). In regard to the first, he does two things. Initially [1] he considers the spendthrift as such. Then [8] he makes a comparison between the spendthrift and the miser, at "We have seen etc." He clarifies the initial point by a twofold distinction. First [1] he shows in what respect the spendthrift is excessive; and next [2], of what nature his act is, at "Since liberality is the mean etc." Although a man may be called liberal when he spends according to his means, he is called extravagant when he spends or gives beyond his means. From this he concludes that tyrants, who have an inexhaustible supply of wealth—usurping as they do public goods for themselves—are not called extravagant. The reason is that it is not easy for tyrants to exceed the amount

of their riches by donations and expenditures because of the great amount of their possessions.

679. Then [2], at "**Since liberality,**" he discloses what the act of the spendthrift is. Because opposites are mutually revealing, he first [2] resumes what was said about the act of the liberal man. Next [7], he shows how the act of the spendthrift is constituted, at "The spendthrift, however, etc." On the first point he proceeds in two ways. First [2] he reviews how the liberal man should conduct himself in the matters principally pertaining to him, i.e., in giving and in the pleasure of giving; and next [3] in matters secondarily pertaining to him, at "Likewise he will accept." He says first that, since liberality is a certain dealing with giving and taking of wealth, the liberal person disposes of his funds by making gifts and disbursements—and this in agreement with right reason—in the proper way, of the proper things, and according to other appropriate circumstances. By this the liberal man is distinguished from the spendthrift; by the fact that he gives both in large and small amounts he is distinguished from the munificent man, who is concerned only with great donations; by the fact that he gives with pleasure he differs from the miser who is saddened by the giving away of his wealth.

680. Next [3], at "**Likewise he will accept,**" Aristotle reviews the way the liberal man should act in matters which secondarily pertain to liberality. He touches first [3] on the liberal man's reaction to taking; and next [4], to sadness at "If it should etc." He says first that the liberal person accepts from the proper sources and observes all proper conditions. Since the virtue of liberality abides by the golden mean in regard to both, i.e., taking and giving, the liberal man will perform both as he ought—worthy acceptance going hand in hand with worthy giving. But acceptance that is not virtuous is contrary to virtuous giving because the two proceed from contrary causes. Virtuous giving proceeds from the fact that a man prefers the reasonable good to the desire for wealth. But dishonorable taking arises from placing the desire of wealth before the reasonable good. Things that go hand in hand exist at the same time in the same subject, but not things that are contrary. Hence virtuous giving and taking that accompany one another are united in the liberal person, but dishonorable taking is not found in him together with virtuous taking, its contrary.

681. Then [4], at "**If it should,**" he explains how the liberal man reacts to sadness arising from the loss of wealth. He develops this point in three steps. First [4] he shows in what manner the liberal person is saddened by disordered giving, affirming that if some of his own money be lost by reason of foolish spending and unfortunate conditions, he becomes sad as any virtuous man is saddened by doing something contrary to virtue. In this sorrow, however, he observes the rule of reason with moderation and as he should. The reason is that it is characteristic of the virtuous person to be delighted and to be saddened by the right thing and in the right manner.

682. Next [5], at "**But the liberal man,**" he shows how the generous person is saddened by the privation of wealth, saying that he is disposed to share his wealth, i.e., is inclined to possess it in common, as it were, with others. He can, without grief, permit someone to injure him in money mat-

ters because he does not attach great importance to wealth.

683. Third [6], at "**He is more grieved,**" he discloses in what manner the liberal man is grieved at inappropriate retention of money, explaining that he is more grieved or saddened over not using his wealth in gifts or expenditures than over spending something which he should not have spent. The reason is that he is more concerned with giving than taking and keeping, although this would not please Simonides, a certain poet, who said we ought to do the opposite.

684. Then [7], at "**The spendthrift, however,**" he explains by the premises how the act of the spendthrift is constituted, saying that the spendthrift sins in all the preceding matters, i.e., not only in giving and accepting but also in taking pleasure and grieving because he is neither delighted nor sad-dened by the right things and in the right way. This will be made clearer by what follows.

685. Next [8], at "**We have seen,**" he compares extravagance to miserliness in regard, first to opposition; and second [Lect. IV] to the gravity of the sin, at "The things that" (1121a16). He affirms, as was noted before (654), that extravagance and miserliness are constituted by excess and defect in two things, viz., taking and giving. He says this because expenditures, which pertain to liberality, are included under giving. And it is precisely in expenditures that the spendthrift and the miser exceed and fall short in opposite things. The spendthrift is excessive in giving and in not taking. But the miser, on the contrary, is deficient in giving and excessive in taking, except perhaps in trifling things that he gives and does not care to take.

LECTURE IV
The Gravity of Extravagance

TEXT OF ARISTOTLE (*1121a16–1121b12*) Chapter 1

1. The things that are proper to extravagance are not increased very much at the same time, because a man cannot easily take nothing and at the same time give with an open hand to everyone. A generous simpleton—such the spendthrift seems to be—is soon separated from his money. A person of this sort, though, is somewhat better than the miser, for he is quickly set right both by age and want.   **1121a16–21; 686–687**

2. He can attain the mean of virtue, for he possesses qualities of the liberal person. He gives and does not take, although he does neither of these things properly and as he ought. If indeed he performs them out of custom or by reason of some change, he will become liberal, for he will then give to the right persons and not take from the wrong sources. For this reason he does not seem to be entirely evil in the moral sense, for it is not characteristic of an evil or vicious person, but of a foolish one, to give excessively and not to take.   **1121a21–27; 688–689**

3. In this way the spendthrift seems to be much better than the miser because of what has been said and because he benefits many people while the miser benefits no one, not even himself.
                                                      1121a27–30; 690

4. But, as we have noted, many spendthrifts take from tainted sources and in this way they are ungenerous.   **1121a30–32; 691**

5. They are inclined to take because they want to spend. But they cannot readily take enough, for their resources quickly vanish forcing them to acquire from others. Likewise they care nothing about what is right, and take from any quarter whatsoever. They want to give presents, so the how and the whence make no immediate difference to them.
                                                      1121a32–1121b3; 692–693

6. For these reasons their donations are not liberal, being good neither in motive nor mode. But they make rich those who would better remain poor. They would give nothing to good men, yet are generous with flatterers and others who provide them with other pleasures.
                                                      1121b3–7; 694

7. Therefore, many of them are intemperate, for being inclined to spend, they waste their resources by intemperance. Moreover, since they do not order their life to good, they turn aside to sensual pleasures.   **1121b7–10; 695**

8. The spendthrift then who will not learn (the way of virtue) suffers consequences. But with effort he may attain the mean and adopt the right attitude.   **1121b10–12; 696**

COMMENTARY OF ST. THOMAS

686. After the Philosopher has explained the opposition between extravagance and miserliness, he now shows that miserliness is the more serious fault for three reasons. The first reason [1] is taken from the mutability of extravagance: although not readily increased it is easily eliminated. Hence he says that the things belonging to extravagance cannot at the same time be increased very much, so that a per-son takes nothing and gives to everyone because resources or riches are quickly exhausted for those who spend recklessly, like the simple and senseless. And spendthrifts seem to be of this type. Since then a vice, which is not increased very much but easily remedied, is not so serious, it follows that the spendthrift is somewhat better, i.e., less evil than the miser.

687. The spendthrift is easily cured

of his vice in two ways. In the first way by age because the older a man grows the more inclined he is to keep things and not give them away. The reason is that riches are desired to supply the needs of man, and as these needs become greater so a man is more prone to husband and not hand out his wealth. Second, the spendthrift is cured by poverty resulting from excessive giving, for poverty prevents extravagant spending both by reason of the impossibility of further giving and the experience of need.

688. At "**He can attain**" [2] he gives the second reason, which is based on the likeness of extravagance to liberality. Hence he says that the spendthrift can easily be directed to the mean of virtue on account of the similarity he has with the liberal man. Since the spendthrift generously gives and does not readily take, he has qualities possessed by the liberal person. But he differs from the liberal man in not doing either of these actions properly and as he ought, i.e., according to right reason. Therefore, if he is induced to perform these things as he ought, either by custom or by some change in age or fortune he will become liberal so that he will give to the right persons and not take from the wrong sources.

689. He concludes from this that the spendthrift does not seem to be evil precisely as it pertains to moral virtue, which directly regards the power of the appetite. It is not characteristic of an evil or perverted appetite or of an effeminate mind to give excessively and not to take. This belongs rather to a kind of stupidity. Thus it seems that extravagance does not belong so much to moral depravity, which regards the inclination of the appetite to evil, as to a lack of common sense.

690. At "**In this way**" [3] he presents

the third reason taken from a defect in extravagance. That the spendthrift is much better than the miser is apparent not only from the two reasons already stated but also from a third, namely, the spendthrift helps many by his giving, although he may hurt himself by giving extravagantly. The miser, on the other hand, benefits no one for he fails in giving; he does not benefit even himself, for he fails in spending.

691. Then [4], at "**But, as we have noted,**" he considers the man who is a blend of spendthrift and miser. First [4] he shows in what manner some spendthrifts have a bit of illiberality. Next [7] he draws some conclusions from what has been said, at "Therefore." On the initial point he first [4] explains how some spendthrifts sin in taking; and then [6] how they conduct themselves in giving, at "For these reasons." In regard to this first, he presents his proposition [4], saying that many who are extravagant in unnecessary donations are also ungenerous in some way, taking as they do from the wrong sources.

692. Next [5], at "**They are inclined,**" he assigns two reasons. The first is that spendthrifts are disposed to take because they want to spend their goods in superfluous gifts and expenditures. They readily succeed in this, for their resources are quickly depleted. Hence, in order that they may satisfy their desire regarding unnecessary gifts and disbursements, they are forced to acquire dishonestly from some other place the means they do not possess.

693. The second reason is that they give rather out of a desire of giving than according to right reason, tending, as it were, to some good. They want to give presents but it makes no difference to them how or whence

these come. Consequently, they do not concern themselves about what is right and so take from any source without distinction.

694. Then [6], at "**For these reasons,**" he explains how spendthrifts may be at fault in making donations. He declares that, because they do not care about what is right, their gifts are neither liberal nor good, either in motive or circumstance. But sometimes they make rich evil men who would be better off poor—men who abuse their riches and thereby cause harm both to themselves and others. Yet they would give nothing to men who regulate their lives according to virtue. Thus they are deficient in giving. They are, however, generous with sycophants or others who give them pleasure in any way whatsoever, e.g., buffoons or panderers. In this way they go to excess in giving.

695. Next [7], at "**Therefore,**" he draws two conclusions from the prem-

ises. The first is that many spendthrifts are intemperate. This is evident first, because (being inclined to spend), they readily waste their substance by intemperance in food and sex, from which many people are restrained by fear of the cost. Second, because they do not order their life to an honorable good, consequently they turn aside to the pleasures of sense. These two (the honorable and the pleasurable) are desirable in themselves—the honorable according to rational desire, the pleasurable according to sensual desire. The useful refers to both.

696. He draws the second conclusion [8], at "**The spendthrift,**" pointing out what is clear from the premises: that if the spendthrift cannot be attracted to virtue, he falls into the previously mentioned vices. But if he possesses zeal for virtue, he will easily attain the mean so that he will give and refrain from taking according to what he ought, as was stated before (688).

LECTURE V
The Incurableness of Illiberality

TEXT OF ARISTOTLE (*1121b12–1122a17*) Chapter 1

1. *Illiberality, however, is incurable for it seems that old age and every other disability make men miserly. Besides, it is more innate to men than extravagance because more men are lovers of wealth than donors of it.*   **1121b12–16; 697–698**

2. *Likewise illiberality can greatly increase, and is very diversified since many species of it seem to exist. It is made up of two elements, namely, deficient giving and needless grasping, which are sometimes found separately and not always together in all subjects. Some indeed are always getting and others never giving.*   **1121b16–21; 699**

3. *All those who are given names like stingy, grasping, close, fall short in giving. But they do not covet the goods of others, nor do they want to acquire them. With some this is due to a kind of moderation and fear of disgrace. They seem to be, or say that they are, careful about this in order not to be forced at times to do anything dishonorable. Among these are the cumin-splitter and anyone of the type designated before by reason of an excessive desire of not giving to anyone. Some again refrain from what is not theirs for fear that their taking of what belongs to others should make it easy for others to take what is theirs. Therefore, they are content neither to give nor to take.*   **1121b21–31; 700–702**

4. *Others again are immoderate in their taking by accepting anything and from any quarter, for example, those who engage in disreputable enterprises, those who live from the proceeds of prostitution, and such like, and usurers who lend small sums and at high rates. All of these receive more than they should and from reprehensible sources. Common to them is sordid gain because they all become infamous for the sake of a little money. People who wrongly take great sums from wrong sources are not called illiberal, for instance, usurers who plunder cities and despoil sacred places but rather wicked, impious, and unjust.*   **1121b31–1122a7; 703**

5. *Among the illiberal, however, we count the gambler, the despoiler of the dead and the robber—shameful profit-makers. For the sake of evil gain, these engage in occupations having the stamp of infamy. Some run the risk of very great danger for gain, while others would take from friends to whom they should give. In both cases, those wishing to enrich themselves are makers of shameful profit. It is clear then that all taking of this kind is opposed to liberality.*   **1122a7–13; 704**

6. *Appropriately then illiberality is said to be the vice opposed to liberality, for it is a graver evil than extravagance. Likewise men sin more by illiberality than by extravagance. So far, therefore, we have discussed liberality and the opposite vices.*   **1122a13–17; 705–706**

COMMENTARY OF ST. THOMAS

697. After the Philosopher has finished the treatise on extravagance, he now treats illiberality, examining it under three headings. First [1] he states a quality of illiberality. Next [2], he distinguishes the modes, i.e., the species of illiberality, at "Likewise etc." Last [6], he makes a comparison of illiberality with its opposite at "Appropriately

then etc." He says first that illiberality is incurable, and assigns two reasons for this. The first reason is that human life, and even earthly things, tend to be defective for the most part. It is obvious from experience that old age and every other disability or defect make a man parsimonious, because it seems to him that he is very much in need.

Therefore, he has a great desire for external things that supply the wants of man.

698. The second reason is this. That to which man is naturally inclined cannot easily be removed from him. But man is more inclined to illiberality than extravagance. A sign of this is that more lovers and custodians of money exist than donors. What is natural is found in the majority of cases. And nature inclines to the love of riches to the extent that man's life is preserved by them.

699. Then [2], at "Likewise," he distinguishes the modes or species of illiberality. On this point he does three things. First [1] he shows that illiberality is considered from two aspects, viz., excess in getting and defect in giving. Next [3], at "All those who," he gives the species which are understood according to deficiency in giving. Last [4], at "Others again," he gives the species that are able to be distinguished according to unnecessary taking. He says first that illiberality is increased greatly; it extends to a multitude of things and is diversified inasmuch as there are many kinds of illiberality. Although illiberality may exist in two forms, defect of giving and excess of taking, not all illiberal people sin in both ways as though they possessed the whole nature of illiberality. But it is found separately in various persons so that some abound in taking who nevertheless do not fall short in dispensing, like the spendthrift previously considered (678). Others, however, fall short in dispensing and, notwithstanding, do not abound in taking.

700. Next [3], at "**All those who,**" he sets down the types of persons who are deficient in giving. He says that some are called stingy who spend very little;

others are called grasping who retain nearly everything from a defect in giving. Still others are called closefisted, or cumin-splitters from an excessive tenacity they manifest in refusing to give the smallest thing without a return. However, these are not excessive in taking because they do not covet the goods of others, nor do they care much about accepting gifts. This happens for two reasons.

701. The first reason is that they pass up these opportunities out of moral consideration and fear of turpitude. They seem to keep what is theirs—they even say so expressly—lest, if they give what they have, they may be forced sometimes to a shameful act because of need. Likewise, they are unwilling to accept the goods of others since they think it dishonorable. They even hesitate lest they be induced to something unseemly by those who gave to them. Among these seem to be the skinflint or the cumin-splitter, so named because he has an aversion to giving anyone even a tiny seed. The same reason holds in all similar cases.

702. The second reason is that some refrain from taking other people's goods because they fear they may have to give, as if it were not easy for men to take the things that belong to others and others not to take the things which are theirs. On this account they are content neither to give nor to take.

703. Then [4], at "**Others again,**" he mentions the species of illiberality in regard first [4], to those who take in a disgraceful way; and next [5], who take in an unjust way, at "Among the illiberal." He says first that certain illiberal persons are immoderate in taking, not caring what or whence they take or profit. Some benefit from cheap and servile operations. Others, like pimps,

make profit from sordid and unlawful dealing, e.g., prostitution and the like. Still others enrich themselves by unjust exaction, for instance, usurers and those who want at least a little gain from a large gift or loan. All these receive from reprehensible sources, i.e., mean or shameful works, or they receive more than they should, like usurers who take more than the interest. All have profit, and this paltry, in common. Those who make enormous profits, and make them by shameful means—they are considered disgraceful for this reason—are not called illiberal but rather wicked, unjust, and impious against God, as if they were criminals. Men of this caliber are not so designated even though they take when they ought not and what they ought not, for example, usurpers who despoil cities and temples.

704. Next [5], at "**Among the illiberal,**" he mentions those who take unjustly, like the gambler who makes money by throwing dice, the fellow who steals from the dead (formerly buried in rich apparel), and the robber who plunders the living. All these are enriched by shameful means, inasmuch as, for the sake of gain, they engage in certain occupations considered disgraceful. This agrees with what was said about those persons just mentioned (703). But in these there is a special reason for turpitude. Some, for

example, the despoiler of the dead and the robber expose themselves to great danger in doing things punishable by law. Others, namely, gamblers want to take something from their friends with whom they play, although it is more appropriate to liberality to give something to friends. It is obvious then that both types, by wanting to enrich themselves from improper sources, are makers of shameful profits. It is necessary, therefore, to say that all the previously mentioned taking or accepting is opposed to liberality.

705. Then [6], at "**Appropriately then,**" he explains illiberality by comparison with the opposite vice, saying that illiberality is fittingly named from the contrast with liberality. It always happens that the worse vice is more opposed to the virtue. But illiberality is worse than extravagance, as was shown before (686–690). Consequently, it remains that illiberality is more opposed to liberality. The second reason is that men commit graver sins by the vice of illiberality than by the vice of extravagance. Therefore, illiberality gets its name from the privation of liberality because liberality is frequently destroyed by this vice.

706. Lastly, he sums up what has been said, stating that so far we have discussed liberality and the opposite vices.

LECTURE VI
Magnificence

TEXT OF ARISTOTLE (*1122a18–1122b18*) Chapter 2

1. It seems logical to pass now to the consideration of magnificence which apparently is a certain virtue concerned with wealth. 1122a18–19; 707

2. Unlike liberality it does not embrace all but only lavish expenditures of money; it is in wealth's magnitude (as the name itself indicates) that magnificence exceeds liberality, although the amount expended is not out of proportion. 1122a20–23; 708

3. But magnitude is a relative term, for the same expenditure is not fit for a captain of a trireme and a leader of a solemn mission to Delphi; it is fitting according to the spender, the thing, and the purpose. 1122a24–26; 709

4. The man, however, who spends small or moderate sums in a becoming manner is not called munificent, for instance, if he makes frequent donations that in the aggregate are large; only he who gives on a grand scale. The munificent man is indeed liberal, but one who is liberal and nothing more is not munificent. 1122a26–29; 710

5. In this matter the habit of defect is called meanness, and of excess banausia (ostentation); the name apirocalia (lack of taste) is given to all other such defects that are not excessive in the sums expended on the right projects but in the wrong circumstances and with a certain vulgar display. We shall discuss these vices afterwards. 1122a29–34; 711

6. A munificent person is like a wise man, for he can judge rightly and spend great sums prudently. (As we said in the beginning, [Bk. II, Ch. 1, 1103b22 sq.] habit is determined by operations and is a product of them.) He makes great and dignified expenditures, and the effects are of a like nature. Thus his expenses will be great and also suited to the work. Therefore, the work must be worth the cost, and the cost equal to or in excess of the work. 1122a34–1122b6; 712–713

7. Things of this kind he spends for the sake of good, and this is common to virtues. 1122b6–7; 714

8. Furthermore, he acts cheerfully and open-handedly, for closeness in reckoning is niggardly. 1122b7–8; 715

9. He plans how the best and most splendid work may be achieved rather than how he may acquire as much for a minimum cost. 1122b8–10; 716

10. Likewise the munificent man is necessarily liberal, since the liberal person makes the right expenditures in the right manner; and it is in this that the greatness of the munificent person lies—a greatness in these matters being a kind of grand liberality. 1122b10–13; 717

11. Besides, for the same cost he will produce a more magnificent work, for the perfection of possession and work does not reside in the same thing. But the perfect possession consists of what is most valued and honored, for example, gold. On the other hand, the perfect work consists of what is great and good, for consideration of it brings about admiration. And truly a magnificent work is a cause of admiration, and the perfection of the work, magnificence, resides in its magnitude. 1122b13–18; 718

COMMENTARY OF ST. THOMAS

707. After the Philosopher has finished the study of liberality, he now begins to consider magnificence, the treatment of which he divides into two parts. In the first part he treats the matter of magnificence and the opposite vices. In the second [6] he explains in what manner magnificence and the

opposite vices operate in their respective matter, at "A munificent person is like a wise man etc." On the first point he does two things. First [1] he shows what the matter of magnificence is; and second [5] what the vices opposed to it are, at "In this matter etc." To clarify the first division he does three things. First [1] he proposes the matter common to magnificence and liberality. Next [2] he explains the difference between the two, at "Unlike liberality etc." Last [4], he proves his proposition, at "The man, however etc." He says first it seems appropriate that the treatise on magnificence should follow that on liberality. The reason is that magnificence, like liberality, is apparently a virtue concerned with wealth.

708. Then [2], at "Unlike liberality," he explains the difference between the matter of magnificence and liberality. He explains this point in a twofold manner. First [2] he proposes the difference. Next [3] he makes clear what he said, at "But magnitude etc." Regarding the first he mentions two differences. The first is that liberality refers to all transactions concerned with money, viz., expenditures, receipts and donations. But magnificence refers only to disbursements or expenditures. The second difference is that in disbursements or expenditures magnificence exceeds liberality in the magnitude of the amount expended. Magnificence deals only in princely outlays, as the name implies, while liberality can be concerned also with moderate or excessive expenditures. Although magnitude indicates a kind of excess, we are not to understand that the munificent person spends on such a grand scale that he exceeds the bounds of reason, but his expenditures are made in amounts that are also in keeping with what is becoming. It is in keeping with both the one who spends and the projects on which the money is spent, as will be pointed out later (721–724).

709. Next [3], at "But magnitude," he explains what he said, i.e., the manner in which the greatness of the expense is becoming to a munificent person. Because the word "great" is predicated relatively, as stated in the *Categories* (Ch. 6, 5b15), it is said here that the greatness of the expenditure is judged in reference to something else, for instance, the thing for which the expenditures are made or the person spending. The reason is that not the same outlay is considered large for a triarch (a commander of galleys having three rows of oars and called a trireme) and for a leader of a solemn enterprise, i.e., the chief superintendent, like a master of a temple or a school. The expenditure must be suitable in comparison with the dispenser and the thing for which the money is spent. Likewise the purpose for which the thing is used must be taken into consideration. Thus if expenses are incurred for the building of a house, we must consider further for whom the house is intended, whether for a public official or a private person, because different expenditures are demanded for different purposes.

710. Then [4], at "The man, however," he proves his statement, i.e., that great expenditure pertains to magnificence. The reason is that one who spends small or even moderate sums in a proper manner is not called munificent, for instance, if he frequently makes many separate disbursements for trifling things, so that all his expenditures taken together would make as great an amount as that which the munificent man spends, nevertheless he would not be called munificent even

though he disbursed these small sums promptly and generously. Because every munificent person is liberal, it does not follow that every liberal person is munificent.

711. At "**In this matter**" [5] he shows what vices are contrary to magnificence. He says that the vice opposed to the habit of magnificence by defect is called meanness; but the vice by excess, *banausia* (ostentation) from *baunos* meaning furnace, because such as have the vice consume all their goods as in a furnace. If other terms of this kind exist, they come under the name *apirocalia* (lack of taste): offenders being, as it were, without experience of what is suitable because they do not know how to do the proper thing. Such names signify excess not because they surpass the munificent person in the amount of disbursements on the right projects, but they are excessive in going beyond right reason, spending, with a certain display, great sums on the wrong things. It is obvious from this that the mean and the extremes in moral virtues are not taken according to absolute quantity but in relation to right reason. He adds that he will discuss these vices afterwards in this book (784-791).

712. Next [6], at "**A munificent person,**" he explains in what manner magnificence and the opposite vices are concerned with the previously mentioned matter. First [6] he treats magnificence, and then [Lect. VII] the opposite vices, at "One who sins etc." (1123a19). On the initial point he does two things. First [6] he assigns to the munificent man certain qualities pertaining to the manner of spending. Then [Lect. VI] he shows on what objects the munificent person makes expenditures, at "Magnificence belongs etc." (1122b19). In regard to the first he

attributes to the munificent person six qualities, the first [6] of which is that he is like a wise man. The reason is that, as it belongs to a wise craftsman to know the proportion of one thing to another, so also it belongs to the munificent man to know the proportion between expenditures and that for which the expenditures are made. In virtue of his habit the munificent man is able to judge what may be proper to spend. Thus he will make grand disbursements in a prudent way because prudent operation is required for every moral virtue.

713. The Philosopher clarifies the statement by what was said in the second book (322), that every habit is determined by operations and objects of which it is the habit, because determined habits have their own proper operations and objects. Since the operations of magnificence are expenditures, and the objects of the operations are the things for which the expenditures are made, it is therefore the duty of the munificent man to consider and expend large and handsome sums, which cannot be done without prudence. In this way the vast outlay will be in keeping with the operation, for instance, the construction of a house or something of this sort. So then the project on which the money is spent must be such that it is worthy of the cost or expense and this ought to be worthy of the work, or in excess of it. It is very difficult to attain the mean; hence if a departure from the mean should occur, virtue always inclines to what has less evil, as the brave man to less fear, the liberal man to giving and so the munificent man to more spending.

714. He gives the second quality [7], at "**Things of this kind,**" which is understood on the part of the end. The munificent person, he says, consumes

grand and proper amounts for an honorable good as for an end. Now, to work for a good is common to all the virtues.

715. At "**Furthermore**" [8] he presents the third consideration, saying that it is characteristic of the munificent man to spend great sums cheerfully and with an open hand, dispensing them promptly and readily. The reason is that great caution in accounting or computing expenses pertains to illiberality.

716. He introduces the fourth quality at "**He plans**" [9], affirming that the munificent person plans how he may accomplish the best and most splendid work rather than how he can spend the least in doing the desired work.

717. He enumerates the fifth quality, at "**Likewise the munificent**" [10] when he says that one who is munificent should be liberal. The reason is that the liberal person should make the right expenditures in the right manner. The munificent man, too, acts in this way, for he makes outlays for great and noble achievements, as was just said (708); and he does this cheerfully,

generously, and for a good purpose. But it is characteristic of the munificent person to do something on a grand scale touching this matter. In fact magnificence is nothing other than a kind of magnified liberality concerning these things.

718. At "**Besides, for the same cost**" [11] he gives the sixth quality. He says that, although the munificent person incurs great expense for some noble work, he produces a more magnificent work with equal expenditure. This is so because excellence (what is ultimate and best) is not the same in possession of money and in a work for which money is spent. Excellence (what is greatest and best) in possessions is found in the most valued object, viz., gold, which men highly honor and prize. But excellence in a work is found in this that a work is great and good; for the contemplation of such a work gives rise to admiration—and this is what magnificence does. So it is evident that the "virtue" of a work, i.e., its greatest excellence corresponds to magnificence involving expenditures on a large scale.

LECTURE VII
The Objects of Magnificence

TEXT OF ARISTOTLE (*1122b19–1123a33*) Chapter 2

1. *Magnificence belongs to those princely outlays we call most honorable, like votive offerings to the gods, preparations, sacrifices and other things pertaining to divine worship. It belongs, also, to any lavish gifts made for the common good, such as a splendid donation for the benefit of all, or the fitting out of a trireme, or the giving of a banquet to the whole community.*
1122b19–23; 719–720

2. *But in all these things, as was just stated, reference is made to the agent—who he is and what possessions he has, for the disbursements must be commensurate with these circumstances and appropriate not only to the work but also to the spender.* **1122b23–26; 721**

3. *For this reason the poor man will not be munificent, since he has not the resources from which he may spend large sums becomingly. If he tries to do so, he is unwise for this would be improper and inopportune. And what is according to virtue is done rightly.* **1122b26–29; 722**

4. *A great expenditure is suitable for those who have wealth themselves, from their parents, or from others transferring it to them; likewise for the noble and those renowned for fame or other similar public acclaim, since all these things have a certain greatness and distinction.*
1122b29–33; 723–724

5. *Such then, especially, is the munificent person, and as we have said, by such expenditures magnificence is exercised in the greatest and most honorable works;* **1122b33–35; 725**

6. *or even in any private affair that happens once, for example, a wedding and the like;*
1122b35–1123a1; 726

7. *or in any event of great interest to the whole city and the dignitaries; or in the reception and departure of foreign guests, in the presentation of gifts and in the repayment of favors. Yet the munificent man does not spend lavishly on himself but donates for the public welfare gifts that have a likeness to those consecrated to God.* **1123a1–5; 727**

8. *It is the privilege of the munificent man to use his riches to build a home which is indeed an ornament, and to spend larger sums on whatever portions are of a permanent nature, for these are best.* **1123a6–8; 728–729**

9. *He will spend in a manner proper to each thing. The same expenditure is not appropriate to gods and men, nor in building a temple and a tomb. He will make an outlay for each thing according to the kind, being most munificent in spending a great amount on a great work. But the expense will be great in comparison with the things. What is great in regard to the work differs from what is great in cost considered in itself. A very pretty ball or jar takes on magnificence when presented as a gift to a child, although the price is trivial and not in the category of liberal. Hence the munificent person has the advantage of performing a great work in any category. And a work, great in its class and reasonable in its cost, can hardly be surpassed. This, then, is a description of the munificent person.* **1123a8–19; 730–731**

10. *One who sins by excess, i.e., the vulgarian, is immoderate in spending contrary to what he ought, as has been pointed out. He expends great sums on paltry things, and his lavishness is out of harmony, figuratively speaking. He banquets buffoons with dishes fit for a marriage feast, gives presents to comedians, and rolls out a red carpet for their entry like the Megarians. In all such affairs he does not act to attain the good but to show off his wealth, hoping in this way for admiration. Where grand outlays are called for, he spends little; where small expenditures are in order, he lays out much.* **1123a19–27; 732**

11. *But the petty person falls short in everything; and after spending very much he will spoil*

the whole good effect for the sake of a trifle. Whatever expenditures he makes, he makes tardily
and he takes care to spend as little as he can. Moreover, he does this glumly and is of the opinion
that he has done more than he should.   **1123a27–31; 733**
12. *These, then, are habits of vice; yet they do not bring shame because they do not injure our*
neighbor and are not very disgraceful.   **1123a31–33; 734**

COMMENTARY OF ST. THOMAS

719. After the Philosopher has shown in what manner the munificent person should be concerned with spending, he now shows the principal object on which the munificent person should spend money. He gives two explanations of this point. First [1] he explains for what things the munificent man should make expenditures; and next [9], how he preserves proportion between the cost and the objects paid for, at "He will spend in a manner proper to each etc." He manifests the initial point in a twofold manner. First [1] he sets forth the principal objects for which the munificent should spend money; and then [6], the secondary objects, at "or even in any private etc." On this first point he does three things. First [1] he discloses what the principal objects are for which the munificent person disburses funds. Next [2], he indicates who should make such expenditures, at "But in all these things etc." Last [5], he sums up his views, at "Such then, especially etc." He says first that the munificent man lays out large amounts for things that are honorable in the highest degree. These sums are of two kinds. The first of them pertains to divine things (for example, the placing of votive offerings in the temples of the gods) and preparations (the building of the temple or some other things of this kind). Even sacrifices come under this heading. The gentiles, however, worshipped not only gods, i.e., certain separated substances, but also demons whom they held to be intermediaries between

gods and men. Therefore, he adds that everything expended on the worship of any demon whatsoever belongs to this same classification. The Philosopher speaks here of a heathen custom that has been abrogated by the plain truth. Hence if someone now spent any money on the worship of a demon he would not be munificent but sacrilegious.

720. The second kind of honorable expenditures are those made for the common good in a sumptuous manner: a person nobly and lavishly gives a becoming donation of something useful to the community; a man, charged with an office by the state like the captaincy of a trireme (a fleet of ships or galleys), makes great expenditures in the execution of that office; or someone gives a banquet for the whole community according to a custom, as is said in the second book of the *Politics* (Ch. 9, 1271a33; St. Th. Lect. XIV, 317).

721. Next [2], at "**But in all these,**" he shows for whom such expenditures are appropriate. Regarding this he does three things. First [2] he explains for whom, in general, such expenditures are appropriate. Then [3], at "For this reason the poor man," he infers for whom, in particular, they are inappropriate. Finally [4], at "A great expenditure etc.," he shows for whom, in particular, they are appropriate. He says first that in all these things that are expended—as was just mentioned (712–713)—we must have regard not only for the objects for which a person spends money (so that we should con-

sider whether the spender is a prince or a private person, a noble or a commoner) but also what possessions, large or small, he may have. Expenditures must be proper, i.e., well proportioned to the wealth and station of the person, so that the expenses may be suited not only to the work for which they are incurred but also to the spender.

722. Then [3], at "**For this reason,**" he infers that such expenditures may not be appropriate. Because of what was just said, the poor man who has little wealth cannot be munificent, for he does not have so great an amount that he can rightly afford to spend much. If he attempts to spend more, he is foolish since it is contrary to good taste and beyond what is proper. So it does not pertain to the virtue of magnificence because, by means of virtue, all things are done correctly, i.e., properly.

723. Next [4], at "**A great expenditure,**" he discloses who may make these expenditures fittingly, understanding this in regard to two things. First he takes it according to the amount of riches. He says that great expenditures should be made by men who are wealthy, i.e., who possess great riches, much of which can be expended becomingly. It makes no difference whether they possess this abundant wealth of themselves, i.e., by acquiring it through their own industry, or have it from their parents (whose heirs they are), or even from any others through whom riches come to them, for example, when they become heirs of those outside the family.

724. Second, he considers the proposition according to the condition of persons. It is becoming that great sums be disbursed by the highborn and the renowned, i.e., those established in

honor and other similar things. Everything of this nature has about it a certain greatness and decorum, so that such splendid donations may be made appropriately.

725. Then [5], at "**Such, then,**" he sums up his views, affirming that the munificent person is of the sort described above, and that magnificence consists in expenditures of this kind—as was stated in 719–720—viz., on things for divine worship and the public welfare, for such are the greatest and most honorable among all human goods.

726. Next [6], at "**or even,**" he shows on what secondary objects the munificent person spends money. He mentions three kinds of objects, the first [6] of which consists in the munificent man spending great sums on affairs pertaining properly to himself and happening only once, like marriage, military service, and so on.

727. He gives the second kind [7], at "**or in any event.**" If the whole city or the rulers are anxious to do something and a man makes great expenditures on this he will be munificent, for instance, if he should honorably receive some guests such as princes or kings, if he should give them great banquets, or even personally offer presents to them, or if he should repay certain favors received; in all these situations, the munificent person will spend large sums. He is not lavish with himself so that he spends much for his own use, but he makes great expenditures for the common good. The splendid gifts bestowed on some resemble those given to God. The reason is that, as offerings are consecrated to God not because He needs them but out of reverence and honor, so also presents are made to distinguished men more on account of honor than any need.

728. Then [8], at **"It is the privilege,"** he mentions the third kind, stating that it pertains to magnificence to build a home in the proper manner with one's own riches, for a decent home adds to a man's distinction. And in constructing buildings the munificent man desires to spend money rather on lasting and permanent parts than on fragile decorations, for instance, on marble columns in the house rather than on glass windows. Things that are more permanent are best.

729. Hence, it is clear from what has been said that the munificent man spends money principally on the things destined for divine worship and the public welfare, but secondarily on things pertaining to private persons under three conditions: first that the things happen once, second that in addition the common good is pursued, third that they are of a permanent nature. These are the requisites making for greatness in private matters.

730. Next [9], at **"He will spend,"** he explains in what way the munificent person maintains the proportion of costs appropriate to the things for which the expenditure is made, spending on each object what is fitting both in kind and quantity. It is obvious that not the same kind and quantity of outlay is suitably offered to gods and men, nor used in the construction of a temple and a tomb. He will see to it that he spends a sum large according to the kind of thing. Hence he will be very munificent when he makes a great expenditure on a great work. But in this work he will make what is great in this class. So, sometimes what is great in regard to the work differs from what is absolutely great in expense. From the fact that someone makes a very pretty globe, i.e., a ball, or a vase (a small

vessel) as a gift to a boy, he is said to possess magnificence in the genus of children's gifts, although the price of the beautiful globe in itself is small, not belonging to the class of generous donations. Obviously, therefore, the munificent person has the advantage of performing a great work in any genus, making expenditures commensurate with the merit of the work. A production of this sort, which is great according to its kind and reasonable in its cost, can hardly be surpassed.

731. Last, he succinctly states the conclusion that the munificent man is such as has been described.

732. Then [10], at **"One who sins by excess,"** he treats the opposite vices: first [10], considering excess; next [11] defect, at "But the petty person etc."; and last [12] what is common to both, at "These, then, are." He says that the man who is immoderate in grand outlays—called *banausos* because he consumes his goods as in a furnace—exceeds the munificent person not in the absolute amount spent but in spending in a way contrary to what he should. The reason is that he uses much money in superfluous expenses, and wants to make lavish expenditures contrary to harmony, i.e., against the right proportion—which is said by way of metaphor—for instance, he entertains buffoons and comedians with nuptial banquets, contributes much to actors, even rolling out the red carpet for their entry, as the Megarians (certain Greek citizens) are in the habit of doing. He does all these and similar things not for some good but for making a show of his riches, thinking that he will be admired for this reason. However, he does not always spend lavishly but sometimes he falls short. Where he ought to spend

much, he spends little; but where little, much. The reason is that he does not keep his eye on the good but on vanity.

733. Next [11], at "**But the petty person**," he considers the vice of defect and states that the petty person falls short in everything, assigning him five traits. The first is that when the petty person does make great expenditures he fails to do well because of a trifle. The second, what sums he expends he expends tardily. The third, he always keeps his mind on how he may spend the least. The fourth, he is a gloomy spender. The fifth, when he lays out everything, he thinks he has done more than he should, for it seems to him that he ought to spend less.

734. Then [12], at "**These, then,**" he considers what is common to either vice. He comes to the conclusion that the two previously mentioned habits are certain vices because they are opposed to virtue by a departure from the mean. However, they are not opprobrious since they do not injure our neighbor in any way, and are not very disgraceful because it is difficult in disbursing large amounts not to depart from the mean.

LECTURE VIII
Magnanimity

TEXT OF ARISTOTLE (1123a34–1224a4) Chapter 3

1. *Judging by the name, magnanimity seems to be concerned with great things the nature of which we should first understand. However, it does not matter whether we consider the habit or the man who operates according to the habit.*   **1123a34–1123b1; 735**

2. *A person seems to be magnanimous in thinking himself worthy of great things when he is worthy.*   **1123b1–2; 736**

3. *But he who presumes this when it is not really so is foolish; yet the man who operates according to virtue in these matters is not unwise or foolish. Consequently, the magnanimous person is such as we have described.*   **1123b2–4; 737**

4. *He who is worthy of small things and considers himself so is temperate, although he is not magnanimous. Magnanimity consists in greatness, as beauty consists in a good build. Short-statured people may be fair and well-proportioned but hardly handsome.*   **1123b5–8; 738**

5. *The person who judges himself worthy of great things and is in fact unworthy is conceited. But one who judges himself worthy of greater things than he merits is not always said to be conceited.*   **1123b8–9; 739**

6. *On the other hand, the man who thinks he deserves lesser things than he deserves—whether the things be great, ordinary, or little—is pusillanimous. This will be especially evident in one capable of splendid achievements. What would he have done if he had not this capability?*   **1123b9–13; 740**

7. *However, the magnanimous man holds an extreme in extension but a mean in appropriateness, for he thinks himself deserving in accord with his worth. Others exceed and fall short of this mean.*   **1123b13–15; 741**

8. *If a man deems himself deserving of great things and especially of the greatest things when he deserves them, then he will be concerned with one particular object. He is said to be deserving in reference to external goods. But we place that external good highest which we attribute to the gods, which is desired most of all by prominent men and is the reward for virtuous action. Such a good is honor, for it is the best of all external goods. Therefore, the magnanimous man will manage honors and dishonors in a manner which is fitting.*
1123b15–22; 742

9. *Even independent of reasoning, the magnanimous seem to be concerned about honors, for the great exalt themselves in dignity principally by honor.*   **1123b22–24; 743**

10. *The pusillanimous person is deficient in regard both to his own merit and the worthiness of the magnanimous man. But one who is presumptuous is excessive respecting his own merit although he does not exceed the merit of the magnanimous person.*   **1123b24–26; 744**

11. *But the magnanimous man as worthy of the greatest goods will be best. Since the better person is worthy of greater things, the best will be worthy of the greatest. Therefore, the magnanimous person must be truly good.*   **1123b26–29; 745**

12. *What is great in every virtue pertains to magnanimity.*   **1123b29–30; 746**

13. *It is never becoming for a magnanimous man to flee one about to give unsought advice, nor to practice injustice. Will not the man who considers nothing great be the one to do disgraceful deeds for gain?*   **1123b31–32; 747**

14. *To an observer of what happens in individual cases, that person will seem altogether ludicrous who thinks himself magnanimous when he is not really virtuous. One who is in fact evil will not be magnanimous nor deserving of honor, for honor is a reward of virtue and is attributed to the virtuous.*   **1123b33–1124a1; 748**

15. *Therefore, it seems that magnanimity is an embellishment of the virtues, since it makes virtue more excellent and does not exist without them. It is difficult to be truly magnanimous because this is not possible without goodness.*   1124a1–4; 749

COMMENTARY OF ST. THOMAS

735. After the Philosopher has finished the treatise on the virtues concerning money, he treats here the virtues having to do with honors. First he considers magnanimity, which regards great honors [Lects. VIII, IX, X, XI]; and then a nameless virtue concerned with ordinary honors [Lect. XII], at "As we remarked in the beginning etc." (1125b1). In the first consideration he does two things. First [I] he investigates the matter of magnanimity and the opposite vices; and second [Lect. IX] their acts and properties, at "For the most part etc." (1124a4). On the first point he does two things. First [1] he sets forth his proposition; and next [2] he explains it, at "A person seems to be etc." He says first: from its name, magnanimity apparently is concerned with great things. But at the beginning we must understand the nature of the things with which it deals. Then he designates the manner of consideration, viz., it does not matter whether we speak of the habit of magnanimity or of the man who is disposed by the habit, i.e., the magnanimous person.

736. Next [2], at "A person seems," he explains his proposition by doing two things. First he exposes the matter of magnanimity generally; and then [8] specifically, at "If a man etc." On the first point he does two (three) things. First [2] he shows that magnanimity refers to great things; and then [5], at "The person who judges etc.," how the opposite vices occur in regard to the same matter. Last [7] he explains how the virtue consists in the mean, at "However, the magnanimous etc." He

treats the first point under three aspects. First [2] he exposes his viewpoint, saying that a person seems to be magnanimous who thinks himself worthy of great things, viz., that he may perform great deeds and that great things should happen to him when in fact he is worthy.

737. Then [3], at "But he who presumes," he teaches that the magnanimous person must be worthy of great things. One who thinks himself worthy of great things contrary to truth, i.e., of which he is not really worthy, is foolish. It is characteristic of a wise man to keep everything in proper order. But the virtuous man is neither unwise nor foolish because virtue operates according to right reason, as was affirmed in the second book (257, 322, 335). Consequently, it is clear that the magnanimous man is the person just described, i.e., one worthy of great things who thinks himself worthy.

738. Finally [4], at "He who is worthy," he shows that the magnanimous man should think himself worthy of great things. One who is worthy of small things and considers himself so, can be called temperate in the sense that temperance is taken for any moderation whatsoever. However, he cannot be called magnanimous because magnanimity consists in a certain size, just as beauty properly consists in a good build. Hence those who are short can be called fair by reason of complexion or well-proportioned members but not handsome because they lack size.

739. Next [5], at "The person who judges," he shows in what manner the opposite vices should be concerned

with great things, first [5] regarding the vice of excess; and then [6] the vice of defect, at "On the other hand etc." Aristotle says first that the man who thinks himself worthy of great things when he is really unworthy is called conceited, i.e., puffed up—we can call him inflated or presumptuous. But the person who is really worthy of great things and thinks himself worthy of still greater things is not always called conceited, because it is difficult to find an exact norm so that someone may judge himself not worthy of great things.

740. Then [6], at "On the other hand," he explains how the vice of defect is concerned with great things, saying that the man who thinks himself worthy of lesser things than he is worthy is called pusillanimous. This is so, whether in fact he is worthy of great, mediocre, or small things. However, the small-souled person is one who refuses to strive after great accomplishments and aims at certain petty undertakings when he is truly capable of what is great. He would bring himself down to affairs more trifling still, except for the fact that he is capable of great things.

741. Next [7], at "However, the magnanimous man," he shows how magnanimity is in the mean, for, treating as it does of great things, magnanimity seems to consist in the extreme. Since the average is the mean between the large and the small, the great has the nature of an extreme. Hence he says that the magnanimous person holds an extreme in reference to great things of which he deems himself worthy. But he holds the mean inasmuch as he does this in an appropriate manner in considering himself deserving according to his worth. The mean of virtue is not judged according to the quantity of the thing but according to right reason. Hence a man is not placed outside the mean of virtue by a work no matter what its size, provided he does not depart from reason. But the opposite vices exceed and fall short of what should be.

742. Then [8], at "If a man deems," he explains the matter of magnanimity specifically, taking up three points. He shows first [8] that magnanimity is concerned with honor; second [10] how the opposite vices should deal with this matter, at "The pusillanimous person etc."; and third [11] in what manner magnanimity is related to other virtues at "But the magnanimous man etc." He explains the first point in two ways. First he reasons that if the magnanimous man deems himself worthy of great things when he is worthy of them, consequently [8] he should deem himself deserving of the greatest things when he is deserving of the greatest. He says further that magnanimity is concerned with one object in particular, for what is predicated by excellence is attributed to one. When someone is said to be worthy of certain things, the worthiness refers to external goods which come to a man as a reward. But that must be placed highest which is attributed to God, which is desired especially by those in eminent positions, and which is the reward of the most noble deeds. Such is honor, for honor is shown to God, is sought by the prominent and is the reward of virtuous action. Obviously then honor is the best of all external goods. Consequently, magnanimity should give the greatest consideration to honors and dishonors, inasmuch as the magnanimous person manages things of this kind in the proper manner.

743. Second [9], at "Even independent of reasoning," he manifests

his proposition by experience, saying that, even without discussion, it is clear that magnanimity has to do with honor for the most part because experience shows the magnanimous deem themselves worthy of honor but not above their deserts.

744. Next [10], at "**The pusillanimous**," he explains in what manner the opposite vices should be concerned with the previously mentioned matter. He says that the small-souled person is deficient in regard to himself because he considers himself deserving of lesser things than he deserves, and also in regard to the worthiness of the magnanimous man because he considers himself deserving of lesser things than a magnanimous man deserves. But the conceited or presumptuous person is excessive in regard to himself because he makes himself greater than his worth, however, not in regard to the magnanimous man because he does not consider himself deserving of greater things than the magnanimous man deserves.

745. Then [11], at "**But the magnanimous**," he compares magnanimity with other virtues: first [11] showing that magnanimity is related to the other virtues; and next [15] drawing certain conclusions from what has been said, at "Therefore it seems." On the first point he does two things: he shows that magnanimity is related to the other virtues, first [11] by a general argument; and then [14] by the things appearing in individual cases, at "To an observer etc." Regarding the first he does two things. First [12] he explains what makes magnanimity a special virtue, at "What is great etc."; and next [13] he rejects an error, at "It is never becoming etc." Aristotle says first that when the magnanimous person deems himself worthy of the greatest goods

and is really worthy of them, it follows that he is best. The better man is always deserving of greater things, and consequently he who is deserving of the greatest must be best. Therefore, the magnanimous man must be truly good, otherwise he would not be deserving of the highest honors.

746. Then [12], at "**What is great**," he shows how magnanimity is a special virtue when it accompanies other virtues. He says that what is great in any virtue seems to pertain to magnanimity because one who does not perform a great act of virtue is not worthy of great honor. So, when that virtue strives for what is proper to itself, it performs an act of another virtue, for example, fortitude intends a courageous action, magnanimity strives for a great deed in the courageous action. Since moral acts take their species from the end to which they tend, it is clear that magnanimity and fortitude differ in species (although they operate in the same matter) because neither virtue follows the same motive.

747. Next [13], at "**It is never becoming**," he rejects an error. Some seem to think that the magnanimous man should rely upon his own opinion and follow the advice of no one. Likewise, that he should not hesitate to do injustice to anyone. The Philosopher, however, says this is false because no one does a shameful deed except for the desire of something. But the magnanimous person does not place so great a value on any external thing that he would wish to do a shameful action for it.

748. Then [14], at "**To the observer**," he explains the clause: "of what happens in individual cases."[1] He says that to someone willing to observe individual cases, that man will seem altogether ridiculous who judges

himself magnanimous without being virtuous. The reason is that if a man is evil he is not deserving of honor, for honor is the reward of virtue. Hence the magnanimous man thinks himself worthy of great honors. Consequently, no evil person is able to be magnanimous.

749. Last [15], at "**Therefore it seems**," he draws two conclusions from the premises. The first is that magnanimity seems to be an ornament of all the virtues because they are made more excellent by magnanimity, which seeks to perform a great work in all the virtues. In this way the virtues increase. Likewise, magnanimity accompanies the other virtues and so seems to be added to them as their ornament. The second conclusion is that it is difficult to be magnanimous because magnanimity cannot exist without the goodness of virtue, and even without great virtue to which honor is due. But it is difficult to attain this. Consequently, it is difficult for a man to be magnanimous.

---

1   In the Commentary the words are *per ea quae in singulis apparent*. The text of Aristotle used here has *secundum singula*.

LECTURE IX
The Acts of Magnanimity

TEXT OF ARISTOTLE (1124a4–1124b6) Chapter 3

1. For the most part the magnanimous man deals with honors and dishonors. **1124a4–5; 750**

2. He takes moderate delight in great and desirable honors, receiving good things as his own ˙ less than his due. In his opinion, honor is not an appropriate tribute to perfect virtue, but still ᵉ accepts it from men who have nothing greater to bestow on him. **1124a5–9; 751**

3. Honors given him by transitory things and for insufficient reasons he values very little as nworthy of him. **1124a10–11; 752**

4. He likewise counts of little value any dishonor that will be imputed to him unjustly. As ˙e have said, then, the magnanimous man for the most part will be concerned with honors. **1124a11–13; 753**

5. Moreover, he will observe moderation about wealth, power, good fortune, and adversity, ᵒ matter what may happen. He will not be exalted by prosperity nor cast down by misfortune, ᵒr does he even regard honor as if it were a very great thing. Power and wealth should be ᵉsirable for the sake of honor; and those who possess them seek to be honored by reason of them. ᵘt a man to whom honor is a trifle will place little value on the other things. For this reason ᵉe magnanimous seem to be disdainful. **1124a13–20; 754–755**

6. The goods of fortune seem to contribute something to magnanimity, for the noble, the ᵒwerful, and the rich are thought to be worthy of honor as possessing goods of great excellence. ᵘt anything that excels in goodness is held in greater honor. For this reason such things make ᵉn more magnanimous, since they are honored by some people, but in fact the good or ˙rtuous man alone is to be honored. However, he who possesses both (virtue and goods of ˙rtune) becomes more worthy of honor. **1124a20–26; 756**

7. Men who possess goods of this kind without virtue are not justified in thinking ᵉemselves worthy of great things, nor are they rightly called magnanimous, for this supposes ᵉrfect virtue. But those having such things become evil by disdaining and harming others, ᵉnce it is not easy to bear the goods of fortune with moderation. They are not able to endure ᵒod fortune gracefully, but thinking themselves more excellent, they look down on others, and ᵒ as they please. Although not similar to the magnanimous man, they imitate him in the way ᵉey can, not by acting according to virtue, but in disdaining others. The magnanimous person ˍstly disdains and properly glorifies others but many do not always act in this manner. **1124a26–1124b6; 757–758**

COMMENTARY OF ST. THOMAS

750. After the Philosopher has in-estigated the matter of magnanimity nd the opposite vices, he now studies ᵉeir acts and properties, first [1] as ᵒuching magnanimity; and then [Lect. I] the opposite vices, at "But the man ᵇho fails etc." (1125a16). On the initial ᵒint he does two things. First [1] he ᵒows how the magnanimous person ᵒould work on matter proper to him. ᵉext [Lect. X] he defines the traits of the magnanimous person, at "The magnanimous man does not run risks foolishly etc." (1124b6). He explains the first point by a twofold procedure. Initially [1] he shows how the mag-nanimous man should conduct him-self toward honors, the matter of magnanimity; and then [5] toward other things, at "Moreover, he will etc." He treats the first in two ways. First [1] he resumes the previous dis-

cussion (735–749) about the matter of magnanimity, reaffirming what was clear from the premises, that someone is called magnanimous especially and principally from the fact that he conducts himself well in regard to honors and the opposites, viz., dishonors. The same virtue is concerned with opposites; fortitude, for instance, deals with fear and rashness.

751. Then [2], at "He takes moderate delight," he shows how the magnanimous man deals with matter of this kind. First [2] he shows the nature and mode of this man's reaction to great honors, saying that great and desirable honors bestowed on the magnanimous for virtuous activity are a source of moderate delight to them. A man might take inordinate pleasure in goods acquired because they come to him unexpectedly, and value them far above their worth. But when the magnanimous person acquires things, he looks upon them as goods peculiarly suitable to him and, besides, less than his due. He judges that no honor outwardly shown to men is a sufficient reward of virtue. The reason is that the good of reason, for which virtue is praised, exceeds all external goods. Nevertheless, he is not displeased because lesser honors are bestowed on him than he deserves. But he accepts them with equanimity considering that men have nothing better to give him.

752. [3], at "Honors given him," he sets forth the way in which the magnanimous person should regard trifling honors. If honors are given him by transitory things and for any other reason than virtue (for example, if he is extolled for riches or the like, or by some insignificant honors), he will despise such honors because he considers himself undeserving of this type of thing. It is not enough for the virtuous to be honored like the rich.

753. Last [4], at "He likewise counts," he explains in what manner the magnanimous man should deal with dishonor, saying that here also he shows moderation. As his mind is not exalted by great honors, so it is not cast down by insults which he considers imputed to him unjustly. Hence it is obvious that the magnanimous person is especially praised in regard to honors.

754. Then [5], at "Moreover, he will observe," he shows in what way the magnanimous person should deal with secondary matters, for example riches and so forth. On this point he does two things. First [5] he explains how the magnanimous man should act in regard to such objects; and next [6] how the objects benefit magnanimity at "The goods of fortune etc." He says first that, although the magnanimous person is concerned with honors principally, nevertheless secondarily he has to do with riches, power, and everything belonging to good fortune inasmuch as someone is honored for these reasons. Likewise he will show moderation about such things and about misfortune, whatever may be the turn of events, so that he will not rejoice exceedingly in prosperity nor grieve unduly in adversity.

755. He proves the point by the argument given before (741–742) that the magnanimous man conducts himself with moderation in regard to honors that are the greatest of all external goods. This is clear from the fact that both power and riches are desired for the sake of honor according as men who have such things want to be honored for them. If then the magnanimous person thinks honor itself of little account so that he does not rejoice in i

exceedingly, for a greater reason he will judge the other things of small moment, so that he will not rejoice in them immoderately. As a consequence, some judge the magnanimous to be disdainful because they despise external goods and value only the internal goods of virtue.

756. Next [6], at "**The goods of fortune**," he shows how external goods of fortune do confer something on magnanimity. He explains first [6] that they increase it when accompanying virtue; and second [7] that without virtue they cannot make a man magnanimous, at "Men who possess." He says that all external goods of fortune seem to add something to magnanimity inasmuch as, for these very things, some are judged worthy of honor, viz., the noble, the powerful, and the rich. All such goods consist of a certain great excellence, just as the noble surpass the baseborn in excellence, and so on. Everything that is surpassing in goodness is honorable in a high degree, for honor is a kind of reverence due to a very excellent good. Since the magnanimous person is worthy of honor, such goods consequently make men more magnanimous accordingly as they are honored by some people who recognize only these goods. But really only the good or virtuous man should be honored because honor is the proper reward for virtue. If someone should possess both at the same time, viz., virtue and the goods of fortune, he will become worthier of honor inasmuch as each matter is honorable. According to truth and opinion, even the goods of fortune are a help to virtuous operations after the manner of instruments.

757. Then [7], at "**Men who possess**," he establishes that goods of fortune without virtue cannot make a man magnanimous. He says that those who have goods of this kind without virtue cannot rightly esteem themselves deserving of great honors. Hence they are not correctly called magnanimous because it cannot happen that a man deserves great things and is magnanimous without perfect virtue, as was pointed out before (749). But because of the excellence of external goods men who lack virtue look down on others, do them injury, and fall into similar evils, since without virtue it is not easy for someone reasonably to bear the goods of fortune. To conduct oneself with moderation among the goods of fortune is a great work of virtue. Those who lack virtue cannot bear good fortune gracefully. Consequently, thinking themselves better absolutely, they despise those whom they exceed in riches. Since they do not consider that any excellence is acquired by virtue, they take no pains to do anything good but do whatever comes to mind.

758. They want to imitate the magnanimous person when in fact they are not like him. They imitate him in the way they can, not I grant in operating according to virtue—a thing the magnanimous man does especially—but in despising others although, not in the same way as he does. The magnanimous person justly despises the wicked, and properly glorifies the virtuous. But many, who are without virtue, manifest disdain and honor indiscriminately, i.e., sometimes despise the virtuous and honor the wicked.

LECTURE X
Properties of Magnanimity

TEXT OF ARISTOTLE (*1124b6–1125a17*) Chapter 3

1. *The magnanimous man does not run risks foolishly, nor is he a lover of danger since he places a high value on few things. But he does undergo danger for things of great worth.*
1124b6–8; 759–76(

2. *When in danger, he exposes his life as if it were altogether unbecoming to continue living.*
1124b8–9; 761

3. *He is good at helping others—which is a mark of the man of excellence, but he shies away from taking favors—a thing characteristic of a man of lesser gifts.*   1124b9–10; 762

4. *He makes lavish recompense, so that the man who gave in the beginning will receive abundantly and become a debtor.*   1124b11–12; 763

5. *The magnanimous person likes to remember those he benefits but not those by whom he is or was treated generously. That man is less noble who gratefully receives benefits than he who bestows them. Hence it is in the bestowal that the magnanimous man wants to be eminent.*
1124b12–14; 764

6. *Likewise he gladly hears of the benefits he has bestowed but not of those he has received. For this reason Thetis did not recount to Jove, nor the Spartans to the Athenians, the favors they had done but the benefits received.*   1124b14–17; 765

7. *The magnanimous person likes to show himself in need of nothing or hardly anything, but to minister to the needs of others promptly.*   1124b17–18; 766

8. *He acts with great dignity toward those in high places and the wealthy but with moderation toward the middle class.*   1124b18–20; 767

9. *To attain excellence among the great is difficult and worthy of reverence, but among the mediocre it is easy. To seek respect from the great is not without nobility, but from the lowly is to make oneself irksome,*   1124b20–22; 768–769

10. *for instance, to display one's power against the weak, and to avoid tasks that are generally honorable or at which others excel.*   1124b22–24; 770

11. *Leisure and slowness are marks of the magnanimous man, but where there is either great honor or great work he performs at least some great and noteworthy operations.*
1124b24–26; 771

12. *Of necessity he is an evident friend or enemy, for to be so in secret smacks of timidity.*
1124b26–27; 772

13. *He cares more for the truth than the opinion of men.*   1124b27–28; 773

14. *He speaks and works in the open, freely divulging things in public, since he pays little attention to others.*   1124b28–29; 774

15. *He is truthful in his speech, excepting what he says in irony, which he uses with the common people.*   1124b30–31; 775

16. *He cannot conform his life to that of another, except perhaps a friend, since this is servile. Because of servility all flatterers are obsequious and lowly people flatterers.*
1124b31–1125a2; 776

17. *Nor is he given to admiration, for nothing seems great to him.*   1125a2–3; 777

18. *Nor is he mindful of injuries, since it is not becoming that a magnanimous person remembers evils at all, but rather despises them.*   1125a3–5; 778

19. *Neither is he a gossip, for he does not speak about himself or others. He is not anxious that he be praised, and he neither blames nor praises others. Therefore, he does not speak evil of his enemies except to ward off injuries.*   1125a5–9; 779

20. *Necessary or trival matters he does not lament or seek help, for this is characteristic of one who cares excessively about these things.*   **1125a9–10; 780**

21. *He is willing to possess unfruitful rather than fruitful and useful goods, for he is somewhat self-sufficient.*   **1125a11–12; 781**

22. *But the movements of the magnanimous man seem deliberate, his voice solemn and his speech measured. He is not hasty since he is concerned about few things. As he considers nothing too important, he is not given to contention from which sharpness of voice and hastiness of speech arise. Such then is the magnanimous person.*   **1125a12–17; 782–783**

COMMENTARY OF ST. THOMAS

759. After the Philosopher has explained how the magnanimous man should work on proper matter, he here considers the traits of the magnanimous person. First [1] he proposes the traits that are taken by comparison with matters of the virtues; and then [17] those according to the inclination of the magnanimous man himself, at "Nor is he given to admiration etc." On the initial point he proceeds in a twofold manner. First [1] he sets forth the traits of the magnanimous person, which are understood in comparison with externally connected things; and next [11] in comparison with human acts, at "Leisure and slowness etc." In regard to the first he makes a triple enumeration. He enumerates the traits of the magnanimous person first [1] by a comparison with external dangers that are the matter of fortitude; then [3] by a comparison with external benefits that properly pertain to liberality, at "He is good at helping others etc."; and last [8] by a comparison with honors that properly pertain to magnanimity, at "He acts with great dignity etc." He passes over the matter of temperance, which does not have any greatness of itself but deals with material common to man and brute, as was stated in the third book (612). Nevertheless magnanimity tends to do what is great in all the virtues—this was pointed out before (746, 749).

760. Touching on the first point he sets forth two traits, the first [1] of which is that the magnanimous man is not *microcindinos*, does not expose himself to dangers for trifles, nor is he *philocindinos*, i.e., a lover of danger, as it were exposing himself to dangers hastily and lightly. This is so because no one lays himself open to danger except for something having considerable value. But it is characteristic of the magnanimous man that he values few things to such a degree that he is willing to expose himself to dangers for them. Hence he does not undergo danger readily nor for insignificant things. However, the magnanimous man is *megalocindinos*, i.e., braves great dangers for great things because he puts himself in all kinds of danger for great things, for instance, the common welfare, justice, divine worship, and so forth.

761. He assigns the second trait [2] at "**When in danger.**" He affirms that the magnanimous person in exposing himself to danger acts ardently, so that he does not spare his own life, as if it were unfitting for him to prefer to live rather than gain great good by his death.

762. Next [3], at "**He is good,**" he enumerates five traits of the magnanimous man, which are understood by comparison with benefits proper to liberality. The first [3] is that the magnanimous person is proficient at doing good for others, i.e., prompt to bestow

benefits, but is ashamed to accept favors from others. To receive favors pertains to one who has lesser gifts, while the magnanimous man tries to surpass others in virtue.

763. At "**He makes lavish recompense,**" he indicates the second trait [4], saying that if the magnanimous person does accept benefits he is anxious to return greater ones. In this way the man who bestowed benefits in the beginning will rather receive them, i.e., becomes the recipient of benefits inasmuch as he receives more than he gave.

764. At "**The magnanimous person likes to remember,**" he gives the third trait [5], which does not follow the choice but the disposition of the magnanimous man—he is so disposed that he cheerfully confers but unwillingly receives benefits. We think often about the things that delight us and consequently remember them. However, we rarely think of things which displease us and consequently hardly ever recall them. Accordingly it seems characteristic of the magnanimous person to remember those for whom he does favors but not those who do favors for him, since this is contrary to his desire of wanting to excel in goodness. That man who is properly receptive, i.e., accepts favors, is less noble than he who grants favors. The magnanimous man does not choose to be unmindful of favors received but is anxious to bestow greater favors, as was just said (763).

765. At "**Likewise,**" he places the fourth trait [6], saying that the magnanimous person cheerfully listens to the benefits he has bestowed but does not enjoy hearing of the benefits he has accepted. He can take delight in the love of him on whom he has conferred benefits but does not find pleasure in the fact that he himself has accepted

benefits. He gives two examples of this. The first is taken from the writings of Homer who represents Thetis (called the goddess of water) approaching Jove (called the king of all the gods). She does not recount the benefits she herself has conferred on Jove, as if this would not be acceptable to him, but rather the benefits she has received from Jove. To this Jupiter listened more willingly. The other example is taken from Greek history in which it is narrated that certain Spartans, when seeking the help of the Athenians, did not recite the favors they had done for the Athenians but the favors received from them.

766. He assigns the fifth trait [7], at "**The magnanimous person likes to show,**" saying that it pertains to the magnanimous man not to show himself in need of anything at all or at least not readily, inasmuch as he does not ask for or take anything, but to be prompt to minister to the needs of others.

767. Then [8], at "**He acts with great dignity,**" he indicates a trait of the magnanimous person by a comparison with honors. He treats the first point in a threefold manner. First [8] he names the trait, saying that it belongs to the magnanimous man to show himself noble and honorable to men of dignity and wealth, but to display a certain moderation with the middle class, not using a grand manner toward them.

768. Second [9], at "**To attain excellence,**" he offers two reasons for what he said. The first is that every virtue strives for what is difficult and honorable. That someone should excel great men in virtue is difficult and worthy of honor, but to excel mediocre men is easy.

769. The second reason is that it is characteristic of a manly soul to show

himself worthy of respect among the great. But to wish respect shown him by men of lowly rank is the attitude of a man who is a nuisance to others.

770. Finally [10], at "**for instance,**" he gives an illustration, stating that such a condition indicates lack of virtue, namely, that a man demonstrates his strength against the weak, and does not undertake difficult and honorable ventures in which others excel.

771. Next [11], at "**Leisure and slowness,**" he distinguishes the traits of the magnanimous person by means of human acts pertaining first [11] to himself; and then [12] to others, at "Of necessity etc." Aristotle says first that the magnanimous man is disposed to be leisurely, i.e., does not engage in many undertakings, and is disinclined, i.e., not readily occupied with business. He devotes himself only to those activities that are connected with some great honor or the accomplishment of some great work. Therefore, the magnanimous person performs at least some great operations that are worthy of the name.

772. Then [12], at "**Of necessity,**" he indicates the traits of the magnanimous person concerned with human acts that are related to another, first [12] in regard to truth; and next [16] in regard to pleasantness, at "He cannot conform." These things are required especially for social intercourse with others, as will be explained later (816–849). To the first he ascribes four traits, the first [12] of which regards internal inclination. The magnanimous man, he says, cannot make a secret of his friends and enemies. The reason is that a secret love or hatred of another arises from some fear, and fear is repugnant to a magnanimous person.

773. At "**He cares more**" [13] he notes the second trait, saying that it is

characteristic of the magnanimous man to be more solicitous about the truth than the opinion of man. He does not depart from what he ought to do according to virtue because of what men think.

774. At "**He speaks**" [14] he gives the third trait, saying that it is a mark of the magnanimous person to speak and work openly because he pays little attention to others. Consequently, he publicly divulges his words and deeds. That a man hides what he does and says arises from the fear of others. But no one fears those he contemns. Therefore, these two things are interchangeable, viz., that a man freely divulge things and that he cares little for others. However, we do not say that the magnanimous man cares little for others in the sense that he despises them—as it were depriving them of proper respect—but because he does not value them above their worth.

775. At "**He is truthful**" [15] he assigns the fourth trait, saying that the magnanimous man does not speak falsehood but the truth, except perhaps that he playfully utters certain things in irony. However, he does use irony in the company of the common people.

776. Next [16], at "**He cannot conform,**" he indicates the trait concerned with pleasure that arises from companionship, saying that the magnanimous person does not easily associate with others; he finds company only with his friends. The servile soul has a tendency to occupy himself with the intimate affairs of everyone. Consequently all flatterers, who want to please everybody without distinction are obsequious, i.e., prepared to be subservient. People of low station who lack greatness of soul are flatterers.

777. Then [17], at "**Nor is he given,**"

he enumerates the traits of the magnanimous man which arise from his natural bent. Aristotle first [17] gives some that exist in the soul; then [19] others existing in speech, at "Neither is he a gossip etc." Last [21], he sets forth those traits that exist in communication with others, at "He is willing etc." In regard to the first he places two traits, the first [17] of which is that the magnanimous person is not quick to show admiration because this is prompted by great things. But there is nothing great for him among the things that can happen externally, because his whole life is busy with internal goods, which are truly great.

778. Next [18], at "**Nor is he mindful**," he says that the magnanimous person is not too mindful of the evils he has suffered, giving two reasons for this. The first is that the magnanimous man refuses to remember many things, just as he refuses to wonder at them. Another reason is that the magnanimous person deliberately determines to forget injuries he has suffered inasmuch as he despises the things by which he could not be disparaged. Hence Cicero said of Julius Caesar that he was in the habit of forgetting nothing but injuries.

779. Then [19], at "**Neither is he a gossip**," he gives two traits of the magnanimous man concerned with speech. First [19] he seldom speaks about men because he does not value highly their particular affairs. But his whole attention is taken up with the goods of the community and God. Consequently, he says little either about himself or others. He is not solicitous that he be praised nor that others be blamed. Hence he does not have much praise for others nor does he speak evil of others, even his enemies,

except to ward off an injury inflicted on him by them.

780. At "**In necessary or trivial**" [20] he assigns a third (second) trait, that the magnanimous person neither complains by lamenting and grumbling about his lack of the necessities of life and other things, nor asks that they be given to him. This is the characteristic of one who is anxious about the necessities of life, as if they were great things, and this view is contrary to magnanimity.

781. Next [21], at "**He is willing**," he indicates the traits that have a relation to external things, and first [21] in regard to external possessions. He says that the magnanimous man is more ready to own certain honorable and unfruitful goods which are profitless than goods which are profitable and useful. The reason is that a self-sufficient man has no need of profit from other quarters.

782. Then [22], at "**But the movements**," he gives the trait of the magnanimous man referring to bodily movements, stating that his movements seem deliberate, his voice solemn, his speech measured and slow. Assigning the reason for these things, Aristotle says that the movements of the magnanimous person cannot be hasty since he is intent on few things. Likewise, he is not contentious because he holds nothing external of value. Now, no one contends except for something of value. But sharpness of voice and hastiness of speech are resorted to because of contention. Therefore, the temperament of the magnanimous man obviously requires a solemn voice together with deliberate speech and movement. The Philosopher says in the *Categories* (Ch. 8, 9b12 ff.) that if someone is naturally

nclined to a passion, for example, bashfulness, he must have by nature that complexion which corresponds to bashfulness. Hence if a man has a natural proneness toward magnanimity, consequently he should have a natural disposition to qualities of this kind.

783. He concludes with the summary observation that the magnanimous man is just as we have described him.

LECTURE XI
Vices Opposed to Magnanimity

TEXT OF ARISTOTLE (*1125a17–1125a35*) Chapter 3

1. *But the man who fails by defect is small-souled, and the man who fails by excess is conceited. These people, however, do not seem to be criminals although they do sin.*
                                                                                        1125a17–19; 784

2. *The small-souled person, although indeed worthy of excellent things, deprives himself of them.*   **1125a19–20; 785**

3. *There seems something bad in such a man because he does not consider himself deserving of good. Besides, he does not really know himself; otherwise he would want the goods of which he is worthy. However, men of this kind are more lazy than stupid.*   **1125a20–24; 786**

4. *This opinion (of themselves) seems to make them worse, for everybody strives after the things they deserve. But, thinking themselves unfitted, they forsake good works and undertakings, and even external goods.*   **1125a24–27; 787**

5. *Conceited people are silly and obviously ignorant of their capability, for they set about those things to which honor is attached and there-upon they are discredited.*   **1125a27–29; 788**

6. *They adorn themselves with clothing and outward show, and such like. They want these goods of fortune to be indicative of themselves. They even talk about themselves in order to receive honor from their conversation.*   **1125a30–32; 789**

7. *But small-mindedness is more opposed to magnanimity than presumption is.*
   As more opposed, it is also worse. Magnanimity then is concerned with great honor, as was said.   **1125a32–35; 790–791**

COMMENTARY OF ST. THOMAS

784. After the Philosopher has finished the treatise on magnanimity, he now begins to treat the opposite vices. Here he does two (three) things. First [1] he determines what is common to each vice. Then [2] he considers each in itself, at "The small-souled person etc." Last [7] he compares the one vice with the other, at "But small-mindedness etc." He says first that the man who falls short of the mean of magnanimity is called small-souled. But he who exceeds the mean is said to be conceited, i.e., puffed up—what we call inflated or presumptuous. These persons are not said to be evil to the extent of being criminals, for they injure no one and do nothing disgraceful. However, they do sin in this: they depart from the mean of reason.

785. At "**The small-souled person**" [2] he considers each vice: first [2] that

which is according to defect; and next [5] that according to excess, at "Conceited people etc." He discusses the first point in a threefold manner. First [2] he states the act proper to the small-souled man, saying that although such a man is worthy of good things, he deprives himself of those he deserves by not attempting to work or obtain things due to him.

786. Next [3], at "**There seems**," he shows the cause of small-mindedness, pointing out that in this cause three things must be taken by turns. That a man deprive himself of goods he is deserving of happens first from the fact that he does not think himself worthy of such goods when in fact he is worthy. This occurs because he is ignorant of his ability. If the small-souled man knew himself, he would strive for the things he deserves because they are

good and desirable, since one's own good is desirable to everyone. Ignorance of this kind does not come from stupidity—for the stupid are not worthy of great things—but rather from a certain laziness by reason of which they are unwilling to engage in great things according to their dignity. This is the third source from which the other two arise.

787. Third [4], at "**This opinion,**" he explains the effect of small-mindedness. A person's opinion that he is unworthy of the goods he really deserves appears to make him worse. Individual men strive for the things befitting their own worth. Hence when they are ignorant of their worth, they suffer a twofold damage to their goodness. First, they abandon works of virtue and the pursuit of speculative truths, as if they were unfitted for and unequal to things of this kind. From this omission of great and good works, they become worse, since it is such actions that make men more virtuous. Second, by reason of this opinion they shirk certain external good works of which they are capable and which instrumentally serve for the performance of virtue.

788. Then [5], at "**Conceited people,**" he discusses the vice of excess under two considerations. First [5], he gives the cause of this vice, saying that the conceited or presumptuous are both stupid and ignorant of their ability not because of laziness like the small-souled but because of stupidity. This is obvious because they attempt to do or attain certain honorable things utterly beyond their ability. So, when they fail in the action or accomplishment they manifestly appear to be discredited.

789. Next [6], at "**They adorn themselves,**" he introduces the act of this vice, which consists in a kind of external glorification, inasmuch as the presumptuous greatly exalt themselves. First, they do this by certain external signs, that is, they wear elegant clothing and set off their figure by walking pompously. Likewise they do other things to show their excellence in the external goods of fortune. Second, they manifest things of this sort by words, as if wishing to achieve honor in this way.

790. At "**But small-mindedness**" [7] he compares these two vices with one another, stating that small-mindedness is more opposed to magnanimity than conceit is. He assigns two reasons for this. The first reason, given in the second book (368), is that the vice, which occurs more frequently because of a stronger inclination of human nature toward it, is more opposed to virtue whose chief purpose is to restrain man's inclination to evil. But some men are obviously more inclined to be small-souled (i.e., to omit the virtuous deeds possible to them) than to extend themselves in the performance of laudable feats beyond them. Hence small-mindedness is more opposed to virtue. The other reason is that small-mindedness is worse from the aspect of making men less virtuous, as was just stated (787). But what is worse is more opposed to virtue. Therefore, it is evident that small-mindedness is more opposed to virtue.

791. He summarily concludes that magnanimity is concerned with great honor, as has been pointed out (346, 742–744, 750, 754).

LECTURE XII
The Virtue Concerned with Ordinary Honors

TEXT OF ARISTOTLE (*1125b1–1125b25*) Chapter 4

1. *As we remarked in the beginning, there appears to be a virtue that deals with honor and is compared to magnanimity as liberality is to magnificence. Neither of these virtues is in any way concerned with what is great, but both rightly dispose us in regard to mediocre and small things.*
1125b1–5; 792

2. *Just as one can take and give small sums of money according to a mean, and also according to excess and defect, so too one can desire honor more or less than he ought, and also from the source he ought and as he ought.* 1125b6–8; 793

3. *We blame the ambitious man because he desires honor inordinately and from the wrong sources. Likewise we blame the unambitious man for not choosing to be honored even for the good that he does. On the other hand, it is a fact that we praise the ambitious person as noble and enamored of what is virtuous, but the unambitious person as moderate and temperate. We indicated this in our earlier discussion of the subject.* 1125b8–14; 794

4. *Clearly, inasmuch as the term lover of honor (or ambitious man) has been used in different contexts, the expression does not always receive the same meaning. But we praise him as more concerned about honor than most people and we blame him for desiring honor more than is right.* 1125b14–17; 795

5. *Since the mean lacks a name, being as it were abandoned, the extremes are not clearly distinguished.* 1125b17–18; 796

6. *Now, where there is an excess and defect, there also is a mean. But people strive for honor more than is becoming and less than is becoming, hence also becomingly.* 1125b18–20; 797

7. *Therefore, this unnamed habit as being a mean concerned with honor is praised. By comparison with ambition it seems to be contempt of honor, but by comparison with lack of ambition, love of honor. But by comparison with each, the habit seems to be one as well as the other. This seems to be true in regard to other virtues also.* 1125b20–24; 798

8. *However, here the extremes appear to be contradictory because the mean has no name.* 1125b24–25; 799

COMMENTARY OF ST. THOMAS

792. After the Philosopher has concluded his study of magnanimity, which treats of honors on a grand scale, he now considers a certain unnamed virtue having to do with ordinary honors. To explain it he does three things. First [1] he points out that such a virtue exists at times. Next [2] he proves his statement, at "Just as one can etc." Last [5], he explains in what manner the mean and the extreme may be considered in this virtue, at "Since the mean lacks a name etc." He says first, as was stated in the second book (346-348), that there appears to be a

virtue concerned with honor. That virtue seems to be related to magnanimity as liberality is to magnificence. Both these virtues, i.e., liberality and the virtue under consideration, are separated from magnificence and magnanimity as from something great. The reason is that magnanimity deals with great honors and magnificence with great expenditures. But the two virtues, liberality and the virtue under consideration, dispose us in regard to small and mediocre things, either honors or riches.

793. Then [2], at "**Just as one can,**" he proves his statement, first [2] by

reasoning from similarity; and second [3] by the general manner of speaking, at "We blame the ambitious man etc." He says that in taking and giving of small or ordinary sums of money there is a mean—and also an excess and defect—as was said before (679, 710–711). Likewise in the desire of small or mediocre honors, it happens that a man strives more or less than he ought, or for improper reasons inasmuch as one desires to be honored for more or greater things than he ought and another for fewer and lesser things. Likewise it happens that a man strives to be honored rightly in all things. So, clearly there is reason to hold for a mean of virtue and extremes of vice in small or mediocre honors as in smaller sums of money.

794. Next [3], at "**We blame the ambitious man**," he explains his proposition by an ordinary use of words. On this point he does two things. First [3] he indicates the ordinary manner of usage; and then [4] he argues from this to the proposition, at "Clearly, inasmuch etc." He says first that sometimes we blame the ambitious man, i.e., the lover of honor, for desiring honor more than he ought and from an improper source. Likewise, we blame at times the unambitious person for not wanting to do those good actions by reason of which he would be honored. On the other hand, we praise at times one who is a lover of honor as being manly or having a noble soul, and as a lover of the good, i.e., virtuous action to which honor is due. Again we praise occasionally a man who does not love honor—as it were regulating and ruling himself—so that he does not exceed his ability, as was stated in the second book (345–348).

795. At "**Clearly, inasmuch**" [4] he draws a conclusion from this manner of speaking, saying that at times we praise then again we blame the lover of honor. But it is obvious that one is called a lover of honor in various senses, and for this reason we do not praise and blame him for the same thing. But we praise the lover of honor according as he is more concerned than the general run of people for the things pertaining to honor. We blame him, however, inasmuch as he desires honors more than is proper. The same line of reasoning applies to one who does not love honor. Consequently, the mean in this matter is praiseworthy according as honor and desire for honor are valued at their true worth. However, the extremes are blameworthy insofar as one desires more than he ought or less than he ought.

796. Next [5], at "**Since the mean**," he treats the mean and the extreme of this virtue. On this point he does two things. First [5] he shows the uncertainty occurring here; and then [8] the consequences of that uncertainty, at "However, here the extremes etc." He discusses the first point under three headings. First [5] he indicates the uncertainty with the observation that, since the mean concerned with desire for honor has no name—and so, because of this lack, appears as if passed over—the extremes do not seem consequently to be clearly drawn, inasmuch as they are sometimes praised, sometimes blamed.

797. Then [6], at "**Now, where there is**," he explains what the truth is concerning mean and extremes. He says that whenever we find an excess and defect, there also we must find a mean. Therefore, since some strive for honor both more and less than they ought, it follows that some strive as they ought—which belongs to the notion of a true mean.

798. Finally [7], at "**Therefore, this unnamed habit etc.,**" he shows the basis for this uncertainty. Because there is reason to accept a mean in regard to honors, the habit of the medium is praised. Likewise, because unnamed, it is designated by the names of extremes, as by a comparison with one of the extremes it seems to have a likeness to the other extreme. By comparison with excessive love of honor, the medium appears to have contempt of honor; but by comparison with contempt of honor, love of honor; by comparison with each it appears to be one as well as the other in some way. This is evident also in other virtues, for the brave man seems reckless by comparison with the timid man but timid by comparison with the reckless man. So, then, in our proposition the extremes considered in themselves are censured but as attributed to the mean they are praised.

799. Then [8], at "**However, here,**" he explains how it follows from this uncertainty that the extremes seem opposed only to one another but not to the mean of virtue because the mean has no name.

LECTURE XIII
Meekness and Its Opposed Vices

TEXT OF ARISTOTLE (*1125b26–1126b10*) Chapter 5

1. *Meekness is a kind of moderation concerned with anger. The mean in the strict sense being without a name (and the extremes nearly so), we refer to meekness as the mean, although it inclines to the defect which is also nameless. However, the excess can be called irascibility.*
1125b26–29; 800

2. *Anger is a passion arising from many and various causes. Hence a man who is angry over the right things, with the right persons, and moreover in the right way, at the right time, and for the right interval is praised. He is a meek man. But if meekness is an object of praise, the meek man seeks to be undisturbed and not controlled by passion, but to be angry at the things and for the length of time that reason directs.*
1125b30–1126a1; 801

3. *However, he seems to sin more on the side of defect, for the meek person is not vindictive but rather forgiving.*
1126a1–3; 802

4. *But the defect—either a certain apathy or something of the kind—is censured, for a man seems to be foolish who does not get angry at the things he should both in regard to the manner, the time, and the persons. Such a one appears not to feel things nor to be pained at them.*
1126a3–6; 803–804

5. *Moreover, he who does not get angry will not stand up for himself;*
1126a6–7; 805

6. *and it is considered slavish to endure insults to oneself and to suffer one's associates to be insulted.*
1126a7–8; 806

7. *The excess can happen in all likely ways, for a man can be angry with the wrong people, at the wrong things, more than he should, more readily than he should, and for a longer time than he should. However, all these excesses do not belong to the same man who certainly would not be able to survive, for evil which is complete destroys itself and would be unendurable.*
1126a8–13; 807–808

8. *Those persons are hot-tempered who become angry too readily, with the wrong people, at the wrong things, and more than they should. They do quiet down quickly—a very commendable trait which belongs to them because they do not retain anger, but in accord with their openness retaliate in a flare-up of temper, and then become tranquil. But the irascible (acrocholi) are intense in their excess, and get angry on every occasion and at every turn. It is from this that the name is derived.*
1126a13–19; 809

9. *However, the sullen are angry for a long time and are mollified with difficulty, for they do not relinquish their anger. But they are appeased when they have taken vengeance. The infliction of punishment calms the surge of anger and brings delight in place of sadness. When this is not done they are glum because they do not externally express their anger, and no one can prevail upon them. In this case time is needed to absorb the anger. Such persons are burdensome to themselves and especially to their friends.*
1126a19–26; 810

10. *We call those persons ill-tempered who are angry at the wrong things, more than they should be, for too long a time, and who are not appeased until they inflict vengeance and punishment.*
1126a26–28; 811

11. *Excess is more opposed to meekness, for it happens more frequently since man is prone to take vengeance, and it makes the ill-tempered worse to live with.*
1126a29–31; 812

12. As was observed in previous discussions and made plain, it is not easy to determine how, at what, and how long one ought to be angry, or when one acts rightly or makes a mistake. Persons, who transgress slightly, either in great or lesser things, are not blamed. In fact, sometimes we praise men as meek who are wanting in anger, and as manly and competent to rule who abound in anger. However, it is not readily ascertainable by reason to what extent and in what manner a transgressor is blameworthy, for judgment is to be made according to sense perception in individual cases.   **1126a31–1126b4; 813**

13. But it is evident in these matters that the mean habit is praiseworthy according to which we are angry with the right people, about the right things, in the right manner, and so on in other circumstances. Likewise, it is evident that excess and defect are blameworthy, in such a way however that if they are slight, they can be tolerated; if greater, then more blameworthy; and if very great, then very blameworthy. But obviously one must adhere to the mean habit. We have now discussed the habits concerned with anger.   **1126b4–10; 814–815**

COMMENTARY OF ST. THOMAS

800. After the Philosopher has finished the consideration of the virtues dealing with external goods, riches, and honors, he now considers meekness, which deals with the external evils which provoke people to anger. On this point he does two things. First [1] he treats meekness and its opposed vices; and then [12] he answers an implied question, at "As was observed." On the initial point he does two things. First [1] he shows how the mean and the extreme are discovered for anger; and then [2] he discusses them, at "Anger is a passion etc." He says first that meekness is a certain mean for anger. However, in this matter the mean taken in the proper sense has received no name. The same can almost be said about the extremes because they are not distinguished by explicit names. The name meekness is taken to signify a mean, although the word implies a lack of anger. People are called meek because they are not violent, as it were like domesticated animals who lose their irascibility. Even the disordered lack of anger has not been given a name. Someone is said to be meek who is not angry for any reason whatsoever, either good or bad. However, the excess is called rage or irascibility.

801. Then [2], at "Anger is a passion," he first [2] treats meekness; and then [4], the opposite vices. He treats the first point from two aspects. Initially [2] he explains what belongs to meekness as it is considered a virtue; and then [3] what belongs to it according to the real meaning of the word, at "However, he seems to sin etc." He says first that irascibility is considered the vice of the extreme because it implies an excess of anger which is a passion arising from many and various causes. So, according to the diversity of these things, a mean and an extreme are found in anger. Consequently, the praiseworthy man is the one who is angry about the right things, at the right people, and in due moderation (since he is angry as he should be, when he should be, and as long as he should be). However, if the word meekness is used as a compliment, it would seem that the meek man is so disposed: first, that he is not disturbed internally in the judgment of reason by anger; second, he is not led by anger in external choice, for reason determines the objects of anger and the length of time within which anger should react.

802. Next [3], at "**However, he seems to sin**," he explains, in accord

with the true meaning of the word, the character of the meek man who (he says) in this respect seems to err more in approaching the defect. When we call a person meek, we signify that he is not inclined to punish but to forgive and remit punishments. This is a thing belonging to a lack of anger which is a desire for vengeance achieved by punishment.

803. At "**But the defect**" [4], he treats the opposite vices, taking up first [4] the vices of defect; and then [7] those of excess, at "The excess etc." Last [11], he compares these two vices with one another, at "Excess is more opposed etc." He says that the defect of the mean in anger is censured whether we call it apathy or any other name whatsoever.

804. Since the Stoics were of the opinion that all anger is censurable, he consequently shows that the defect of anger sometimes is censurable for three reasons [4]. He proposes the first reason at "**a man seems to be foolish etc.**" Whatever indicates a lack of wisdom is blameworthy because virtue is praised for working in accord with the right understanding of prudence. But for a man to fail to be angry at the things, in the manner, at the time, and with the persons he should be angry seems to denote a lack of wisdom. It is evident that anger is caused by sadness. But sadness is a feeling of injury. If then someone fails to be angry at the things he should, he does not grieve for them and so does not feel they are evil. This pertains to a lack of wisdom. Therefore it is clear that a defect of anger is blameworthy.

805. He gives the second reason [5] at "**Moreover, he who does not get angry.**" Anger is a desire for vengeance. Hence one who is not angry at the things he should, accordingly does not

punish the actions he ought to punish. This is blameworthy. However, this explanation is not to be understood as if another vengeance cannot be taken according to the judgment of the reason without anger, but as if the movement of anger stirred up by the judgment of the reason makes one more prompt to take vengeance in the right way. If the sensitive appetite did not help to carry out the judgment of the reason, it would be useless in human nature.

806. He introduces the third reason [6] at "**and it is considered,**" saying only a cringing man suffers his household to be insulted and permits others to injure him without repelling the injury with due force. This follows from a defect of anger which renders a man slothful and remiss in warding off injury. Hence it is evident that the defect of anger is blameworthy.

807. Then [7], at "**The excess can happen,**" he treats the excess of anger. First [7] he shows that this vice takes place in many ways; and second [8] he considers its species, at "These persons are hot-tempered etc." He says first that excess of anger can occur according to all the circumstances. It happens that someone is angry with the wrong people and in the wrong things, that he is provoked too much and too easily angered, that he is angry too long. However, all these excesses are not found in one man, both because of the trouble he himself would suffer from his own anger, and also because, being burdensome to all, he could not live with others.

808. This is universally true of evil—if it were complete, it would destroy itself. It could not continue to exist in taking away the subject by which it must be sustained if it is to continue to be. What does not exist can hardly be

called evil, because evil is a privation of good. But every being precisely as existing is good. Obviously then evil does not take away good entirely, but some particular good of which evil is a privation. In such a way blindness takes away sight but does not destroy the animal. If the animal were destroyed, blindness would cease to exist. Manifestly, then, evil cannot be complete because in so taking away the good entirely, it would destroy itself.

809. Next [8], at "**Those persons,**" he presents three kinds of excess in anger. The first [8] is that of those called hot-tempered, those easily aroused to wrath, readily becoming angry both with the wrong persons, and at the wrong things, and too vehemently. However, their anger does not last long but quickly subsides. This is very fortunate in a way for them that anger is not retained internally in their heart, but immediately bursts forth externally because they either take vengeance at the time or show their anger in some other way by clear indications with a burst of temper. In this way, when their anger is expressed they quiet down. So, also, heat which is shut up is kept at a higher degree, but when dispersed in vapor it disappears rather quickly. To this kind of anger the choleric seem disposed most readily by reason of the subtletly or speed of the bile. It is from this speed that excess is acquired by the irascible or *acrocholi,* i.e., those excessive in anger, from *acros* meaning extreme and *cholos* meaning anger, because they are intense and quick in anger.

810. He presents the second kind (of anger) [9], at "**However, the sullen,**" saying that some are called sullen whose anger is dispelled with difficulty and lasts a long time because they

keep it pent up in their hearts. But they cease to be angry only when they have satisfaction for the injury inflicted. Punishment calms the surge of passion when the previous sadness is replaced by delight, inasmuch as a man takes pleasure in vengeance. But if this does not happen, that is, if punishment is not inflicted, they are sorely grieved inwardly, since they do not show their anger. No one can persuade them to moderate this wrath that is not indulged. But the dissolution of anger requires a long time in which the fire of wrath may cool off gradually and be extinguished. Such persons who retain anger for a long time are a trial to themselves and especially their friends with whom they cannot live pleasantly. For this reason they are called sullen. To this kind of excess, the melancholic seem particularly inclined because the influence received from the coarseness of the humor lasts a long time in them.

811. He introduces the third kind (of anger) [10], at "**We call those persons,**" saying that some are called ill-tempered or morose who are angry at improper things, in an improper degree and for an improper length of time, and do not leave anger until they wreak vengeance on or punish those with whom they are angry. Indeed their anger lasts long not because of a retention alone that can be dissolved in time but because of a firm resolve to inflict punishment.

812. Then [11], at "**Excess is more opposed,**" he compares the things just treated with one another, stating that the excess of anger is more opposed to meekness than the defect is. He proves this by two arguments: first, it is the usual occurrence. Man is inclined more naturally to inflict punishment after suffering an injury to himself, while he is naturally inclined to meek-

ness when he has not suffered any injury. The second reason is that the excessive in anger are more difficult to live with and to this extent are worse. Hence they are more in opposition to the good of virtue.

813. Next [12], at "**As was observed**," he answers an implied question, namely, at what things and in what manner ought a man be angry. On this point he does two things. First [12] he affirms that this cannot be determined with certitude; and second [13] he states what is clear in this matter, at "But it is evident etc." He says first that, as was observed in the second book (379) and there made clear, it is not easy to determine in what manner one should be angry, i.e., at things of what nature, for how long a time, and up to what point one acts correctly or errs in becoming angry. One who departs a little from the mean, either in great or small matters, is not blamed. In fact, at times we praise those who are somewhat deficient in anger and call them meek, but those who are a little excessive we call manly, as if able and qualified to rule by reason of their promptness for vengeance, which is appropriate to rulers. It is not easy to determine by reason the extent and kind of deviation from the mean for which a man should or should not be blamed. The reason is that judgment in this case depends on particulars and on sense perception which is more an interior than an exterior evaluation.

814. At "**But it is evident**" [13] he shows what is obvious in these matters, saying it is evident that the mean according to which we are angry with the right persons, at the right things, and so on with regard to the other circumstances, is praiseworthy. Likewise, it is evident that excess and defect are blameworthy, in such a way however that if they are slight they can be tolerated; if they are greater, they are more blameworthy; and if very great, they are blameworthy in the highest degree. Hence a man ought to draw himself towards the mean.

815. Last, he says in the epilogue that we have discussed the habits that deal with anger.

LECTURE XIV
Amiability

TEXT OF ARISTOTLE (1126b11–1127a12) Chapter 6

1. *Some men seem to be obsequious in association with others and in interchange of words and deeds. They praise everything for the sake of pleasantness, and never contradict anyone, being of the opinion that unpleasantness ought to be avoided.*   **1126b11–14; 816**

2. *Others, on the contrary, always find fault, taking care to emphasize anything unpleasant. They are called perverse and quarrelsome.*   **1126b14–16; 817**

3. *These habits being reprehensible, obviously the mean habit is laudable—that habit according to which a person approves what he should and also disapproves what he should.*
1126b16–19; 818

4. *This mean habit has not been given a name.*   **1126b19–20; 819**

5. *But it has a remarkable resemblance to friendship, for the man who is disposed according to the mean habit is a man worthy of friendship, assuming that he loves us.*   **1126b20–22; 820**

6. *However, since this virtue is without passion or affection for people with whom we associate, it differs from friendship. A man does not take particular things as becoming because he is influenced by love or hatred but because he is disposed in this way. He will act similarly with strangers, intimates, and outsiders.*   **1126b22–26; 821**

7. *Nevertheless, in particular cases, he does the proper thing; it is not becoming to treat intimates and strangers in the same way, nor similarly to show displeasure toward them.*
1126b26–28; 822

8. *Therefore, as has been pointed out, he always communicates with others in an amiable manner.*   **1126b28; 823**

9. *Considering it honorable and useful, he aims to cause no offense, and even to give pleasure, for he is concerned with pleasure and sadness which occur in social intercourse.*
1126b28–31; 824

10. *Any virtuous man of this type will refuse to give pleasure and will choose to cause pain over what is dishonorable and harmful to himself or to the person doing an injury or a great wrong. Although his opposition brings not a little offense, he will disregard it.* **1126b31–35; 825**

11. *He converses differently with persons in high places and with others, with friends, and with acquaintances. Likewise, according to other differences he attributes what is becoming to each.*   **1126b36–1127a2; 826**

12. *He primarily strives to give pleasure and declines to inflict pain, considering that future events may be of greater importance. (I speak of what is honorable and useful.) But he will cause grief especially in a slight degree for the sake of a pleasure in a good that is to come. The mean then is of this nature but is nameless.*   **1127a2–7; 827**

13. *Of those who are agreeable, the man who aims at being pleasant without personal profit is called affable, but he who does so for money and things valued in terms of money is called a flatterer.*   **1127a7–10; 828**

14. *But the individual who is a trial to everyone is called quarrelsome and perverse, as has been stated.*   **1127a10–11; 829**

15. *However, the extremes seem to be mutually opposed because the mean is nameless.*
1127a11–12; 830

COMMENTARY OF ST. THOMAS

816. After the Philosopher has considered virtues relating to external things, now he considers the virtues that relate to human actions. First he

treats the serious; and then [Lect. XVI] the humorous actions, at "Since recreation should have a place etc." (1127b33). In the investigation of the serious actions, he examines pleasantness and veracity. First [1] he investigates the virtue concerned with pleasantness and sadness arising from the serious actions of men; and then [Lect. XV] the virtue concerned with veracity, at "Likewise, the mean opposed to boasting etc." (1127a13). He develops the first point in a twofold fashion. Initially [1] he shows that a mean and extremes are found in regard to pleasantness and sadness in human acts; and then [4] he examines these, at "This mean habit has not etc." He discusses the first from three aspects. First [1] he presents the vice pertaining to the excess of pleasantness. He says that in human conversation (by which men especially associate with one another according to a natural tendency) and generally in all human companionships (made possible by the fact that men communicate with one another in words and deeds) some seem to be obsequious, as it were straining to please men. Wherefore, they praise everything that others say and do for the purpose of making themselves agreeable. They never contradict people for fear of giving offense, thinking they must live without causing pain to anyone.

817. Second [2], at "**Others, on the contrary,**" he introduces the vice that pertains to the defect in such matters. He states that people who are crossgrained wish to be contrary to everything said or done as if trying to make others sad and taking care to emphasize anything that will make life unpleasant for others. These persons are called perverse or quarrelsome.

818. Last [3], at "**These habits,**" he draws the conclusion that the mean is praiseworthy, saying that these habits, which consist in an extreme, are unworthy of praise. Obviously, then, the mean habit is worthy of praise—that habit by which a man accepts what others say or do, or rightly rejects and contradicts it.

819. Next [4], at "**This mean habit,**" he defines the previous matter: first [1] the mean; and then [13] the extremes, at "Of those who are etc." He handles the initial point in a twofold manner. First [4] he treats the name of the mean habit; and then [8] its properties, at "Therefore, as has been pointed out." He considers the name under three headings. First [4] he states that the mean habit has no name.

820. Second [5], at "**But it has,**" he gives the habit a name from a resemblance to friendship. This virtue, he says, is very much like friendship because there is agreement in the external act which is especially proper to friendship, viz., to live amicably with friends. That person, who is disposed according to the mean habit of this virtue, conducts himself in agreeable association with others in a manner becoming to a friend whose friendship is moderated by reason—a thing that pertains to honorable friendship. Not every friendship is virtuous, as will be pointed out later (1574–1577). If the man who has this virtue should love those with whom he lives, his friendship will be entirely virtuous.

821. Last [6], at "**However, since,**" he shows how this virtue differs from friendship. He treats this point in a twofold manner. First [6] he presents the difference; and then [7] rejects a false understanding of it, at "Nevertheless, in particular cases etc." He says first that, since this virtue is without love (which is a passion of the sen-

sitive appetite) and without affection (which pertains to the intellective appetite) for those with whom we associate, it differs from true friendship. A man does not take the particular things said or done by others as becoming, because he is influenced by hatred or love of them but because he is disposed in this way by habit. This is proved by the fact that he observes the same not only with friends but generally with all acquaintances and strangers, intimates and outsiders. Liberality is like this. A friend gives gifts to his friends because he loves; the liberal man however gives not because he loves but because his nature is to be a free spender.

822. Then [7], at "**Nevertheless,**" he rejects a false understanding of these things. Since he just stated (821) that this virtue is practiced alike toward strangers and acquaintances, a man might consider this likeness as extending to everything. But the previously mentioned likeness must be taken as referring to this common characteristic, which is to live agreeably with others. There is a difference in regard to the special ways of living with others. The reason is that the virtue affects the proper actions in particular cases, for a person should not delight or displease intimates and outsiders in the same way.

823. At "**Therefore, as has been**" [8], he enumerates the five properties of this virtue; the first [8] of which is taken from the manner of communicating with others. As has been noted (821), one having this virtue always communicates with others in a becoming way.

824. At "**Considering,**" Aristotle gives the second property [9], which is understood on the part of the end, saying that one having this virtue aims at living with others without offense or even with pleasure. This end pertains to a good that is honorable and advantageous, i.e., useful, because it is concerned with pleasure and sadness occurring in associations in which human companionship principally and fittingly consists. This is proper to men in contrast to animals who share food and the like in common.

825. At "**Any virtuous man,**" he introduces the third property [10], which is understood by comparison with pain, saying that the man who possesses this virtue sometimes refuses to give pleasure to another, in fact sometimes chooses to cause pain. This may take place in two ways. In one way it can happen on his part: if a thing is not honorable to him, for instance, another uses indecent language; or if a thing is harmful to him, for instance, another injures him in word. In the other way, it can happen on the part of the person he lives with. This person may say or do something pertaining to his own great disgrace, or he may be greatly harmed. By reason of the fact that he is contradicted he is grieved to some extent. So the virtuous man will not take what is said by others, or if he does he will nonetheless reprove them.

826. At "**He converses differently**" he introduces the fourth property [11], which is understood by comparison with different persons. He says that a virtuous man speaks and converses in a different way with persons in high places and with private persons, with friends and with acquaintances, and so on according to other distinctions of persons, ascribing to each individual what is appropriate.

827. At "**He primarily strives,**" he presents the fifth property [12] which is taken by comparison of pleasure with pain. He affirms that the virtuous man primarily strives to give pleasure and declines to inflict pain. However,

at times he causes some grief considering that future events will outweigh the existing affliction in what concerns decency and utility or even a future important consideration, the evidence for which is provided by the present distress. He concludes that the mean habit is like this but is without a name, although we can call it affability.

828. Then [13], at "**Of those who,**" he defines the opposite vices, doing three things. First [13] he treats the vice belonging to the excess of pleasantness. He says that the man who is immoderate in being pleasant—if he does not act for something else—is called obsequious. But if he acts to acquire money or any other thing computable in money, he is called a sycophant or a flatterer.

829. Next [14], at "**But the individual,**" he refers to the opposite vice, saying that the individual who is a trial to everyone is called contentious and perverse, as has been stated previously (817).

830. Finally [15], at "**However, the extremes,**" he compares the two vices one with the other, saying that the extremes seem to be opposed to one another but not to the virtue because the mean of the virtue is nameless.

LECTURE XV
Veracity

TEXT OF ARISTOTLE (1127a13–1127b32) Chapter 7

1. *Likewise, the mean opposed to boasting treats of almost the same subject, and it too is nameless.*   **1127a13–14; 831**

2. *It is not a loss to examine these matters, for in making the investigation we will learn more about particular habits.*   **1127a14–16; 832**

3. *Observing what is so in all cases, we are assured that virtues are certain median states.*
1127a16–17; 833

4. *We have already discussed the people who cause pleasure or pain in their association with others. In like manner we will now investigate those persons who manifest truth and falsehood by words, operations, and pretense.*   **1127a17–20; 834**

5. *The boaster simulates non-existent qualities, or claims a greater distinction than he really has. On the contrary, the dissembler denies or minimizes the qualities he has. But the man who observes the mean is admirable, being truthful both in life and speech, acknowledging that his own qualities are neither more nor less excellent than they really are.*   **1127a20–26; 835**

6. *Each of these acts may be done both for the sake of something else and for nothing other than itself. As a man is, so he speaks, acts, and lives, unless some other cause affects him.*
1127a26–28; 836

7. *A lie is intrinsically evil and to be avoided but the truth is both good and to be praised. So, the man who speaks the truth is worthy of praise as being better, while the above two who do not tell the truth are worthy of blame, more especially the boaster.*   **1127a28–32; 837**

8. *We will discuss both, but first the truthful man. We are not going to investigate the person who speaks the truth in his agreements nor on any subject pertaining to right or its violation, for this belongs to another virtue. But we do intend to study the person who manifests the truth by his conversation and way of living (insofar as he does this from habit) in matters not touching justice and injustice.*   **1127a32–1127b3; 838**

9. *Such a man seems to observe moderation, for he is a lover of the truth and, being truthful where it makes little difference, he will speak the truth all the more where it does matter. He will fear a lie as disgraceful because he feared it in itself. Such a man is worthy of praise.*
1127b3–7; 839

10. *He turns aside from the truth more by understatement, for this seems rather prudent since overstatements are irritating.*   **1127b7–9; 840**

11. *The person who boasts more excellent talents than he possesses for no ulterior motive has a semblance of evil; otherwise, he would not find pleasure in lying. He is really, though, more vain than evil. But one who boasts for something else, like glory or honor, does not deserve great blame. However, the man who boasts for the sake of money or objects valued in money is more vicious.*   **1127b9–13; 841–842**

12. *A boaster is constituted not by capability but by choice. He is such in accordance with a habit, as is the case with the liar who finds pleasure in lying itself, or the one who lies because he desires glory or profit.*   **1127b14–17; 843**

13. *Therefore, people who boast for the sake of fame simulate qualities that win praise and admiration. Those who boast for the sake of gain pretend things more closely connected with profit and things whose absence is not clearly apparent. For this reason many braggarts pretend to be doctors, soothsayers, or wise men, for the qualities mentioned are verified in them.*
1127b17–22; 844–845

14. Dissemblers, however, who say less than what is true seem to be more gracious. For they apparently speak not to acquire gain but to avoid offense and vanity.   **1127b22–24; 846**

15. Some people especially deny qualities about themselves that bring renown, as Socrates did. Others, who disclaim insignificant and obvious things are called affected humbugs (blato-panurgi). They are readily despised; and at times they seem guilty of ostentation, like the Spartans by their clothing. For this reason excess and immoderate deficiency seem characteristic of the boastful. Still others who moderately employ dissimulation, even dissembling about things obvious and ready at hand, seem rather agreeable.   **1127b25–31; 847–848**

16. As being more vicious, the boaster seems more opposed to the truthful man.

1127b31–32; 849

COMMENTARY OF ST. THOMAS

831. After the Philosopher has finished the treatise on the virtue possessing the mean in human actions in regard to amiability, he now treats a virtue called veracity, which possesses a mean in the same human actions. First [1] he explains his intention; and then [5] he defines his proposition, at "The boaster simulates etc." He develops the first point in three ways. First [1] he discloses that a certain virtue is a mean opposed to boasting. Next [2], at "It is not a loss etc.," he shows that we must treat this virtue. Last [4], at "We have already discussed etc.," he explains the difference between this and the preceding virtue. He says first that the mean opposed to boasting treats about nearly the same subject as the previous virtue. The reason is that it is concerned with human actions, but not in relation to the same thing, since it does not regard pleasantness but another topic to be discussed shortly (838). As in the case of the previous virtue, this mean too is nameless.

832. Then [2], at "It is not a loss," he explains why it is necessary to investigate this virtue, giving two reasons. First [2] he says that it is not profitless but in fact useful to moral science to treat the virtues as we go along. In this way we will learn better what pertains to morals if, as we proceed, we treat the material pertaining to individual habits. The reason is that the science of moral matters is completed by a knowledge of particulars.

833. At "Observing what," he presents the second reason [3]. We shall be assured that the virtues are kinds of median states by seeing how this is the case in the individual virtues.

834. Next [4], at "We have already," he defines the difference between this and the preceding virtue. He states that we have already considered (816–830) the people who in some way give pleasure or pain in their association and conversation with others. But we must still discuss those people who are truthful or deceitful in their words and actions or who simulate these qualities by their deeds.

835. Then [5], at "The boaster simulates," he treats the virtues and vices. First [5] he presents the virtue and the opposite vices; and then [8], at "We will discuss both etc.," he investigates them. He handles the first point from three aspects. First [5] he shows what belongs to the mean and extremes in this matter. Next [6], at "Each of these etc.," he explains how the things which were discussed pertain to the median habit and the extremes. Third [7], at "A lie is intrinsically etc.," he reveals that the mean habit is praiseworthy but the extremes, vicious. He says first that the boaster who sins by excess pretends

certain praiseworthy qualities, and this in two ways. In one way he pretends to have some distinctions that he does not possess. In the other way, he claims distinctions greater than they really are. But the person who sins by defect is called a dissembler. However, the man who possesses the mean is said to be *autocastos*, i.e., admirable in himself, because he does not seek to be admired more than becomes him. He is also said to be *autophastos*, i.e., essentially sincere, manifesting himself to be what he is. He is truthful inasmuch as the things he divulges about himself are true. He does this not only by word but also by his manner of living, according as his exterior conduct and his speech conform to his nature.

836. At "**Each of these**" [6], he explains how these things pertain to the three specified habits, saying that each of the above-mentioned acts may happen in two ways. In one way, it may be done for the sake of something else, for instance, a man denies that he is what he is because of fear; in the other way, not for the sake of something else but because he takes delight in the act itself. This property belongs to a habit, since everyone speaks, acts and lives according to the quality of his habit. Of course at times he may act differently because something else arises.

837. Then [7], at "**A lie is intrinsically etc.**," he discloses what deserves praise and what blame in the habits mentioned, saying that a lie is essentially evil and to be avoided, but truth is good and to be praised. Signs were instituted to represent things as they are. Therefore, if a person represents a thing otherwise than it is by lying, he acts in an inordinate and vicious manner. But if he speaks the truth, he acts in an orderly and virtuous manner. Now, it is clear that the man who

speaks the truth possesses the mean because he designates a thing as it is. The truth consists in an equality that is a mean between great and small. But the person who lies stands in an extreme either by excess because he affirms more than really is, or by defect because less than really is. Hence, it is evident that both are blameworthy. But the boaster who sins by excess deserves more blame since he departs farther from the truth; for the less, not the more, is found in the mean.

838. Next [8], at "**We will discuss both**," he investigates the previously mentioned habits, treating first [8] the virtue and then [11] the opposite vices, at "The person who boasts etc." He treats the first point in a threefold manner. First [8] he determines what truthful person we are discussing. Next [9], at "Such a man etc.," he shows what is especially characteristic of this person. Third [10], at "He turns aside etc.," he explains to what extreme the person is more inclined. He says first that we must talk about these habits, but first about the truthful man. However, we do not have in mind now the person who speaks the truth in judicial testimony, for example, a witness who reveals the truth when questioned by a judge; nor the person who speaks the truth in any matter touching right—this pertains to another virtue, viz., justice. But we are directing our attention to that truthful man who manifests the truth in his life and conversation in matter not having distinction of justice and injustice. However, he manifests the truth only by reason of the disposition of the habit, as was said before about a previous virtue (821) that it aims at living pleasantly with others, not by reason of love but by reason of its habit. So, too, this virtue shows the truth not on account of the observance

of justice but on account of the inclination it has to manifest the truth.

839. At "**Such a man**" [9], Aristotle explains what particularly pertains to the truthful man we have in mind, saying he is one who apparently observes moderation in his actions, avoiding excess and defect. He loves truthfulness and the truth even where damage or profit is of little importance. The reason is that he hates a lie as something shameful in itself, and not only because it injures another. A person of this kind is to be commended.

840. Then [10], at "**He turns aside,**" he explains to what extreme the truthful man more inclines, affirming that since sometimes it is quite difficult to tell the exact truth, he wishes to lean towards understatement rather than overstatement. This seems to pertain more to prudence since men tend to excess, and when speaking about themselves, they become tiresome to others. The reason for annoyance is that they seem in this to prefer themselves to others.

841. Next [11], at "**The person who boasts,**" he examines the opposite vices. He considers this point under three aspects. First [11] he investigates the vice pertaining to excess; next [14] the vice pertaining to defect, at "Dissemblers, however etc."; and last [16] the opposition of vices among themselves, at "As being more vicious etc." He treats the first point in a threefold manner. First [11] he shows in how many ways we may commit the vice of boasting which is an extreme by excess. Second [12], at "A boaster is constituted etc.," he explains in what respect we may especially take into account the vice of boasting. Finally [13], at "Therefore, people who etc.," he shows in what things we may principally commit the vice of boasting.

842. He states first that sometimes a man says boastfully about himself things that are untrue or exaggerated, not for some other purpose but for the enjoyment he gets out of it. Such a man is said to have a semblance of evil, otherwise he would not find pleasure in lying, for this arises from a disordered soul. However, he is not at all evil since he does not intend any malice; he is only vain for taking pleasure in a thing which is really neither good nor useful. In another way, a person speaks boastfully about himself because he wants glory or honor. This person really ought not to be blamed since glory and honor have a certain relationship to honorable things for which people are praised and honored. In still another way, people brag about themselves for the sake of money or some other thing that can be valued in money. An individual belonging to this class is more vicious because he lies for an inferior good.

843. At "**A boaster is constituted**" [12], he explains in what respect we may take boasting into account, saying that a man is not considered a boaster from the fact that he has or has not the capability, but from the fact that he chooses to boast. He is called a boaster according to the habit that this choice follows. It is the same with any liar who is such in choosing to lie, or finding pleasure in lying, or lies out of his desire for fame or profit.

844. Then [13], at "**Therefore, people who,**" he explains the things that people usually boast about. Obviously, persons who find enjoyment in boasting boast indiscriminately. But those who boast for the sake of fame pretend things that seem worthy of praise, like virtuous works, or that have reference to good fortune, like the dignity of wealth and so on. Those,

however, who boast for the sake of profit pretend things in which others find pleasure, otherwise it would profit them nothing. Again, when the things they boast about are not true, they take care that this fact can be hidden so their lie may not be discovered.

845. He takes an example from two fields: first, from things belonging to medicine, since everyone wants health and no one can find out whether the doctor makes a mistake; second, from divination, which naturally disturbs men and where they cannot easily discover a lie. For this reason people who boast for profit especially pretend to be doctors or men wise in foretelling the future. Perhaps his use of the word "wise" can be referred to this that these men boast that they have a knowledge of divine things that is desirable and hidden.

846. Next [14], at "**Dissemblers, however,**" he considers the vice belonging to the defect. On this point he does two things. First [14] he compares this vice with boasting; and then [15] points out its difference at "Some people especially etc." He says first that dissemblers who minimize the truth about themselves seem to have more pleasing ways than boasters, because they apparently do not speak this way for the sake of gain but as if fleeing from vanity.

847. At "**Some people especially**" [15] he explains how this vice is practiced in different ways, saying there are some who especially deny about themselves things pertaining to great

renown, for example, Socrates denied that he was wise. There are others who want to show by certain insignificant and obvious things that they do not pretend more excellent things about themselves than they possess. Such are called *blato-panurgi,* i.e., men who have their delight in a certain cunning pretense. *Panurgi* is a Greek word for "cunning fellow," while *blaton* means something done amusingly. These, he says, are readily despised because their pretense is too obvious. A defect of this nature in external things sometimes seems to pertain to boasting when in this way they want to appear better and more observant of moderation, like the Spartans who wore clothing humbler than became their state. For this reason an excess and an immoderate deficiency in externals seem to pertain to boasting precisely because a certain singularity in a man is displayed in case of each.

848. Still others exercise this vice in a mitigated form, since they neither altogether deny famous deeds done by themselves nor do they even attribute to themselves negligible qualities, practicing the vice in matter obvious and at hand. People like this seem to be pleasing, as was just said (846).

849. Then [16], at "**As being more vicious,**" he considers the opposition between the vice and the virtue, saying that the boaster is more in opposition to the truthful man because more vicious, as we have already noted (837). The worse vice is always more opposed to virtue.

LECTURE XVI
Amusement

TEXT OF ARISTOTLE (*1127b33–1128b9*) Chapter 8

1. *Since recreation should have a place in our life and our social living by means of playful conversation, this would be a suitable time for a discussion of what things are proper to say and hear. In matters of this nature, speaking and listening are different, but it is clear that we have both excess and defect in respect to the mean.* 1127b33–1128a4; 850–851

2. *People who engage in too much derision are buffoons and nuisances wanting laughter at any cost. They try more to get a laugh than to converse politely and avoid offending the persons they mock.* 1128a4–7; 852

3. *On the other hand, persons who say nothing funny and are disagreeable to those who do, seem uncultured and rude.* 1128a7–9; 853

4. *But men indulging in jest with good taste are called witty, like those who give a humorous turn to things.* 1128a9–10; 854

5. *Actions of this kind seem to belong to character, for as bodies are judged from their movements, so too are characters.* 1128a10–12; 855

6. *Since laughter is quite popular, most people take more pleasure in fun and in joking reproach of others than they should. Hence they are pleased with buffoons who are called witty. However, from what has been said it is obvious that buffoons are quite different from persons of wit.* 1128a12–16; 856

7. *Tact belongs to the mean habit of this virtue. It is characteristic of a tactful person to tell and listen to such tales as become a decent and liberal man.* 1128a16–19; 857

8. *Now, the witty person speaks and listens to what is becoming in jest. But the jesting of the liberal man differs from that of the servile man; the jesting of the cultured man from that of the uncultured.* 1128a19–22; 858

9. *Anyone can see this in the comedies of the ancient and modern authors. In the earlier plays obscene language appears and is an object of laughter; in the later it is rather implied. This difference towards obscenities is of no small importance for decency.* 1128a22–25; 859

10. *We must determine, then, whether a man is good at raillery because he says what becomes a liberal man, or because he does not offend his listener, or because he even delights him.* 1128a25–28; 860

11. *This norm is indefinite to the extent that what is hateful to one person is pleasing to another. But each will listen to the things which give him pleasure, while he seems to encourage the things which he permits.* 1128a28–29; 861

12. *The virtuous person will not employ every kind of jest, for some jokes are in fact an insult. But legislators forbid the making of some insulting remarks. Actually they should forbid all reviling. Here the pleasing and liberal man will be as it were a law unto himself. Therefore, either the witty or the tactful person possesses the mean in this matter.* 1128a29–33; 862–863

13. *However, the buffoon, less vicious than the derider, spares neither himself nor others for the sake of a laugh. Likewise, he says such things as the polite person would never think of saying—would not in fact listen to.* 1128a33–1128b1; 864

14. *But the lout is useless at these conversations, contributing nothing and making everyone uncomfortable. Nevertheless, recreation and jest seem to be necessary for human life.* 1128b1–4; 865

15. *In human living there are three median courses, all of which regard communication in speech and action. They differ, however, for one deals with truthfulness and the others with*

what is pleasing. Of this second class, one concerns pleasure taken in amusements, the other concerns pleasure in things according to another aspect of life, viz., conversations.

1128b4–9; 866

COMMENTARY OF ST. THOMAS

850. After the Philosopher has finished the consideration of the virtues dealing with human actions of a serious nature, he now considers a certain virtue which deals with amusement. He develops this point in three ways. First [1] he shows there can be a virtue and vice having to do with amusement. Next [2], at "People who engage in too much etc.," he treats the virtue and the opposite vices concerned with amusement. Third [15], at "In human living there are etc.," he explains the difference between this and those virtues already considered. In regard to the first we must consider that, as has been shown (329), there can be no corresponding virtue and vice concerned with what is intrinsically evil and incapable of having an aspect of good. Consequently, if no aspect of good can be found in amusement there will be no virtue connected with it.

851. But amusement does have an aspect of good inasmuch as it is useful for human living. As man sometimes needs to give his body rest from labors, so also he sometimes needs to rest his soul from mental strain that ensues from his application to serious affairs. This is done by amusement. For this reason Aristotle says that, since there should be some relaxation for man from the anxieties and cares of human living and social intercourse by means of amusement—thus amusement has the aspect of useful good—it follows that in amusement there can be a certain agreeable association of men with one another, so they may say and hear such things as are proper and in the proper way. Yet, in matters of this

kind, talking and listening are very different, for a man properly listens to things he could not properly say. But wherever difference exists between the things that ought to be done and ought not to done, there is found not only a mean but also excess and defect in regard to this mean. Hence we have a virtuous mean and extremes concerned with amusement.

852. At "**People who engage**" [2] he considers the mean and the extremes. First [2] he speaks about the nature of each habit; then [7], at "Tact belongs etc.," he shows what is proper to each habit. He discusses the first point in a threefold manner: initially [2] he explains what the mean and the extremes in amusement are; then [5] at "Actions of this kind etc.," he shows that they belong to a difference of character; last [6], at "Since laughter is quite etc.," he discloses that the extreme is sometimes taken for the mean. He treats this first point from three aspects. In the beginning [2] he shows what belongs to excess, saying that those who indulge excessively in playful derision are *bomolochi* or temple plunderers because of a resemblance to birds of prey who used to fly over the temple to pounce upon the entrails of sacrificed animals. In that way these people lie in wait so they can pounce upon something to turn into a laugh. On this account persons of this kind are a nuisance because they want to make laughter out of everything. They make more effort to do this than to engage in becoming or polite conversation and avoid disturbing the man they heap with playful reproach. They would rather tell scan-

dalous stories, even at the risk of offending others, than (not) cause men to laugh.

853. Second [3], at "**On the other hand,**" he explains the nature of the vice by defect, stating that men who never want to say anything funny and are disagreeable to the people who do (these being reasonably disturbed) seem to be uncultured or boorish and coarse, like those who are not mellowed by amusing recreation.

854. Third [4], at "**But men indulging,**" he explains the nature of the mean in amusement, saying that men who devote themselves to amusement in moderation are called witty (*eutrapeli*), as it were, good at turning because they becomingly give an amusing turn to what is said and done.

855. Then [5], at "**Actions of this kind,**" he shows that the actions just mentioned belong to different habits. He says that these movements by which a person wishes to amuse others too much, or too little, or in a moderate way are indications of internal dispositions of habit. As external movements of bodies clearly indicate their internal dispositions, so external actions manifest internal characters.

856. At "**Since laughter is quite**" [6], he explains how the extreme sometimes is taken for the mean. He says that many people bubble over with laughter and take more pleasure than they should in jest and in joking reproach of others. Hence, they give the name witty to buffoons who please them by excessive indulgence in jest which the majority of men love immoderately. Nevertheless, as is clear from what was said before (852–854), buffoons are quite different from witty people.

857. Next [7], at "**Tact belongs,**" he shows what properly belongs to the preceding habits. First [7] he explains what is peculiar to the mean of the virtue; and then [13], at "However, the buffoon etc.," what is proper to the extreme by excess. Finally [14], at "But the lout etc.," he discloses what pertains to the extreme by defect. He handles the initial point from two aspects. First [7] he shows how the witty person conducts himself in general with reference to fun; and then [10], at "We must determine etc.," how he acts especially in friendly banter. He considers this first in a threefold way. In the beginning [7] he brings out that the use of clean fun pertains to the mean habit. He affirms that what is characteristic of a tactful person (*epydexiotis*), i.e., of a man well-fitted and prepared to engage in conversation with others, belongs to the mean habit of this virtue. It is proper to men of this sort to narrate and listen to such amusing incidents as become a decent and liberal man who possesses a soul free from slavish passions.

858. Next [8], at "**Now, the witty person,**" he gives a reason as proof for what he has said, viz., that wherever something is found that can be done in a becoming manner, there is a thing that belongs to virtue. But it happens that a witty person says and listens to what is becoming. This is obvious from the different kinds of jest. The jesting of the liberal man who spontaneously strives to act virtuously differs from the jesting of the servile man who is engaged in disreputable activities. The jesting of the cultured man who has been instructed how he should recreate differs from the jesting of the uncultured man who has not been trained by any instruction in jesting. Hence, it is clear that it pertains to the mean habit of virtue to speak and listen to what is becoming in jesting.

859. Last [9], at "**Anyone can see,**" he introduces a proof for the previous statement that the jesting of the cultured and the uncultured person differs. This, he says, is particularly evident in considering the conversation of the players with one another in the old and new comedies or plays. The evidence is that where these narratives in places contain obscene language, some create derision when they turn the obscene words into laughter; but others create a suspicion when they imply that those who were speaking in an obscene manner had evil in their hearts. However, obviously it is of great importance to human decency whether a man in playful conversation speaks obscenely or properly.

860. At "**We must determine**" [10], he explains how the virtuous man conducts himself regarding jesting insults. On this point Aristotle does three things. First [10] he asks the question whether we must decide that a person does well at raillery by reason of the things which he says, i.e., because he says what is becomingly said by a liberal man who is virtuous and decent; or that he is not determined according to this but rather by reason of the end or effect, i.e., because he aims not to offend his listener; or, what is more, aims to give him pleasure.

861. Then [11], at "**This norm is indefinite,**" he answers the second part of the question, saying that it is indeterminate what may offend or please the listener because different things are odious and pleasant to different people. Everyone will gladly listen to what pleases him. And, as long as no offense is intended, a man seems to promote those things which he patiently hears by co-operating in them with others.

862. Third [12], at "**The virtuous person,**" he shows that something is settled as to the first part, viz., as to affronts that are offered. It is clear that the virtuous man does not make use of every reproach, since reproach is a kind of insult. Besides, legislators forbid the hurling of any insult that defames a man. They do not forbid reproachful remarks that are fittingly uttered for amusement or for a man's correction (a thing to be managed without loss of good name). That man who acts in a pleasing and polite manner in raillery seems to be a law unto himself, provided that by his own choice he avoids the things forbidden by the law and makes use of the things sanctioned by the law.

863. Finally, he comes to the conclusion that the man possessing the mean is such as was described, whether he is called *epidexios*, i.e., tactful, or *eutrapelos*, i.e., witty.

864. Next [13], at "**However, the buffoon,**" he explains the viciousness of the excess, saying that the buffoon is less vicious than the mocker because the mocker tries to put another to shame while the buffoon does not aim at this but only at getting a laugh. The latter spares neither himself nor others in attempting to create laughter, since he makes fun both of his own tales and of the sayings and deeds of others. Besides, he says things that a polite and virtuous person would not say, and some that he should not say and should not even listen to.

865. Then [14], at "**But the lout,**" he treats the vice by defect, saying that the man who is uncultured, i.e., boorish, is useless at these witty conversations. He contributes nothing to them but is disagreeable to everyone. He is vicious in that he completely abhors jest, which is necessary for human living as a kind of recreation.

866. Next [15], at **"In human living there are,"** he deduces the difference between this virtue and the two previously discussed, stating that in human life there are the three median states mentioned, all of which regard communication in words and works. But they differ among themselves, since one of them deals with truthfulness in speech and action, while the others pertain to what is pleasing. One of these concerns pleasure taken in amusement; the other concerns pleasure taken in conversation according to our usual way of living, i.e., in serious matters.

LECTURE XVII
Shame

TEXT OF ARISTOTLE (*1128b10–1128b35*) Chapter 9

1. *Shame is not properly spoken of as a virtue because it is more like a passion than a habit.*
1128b10–11; 867

2. *In any case shame is defined as fear of disgrace.*   1128b11–12; 868

3. *Like fear, shame is brought about by reason of danger, for people who feel ashamed blush, and those who fear death grow pale. Both qualities are in some measure modifications of the body, and so pertain rather to passion than habit.*   1128b12–15; 869–870

4. *This passion is not becoming to persons of every age but only to the young.*
1128b15–16; 871

5. *We are of the opinion that it is well for the young to feel shame because, living according to their emotions, many of them would fall into sin but are restrained by shame. Moreover, we are in the habit of praising youngsters who have a sense of shame.*   1128b16–19; 872

6. *But no one praises an old man because he is shamefaced, for we think it unbecoming of him to commit acts giving rise to shame.*   1128b19–21; 873

7. *Likewise, shame is not characteristic of a virtuous person but follows evil actions such as must not be done.*   1128b21–23; 874

8. *If some actions are shameful in fact and others only considered such, this does not matter for neither kind should be done, and so should not be objects of shame. The wicked, however, perform disgraceful actions of this kind.*   1128b23–25; 875–876

9. *It is unreasonable to hold that if a man is so constituted that he is ashamed if he does a disgraceful action, he is considered virtuous on this account. Shame is felt because of acts voluntarily done, and no virtuous man voluntarily does evil.*   1128b25–29; 877–878

10. *Shame will be a virtue resulting from the supposition of something else, viz., if a man did such an act, he would be ashamed. But virtue does not work this way.*   1128b29–31; 879

11. *But, if shamelessness and the absence of shame at doing dishonorable actions is evil, it is not on that account virtuous to be ashamed to do things of this kind.*   1128b31–33; 880–882

12. *Likewise, continence is not a virtue but has a mixture of virtue. Hence, we shall consider this in a later treatise, but now we must treat justice.*   1128b33–35; 883–884

COMMENTARY OF ST. THOMAS

867. After the Philosopher has completed the treatise on the median qualities that are virtues, he now treats a median quality that is not a virtue, viz., shame. First he shows that shame is not a virtue. Then [7], at "Likewise, continence is not etc.," he says a similar thing about continence, which, although laudable, is not a virtue. He discusses the first point from two aspects. First [1] he investigates the genus of shame; and then [4], at "This passion is not etc.," he examines its subject. He treats this first in a twofold

manner. Initially [1] he presents his proposition, saying that shame is not properly called a virtue. But shame is more like a passion than a habit which is the genus of virtue.

868. Next [2], at "**In any case,**" he proves his proposition in two ways: first [2] by means of a definition of shame. Shame is said to be fear of disgrace or confusion which is the opposite of glory. But fear is a certain passion. Consequently, shame belongs to the genus of passion.

869. Then [3], at "**Like fear,**" he

proves the same thing by the effect of shame. In this regard we must consider that passions are movements of the sensitive appetite that uses bodily organs. Hence all the passions are accompanied by some corporeal change. Shame and fear—which is concerned with the danger of death—have a general resemblance in that each passion is judged by a change in the color of the body.

870. But they have particular differences, since people who are ashamed blush, while those who fear death turn pale. The reason for this difference is that the spirit and the humors naturally rush to the place feeling the need. Now, the seat of life is the heart, and so when danger of death is feared, the spirit and the humors speed to the heart. Consequently, the surface of the body, being as it were deserted, grows pale. On the other hand, honor and confusion are numbered among external things. Therefore, since a man fears the loss of honor by shame, he blushes as the humors and spirits stream back to the surface. It is evident then that both shame and fear of death are certain alterations of the body inasmuch as they are accompanied by a change. Because this apparently belongs rather to passion than habit, it is obvious that shame is not a virtue.

871. At "**This passion**" [4], he discloses what is the fitting subject of shame. First [4] he shows at what age it is becoming; and then [7], at "Likewise, shame is not etc.," for what condition. He develops the first point in a threefold fashion. First [4] he presents his proposition, viz., that it is not becoming to persons of every age but to the young.

872. Then [5], at "**We are of the opinion,**" he proves in two ways that shame is becoming to adolescence. In one way he shows this from the peculiar nature of youth, namely, that on account of the intense desires of their age they live according to their emotions. For that reason they are inclined to sin in various ways. But they are restrained from this because of shame by which they fear disgrace. Therefore, shame is becoming to youth. In the other way he gives evidence of the same thing from usage. We are accustomed to praise young people who have a sense of shame.

873. Third [6], at "**But no one praises,**" he explains that shame is not becoming to another period of life, i.e., old age, saying that no one praises an old man for feeling shame. The reason is that we think it unbecoming of him to do any shameful deed from which shame usually arises. Besides, we think both that old men have been proved by their years and that they ought not to do any shameful act from passion after the fire of youth has subsided.

874. Next [7], at "**Likewise, shame is not,**" he shows to what condition shame is or is not becoming. He handles this point under two headings. First [7] he explains that it is not becoming to the virtuous person. Then [8], at "If some actions etc.," he answers certain frivolous objections against his thesis. He says that shame does not belong to the man of virtue, for it occurs in regard to evil deeds. But the virtuous man does not do wicked actions because virtue is a quality which makes good both its possessor and his work. Therefore, shame is not becoming to a virtuous person.

875. Then [8], at "**If some actions,**" he answers three objections dealing with what has just been said. The first [8] is that someone might say that shame arises not only from truly dis-

graceful acts, which are contrary to virtue, but also from actions believed to be disgraceful.

876. But Aristotle says that it does not make any difference for our thesis, since the morally good man must not do things shameful either according to truth or opinion, and so is not in danger of being ashamed of anything. But the wicked person characteristically is of the sort who perform acts certainly disgraceful or held to be such.

877. He introduces a second objection at "**It is unreasonable**" [9]. A person could say that, although the man of virtue does not have anything to be ashamed of, nevertheless he is so disposed that if he did something of the kind, he would be ashamed of it. Therefore, in case anyone should think on this account that shame belongs to the virtuous person, he proves in two ways that this is untenable.

878. First [9] he says that shame, strictly speaking, regards only voluntary failings for which blame is due. But it is inconsistent with virtue that someone should voluntarily do evil. Therefore, shame does not belong to virtue for the reason just given. The case would be otherwise if shame were among the things which can happen involuntarily like sickness. Hence, it can be proper for the virtuous man even when well to be solicitous about a doctor on account of the sickness that can happen.

879. Second [10], he excludes the preceding objection at "**Shame will be.**" He says that if the objection were valid, shame would be a certain conditional virtuous state, for the virtuous man would be ashamed if he were to do wrong. But a conditional state (that a man would be ashamed) is not one of the qualities that properly belong to virtuous people. Rather, it belongs to

them absolutely, as is the case of all the virtues. We must conclude then that shame is not a special quality in a virtuous person.

880. At "**But if shamelessness**" [11] he gives a third objection. Someone could draw the conclusion that, because shamelessness and the absence of shame concerning a disreputable operation is an evil thing, for this reason shame is virtuous.

881. But Aristotle says that this is not a necessary inference because both shame and shamelessness suppose a dishonorable act which is not attributable to a morally good man. On this basis it is more reasonable that a man should reject the disgraceful operation by reason of shame than not care about it by reason of shamelessness. From this it is clear also that shame is not a virtue, for if it were a virtue it would exist in a virtuous person.

882. We must take into account that the Philosopher previously (356) treated the praiseworthy passion of righteous indignation (*nemesis*), and that here he does not mention it because it is not his intention to treat these passions on this occasion. This matter pertains rather to rhetoric, as is clear from the second book of the *Rhetoric* (Ch. 9, 1386b9 sq.). Hence, neither does he here consider shame except to show that it is not a virtue. He leaves the same thing to be understood about righteous indignation.

883. Then [12], at "**Likewise, continence,**" he introduces something similar concerning continence which, although laudable, is not a virtue but has an admixture of virtue. Certainly, the continent man follows right reason, and this pertains to virtue. Nevertheless, he suffers vehement and evil desires, and this pertains to lack of virtue. We will discuss these subjects af-

terwards in the seventh book (1435–1454). It is enough that he brings out in a fitting manner shame's resemblance to continence because shame is especially necessary where evil passions abound, as they do in continent peo-ple. We have already remarked this (873).

884. Finally, he makes a connection with what follows, saying that we must next discuss justice. With this the teaching of the fourth book comes to an end.

BOOK FIVE
JUSTICE
LECTURE I
Justice

TEXT OF ARISTOTLE (*1129a3–1129b11*) Chapter 1

1. We must give our attention to justice and injustice so as to determine what is the nature of the actions done, what is the mean of justice, and between what extremes the just action is a mean.   **1129a3–5; 885–886**

2. It is our intention to proceed according to the same method we used with the virtues just studied.   **1129a5–6; 887**

3. Apparently everyone wants to call justice that habit by which men are disposed to just works, and by which they actually perform and will just deeds. We must speak in a similar way about injustice, viz., that it is a habit by which men are disposed to unjust deeds and by which they do and will unjust actions. For that reason we must presuppose what is said here in outline (in typo).   **1129a6–11; 888–889**

4. Likewise, the same is not true in regard to sciences and potencies as in regard to habits, for contraries belong to the same potency and the same science, but with a habit contrary things are not referred to it. We see, for example, that things contrary to health do not proceed from health, but only things in keeping with it. Thus we say that a man walks in a healthy way when he walks like a healthy man.   **1129a11–17; 890–891**

5. Oftentimes, then, one contrary habit is known by another, and oftentimes by its subject. If a healthy condition is known, then an unhealthy condition also becomes known. But from the things that make a man healthy a healthy condition is known, and the things themselves from the condition. If firmness of flesh is a sign of good condition, then flabbiness is necessarily a sign of bad condition. Likewise, what makes a man healthy necessarily makes his flesh firm.   **1129a17–23; 892**

6. It follows in most instances that if one of opposites is spoken of in various ways then the other also can be, as is the case with what is just and unjust.   **1129a23–26; 893**

7. Justice and injustice can be spoken of in various ways but the different meanings lending themselves to equivocation are not immediately apparent, and are not so evident as in the things which are widely separated. In these there is a great difference in concept, for instance, the name key is used equivocally both for the clavicle in the shoulder of animals and for the instrument which locks doors.   **1129a26–31; 894**

8. The unjust man should be understood in as many ways as he is designated. He is spoken of as lawbreaking, as covetous and as unfair. It is clear then that the just man will be taken as law-abiding and fair. Hence what is just is according to law and fair, but what is unjust is contrary to law and unfair.   **1129a31–1129b1; 895–896**

9. Since the unjust man is covetous, he will be concerned not about all goods but about whatever pertains to fortune and misfortune. Goods of this kind are always good in themselves but not always for a particular man. They are objects of his prayers and pursuits. This ought not to be so, but a man should pray that the things that are good in themselves become good for him, and should choose such as are good for him.   **1129b1–6; 897**

10. But the unjust man does not always choose too much, rather sometimes too little of the things burdensome in themselves. However, because a lesser evil apparently is in some way a good—covetousness is concerned with a good—therefore it seems that this type of man is covetous. But he is unfair—a term which contains both and is common.   **1129b6–10; 898**

11. *Besides, the unjust man is lawbreaking, but this lawlessness or inequality contains all injustice and is common in respect of all kinds of injustice.*   **1129b10–11; 899**

COMMENTARY OF ST. THOMAS

885. After the Philosopher has finished the consideration of the moral virtues dealing with the passions, he now begins to consider the virtue of justice dealing with actions. He divides the inquiry into two parts, in the first of which he examines justice in the proper sense; and then [Lect. XVII], at "Whether or not it is possible etc." (1138a4), in the metaphorical sense. He discusses the first point under two headings. Initially [1] he investigates the virtue of justice; and then [Lect. XVI], at "Next we will treat equity etc." (1137a31), a certain virtue, namely, equity that gives direction to ordinary justice. He handles the initial point in a twofold manner. First [1] he indicates what he intends to treat; and next [3], at "Apparently everyone wants to call etc.," he carries out his intention. He considers the first under two aspects. Initially [1] he shows what subject he intends to consider, viz., justice and injustice. Concerning justice he proposes for consideration three differences existing between justice and the previously mentioned virtues.

886. The first difference is touched upon when he says that we must aim at such operations as are done by justice and injustice. The virtues and vices discussed before (649–884) are concerned with the passions, for there we consider in what way a man may be internally influenced by reason of the passions; but we do not consider what is externally done, except as something secondary, inasmuch as external operations originate from internal passions. However, in treating justice and injustice we direct our principal attention to what a man does externally;

how he is influenced internally we consider only as a by-product, namely, according as he is helped or hindered in the operation. The second difference is touched upon when he says "what is the mean of justice and the just action," i.e., the object of justice. In the virtues previously treated we took the mean of reason and not of the thing. But in justice the mean of the thing is used, as will be determined later (932–977). The third difference is touched upon when he says "and between what extremes the just action is the mean." Each of the afore-mentioned virtues is a mean between two vices, but justice is not a mean between two vices, as will be clear afterwards (993–994).

887. Then [2], at "It is our intention," he shows by what method we are to examine the differences just mentioned. He says that we intend to investigate justice in the same way as we investigated the virtues just discussed, i.e., according to type and so on.

888. Next [3], at "**Apparently everyone etc.**," he begins the investigation of justice. First [3] he distinguishes particular from legal justice. Then [Lect. IV], at "One species of particular etc." (1130b30), he considers particular justice, his principal concern. He discusses the first point in a threefold manner. First [3] he divides justice into legal and particular. Second [Lect. II], at "Since it was said that etc." (1129b12), he shows what the nature of legal justice is. Third [Lect. III], at "We are now investigating etc." (1130a14), he explains that, besides legal justice, there is a particular justice. He treats the initial point in a twofold manner. First [3] he shows what the names, jus-

tice and injustice, signify; and then [6], at "It follows in most instances etc.," he distinguishes the two concepts. He develops the first under three headings. At the outset [3] he explains justice and injustice. Next [4], at "Likewise the same etc.," he shows that the explanation is reasonable. Last [5], at "Oftentimes then etc.," he infers a corollary from the premises. He says in the beginning that all seem to contend that justice is the sort of habit that brings about three effects in man. The first is an inclination to a work of justice in accord with which a man is said to be disposed to just works. The second is a just action. The third is that a man wants to perform just operations. We must say the same about injustice, namely, that it is a habit by which men are disposed to unjust deeds and by which they do and will unjust actions. For that reason we must presuppose these things about justice as apparently typical in such matters.

889. Likewise, we must take into consideration that he properly explained justice after the manner of a will, which does not have passions but nevertheless is the principle of external actions. Consequently, the will is a proper subject of justice, which is not concerned with the passions.

890. At "Likewise, the same" [4] he shows that the preceding explanations are reasonable in this respect, viz., that justice is explained by the fact that its purpose is to will and perform just actions, and injustice to will and perform unjust actions. What is true of sciences and potencies is not true of habits, for contraries belong to the same potency (for example, white and black to sight) and to the same science (for instance, health and sickness to medicine). But in regard to habits, contrary things are not referred to them.

891. He takes an example from habits of the body. Not the things that are contrary to health but only those in keeping with health proceed from health. In this way we say that a man walks with a vigorous step who is vigorous in health. Hence science itself, as it is a kind of knowledge, refers to contraries inasmuch as one of contraries is the reason for knowing the other; nevertheless, inasmuch as science is a certain habit, it is attributed to one act only (which is knowing the truth) and not to the contrary error. So then it was properly said that by justice we do just actions; by injustice, unjust actions.

892. Then [5], at "Oftentimes, then," he infers a corollary from the premises. Since contrary habits belong to contraries, and one act belongs to one object in a fixed manner, it follows that frequently one contrary habit is known by another and oftentimes by its object which is, as it were, matter subject to the operation of the habit. He illustrates this by an example. If *evexia* or a healthy condition is known, *cachexia* or an unhealthy condition is also known. In this way a habit is known by its contrary. Likewise it is known from its object because from the things that make a man healthy, a healthy condition becomes known. This is further illustrated in a more particular way. If the fact that a man has very firm flesh is a characteristic of a healthy condition, then the fact that he has flabby flesh—as it were loosely compressed by reason of disordered humors—is necessarily characteristic of an unhealthy condition. Again, that which makes a man healthy is necessarily a condition making him have firm flesh.

893. Next [6], at "It follows in most instances," he distinguishes justice and injustice. First [6] he gives the di-

vision; and then [9], at "Since the unjust man etc.," the parts of the division. He treats the first point in three ways. At the outset [6] he shows that various meanings of injustice indicate various meanings of justice. The reason is that it follows in most instances that if one of opposites may be spoken of in diverse ways, then the other can be. This is the case, too, with what is just and unjust.

894. Second [7], at "**Justice and injustice**," he explains the nature of their various meanings. He says that both justice and injustice can be spoken of in diverse ways, but their many meanings lie concealed because the things making for equivocation are close to one another in their agreement among themselves. But in widely separated things equivocation is evident, if the same name be given them, because their great difference in concept, i.e., in the essential element of the proper species, is immediately apparent. In this way the name key is used equivocally of an instrument which locks doors and of the clavicle (clavicula i.e. little key) which covers the artery in the shoulder of animals.

895. Third [8], at "**The unjust man,**" he explains in how many ways the previously mentioned habits may be signified, saying that first we must consider the unjust man in as many ways as he is designated. He is spoken of in three ways: in one way as the lawbreaking man, i.e., one who acts contrary to the law; in another way as the covetous man who wants too much prosperity; in the last way as the unfair man who determines to have too few burdens.

896. It is obvious then that the just man is taken in two ways: in one way as a law-abiding person, i.e., as one who observes the law; in the other way as the fair person who is willing to have the smiles and frowns of fortune in equal measure. The equal is opposed to both, i.e., to what is excessive and to what is deficient. From this he draws a further conclusion that what is just is said to be according to the law and fair; and what is unjust, contrary to the law and unfair inasmuch as objects are made known by habits, as was said before (892).

897. At "**Since the unjust man**" [9] he makes clear the parts of the division just given. First [9] he shows in what way the covetous man is said to be unjust. He affirms that since the covetous person who wants to have too much is unjust, it follows that he will be concerned about an abundance of goods which men desire. However, he will not be solicitous about all goods but only those pertaining to fortune and adversity. Goods of this kind are beneficial if we do not make qualification, i.e., they are good considered independently and in themselves. But they are not always beneficial for an individual because they are not always proportionate to him nor always expedient for him. However, men seek these goods from God, and pray for and desire them as if such things were always beneficial. By reason of this they become covetous and unjust. It should not be this way, but a man ought to pray that those things that are in themselves good be made good for him, so that each may choose what is good for him, i.e., the proper exercise of virtue.

898. Then [10], at "**But the unjust man,**" he shows how the unjust person is said to be unfair, stating that a man is not always called unjust because he chooses too much but because he chooses too little of the things that simply and considered in themselves are

burdensome—like labors, lack of necessities, and so on. However, since lesser evil apparently is in some way a good precisely as it is eligible—covetousness regards a good as was just said (897)—it seems for this reason that a person who desires too little of what is arduous is in some way covetous. But it is nearer the truth to say that he is unfair—a term that contains both and is common to excess and defect.

899. Last [11], at "**Besides, the un-just,**" he explains how the unjust man is said to be lawbreaking, affirming that he who is unlawful is also called unjust. A person is designated a lawbreaker by reason of unlawfulness which is also an inequality inasmuch as a man is not equal to the norm of the law. This unlawfulness contains in general all injustice and something common in respect of every kind of injustice, as will be made clear later (911, 919, 922).

LECTURE II
Legal Justice

TEXT OF ARISTOTLE (*1129b11–1030a13*) Chapter 1

1. *Since it was said that the lawless person is unjust and the law-abiding person just, obviously lawful acts are in some measure[1] just acts. Likewise, what is determined by the positive law is lawful, and we say that such a determination is just.*   1129b11–14; 900–901

2. *But laws aim to touch on everything which contributes to the benefit of all, or of the best, or of the rulers, either on account of virtues or something else. Therefore, for one such reason we call those laws just that bring about and preserve happiness and the things that make for happiness in the civic community.*   1129b14–19; 902–903

3. *A law commands deeds of bravery, for instance, that a soldier should not leave the battle line nor throw away his arms. It commands things belonging to temperance, for example, that no one should commit adultery, that no one should be guilty of outrage. It commands things that pertain to meekness: no one should strike another, no one should contend with another. It is the same with other virtues and vices, the law ordering the former and forbidding the latter. In accord with this, a law rightly drafted will be excellent but one insufficiently considered will be bad.*   1129b19–25; 904–905

4. *Justice itself then is a perfect virtue, not in itself but in relation to another. For this reason justice seems to be the most excellent among the virtues. Hence we have the proverb: "neither evening star nor morning star is so wonderful as justice."*   1129b25–29; 906

5. *But under justice every virtue is included at the same time, and it is especially the perfect virtue because it is the exercise of perfect virtue.*   1129b29–31; 907

6. *Legal justice is perfect because the person who has this virtue can exercise it in relation to another and not in relation to himself alone. Some people can apply virtue to their own affairs but not to affairs pertaining to others. Because of this, the saying of Bias seems to be commendable that authority tests a man, for the prince is already engaged in communication with others. Therefore, justice alone among the virtues seems to be another's good because it refers to another. It produces goods useful to another, viz., the prince or the common good. Consequently, the man who practices vice in regard to himself and his friends is most wicked. On the other hand the man who practices virtue in regard to himself and toward others—a difficult thing to do—is most honorable.*   1129b31–1130a8; 908–910

7. *This virtue, therefore, is not a particular but a general virtue. Likewise, the opposite injustice is not a particular vice but a general one.*   1130a8–10; 911

8. *How virtue and justice differ from one another is evident from what has been said, for they are the same in substance but different in concept. Virtue as related to another is justice; as this kind of habit it is virtue without qualification.*   1130a10–13; 912

COMMENTARY OF ST. THOMAS

900. After the Philosopher has given the division of justice, he now considers legal justice. First he treats the legally just itself, which is the object of legal justice. Second [4], at "Justice it- self then etc.," he considers legal justice. He discusses the first point in a twofold manner. First [1] he shows that the legally just is determined by law. Now [2], at "But laws aim etc.," he

---

1   The text used by St. Thomas had *aliqualiter* not *aequaliter*.

explains the nature of legal enact-ments. He affirms first that, since it was said above (895–896, 899) that the law-less man is unjust and the law-abiding man just, it clearly follows that all law-ful acts are just in some measure.

901. He says "in some measure" be-cause every law is determined in rela-tion to some state. Now, not every state possesses what is simply just but some states have only what is partially just, as is evident in the third book of the *Politics* (Ch. 9, 1281a10; St. Th. Lect. VII, 413). In a democratic state where all the people govern, what is partially just is observed but not what is simply just, so that because all the citizens are equal in one respect (i.e., in liberty), therefore they are considered equal in every respect. Consequently, acts that are prescribed by law in a democracy are not simply but only in some meas-ure just. But Aristotle says that those enactments are lawful that have been fixed and determined by positive law, which is within the competence of leg-islators, and that each enactment so decreed is said to be just in some way.

902. Next [2], at "**But laws aim,**" he explains with what the decrees of law are concerned. He considers this point from two aspects. First [2] he shows for whose sake a law is enacted. Then [3], at "A law commands," he shows on what matters laws are made. He says first that laws touch on everything that can be of any possible utility for the community (as in the ideal states where the common good is kept in mind), or for the utility of the best (i.e., certain elders of the state who govern it and are called nobles), or for the utility of the rulers (as happens in states ruled by kings and tyrants). In the framing of laws attention is always given to what is useful to the affair of chief importance in the city.

903. Some may be considered as best or as ruling either because of virtue (as in an aristocratic state where certain ones rule on account of virtue), or for the sake of something else (as in an oligarchy where the few rule on ac-count of riches or power). Since human utility of every kind is finally ordered to happiness, obviously the legal en-actments that bring about happiness and the means to it (i.e., the things that are ordered to happiness either princi-pally, like the virtues, or instrumen-tally like riches and other external goods of this kind) are called just in some fashion. This is by comparison with the civic community to which the framing of a law is directed.

904. At "**A law commands**" [3] he explains on what matters laws are made, saying that a law commands what belongs to individual virtues. It commands deeds of bravery, for in-stance, that a soldier should not leave the battle line, nor take flight, nor throw away his arms. Likewise, it com-mands things pertaining to temper-ance, for example, that no one should commit adultery, that no one should dishonor the person of a woman. Also it commands the things belonging to meekness: no one should strike an-other in anger, no one should contend with another by insults. It is the same with other virtues whose acts the law commands, and with other vices whose acts the law forbids.

905. If the law is rightly drafted ac-cording to this, it will be declared an excellent law. Otherwise it is called *aposchediasmenos* (from *a* meaning without, *poschedias* meaning knowl-edge, and *menos* meaning a searching) as if the law was drafted without a thorough knowledge, or the expres-sion may come from *schedos* signifying a decree published without being thor-

oughly scanned, from which we have *schediazo*, i.e., I am doing something off-hand. Hence a law is said to be *aposchediasmenos* which lacks proper forethought.

906. Then [4], at "**Justice itself then**," he determines how legal justice is constituted, showing first [4] the nature of legal justice; and then [5], at "But under justice," in what way it is related to the virtues. He says first that justice itself is a certain perfect virtue not in terms of itself but in relation to another. Since it is better to be perfect not only in oneself but also in relation to another, therefore it is often said that this justice is the most excellent among all virtues. This is the origin of the proverb that neither Hesperus nor Lucifer, the brightest of the morning and evening stars, shine with such brilliance as justice.

907. Next [5], at "**But under justice**," he shows from our discussion thus far how legal justice is related to the virtues. He treats this point under three headings. First [5] he sets forth his intention. Then [6], at "Legal justice is perfect etc.," he explains his proposition. Lastly [8], at "How virtue and justice etc.," he settles a point which could be called in question by the present discussion. He states first that justice itself comprehends every virtue at the same time and is even the perfect virtue in a special way. The reason that legal justice consists in the exercise of virtue having to do with another and is in agreement with every virtue prescribed by the law.

908. At "**Legal justice is perfect**" [4] he explains what was set forth: first [4] that legal justice is an especially perfect virtue; and then, at "This virtue, therefore" [7], that it includes every virtue. He says first that legal justice is a perfect virtue because a man who has this virtue can employ it in relation to another and not to himself only—something not characteristic of all virtuous people. Many can practice virtue in things pertaining to themselves but not in the things pertaining to others. To make clear the previous statements he introduces two common sayings or proverbs.

909. Bias, one of the seven wise men, said that authority tests whether a man is perfect or deficient. The man who rules is already engaged in communication with another because it is his business to arrange the things which are ordered to the common good. So from this we see that the perfection of virtue is indicated by the fact that one person is in touch with another. He proposes another saying to show that legal justice refers to another. For this reason legal justice alone seems to be the good of another (that is, relates to our neighbor) inasmuch as it aims to perform actions useful to another, viz., to the community or the ruler of the community. But some virtues aim to achieve an individual's good, for instance, temperance strives to quiet the disgraceful desires of the soul. The same is true of other virtues.

910. He draws the conclusion that, as that man is most wicked who practices vice not only in regard to himself but also in regard to his friends, so that man is most honorable who practices virtue in relation not only to himself but also to others. This is especially difficult. So then it is clear that the law-abiding just man is most virtuous and legal justice is the most perfect of virtues.

911. Then [7], at "**This virtue, therefore**," he infers that legal justice embraces every virtue, for it pertains to legal justice to exercise virtue in regard to another. But a person can practice

every virtue in his relation with another. Hence obviously legal justice is not a particular virtue but has a connection with virtue in general. Likewise, the opposite vice is not a particular vice but a general vice, since in a similar way man can exercise every vice in his relations with his neighbor.

912. Next [8], at "**How justice and virtue,**" he clarifies something that may be doubtful from the premises. He says that it is clear, from what has been said, the way in which virtue and legal justice differ since they are the same in substance but different in concept.

However, virtue in its relation to another is called justice, but precisely as it is a habit operative of such good, it is a virtue simply. This must be understood in regard to the act itself of justice and virtue, for an act identical in subject but diverse in concept is produced by legal justice and by virtue simply so called, for instance, not to commit adultery. But where a special formal aspect of an object exists even in general matter, there a special habit must be found. For this reason it follows that legal justice is a definite virtue taking its species from this, that it tends to the common good.

LECTURE III
Particular Justice

TEXT OF ARISTOTLE (1130a14–1130b29) Chapter 2

1. We are now investigating that justice which is a part of the general virtue. As we have remarked, there is such a virtue. We also intend to speak in a similar way about particular injustice.   **1130a14–16; 913**

2. The proof for the existence of a particular justice is that a man who practices other vices acting unjustly, nevertheless does not act covetously, for example, one who throws away his shield out of cowardice, or who speaks ill of another out of anger, or who refuses financial help because of stinginess. On the other hand, a person often sins by covetousness, although not by one or all of the other vices, but he does sin by this particular vice, for we reproach him for being unjust. There is then another kind of injustice, a part of injustice in general. Likewise, there is a certain unjust thing that is a part of that which is legally unjust.   **1130a16–24; 914–915**

3. Moreover, if one man commits adultery for the sake of gain and makes money by this act, while another commits adultery for the sake of concupiscence and pays, thus sustaining a loss; the second man seems to be more lustful than the first who is unjust rather than lustful, for obviously he acted for gain.   **1130a24–28; 916**

4. Yet in all other kinds of injustice[2] there is always a reference to some particular vice, for instance, if a man commits adultery it is ascribed to lust. If a soldier deserts his leader, it is referred to cowardice. If anyone strikes another, it is attributed to anger. But if a person makes an exorbitant profit, it is not reduced to any other vice but only to injustice. Hence it is clear that over and above general justice, there is a particular justice.   **1130a28–33; 917**

5. This justice has the same name because defined under the same genus, since both agree in a relation to another.   **1130a33–1130b2; 918**

6. But particular justice is concerned with honor, money, security, and all other things of this kind whatever name they may have, and also with the pleasure that follows upon possession. But general justice touches upon everything by reason of which a man can be called virtuous.   **1130b2–5; 919**

7. Obviously then there is more than one justice, there is another justice besides the general virtue. What this other justice is and its characteristics will be considered now.   **1130b6–8; 920**

8. We have determined that the unjust thing is both the illegally unjust and the unjust simply, but the just thing is both the just corresponding to the law and the just that is equal or fair.   **1130b8–9; 921**

9. Therefore, in accord with the illegally unjust thing, there is an injustice that we previously discussed. Now, the unjust thing that consists in a desire for inequality is not the same, but is related to the other as a part to the whole, for every unjust thing consisting in a desire for inequality is an illegally unjust thing but not the reverse. Besides, the excessive is unequal but not the reverse. Because one unjust thing is not the same as another, so also one injustice is not the same as another but different from it as a part from the whole. The same comparison holds for one injustice with the other.   **1130b9–16; 922**

10. We must then discuss particular justice and injustice, and also the just and the unjust thing taken in the same sense.   **1130b16–18; 923**

11. Justice that corresponds to all of virtue and injustice that corresponds to all of vice, as

---

2   Justificationes in the text should be injustificationes or injustitias.

their exercise pertains to our neighbor, are both to be passed over for the present. It is evident in these cases how the just thing must be determined. Nearly all legal enactments are prescribed by the general virtue, for the law commands us to live according to every virtue and forbids us to live according to any vice.   **1130b18–24; 924**

12. However, positive laws are productive of virtue in general in regard to instruction which pertains to the common good. But that instruction according to which a man is good simply, whether it belongs to political science or some other science, must be determined afterwards. Perhaps, to be a good man and to be a good citizen are not the same thing in any state.

                    1130b25–29; 925–926

COMMENTARY OF ST. THOMAS

913. After the Philosopher has shown what is the nature of legal justice, which is a general virtue, now he shows that besides this there is a particular justice. He treats this point under three headings. First [1] he indicates his proposition; and then [2], at "The proof for etc.," he explains it. Last [7], at "Obviously then etc.," he sums up what has already been said and shows what remains to be discussed. He says first that, while legal justice is a general virtue, we are not principally investigating this at present, but that which as a part of the general virtue is a particular virtue. As is commonly held, there is such a virtue. Also we intend to speak about particular injustice in a similar manner.

914. Then [2], at "**The proof for,**" he explains the proposition. He discusses this point from two aspects. First [2] he shows that besides legal justice, which is a general virtue, there is a justice that is a particular virtue. Next [5], at "This justice etc.," he assigns the reason why it has a name in common with legal justice. On this question we must consider that to prove there is a justice that is a particular virtue, he takes for granted that there is an injustice that is a particular vice, for we said above (892) that habits are made known by their contraries. He proposes three arguments for this. The first argument [2] is taken according to the real dis-

tinction of injustice from other vices inasmuch as injustice is found without the others and conversely. From this it is evident that injustice is a particular vice distinct from other vices.

915. He says that we have this proof that there is a particular justice and injustice because a man, who practices other particular vices acting unjustly according to legal injustice, nevertheless does not act covetously in taking something from his neighbor, for example, when a soldier throws away his shield because of cowardice, or a man casts opprobrium on someone because of anger, or a person refuses financial help to a friend because of the vice of stinginess. So other vices can exist without covetousness which is a special kind of injustice. Sometimes, on the contrary, it happens that a person sins by covetousness in taking another's goods; although he does not sin by some one or all of the other vices, he does sin by a particular vice. This is clear because he is reproached as unjust for that reason. Hence obviously there is another justice—a part of the virtue—that is a special virtue. So evidently there exists also a certain unjust thing that is a part of what is legally unjust—the legally unjust being the unjust thing in general.

916. At "**Moreover, if one man**" [3] he gives the second argument, which is taken from the order to the end.

Clearly, if a vicious or evil act is ordered to another unbecoming end, from this fact it will obtain a new species of vice. This is so when a man commits adultery for the sake of gain, for example, to rob a woman or to take from her in any way whatsoever. Also it happens sometimes that a man commits adultery entirely because of concupiscence, so that he not only does not gain but rather gives something of his own and suffers a loss of his goods. A man of this sort seems to be lustful, essentially speaking (*per se*), since the vice of lust is strictly ordered to the satisfaction of concupiscence. But the man who commits adultery to take a woman's goods does not seem to be lustful, absolutely speaking, because he does not intend lust as his end. He seems rather to be unjust since he sins against justice for the sake of gain. So it is clear then that injustice is a special vice.

917. At "**Yet in all**" [4] he assigns the third argument, which is taken by comparison with legal justice. As nothing is contained in a genus that is not contained in some species, so anything that is done according to legal injustice is reduced to a particular vice. If a man acts contrary to legal justice by committing adultery, this will be referred to the vice of lust. If a soldier deserts his general in battle, this will be attributed to the vice of cowardice. If anyone immoderately strikes his neighbor, this will be ascribed to the vice of anger. But if a person inordinately enriches himself by pilfering another's goods, this will not be ascribed to any other vice except injustice. Hence it remains that there is a particular injustice over and above the other injustice that is a general vice. For a like reason there is another particular justice besides legal justice that is a general virtue.

918. Then [5], at "**This justice has,**" he shows why a particular virtue of this kind is also named justice. First [5] he assigns the reason for this from the agreement of particular with legal justice. Next [6], at "But particular justice," he explains the difference between them. He says first that particular justice is univocal, that is, has a common name with legal justice. The reason is that they agree in definition according to the same genus inasmuch as both are concerned about what relates to another. However, legal justice is taken into account in relation to what is the common good, while particular justice is ordered to another as pertaining to a private person.

919. Next [6], at "**But particular justice,**" he explains the difference between justice and injustice on part of the matter. He says that particular justice regards those things that take into account social intercourse, like honor, money, whatever pertains to the safety or harm to the body, and so on. Likewise, particular justice is concerned not alone with external things but also with pleasure consequent on the profit by which a man takes his neighbor's goods beyond what he ought. But legal justice and injustice treat all moral matters in general in whatsoever way a man may be said to be good or virtuous about a thing.

920. At "**Obviously then**" [7] he summarizes what has been said and shows what remains to be discussed. First [7] he sets this forth in a general way; and then [8] at "We have determined etc.," he takes it up in a specific way. He says first that it is clear from the premises (913–919) that there is more than one justice, viz., legal justice and justice aiming at equality, and that over and above legal justice, as a general virtue, there is a particular justice.

But we must determine later on (927–1077) the nature and characteristics of particular justice.

921. Then [8], at "**We have determined,**" he shows in detail what has been treated and what remains to be discussed. First [8] he resumes what was said about the distinction between justice and injustice. He affirms that we have determined that the unjust thing is called illegal and unequal either by excess or defect. On the contrary, the just thing is called legal and equal.

922. Next [9], at "**Therefore, in accord with,**" he resumes what he has said, viz., that as there is a twofold just thing, so there is a twofold justice. He affirms that in accord with the illegally unjust thing there is a certain injustice, previously discussed (911, 919), which is a general vice. Likewise, in accord with the just corresponding to the law, there is a certain justice that is a general virtue. Now, the unjust thing consisting in a desire for inequality and the illegally unjust thing are not altogether the same, but one is related to the other as a part to the whole so that every unjust thing consisting in a desire for inequality is an illegally unjust thing, but not the reverse. Again, every thing that is excessive is unequal but not the reverse, since there is a certain illegal injustice in having too few burdens. Because (I say) one unjust thing is a part of the other unjust thing, and they are not entirely the same; in a similar way, therefore, the injustice called inequality is not entirely the same as illegal injustice but is compared to it as a part to the whole. Also the justice aiming at equality is compared to legal justice in a similar manner.

923. Last [10], at "**We must then,**" he shows which of these things we must discuss. On this point he does three things. First [10] he says that we must

treat particular justice after this (927–1077), and similarly the just and the unjust thing particularly so called.

924. Then [11], at "**Justice that corresponds,**" he explains that here we are not going to treat legal justice. He affirms that legal justice—which conforms to all of virtue inasmuch as the use of the whole of virtue referring to our neighbor pertains to it—is to be passed over for the present. Likewise, the opposite injustice (inasmuch as the use of the whole of vice pertains to it) is to be passed over. It is clear how what is just and unjust ought to be determined according to justice and injustice of this kind, because they are the precepts as laid down by the law. The greater part of legal prescriptions are enjoined in agreement with the whole of virtue inasmuch as the law commands us to live according to every virtue and forbids us to live according to any vice. However, there are certain determinations of the law that do not belong directly to the exercise of any virtue but to some disposition of external goods.

925. Last [12], at "**However, positive law,**" he raises a doubt. It is evident that positive laws are productive of virtue in general by the instruction given a man in reference to the common good. But there is another kind of instruction by which a man is trained in virtuous actions as applicable to him individually, i.e., to his proper good inasmuch as in this way a man becomes virtuous in himself. Therefore, there can be a doubt whether instruction of this kind should belong to political science or to some other science.

926. He says that this question must be settled afterwards in the work on *Politics*. It is proved in the third book of the *Politics* (Ch. 4, 1276b16–1277b33; St. Th. Lect. III, 365–377) that to be a good

man simply and to be a good citizen are not the same in every state. There are some states not worthy of honor in which a person can be a good citizen yet not be a good man. But in the most worthy state no one is a good citizen who is not a good man.

LECTURE IV
Distributive and Commutative Justice

TEXT OF ARISTOTLE (1130b30–1131a29) Chapter 2

1. One species of particular justice—and of the just thing corresponding to it—consists in the distribution of honor, money, and other common goods that are to be apportioned to people sharing in social community, for in these matters one man as compared with another may have an equal or unequal share. 1130b30–33; 927

2. Another species gives directions for use in private transactions. 1130b33–1131a1; 928

3. There are two parts of this species, as some types of transaction are voluntary and others involuntary. Examples of the voluntary are selling, buying, bail, loan, deposit, rent. They are called voluntary because the origin of these exchanges is voluntary. 1131a1–5; 929

4. Some kinds of involuntary transaction are occult, like theft, adultery, poisoning, procuring,[3] enticement of a slave, assassination, false testimony. Others are done with manifest violence, for example, beating, imprisonment, murder, robbery, despoiling parents of children, reproach, outrage. 1131a5–9; 930–931

Chapter 3

5. Since the unjust person is unfair and the unjust thing is unequal, it is clear that there is a mean corresponding to what is unjust. This is the equal, for in operations of this kind where there is more or less, there is also an equal. Therefore, if the unjust thing is the unequal and, the just thing the equal—and this is evident in all situations without need of proof—then the just thing will be the mean since the equal is the mean. 1131a10–15; 932–933

6. However, the equal implies at least two things. Therefore, since the just thing is both a mean and an equal, it necessarily is related to another and pertains to certain matters of equality. As a mean it will be between two things which are more and less. As it is an equal it will be between two things. As it is a just thing it will concern matters in relation to other persons, for justice regards another. Therefore, the just necessarily involves at least four objects, viz., two persons by whom justice is observed and two things about which justice is done. There will be the same equality between persons and between things in such a way that, as things are related to one another, so are persons. If they are not equal they will not have equal shares, and from this source quarrels and complaints will arise when, either persons who are equal do not receive equal shares in distribution, or persons who are not equal do receive equal shares. 1131a15–24; 934–935

7. Moreover, this is clear from the fact that bestowal should be made according to merit, for the just thing in distribution has to be done according to a certain merit. But all do not agree that merit consists in the same thing. People of a democracy place it in a condition of freedom, people of an oligarchy in one's riches or nobility of birth, and people of an aristocracy in a state of virtue. 1131a24–29; 936–937

COMMENTARY OF ST. THOMAS

927. After the Philosopher has differentiated particular justice from legal justice, he now begins to investigate particular justice without treating legal justice. He divides the investigation into two parts. In the first part he considers particular justice in a general way by comparison with its proper ob-

---

3   Proagogia in the text, but paragogia in the Commentary.

ject, and in the second part [Lect. XI], at "Since someone etc." (1134a16), he considers it in its application to the subject. In regard to the first part, he does two things. Initially [1] he makes a division of particular justice. Next [5], at "Since the unjust person etc.," he explains how a mean may be taken in this virtue. He discusses the initial point from three aspects. First [1] he indicates a species of particular justice. He says that one species—the same holds for the unjust thing corresponding to it—consists in the distribution of certain common goods (either honor or money or any other thing belonging to external goods or even to external evils, like labor, expenses and so on) that are to be apportioned among people who share in social community. He proves that this should belong to particular justice because in matters of this kind, equality and inequality—which belong to particular justice and injustice, as was stated before (922) of one person to another are taken into consideration.

928. Next [2], at "**Another species,**" he gives a second kind of particular justice. He says that another species establishes a measure of justice in transactions, by which a thing is transferred from one person to another—in the first species the transfer of a thing from the community to the individual was considered.

929. Last [3], at "**There are two parts,**" he subdivides commutative justice according to the different kinds of transactions, making a twofold division. He says first [3] that there are two parts of commutative justice because there are two kinds of transactions. Some are voluntary, others involuntary. The voluntary are so-called because the principle of transaction is voluntary in both parties, as is evident

in selling and buying, by which one man transfers the dominion over his own property to another as compensation for a price received; *in barter,* by which someone gives what is his to another for something of equal value; *in bail,* by which a person voluntarily appoints himself a debtor for another; *in a loan,* by which a man grants the use of his property to another without recompense but reserves ownership of the thing to himself; *in a deposit,* by which one commits something of his to the custody of another; *in rent,* by which a person accepts the use of something belonging to another for a price.

930. Then [4], at "**Some kinds of involuntary,**" he subdivides the other division of transactions, saying that some involuntary transactions are occult: like theft, by which one takes a thing belonging to another who is unwilling; adultery, by which a man secretly approaches the wife of another for sexual intercourse; poisoning, by which a person poisons another with intent either to kill or injure in some way. Also they are especially called poisoners who by some sorcery bring about murder or harm. *Paragogia* is a derivation or a leading away, for example the occult diversion of a stream belonging to one person to the property of another. The enticement of a slave takes place when someone induces another's slave to flee from his master. Assassination is that slaying which happens from wounds inflicted by trickery. Testimony is false in which a person conceals the truth by lying. Other transactions are involuntary and done by manifest violence. Thus a man may use violence either upon a person by beating, fettering, murdering, or upon things by robbing another of his goods, by despoiling parents of their children through murder. Likewise, a

man may use violence through infamy by using reproachful words, or through injury by inflicting outrage.

931. We must consider that the voluntary and involuntary in transactions make a difference in the species of justice because voluntary transactions cause the subtraction of only a thing which must be repaid according to the equality of justice. But involuntary transactions cause a certain injury. Hence the robber is forced not only to return the thing plundered but to undergo punishment because of the affront inflicted. Since the involuntary is twofold, viz., arising from force and from ignorance, he divides involuntary transactions into those which are occult, as it were through ignorance, and those that are done openly through violence.

932. Next [5], at "**Since the unjust person,**" he shows how a mean is understood in these matters. He discusses this point from two aspects. First [5] he explains how the just thing is a mean; and then [Lect. X], at "From these discussions etc." (1133b30), how justice is a mean. He treats the first point in a twofold manner. First [5] he shows in what way the just thing, consisting in a mean according to either justice, may be determined. Next [Lect. VIII], at "Some philosophers seem to think etc." (1132b21), he rejects an error. He further discusses the first point in two stages. First [5] he explains how the just thing may be taken as a mean according to distributive justice; and second [Lect. VI], at "There remains another etc." (1131b25), according to commutative justice. He considers the first point in two ways. First [5] he proves that the mean of distributive justice should be taken according to a certain relationship of proportions. Next [Lect. V], at "Therefore, the just

thing etc." (1131a30), he shows what the nature of that relationship of proportions is. On the initial point he does two things. First [5] he proves the proposition from the very concept of justice; and then [7], at "Moreover, this is clear etc.," from the concept of merit. He treats the first point under two headings. First [5] he shows from the very notion of justice that the just thing is a certain mean. Second [6], at "However, the equal etc.," he explains that the mean is according to a certain relationship of proportions.

933. He says first that, as was said previously (898, 921), the unjust man is one who desires an inequality of good and evil, and the unjust thing is that which consists in an inequality, and concerns both too much and too little. But wherever there is more and less, there the equal must be found, for the equal is the mean between the greater and the less. Hence wherever we find equality, there we find a mean. It is clear then that the unjust thing is a kind of unequal thing, and the just thing is a kind of equal thing. That the just thing is a kind of equal thing is obvious to everyone without any proof. Therefore, since the equal is a mean between more and less, as has been shown (310, 896, 898), it follows that the just thing is a kind of mean.

934. At "**However, the equal**" [6] he explains that the just thing is a mean according to a certain relationship of proportions. To prove this he takes for granted that the equal consists in at least two things between which an equality is considered. Therefore, since the just thing is both a mean and an equal, inasmuch as it is just, it is necessarily a relation to something, i.e., with respect to another, as is evident from what has been indicated (922); but inasmuch as it is an equal it pertains to

certain matters in which equality between two persons is taken into account. Thus it is evident that if we consider the just thing precisely as a mean, it will then be a mean between two things that are more and less. But precisely as the just thing is an equal, it must be between two things (as a just thing, of course, it must concern some matters in relation to other persons, because justice regards another person). However, justice insofar as it is a mean, an extrinsic thing, considers more or less; but as something intrinsic it considers two things and two persons in which justice is established. So it is clear that what is just, necessarily consists in at least four objects, viz., two persons by whom justice is observed and two things about which justice is done.

935. In the concept of justice there must be the same equality between persons who practice justice and between things about which justice is done, so that as the things are related to one another, so are the persons. Otherwise they will not have shares proportional to themselves. But, by reason of this, quarrels and complaints arise as if justice had been neglected because, either persons who are equal do not receive equal shares in the distribution of common goods or persons who are not equal do receive equal shares, for example, if laborers are paid wages for doing an unequal amount of work, or are paid unequal wages for doing an equal amount of work. So then it is

evident that the mean of distributive justice is taken according to a certain relationship of proportions.

936. Then [7], at "**Moreover, this is,**" he shows that it is obvious also by reason of merit that the just thing consists in a certain relationship of proportions. In this way a thing is said to be just in distributions inasmuch as allotment is made according to merit as each is worthy to receive. A certain relationship of proportions is designated by this—that as one person is deserving of one thing, so another is deserving of another thing.

937. However, all do not judge merit in distribution in agreement with the same norm. In a democratic state where everyone governs, they judge merit according to a condition of freedom. Because the common people are the equal of others in freedom, therefore they think it proper that equal distribution be made to them. In an oligarchy where some few rule, they measure merit according to a man's riches or according to nobility of birth, so that men who are more eminent by birth or riches should have more of the common goods. In an aristocracy where certain men govern because of their virtue, they measure merit according to a state of virtue, so that a man should have more who practices virtue more perfectly. Thus it is clear that the mean of distributive justice is understood according to a relationship of proportions.

LECTURE V
Proportionality

TEXT OF ARISTOTLE (*1131a29–1131b24*) Chapter 3

1. *Therefore, the just thing is something belonging to proportion, for the proportional is proper not only to abstract number but to all enumerations. Proportionality is an equality of ratios.*   **1131a29–31; 938–939**

2. *Proportionality consists of four parts at least. It is clear that discrete proportionality has four terms, but so does continuous proportionality, for we use one term in two different aspects and state it twice, for example, A is in proportion to B as B is to G. So B has been stated twice. Wherefore if B is used twice there will be four proportioned terms.*   **1131a31–1131b3; 940**

3. *Like proportionality, what is just is also found in four terms at least, for both the things and persons are divided according to a similar proportion. Therefore, as the term A will be to B, so G will be to D. Hence, alternating, as A is to G, B will be to D. Therefore, the whole will be related to the whole, and this is what distribution conjoins.*

If adjustment be made in this way, it will be justly done. Therefore, the union of term A with G, and of B with D will be the just thing and the mean guiding distribution. But the unjust thing is outside of what belongs to proportion, for the proportional is a mean and the just thing belongs to proportion.   **1131b3–12; 941–943**

4. *Mathematicians call this proportionality geometrical, for in geometry it happens that the whole is compared to the whole as part to part.*   **1131b12–15; 944**

5. *But this proportionality is not continuous because there is no numerically common term for the person and the thing.*   **1131b15–16; 945**

6. *This just thing then is a proportional. But the unjust thing is outside the proportional either by excess or defect. This occurs in distributions where a man acts unjustly when he accepts too much and a man suffers unjustly when he has too little of good. The reverse is true in regard to evil. By comparison with a greater evil a lesser evil has the aspect of good, for a lesser evil is preferable to a greater one. Good is preferable, and a greater good is more to be preferred. This then is one kind of the just thing.*   **1131b16–24; 946**

COMMENTARY OF ST. THOMAS

938. After the Philosopher has shown that the mean of distributive justice is taken according to proportionality, he now shows according to what proportionality and in what way it is understood. He considers this point in a twofold manner. First [1] he explains in what way the just thing should be taken according to a certain proportionality. Second [6], at "This just thing etc.," he shows how the unjust thing is outside that proportionality. He discusses the initial point under three aspects. First [1] he presents in advance some general comments about proportionality. Then [3], at

"Like proportionality etc.," he explains how the just thing consists in a certain proportionality. Last [4], at "Mathematicians call etc.," he shows the nature of proportionality by which a thing is judged just in distributive justice. On the first point he premises two comments. The first [1] is that the just thing is fittingly said to be according to proportionality, because proportionality is found not only in the enumeration of units (which is number simply taken and here called abstract number), but the quality of being proportionate is met with wherever number is found.

939. This is so because proportional-

ity is simply geometrical equality, i.e., this to this and that to that contains the proportion of equality. Proportion is only a relation of one quantity to another. But quantity has the nature of a measure. It is found in numerical unity and is transferred from there to every kind of quantity, as the tenth book of the *Metaphysics* indicates (Ch. 1, 1052b20 sq.; St. Th. Lect. II, 1938). Therefore, number primarily is found in the enumeration of units, and thence is attributed to every genus of quantity which is measured according to the idea of number.

940. He makes the second comment at "**Proportionality consists**" [2], saying that every proportionality consists of four parts at least. It has a twofold division, one of which is a disjunctive proportionality and the other a continuous proportionality. The disjunctive proportionality is an equality of two proportions not alike in any term. Therefore, when any proportion exists between the two, it is evident that the disjunctive proportionality consists of four terms, as when I say: as six is to three so ten is to five. There is a double proportion on both sides. The continuous proportionality is an equality of two proportions alike in one term, for instance, if I say: as eight is to four so four is to two. There is a double proportion on both sides. Therefore in this continuous proportionality there are in some measure four terms inasmuch as we use one term in two different aspects, declaring it twice, i.e., in either proportion as when I say: the proportion of A to B (or eight to four) is the same as the proportion B to C (or four to two). There is a double proportion from both sides. In this way B is used twice. Hence, although B is one in subject, nevertheless because it is taken in

two different aspects there will be four proportioned terms.

941. Then [3], at "**Like proportionality**," he shows how the mean of distributive justice is taken according to proportionality. He says that, like proportionality, the just thing is found in four terms in which the same proportion is observed, because the things that are distributed and the persons to whom distribution is made are divided according to the same proportion. Therefore, let A be one term, for example, two pounds, and B one pound. But let G be one person, for example, Socrates who has worked two days, and D, Plato, who has worked one day. Therefore, as A is to B so G is to D, because a double proportion is found on the one side and the other. Hence by alternation, as A is to G, so B is to D. Whatever things are proportionable one to another are proportionable by alternation, as is evident in the preceding example (940), for instance, as ten is to five so eight is to four. Therefore, by alternation, as ten is to eight, so five is to four, for there is a ratio of five to four on one side and the other. In this way then, by alternation, it will be true to say that as A is to G, i.e., two pounds to the man who worked two days, so B is to D, i.e., one pound to the man who worked a day.

942. In such matters we must also consider that in the things proportionable in this way, the ratio of one to the other is the ratio of the whole to the whole. For example, if the ratio ten to eight is the same as five to four, it follows further that the ratio ten to eight and five to four will be the same ratio as ten and five taken together, i.e., fifteen to eight and four taken together, i.e., twelve. The reason is that here we

have also the ratio of five to four. How does this happen? Because fifteen contains twelve and its fourth part, i.e., three.

943. In the proposition it follows that, if as this thing is to this person, so that thing is to that person, then also the whole will be to the whole in the same way, i.e., both things taken together will be to both persons taken together. This is as distribution connects them. If in distribution man unites the things to the persons in this way, he acts justly. It is plain then that the union of A with G, i.e., of a thing doubled with a person doubly more deserving, and of B with D, i.e., of a half thing with a person deserving only half is the just thing in distribution and such a just thing is a mean. But the unjust thing is outside this proportionality. The proportional is a mean between excess and defect because the proportionality is an equality of proportion, as has been remarked (939). So the just thing is a mean since it is a certain proportional.

944. At "**Mathematicians call**" [4] he explains the nature of proportionality according to which this just thing is understood. On this point he does two things. First [4] he says that the abovementioned proportionality, which is considered according to the equality of proportion, is called geometrical by mathematicians. In this it happens that as the whole is to the whole so one part is to another, as we have pointed out in previous discussions (939–940). But this does not take place in arithmetical proportionality, which we will treat later (950).

945. Next [5], at "**But this,**" he says that this proportionality, which is observed in distributive justice, cannot be continuous because on one side are the things and on the other the persons. So it is not possible to take for a common term a person to whom distribution is made and the thing which is distributed.

946. Then [6], at "**This just thing,**" he considers what is unjust in distributions. He says that, since the just thing is proportionable, it follows that the unjust thing is outside the proportionable. This happens either by reason of more or less than the equality of proportion demands, as is evident in the very operations of just and unjust distribution. That man acts unjustly who accepts for himself too many goods, but he suffers unjustly who has too few. The reverse is true in regard to evils. Since a lesser evil has the aspect of good by comparison with a greater evil, the lesser evil is more to be preferred than the greater evil. Everything is chosen under the aspect of good, and for this reason the thing which has the aspect of greater good is more to be preferred. So then this is one species of justice that has been discussed.

LECTURE VI
The Mean of Commutative Justice

TEXT OF ARISTOTLE (1131b25–1132a25) Chapter 4

1. There remains another kind of justice directive of what is done both in voluntary and involuntary transactions.   1131b25–26; 947

2. This differs in species from the preceding justice.   1131b26–27; 948

3. What is just in the distribution of common goods is always in conformity with proportionality previously discussed, for when distribution is made of common wealth, it will be made according to the proportion contributed by each one. On the other hand the unjust thing opposed to this just thing is outside the proportional.   1131b27–32; 949

4. However, in transactions the just thing is an equal—and the unjust thing an unequal—not according to geometrical but according to arithmetic proportion. Here it does not matter whether the good man steals from the wicked man or the wicked from the good, whether the good or wicked man commits adultery. But the law looks at only the nature of the damage done, and treats the parties as equals, if indeed one does an injustice and the other suffers an injustice, if this one injures and that one is injured. Therefore, the judge attempts to reduce to equality the unjust thing which has an inequality.   1131b32–1132a7; 950–951

5. If one of two contestants receives a wound and the other inflicts a wound or even one commits murder and the other is murdered the division of action and passion brings about inequality. However, a judge tries to remove inequality by awarding damages.   1132a7–10; 952

6. In the interest of plain talk, we speak of gain in these matters, even though the name is not appropriate to some cases, for example, to the person who strikes another or to the person injured. But when passion is measured, one thing is called loss and another gain.
                                                                           1132a10–14; 953

7. Therefore, that which is just is an equal, a mean between more and less in such a way that gain is taken as more, and loss as less. Gain is understood in contrary ways, for it is more in relation to good and less in relation to evil, while the opposite is true of loss. Between gain and loss stands a mean, the equal which we call the just. This then is a directive, and will be the mean between gain and loss.   1132a14–19; 954

8. For this reason when men are in doubt they have recourse to a judge. But going to a judge is going to justice, for a judge ought to be living justice. Men approaching a judge are seeking an intermediate, and this is why judges are called intermediaries or mediators, as if they touch the mean when they attain what is just. Therefore, the just thing is a mean as also is the judge who brings about an equality.   1132a19–25; 955

COMMENTARY OF ST. THOMAS

947. After the Philosopher has shown how the mean should be taken in distributive justice, he now explains in what way the mean should be understood in commutative justice. He discusses this point under three aspects. First [1] he shows there is a species of justice in addition to distributive. Then [2], at "This differs etc.," he says this differs from the other

justice. Third [Lect. VII], at "It is as though etc." (1132a25), he shows how a mean should be understood in this kind of justice. He says first that in addition to the preceding species of justice which exists in distributions, there remains one that is directive of transactions both voluntary and involuntary.

948. Then [2], at "This differs," he

shows the difference between this species and the preceding. He treats this point under two headings. First [2] he sets forth his proposition, saying that the just thing existing in transactions belongs to another species than distributive justice.

949. Second [3], at "What is just," he presents the difference. First [3] he reviews something relevant to distributive justice. Then [4], at "However, in transactions etc.," he shows what pertains to commutative justice. He says first that the justice mentioned before always directs the distribution of common goods in conformity with proportionality, i.e., the geometrical which is observed in the equality of proportion. This is clear because if wealth belonging to the city or to certain men must be distributed to individuals, the distribution will be made in such a way that each may receive from the community in that ratio according to which he contributed to the community. We suppose in business ventures that the more a man invests in a company the greater is his return. As the just thing directing distributions consists in this proportionality, so the opposite unjust thing consists in disregarding proportionality of this kind.

950. At **"However, in transactions"** [4], he shows what pertains to commutative justice. He gives a threefold consideration of this notion. First [4] he explains a fact relative to commutative justice. Next [5], at "If one of two contestants etc.," he clarifies this by an example. Third [7], at "Therefore, that which etc.," he deduces some corollaries from the premises. He says first that the just thing that exists in transactions agrees somewhat with the just thing directing distributions in this—that the just thing is equal, and the unjust thing, unequal. But they differ in the fact that the equal in commutative justice is not observed according to that proportionality, viz., geometrical, which was observed in distributive justice, but according to arithmetical proportionality which is observed according to equality of quantity, and not according to equality of proportion as in geometry. By arithmetical proportionality six is a mean between eight and four, because it is in excess of the one and exceeds the other by two. But there is not the same proportion on the one side and the other, for six is to four in a ratio of three to two while eight is to six in a ratio of four to three. On the contrary by geometrical proportionality the mean is exceeded and exceeds according to the same proportion but not according to the same quantity. In this way six is a mean between nine and four, since from both sides there is a three to two ratio. But there is not the same quantity, for nine exceeds six by three and six exceeds four by two.

951. Therefore, in commutative justice the equal is observed according to arithmetic proportion. This is clear from the fact that here the different relations of persons are not considered. It does not matter, insofar as commutative justice is concerned, whether a good man has stolen or robbed an evil man of his property or an evil man has done it to a good citizen. Likewise, it does not matter whether a good or evil man commits adultery. The law takes into account only the nature of the injury, so that the man who has done more damage, whatever his condition, must make more restitution. So it is evident that if one of two contestants does an injustice and the other suffers an injustice, one injures and the other is injured, the law treats them as equals, however much they may be unequal. Hence a judge, who is a dis-

penser of the law, attempts to reduce that injustice—by which one man injures another and which has a certain inequality—to an equality by establishing an equality in the very quantity of things and not according to the relation of different persons.

952. Next [5], at "**If one of two contestants,**" he clarifies what he had said, by an example. First [5] he presents the example; and then [6], at "In the interest of plain talk etc.," he resolves a doubt. First he sets forth the example of a personal injury about which too little is clear. He says that if one of two contestants receives a wound and the other inflicts it, or even if one commits murder and the other is murdered, this division of action and passion brings about inequality because the assailant and the murderer have more of what is esteemed good, inasmuch as they have done their own will and so seem as it were to have gained. But the man who is wounded or murdered has more of evil insofar as he is deprived against his will of well-being or life, and so he seems as it were to have suffered loss. The judge tries to equalize this by subtracting from the gain and allotting compensation for the loss, inasmuch as he takes away something from the assailant and the murderer contrary to their will and bestows it to the gain or honor of the person wounded or murdered.

953. Then [6], at "**In the interest of plain talk,**" he resolves a certain doubt that could arise from the words "gain and loss." He says that, in the interest of plain talk, the terms "gain and loss" are used in matters where a person has more or less. Strictly these words refer to what we possess, and sometimes they do not seem suitable, for example, in the case of personal injuries (as when one person receives a blow and

another inflicts it, some injury results) because a fixed measure of action and passion cannot be taken in injuries of this kind so that what is more can be called gain and what is less, loss. But when passion is measured, i.e., according to the measure of justice, then what is more is called gain and what is less, loss.

954. At "**Therefore, that which is just**" [7], he deduces two conclusions: the first [7] on the part of the just thing itself; and the second [8], at "For this reason etc.," on the part of the judge. He says first that the just thing in transactions is a kind of equal that is a mean between more and less in such a way that gain is taken as more and loss as less. However, they are understood in different ways in good and evil, for to have more of good and less of evil belongs to the nature of gain. But the contrary pertains to the idea of loss. Between these two, gain and loss, stands a mean, that equal which we call the just thing. Consequently that just thing, which gives directions in transactions, is a mean between gain and loss as both these terms are commonly understood.

955. Next [8], at "**For this reason,**" he draws a conclusion on the part of the judge of whom it was said (952) that he tries to bring about an equality. Aristotle affirms that because the just thing is a mean between gain and loss, it follows that when men are in doubt about the mean they have recourse to a judge. A judge ought to be, as it were, living justice, so that his soul is entirely possessed by justice. But the people who go to a judge seem to be seeking a mediator between parties who quarrel. Consequently, judges are called intermediaries or mediators as if they may attain the intermediate or the mean, and lead the way to what is just. So

hen it is evident that what is just, the subject of our discussion, is a certain mean because the judge, who determines this just thing, is the middle inasmuch as he proposes what is equal between the parties. But the equal is the mean or middle between more and less, as we have pointed out (310, 933).

LECTURE VII
Finding the Mean of Commutative Justice

TEXT OF ARISTOTLE (1132a25–1132b20) Chapter 4

1. *It is as though the judge were dealing with a line divided into unequal sections, and took from the greater section the length exceeding the half and added it to the smaller section. When a whole belonging to two men is divided by the dicha or measure, then it is said that each has what is his inasmuch as each receives an equal portion—the equal portion being a mean between something greater and something less according to arithmetic proportionality.*

1132a25–30; 956–957

2. *Therefore, this mean is called dicheon (dikaion)—since it is a dicha (measure)—in the way they say dicheon (just thing) and dichastes (just man) and dichaste (justice).*[4]   **1132a30–32; 958**

3. *If there are two equals and the half of one is taken from it and added to the other, the other will exceed it by two. But if what was taken away was not added to the other, the other would exceed the half by one. Therefore, the half taken is equal to one, and the half from which subtraction was made is equal to one. From this we know both what must be taken from the person with too much, and what must be added to the one with too little. The amount exceeding the mean must be awarded to the man with too little and taken from the one with too much.*

1132a32–1132b6; 959–960

4. *Let us take three equal lines and mark them by the terms A A, B B and G G. Subtract A E (the half of A) from A A, and add it to G G and call it G D. Therefore the whole line D G G exceeds the line A E by that which is G D and by that which is G B (the half of G),*[5] *1 but it exceeds line B B by that which is G D.*   **1132b6–9; 961**

5. *This is true also in other arts, for they would be destroyed if the craftsman doing the quality and quantity of work which he should is not supported accordingly.*   **1132b9–11; 962**

6. *The names, gain and loss, have their origin in voluntary transactions. When a man owns more than he did own he is said to have profit, but when less he is said to have loss, as in buying, selling, and other exchanges permitted by law. However, when men have neither more nor less but the same after their transactions they are said to have what is theirs, neither gaining profit nor suffering loss. Therefore, justice is a mean between some kind of gain and loss arising in involuntary transactions; it is having an equal amount of these both before and after the transaction.*   **1132b11–20; 963–964**

COMMENTARY OF ST. THOMAS

956. After the philosopher has shown the difference between the mean of justice regulating transactions and the mean of justice regulating distributions, now he shows how the mean of that justice which regulates transactions is understood. He handles this point in a twofold fashion. First [1] he discloses his proposition. Then [6], at "The names etc.," he explains the origin of the names, gain and loss, which he has used. He discusses the

---

4   Thus St. Thomas seems to have understood the sentence. W. D. Ross translates it: "It is for this reason also that it is called (*dikaion*), because it is a division into two equal parts (*dicha*), just as ii one were to call it (*dichaion*); and the judge (*dicastes*) is one who bisects (*dichastes*)." (New York: Random House, page 1009.)

5   "B" is evidently "3." See diagram in n. 961.

nitial point from two aspects. First [1] he shows how we may discover the mean of commutative justice in these things; next [5], at "This is true etc.," how we may discover it in the matter of the different arts. He treats the first point in two ways. First [1] he introduces an example to show how the mean is applied in commutative justice. Then [3], at "If there are etc.," he clarifies what he has said. In regard to the initial point he first [1] gives the example to explain his proposition. Then [2], at "Therefore, this mean etc.," he shows the appropriateness of the example from the very manner of speaking.

957. Aristotle says that this is the way a judge expresses a reduction to equality. If he wishes to reduce to equality a line divided into unequal parts, he takes away from the larger part that portion by which it exceeds the half of the whole line and adds it to the smaller part so that the half of the whole line is a certain *dicha*, i.e., rule or measure for reducing unequal portions to an equality. So when a whole thing belonging to two men is divided by such a *dicha* or measure, then it is said that each one has what is his inasmuch as he receives equality—which is the mean between more and less—according to arithmetic proportionality. The reason is that the mean of justice is exceeded by the one with more to the extent that it exceeds the person with less—this pertains to arithmetic proportionality, as we pointed out before (944, 950).

958. Then [2], at "**Therefore, this mean,**" he shows that the preceding example is suitable according to Greek usage. He says that since the mean of this justice is a certain *dicha*, hence it is that the just thing is called *dicheon* by the Greeks, as if a person wanting to

vary the names should say that *dicheon* is the just thing, *dichastes* the just man, and *dichaste* justice.

959. Next [3], at "**If there are two equals,**" he makes clear what he has said, viz., that it is necessary to take from one with more in the amount exceeding the mean and to give to one with less. First [3] he explains his statement; and then [4], at "Let us take etc.," he expresses it by terminals. He says first, let us take two equal lines both of which are two measures long, for example, two palms breadth or two feet; let us subtract half from one line and add it to the other. Obviously, the line receiving the addition exceeds the other by two units because the line from which the subtraction was made has only one unit remaining, and the line to which the addition has been made has three units. But if the section subtracted from one line is not added to the other, there will be an excess of only one unit. By that line, to which nothing is added or from which nothing is subtracted, we understand the mean of justice, having as it does neither more nor less than what belongs to it. By the line to which addition has been made we understand the person who has too much. By the line from which subtraction has been made we understand the person who has too little.

960. In this way then it is evident that the man who has too much exceeds the mean by one unit, which has been added to it over and above, but the mean exceeds by one—which has been taken from it—that from which subtraction has been made. Therefore, we will know by this mean what we ought to take from him who has more and give to him who has less. Besides, we will know that we ought to take from the greater, i.e., from him who has more, the amount by which he ex-

ceeds the mean because we ought to give him who has less in the amount the mean exceeds him.

961. At "**Let us take**" [4] he sets forth in figure what was said. Let us take three equal lines and mark the terminations of one A A, of another B B, of the third G G. Then let B B remain undivided, but divide A A in half at the point E, and divide G G in half at the point 3. Next, take away from line A A a section A E, add it to the line G G and call the addition G D. It is clear then that the whole line D G exceeds the line A E by two units, viz., by that which is G G and by that which is G D, but it exceeds the line B B by one unit only, viz., G D. Therefore, obviously, that which is longest exceeds the mean by one unit and the shortest by two units after the manner of arithmetic proportionality.

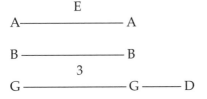

962. Then [5], at "**This is true**," he shows that what has been said must be observed in transactions having to do with the different arts. The arts would be destroyed if the craftsman, who works at some handicraft, would not be supported, i.e., would not receive for his workmanship according to the quantity and quality of what he produced. For that reason the work of one craftsman must be commensurate with the work of another to the extent that there is a just transaction.

963. Next [6], at "**The names**," he explains the origin of the names, gain and loss, saying that they come from voluntary transactions in which names of this kind were first used. When a man owned more than he previously had owned, he was said to have gained; but when less, he was said to have suffered loss, as in buying, selling and in all other transactions which are permitted by law. However, when men have neither more nor less than they had in the beginning, but bring back in equal quantity the same as they had taken by their transactions, then they are said to have what belongs to them, neither gaining nor losing.

964. He draws the final inference that he had principally intended. It is evident from the premises that the justice we are now discussing is a mean between gain and loss, that justice is simply the possession of an equal amount before and after a transaction even an involuntary one, as we see in the person who, when constrained by a judge, restores to another what he had in excess.

LECTURE VIII
The Opinion of Pythagoras

TEXT OF ARISTOTLE (*1132b21–1133a18*) Chapter 5

1. *Some philosophers seem to think that, generally speaking, justice is reciprocation, as the Pythagoreans held; in this way they defined justice without qualification.* **1132b21–23; 965**

2. *However, reciprocation does not belong to distributive justice.* **1132b23–24; 966**

3. *Likewise, it is not suited to the justice that regulates all transactions, although Rhadamantus wished to say that it was, holding that if a man suffers what he himself did to another, justice is attained.* **1132b24–27; 967**

4. *Such justice is at variance with true justice in many situations, for example, if a prince strikes another it is not required that the prince be struck, but if another strikes a prince such a man should not only be struck but also punished in addition.* **1132b28–30; 968–969**

5. *Moreover, it makes a great deal of difference whether the offender acts voluntarily or involuntarily.* **1132b30–31; 970**

6. *But in dealings of exchange justice is such that it includes reciprocation according to proportionality but not according to equality.* **1132b31–33; 971–972**

7. *By reason of proportional reciprocation the state continues to exist, for either the citizens seek to return evil (for evil)—if not, a kind of servitude seems to be present when revenge may not be taken—or they seek to return good (for good) and if not, proper recompense will not be made. It is by return of favors that men live together. Because of this they promptly express gratitude as if it were a sacred duty to make repayment—a thing characteristic of gratitude. It is fitting that a man should be of service to one who has done him a favor and in return begin to do a greater favor.* **1132b33–1133a5; 973–974**

8. *A conjunction by means of a diagonal shows how to make that compensation which is according to proportionality. Let A be a builder, B a shoemaker, G a house, and D a sandal. It is necessary that a builder should take from the shoemaker his product and in return give what he himself makes. If first an equality according to proportionality be found and then reciprocation be made, it will be as we have said. But if not, there will not be an equality—and the state will not continue to exist—because nothing hinders the work of one craftsman from being of more value than the work of another. Therefore these things must be equated.* **1133a5–14; 975–976**

9. *This is to be observed also in the other arts, for they would be destroyed if a workman did not receive according to the quantity and quality of what he produced. Between two doctors an exchange does not take place but between a doctor and a farmer who are altogether different and unequal. These then must be equated.* **1133a14–18; 977**

COMMENTARY OF ST. THOMAS

965. After the Philosopher has shown how the mean should be understood in both kinds of justice, now he rejects a false opinion about the understanding of the mean of justice. He discusses this point under three headings. First [1] he states the erroneous opinion. Next [2], at "However, reciprocation etc.," he rejects it. Third [6], at "But in dealings etc.," he shows where and

how the truth may be found. He says first it seems to some that, generally speaking, justice is nothing other than reciprocation, viz., that a man should suffer according to what he has done. This was the opinion of the Pythagoreans who decided that justice is the same as reciprocation.

966. Then [2], at "**However, reciprocation,**" he rejects this opinion on two

accounts; and first [2] in regard to distributive justice, he says that reciprocation does not correspond to what is just distributively. The reason for this is evident. The just thing in distributions is not judged according to what one of two, who must be equated by justice, does against the other or suffers from the other. This is necessary for the nature of reciprocation; but in distribution a share of the common goods is given to each by an equality of proportion.

967. Next [3], at "**Likewise, it is not**," he rejects the preceding error in the case of commutative justice. First [3] he proposes what he intends to do with commutative justice. He says that reciprocation does not coincide with all the processes in justice that regulate transactions, although the philosophers who expressed the foregoing opinion meant that in transactions justice is the same as reciprocation. This is clear from the fact that a legislator named Rhadamantus maintained that this justice is of such a nature that if a man suffers those very things he inflicted on others, justice is vindicated.

968. Then [4], at "**Such justice,**" he rejects this view for two reasons. In regard to the first [4] he says that in many situations vengeance of this kind is found to be at variance with true justice, for instance, if a ruler strikes a private person justice does not require that the ruler be struck. But if a person strikes a ruler it is necessary that such a person not only be struck but be more gravely punished.

969. This seems to contradict what the Philosopher said before (951) that in commutative justice the different rank of persons is not taken into account—all being equal under the law. But it should be noted what the Phi-

losopher had said was this: in commutative justice the law considers only the nature of the damage. It is clear that when damage is considered in the taking of an external thing—money for instance—the amount of damage does not vary according to a person's rank. Still when the injury is personal, the extent of the injury necessarily changes according to the rank of the person. Obviously, worse damage is done when someone strikes a ruler, by reason of the fact that injury is done not only to the person of the ruler but also the whole commonweal. Therefore, reciprocation simply taken is not suitable for justice in matters of this kind.

970. At "**Moreover, it makes**" [5] he gives the second reason. He says in the matter of imposing punishment, it makes a great deal of difference whether the offender inflicted the injury voluntarily or involuntarily, i.e., because of ignorance or violence or fear. The man who sinned voluntarily ought to be punished more severely than the man who sinned involuntarily, for two reasons. First, because in regard to punishments, consideration is given to the restoration of equality of justice not only by a person restoring what he has taken but also by his being punished for the crime. For this reason some are punished by law even for sins causing no injury or damage to another. Likewise a thief is compelled not only to restore what he took—by which the equality of justice is reestablished—but beyond that he is punished for the offense perpetrated. But the offense is increased or diminished by the fact that a man sins voluntarily or involuntarily. Hence the voluntary offender is punished more severely than the involuntary offender. The second reason is that the injury of the

deliberate transgressor is greater, for internal contempt is added to the external damage.

971. Next [6], at "**But in dealings,**" he explains in what matter and manner the statement is true that reciprocation is justice. He discusses this point from three aspects. First [6] he shows that there must be reciprocation in exchanges according to proportionality. Then [8], at "A conjunction by means etc.," he explains the form of this proportionality. Last [Lect. IX], at "Therefore all etc." (1133a18), he shows how such a form can be observed. On the initial point he does two things. First [6] he states his intention. Next [7], at "By reason of proportional etc.," he proves his statement. He says that in dealings of exchange it is true that justice is of such a nature that it includes reciprocation not according to equality but according to proportionality.

972. It seems this is contrary to what was said before (950), that in commutative justice the mean is taken not according to geometrical proportionality, which consists in an equality of proportion, but according to arithmetic proportionality, which consists in a quantitative equality. We must say that, in regard to commutative justice there should always be an equality of thing to thing, not, however, of action and passion, which implies corresponding requital. But in this, proportionality must be employed in order to bring about an equality of things because the work of one craftsman is of more value than the work of another, e.g., the building of a house than the production of a penknife. Hence, if the builder exchanged his work for the work of the cutler, there would not be equality of thing given and taken, i.e., of house and penknife.

973. Then [7], at "**By reason of proportional,**" he proves his statement, saying that justice in exchanges includes reciprocation according to proportionality. This can be shown by the fact that the citizens live together amicably because they have a proportionate kindliness towards one another. Accordingly, if one does something for another, the other is anxious to do something in proportion in return. Obviously, all citizens desire that reciprocation be done to them proportionately. By reason of this all men can live together because they do for one another what they themselves seek. Therefore, they never seek in regard to evil that corresponding requital be done to them proportionately. But if they do not seek this in regard to evil, for example, when one man does not take vengeance on another who injures him, a kind of servility seems to result. Indeed it is servile when a man cannot gain by his own activity something that he does not desire in an evil way.

974. We may even say that men not only do not desire that corresponding requital, when unjust, be done to them proportionately, but they do not desire that it be done when just. In this way if corresponding requital is not done them in a proportionate way, proper retribution will not be effected. But men live together because one makes a return to another for the favors he has received. So it is that virtuous men promptly express gratitude to their benefactors as if it were a sacred duty to make them a return in this way—repaying a favor is characteristic of gratitude. It is fitting that a man should be of service to one who has done him a favor, i.e., bestowed a gratuitous kindness, and that he be not content to give only as much as he received but that in

return he begins to offer more than he got so that he himself may do a favor.

975. Next [8], at "**A conjunction by means,**" he makes known the form of proportionality according to which reciprocation ought to be made. First [8] he gives an example in the shoemaker and the builder; then [9], at "This is to be observed etc.," he shows that the same is found in other arts. He says first that a conjunction by means of a diagonal shows how to make compensation or reciprocation according to proportionality. To understand this draw A B G D, make two diagonals intersecting one another, viz., A D and B D. Let A represent a builder, B a shoemaker, G a house that is the work of the builder, and D a sandal that is the work of a shoemaker. It is necessary at times that the builder should take from the shoemaker his product, a sandal. But the builder himself ought to give his product as a recompense to the shoemaker.

976. Therefore, if first an equality according to proportionality is found so that on one side a certain number of sandals be fixed as equal to one house (for a builder incurs more expense in building one house than a shoemaker in making one sandal), next, corresponding reciprocation is had so that the builder may receive many sandals equal to one house and the shoemaker one house, there will be recompense—as was said—made according to proportion by a diagonal conjunction.

The reason is that a proportionate number of sandals are given to the builder, and the house to the shoemaker. But if compensation is not made in this way, there will not be an equality of things exchanged—and so men will not be able to live together—since nothing hinders the work of one

BUILDER   SHOEMAKEI

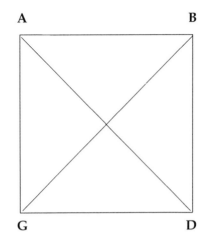

A   B

G   D

HOUSE   SANDAI

craftsman from being worth more thar the work of another, a house than a sandal. For this reason these thing: must be equated one with the othe. according to the previously mentionec proportionality, so that a just exchang may take place.

977. Then [9], at "**This is to be ob served,**" he shows that the same thin; is found in the other arts. He affirm: that what was said (975, 976) about the builder and the shoemaker must be observed also in the other arts, so tha reciprocation and exchange may take place according to diagonal propor tionality. Indeed the arts would be de stroyed if a workman did not receive according to the quantity and quality of what he produced—a thing tha must be discovered in the way indi cated. It is not common for men prac ticing one art, for example, two doctors, to communicate their work with one another, but very often mer practicing different arts do, for in stance, a doctor and a farmer, both en tirely different and unequal. These must be equated in the preceding way

LECTURE IX
Money

TEXT OF ARISTOTLE (*1133a19–1133b29*) Chapter 5

1. *Therefore all things capable of exchange ought to be compared in some way. For this purpose money was invented and became a kind of medium measuring everything including excess and defect.*   **1133a19–21; 978–979**

2. *A certain number of sandals are equal in value to a house or to a quantity of food. Therefore, as many sandals must be exchanged for a house or a quantity of food in proportion as the builder contributes more than the shoemaker (or the farmer). If this is not observed, there will be neither exchange nor sharing. But this reciprocation will not be possible unless things are equated.*   **1133a21–25; 980**

3. *Therefore, it is reasonable to measure all things by one norm, as has been pointed out previously. This norm in reality is demand which connects all things. If men were not in need there would be no exchange, or if they did not have a similar demand, exchange would not be the same. Money originated by agreement on account of necessary exchange. Hence money (numisma) has the name because it is a norm not by nature but by law (nomos). We have the power to change money and to make it useless.*   **1133a25–31; 981–982**

4. *When things have been equated there will be reciprocation, so that as the farmer is to the shoemaker, the amount of the shoemaker's work is to the amount of the farmer's work. When things are to be exchanged they ought to be represented in a figure showing proportionality. If this is not done one extreme will have both excesses, but when all have what is theirs they will be equal and will do business with one another because this equality can be brought about for them.*   **1133a31–1133b4; 983**

5. *Let A represent the farmer, G the food, B the shoemaker and D his equated work. If there is no such reciprocation, there will not be any sharing of goods.*   **1133b4–6; 984**

6. *That human demand connects everything as by a kind of measure is evident because when men are so mutually situated that both or at least one is not in need, they do not exchange their goods. But they engage in exchange when one needs what the other has, e.g., wine, and they give grain for it. An equation then must be made between these goods.*   **1133b6–10; 985**

7. *For future exchanges money is as it were a guarantee that a man, who has no present need, will be helped when he is in want later on. The man who offers currency should receive what he needs. However, currency suffers like other things, for it is not always of the same value; although it tends to be more stable than other things.*   **1133b10–14; 986–987**

8. *Everything then must be evaluated in money, for in this way exchange will always take place and consequently association among men. Money equates goods making them commensurate after the manner of a measure. Indeed association is not possible without exchange, nor exchange without equality which cannot exist unless there is commensuration.*   **1133b14–18; 988**

9. *It is impossible that things so greatly different be made commensurate according to reality, but they agree sufficiently by comparison with the needs of man, and so there must be one measure determined by man. And this is called money, which makes all things commensurate inasmuch as they are measured by money.*   **1133b18–23; 989**

10. *Let A represent a house and B five minae. Let G represent a bed worth one mina. The bed then will be one fifth the value of the house. Therefore it is obvious how many beds equal a house, viz., five. Likewise it is obvious that barter took place before money existed. But it makes no difference whether five beds or the value of five beds are given.*
We have now discussed the nature of what is just and what is unjust. **1133b23–29; 990–991**

COMMENTARY OF ST. THOMAS

978. After the Philosopher has proposed the form of proportionality, with which reciprocation is identified in exchange, he now shows in what way this form of proportionality can be observed. First [1] he explains his intention. Then [6], at "That human demand etc.," he clarifies the previous statements. He discusses the initial point in a twofold manner. First [1] he shows that to preserve the form of proportionality perfectly it is necessary to make everything commensurate. Next [4], at "When things have been etc.," he explains how a just reciprocation in exchanges may be effected by a commensuration of this kind. He treats the first point under three aspects. Initially [1] he explains the nature of that which measures all things. Then [2], at "A certain number etc.," he shows how such a commensuration is established in exchanges. Last [3], at "Therefore, it is etc.," he indicates the nature of this commensuration.

979. He says first, in order that the products of the different workmen be equated and thus become possible to exchange, it is necessary that all things capable of exchange should be comparable in some way with one another so that it can be known which of them has greater value and which less. It was for this purpose that money or currency was invented, to measure the price of such things. In this way currency becomes a medium inasmuch as it measures everything, both excess and defect, to the extent that one thing exceeds another, as was pointed out before (955, 959–960). It is a mean of justice—as if someone should call it a measure of excess and defect.

980. Next [2], at "**A certain number**," he shows how exchange takes place according to the preceding commensuration. Although a house is worth more than a sandal, nevertheless a number of sandals are equal in value to one house or the food required for one man during a long period. In order then to have just exchange, as many sandals must be exchanged for one house or for the food required for one man as the builder or the farmer exceeds the shoemaker in his labor and costs. If this is not observed, there will be no exchange of things and men will not share their goods with one another. But what has been said, that a number of sandals are exchanged for one house, is not possible unless the sandals are equated with the house in some way.

981. At "**Therefore, it is**" [3] he indicates the nature of this commensuration made by means of money. He states that for this reason it is possible to equate things because all things can be measured by some one standard, as was pointed out (957). But this one standard which truly measures all things is demand. This includes all commutable things inasmuch as everything has a reference to human need. Articles are not valued according to the dignity of their nature, otherwise a mouse, an animal endowed with sense, should be of greater value than a pearl, a thing without life. But they are priced according as man stands in need of them for his own use.

982. An indication of this is that if man were not in need there would be no exchange, or if they did not have a similar need, i.e., of these things, exchange would not be the same because men would not exchange what they have for something they did not need. That demand really measures every-

thing is evident from the fact that money originated by arrangement or a kind of agreement among men on account of the necessity of exchange, i.e., exchange of necessary goods. There is an agreement among men that what a person needs will be given him in exchange for currency. Hence currency is called money (*numisma*)—*nomos* means law—since currency is not a measure by nature but by law (*nomo*). It is in our power to change currencies and make them useless.

983. Then [4], at "**When things have been**," he shows how just reciprocation takes place in exchanges according to the preceding commensuration. First [4] he explains his proposition; and then [5], at "Let A represent etc.," puts it in a diagram. He says first that the norm measuring all things by need according to nature and by currency according to human convention will then become reciprocation when everything will be equated in the way just mentioned. This is done in such a manner that as the farmer (whose work is raising food for men) excels the shoemaker (whose work is making sandals), in the same proportion the work of the shoemaker exceeds in number the work of the farmer, so that many sandals are exchanged for one bushel of wheat. Thus when exchange of things takes place, the articles to be exchanged ought to be arranged in a proportional figure with diagonals, as was stated previously (957). If this was not done, one extreme would have both excesses; if a farmer gave a bushel of wheat for a sandal, he would have a surplus of labor in his product and would have also an excess of loss because he would be giving more than he would receive. But when all have what is theirs, they are in this way equal and do business with one another because

the equality previously mentioned is possible for them.

984. Next [5], at "**Let A represent,**" he puts in a diagram what has been said about the proportional figure. Take then (as in the previous example) a square A, B, G, D, and two diagonals A D and B G intersecting one another. Let A represent the farmer and G the food, his product, e.g., a bushel of wheat. Let B represent the shoemaker and D his equated product, i.e., as many sandals as have the value of a bushel of wheat. There will then be a just reciprocation if A be joined with D and B with G. If there is not such a compensation men will not share their goods with one another.

FARMER   SHOEMAKER
A   B

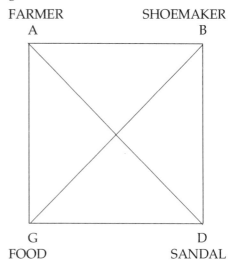

G   D
FOOD   SANDAL

985. At "**That human demand**" [6] he explains more fully what has already been mentioned. First [6] he shows how things are made commensurate; and next [8], at "Everything then," how the things made commensurate may be exchanged. He discusses the first point from two aspects. First [6] he shows that necessity is a measure according to reality; and then [7], at "For future exchanges etc.," how currency is a measure according to the

provision of law. He says first the statement (981–982) that human need contains everything as a certain measure is explained in this way. When men are so situated among themselves that either both, or at least one, do not need a thing possessed by the other, they do not engage in mutual exchange. But exchange does take place when a man owning grain is in need of wine which his neighbor has, and thus gives the grain for the wine, so that a quantity of grain is alloted according to the value of the wine.

986. Then [7], at "**For future exchanges**," he shows clearly how currency serves as a measure. On this point we must consider that if men always needed immediately the goods they have among themselves, they would have no need of any exchange except of thing for thing, e.g., wine for grain. But sometimes one man (who has a surplus of wine at present) does not need the grain that another man has (who is in need of wine), but perhaps later he will need the grain or some other product. In this way then for the necessity of future exchange, money or currency is, as it were, a surety that if a man has no present need but may want in the future, the thing he needs will be available when he presents the currency.

987. The particular virtue of currency must be that when a man presents it he immediately receives what he needs. However, it is true that currency also suffers the same as other things, viz., that it does not always obtain for a man what he wants because it cannot always be equal or of the same value. Nevertheless it ought to be so established that it retains the same value more permanently than other things.

988. Next [8], at "**Everything then**,"

he explains how, by the measure of currency, there is exchange of things which are made commensurate in currency. He discusses this point from three aspects. First [8] he shows in what manner there is exchange of goods that are measured in currency. Then [9], at "It is impossible," he discloses under what aspect currency serves as a measure. Last [10], at "Let A represent a house," he puts in terminals what was said. He states first that, because currency as a measure ascertaining quantity retains its value longer, all goods must be evaluated in currency. In this way exchange of goods can take place and, consequently, association among men. Money equates commutable goods, as a certain measure making them commensurate. He clarifies what has been said by stating that association is not possible if there is no exchange. But exchange is impossible unless an equality is established in goods, which in turn cannot exist without commensuration.

989. Then [9], at "**It is impossible**," he shows in what way currency is used as a measure. He says that it is impossible that things so greatly different be made commensurate according to reality, i.e., according to the peculiar nature of the things themselves. But they can be sufficiently contained under one measure by comparison with the needs of men. Hence there must be some one criterion that measures all things of this kind and is not a measure by reason of nature but because so fixed by men. Therefore, this is called money owing to the fact that it makes all things commensurate insofar as they are measured by money.

990. At "**Let A represent a house**" [10] he explains in terminals what has been said, stating: let A be a house

worth five minae, B a bed worth one mina, and in this way the bed will be one fifth the value of the house. Hence it is obvious how many beds are equal in value to one house, viz., five. Likewise it is obvious that barter took place before there was currency, since five beds have been exchanged for one house. But it makes no difference whether five or the value of five beds are given.

991. He concludes saying that we have now discussed the nature of what is just and what is unjust.

LECTURE X
Just Action as a Mean

TEXT OF ARISTOTLE (*1133b30–1134a16*) Chapter 5

1. From these discussions it is clear that a just action is a mean between doing what is unjust and suffering what is unjust. To be unjust is to have too much, to be injured is to have too little.   **1133b30–32; 992**

2. But justice is a mean, not in the same way as the preceding virtues but in the sense that it produces a mean. However, injustice pertains to extremes.   **1133b32–1134a1; 993**

3. Justice is also a habit by which the just man is said to operate by choosing what is just and to distribute both to himself in relation to his neighbor and to one man in relation to another.

1134a1–3; 994–995

4. He does not act in such a way that he bestows more desirable things on himself and less desirable things on his neighbor, and on the contrary less hurtful things on himself than on his neighbor, but he distributes equally according to proportion. Likewise, he observes a rule regarding one man in relation to another. On the other hand injustice is a habit operative of what is unjust. This takes place by excess and defect of useful or hurtful things contrary to what is proportional. Hence injustice is called excess and defect because it brings about excess and defect, the unjust man assigning himself an excess of what is simply useful and a deficiency of what is harmful. In a similar way he attributes both an excess and a deficiency to others. But this too is contrary to what is proportional in whatever way it takes place.   **1134a4–12; 996**

5. One injustice, which is to have too little, is to suffer what is unjust. Another injustice, which is to have too much, is to do what is unjust.   **1134a12–13; 997–998**

6. We have then discussed justice and injustice, and the nature of both. Likewise we have treated in a general way what is just and unjust.   **1134a14–16; 999**

COMMENTARY OF ST. THOMAS

992. After the Philosopher has shown how the just thing is a mean, now he shows how justice is a mean. On this point he does three things. First [1] he states his intention. Then [3], at "Justice is also etc.," he proves his statement. Finally [6], at "We have then discussed etc.," he recapitulates what has been said. Since habits are known by acts, he treats two aspects of the initial point. First [1] he proposes that the operation of justice is a mean; and second [2], at "But justice etc.," how justice itself is a mean. He says first that, from previous considerations (978–991), it is evident that a just operation, that is, an operation of justice, is a mean between doing what is unjust and suffering what is unjust. The first is to have more than is due to

oneself, i.e., to do an unjust action; but the other, viz., to suffer an unjust thing, is to have too little by reason of the fact that a person has been deprived of what is due him. The act of justice is to do what is equal, i.e., the mean between too much and too little. Obviously then it follows from the premises that a just action is a mean between doing what is unjust and suffering what is unjust.

993. Then [2], at "**But justice**," he explains how justice is a mean, saying that justice is not a mean in the same way as the other moral virtues. Their mean lies between two vices; liberality is a mean between parsimony and extravagance. But justice is not a mean between two vices. However, it can be called a mean by reason of its effect

inasmuch as it constitutes a mean, since its act is a just operation which is a mean between doing what is unjust and bearing the unjust. The first of these, active injustice pertains to a vice of injustice which is a habit of extremes inasmuch as it takes for itself too many goods and too few evils. But the other, i.e., the toleration of the injustice is not a vice, but a suffering.

994. Next [3], at "**Justice is also,**" he proves what was said, viz., that justice is not a middle course between two vices, as is the case with other moral virtues. He treats this point in a two-fold manner. First [3] he takes up the nature of justice; then [5], at "One injustice etc.," he adds some remarks to bring his subject to a conclusion. He discusses the first point from two aspects. Initially [3] he states what justice is; and next [4] at "He does not act etc.," what injustice is. He says first that justice is a habit by which the just man does the just thing—and this by deliberate choice because, as was previously pointed out in the second book (305, 308, 382), a moral virtue is a habit of correct choice. Doing the just thing can be referred to justice directing exchanges, in which the nature of justice is more apparent by reason of the equality of the thing. Hence he adds "and to distribute" in order to include also distributive justice, which consists in the equality of proportion.

995. A man can do the just thing by choice, both in exchanges and in distributions, in two ways. In one way he does this between himself and another, and touching this point Aristotle says "both to himself in relation to his neighbor." In the second way a man does this between two others—this pertains to a judge or an arbiter—and so the Philosopher adds "and to one man in relation to another." He ex-plains, by exclusion of the contrary, how the just man does a just deed. He adds that the just man does not so act that in regard to desirable things (for example, riches and honors) he bestows more on himself and less on his neighbor, and in regard to harmful things (i.e., burdensome and painful), on the contrary, more on his neighbor than himself; but he makes an equal distribution according to proportion—a thing he observes not only between himself and another but also between two others.

996. At "**He does not act**" [4] he presents the nature of injustice. He affirms that on the contrary injustice is a habit which does by choice what is unjust. This happens by excess or defect of useful or harmful things which the just man accepts according to due proportion. Hence, as justice is called a mean because it produces a mean, so also injustice is called excess and defect because it produces excess and defect in such a way that the unjust man bestows on himself an excess of things which are simply useful but a deficiency of things which are harmful. In a similar way he attributes to others both excess and defect, however not of the same things, but a defect of the useful and an excess of the harmful. Nevertheless, it has not been determined in what way injustice may depart from the proper proportion, i.e., how much more or how much less it may accept than is due. But injustice does this, howsoever it may happen.

997. Next [5], at "**One injustice,**" he adds some remarks required to conclude the subject. He says there is a twofold injustice: one consists in a lack of beneficial things, and indicates an excess of onerous things—which amounts to the same. This is to suffer what is unjust. The other injustice is to

have an excess of beneficial things and a lack of onerous things—and this is to do an injustice.

998. From what has been said we can come to three conclusions. To do an unjust act pertains to injustice. However, to have a lack of benefits or an excess of burdens is not to do what is unjust but to suffer what is unjust. Therefore this does not pertain to the vice of injustice. But justice is a mean between having too much and too little, as was pointed out before (992, 993). Consequently, injustice is not a mean between two vices.

999. Then [6], at "We have then discussed," he concludes by recapitulating what has been said. He affirms that we have discussed justice and injustice and the nature of both. Likewise we have treated what is just and what is unjust in a general way, for he will determine afterwards (1000–1108) certain particular modes of what is just and unjust.

LECTURE XI
The Unjust Man

TEXT OF ARISTOTLE (*1134a17–1134b18*) Chapter 6

1. *Since someone doing an unjust act may not be unjust himself, we will investigate the nature of the unjust actions that show the doer—for example, a thief or an adulterer or a robber—already unjust according to the injustice proper to each case. Or does not this make any difference? If a man having sexual intercourse with a woman knows with whom he sins and acts not by choice but by passion, he does an unjust act but is not unjust. So neither is a man a thief although he steals, nor an adulterer although he commits adultery. The same is true in other cases* **1134a17–23; 1000–1001**

2. *We have previously discussed how reciprocation is related to what is just.*
1134a23–24; 1002

3. *We must not forget that we seek what is just in the absolute sense and political justice.*
1134a24–26; 1003

4. *The latter consists in a community of life for the purpose of having a self-sufficiency among free men equal according to proportionality or arithmetical equality.*
1134a26–28; 1004–1005

5. *Therefore, among those persons in whom this does not exist we find not political justice but a special kind of metaphorical justice.* **1134a28–30; 1006**

6. *For justice exists between those very persons whose relations are governed by law. But the law is enacted for those among whom injustice is found, because punishment is a judgment of what is just and what is unjust. Among these there is unjust action, but injustice does not exist in everyone who does an unjust action, which is to attribute to oneself too many of the things good in themselves and too few of the things onerous in themselves.* **1134a30–34; 1007–1008**

7. *For this reason we do not permit the rule of man but of reason, for a man rules for himself and becomes a tyrant. But a prince is the guardian of justice and of equality.*
1134a35–1134b2; 1009

8. *Since a prince, if he is just, attributes nothing excessive to himself, it follows that he does not give himself more of what is simply good, except according to proper proportion, and on this account he works for others. Therefore it is said that justice is the good of another, as was previously pointed out.* **1134b2–6; 1010**

9. *Consequently a reward should be allotted to him, namely, honor and glory. Rulers who are not satisfied with these are tyrants.* **1134b6–8; 1011**

10. *However, the justice of a master and of a father are not the same as but similar to those we have examined.* **1134b8–9; 1012**

11. *Toward one's own things injustice does not exist in an unqualified manner. But a chattel and a son, until he is a certain age and acts in his own right, are as it were a part of a man. Now no one chooses to injure himself. Therefore, there is no injustice done to oneself, and consequently no injustice simply speaking.* **1134b9–13; 1013**

12. *Nor is political justice observed here which is according to the law and is found in men naturally bound by the law. Such are the persons who have equality in regard to ruling and being ruled.* **1134b13–15; 1014**

13. *Hence justice concerns rather a wife than children and chattels. In the first there is domestic justice, and this is also different from political justice.* **1134b15–18; 1015**

COMMENTARY OF ST. THOMAS

1000. After the Philosopher has treated justice and the unjust thing in themselves together with their opposites, now he treats them in comparison with their subject, showing how a man in doing an unjust action becomes unjust. He handles this point under two headings. First [1] he determines the truth. Then [Lect. XIV], at "Someone may raise etc." (1136a10), he raises some doubts about matters previously settled. He discusses the initial point from three aspects. First [A] he asks a question. Next [3], at "We must not forget etc.," he interposes some subjects necessary for a solution of the question. Finally [Lect. XIII], at "Since just and unjust etc." (1135a15), he answers the question. He treats the first point in a twofold manner. First [1] he presents the question. Then [2], at "We have previously etc.," he shows that another question was settled previously. He says first that a person who does an unjust action still may not be unjust. Therefore, we must inquire into the characteristics of injustice, i.e., the actions of unjust men must be of such a type that the man who does unjust deeds is already unjust in that particular species of injustice, for example, theft or adultery or robbery. Or, passing over the cases just mentioned, can it be said that for a man to be unjust it makes no difference in what actions he may act unjustly?

1001. For this reason we ask with what kind of injustice it occurs, because the doing of an unjust action takes place in many ways. A man may have sexual intercourse with a woman, the wife of another, and not be ignorant who the person is (ignorance could cause an involuntary) but know with whom he is having intercourse,

and still not perform the act by deliberate choice but by passion. Such a man does an unjust act although he does not seem to be unjust because he does not act by deliberate choice. So also we can say in a particular case that a man is not a thief although he has stolen, since he did not commit theft by deliberate choice. In a similar way a man is not an adulterer although he has committed adultery. The same idea is found in other matters.

1002. Then [2], at "We have previously," he shows that a particular doubt has already been solved, viz., in what way reciprocation is related to justice—a point we discussed previously (971–972).

1003. Next [3], at "We must not forget," he interposes some subjects that are necessary for the solution of the proposed question: first [3] what is justice in the absolute sense; and second [Lect. XII] at "There is a difference etc." (1135a9), what is unjust action. He handles the initial point in a twofold fashion. First [3] he states his intention. Then [4] at "The latter consists etc.," carries out his intention. He says first that for a clear understanding of the question (in which we seek by what actions a man who does a just or an unjust act is said to be just or unjust) we must not forget the fact that the justice sought is justice in the absolute sense which is political justice.

1004. Then [4], at "The latter consists," he carries out his intention. First [4] he shows what political justice is. Then [Lect. XII], at "One kind of political justice etc." (1134b18), he divides it. He treats the initial point under two aspects. First [4] he proposes what he intends, viz., what political justice is. Next [6], at "For justice exists etc.," he explains his intention. He discusses the first point under two headings. Initially [4] he shows what political justice is. Second [5], at "Therefore, among those persons etc.," he concludes that there are other kinds of justice differing from this. He says first that political justice consists in a community of life that is ordered to a self-sufficiency of the things pertaining to human living. And the state-community should be such that everything sufficient for the needs of human life is found in it. This justice is found in free men, not slaves, because masters exercise towards slaves not political justice but the justice of dominion, of which more later (1006–1012). However, political justice is encountered with persons who are equal, i.e., one of whom is not subject to the other in the natural or political order, as a son to a father between whom there is no question of political justice but of paternal right.

1005. This political justice is either according to proportionality, i.e., proportional equality pertaining to distributive justice, or numerical equality, i.e., the equality of numerical quantity pertaining to commutative justice.

1006. Next [5], at "**Therefore, among those persons,**" he concludes there are other kinds of justice differing from that just mentioned. He states that—since political justice exists among the free and equal—in people who do not have this (that they are free and equal) there is not found political justice, which is unqualified justice, but a peculiar justice, viz., of a master or father, which is a qualified justice inasmuch as it has some likeness to political justice.

1007. At "**For justice exists**" [6], he clarifies his statement: first [6] in regard to political justice, which is unqualified justice; second [10] in regard

to justice of a master or a father, which is qualified justice, at "However, the justice of a master etc." First [6] he clarifies his statement, viz., that political justice is in free and equal persons. Next [7], at "For this reason we do not etc.," he draws some corollaries from the premises. He says first—as has been pointed out (1004)—that political justice is in the free and equal because, being determined by law, it necessarily is found in those for whom the law is enacted. But law is enacted principally not for slaves who are restrained by masters nor for children who are restrained by fathers but for the free and equal. That political justice exists in men of this kind, for whom law is enacted, is obvious from this that justice and injustice exist in them. Now, law extends to persons in whom there can be injustice. This is clear from the fact that punishment, which is fixed by law, is nothing other than a judgment about what is just and unjust.

1008. From this statement—the law exists for those between whom justice exists—it follows that it is for those between whom there is unjust action and for those between whom there is just action. The reason is that in whomsoever there is injustice, in these the performance of an unjust act is found but not the reverse. It was pointed out in the second book (252–253) that the doing of a virtuous action may take place without virtue, and likewise the doing of vicious actions without the habit of vice. An unjust act arises from the fact that a person should attribute to himself too many of those things which are absolutely and of themselves good, like riches and too few of those things which are simply and of themselves evil, as the opposite of these.

1009. Next [7], at "**For this reason**

we do not permit," he draws three corollaries from the premises. First [7] he says that because injustice consists in this that a man attributes to himself too many of the benefits and too few of the burdens, it follows that in good government of the multitude we do not permit that men should rule, that is, according to whim and human passion but that the law, which is a dictate of reason, should rule man, or that man who acts according to reason should rule. The explanation is that if a prince follows human passions he will do this for himself; he will take more of the good things and less of the burdensome and so become a tyrant, although this is contrary to the concept of a prince. A prince was given the office to observe justice, and consequently equality, which he passes over when he usurps for himself too many beneficial and too few onerous things.

1010. He gives the second corollary [8] at **"Since a prince."** He affirms that since a prince—if he is just—attributes no more of the good things to himself than to others (unless perhaps according to a proper ratio of distributive justice), it follows that he does not labor for the advantage of himself but of others. Because of this it was said before (909) that legal justice, by which the prince rules the multitude of the people, is the good of another.

1011. He presents the third corollary at **"Consequently a reward"** [9]. It is clear that everyone should reward the man who labors for him. Therefore, since the prince labors for the multitude, a reward should be given by the multitude, namely, honor and glory, which are the greatest goods that can be offered by men. But if there are some princes who are not satisfied with these for a reward but seek wealth, they are unjust and tyrannical.

Over and above this reward proffered by man, good princes look for a reward from God.

1012. Then [10], at **"However, the justice of a master,"** he explains what was indicated previously about the fact that this is not justice in the absolute sense but by similitude. First [10] (he explains) in regard to the justice of a master and of a father; and second [13], at "Hence justice concerns etc.," in regard to justice which belongs to a husband in relation to a wife. On the prior point he does three things. First [10] he proposes what he intends, saying that the justice of a master, i.e., of a lord over a slave, and paternal justice, i.e., of a father over a son, are not the same as political justice but have some likeness to it according as it has a relation to another in a way.

1013. Second [11], at **"Toward one's own things,"** he explains what was pointed out regarding this that the justice of a master or of a father is not justice without qualification. It is evident that injustice cannot exist in an unqualified way for a man in regard to the things belonging to him, and neither can justice, because both have a relation to another. But the slave belongs to the master as a chattel, and a son is—so to speak—a part of the father until he is a certain age or mature and separated from the father by emancipation. That there is no injustice toward oneself is clear from the fact that no one chooses to injure himself. Hence it is obvious that absolutely speaking there is no justice or injustice towards a son or a slave.

1014. Third [12], at **"Nor is political justice,"** he explains that even if the justice of a master and of a father would be justice without qualification, it would not be political justice because political justice is according to the law and in those for whom the law is designed by its nature. Such are those persons who have equality in regard to ruling and being ruled; but of these one is subject to another, e.g., a slave to a master and a son to a father. Hence political justice does not exist in these matters.

1015. Then [13], at "**Hence justice concerns,**" he treats justice pertaining to a wife. He says that because a wife is less subject to a husband than a slave to a master or a son to a father, therefore the relation of a husband to a wife has more of the nature of justice than the relation of a father to his children, and of a master to his chattels or slaves. The justice that belongs to a husband in regard to a wife is domestic because the husband is the head of the home, as the prince of the state. However, domestic justice is different from political, as the home is different from the state.

LECTURE XII
A Division of Political Justice

TEXT OF ARISTOTLE (1134b18–1135a15) Chapter 7

1. One kind of political justice is natural and the other is legal.   1134b18–19; 1016–1017

2. Natural justice is that which has the same force everywhere and is not affected by what men may or may not think.   1134b19–20; 1018–1019

3. That is called legal justice which in the beginning is indifferent about a thing being done this way or that. But when something just is decreed a difference arises, for example, a mina for redeeming a captive, a goat but not two sheep for sacrifice; also when things are mentioned individually in the law, for instance, sacrifice to Brasidas; and again when sentences are passed by judges.   1134b20–24; 1020–1024

4. Some people were of the opinion that all justice is of this kind because what is by nature is unchangeable and has the same force everywhere (fire, for instance, burns both here and in Persia). But just things are looked upon as variable.   1134b24–27; 1025

5. However, that opinion is not true universally but in some respect, although there may be no change at all among the gods. But with us there is something natural and this is changeable because everything in us is changeable. Moreover, there is in us something natural and something not natural.   1134b27–30; 1026

6. Among the things subject to change, what kind is just by nature and what kind is just not by nature but by law and agreement, if both kinds are changeable in a similar way?   1134b30–32; 1027

7. Obviously, the same determination applies to other natural things. Now by nature the right hand is stronger, although some people are ambidextrous.   1134b32–35; 1028–1029

8. Those things that are just according to agreement and utility are similar to the measures of commodities. But the measures of wine and grain are not equal everywhere, for where these articles are bought (wholesale) the measures are greater, where sold (retail), smaller. Likewise, things just not by nature but by agreement among men are not the same everywhere, as neither is the form of government. But one form only is best everywhere by nature.   1134b35–1135a5; 1030

9. Particular just and legal things hold the place of universals in regard to singulars, for there are many actions performed but each of the just things is one and a universal.   1135a5–8; 1031

10. There is a difference between an unjust action and an unjust thing, between a just action and a just thing. The unjust thing is something unjust by nature or ordinance of man, but when it is performed it becomes an unjust action. Before a thing has been done it is not an unjust action but something unjust.   1135a8–11; 1032

11. It is the same with just action. In general it is more often called the doing of a just thing (diceopragma) but it means the correction of unjust action. In regard to each of these we must see afterwards of what nature they are, what are their species and how many they are.   1135a11–15; 1033–1034

COMMENTARY OF ST. THOMAS

1016. After the Philosopher has shown the nature of political justice, i.e., unqualified justice, now he makes a division of it. First [1] he divides po-litical justice into species. Then [9], at "Particular just and legal things etc.," he touches upon the division of this justice into individual parts. He dis-

:usses the first point from three aspects. First [1] he proposes the division. Next [2], at "Natural justice etc.," he explains it. Last [4], at "Some people were etc.," he rejects an error opposed to the division. He says first that there is a twofold division of political justice: natural justice, and legal justice. This is the same as the division that the jurists make, namely, that one kind of right is natural and the other positive. They call right the very thing that Aristotle calls the just object. Isadore too says in *Libri Etymologiarum* (Bk. V, Ch. III) that right is as it were what is just. But there seems to be inconsistency in that political is the same as civil. In this way what the Philosopher considers the whole division seems to be considered by the jurists as a part of the division, for they make civil law a part of positive law.

1017. But we must take into account that political or civil is taken here in one way by the Philosopher and in another way by the jurists. The Philosopher here calls justice political or civil from the usage the citizens are accustomed to, but the jurists call right political or civil from the cause, viz., that some city has decreed for itself. For this reason the Philosopher appropriately designates legal or posited by law that which they call positive. Political justice then is properly divided by means of these two, for the citizens use justice to the extent that it is imparted to the human mind by nature and to the extent that it is posited by law.

1018. Then [2], at "**Natural justice,**" he indicates the parts of the preceding division. First [2] he explains natural justice in two ways: in one way according to its effect or power, saying that that justice is natural which everywhere has the same force and power to induce to good and prevent evil. This

happens because nature, the cause of this justice, is the same everywhere among all men. But justice by the decree of a state or prince has force only among those who are subject to the jurisdiction of that state or prince. In the other way he explains this justice according to its cause, when he says that natural justice does not consist in what seems or does not seem to be, i.e., it does not arise from human conjecture but from nature. In speculative matters there are some things naturally known, like indemonstrable principles, and truths closely connected with them; there are other things discovered by human ingenuity, and conclusions flowing from these. Likewise in practical matters there are some principles naturally known as it were, indemonstrable principles and truths related to them, as evil must be avoided, no one is to be unjustly injured, theft must not be committed and so on; others are devised by human diligence which are here called just legal enactments.

1019. We must consider that that justice is natural to which nature inclines men. But a twofold nature is observed in man. One, is that which is common to him and other animals. The other nature belongs to man properly inasmuch as he is man, as he distinguishes the disgraceful from the honorable by reason. However, jurists call only that right natural which follows the inclination of nature common to man and other animals, as the union of male and female, the education of offspring, and so forth. But the right which follows the inclination proper to the nature of man, i.e., precisely as he is a rational animal, the jurists call the right of the peoples (*jus gentium*) because all people are accustomed to follow it, for example, that agreements are to be kept, legates are safe among enemies, and so on. Both of these, though, are included under natural justice as it is here taken by the Philosopher.

1020. Next [3], at "That is called legal justice," he explains legal justice and seems to give three differences in justice of this kind. The first is this: when something is universally or commonly imposed by law it becomes legal. Regarding this he says that that justice is called legal which in the beginning, i.e., before it becomes law, is indifferent whether something is done in this way or that, but when it is laid down, i.e., enacted into law, then a difference arises because observing it is just, disregarding it is unjust. Thus in some state it has been decreed that a prisoner may be redeemed at a fixed price and that a goat should be offered in sacrifice but that two sheep are not to be sacrificed.

1021. The second difference in legal justice is that something is stated by law in a particular case, for instance, when a state or a prince grants some privilege—called a private law—to an individual person. Touching this point he says there are also legal enactments, not those that are decreed in a general way but whatever are prescribed by legislators as law in individual cases. It was enacted, for example, in a particular state that sacrifice should be offered to a man named Brasidas who rendered great service to the state.

1022. The third difference in legal justice is that sentences passed by judges are called a kind of legal justice. In regard to this he adds that the decrees of judges are also legal enactments.

1023. But here we must take into consideration that legal or positive jus-

tice always has its origin in natural justice, as Cicero says in his *Rhetoric*. [*Rhetorica, De Inventione,* Lib. II, Cap. LIII.] Origin from natural right can occur in two ways: in one way as a conclusion from a principle, and in such a manner positive or legal right cannot originate from natural right. The reason is that once the premises are stated the conclusion necessarily follows. But since natural justice exists always and everywhere, as has been pointed out (1018), this is not applicable to legal or positive justice. On this account it is necessary that whatever follows from natural justice as a conclusion will be natural justice. Thus, from the fact that no one should be unjustly injured it follows that theft must not be committed—this belongs to natural justice. In the other way something can originate from natural justice after the manner of a determination, and thus all positive or legal justice arises from natural justice. For example, that a thief be punished is natural justice but that he be punished by such and such a penalty is legal justice.

1024. Also we must consider here that legal justice has its origin in two ways from natural justice in the preceding manner. In one way it exists with an admixture of some human error, and in the other without such error. Aristotle explains this by examples. It is natural justice that a citizen who is oppressed without any fault on his part should be aided, and consequently that a prisoner should be ransomed, but the fixing of the price pertains to legal justice which proceeds from natural justice without error. Likewise it is natural justice that honor be bestowed on a benefactor but that divine honor be given him—that he be offered sacrifice—arises from human error. But the just decrees of judges are applications of legal justice to particular cases.

1025. At "**Some people were of the opinion**" [4] he rejects an error opposed to this division. On this point he does three things. First [4] he proposes the error together with the reason for it. Second [5], at "However, that opinion etc.," he refutes it. Last [6], at "Among the things etc.," he asks a question occasioned by the refutation. He says first that some were of the opinion that all justice is that which is established by law and there is then no natural justice. This was the opinion of the followers of the Socratic philosopher Aristippus. They were influenced by this reason: that which is according to nature is invariable, and wherever it is it has the same force, as is obvious fire burns in Greece as well as in Persia. Apparently this is not true of justice because all just things seem to be changed at times. Nothing seems to be more just than that a deposit should be returned to the owner. Nevertheless the return must not be made to a madman demanding his sword or to a traitor to his country demanding money for arms. So then it seems that there is nothing just by nature.

1026. Then [5], at "**However, that opinion**," he provides a refutation, saying that the statement that natural things are unchangeable is not so universally but is true in some respect. The reason is that the nature of divine things never changes, for example, the nature of separated substances and of the heavenly bodies, which the ancients called gods. But with us humans, who are counted among perishable things, there is something according to nature and yet whatever is in us is changeable either intrinsi-

cally or extrinsically. Moreover, there is in us something natural like having two feet, and something not natural like having a coat. Undoubtedly all the things that are just among us are variable, although some of them are naturally just.

1027. Next [6], at "**Among the things**," he raises a doubt occasioned by the preceding refutation. He handles the first point in a twofold manner. First [6] he asks the question. Then [7], at "Obviously, the same," he answers it. First he proposes this question. If all just human things are changeable the question remains: of the things that change, what kind is just by nature and what kind is just not by nature but by the decision of the law and agreement among men, if both are changeable in a similar way?

1028. At "**Obviously, the same**" [7] he answers the question just asked. He considers this point in a twofold manner. First [7] he shows how things just by nature are changeable. Then [8], at "Those things that are," he shows how things just by law are changeable. He says it is obvious that the arrangement found in other natural things, likewise applies to things just by nature. Those things that are natural with us occur in the same way in the greater number of cases but fail in a few. Thus it is natural that the right hand is stronger than the left, and this is so in the greater number of instances, although it happens occasionally that some men are ambidexterous since their left hand is as strong as their right. So also the things that are just by nature, for example, that a deposit ought to be returned must be observed in the majority of cases but is changed in the minority.

1029. However, we must keep in mind that the essences of changeable things are immutable; hence whatever is natural to us, so that it belongs to the very nature of man, is not changeable in any way, for instance that man is an animal. But things that follow a nature, like dispositions, actions, and movement, are variable in the fewer instances. Likewise those actions belonging to the very nature of justice cannot be changed in any way, for example, theft must not be committed because it is an injustice. But those actions that follow (from the nature of justice) are changeable in a few cases.

1030. Then [8], at "**Those things that are**," he shows how the legally just are changeable without exception. He says that regulations that are just according to arrangement and advantage, i.e., by what is agreed among men for some utility, are similar to measures of salable commodities, wine and wheat. These are greater where products are bought wholesale but smaller where products are sold retail. So also things that are not naturally just but fixed by men are not the same everywhere, thus the same punishment is not inflicted everywhere for theft. The reason is that civil life and the administration of the state are not the same everywhere. All laws are framed as they are needed for the end of the state, although only one form of government is everywhere best according to nature.

1031. Next [9], at "**Particular just and legal things**," he treats the division of justice in regard to the individual parts. He says that each particular just and legal thing is related to human affairs as a universal to singulars. The

reason is that actions which are done according to justice are many but each just thing is one, as it were a kind of universal. Thus, that a deposit must be returned is one which has a reference to many cases.

1032. At "**There is a difference**" [10] he shows what just action and unjust action are. First [10], what unjust action is. Then [11], at "It is the same etc.," what just action is. He says first that unjust action and unjust thing differ, for an unjust thing is something that is contrary to justice either by nature or by human decree, as theft. But the doing of an action by someone, for instance, stealing is called unjust action, the execution of injustice so to speak. However, before this is done by anyone it is not called an unjust action but an unjust thing.

1033. Then [11], at "**It is the same**," he shows what just action is. He says that in a similar way just action is present when a person does a thing which is just by nature or by regulation of law. But with the Greeks the doing of a just thing in general is rather called *dicaeopragma* or doing of what is just, but every doing of a just thing does not seem to be called justifying action but only when a person is corrected in the justifying action, i.e., by restoring what is unjust to justice.

1034. Finally, he says that we must discuss later, in the *Politics* (Bk. I, Ch. 6, 1255a3–1255b15; St. Th. Lect. IV, 75–88), the nature, the number, and the species of each type of justice, viz., natural and legal.

LECTURE XIII
Actions Which Make a Man Just or Unjust

TEXT OF ARISTOTLE (*1135a15*) Chapter 8

1. *Since just and unjust acts are such as have been described, a man acts unjustly or justly when he acts voluntarily. But when he acts involuntarily he works neither injustice nor justice except incidentally, for it is incidental that the actions are just or unjust. An act of justice and a just action are indicated by reason of a voluntary and an involuntary. When a voluntary is done and a person is blamed, then there is at the same time an unjust action. Wherefore something unjust may be present but an unjust action never exists if there is no voluntary.*
1135a15–23; 1035–1036

2. *As has been pointed out previously, I call voluntary any of the actions within a man's power, which he does knowingly and without ignorance of the what, how and why; for example, whom he struck, with what instrument, and with what intention—none of these being unintentional. Also the act must be done without violence, thus when one takes a person's hand and strikes another, that person does not act voluntarily because it was not in his power to hinder this. It can happen that the one struck is the man's father, the striker knowing the person is a human being or someone present but not recognizing his father. Likewise the same should be determined in what concerns the intention and the whole operation. Certainly the act done without knowledge, or knowingly and not being in our power, is like an involuntary. We knowingly do and experience many natural things none of which are either voluntary or involuntary, for example, growing old and dying.*
1135a23–1135b2; 1037–1038

3. *The same is true even when the act is just or unjust incidentally, because if someone restores a deposit unwillingly and on account of fear his act is not said to be just, nor is it an act of justice except incidentally. In a similar way a person forced against his will to not restore a deposit is said to do an unjust thing or an act incidentally unjust.*
1135b2–8; 1039

4. *We perform some voluntary actions by choice and others without deliberation. When we make a choice of anything we first deliberate, but things we do without choice[6] are without previous deliberation.*
1135b8–11; 1040

5. *Injury may occur in dealings among men in three ways. Through ignorance sins are committed in which neither the person against whom, nor the what, nor the how, nor the end are known, and they take place for an end not considered, for example, a man intends not to wound but to tap, not this person or not in this way. When therefore (1) injury is inflicted unintentionally, we have an unfortunate accident, but when (2) the injury is not unintentional although without evil intent, we have a sin certainly since the principle of the cause is in the agent. But what happens incidentally has an external cause.*
1135b11–19; 1041–1043

6. *However, when (3) injury is inflicted knowingly but without deliberation, we have unjust action, thus whatever is done through anger or other passions which are necessary or natural to man. Under these circumstances persons sinning and injuring others act unjustly and their actions are unjust but they are not unjust or evil on account of this, for they do not inflict injury from wickedness.*
1135b19–24; 1044

7. *But when injury is inflicted by choice the perpetrator is unjust and evil.*   **1135b25; 1045**

8. *Therefore, it is in their favor that the things done out of anger are judged not to arise from*

---

6   The text used by St. Thomas evidently had the word *ineligibilia* and not *intelligibilia* as given in the Pirotta and Spiazzi editions.

premeditation, for it is the man who gave the provocation that began it and not he who acted in sudden anger. **1135b25–27; 1046**

9. *Besides, it is not a question of whether the act is done but whether it is done justly, for anger indicates some injustice which is obvious. The case is different when the fact is questioned as in transactions where the alternative is necessarily evil if the action is not done through forgetfulness. But angry people, acknowledging the fact, are uncertain in what way there is injustice. However, those who act deviously are not ignorant on this point. Therefore the cunning, but not the angry, know that the injured party suffered unjustly.*

1135b27–1136a1; 1047

10. *If a man inflicts injury by deliberate choice, he acts unjustly and he is now called unjust because of those unjust acts since they are contrary to the proportional or the equal. In a similar way a person is called just when he acts justly by deliberate choice, but he is said to be a doer of a just act only if he acts voluntarily.* **1136a1–5; 1048**

11. *Some involuntary acts deserve pardon, others do not. Whatever sins men commit not only in ignorance but also because of ignorance are excusable. However, the sins they commit not by reason of ignorance but in ignorance because of passion, which is neither natural nor human, are inexcusable.* **1136a5–9; 1049**

COMMENTARY OF ST. THOMAS

1035. After the Philosopher has shown what justice in itself is, and what just action and unjust action are, now he answers a question that he previously asked, viz., by what just or unjust actions may a man become just or unjust? He treats this point in a two-fold manner. First [1] he explains his plan. Then [11], at "Some involuntary acts etc.," he introduces a division to explain things mentioned previously. He discusses the initial point from two aspects. First [1] he shows when a just or unjust thing may exist without a just or unjust action. Next [4], at "We perform some voluntary etc.," he shows that there is just or unjust action without the agent being just or unjust. He discusses the first point under two headings. Initially [1] he explains his intention. Second [2], at "As has been pointed out etc.," he clarifies what he said. He affirms first that since just and unjust acts are such as have been described before (1000–1001), then a man acts unjustly or justly in this way: there is an act of injustice or a just action when he voluntarily does these very

things, i.e., what is just and unjust. But when a man does them involuntarily he does not act justly or unjustly except perhaps incidentally; it happens contrary to his intention that the acts he does are just or unjust.

1036. Those things that we intend to do are said to be done in themselves and not incidentally. However, nothing is specified by what is incidental but only by what is in itself (*per se*). Therefore the act of justice and the *dicaeopragma* or the just operation, and likewise the act of injustice are indicated by a voluntary or involuntary, in such a way that when something is voluntary a person is praised or blamed. Hence, obviously, on the part of the thing done there will be something unjust, but there will not be an unjust action as regards the species of the operation if there is not a voluntary on the part of the agent. The same holds for just action.

1037. Then [2], at "**As has been pointed out**," he clarifies some things that have been said, what a voluntary and an involuntary are. He handles this point in a twofold fashion. First [2] he indicates his intention. Second [3], at "The same is true etc.," he shows that the previous explanation is applicable to both just and unjust acts. He says first that a voluntary, as has been pointed out in the third book (382, 391, 427, 435, 436), is said to be present when a person knowingly does a thing that is in his power and is not ignorant either of what is done, or by what means, or for what end he does this. For example, he knows whom he struck, how he delivered the blow—as by an instrument—and the purpose of it; so too he knows each of these in themselves and not incidentally. In order that there be a voluntary it is necessary that the thing not happen by violence, for instance, if one takes a person's hand by force and strikes another, he whose hand it is does not do this voluntarily, because it is not in his power to avoid being forced.

1038. After this, he explains how a thing may be known incidentally. It is possible that the man struck is his father. He who delivers the blow knows that a human being or someone present was struck but not that his father was; thus he knows incidentally that this was his father inasmuch as he knows that the person to whom this happened was his father. As we have discussed the man who delivers the blow, similarly we must investigate the purpose of the whole operation, i.e., all the circumstances of the operation. From the statement of what the voluntary is we can know what the involuntary is. The reason is that if something is done through ignorance or (after ignorance has ceased) is not in the power of the agent, or still more is done through violences it will be an involuntary. On this account it was added "by violence" because many

things that are in us are not involuntary, for there are many natural things we knowingly do and experience, for example, growing old and dying. Nevertheless none of these is voluntary or involuntary because each one of them concerns the things which are in us by nature. But if it happens through violence that one of them is not in us, then it is called an involuntary.

1039. Next [3], at "**The same is true**," he explains what was said about just and unjust acts. In regard to just acts, for example, if a man hands over a deposit to its owner not willingly but on account of fear, we do not say there is just action in this case except incidentally. Likewise if a person forced against his will abstains from restoring a deposit, we say he does an unjust thing or acts unjustly by accident.

1040. At "**We perform some voluntary actions**" [4] he shows when there is just or unjust action and yet the agent himself is not just or unjust. First [4] he premises a division necessary to explain the statement. Next [5], at "Injury may occur etc.," he explains the statement. Last [8], at "Therefore, it is etc.," he clarifies some things that have been said. He states first that we do some voluntary actions by deliberate choice and others without deliberate choice. Whatever we do by deliberate choice we do with preceding counsel or deliberation; but whatever is not subject to choice or is performed without choice we do without previous counsel or deliberation.

1041. Next [5], at "**Injury may occur**," he explains the statement. First [5] he repeats when there may be an unjust thing without an unjust action. Then [6], at "However, when etc.," he restates when there is unjust action without the agent being unjust. Last [7], at "But when injury etc.," he shows when one is unjust by the injustice and wickedness of the agent. He says first, as appears from what has been stated previously (1037–1038), that injury may occur in dealings among men in three ways: in one way by ignorance and involuntarily, in another way voluntarily but without choice, and in a third way voluntarily and with choice.

1042. Those sins are committed through ignorance that are done by a man who does not know what he is doing, nor against whom he acts, nor with what means, nor for what end even if he was aware of performing an act. Thus a man thought that he landed a blow not with this instrument, e.g., a piked lance but with a rounded one; or he thought that he struck not this man, viz., not his father but an enemy; or he did not think he was about to strike for this objective but an objective was achieved he did not think of, for example, when he intended to strike not to wound but to tap. The case is similar when ignorance exists in regard to the way a man landed a blow, mightily or lightly.

1043. But on this point we must consider that when injury is inflicted unintentionally, i.e., contrary to plan or intention, then an altogether unfortunate accident happens. For instance, a man means to brandish a spear and instead throws it. But when someone inflicts injury not unintentionally, that is, not without the intention of injuring but without malice in the sense that he does not mean to injure much or injure such a person, then there is some sin, although not so great a one. A man sins when the principle of an inordinate act is in his power in this that he intends to perform the act. But when the principle of operation is entirely external so that it works contrary to the intention, then an unfortunate accident occurs

since fortune is an intellectual cause acting outside of reason, as is explained in the second book of the *Physics* (Ch. 5, 196b10–197a8; St. Th. Lect. VIII, 210–216).

1044. Then [6], at "**However, when,**" he shows when there may be unjust action without wickedness or injustice of the agent. He says that when a man inflicts injury knowingly but not with previous counsel, i.e., without deliberation, then there is a kind of injustice, as there is in any action that a person commits through anger and other passions—provided these passions are not natural and necessary to men, like desire for food and drink in extreme necessity which excuses the taking of what belongs to another. Therefore, those who injure others because of these passions sin and do an unjust thing and their acts are unjust actions. Nevertheless by reason of this they are not unjust and evil because they do not inflict injury from wickedness but from passion. Such people are said to sin from weakness.

1045. At "**But when injury**" [7] he shows when there may be unjust action with injustice on the part of the agent. He says that when a man by deliberate choice causes injury to another, he is unjust and evil. Such a one is said to sin out of sheer wickedness.

1046. Next [8], at "**Therefore, it is,**" he clarifies what has been said. Because the first of the three things mentioned previously (which treats of what is done from ignorance) was commented on before (1042–1043), in the beginning [8] he explains the second, which deals with what is done from weakness or passion. Then [10], at "If a man inflicts injury by choice etc.," he explains the third, which treats of what is done by deliberate choice. He says first that when people sin from anger they are not evil or unjust because of this. Therefore we are well able to judge from this proof of previous statements that what is done from anger is not considered to be done with premeditation. He proves this afterwards, at "for it is the man" [8], by two reasons. The first is this, that it is not the man himself who does something in anger that begins the process of injuring but the person who provoked him. So it does not seem that the injury arose with premeditation.

1047. Then [9], at "**Besides, it is not,**" he gives the second reason. He says that when a man inflicts injury in anger there is no question whether he does the act or not but whether he does it justly, for by anger some injustice is obvious, i.e., operates openly. And the angry man wishes the punishment to be obvious but it seems to him that he is justly provoked. It is not the same thing with unjust dealings, like theft and so forth in which there is doubt whether the act should have been done. One of the things must be evil, for instance, giving or not giving; for we sin sometimes by omission, other times by transgression unless we are excused by reason of forgetfulness, as when a person forgets to pay a debt to a creditor at an agreed time. But people acting in anger admit the thing, or the fact, but doubt whether what they did is unjust. This does not happen to those who act deviously by choice and are not ignorant that they act unjustly. Wherefore, the insidious person judges that the man he injured suffers unjustly; but the angry person does not think this. So it is evident that he who

does an unjust thing in anger does not act with premeditation.

1048. At "**If a man inflicts injury**" [10] he explains the third reason concerned with acts done by deliberate choice. He says that if a man inflicts injury by deliberate choice, it is obvious that absolutely speaking he acts unjustly, because he operates voluntarily. He who acts according to an injustice of this kind is called unjust since this action is contrary to the proportional, i.e., against distributive justice, or contrary to the equal, i.e., against commutative justice. In a similar way a man is called just when he acts justly by deliberate choice. However, if he should act voluntarily and not by choice he will be called the worker or doer of what is just.

1049. Then [11], at "**Some involuntary things,**" he gives a division to explain things mentioned previously. He says that some involuntary acts are venial, i.e., deserving of pardon, and others are not. Those sins deserve pardon that men commit not only in ignorance, that is, when they have concomitant ignorance, but on account of ignorance, viz., when ignorance is the cause so to speak—this happens to those who are sorry when they become aware. But those sins do not deserve pardon that men commit not on account of causative ignorance but in ignorance because of passion, which is neither natural nor human nor according to right reason. In actions of this kind passion is the cause of ignorance and sin; these have been more fully treated in the third book (406–424).

LECTURE XIV
Suffering Injustice Is Involuntary

TEXT OF ARISTOTLE (*1136a10–1136b14*) Chapter 9

1. *Someone may raise a doubt whether suffering and doing injustice have been treated sufficiently. Does Euripides speak the truth when he unseemly says: "I killed my mother: briefly, willingly or unwillingly I killed her who was willing to be put to death?"*
1136a10–14; 1050

2. *Is it true or not that a person willingly suffers injustice? Or is this an involuntary, as every doing of injustice is a voluntary?*
1136a15–16; 1051

3. *Is suffering injustice always voluntary or always involuntary, or is it sometimes voluntary and sometimes involuntary? The same question can be asked about the reception of justice.*[7]
1136a16–19; 1052

4. *Every doing of justice is a voluntary. Therefore it is reasonable that suffering injustice and the reception of justice, in a similar way, are opposed according to both, viz., the voluntary and the involuntary (so that all of the one are voluntary, and all the other are involuntary).*
1136a19–21; 1053

5. *It seems unreasonable that every suffering of injustice is voluntary, for some people unwillingly suffer injustice.*
1136a21–23; 1054

6. *Wherefore, doubt can arise whether a person who has undergone damage suffers injustice.*
1136a23–25; 1055

7. *In regard to what is incidental the same holds for receiving as for doing, since clearly we take one for the other in matters concerning justice and injustice alike. Acting unjustly is not the same as doing something unjust, nor is suffering unjustly the same as suffering something unjust. Likewise, doing an unjust thing and suffering an unjust thing are not the same. It is impossible to suffer unjustly without someone doing what is unjust, or receive justice without someone doing what is just.*
1136a25–31; 1056

8. *Doing an injustice in itself is present when a man voluntarily inflicts injury, that is, knowing who is injured, by what means, and in what manner.*
1136a31–32; 1057

9. *The incontinent person who voluntarily injures himself also voluntarily suffers an injustice and does an injustice to himself.*
1136a32–34; 1058

10. *But this is one of the doubtful points whether it is possible for a man to do an injustice to himself.*
1136a34–1136b1; 1059

11. *Moreover, it happens by reason of incontinence that a man is voluntarily injured by another acting voluntarily. Hence someone willingly suffers an injustice.*
1136b1–3; 1060

12. *Perhaps the definition is not correct, and we should add to the words "knowing who is injured, by what means, and in what manner" the further qualification "contrary to the will of the injured person." Anyone, then, can have an unjust thing done to him voluntarily, but no one can suffer injustice voluntarily.*
1136b3–6; 1061

13. *No one wants to suffer injustice—not even the incontinent person unless he acts contrary to his will. No one wishes what he does not think is good. But the incontinent person performs actions he thinks he ought not to perform.*
1136b6–9; 1062

14. *Anyone who gives what is his, as (according to Homer's story). Glaucus gave Diomede golden armor for brass armor and a hundred oxen for nine oxen, suffers no injustice. It is in this*

---

7   *Justum* seems called for in place of *injustum*. Cf. Commentary.

man's power to give but not in his power to suffer injustice—there must be someone who inflicts the injustice. Therefore it is obvious that suffering injustice is not voluntary.

1136b9–14; 1063–1064

COMMENTARY OF ST. THOMAS

1050. After the Philosopher has shown by what just actions a person may be called just or unjust, now he raises some doubts about the questions just discussed. He treats this point from two aspects. First [1] he raises the doubts and solves them. Then [Lect. XV], at "Men are of the opinion etc." (1137a5), he refutes the errors of some philosophers about these subjects. The first part is divided into two according to the two questions he answers. The second part begins at [Lect. XV] "There are still etc." (1136b15). He handles the initial part under two headings. First [1] he proposes the question. Then [4], at "Every doing of justice," he follows up the question. He discusses the first point in a twofold manner. First [1] he proposes the matter of the question. Next [2], at "Is it true or not etc.," he puts the questioning into form. In the first place the matter of the question is taken from material that was settled earlier (1035–1049). Hence he says that someone can raise a doubt whether suffering and doing of injustice have been sufficiently discussed by reason of what has been said already. It was stated (1035) that doing justice is voluntary. So it can be questioned whether this must be referred to suffering injustice. In the second place the matter of the doubt is taken from the words of the poet Euripides who somewhat unbecomingly introduced a character saying: "I killed my mother—to make the story short, either I voluntarily killed her who wished to be put to death or else I killed her involuntarily." In either case

we understand that the mother had expressed a wish to be killed.

1051. Then [2], at "**Is it true or not**," he puts the questioning into form. He considers this in two ways. First [2] he proposes one question, viz., whether it is really proper to say that a man voluntarily suffers injustice or whether this is untrue, but that every suffering of injustice is involuntary, as every doing of injustice is voluntary.

1052. Second [3], at "**Is suffering injustice**," he proposes another question. The question is whether every suffering of injustice is constituted in this way or in such a way that every suffering of injustice is either voluntary or involuntary. As this question can be asked about doing injustice—whether every such action is voluntary or whether some are voluntary and others involuntary—so in a similar way the same question can be asked about the reception of justice.

1053. Next [4], at "**Every doing of justice**," he follows up the question previously asked. He develops this in a threefold fashion. First [4] he argues that every reception of justice is voluntary or every reception is involuntary. Then [5], at "It seems unreasonable," he argues that not every suffering of injustice is voluntary. Last [8], at "Doing an injustice," he argues that not every suffering of injustice is involuntary. He argues in this way for the first point. Every doing of justice is voluntary, as is clear from what has been pointed out (1035). But doing justice is the opposite of receiving justice. Therefore it seems reasonable that receiving justice or injustice should be opposed similarly according to both, i.e., voluntary and involuntary, so that all of the one is voluntary and all of the other involuntary.

1054. At "**It seems unreasonable**" [5] he argues that not every suffering of injustice is voluntary. He treats this point from three aspects. First [5] he argues for the proposition, saying it seems unreasonable to hold that every suffering of injustice is voluntary. Obviously some people unwillingly suffer injustice, like those who are flogged or whose possessions are taken by others.

1055. Second [6], at "**Wherefore, doubt can arise**," he asks a question on this point: whether everyone who suffers injustice materially and incidentally can be said to suffer injustice formally and in itself. Thus someone may readily object that the man who unwillingly suffers robberies or blows, suffers injustice incidentally, nevertheless he is not, so to speak, simply a victim of injustice.

1056. Last [7], at "**In regard to what is incidental**," he answers the objection. He says that the same holds for doing as for receiving. The reason is that in both cases it is possible to take one for the other: to understand what is incidental about justice in a similar way to what is incidental about injustice. He gives this explanation, that performing acts incidentally unjust is not the same as doing an act unjust in itself. It was pointed out (1035–1036) that sometimes a person in ignorance does by chance what is unjust, nevertheless, absolutely speaking, he does not act unjustly. Similarly, undergoing things that are incidentally unjust is not the same as undergoing what is simply unjust. Likewise it is impossible that these things are the same in the

doing of justice and in receiving justice; and that the same reason holds for the doing and receiving both in regard to just things and unjust things. He explains this afterwards by the fact that it is not possible to suffer something just or unjust simply speaking because passion is an effect of action. If then a man does what is unjust incidentally and does not become unjust simply, it follows that neither does he suffer injustice simply who suffers an unjust thing. The same argument holds for justice.

1057. Then [8], at "**Doing an injustice**," he argues against the idea that suffering injustice is involuntary. First [8], he argues for the proposition. Second [12], at "Perhaps the definition etc.," he solves the proposition. Concerning the initial point he offers two reasons. In regard to the first [8] of these he presents three considerations. First [8] he gives a definition of doing injustice, which was defined previously (1035, 1045): doing injustice simply and in itself is simply the voluntary inflicting of injury. By voluntary is meant that one knows who is injured, what inflicts the injury, and how, i.e., in what manner together with other circumstances of this kind.

1058. Second [9], at "**The incontinent person**," he argues from the definition given. It is obvious that the incontinent person voluntarily injures himself, inasmuch as he does voluntarily what he knows is harmful to him. If then suffering injustice resembles doing injustice, it follows that the person acting voluntarily himself may suffer injustice from himself, so it is possible for someone to do injustice to himself. Thus it follows that not every suffering of injustice is involuntary.

1059. Third [10], "**But this is one**," he asks an incidental question:

whether in fact someone can do an injustice to himself. But he takes up this question later (1091–1108).

1060. At "**Moreover, it happens**" [11] he gives the second reason. If it happens that anyone by reason of incontinence is knowingly and willingly injured by another (for example, a man ensnared by love of a prostitute allows himself to be robbed) then it is possible that a person may willingly suffer injustice. So, not every suffering of injustice is involuntary.

1061. Then [12], at "**Perhaps the definition,**" he gives the solution. He discusses this point from three aspects. First [12] he corrects the definition of doing injustice given above (1057), and from it he infers the truth of the question. He says that the definition of doing injustice, stated without qualification, is not correct. But the statement should be added that doing injustice is present when someone with a knowledge of the circumstances inflicts injury on another against his will. From this it follows that although a person voluntarily may be injured and suffer incidentally what is unjust; nevertheless, no one voluntarily suffers injustice, absolutely speaking, because in itself doing injustice is to inflict harm on another against his will.

1062. Next [13], at "**No one wants,**" he answers the first reason. No one wishes with a complete will to suffer injustice, not even the incontinent person, although he does things harmful to himself against his will. Essentially he wills good, but by concupiscence he

is drawn to evil. Aristotle proves this statement from the fact that, since the will desires what appears good, no one wills what he does not think is good. But the incontinent person in a passionless moment does not think what he does is good and therefore he does not will it absolutely; nevertheless he does what he thinks he ought not to do, on account of concupiscence which is in the sensitive appetite, the will being in the reason.

1063. Last [14], at "**Anyone who gives,**" he answers the second reason concerning the person who is willingly injured by another. He says that a man does not suffer injustice absolutely speaking who voluntarily gives what is his own, as Homer narrates[8] about an individual named Glaucus that he gave Diomede golden armor for brass armor and a hundred oxen for nine oxen. Therefore this type does not suffer injustice because it is in the man's power to give what belongs to him. However, suffering injustice is not in the power of him who suffers injustice, but there must be someone who does the injustice. Consequently suffering injustice is involuntary, and doing injustice is voluntary because the principle of action is in the agent—this belongs to the nature of a voluntary. However, the source of suffering is not in the patient but in another—and this belongs to the nature of an involuntary.

1064. He concludes by way of summary that suffering injustice obviously is involuntary.

---

8   *Iliad* vi. 236.

LECTURE XV
Who Does Injustice in Distributions?

TEXT OF ARISTOTLE (*1136b15–1137a30*) Chapter 9

1. There are still two questions we wish to discuss. Who does an injustice, he who distributes more than one's share or he who receives it? And does a person do injustice to himself?

1136b15–17; 1065

2. If the first proposal is true, viz., he who distributes but not he who receives commits injustice; then when a person knowingly and willingly gives more to another than to himself, he does injustice to himself, as moderate men seem to do, for the person who keeps within measure takes what is of less value for himself.

1136b17–21; 1066

3. But it does not seem entirely true, for in this case he abounds in another good, namely, glory or moral good.

1136b21–22; 1067

4. Again we can answer in accord with the definition of doing injustice, for the distributor suffers nothing contrary to his will. Therefore he does not suffer injustice by reason of this but only damage.

1136b23–25; 1068

5. However, it is obvious that he who distributes too much, but not always he who receives it, does an injustice.

1136b25–26; 1069

6. Not the man in whom the unjust thing exists does injustice but the man who wills to do it. He is the one who is the principle of action. This is in the distributor, not in the recipient.

1136b26–29; 1070

7. Action is said to occur in various ways: in one way as inanimate things or the hand or servant of the owner are said to take life. These do not act unjustly but do unjust things.

1136b29–31; 1071

8. Moreover, he who has formed a judgment through ignorance of what is legally just does not do an injustice nor is his judgment unjust but it resembles injustice, for legal justice differs from primary justice. But if a person knowingly forms an unjust judgment, he acts covetously to obtain favor or avoid punishment. Hence—just as if he shares in the injustice—the man, who judges unjustly for that purpose, has more than his due; for in such cases the man who awards a field does not receive a field but silver.

1136b32–1137a4; 1072–1073

9. Men are of the opinion that they are unjust when they do what is unjust, and for this reason they think it easy to become unjust. But this is not true. It is easy and within their power to have carnal intercourse with a neighbor's wife, to strike another, and to hand over silver, but doing these things as a habit is not (immediately) in their power.

1137a4–9; 1074

10. Similarly, some people think that no wisdom is needed to know what things are just and unjust because it is not difficult to understand what the law says. However, these things are only incidentally just but become truly just when done and distributed in a particular way. Now to know this way is a more difficult task than to know the things that are healthful because there it is easy to know the virtue of honey, wine, and hellebore, to know the effect of cautery and surgery, but how they ought to be prescribed for health, for what patient, and when is as great an accomplishment as that of being a doctor.

1137a9–17; 1075

11. For this very reason it is thought also that the just man is not less able to do injustice but rather can do any unjust thing: for example, he can have carnal intercourse, strike a blow, and a brave man can throw away his shield, can turn and run away. However, perpetration of a cowardly action or of something unjust is doing these things only incidentally, but the doing is absolute for one having the permanent facility, just as healing and restoring to health do not consist in cutting or not cutting, in giving medicine or not giving it, but in prescribing these things as they should be.

1137a17–26; 1076

12. *Just acts are found among people who participate in things good in themselves but have both defect and excess of them. For some persons there is no excess in regard to such goods (possibly so with the gods). For others, the hopelessly evil, no particle of these goods is useful but every one of them is harmful. In still others the goods become harmful at a determined point; and this is human.*   **1137a26–30; 1077**

COMMENTARY OF ST. THOMAS

1065. After the Philosopher has solved one doubt, now he comes to another. First [1] he proposes it, then [2], at "If the first proposal etc.," he follows it up. He says first that in the matter of justice and injustice two questions still remain which he wishes to treat in preference to others. The first of these is, which of the two persons does an injustice in regard to distribution: he who gives to someone without regard to worth or he who accepts? The second—Can a person do injustice to himself?—is a question he asked before (1059) and resolves later (1091–1108).

1066. Then [2], at "**If the first proposal,**" he follows up the question previously asked. First [2] he objects to the false part. Next [3], at "But it does not seem," he solves it. Last [5], at "However it is," he determines the truth. He says first that if what was just said (1065) is true, viz., that the dishonest distributor does injustice and not he who receives too much, something inappropriate seems to follow. It can happen that a person knowingly and willingly gives more to another than to himself, and so it seems that he may do injustice to himself—a thing that is inappropriate. The reason is that moderate men apparently do this, as they retain things of less value for themselves. It is characteristic of the virtuous man that he belittles himself, i.e., accepts things of less value for himself.

1067. Next [3], at "**But it does not seem,**" he solves this by two reasons. The first is that sometimes it is not entirely true that the distributor retains things of less value for himself. Although he keeps the less valuable external goods for himself, he nevertheless has an abundant share of another good, viz., glory, and of moral or honorable good.

1068. At "**Again we can answer**" [4] he gives the second reason proceeding from the definition of doing justice given before (1061). To this an addition was made indicating that it is contrary to the will of him who suffers. But the distributor suffers nothing contrary to his will. Consequently he does not suffer injustice but only undergoes some damage.

1069. Then [5], at "**However it is obvious,**" he determines the truth. He says that obviously the man who distributes more than one's share does an injustice, yet this is not always true of him who accepts too much but only when he works to bring about this object.

1070. Next [6], at "**Not the man in whom,**" he proves the proposition by three reasons. The first [6] is that the man in whom the unjust thing exists is not said to do injustice, because in this way the one who is injured would do injustice; but he does injustice who wills to do it—he is the principle of action. This is the case of the person who distributes but not so with the recipient. Therefore the distributor does injustice and not the receiver.

1071. Aristotle gives the second reason at "**Action is said**" [7], affirming that a man is said to act in various ways. In one way he acts as a principal agent, and in another, as instruments act. In the latter way it can be said that inanimate things, like stones, swords, or arrows cause death, and that the hand or the servant of the one who commands brings about death. None of these, absolutely speaking, does injustice although they are the means by which unjust actions are done. The reason is that doing injustice, since it is voluntary, is attributable to the agent in whom the principle of action lies, as has been pointed out (1063). But it is clear that in distribution the distributor holds the place of the principal agent while the recipient holds the place of an instrument after the manner of one obeying. Hence it remains that the distributor does the injustice.

1072. At "**Moreover, he has formed**" [8] he gives the third reason. He says that if a person by reason of ignorance of legal justice wrongly judges, he does not do injustice, absolutely speaking, nor is the judgment by which his action is done unjust in itself; but it is unjust in a way because the thing judged is unjust. Therefore we spoke of legal justice because one kind of justice is legal which can be unknown, another is natural which cannot be unknown because it is impressed by nature on the human mind. But if someone knowing legal justice judges unjustly, then he acts greedily, that is, unjustly either for the sake of acquiring the favor of another or to avoid a penalty.

1073. If a man wishes to share injustice in unfair portions, he who judges unjustly to curry someone's favor has more good than belongs to him. So he acts greedily, although he may not have more of that good in which he injured another. The reason is that in such affairs a man who unjustly

awarded a field to someone obviously for profit, did not get the field but money. And so a distributor is situated in distribution as a judge in exchanges. Therefore as a judge wrongly judging with full knowledge does an injustice, so too does he who distributes unjustly.

1074. Then [9], at "**Men are of the opinion**," he refutes some errors. Regarding this he does two things. First [9] he refutes some false opinions concerned with one doing justice or injustice. Next [12], at "Just acts are found," he shows in whom just and unjust acts exist. In regard to the first point he refutes three false opinions. The first of these [9] concerns the facility in becoming unjust. He says that many people are of the opinion that they are ready to do even injustice immediately. Hence they think that it is easy to be habitually unjust. Certainly it is easy, and immediately in a man's power, to do unjust things: to have sexual intercourse with his neighbor's wife, to strike his neighbor, to take money from the hand of another, or to hand over money to have murder or some crime done. But that men should do actions of this kind in such a way that they act promptly and with pleasure is not easily nor immediately in a man's power, but they come to this point through persistent habit.

1075. Second [10], at "**Similarly, some people**," he refutes a false opinion about the knowledge of just and unjust things. He says some people think great wisdom is not needed for a man to discern just and unjust acts because it is not difficult to understand the decrees of the law determining legally just acts. However, such people are self–deceived because these acts simply considered are just only accidentally inasmuch as it is an accident

hat such things are just. But they be-
ome genuinely just when in some way
hey are performed and distributed
i.e., attributed) in some way to affairs
nd persons. But proper adaptation to
ffairs and people is more laborious
nd difficult than knowing remedies in
vhich the whole art of medicine con-
ists. There is a greater diversity
mong voluntary acts about which jus-
ice is concerned than among the hu-
nors about which health is concerned.
Also it is easy to know the virtue of
1oney, wine, and hellebore, and the
ffect of cautery and surgery, but to
1rescribe these things for the restora-
ion of health in the right way, for the
ight person, and at the right time is as
great an accomplishment as being a
loctor, for one who has this knowl-
1dge is a doctor.

1076. Third [11], at "**For this very
1eason,**" he refutes a false opinion con-
1erning facility in doing justice and un-
1ust things. He affirms that, on account
1f what has been said, people also are
1f the opinion that the just man can do
njustice as readily as anyone else, be-
1ause from the fact that he is just he
1nows not less but more and can do
1ny one of the things called unjust, like
1aving sexual intercourse with an-
1ther's wife, striking another, throw-
1ng away his shield in battle; and a man
1an attack anyone he pleases. But they
1eceive themselves because the perpetration of cowardly actions and the doing of what is unjust is doing these
things only incidentally inasmuch as it
happens that the acts are unjust, but to
do what is simply unjust is for someone to do these things in such a way
that he is willing and prompt at it. So
it is in medicine—healing and restoring to health do not consist in operating or not operating, in prescribing or
not prescribing a drug, i.e., a laxative,
but in a person prescribing them as he
ought.

1077. Then [12], at "**Just acts are
found,**" he shows to whom they are
attributable. We say that just acts are
attributable to the people among
whom are found things simply and in
themselves desirable, like riches and
so on, although these persons (as is
common among men) have excess and
defect in this matter. For some there is
no excess in such things that are used
most laudably, as becomes men perfect
in virtue and perhaps the gods (according to the error of people who
hold that gods use things of this nature). For others, viz., the very wicked
and the incurably evil no particle of
these goods is useful but everything is
harmful. For still others not everything
is harmful but it becomes so at a certain
fixed point. Hence it is evident that
justice is a human good because it regards the general condition of man.

LECTURE XVI
Equity

TEXT OF ARISTOTLE (*1137a31–1138a3*) Chapter 10

1. Next we will treat equity and the equitable thing; we will consider in what way equity is related to justice, how the equitable is related to the just thing.   **1137a31–33; 107**

2. When we stop to think of it, they are not absolutely the same nor do they altogether differ in kind. Sometimes we praise a thing and a man as equitable, and hence transfer "equitable" as a greater good to the things we praise, showing that it is better. Other times it seems unfitting, to those following reason, that the equitable—as something beyond the just—is praise-worthy. Either the just thing or the equitable (which is other than the just) is not good. Or if both are good then they are the same. The doubt generally arises because of the things said about the nature of what is equitable.   **1137a33–1137b6; 1079–108**

3. Everything said is true in a certain way and contains no latent contradiction. The equitable is something just and is better than some other just thing, but it is not better as another genus separated from the just. Therefore the equitable is the same as the just thing and when both are good the equitable is better.   **1137b7–11; 108**

4. What raises the doubt is that the equitable is a just thing, yet it is not something legal but is a directing of the legally just.   **1137b11–13; 108**

5. The reason for this is that every law is proposed universally, but it is not possible to deal with some things in a universal way. Where the necessary exists we can speak universally but it is impossible to apply this rightly where the law understands the application to be valid in the majority of cases, while being clearly aware that a defect is present.   **1137b13–16; 1083–108**

6. Nevertheless the law is good, for the defect is not in the law nor the making of it but in the nature of the thing. And clearly the matter of human actions is such that they are not always done in the same way.   **1137b17–19; 108**

7. Therefore, when the law proposes something universally and a particular thing happens contrary to this, then, where the legislator has left a gap and erred in speaking absolutely, it is right to correct what is deficient. The legislator would have spoken on the point in this way if he had been present, and if he had known he would have filled this gap in the law.
          1137b19–24; 108

8. For this reason what is equitable is just and is something more excellent than one kind of just thing, not better than that which is absolute but better than that which errs by reason of being proposed absolutely. This thing that is the equitable is the directing of the law where there is deficiency because of faulty universal application. The reason why everything cannot be judged according to the law is that it is impossible to make a law for certain cases. Hence there is need of passing judgment, for the rule of indeterminate matter is itself flexible, like the leaden rule used by builders in Lesbos; just as that rule conforms to the shape of the stone, and does not remain the same, so also the sentence is adapted to the conditions. In this way then it has been made clear what the equitable is, that it is both the just and better than the just thing.
          1137b24–34; 1087–1088

9. From this it is obvious who the equitable man is. He is one who chooses and does the things spoken of; he is not a zealous enforcer of justice in the worse sense, but a mitigator although he recognizes the law as a deterrent.   **1137b34–1138a2; 1089**

10. And this habit of equity is a species of justice and not another kind of habit.
          1138a2–3; 1090

COMMENTARY OF ST. THOMAS

1078. After the Philosopher has finished the consideration of justice in general, he now begins to consider equity which is a general directive of justice. First [1] he indicates his intention. Then [2], at "When we stop to think etc.," he proceeds with his proposition. He says first that following what has been said, we should discuss equity that designates a certain habit and the equitable thing that is its object. In the discussion we should declare how equity is related to justice and how its object, which is called the equitable thing, is related to the just thing, the object of justice. In Greek *epiiches* is understood as what is reasonable or becoming; it is derived from *epi* meaning "above" and *ikos* meaning "obedient," because by equity a person is obedient in a higher way when he follows the intention of the legislator where the words of the law differ from it.

1079. Then [2], at "**When we stop to think,**" he proceeds with his proposition. He discusses it under three headings. First [2] he determines the object of equity. Second [9], at "From this it is obvious etc.," the subject of it. Last [10], at "And this habit etc.," he determines the habit. He considers the initial point in a twofold manner. First [2] he raises a doubt; then [3], at "Everything said is true," he solves it. He says first that if we look closely, it does not seem that the equitable thing is absolutely the same as the just, because the equitable sometimes departs from what is legally just; nor does it seem to be altogether different in species from what is just. He assigns a reason for these things: sometimes we praise what is equitable and declare that it is well

done. Likewise we praise the kind of man who does it—we even call him a manly and perfect individual. So it is evident that, when we transfer praise to what is equitable, or to a person, as if to a greater good, we show what is equitable as something better than what is just. Hence the equitable does not seem to be the same absolutely as the just thing.

1080. On the other hand (if we wish to follow reason) it seems inappropriate if what is equitable is praiseworthy and something over and above the just. It seems necessary that either the just thing is not desirable, i.e., good, or that if what is equitable is different from the just, it is not good because good (in the law) is achieved in one way, as was pointed out in the second book (319–321); or it is necessary that if both are good, they are identical. So he infers that a doubt arises about what is equitable on account of the things just stated. On the one hand it seems that it is not the same inasmuch as it is praised as better than the just thing, on the other it seems that it is the same as the just thing, for what is beyond the just apparently is not good and praiseworthy.

1081. Next [3], at "**Everything said is true,**" he solves the question raised. He handles this point in two ways. First [3] he sets forth the truth. Then [4], at "What raises the doubt etc.," he assigns the reason. He says first that everything that has been said for either side of the doubt is in some way right, and if correctly understood no opposition lies hidden there. It is true that what is equitable is one kind of just thing and is better than another just thing because, as was noted before

(1016–1017), justice which citizens practice is divided into natural and legal. But what is equitable is better than what is legally just but is contained under the naturally just. Consequently it is not said to be better than the just thing as if it were some other kind of norm distinct from the genus of just things. Although both, viz., the legally just thing and the equitable, are good, the equitable is better.

1082. At "**What raises the doubt**" [4] he assigns the reason, treating it in a threefold manner. First [4] he assigns the reason for doubt. Second [5], at "The reason for this etc.," he indicates the reason for the truth proposed. Third [8], at "For this reason what is equitable etc.," he infers the truth intended. He says first that this is what raised the doubt: that the equitable is a just thing, yet it is not something legal. But it is a certain directing of legal justice, for we said (1023) that it was contained under natural justice from which legal justice has its origin.

1083. Then [5], at "**The reason for this,**" he assigns the reason for the truth proposed, i.e., why legal justice has need of direction. He discusses this point from three aspects. First [5] he points out a defect in legal justice. Next [6], at "Nevertheless the law," he shows that this defect does not destroy the rectitude of legal justice. Last [7], at "Therefore, when," he infers the necessity for direction. He says first that the reason why legal justice has need of direction is that every law is proposed universally. Since particulars are infinite, our mind cannot embrace them to make a law that applies to every individual case. Therefore a law must be framed in a universal way, for example, whoever commits murder will be put to death.

1084. It is evident that our intellec can predicate something universally true about some things, in the case o what is necessary where no defect car occur. But about other things it is no possible that something true be predicated universally, in the case of what is contingent. Here even though something is true in most instances, never theless it errs as we know in a few instances. And of such a nature are human acts about which laws are framed. In these things the legislato necessarily speaks in a universal way on account of the impossibility of comprehending particulars; however, he cannot be correct in all the situations for which he legislates since error arises in some few cases. For this reason the legislator accepts what happens in most cases, and nevertheless he is not ignorant that defect is possible in some cases. Thus the anatomist says that man has five fingers, although he knows that by a mistake of nature it happens that man has more or less in rarer cases.

1085. Next [6], at "**Nevertheless the law,**" he shows that the previously mentioned defect does not destroy the rectitude of law or of legal justice. He says that, although a fault may be committed in some cases by the observance of the law, nevertheless the law is good because that fault is not on the part of the law (since it was made according to reason) nor on the part of the legislator (who legislated according to the condition of the material), but the fault arises from the nature of the thing. Such is the nature of human actions that they are not done always in the same way but are done otherwise in certain infrequent instances. For example, the return of a deposit is in itself just and good, as it happens in most cases, but in a particular situation it can be bad, for instance, if a sword is returned to a madman.

1086. At "**Therefore, when**" [7] he infers the necessity for directing legal justice. He says that when the law proposes something in a universal way, and the observance is not beneficial in a special instance, reason rightly dictates that a person should correct what is deficient in the law. Where the legislator evidently left indeterminate a particular case (in which the law falls short) he is at fault, i.e., he proposed a defective proposition in speaking absolutely or universally. The reason is that even the legislator himself, had he been present where such a case happened, would have determined in this way and the correction would have been made. Moreover, had he foreseen this from the beginning he would have put it in the law. But he could not comprehend all particulars; in a certain city it was decreed under penalty of death that strangers were not to climb the walls of the city for fear they would usurp the civil government. But during an enemy invasion some strangers by climbing the walls defended the city from the invaders. They do not deserve to be punished by death; it would be against the natural law to reward benefactors with punishment. Therefore in this case legal justice must be directed by natural justice.

1087. Then [8], at "**For this reason what is equitable,**" he infers the truth intended, affirming that by reason of what has been said it is clear what the equitable is. It is a just thing and it is better than one kind but not better than what is naturally just that is laid down absolutely, that is, universally. Hence the nature of the equitable is that it be directive of the law where the law is deficient for some particular case. Indeed the law does fail in particular cases. The reason why not everything can be determined according to the law is that the law cannot possibly be framed to meet some rare particular incidents, since all cases of this kind cannot be foreseen by man. On account of this, after the enactment of the law, a decision of the judges is required by which the universal statement of the law is applied to a particular matter. Because the material of human acts is indeterminate, it follows that their norm, which is the law, must be indeterminate in the sense that it is not absolutely rigid.

1088. He offers an example of a norm for building in Lesbos. In this island there are certain hard stones that cannot easily be dressed by chisel so they may be arranged in an entirely correct position. Therefore the builders there use a leaden rule. Just as this leaden rule conforms to the shape of the stone and does not stay in the same form, so the sentence of the judge must be adapted to things according to their suitableness. In this way then he ends by way of summary that it is clear from the premises what the equitable thing is, that it is something just which is better than one kind of just thing, viz., the legally just.

1089. Next [9], at "**From this it is obvious,**" he determines the subject of equity. He affirms that it is evident from what has been proposed (1078–1088), who the equitable man is: he who chooses and does the things which have been discussed. He lays down a certain characteristic of this kind of virtuous person. He says that such a one is not *acribodikaios*, i.e., a zealous enforcer of justice in the worse sense, for vengeance, like those who are severe in punishing, but rather like those who mitigate the penalties although they may have the law on their side in punishing. The legislator does not intend punishments in themselves but as a kind of medicine for offenses. Therefore the equitable person does not add more punishment than is sufficient to prevent violations.

1090. At "**And this habit**" [10] he determines the habit of virtue. He says that this habit, called equity, is a particular species of justice and is not a habit different from legal justice; we said the same about its object, for habits are known by reason of their objects.

LECTURE XVII
Injustice to Oneself
TEXT OF ARISTOTLE (*1138a4–1138b14*) Chapter 11

1. *Whether or not it is possible to do injustice to oneself is clear from what has been discussed.* **1138a4–5; 1091**

2. *There are certain just acts arising from every virtue that are ordained by law. Hence, for example, the law never commands a man to kill himself. But what it does not command it forbids.* **1138a5–7; 1092**

3. *Again, however, when someone inflicts damage contrary to the law (it being not against one resisting injury from another) he voluntarily does injustice. By "voluntary" is meant the agent knows both the nature of what he does and the circumstances. But the man who voluntarily kills himself in anger does an act contrary to a just law by willing what the law does not permit. Therefore he does an injustice.* **1138a7–11; 1093**

4. *But to whom? Does he not injure the state rather than himself?* **1138a11; 1094**

5. *He voluntarily suffers what is unjust but no one voluntarily suffers injustice.* **1138a12; 1095**

6. *For this reason the state imposes punishment and a certain disgrace on the person who commits suicide as on one who does an injustice to the state.* **1138a12–14; 1096**

7. *Besides, inasmuch as a man is called unjust not as being entirely evil but only as performing particular injustice, he does not do injustice to himself. This is different from the other kind of injustice because a person unjust in a limited way—like the coward is evil—does not possess total perversity. Hence he does not do injustice to himself according to this injustice.* **1138a14–18; 1097**

8. *Indeed something will be given to and taken from one and the same person at the same time. This is impossible, for it is necessary that justice and injustice be found in different persons.* **1138a18–20; 1098**

9. *Again, doing injustice is voluntary and with choice and happens previous to suffering injustice. A man who first suffers injustice and resists it does not seem to do an injustice. But the person receiving injustice from himself suffers and does the same injustice at the same time.* **1138a20–23; 1099**

10. *Moreover, he will be voluntarily suffering injustice.* **1138a23–24; 1100**

11. *Besides, no one does injustice to himself in regard to particular injustice. No one, for example, commits adultery with his own wife, nor breaks into his own home, nor steals his own goods.* **1138a24–26; 1101**

12. *This question of doing injustice to oneself is completely solved according to the definition that suffering injustice is contrary to the will.* **1138a26–28; 1102**

13. *Obviously both are evil, that is, suffering injustice and doing injustice—for the former is to have less and the latter to have more than the mean, (this corresponds to what produces health in medicine and good condition in physical training.)* **1138a28–31; 1103**

14. *However, to do injustice is worse because it is blameworthy and wicked either completely and absolutely, or for the most part (not every voluntary injury takes place with injustice). But a man suffers injustice without being guilty of wickedness or injustice. Therefore in itself suffering injustice is a lesser evil,* **1138a31–35; 1104**

15. *although nothing hinders it from being by chance a greater evil. But art does not care about what is by chance, for example, medicine considers pleurisy a worse ailment than an*

injured foot, even if it should happen that the latter may be worse. An example of this would be the case when the one so injured falls and so is captured and put to death by enemies.

1138b1–5; 1105

16. By metaphor and likeness, there is justice not of a man toward himself but among the parts of man toward one another. However, not every kind of justice is found here but the justice of master or administrator. According to these concepts, one part of the soul has been divided as against the irrational part (irascible and concupiscible). Looking at these, some people think that injustice to oneself is present because in them it is possible to suffer something contrary to one's own desire. Here a kind of injustice is found as between master and slave. We have, then, finished the treatise on justice and the other moral virtues according to the preceding plan.

1138b5–14; 1106–1108

COMMENTARY OF ST. THOMAS

1091. After the Philosopher has finished the treatise on justice in the proper sense, he now intends to treat justice in the metaphorical sense. Because justice of this kind exists in things that relate to oneself, therefore, he first [1] shows that no one, properly speaking, can do himself an injustice. Second [16], at "By metaphor etc.," he shows how this takes place in a metaphorical sense. He develops this point in a twofold manner. First [1] he shows that no one can do himself an injustice nor suffer an injustice from himself. Then [13], at "Obviously both are evil etc.," he shows whether it is worse to do an injustice or suffer an injustice. He considers the first under three aspects. Initially [1] he suggests that a question of this kind can be settled from what has been said before. Next [2], at "There are certain just acts etc.," he proposes certain grounds on which it seems that a person can do himself an injustice. Last [4], at "But to whom? etc.," he determines the truth. He says first that from the premises it can be made clear whether a man may do an injustice to himself. He raised this question before (1059–1064). But here he follows it up because of the connection it has with an understanding of justice taken in a metaphorical sense.

1092. Then [2], at "There are certain just acts," he gives two reasons from which it seems that someone can do himself an injustice. The first is this [2]. Obviously from what has been said before, the things that are just according to any virtue are ordered by law. Hence what is not ordered at all by law does not seem to be just in terms of any virtue and hence is unjust. In no case does the law command a man to take his own life. But those acts that the law does not command as just, it forbids as unjust. This is not to be understood as if no mean exists between the command and the prohibition of the law, since there are many acts that are neither commanded nor forbidden by the law but are left to man's will, for example, buying or not buying a particular thing. But this is to be understood in the sense that it is only those things which are forbidden as unjust in themselves that the law in no case commands. So it seems that to take one's own life is of itself unjust, since the law never commands it.

1093. At "**Again, however**" [3] he gives the second reason, saying that one who injures another contrary to the precept of the law (as when the law commands that an action be punished provided it is not against a person defending himself, i.e., resisting injury inflicted on oneself by another), such a one, I say, willingly does injustice. When I say "willingly," it is understood the person should know what he does, in what manner, and the other circumstances. But he who takes his own life because of anger acts contrary to a good law in willing something the law does not permit. Therefore he does injustice. Consequently it seems that a man can do himself an injustice.

1094. At "**But to whom**" [4] he solves the previously mentioned doubt. First [4] he presents and confirms the solution. Second [12], at "This question," he gives the root of the solution. He treats the first point in two ways. Initially [4] he solves the doubt raised before, regarding legal justice. Second [7], at "Besides, inasmuch etc.," he solves the doubt regarding particular justice. On the initial point he does two (three) things. First [4] he proposes the solution saying that the man who commits suicide does some injustice. But we must consider against whom he acts unjustly. Certainly he does an injustice to the state, which he deprives of a citizen, even if he does no injustice to himself.

1095. Next [5], at "**He voluntarily suffers**," he confirms the solution given; first [5] in regard to the fact that one does not do himself an injustice. He may willingly endure the slaying but no one willingly suffers injustice, as was said before (1094). Therefore this person does not suffer an injustice and does not do himself an injustice.

1096. Then [6], at "**For this reason**," he confirms the solution in regard to the injustice to the state—this by a certain sign. We see that the state imposes what punishment is possible, dishonor or censure on the suicide; that it has his body dragged or left unburied. In this way we are given to understand that this man committed injustice against the state.

1097. At "**Besides, inasmuch**" [7] he shows that no one does himself an injustice according to particular justice. First [7] he proposes what he intends. He says that inasmuch as a person is called unjust not as being completely perverse in evil but only as doing particular injustice, according to this injustice it is not possible for a person to do injustice to himself. This particular injustice, which we discussed before (913–926), is different from legal injustice. A man may be called unjust in some measure not as being completely evil but as being partially evil, for example, someone is called cowardly according to a particular evil. Hence neither according to particular injustice can anyone do injustice to himself.

1098. Next [8], at "**Indeed something**," he proves the proposition by four reasons. The first [8] is that one who does injustice according to particular injustice has more than is due him, and he who suffers injustice has less. If then someone could do injustice to himself, it would follow that something could be taken from him and added to him at one and the same time—things that are opposites. Therefore it is impossible for the same person to be the one doing injustice and suffering injustice from himself. But justice and injustice necessarily implies more than one person.

1099. At "**Again, doing injustice**" [9] he gives the second reason saying that doing injustice must be voluntary and with choice, and must be previous to suffering injustice. That man, who first has suffered injustice and reacts against it according as the law allows, does not seem to do injustice, for example, if he repossesses a thing taken from him. But if a person injures himself, he suffers and inflicts the same act at the same time. Therefore he does not seem to do injustice to himself.

1100. Then [10], at "**Moreover, he will**," he offers the third reason. Certainly a person voluntarily does harm to himself. If then such a one suffers injustice from himself, it follows that suffering injustice is a voluntary. This we disproved before (1094–1096).

1101. Next [11], at "**Besides, no one**," he gives the fourth reason. If we look at particular injustice, that is, the species of particular injustice, it is apparent that no one does himself an injustice. One particular species of injustice is fornication, i.e., adultery. But no man fornicates or commits adultery with his own wife. No one is called a burglar—burglary belongs to another species of injustice—because he breaks into his own home, nor a thief if he secretly takes his own goods. Obviously then it is not possible to do oneself injustice.

1102. At "**This question**" [12] he gives the principal root of the previously mentioned solution. He says that this question about doing injustice to oneself is completely solved in accord with what was determined before (1063, 1071, 1099) on the point that it is impossible to suffer any injustice voluntarily. From this it clearly follows that no one unwillingly does injustice, since doing injustice is a voluntary, as was pointed out previously (1063, 1071, 1099).

1103. Then [13], at "**Obviously both**," he compares these two things with one another. In regard to the comparison he takes up three points. First [13] he shows that both of them are

evil. Next [14], at "However, to do injustice etc.," he shows that in itself it is worse to do injustice. Last [15], at "although nothing hinders etc.," he shows that by chance the contrary can be true. He says first that both, doing injustice and suffering injustice, are evil. He proves the statement from the fact that to suffer injustice is to have less than the mean of justice requires. But the first, to do injustice, is to have more than the measure of justice. Now the mean of justice, called the just thing, is related to exchanges and distributions as the healthful is to medicine and the well-conditioned to gymnastics. Consequently, as in medicine and gymnastics what is too much or too little is evil, so also in regard to justice.

1104. Next [14], at "**However, to do injustice**," he shows that it is worse to do injustice than to suffer injustice. This he proves from the fact that to do injustice is blameworthy and evil—a thing that is to be understood either as complete and absolute evil (for instance, when someone does injustice not only voluntarily but by choice) or as coming close to complete evil (evident in the person who acts unjustly not by choice but by anger or some other passion). It has been explained before (1041) that not every voluntary accompanies injustice, because sometimes a man does an unjust act and nevertheless is not unjust, although he is blameworthy. But a person's suffering injustice is entirely without evil and injustice, for he who suffers injustice can in no way be considered unjust or evil. But, obviously, that by which a man is called evil is worse than that by which he is not called evil, an actual whiteness by which a person is called white is whiteness in a greater degree than potential whiteness by which a person is not called white. It follows then that suffering injustice is in itself less evil than doing injustice.

1105. At "**although nothing hinders**" [15], he shows that the contrary can be true by chance. He says nothing prevents suffering injustice from being more evil by chance than doing injustice, as when a man is provoked to do greater injustice by the fact that he suffers unjustly. But this is by chance, and art does not care about what is by chance but judges only according to what is essential. Thus the art of medicine calls pleurisy, a dangerous and deadly abscess under the ribs, a worse ailment than a sore foot that nevertheless can by chance be worse, for instance, when a man falls because of an injured foot and so by accident is captured and slain by an enemy.

1106. Next [16], at "**By metaphor and likeness**," he shows of what nature metaphorical justice is. He says that by a kind of metaphor and likeness, it is possible to have, not justice or injustice of the whole man toward himself, but a certain species of justice among the parts of man. However, this is not justice in the full sense but only the justice of a master or an administrator (viz., the head of a household), because corresponding to these reasons of dominion and administration the rational part of the soul seems to be distinguished from the irrational part, which is divided into irascible and concupiscible. The reason is master of the irascible and concupiscible parts and governs them.

1107. In view of such consideration some people think that a man's justice extends to himself because, by reason of these parts, he can suffer from his own desires, for instance, when he acts against reason out of anger or concupiscence. Hence, among the parts a kind of justice and injustice is found, as between one who commands and one who obeys. However, it is not genuine justice because it is not between two, but it has a resemblance to justice inasmuch as the diversity in the soul is like the diversity between persons.

1108. Finally, as a summary, he concludes that we have finished the treatise on justice and the other moral virtues according to the preceding plan. With this the teaching of the fifth book is completed.

BOOK SIX
INTELLECTUAL VIRTUES
LECTURE I
Right Reason

TEXT OF ARISTOTLE (*1138b18–1139a15*) Chapter 1

1. *But since we previously said that we ought to choose a mean, rejecting excess and defect, and that the mean is determined according to right reason, we may now make a division of right reason.*　　**1138b18–20; 1109**

2. *In all habits previously considered and in other matters, there is some mark on which the man who possesses right reason keeps his eye, straining and relaxing; and this is the limit of the middle courses that we say are a mean between excess and defect in accord with right reason.*　　**1138b21–25; 1110**

3. *It is true indeed to say this, but nothing is made clear by it. In all occupations in which science is at work, it is true to say that neither too much nor too little ought to be done or passed over but what is moderate and as reason determines. But a man possessing only this knowledge will not know how to proceed further, for instance, what remedies must be given for the body, if someone suggests that it should be whatever medical art, as possessed by the doctor, prescribes.*　　**1138b25–32; 1111**

4. *For this reason, not only must this true statement be made about the habits of the soul but also the nature of right reason and its limits must be determined.*　　**1138b32–34; 1112**

5. *We have, however, already divided the virtues of the soul, stating that some are moral and others intellectual. The moral virtues we have discussed, and the others we will now treat, after first speaking of the soul.*　　**1138b35–1139a3; 1113**

6. *We said before that there are two parts of the soul: rational and irrational.*　　**1139a3–5; 1114**

7. *Now we will speak of the rational part in the same way. Let us suppose two parts of the rational soul: one by which we consider the kind of things whose principles cannot be otherwise; the other by which we consider contingent things.*　　**1139a5–8; 1115**

8. *To the objects, which differ in kind, correspond different kinds of parts of the soul,*　　**1139a8–9; 1116**

9. *since indeed the knowledge of the objects exists (in the parts) according to a certain species and reality.*　　**1139a9–11; 1117**

10. *Let one of these be called scientific but the other estimative, for deliberating and estimating are the same. No one deliberates about things that do not take place any other way. Therefore the estimative element is one part of the rational soul.*　　**1139a11–15; 1118–1123**

COMMENTARY OF ST. THOMAS

1109. After the Philosopher has completed the explanation of the moral virtues, he begins in the sixth book to explain the intellectual virtues. First [1] by way of introduction, he speaks of what he proposes. Then, at "We said before etc," [6] he explains his proposition. On the first point he does three things. Initially, he states that we must discuss right reason. Next, at "In all habits previously considered etc.," [2] he shows what we must discuss about it. Last, at "We have, however, already divided etc.," [5] he continues with what precedes. He says first that it was stated before (317) we must choose a mean, and reject excess and defect in the moral virtues that we have just discussed (245–1108); that the mean is determined according to right reason, as was decided in the second book (322). Consequently, we should divide right reason, an intellectual virtue that is rectitude of the reason, into its species, as in a similar fashion we have already divided the moral virtues.

1110. Then [2], at **"In all habits previously considered"** he shows what has to be discussed about right reason. On this point he does three things. First he shows what can be understood from the things that were said before. Next at "It is true indeed etc.," [3] he discloses that this is not sufficient. Last, at "For this reason etc.," [4] he infers what should be added. He says first that in all habits previously considered, i.e., the moral virtues—as in other things, for example, the artistic—there is an object, as it were a mark, on which the man with right reason keeps his eye; and according to this he strives and makes modifications (i.e., he adds or subtracts) or considers by this mark what the limit of the middle course is, how it ought to be ascertained in each virtue. Such a middle course we say is a certain mean between excess and defect, and in accord with right reason. This mark, holding for the virtuous man the place of a rule for the craftsman, is what is becoming and fitting, that which we must not fall short of, nor add to; this is the mean of virtue. These matters have been clarified in the second book (327).

1111. Next [3], at **"It is true,"** he shows that it is not enough to know this about right reason. He states that what was said (1110) is certainly true but does not make sufficiently clear what is required for the use of right reason; it is something common verified in all human occupations in which men operate according to a practical

science, for instance, in strategy, medicine, and the various professions. In all these it is true to say that neither too much nor too little ought to be done or passed over but that which holds the middle and is in accord with what right reason determines. But the man, who considers the common feature alone, will not know how to proceed to action by reason of this generality. If a person were to ask what ought to be given to restore bodily health, and someone advised him to give what is prescribed by medical art and by one who has this art, i.e., a doctor, the interrogator would not know from such information what medicine the sick man needs. But as the right plan of prudence is the guide in moral matters so the right plan of art is the guide in art. Hence it is evident that the principle discussed is insufficient.

1112. At **"For this reason"** [4] he concludes by like reasoning that a general statement on the soul's habits is insufficient; a precise definition of the limits of right reason and its norm must be determined.

1113. Then [5], at **"We have, however, already divided etc.,"** he continues with a previous discussion. He says that in making the division at the end of the first book (234), we spoke of the virtues of the soul as being either intellectual or moral. Since we have completed the investigation of the moral virtues (245–1108), it remains for us to examine the intellectual virtues in accord with which reason itself is regulated, prefacing this with a discussion of certain things about the soul (for without this knowledge the virtues of the soul cannot be known), as was noted previously at the end of the first book (228).

1114. Next [6], at **"We said before,"**

he begins to follow up his proposition. First he explains what is to be discussed about the soul. Then [Lect. II] at "We must, then etc.," he pursues the intellectual virtues (1139 a 16). On the initial point he does three things. First he resumes the division of the parts of the soul given previously at the end of the first book. Second [7], at "Now we will etc.," he subdivides one member. He says first it was previously stated that there are two parts of the soul: one is rational, the other irrational. It has been explained before (243) that the part which is essentially rational is perfected by the intellectual virtues. But the irrational part, which, however, participates in rationality, is perfected by the moral virtues.

1115. At "**Now we will**" [7] he subdivides one member of this division. On this point he does three things. First he proposes the division. Next [8], at "To the objects, which differ etc.," he explains the members of the division. Last [10], at "Let one of these be called etc.," he names the members of the division. He says first that, since we have in mind the intellectual virtues that perfect the rational part of the soul, in order to distinguish the intellectual virtues we must divide the rational part in the same way as we have previously divided the parts of the soul (229)—not as it were by reason of its principal aspect but in a way sufficient for our purpose. Let us suppose, then, that the organ of reason is divided into two parts: one by which we consider those necessary things whose principles cannot be otherwise; the other, by which we consider contingent things.

1116. Then [8], at "**To the objects, which differ**," he explains the afore-mentioned division by this reasoning. It is necessary that different kinds of

parts of the soul should correspond to objects differing in kind. But obviously the contingent and the necessary differ in kind, as is noted concerning the corruptible and incorruptible in the tenth book of the *Metaphysics* (Ch. 10, 1058b26 sq.; St. Th. Lect. XII, 2136–2145). Therefore we conclude that by a differentiation of parts the rational soul knows necessary and contingent things.

1117. Next [9], at "**since indeed,**" he explains the major proposition in this way. Knowledge exists in parts of the soul according as they have a certain likeness to the things known. By this we do not mean that the thing actually known is in the substance of the knowing faculty (as Empedocles held: that we know earth by earth, fire by fire, and so on) but inasmuch as each power of the soul according to its peculiar nature is proportioned to know objects of this kind, as sight to see color and hearing to perceive sound. But in things that are similar and proportioned to one another the same reason for distinction exists. Therefore, as the things known by reason differ in kind, so also the parts of the rational soul differ.

1118. At "**Let one of these be called**" [10], he names the afore-mentioned parts. He says that, of these parts of the rational soul, the one that considers necessary things may be called the scientific kind of soul because its knowledge is of the necessary. But another part may be called the estimative kind (*ratiocinativa*) according as estimating and deliberating are taken for the same thing. He calls deliberation a certain inquiry not yet concluded, like argumentation. This indetermination of mind happens especially in regard to contingent things that are the only subjects of deliberation, for no one deliberates about things that take place in one fixed mode. So, then, it follows that the estimative element is one part of the rational soul.

1119. What the Philosopher here determines seems to be doubtful. In the third book *De Anima* (Ch. 4, 429a10 sq.; St. Th. Lect. VII, 671 sq.) he divides the intellect into two parts, viz., the active and the potential. He says that the active intellect is the power of operating on all things; and the potential, the power of becoming all things. So, then, both the active intellect and the potential by their very nature are in touch with all things. Therefore, it would be contrary to the nature of each intellect, if there was one part of the soul that understood necessary things, and another contingent things.

1120. Again, the true in necessary matter and the true in contingent matter resemble perfect and imperfect in the genus of what is true. But by the same power of the soul we know both perfect and imperfect things of the same genus, for example, sight perceives bright and dark objects. Much more, then, the same intellective power knows necessary and contingent things.

1121. Likewise, the intellect touches intelligible objects in a more universal way than the senses touch sensible objects. Now the nobler the power the more united is its activity. But the sense of sight shares in both incorruptible (heavenly) bodies and corruptible (lower) bodies, to which the necessary and contingent proportionately correspond. For a far greater reason, then, the intellective power knows both necessary and contingent.

1122. Moreover, the proof that he presents does not seem to be convincing. Not every difference in the classi-

fication of the object requires different powers (otherwise we would not see plants and other animals by the same power of sight) but that difference regarding the formal reason of the object. For instance, if there were a different genus of color or light there would have to be different powers of sight. But the proper object of the intellect is that which exists, something common to all substances and accidents, although not in the same way. Hence we know both substances and accidents by the same intellective power. Therefore, by the same token the difference in the classification of necessary and contingent things does not require different intellective powers.

1123. This doubt is easily solved by considering that contingent things can be understood in two ways: in one way according to their universal concepts (rationes), in the other way as they are in the concrete. Accordingly, the universal concepts of contingent things are immutable. In this way demonstrations are given about contingent things, and the knowledge of them belongs to the demonstrative sciences. Natural science is concerned not only with necessary and incorruptible things but also with corruptible and contingent things. Hence it is evident that contingent things considered in this way belong to the same part of the intellective soul (called scientific by the Philosopher) as necessary things, and the reasons presented proceed with this understanding. In the other way contingent things can be taken as they are in the real order. Thus understood they are variable and do not fall under the intellect except by means of the sensitive powers. So, among the parts of the sensitive soul we place a power called particular reason or the sensory power of judgment, which collates particular impressions. It is in this sense that the Philosopher here understands contingent things, for thus they are objects of counsel and operation. For this reason he says that necessary and contingent things, like speculative universals and individual operable things, belong to different parts of the rational soul.

LECTURE II
Function Proper to Each Part of the Soul

TEXT OF ARISTOTLE (*1139a17–1139b13*) Chapter 1

1. *We must, then, ascertain what is the most excellent habit of each of these parts, for this is their virtue.*

Chapter 2

But virtue is directed to the work that is proper.   **1139a17–18; 1124–1125**

2. *Three things in the soul seem to have power over action and truth: the senses, intellect, and appetitive faculty.*   **1139a18–19; 1126**

3. *But one of these, viz., the senses is not a principle of any action. This is obvious because dumb animals have senses but do not share in action.*   **1139a19–20; 1127**

4. *Now, affirmation and negation are in the mind, and corresponding to these in the appetitive faculty are pursuit and flight.*   **1139a21–22; 1128**

5. *Therefore, since moral virtue is a habit of free choice, and choice is the appetitive faculty deliberating, then reason must be true and the appetitive faculty right if choice is to be good; and the same things that reason affirms, the appetitive faculty pursues. Hence this mind and its truth are practical.*   **1139a22–27; 1129**

6. *However, it is the function of the speculative mind (but not the practical) as it operates in good or faulty fashion, to express truth and falsity. This belongs to every intellect but the good of the practical intellect is truth conformable to a right appetitive faculty.*
                                          1139a27–31; 1130–1132

7. *Choice, then, is a principle of action, and so of motion but not as a final cause. But, for choice itself the principles are the appetitive faculty and the reason which is terminative. Hence choice does not exist without intellect and mind, nor without moral habit, for good and bad actions cannot exist without the intellect or mind and moral disposition.*
                                          1139a31–35; 1133–1134

8. *Still, mind itself does not move anything, but the mind that has a purpose and is practical does so, for it governs even the operation which fashions some product. Indeed every worker produces for the sake of something—he is not induced to act for an end in general but for a particular thing made for some use; he does not act merely for the sake of acting. The good action itself is an end but the appetitive faculty is for some particular end.*
                                          1139a35–1139b4; 1135–1136

9. *Therefore, choice is either the appetitive intellect or the intellective faculty of appetition, and man is this kind of principle.*   **1139b4–5; 1137**

10. *What has already taken place is not now an object of choice, e.g., no one now chooses to have captured Ilion. Nor does anyone give advice about something past, but about a future and contingent event. It is not possible that what has taken place did not occur. Therefore Agathon was right, for God lacks only this—to undo things already done.*   **1139b5–11; 1138–1139**

11. *In any case the work of each of the intellect's parts is the knowledge of the truth.*
                                          1139b12; 1140

13. *These habits according to which each part especially manifests the truth are the virtues of both divisions of the intellect.*   **1139b12–13; 1141**

COMMENTARY OF ST. THOMAS

1124. After the Philosopher has divided the parts of the rational soul as
required for his purpose, he now be-

gins to examine the intellectual virtues
themselves by which each part of the
rational soul is perfected. First he con-

siders the particular intellectual virtues. Then [Lect. X], at "Someone may raise a doubt etc." (1143b17), he expresses a certain doubt about their utility. On the first point he does two things. First he investigates the ways of understanding the intellectual virtues. Next [Lect. III], at "Introducing again the subject etc." (1139b14), he sets himself to examine them. On the initial point he does three things. First [1] he proposes the common notion of virtue as stated in the beginning (65, 81): that which renders the work of a thing good is its virtue. Then [2], at "Three things in the soul etc.," he inquires what the good of the rational soul is in regard to each part. Last [13], at "These habits according to which etc.," he infers the nature and quality of the virtues of each part.

1125. He says first that, because we have assigned two parts of the rational soul (to which the intellectual virtues are ascribed), we must understand which is the most excellent habit of each of these two parts. The reason is that each habit is necessarily a virtue of each part. It has been noted (308, 536) that the virtue of anything is directed to its characteristic operation, for this is perfected by virtue. Such a habit would be best when it insures that an action is performed in the best way.

1126. Then [2], at "**Three things in the soul,**" he inquires what the proper good of each of these parts is. On this point he does three things. First he shows what the principles of human acts are. Next [6], at "However, it is the function etc.," he seeks what the proper work of reason is. Last [11], at "In any case the work etc.," he draws the conclusion he sought to establish. On the initial point he does three things. First [2] he proposes three ingredients that are called principles of human acts.

Then [3], at "But one of these etc.," he excludes one of them. Finally [4], at "Now, affirmation and negation etc.," he shows how the remaining two can harmonize with each other. In regard to the first we must consider that two works are said to be proper to man, namely, knowledge of truth and action, inasmuch as man assumes mastery of his own action (and as moved or led by something). Over these two, then three things in the soul: senses, intellect, and appetitive faculty, seem to have mastery and power. It is by the same three that animals move themselves, as was noted in the third book *De Anima* (Ch. 10, 433a9 sq.; St. Th. Lect. XV, 818–819).

1127. Next [3], at "**But one of these,**" he excludes one of them, viz., the senses, from further consideration. It is certainly obvious that truth pertains neither to the senses nor to the appetitive faculty. He adds further that one of the three, the senses, is not a principle of any action, in such a way that mastery of the action can be established. This is clear from the fact that dumb animals have senses but do not have social action because they are not masters of their own action; they do not operate from themselves but are moved by natural instinct.

1128. At "**Now, affirmation and negation**" [4], he shows how the work of the remaining two, namely, intellect and appetitive faculty, can harmonize one with the other. First he shows how their actions are proportionable. In judging, the intellect has two actions, viz., affirmation by which it assents to what is true, and negation by which it dissents from what is false. To these two correspond proportionately two acts in the appetitive faculty, namely, pursuit by which the appetitive faculty tends and adheres to good, and flight by which it withdraws and dissents from evil. In this manner the intellect and the appetitive faculty can be brought into harmony inasmuch as what the intellect declares good the appetitive faculty pursues, and what the intellect denies to be good the appetitive faculty seeks to avoid.

1129. Then [5], at "**Therefore, since moral virtue**," he shows how these actions of the intellect and appetitive faculty—touching the moral virtues—are in agreement. Moral virtue is a habit of free choice, as was said in the second book (305, 308, 382). Choice is the appetitive faculty deliberating inasmuch as the appetitive faculty takes what was preconsidered, as was stated in the third book (435, 436, 457). But to counsel is an act of one part of the reason, as was previously shown (473, 476, 482, 1118). Since then reason and appetitive faculty concur in choice, if choice ought to be good—this is required for the nature of a moral virtue—the reason must be true and the appetitive faculty right, so that the same thing which reason declares or affirms, the appetitive faculty pursues. In order that there be perfection in action it is necessary that none of its principles be imperfect. But this intellect or reason (which harmonizes in this way with the right appetitive faculty) and its truth are practical.

1130. Next [6], at "**However, it is the function**" he explains what the work of the rational soul is in terms of each part. First he shows how each part is related to truth. Then [7], at "Choice, then, is etc.," he shows how each part is related to action. He says first that the work of a good or faulty mind (i.e., intellect or reason), in the speculative rather than practical order, consists simply in the true and false, in such a way that the absolutely true is its good and the absolutely false is its evil. To

express the true and the false is an essential function of every intellect. But the good of the practical intellect is not absolute truth but the "conformable" truth, i.e., corresponding to a right appetitive faculty, as has been shown (322, 326, 548), because on this point the moral virtues are united.

1131. However, there seems to be some difficulty here. If the truth of the practical intellect is determined by comparison with a right appetitive faculty and the rectitude of the appetitive faculty is determined by the fact that it agrees with right reason, as was previously shown, an apparent vicious circle results from these statements. Therefore, we must say that the end and the means pertain to the appetitive faculty, but the end is determined for man by nature, as was shown in the third book (524, 525). On the contrary, the means are not determined for us by nature but are to be investigated by reason. So it is obvious that rectitude of the appetitive faculty in regard to the end is the measure of truth for the practical reason. According to this the truth of the practical reason is determined by agreement with a right appetitive faculty. But the truth of the practical reason itself is the rule for the rectitude of the appetitive faculty in regard to the means. According to this, then, the appetitive faculty is called right inasmuch as it pursues the things that reason calls true.

1132. A further confusion arises here from the manner in which he connects the speculative and practical intellect—as with the two parts given above (1118): the scientific and the estimative—since he stated previously (1123) that the scientific and estimative were different parts, a thing he denies about the speculative and practical intellect in the third book De Anima (Ch. 10,

433a15 sq.; St. Th. Lect. XV, 820–821). Therefore, we must say that the practical intellect has a beginning in a universal consideration and, according to this, is the same in subject with the speculative, but its consideration terminates in an individual operable thing. Hence the Philosopher says in the third book *De Anima* (Ch. 11, 434a16 sq.; St. Th. Lect. XVI, 845–846) that universal reason does not move without the particular. In this way the estimative is considered a different part from the scientific.

1133. At "**Choice, then, is the principle**" [7], he shows that each reason has a relation to action. On this point he does three things. First he explains that the mind is a principle of action. Second [8], at "Still, mind itself etc.," he shows of what mind he speaks. Third [10], at "What has already taken place," he explains about what kinds of objects the mind is the active principle. First he concludes from what was just said (1129) that because choice is the appetitive faculty deliberating, consequently it is a principle of action, and so of motion, i.e., in the manner of an efficient cause but not for the sake of something, i.e., in the manner of a final cause. We have already said in the third book *De Anima* (Ch. 10, 433b27–31; St. Th. Lect. XV, 836–837) that the appetitive faculty is a source of movement in animals. But, for choice itself the principles are the appetitive faculty and the reason that is purposive, i.e., which is ordered to a practical thing as to an end, for the choice of the appetitive faculty is concerned with the things that are for the end. Hence reason proposing an end and thereupon proceeding to think discursively about it, and the appetitive faculty tending to the end, are compared to choice as a cause. So it is that choice depends on

the intellect (or mind) and on the moral habit that perfects the appetitive power in such a way that it does not exist without either of them.

1134. He gives a sign in proof of this, for the effect of choice is action, as was pointed out. But the action that is good, and its direct opposite in action (i.e., the action that is evil) cannot exist without the mind and disposition or moral condition, i.e., some inclination belonging to the appetitive faculty. Hence neither does choice, good or bad, exist without disposition and mind.

1135. Then [8], at "**Still, mind itself,**" he shows what mind or reason is the principle of action. First he explains the proposition. Next [9], at "Therefore, choice is either etc.," he infers a corollary from what has been discussed. He says first that, although the mind is a principle of action, nevertheless the mind simply considered in itself (or the speculative reason) does not move anything because it prescribes nothing about pursuit or flight, as was stated in the third book *De Anima* (Ch. 9, 432b27–33; St. Th. Lect. XIV, 812–815). Hence it is not the speculative mind that is a principle of action but the mind having a purpose or ordained to an individual operable thing as an end. This is the practical reason or mind, and it governs not only active operation, which does not pass into external matter but remains in the agent—like desiring and becoming angry—but also "factive" operation which does pass into external matter—burning and cutting for instance.

1136. He proves this by the fact that every worker, say the carpenter or builder, makes his product for the sake of something, i.e., for an end—not an abstract one but with a view to some particular thing that is made or established in external matter, for instance, a knife or a house. Moreover, the end is not something done, i.e., a practicable thing existing in the agent, like rightly desiring or becoming angry. Every worker acts for the sake of something belonging to a thing, i.e., which has some use, as the use of a house is habitation. This then is the end of the worker, viz., something made and not a thing done. Therefore, it is not something done, since in immanent actions the good action itself is the end, for example, rightly desiring or justly becoming angry. As the practical mind is for the sake of this end, either a thing made or an action, so also the appetitive faculty is for the sake of some particular end.

1137. Next [9], at "**Therefore, choice is either,**" he draws a corollary from the premises. Because choice is a principle of action, and the principles of choice are the appetitive faculty and reason (i.e., intellect or mind), which by means of choice are principles of action, it follows that choice is of the appetitive intellect (in such a way that choice is essentially an act of the intellect according as it orders the appetitive faculty) or it is of the intellective faculty of appetition (in such a way that choice is essentially an act of the appetitive faculty according as it is directed by the intellect). The latter is nearer the truth, as is clear from the objects. The object of choice, as also of the appetitive faculty, is good and evil but not true and false which pertain to the intellect as such. A principle of this kind is man, viz., an agent choosing by means of intellect and appetitive faculty.

1138. At "**What has already taken place**" [10] he explains the kinds of objects the mind is concerned with as the principle of action by power of

choice. He says that nothing over and done with, i.e., nothing past is an object of choice, for instance, no one chooses Ilion, that is, to have captured Troy. The reason is that choice belongs to the deliberating faculty of appetition, as already noted (1129, 1133). But no one takes counsel about something done, i.e., about a past event but about a future and contingent one. He proves this from the fact that counsel is given only about a contingent event, as shown previously (460–472). Now what was done is not contingent, since it is not possible that the thing becomes undone, i.e., that it did not take place. Here he introduces the words of Agathon who rightly remarked: God lacks only this power—to cause things to be unproduced, i.e., not to be made which are already made. This was well said.

1139. Everything that can be contained under the proper object of any cause's capacity is necessarily subjected to the influence of that cause, for instance, fire can heat anything capable of becoming hot. But the power of God, who is the universal cause of being, extends to the totality of being. Hence that only is withdrawn from the divine power which is inconsistent with the nature of being, as something which implies a contradiction. That a thing done be undone is of this kind, because it involves the same formality for a thing to be (i.e., will be) while it is, and to have been (i.e., was to have been) while it was; and for what is, not to be—and what was, not to have been.

1140. Next [11], at "**In any case the work,**" he infers from the premises that knowledge of the truth is the work of each part of the intellect, namely, the practical and the speculative or the scientific and the estimative (*ratiocinativi*).

1141. Then [13], at "**Those habits**

according to which," he deduces lastly that those habits by which the truth—the good of the intellective part—is manifested, are virtues of both divisions of the intellect.

LECTURE III
An Enumeration of the Intellectual Virtues; Every Science Can Be Taught

TEXT OF ARISTOTLE (*1139b14–1140a23*) Chapter 3

1. Introducing again the subject treated above, let us discuss it further. There are five habits by which the soul expresses the truth by affirming or denying. They are: art, science, prudence, wisdom, and understanding; but not suspicion and opinion, which can express falsehood.
1139b14–18; 1142–1143

2. From this then it can be made clear what science is, if it is proper to science to know with certitude and not follow approximations to the truth. Indeed we all suppose that what we know scientifically cannot be in any other way. But contingent things are not of this kind, for when they pass from observation it is not known whether they exist or not. The object of science then concerns necessity, and therefore is eternal, because everything that is of necessity without qualification is eternal. Eternal things, however, are unproduced and indestructible.
1139b18–24; 1144–1146

3. Besides, every science can be taught and every object of science can be learned. But all teaching comes about by reason of previous knowledge, as we have indicated in the Analytics; one kind is by induction, the other by syllogism. Induction then gives us a first principle and a universal assent, but the syllogism proceeds from universals. Therefore, there are principles from which the syllogism proceeds—principles not derived from the syllogism, and consequently arising from induction. Science then is a demonstrative habit having all the other requirements determined in the Analytics. When a man knows scientifically, he assents to and understands principles in some way; indeed, if he does not know them more than the conclusion, then he has science only incidentally. In this way, therefore, the question of science has been settled.
1139b25–36; 1147–1149

Chapter 4

4. The contingent is both something to be made and something to be done; and making is one thing and action another. We assent to these things even by proofs outside the science. For this reason the habit that is active under reason's guidance is different from the habit that is productive through reason. Likewise action and making are not contained under one another, for action is not making, nor is making action.
1140a1–6; 1150–1152

5. However, since architecture is a kind of art and also a kind of habit productive through reason, and no art is found that is not a habit of this sort; and again there is no such habit that is not an art, art then will be the same as a habit concerned with making, under the guidance of true reason.
1140a6–10; 1153

6. But every art is concerned with realization, an artifact and observation; it considers particularly how contingent things may be made, and indicates that their principle is in the craftsman but not in the thing made.
1140a10–14; 1154–1155

7. Art, however, does not deal with things that exist necessarily or come into being by necessity;
1140a14–15; 1156

8. nor with things that are according to nature, for they have these principles in themselves.
1140a15–16; 1157

9. Since making and action differ from one another, art necessarily directs making and not action.
1140a16–17; 1158

10. In some manner art and chance are concerned with the same things, as Agathon remarked: Art highly esteems chance, and chance art.
1140a17–20; 1159

11. Art then, as was previously noted, is a kind of habit productive under the guidance of genuine reason. On the contrary, however, unskillfulness is a habit productive under the guidance of incorrect reason operating on contingent matter. **1140a20–23; 1160**

COMMENTARY OF ST. THOMAS

1142. After the Philosopher has investigated the way in which the intellectual virtues are to be understood, he begins now to discuss the intellectual virtues themselves. First he discusses the principal intellectual virtues. Then [Lect. VIII], at "Now we must consider etc." (1142a32), he defines certain virtues connected with one of them, namely, prudence. On the initial point he does two things. First [1] he enumerates the intellectual virtues. Next [2], at "From this then it can be made clear etc.," he discusses each of them. He says first—after the way of understanding the intellectual virtues has been given—we ought to begin again from what has been settled before (1115), so that we may treat the intellectual virtues themselves.

1143. It was previously pointed out (1125) that the intellectual virtues are habits by which the soul expresses the truth. But there are five habits by which the soul always expresses the truth by either affirming or denying, viz., art, science, prudence, wisdom, and understanding. Clearly then these are the five intellectual virtues. He omits suspicion, which is brought about by some conjectures concerning any particular facts, and opinion, which is brought about by some conjectures concerning any general things. Although these two sometimes do express the truth, nevertheless at other times it happens that they express falsehood, which is the evil of the intellect just as truth is the good of the intellect. But it is contrary to the nature

of virtue to be the principle of an evil act. Obviously then suspicion and opinion cannot be called intellectual virtues.

1144. Then [2], at "**From this then it can be made clear,**" he determines the intellectual virtues just enumerated. First [2] he discusses each of them. Next [Lect. VI], at "As having supremacy" (1141a20), he shows which is the principal one among them. On the initial point he proceeds in two ways. First he discusses the intellectual virtues perfecting the intellect regarding the things which are derived from principles. Second [Lect. V], at "Since science is an evaluation etc." (1140b31), he discusses the intellectual habits perfecting the intellect in regard to first principles. On the first point he does two things. Initially he defines the science which perfects the intellect in regard to necessary things. Then [4], at "The contingent is both etc.," he defines the habits perfecting the intellect in regard to contingent things. On the initial point he does two things. First [2] he explains science on the part of the matter. Next [3], at "Besides, every science can be taught etc.," he explains it on the part of the cause.

1145. He affirms first that it can be made clear what science is from what has been said, if it is proper to science to know with certitude and not follow approximations to the truth, for in this latter way we are sometimes said to know sensible things about which we are certain. But a well-founded notion of science is taken from the fact that we all agree that what we know cannot be in any other way; otherwise we would have the doubt of the guesser and not the certitude of the knower. However, certitude of this kind, viz., that cannot be in any other way, is not possible about things that can be in some other way, for in that case certitude can be attained about them only when they fall under the senses. But when they pass from observation, that is, cease to be seen or felt, then their existence or non-existence escapes us, as is obvious in the fact that Socrates is sitting. It is evident then that everything known by science is of necessity. From this he infers that it is eternal because everything which is of necessity without qualification is eternal. But things of this kind are neither produced nor destroyed. Therefore, it is about such things that science is concerned.

1146. There can even be a science about producible and perishable things, for example, natural science; yet it cannot be based on particulars that are subject to generation and destruction, but on universal reasons which are necessary and eternal.

1147. Next [3], at "**Besides, every science,**" he explains science by its cause, saying that every science seems to be teachable. Hence it is stated in the first book of the *Metaphysics* (Ch. 2, 982a14; St. Th. Lect. II, 39) that a characteristic of the one possessing science is his ability to teach, for a thing is led from potency to actuality by another which is actual. For the same reason every knowable thing can be learned by a man who has the potentiality. But all teaching or science must come about by reason of some previous knowledge, as was indicated in the beginning of the *Posterior Analytics* (Bk. I, Ch. 1, 71a; St. Th. Lect. I, 8). We cannot arrive at the knowledge of an un-known thing except by means of something known.

1148. There is a twofold teaching by means of things known: one by induction and the other by syllogism. Induction leads us to perceive some principle and something universal at which we arrive by experiments with singulars, as is noted in the first book of the *Metaphysics* (Ch. 1, 980b25–981 a 12; St. Th. Lect. I, 17–19). But the syllogism proceeds from universal principles previously known in the aforementioned manner. Therefore, it is evident from this that there are certain principles from which the syllogism proceeds and which are not attested as accurate by the syllogism. Otherwise there would be a process to infinity in the principles of syllogisms—which is impossible, as is proved in the first book of the *Posterior Analytics* (Ch. 3, 72b25–73 a 20; St. Th. Lect. VIII, 68–75. Ch. 19–22, 81b10–84b2; St. Th. XXXI–XXXV, 255–307). So then it remains that the principle of the syllogism is induction. But not every syllogism is productive of knowledge, i.e., causes science, but only the demonstrative, which infers necessary things from the necessary.

1149. So, obviously, science is a demonstrative habit, i.e., produced by demonstration, taking into consideration what has been noted about science in the *Posterior Analytics*. In order that a man may have science it is necessary that the principles by which he knows be assented to in some way and understood even more than the conclusions which are known. Otherwise he will not have science per se but only incidentally, inasmuch as it can happen that he knows this conclusion through certain other principles and not through these which he does not know better than the conclusion. The cause, certainly, must be more powerful than the effect. Hence that which is the cause of knowing must be more known. In this way then the question of science has been settled.

1150. Next [4], at "**The contingent is both,**" he defines the habits which perfect the intellect in regard to contingent things. On this point he does three things. First [4] he shows that there are two habits concerned with contingent things. Second [5], at "However, since architecture etc.," he defines one of these. Third [Lect. IV], at "Let us now investigate etc.," he defines the other, viz., prudence. He says first that the contingent is divided into two sections: something to be done, and something to be made. Thus we know that the one is an action and the other a making.

1151. We can assent to these things by external reasons, i.e., by what has been determined outside this science, viz., in the ninth book of the *Metaphysics* (Ch. 8, 1050a23–1050 b; St. Th. Lect. VIII, 1862–1865). There the difference between action and making has been explained. Action is an operation remaining in the agent, like seeing, understanding, and willing. But making is an operation passing into external matter to fashion something out of it, like constructing and sawing. Since habits are distinguished according to the object, it follows that the habit that is active by means of reason, i.e., prudence, is different from the habit that is productive through reason, i.e., art. It follows also that one of these is not contained under the other, as action and making are not contained under one another, since neither is action making nor is making action. They are distinguished by opposing differences, as is clear from what has just been said.

1152. We must consider that the knowledge of contingent things cannot possess the truth's certitude rejecting untruth. Therefore, where there is question of knowledge alone, contingent things are passed over by the intellect which is perfected by the knowledge of the truth. But the knowledge of the contingent is useful according as it gives direction to human operation which is concerned with what is contingent. For that reason he makes the division of contingent things—when treating the intellectual virtues—only as they are subject to human operation. Hence, also, only the practical sciences are concerned with contingent things precisely as they are contingent, viz., in the area of the particular. The speculative sciences, on the other hand, do not deal with contingent things except according to universal reasons, as was noted before (1146).

1153. Then [5], at "**However, since architecture,**" he defines art. First he defines art in itself, and second [1140a20] at "Art then etc.," by comparison with its opposite. On the initial point he does two things. First [5] he shows what art is. Next [6], at "But every art is concerned etc.," he shows what the subject matter of art is. He makes the first point by induction. We see architecture as a kind of art, and also as a kind of habit for making something through reason. Likewise, every art is so constituted that it is a habit, concerned with making, under the guidance of reason. Likewise, no productive habit of this kind, i.e., directed by reason, is found which is not an art. Hence it is evident that art is the same as a habit concerned with making under the guidance of true reason.

1154. Next [6], at "**But every art,**" he considers the subject matter of art. On this point he does three things. First [6] he proposes the subject matter of art. Second [7], at "Art, however, does not," he shows from what things art differs according to its subject matter. Third [10], at "In some manner etc.," he shows with what it agrees in subject matter. We should consider two things about the subject matter of art: the very operation of the craftsman which is directed by the art, and the product manufactured. Now, there is a threefold operation of art: the first is to consider how an artifact is to be produced; the second is to operate on the external matter; the third is to accomplish the work itself. For this reason he says that every art is concerned with the creation, or the achievement and completion of the work which he places as the end of art. It is concerned also with the artistic, i.e., with the operation of art that disposes the material, and with observing how a thing may be made by art.

1155. On the part of the work itself we should consider two things. The first of these is that the things that are made by art are contingent—can be or not be. This is evident from the fact that when they are made they begin to be in a new form. The second is that the principle of the creation of artistic works is in the craftsman alone, as it were, in something extrinsic to the artifact but is not in the thing made as something intrinsic to it.

1156. Then [7], at "Art, however, does not," he explains what was just said (1154–1155), showing how art differs from three other areas of knowledge. First in relation to the divine sciences and mathematics dealing with those things that exist or come into

being by necessity; about these subjects there is no art.

1157. Next [8], at "nor with things," he shows the difference in relation to natural science which treats of those things that are according to nature, and about which there is no art. The things that are according to nature have the principle of motion in themselves, as was stated in the second book of the *Physics* (Ch. 1, 192b15; St. Th. Lect. I, 142). This does not belong to the works of art, as we just pointed out (1155).

1158. Third [9], at "Since making," he shows how art differs from prudence. He says that since action and making differ from one another, art is restricted to giving directions to making and not to action that prudence directs.

1159. At "In some manner" [10], he shows that with which art is in material agreement. He says that chance and art have to do with those things that are done by intellect: art in company with reason, and chance without reason. Agathon indicated this agreement when he said that art values chance and chance art, inasmuch as they agree in matter.

1160. Then [11], at "Art then," he considers art by comparison with its opposite. He says that as art—this was previously noted (1153)—is a certain habit concerned with making under the guidance of true reason, so a technia or unskillfulness, on the contrary, is a habit concerned with making directed by incorrect reason regarding what is contingent.

LECTURE IV
Prudence

TEXT OF ARISTOTLE (*1140a24–1140b30*) Chapter 5

1. *Let us now investigate prudence in this way, considering who are called prudent.*
1140a24–25; 1161

2. *It seems to pertain to the prudent man that he can give good advice about proper goods useful not for one aspect of life—as an example, what are useful for health or bodily strength—but for the benefit of the total life of man.*
1140a25–28; 1162

3. *A sign of this is that we call men prudent in a particular matter when they can rightly conclude what is useful for a determined good end in things that do not belong to art. Therefore, a man will be absolutely prudent who gives advice about the whole of life.*
1140a28–31; 1163

4. *But no one takes counsel about things that either are incapable of being in any other way or are not within his power. Therefore, let us consider that science comes about by demonstration, and a demonstration is not possible in things whose principles can be in some other way—otherwise all the conclusions could be different; also, that counsel is not about matters which are necessarily so. Prudence then will be neither a science nor an art. It is not a science because the thing to be done is contingent; it is not an art because the genus of action and making differ.*
1140a31–1140b4; 1164–1165

5. *It remains, therefore, that prudence is a genuine habit concerned with action under the guidance of reason, dealing with things good and bad for man.*
1140b4–6; 1166

6. *Indeed the end of making is something other than itself. This is not always true in regard to action, for sometimes a good operation is its own end.*
1140b6–7; 1167

7. *For this reason we think Pericles and others like him are prudent, because they can reckon what things are good both for themselves and others. We look upon stewards or dispensers of goods and statesmen or rulers of cities as men of this kind.*
1140b7–11; 1168

8. *Hence we call temperance by the name sophrosyne, as it were, a thing preserving prudence. Prudence does preserve an estimation of the kind mentioned, for while pleasure and pain do not distort or pervert all judgments (for example, that a triangle has or has not three angles equal to two right angles), they do affect those dealing with the practicable. The principles of practicable things are the ends for which they are done. But the principle is not clear to a man corrupted by pleasure or pain, nor does he see the obligation to choose and do everything for the sake of it and on account of it, for vice is corruptive of principle. Consequently, prudence is of necessity a habit concerned with action, under the direction of correct reason, regarding things good for man.*
1140b11–21; 1169–1171

9. *Nevertheless, virtue is required for art but not for prudence.*
1140b21–22; 1172

10. *Likewise in art a man who makes a deliberate mistake is the more acceptable, but in prudence, as in the virtues, it is the reverse. It is clear, therefore, that prudence is a particular kind of virtue and not an art.*
1140b22–25; 1173

11. *But since there are two parts of the reasoning soul, prudence will be a virtue of the second part, viz., the estimative (opinativae), for opinion deals with the contingent as prudence does. Nevertheless, prudence is not a habit connected with reason alone, and a sign of this is that such a habit can be forgotten. But this is not true of prudence.*
1140b25–30; 1174

COMMENTARY OF ST. THOMAS

1161. After the Philosopher has finished his investigation of art, he begins now to investigate prudence. First [1]

he shows what prudence is. Then [4], at "But since there are two parts etc.," he shows what its object is. On the first point he does two things. First [1] he shows the nature of prudence. Next [9], at "Nevertheless, virtue etc.," he shows how it differs from art. On the initial point he does two things. First he shows who is prudent. Second [4], at "But no one takes counsel etc.," he shows what prudence is. On the first point he does three things. Initially he determines the method of procedure, saying that we must accept what prudence is from a consideration of people classed as prudent.

1162. Second [2], at "**It seems to pertain,**" he shows who are prudent. He says that it seems to pertain to the prudent man that he can, by the power of habit, give good advice about proper and useful goods, not only in some particular matter—for example, what things are useful for health or bodily strength—but also about things good and useful for the benefit of the total life of man.

1163. Last [3], at "**A sign of this is etc.,**" he gives a probative sign for his assertion. People are called prudent not absolutely but in a particular matter who can infer correctly what things are good or useful for some determined end. We suppose the end is good because to make deductions about things in reference to an evil end is contrary to prudence. We suppose likewise that there is question of things to which art does not apply because to conclude rightly in such matters (which are the concern of art) belongs not to prudence but to art. Therefore, if a man who is capable of giving good advice for a particular incident is presumed prudent in some matter, it follows that he will be absolutely prudent who gives good counsel about things touching the whole of life.

1164. Then [4], at "**But no one takes counsel,**" he shows what prudence is.

First [4] he gives the definition. Next [7], at "For this reason we think etc.," he makes it known by signs. On the initial point he does three things. First he shows in this context the difference between prudence and other habits given above (1142–1160), viz., science and art. Second [5], at "It remains etc.," he infers the definition of prudence. Third [6], at "Indeed the end of making etc.," he assigns the reason for a statement he has made. He remarks first that no one deliberates either about things that absolutely cannot be in any other way, or about things not within his power. Let us then take the things stated above (1148–1149), viz., that science comes about by demonstration, and again that a demonstration is not possible in matter whose principles can be in some other way, otherwise all the conclusions from those principles could be different. It is not possible that principles should be weaker than the inferences drawn from the principles. But let us now join to these observations what has just been said, viz., that counsel is not about matters that are necessarily so, and that prudence is concerned with things worthy of deliberation, since it was previously stated (1162, 1163) that the prudent man's special function is to give good counsel. From all this it follows that prudence is neither a science nor an art.

1165. That it is not a science is evident from the fact that things to be done, about which counsel is given and prudence is concerned, are contingent; and there is no science about matters of this kind. But that it is not an art is evident because the genus of action and making are different. Consequently, prudence, which deals with action, differs from art, which deals with making.

1166. Next [5], at "**It remains then,**"

ie infers the definition of prudence rom the premises. He says that, inasmuch as prudence is not a science (a habit of demonstration concerning necessary things) nor an art (a habit concerned with making under the guidance of reason), it follows that it is a habit dealing with action directed by genuine reason and is concerned not about things to be made—which are outside man—but about things good and bad for man himself.

1167. At "**Indeed the end of making**" [6] he assigns the reason for his statement (1166), that prudence is a habit dealing with action and concerned with things good and bad for man. Obviously the end of making is always something other than the making itself, as the end of building is a constructed edifice. Consequently, the good of making is not in the maker but in the thing made. So then art, which deals with making, is not concerned with the good and bad of man but with the good and bad of things wrought by art. But the end of action is not always something other than the action because sometimes eupraxia or good operation is its own end, i.e., for itself, or even for the agent; this, however, is not always so. Nothing prevents one action from being ordered to another as an end, for example, the consideration of effects is ordered to a consideration of the cause, but the end of each is a good. Clearly then the good of action is in the agent himself. Hence prudence, which deals with action, is said to be concerned with the goods of man.

1168. Then [7], at "**For this reason,**" he gives two signs indicating the validity of the proposed definition. The first of these is that, since prudence is concerned with things good and bad for man, therefore Pericles and others like him are thought to be prudent because they can consider what are the good things not only for themselves but also for others. Likewise, we think of stewards or dispensers of goods and of statesmen or governors of cities as men of this kind, viz., who can reckon good things for themselves and others.

1169. At "**Hence we call**" [8] he presents the second sign. He says that because prudence is concerned with good and bad things to be done, for this reason temperance is called in Greek *sophrosyne* (as it were, a thing preserving the reason) from which prudence gets the name phronesis. But temperance, precisely as it moderates the pleasures and pains of touch, preserves an estimation of this kind, namely, concerned with things to be done that are good or bad for man. Likewise this is made clear from the converse, since pleasure and pain—which temperance moderates—do not altogether distort (nor pervert by bringing about the exact opposite) every estimation, for example, the speculative judgment whether a triangle has or has not three angles equal to two right angles. But pleasure and pain do distort and pervert estimations that have to do with the practicable.

1170. Subsequently, he shows how this distortion comes about. It is evident that the principles of practicable things are the ends for the sake of which the practicable are done; these are in practicable matters like principles in demonstrations, as is stated in the second book of the *Physics* (Ch. 9, 200a15–b10; St. Th. Lect. XV, 273–274). But to a man experiencing intense pleasure or pain that thing appears best by which he attains pleasure and avoids pain. So, when the judgment of his reason is distorted, a man does not see clearly the end which is the principle of prudence regarding the practicable, nor does he desire the end; likewise it does not seem to him necessary to choose and do everything on account of the true end but rather on account of pleasure. Every vice or bad habit distorts the principle inasmuch as it distorts the correct estimation of the end. However, this distortion is prevented to a great degree by temperance.

1171. Thus he comes to the conclusion from the foregoing signs that prudence is necessarily a habit of action with correct reason regarding the good of man.

1172. Next [9], at "**Nevertheless, virtue,**" he shows a twofold difference between art and prudence from the nature of virtue. The first is that in the art a moral virtue regulating its use is required, for it is possible for a man to have the use of art enabling him to build a good building but not will it because of some other vice. But moral virtue, for instance, justice, causes a craftsman rightly to use his art. On the other hand, in the use of prudence an additional moral virtue is not required, for it was said (1170) that the principles of prudence are ends in regard to which rectitude of judgment is preserved by the moral virtues. Hence prudence, which is concerned with things good for man, necessarily has joined with it the moral virtues preserving its principles. This is not true of art, which deals with external goods, but, after art is acquired, moral virtue is still necessary to regulate its use.

1173. He presents the second difference at "**Likewise in art**" [10]. Obviously if a man deliberately makes a mistake in art, he is considered a better artist than if he does not do this of his own will, because then he would seem

to act out of ignorance of his art. This is evident in those who deliberately make grammatical errors in their speech. But in the case of prudence a man who willingly sins is less commended than one who sins against his will; the same is true of the moral virtues. This is true because for prudence there is required a rectitude of the appetitive faculty concerning the ends, in order that its principles be preserved. Thus it is clear that prudence is not an art consisting, as it were, only in the truth of reason, but a virtue requiring rectitude of the appetitive faculty after the manner of the moral virtues.

1174. Then [11], at "**But since there are two parts,**" he shows what the subject of prudence is. He says that since there are two parts of the rational soul—one of which is called scientific and the other estimative or conjectural (*opinativum*)—it is clear that prudence is a virtue of the second of these, viz., the conjectural. Opinion indeed deals with contingent things, as prudence does. Nevertheless, although prudence resides in this part of the reason as in a subject—because of this it is called an intellectual virtue—it is not connected with reason alone, as art or science, but it requires rectitude of the appetitive faculty. A sign of this is that a habit in the reason alone can be forgotten (for example, art and science), unless the habit is a natural one like understanding. Prudence, however, is not forgotten by disuse, but it is destroyed by the cessation of right desire which, while remaining, is continually engaged with the things belonging to prudence, so that oblivion cannot come along unawares.

LECTURE V
Understanding, the Habit of First Principles; Wisdom

TEXT OF ARISTOTLE (*1140b31–1141a19*) Chapter 6

1. *Since science is an evaluation of universal and necessary truths, and since there are principles of demonstrable things and of every science (science is accompanied by demonstrative reason), the principle of the knowable is neither a science nor an art nor prudence. What is knowable is demonstrable, but these, viz., art and prudence, deal with contingent things. Likewise, wisdom does not treat these principles because it is the business of the man of wisdom to furnish demonstrations about some things. If intellectual habits are science, prudence, wisdom, and understanding—by which we have the truth and are never deceived about contingent or necessary things—and none of the three (viz., prudence, science, and wisdom) is concerned with those principles, it remains then that understanding treats them.*

1140b31–1141a8; 1175–1179

Chapter 7

2. *We attribute "wisdom" to the most certain arts; accordingly we call Phidias a wise sculptor, and Polycletus a wise statuary. Here then by wisdom we mean nothing more than the excellence of the art.* **1141a9–12; 1180**

3. *But we consider some men wise in an unqualified sense and not just in a particular area or in some other way, as Homer says in his Margites: "The gods made this man neither a miner nor a farmer, nor wise in any other particular way." It is clear then that wisdom is the most perfect of the modes of knowledge.* **1141a12–15; 1181**

4. *Therefore, the wise man must not only know the conclusions drawn from the principles but he must declare the truth about the principles. Hence wisdom will be a combination of understanding and science.* **1141a16–19; 1182–1183**

COMMENTARY OF ST. THOMAS

1175. After the Philosopher has treated the intellectual virtues that perfect the intellect in respect to the things derived from principles, he will now consider the intellectual virtues perfecting the intellect in relation to the principles themselves. He does two things. First he discusses understanding which deals with the principles of demonstration. Second [1141a9], at "We attribute wisdom etc.," he considers wisdom which deals with the principles of being. He shows first that, over and above the other intellectual virtues, there must be understanding concerning the principles of demonstration. Science is a certain evaluation of universals and things existing of necessity, for particulars and contingents cannot attain the certitude

of science since they are only known insofar as they fall under the senses.

1176. In regard to the science of the things that are demonstrated, we must consider that there are some principles of the science itself necessarily dealing with demonstrable things. This is clear from the fact that science is founded on demonstrative reason proceeding from principles to conclusions. Since this is the case with science, the principle of the science necessarily is neither a science, nor an art, nor prudence—which we have just discussed (1142–1174).

1177. Obviously it is not a science because the subject matter of science is demonstrable. But the first principles of demonstrations are indemonstrable, otherwise we would proceed to infinity. That art and prudence have nothing to do with these principles is evident from the fact that these two virtues deal with contingent things. This cannot be said of the principles of demonstration, for principles must be more certain than necessary conclusions. Likewise it is clear that wisdom, another intellectual virtue which we will discuss subsequently (1180–1181), does not treat these principles. The reason is that it pertains to the wise man to frame a demonstration about some things, viz., the ultimate causes of being. But principles are indemonstrable, as has been said (1148).

1178. If then the intellectual virtues—about which we so truly say that falsehood never underlies them whether concerned with necessary or contingent things—are these habits: science, prudence (under which he includes art which also has to do with what is contingent), and, besides, wisdom and understanding, it remains that understanding treats these principles since none of the three, prudence, wisdom, or science, can be concerned with indemonstrable principles, as is clear from the foregoing.

1179. Understanding is not taken here for the intellect itself but for a particular habit by which a man in virtue of the light of the active intellect, naturally knows indemonstrable principles. The name is suitable enough, for principles of this kind are immediately understood from a knowledge of their terms. Once we know what a whole and what a part is, we grasp immediately that every whole is greater than its part. It is called understanding (intellectus) because it reads (legit) within, observing the essence of a thing. Hence his third book De Anima (Ch. 4, 429b5–23; St. Th. Lect. VIII, 700–719) says that the proper object of the intellect is the essence of a thing. So the knowledge of principles, which immediately become known when the essence of the thing is understood, is suitably called "intellect" or understanding (intellectus).

1180. Next [2], at "We attribute wisdom," he considers wisdom. First [2] he shows what wisdom is. Then [4], at "Therefore, the wise man etc.," he infers a corollary from what was said. On the initial point he does two things. First [2] he shows what wisdom, understood in a special sense, is called. Second [3], at "But we consider some etc.," he shows what wisdom in the unqualified sense is. He says first that in the arts we attribute the name wisdom to the most certain ones—those which, knowing the ultimate causes in some category of handicraft, direct other arts concerned with the same category, for example, an architectonic art directs technical workers. In this way we say Phidias was a wise sculptor and Polycletus a wise statuary, i.e., a carver of statues. Here we call wisdom nothing other than the excellence of the art (i.e., its ultimate perfection) by which a man attains what is ultimate and most perfect in the art. In this the excellence of each thing consists, as was pointed out in the first book De Coelo (Ch. 11, 281a7–15; St. Th. Lect. XXV, 248–249).

1181. Then [3], at "But we consider," he shows what wisdom in the unqualified sense is. He says that, as we consider some men wise in a particular handicraft, so too we consider others completely wise, i.e., with regard to the whole category of beings and not just a part of them, even though they are not wise in a particular handicraft. Thus Homer remarks that the gods did not make a certain man a miner or a farmer, nor make him gifted in any craft but simply made him wise. Hence it is clear that, as the man who is wise in some handicraft is most sure in that art, so that knowledge which is wisdom in an unqualified sense is the most certain of all modes of knowledge inasmuch as it treats first principles of being—in themselves most known, although some of them, the immaterial, are less known in regard to us. But the most universal principles are also more known in regard to us, for example, those belonging to being as being—the knowledge of which pertains to wisdom taken in this sense, as is evident in the fourth book of the *Metaphysics* (Ch. 1, 1003a21–22; St. Th. Lect. I, 529–531).

1182. At "**Therefore, the wise man**" [4] he infers a corollary from this: because wisdom is most certain and the principles of demonstrations more certain than the conclusions, the wise man should not only know the things in-ferred in the matter that he is considering but he should also declare the truth about first principles themselves not to prove them but to explain common notions, e.g., whole and part, equal and unequal, and suchlike—a function proper to a philosopher. When these common notions are known, the principles of demonstrations are clear. Hence the concern of such a man is to argue against those denying principles, as is evident in the fourth book of the *Metaphysics* (Ch. 3, 1005a19–b8; St. Th. Lect. V, 588–595).

1183. Finally, he draws a further conclusion that wisdom, in declaring the truth about principles, is understanding; but in knowing the things inferred from the principles, it is science. However, wisdom is distinguished from science, taken in the usual sense, by reason of the eminence which it has among other sciences; it is a kind of perfection of all sciences.

LECTURE VI
Wisdom, the Principal Intellectual Virtue

TEXT OF ARISTOTLE (*1141a19–1141b23*) Chapter 7

1. As having supremacy it is the science of the most honorable things,   **1141a19–20; 1184**

2. for it is unreasonable to consider political science or prudence the best of the sciences if man is not the most excellent thing in the world.   **1141a20–22; 1185–1186**

3. What is healthful and what is good for men and fishes are different, but white and straight are always the same; and everyone would say that in godlike things what is wise is always the same. However, what is prudent may be different, for the man who can properly consider individual things pertaining to himself is called prudent and we entrust such matters to him. For this reason people call prudent all dumb animals who seem to have the ability to care for themselves. It will certainly be evident then that wisdom is not the same as political science. If people call wisdom that science dealing with things useful to themselves, there will be many kinds of wisdom, for there is not one consideration regarding the good of all animals but there is a different consideration for individual animals. Likewise there is not one medicine for all beings.   **1141a22–33; 1187–1188**

4. That man is the most excellent of all animals makes no difference, because there are other creatures more divine by their nature, for instance, the very evident things that constitute the universe.   **1141a33–1141b2; 1189**

5. From what has been said it is obvious that wisdom is both science and understanding about the things most honorable by their nature.   **1141b2–3; 1190**

6. For this reason people say Anaxagoras and Thales, and others like them, are wise but not prudent: men, seeing them ignorant of what is useful to themselves, assert they know superfluous and wonderful things both difficult and divine, but that this knowledge is useless because they do not seek human goods. Prudence has to do with human goods about which we deliberate, for skillful deliberation seems to be the special work of the prudent man. But no one deliberates about things that cannot be in any other way, nor about whatsoever is not ordered to some end—and this a practicable good. Moreover, that man is a good counsellor absolutely speaking who can conjecture, by reasoning, what is best for man to do.   **1141b3–14; 1191–1193**

7. Prudence not only considers universals but must also know singulars, for it is active, and action is concerned with singulars. Hence some men not informed scientifically but expert in different particulars are more effective than other men with scientific knowledge. Certainly, if a doctor knows that light meats are easily digestible and healthful but does not know what meats are light, he will not make people well. But if he knows that the flesh of fowls is light and healthful he will be better able to effect a cure. Since prudence is concerned with action, therefore, it must have both kinds (of knowledge) but especially the latter (of particulars).   **1141b14–22; 1194**

COMMENTARY OF ST. THOMAS

1184. After the Philosopher has defined the individual intellectual virtues, he now explains the principal one among them. First he shows which is absolutely principal. Then [Lect. VII], at "But there will be etc." (1141b22), he shows which is principal in the genus of the practicable in reference to man. On the first point he does two things. First [1] he shows that wisdom is principal among all without qualification. Next [6], at "For this reason etc.," he infers a corollary from the premises, clarifying what has been said, by a ign. On the initial point he does three things. First [1] he proposes what he intends. Then [2], at "for it is unreasonable etc.," he rejects the opposite error. Last [5], at "From what has been said etc.," he infers the truth. He says first that wisdom is not science of any sort whatever but the science of the most honorable and divine things, inasmuch as it has the essential elements to be head of all sciences. As the senses located in the head direct the movements and operations of all the other members, so wisdom directs all the other sciences since they take their principles from it.

1185. Then [2], at "**for it is unreasonble,**" he rejects the error of certain philosophers who, considering usefulness rather than the dignity of science, assign primacy of the sciences to political science by which the multitude is governed, or to prudence by which a man governs himself. As was pointed out in the beginning of the *Metaphysics* Bk. I, Ch. 1, 981b13–25; St. Th. Lect. I, 31–33), the speculative sciences are not sought as useful for some further end but simply as honorable in themselves. Hence he does two things on this point. First [2] he rejects this error. Next [4], at "That man etc.," he dismisses an objection raised. For the first statement he gives two reasons.

1186. Concerning the first of these he says that [2] it is unreasonable for a man to consider political science or prudence the most desirable science, i.e., the best of the sciences. This could not be unless man were the most excellent of all things in the world, for one science is better and more honorable than another because it deals with better and more honorable subjects—as is said in the first book *De Anima* (Ch. 1, 402a1–5; St. Th. Lect. I, 4–5). But it is false to say that man is the most excel-

lent thing in the world. Consequently, neither political science nor prudence—both dealing with human affairs—are the best among the sciences.

1187. At "**What is healthful etc.**" [3] he gives the second reason. It arises from this, that there are certain things whose prime characteristic consists in a proportion and relation to another. For this reason such things cannot be the same in reference to all objects. Thus it is clear that what is healthful and what is good are not identical for men and fishes. But other things are predicated without limitation, for example, white of colors and straight of figures. Because wisdom is one of the things which are such simply and in themselves (it is numbered among the primary entities), everyone must say that what is wise is the same in all things and that wisdom is the same without qualification in relation to everything. But what is prudent must be a thing that may be different in different subjects, because prudence is predicated according to a proportion and a relation to something. The man who can properly consider each thing pertaining to him is said to be prudent and to such a one we grant or attribute prudence. Hence by a kind of analogy men say that certain dumb animals are prudent, viz., those that seem to be able to care for themselves, not however by means of reason which properly belongs to prudence. So then it is evident that wisdom, which is a particular virtue, is not the same as political science.

1188. If we would hold that a science such as politics, which deals with useful things, was wisdom—the chief of all the sciences—it would follow that there would be many kinds of wisdom. Certainly there cannot be one identical formality in the things which are good for all animals, but a different consideration must be accorded to individual animals, taking into account what is good for each. A similar reason holds for medicine that cannot be the same for all. It was just said (1187) that what is healthful and what is good differ for men and fishes. But there must be only one wisdom because its function is to consider things which are common to all entities. So it remains that political science, which governs a human multitude, cannot be wisdom without qualification; much less can ordinary prudence which governs one man.

1189. Then [4], at "**That man,**" he answers a certain objection. Someone could say that political science or (practical) prudence, treating as it does of human affairs, is the principal science because man is more excellent than other animals. But this has no relevance to our proposition because certain other things are by their nature more divine than man by reason of their excellence. And—as we may not treat of God and separated substances, for they do not come under the senses—even the objects most evident to the senses and constituting the universe, namely, the heavenly bodies, are better than men. This is so whether we compare body to body, or the moving substances to the human soul.

1190. Next [5], at "**From what has been said,**" he infers the truth, viz., that wisdom is science and understanding—as was previously pointed out (1183)—not of all possible things but of the most honorable. This is evident from the preceding, because if any science was more honorable it would be especially political science or prudence, and this view has just been rejected (1186–1188).

1191. At "**For this reason**" [6] he infers from the premises a corollary by which some things previously dis-

cussed are clarified. On this point he does two things. First he introduces the corollary. Then [7], at "Prudence not only considers etc.," he manifests one aspect of it. He says first that, because prudence deals with the goods of man but wisdom with the things that are better than man, accordingly people call Anaxagoras and Thales the philosopher—and others like them—wise but not prudent. This is because men see these philosophers ignorant of things useful to themselves, but admit they know useless truths that are wonderful (as it were exceeding the common knowledge of mortals), difficult (needing careful investigation), and divine by reason of their exalted character.

1192. He gives in particular the example of Thales and Anaxagoras because they are especially censured on this point. When Thales was leaving his house to look at the stars he fell into a ditch; while he was bewailing the fact an old woman remarked to him: "You O Thales, cannot see what is at your feet and you expect to see what is in the heavens?" And Anaxagoras, though noble and wealthy, left his family possessions to his relatives and devoted himself to the investigation of natural phenomena; taking no interest in civic affairs, he was consequently blamed for his negligence. When someone asked him: "Do you not care about your country?" He answered: "I will have great concern for my country after I have explained the heavens."

1193. Therefore people say they know useless things, since they do not seek human goods; on this account too, they are not called prudent, for prudence deals with human goods about which we deliberate. Now, to deliberate well seems to be the special work of the prudent man. But no one deliberates about necessary things which cannot possibly be in any other way; and the divine things, which these wise men consider, are necessary. Likewise deliberation is not possible about things in general that are not ordered to some end, i.e., to a practicable good—things that the speculative sciences consider, even when they treat what is corruptible. That man is a good counsellor without qualification, and consequently prudent, who can conjecture by reasoning what is best for man to do.

1194. Then [7], at "**Prudence not only considers**," he makes clear something he had said, assigning the reason why the prudent man is concerned about practicable things. Prudence not only considers universals, in which action does not occur, but must know singulars because it is active, i.e., a principle of doing. But action has to do with singulars. Hence it is that certain people not possessing the knowledge of universals are more effective about some particulars than those who have universal knowledge, from the fact that they are expert in other particulars. Thus if a doctor knows that light meats are easily digestible and healthful but does not know which meats are light, he cannot help people to get well. But the man who knows that the flesh of fowls is light and healthful is better able to effect a cure. Since then prudence is reason concerning an action, the prudent person must have a knowledge of both kinds, viz., universals and particulars. But if it is possible for him to have one kind, he ought rather to have the latter, i.e., the knowledge of particulars that are closer to operation.

LECTURE VII
Prudence, the Principal Virtue in Human Affairs

TEXT OF ARISTOTLE (*1141b22–1142a30*) Chapter 7

1. *But there will be a certain architectonic knowledge even here.*   1141b22–23; 1195

Chapter 8

2. *However, civic prudence and prudence as such are really the same habit although they differ from one another.*   1141b23–24; 1196

3. *One part of the habit dealing with the whole state is as it were architectonic prudence and is denominated legislative; the other part concerned with individual practicables goes by the general name of civic prudence. The latter is operative and deliberative, for a decree has to do with the practicable as a singular ultimate. Hence only those with civic prudence are said to be engaged in civic affairs because they alone are active like manual workers.*
1141b24–29; 1197–1198

4. *But that which is concerned with oneself seems to be prudence in a special way. This retains the general name, prudence; but of the others, one is called domestic, another legislative, and a third executive. Each of these is divided into consultative and judicial.*
1141b29–33; 1199–1201

5. *Therefore, to know what is to one's advantage is a certain kind of human knowledge differing much from other human knowledge.*   1141b33–34; 1202

6. *Moreover, that man seems to be prudent who knows and diligently cultivates the things pertaining to himself, but public officials seem to be busy about many affairs.*   1142a1–2; 1203

7. *For this reason Euripides says: "How could I be prudent—I who have neglected to take care of myself and now share equally with many others in military service?"*   1142a2–6; 1204

8. *They (public officials) seem to be intent on superfluous things and to do more than is necessary. But men generally seek what is good for themselves and think they must work to secure it. Hence in this opinion only such men are prudent.*   1142a7–9; 1205

9. *It may be, though, that the individual's good cannot be attained without domestic prudence or civic virtue. But still it is not evident how the things pertaining to him are to be disposed, and this must be given attention.*   1142a9–11; 1206–1207

10. *In evidence of this it may be noted that youths become geometricians and scientists and are learned in studies of this kind, yet do not seem to become prudent. The reason is that prudence deals with particulars that are known by experience. But a young man does not have experience, which requires a great deal of time.*   1142a11–15; 1208

11. *Here someone may ask why a boy can become a mathematician but not a philosopher or a scientist. The reason is that the truths (belonging to mathematics) are known by abstraction but the principles (of nature) are learned by experience. Then too these things (pertaining to wisdom) are mouthed but not grasped by youths while the nature of mathematics is not obscure to them.*   1142a15–20; 1209–1211

12. *Moreover, error in deliberating can happen either regarding a universal or a particular proposition, because a man can err, for example, about all sluggish waters being unhealthy or about this water being sluggish.*   1142a20–23; 1212

13. *It is plain that prudence is not science because prudence deals with a singular ultimate, as was pointed out, and the practicable is of this nature.*   1142a23–25; 1213

14. *They (science and prudence) have some agreement with understanding. Understanding indeed concerns those principles requiring no proof. But prudence deals with a singular ultimate, an object not of scientific knowledge but of a kind of sense—not that by which we perceive proper sensibles—but the sense whereby in mathematics we perceive the external*

iangle (to which we conform our reasoning). This, however, is perception rather than rudence although it is another kind of perception. **1142a25–30; 1214–1215**

Chapter 9

15. But inquiry and deliberation differ, for deliberation is a kind of inquiry.

1142a31–32; 1216

COMMENTARY OF ST. THOMAS

1195. After the Philosopher has shown what is absolutely primary among all the intellectual virtues, he now shows what is primary in human affairs. First [1] he explains his proposition. Then [10], at "In evidence of this etc.," he makes known something that he had stated above. On the initial point he does three things. First, he proposes his objective. Next [2], at "However, civic prudence etc.," he makes known his proposition. Finally [6], at "Moreover, that man etc.," he rejects an error. He says first that although wisdom, which is absolutely primary, does not consist in the knowledge of human things, nevertheless there is a certain architectonic (i.e., guiding and governing) reason or knowledge here, viz., in the order of human affairs.

1196. Then [2], at "**However, civic prudence**," he makes known his proposition, distinguishing the things which pertain to a knowledge of human affairs. First he distinguishes civic prudence from prudence as such. Next [3], at "One part of the habit etc.," he defines civic prudence. Last [4], at "But that which is etc.," he defines prudence. He says then that prudence and civic prudence are substantially the same habit because each is a right plan of things to be done about what is good or bad for man. But they differ specifically (*secundum rationem*), for prudence as such is the right plan of things to be done in the light of what is good or bad for one man, that is, oneself. Civic prudence, however, deals with things good or bad for the whole civic multitude. Consequently, civic prudence is to prudence simply as legal justice to virtue, as was indicated heretofore in the fifth book (906–910). When the extremes have been stated, we see the median, i.e., the prudence of the household, which holds a middle place between that regulating one man and the state.

1197. Next [3], at "**One part of the habit**," he defines civic prudence. He divides it into two parts, noting that one part of the habit dealing with the whole state is, so to speak, architectonic or legislative prudence. The name architectonic derives from its role, to determine for others what is to be done. Hence rulers imposing a law are in civic matters as architects regarding things to be built. Because of this, positive law itself (that is, right reason according to which rulers frame just laws) is called architectonic prudence. But the other part of civic prudence, namely, that which is concerned with individual operable things, goes by the general name, civic prudence. In fact, the laws are compared to works of man as universals to particulars, as the fifth book stated about legally just things (902–903). Likewise, as legislative prudence gives the precept, so also civic prudence puts it in effect and conserves the norms stated in the law.

1198. Obviously it belongs to executive civil prudence to frame a decree that is simply the application of universal reason to a particular practicable, for it is called a decree only in regard to some practicable. Moreover, since every practicable is individual, it follows that a decree concerns some singular ultimate, i.e., an individual norm or precept—it is called an ultimate because our knowledge begins from it, proceeding to universals, and terminates at the ultimate itself by way of descent. Likewise the decree itself can be called ultimate because it is the application of a law, universally stated, to an individual practicable. Because this executive prudence of positive law retains for itself the general name of civic prudence, it follows that only those who see to the execution of the enacted laws are said to be engaged in civil affairs since they alone are active among the people like *chirotechnae*, i.e., manual workers in things to be built; and legislators bear the same relation to them as do architects to those who execute their plans.

1199. At **"But that which is"** [4] he treats prudence. First [4] he shows what should be called prudence. Then [5], at "Therefore, to know etc.," he infers a corollary from what has been said. He says first that although civic prudence, both legislative and executive, is prudence, nevertheless, that which is concerned with one person only, oneself, seems to be especially prudence. And reason of this type directive of oneself retains the general name prudence, since the other parts of prudence are qualified by particular names. One of these is called domestic, that is, the prudence that administers a household. Another is called legislative, that is, the prudence in making laws. Still another is civic, that is, the prudence in executing the laws. Each of these is divided into consultative and judicial; for in things to be done we must first investigate something by the inquiry of counsel, then judge the feasibility of the thing investigated.

1200. As has been noted previously (1174), we must consider that prudence is not only in the reason but has a function likewise in the appetitive faculty. Therefore, everything mentioned here is a species of prudence, to the extent that it does not reside in the reason alone but has ramifications in the appetitive faculty. Inasmuch as they are exclusively in the reason they are called certain kinds of practical science, viz., domestic ethics and political science.

1201. Likewise, we must consider that, because the whole is more important than the part, and consequently the city than the household and the household than one man, civic prudence must be more important than domestic and the latter more important than personal prudence. Moreover, legislative prudence has greater importance among the parts of civic prudence, and without qualification is absolutely principal about action which man must perform.

1202. Then [5], at **"Therefore, to know,"** he infers a corollary from what has been discussed. He says that, because individual prudence is a part of general prudence, it follows that to know the things good for oneself—which belongs to this prudence—is a particular kind of human knowledge unlike others by reason of the diverse things pertaining to one man.

1203. Next [6], at **"Moreover, that man,"** he rejects an error. First [6] he presents it. Then [7], at "For this reason," he gives a proof for it. Last [9], at "It may be, though etc.," he excludes the error by disproving it. He says first that, to some people, only that man seems prudent who knows and dili gently cultivates the things having to do with himself. However, those who are public officials do not seem to be prudent but rather *polipragmones*, i.e., busy with a variety of affairs pertaining to the multitude.

1204. At "**For this reason**" [7] he gives a proof of the foregoing error. He does this first by a statement of Euripides the poet who has one of his characters, a soldier fighting for his country, say: "How could I be prudent when I have neglected to take care of myself, i.e., I did not attend to my own affairs but, one of many, I am sharing military service equally with them."

1205. Then [8], at "**They (public officials),**" he proposes a reason for this notion. He says that some people affirm that public officials are not prudent, since they are intent on superfluous or vain things and are doing something more than their individual concern. Because of the inordinateness of their hidden self-love, men seek only what is good for themselves; and they are concerned that each one must do only what is good for himself. From this opinion of theirs it follows that, for some men, only those are prudent who are intent on their own affairs.

1206. Next [9], at "**It may be, though,**" he rejects this error. He says that the particular good of each individual person cannot be attained without domestic prudence, i.e., without the proper administration of the household, nor without civic virtue, i.e., without the proper administration of the state, just as the good of the part cannot be attained without the good of the whole. Hence it is evident that statesmen and household stewards are not intent on anything superfluous but on what pertains to themselves.

1207. Nevertheless, civic and domestic prudence are not sufficient without personal prudence. The reason is that when the state and the household have been properly arranged, it is still not evident how one's own personal affairs must be disposed. Therefore, it is necessary to attend to this by the prudence dealing with an individual's good.

1208. At "**In evidence of this**" [10] he clarifies a previous assertion (1194): that prudence is not only concerned with universals but also with particulars. On this point he does two things. First]10] he explains his proposition. Next [13], at "It is plain that prudence," he compares prudence with science and understanding. For the initial point he offers two reasons. In regard to the first he does two things. First [10] he gives a confirmation of the proposition. Then [11], at "Here someone etc.," he brings up a particular question on this heading. He states first that a sign of the previous assertion (1194), that prudence is concerned not only with universals but also particulars, is that youths become geometricians and scientists, i.e., learned in the speculative sciences and in mathematics; they are erudite in studies of this kind, and attain perfection in these sciences. However, it does not seem that a youth can become prudent. The reason is that prudence deals with particulars which are made known to us by experience. But a lad does not have experience because much time is needed to get experience.

1209. Then [11], at "**Here someone,**" he raises a question about why a boy can become a mathematician but cannot become wise, i.e., a metaphysician or natural philosopher. To this the Philosopher answers that the principles of mathematics are known by abstraction from sensible objects (whose understanding requires experience); for this reason little time is needed to grasp them. But the principles of nature, which are not separated from sensible objects, are studied via experience. For this much time is needed.

1210. As to wisdom, he adds that youths do not believe, i.e., grasp, although they mouth, things pertaining to wisdom or metaphysics. But the nature of mathematics is not obscure to them because mathematical proofs concern sensibly conceivable objects while things pertaining to wisdom are purely rational. Youths can easily understand whatever falls under imagination, but they do not grasp things exceeding sense and imagination; for their minds are not trained to such considerations both because of the shortness of their lives and the many physical changes they are undergoing.

1211. Therefore, the proper order of learning is that boys first be instructed in things pertaining to logic because logic teaches the method of the whole of philosophy. Next, they should be instructed in mathematics, which does not need experience and does not exceed the imagination. Third, in natural sciences, which, even though not exceeding sense and imagination, nevertheless require experience. Fourth, in the moral sciences, which require experience and a soul free from passions, as was noted in the first book (38–40). Fifth, in the sapiential and divine sciences, which exceed imagination and require a sharp mind.

1212. He gives the second reason at "Moreover" [12]. It was said (1164) that the work of prudence is to deliberate well. But in deliberating a twofold error can happen. One concerns the universal, e.g., whether it is true that all sluggish waters are unhealthy. The other concerns the particular, e.g., whether this water is sluggish. Therefore, prudence must give direction in regard to both universals and particulars.

1213. Then [13], at "It is plain that prudence," he compares prudence with the things mentioned above: first, with science and next, with understanding at "They (science and prudence) etc." [14]. He says first, it is evident from the premises that prudence is not science, for science has to do with universals, as was stated before (1145–1175). But prudence deals with a singular ultimate, viz., the particular, since it is of the nature of the practicable to be particular. So it is clear that prudence is not science.

1214. Next [14], at "They (science and prudence)," he compares prudence with understanding. First [14] he shows the agreement. Second [15], at "But inquiry and deliberation," he shows the difference. He says first that both science and prudence are receptive of, or in contact with (according to another text), understanding, i.e., have some agreement with it as a habit of principles. It was previously pointed out (1175–1179) that understanding concerns certain principles or ultimates, that is, indemonstrable principles for which there is no proof, because they cannot be established by reason but immediately become known by themselves. But prudence is concerned with an ultimate, i.e., a singular practicable that must be taken as a principle in things to be done. Yet there is no scientific knowledge of the singular ultimate, for it is not proved by reason; there is, though, sensitive knowledge of it because this ultimate is perceived by one of the senses. However, it is not apprehended by that sense which perceives the species of proper sensibles (for instance, color, sound, and so on—this is the proper sense) but by the inner sense which perceives things sensibly conceivable. Similarly, in mathematics we know the exterior triangle, or the triangle conceived as singular, because there we also conform to a sensibly conceivable singular, as in the natural sciences we conform to a sensible singular.

1215. Prudence, which perfects particular reason rightly to judge singular practicable relations, pertains rather to this, i.e., the inner sense. Hence even dumb animals who are endowed with an excellent natural estimative power are said to be prudent. But that sense which is concerned with proper sensibles has a certain other perfecting quality, viz., a skill in discerning shades of color or taste and the like. So prudence agrees with understanding in this that it deals with an ultimate.

1216. Then [15], at "**But inquiry and deliberation,**" he shows the difference between prudence and understanding. Understanding is not given to inquiring, but prudence is, because it is deliberative. To deliberate and to inquire differ as proper and common, for deliberation is a kind of inquiry—as was said in the third book (473, 476, 482).

LECTURE VIII
Eubulia (Excellence in Deliberating)

TEXT OF ARISTOTLE (*1142a32–1142b33*) Chapter 9

1. *Now we must consider the nature of eubulia. Is it science, or opinion, or eustochia (the virtue of conjecturing well in practical matters), or does it belong to some other genus?*

1142a32–34; 1217

2. *Certainly it is not science, for men do not inquire about things they already know. But eubulia is a kind of counsel that is given to inquiry and discursive thinking.*

1142a34–1142b2; 1218

3. *However, it is not eustochia because eustochia exists without the inquiry of reason and is instantaneous, while eubulia requires much time for those who deliberate. As the proverb goes: Be slow to come to a decision; but when you have decided, act quickly.*   **1142b2–5; 1219**

4. *Furthermore, quickness of mind and eubulia differ, for the former is a kind of eustochia.*

1142b5–6; 1220

5. *Nor is eubulia opinion in any sense whatever.*   **1142b6–7; 1221**

6. *But because the man errs who deliberates badly and the man who deliberates well does so rightly, it is evident that eubulia is a kind of rectitude,*   **1142b7–9; 1222**

7. *although not pertaining to either science or opinion,*   **1142b9; 1223**

8. *for rectitude, like error, is not applicable to science,*   **1142b10; 1224**

9. *while truth is the rectitude of opinion.*   **1142b11; 1225**

10. *Likewise, everything that is a matter of opinion has already been determined. Nevertheless eubulia is not without discursive knowledge, and so differs from opinion; it is not at all a declaration. And opinion is not an inquiry but a sort of declaration already made. However, the man who deliberates, well or badly, inquires and thinks discursively about a subject.*   **1142b11–15; 1226**

11. *But eubulia is a certain rectitude of deliberation. Therefore, we must inquire what deliberation is and about what it is concerned.*   **1142b16–17; 1227**

12. *Obviously, rectitude is taken in various senses because not every rectitude is eubulia. Indeed the incontinent and evil man will acquire by reasoning what he sets out to know. Wherefore one who keeps in view even some great evil will be said to deliberate rightly. But to deliberate well seems to be a good. And this rectitude of deliberation by which someone obtains a good end is eubulia.*   **1142b17–22; 1228–1229**

13. *But it is possible sometimes to determine this even by a false syllogism, so that we arrive at what we ought to do but not by the means we ought—the middle term being false. Therefore that, by which we attain what we ought but not in the way we ought, is not eubulia in the full sense.*   **1142b22–26; 1230–1231**

14. *Besides, it happens that one man deliberates too slowly but another too quickly. Hence genuine eubulia is found not in these exaggerations but in rectitude, which acts according to what is useful and proper in regard to the end, the manner, and the time.*   **1142b26–28; 1232**

15. *Again, one person may deliberate well in the unqualified sense and another may simply concern himself about a particular end. Therefore eubulia without qualification will be that which directs deliberations in relation to an absolute end; but eubulia in a limited sense, that which directs deliberations in relation to a particular end. If indeed to deliberate well belongs to prudent people, eubulia will be rectitude conducing to that end about which prudence gives the true evaluation.*   **1142b28–33; 1233–1234**

COMMENTARY OF ST. THOMAS

1217. After the Philosopher has defined prudence and the other principal intellectual virtues, he now investigates certain virtues connected with prudence. First [1] he defines them individually, each in itself. Then [Lect. IX], at "All the preceding habits tend etc." (1143a25), he compares them with one another and with prudence. On the first point he does three things. First he investigates the genus of *eubulia*. Next [Lect. IX], at "Nor is synesis etc." (1142b34), he investigates *synesis*. Last [Lect. IX], at "The virtue called gnome etc." (1143a19), he investigates *gnome*. Regarding the initial point he does three things. First [1] he examines the genus of *eubulia*, showing that it is a kind of rectitude. Then [7], at "although not etc.," he shows to what rectitude is linked. Last [12], at "Obviously, rectitude etc.," he shows what kind of rectitude he is discussing. On the first point he does two things. First [1], he explains his intention. Next [2], at "Certainly it is not etc.," he carries it out. He says first that, after the tract on the principal intellectual virtues (1142–1216), he must treat the nature of *eubulia* (excellent deliberation) in order to have a complete knowledge of these virtues. Is it a kind of science, or at least opinion, or even *eustochia*—shrewd conjecturing? Or in what other genus is it?

1218. Then [2], at "**Certainly it is not**," he shows what the genus of *eubulia* is. First [2] he shows where it does not belong. Next [6], at "But because the man etc.," he determines its genus. On the first point he does three things. First [2] he shows that eubulia is not science. Then [3], at "However, it is not etc.," he shows that it is not *eustochia*.

Last [5], at "Nor is eubulia etc.," he shows that it is not opinion. He says first that eubulia is not science. This is clear from the fact that men already possessing science do not inquire about those things which they know, but have certain knowledge about them. But *eubulia* being a kind of deliberation is joined with some sort of inquiry, for the man who deliberates inquires and thinks discursively. But discursive knowledge is attained at the end of an inquiry. Therefore *eubulia* is not science.

1219. At "**However, is it not**" [3] he shows that *eubulia* is not *eustochia*, for two reasons. The first is this. *Eustochia* or happy conjecture exists without the inquiry of reason and is instantaneous. It is innate in some men, who, by reason of acuteness of powers, richness of imagination and sensitivity of the external senses, come to a prompt judgment based on intellect or sense whereby they correctly evaluate a situation. Wide experience also develops this. And these two things are lacking in *eubulia*, which is associated with the inquiry of reason, as was just mentioned (1218). Besides, *eubulia* is not instantaneous but rather takes time for those who deliberate so they may thoroughly explore everything touching the subject. Hence too the proverb saying that the matters of counsel ought to be carried out quickly but deliberated slowly. So, obviously, *eubulia* is not *eustochia*.

1220. At "**Furthermore, quickness etc.**" [4] he gives the second reason. If *eubulia* was identical with *eustochia*, then whatever was contained under *eubulia* would be contained under *eustochia*. But quickness of mind is a certain kind of eustochia; it is a rapid conjecture about finding a means. However, quickness of mind differs from eubulia since *eubulia* is not concerned with the end which in practical matters holds the place of the middle term in syllogisms, for counsel is not taken about the end, as was indicated in the third book (473–474). Therefore *eubulia* is not the same as *eustochia*.

1221. Next [5], at "**Nor is eubulia,**" he shows that eubulia is not opinion in such a way that not only is not every opinion *eubulia* but neither is any opinion *eubulia*. This is evident for the same reason stated previously (1145, 1165) about science, for although a man who holds an opinion is not certain, nevertheless he has already limited himself to one viewpoint—something that is not true of a man deliberating.

1222. Then [6], at "**But because the man,**" he shows what is the real genus of *eubulia* from the fact that the man who deliberates badly is said to err in deliberating, but the man who deliberates well is said to deliberate rightly. The latter is *eubuleos* (i.e., correct in deliberation). Hence it is plain that *eubulia* is a kind of rectitude.

1223. At "**although not**" [7] he shows to what rectitude is linked. First [7] he shows whence it does not arise, and then [11] at "But eubulia is etc.," whence it does arise. On this (first) point he does two things. First he proposes what he intends, saying that *eubulia* is rectitude neither of science nor of opinion.

1224. Next [8], at "**for rectitude,**" he establishes his proposition: first in regard to science. In an area where error is possible, rectitude appears necessary. But error does not apply to science, which always has to do with true and necessary things. Therefore *eubulia* is not rectitude of science.

1225. Then [9], at "**while truth,**" he establishes his proposition in regard to opinion, by two arguments. The first is this. Since error is possible in opinion, rectitude is applicable to it. However, its rectitude is not called goodness but truth, just as its defect is called falsity. Therefore *eubulia*, which takes its name from goodness, is not rectitude of opinion.

1226. He gives the second argument at "**Likewise**" [10], saying that everything which is a matter of opinion is already determined so far as concerns the one holding it, but not in reality. On this point eubulia, since it is not without the inquiry of reason, differs from opinion. *Eubulia* is not a declaration of something but an inquiry. On the contrary, however, opinion is not an inquiry but a kind of declaration of the man holding it, for a person expressing an opinion states what he imagines to be true. But the man who deliberates, well or badly, seeks something and thinks discursively about the subject; hence he does not yet declare it is or is not so. Therefore *eubulia* is not rectitude of opinion.

1227. Then [11], at "**But eubulia,**" he shows of what subject *eubulia* is rectitude. He says that, since eubulia is not rectitude of science nor opinion, we conclude that it must be a certain rectitude of deliberation, as the very name (*eubulia*) indicates. Consequently to have a perfect notion of *eubulia* we must inquire what deliberation is and about what it is concerned. These questions have been discussed before in the third book (458–482); so there was no need that they be resumed here.

1228. Next [12], at "**Obviously, rectitude,**" he shows what kind of rectitude *eubulia* is. On this point he determines four conditions by turns. He says first that rectitude is used in various senses: in one sense properly, in another figuratively. Properly it is used in reference to good things but figuratively it is applied to evil things, just as if we should say that a man is a real burglar, as we do say he is a good burglar.

1229. Obviously, not every rectitude of deliberation is eubulia, for rectitude of deliberation does not refer to evil things but to good things only. The incontinent and evil man sometimes attains what he sets out to know by his reasoning, for example, when he finds out the way he can commit sin. Hence figuratively he is said to deliberate correctly inasmuch as he discovers a way effectively leading to an evil end. However, he takes some great evil for his end, e.g., theft or adultery. But to deliberate well—the name *eubulia* means this—seems to be something good. Hence it is evident that this rectitude of deliberation is *eubulia* by which a man attains a good end.

1230. At "**But it is possible**" [13], he explains the second condition, that sometimes in syllogistic arguments a true conclusion is drawn by a false syllogism. So also sometimes in practical matters we arrive at a good end by some evil means. This is what he means by saying that sometimes we determine a good end as it were by a false syllogism; thus a man by deliberating arrives at what he ought to do but not at the means he ought to use, for example, when someone steals to help the poor. It is as if a man in reasoning would take some false middle term to arrive at a true conclusion.

1231. Although the end in the order of intention is like the principle and the middle term, nevertheless, in the order of execution, which the counsellor seeks, the end takes the place of the conclusion and the means the place of the middle term. Obviously, the man who draws a true conclusion by means of a false middle term is not reasoning correctly. Consequently eubulia is not genuine insofar as a man attains the end he ought but not in the way he ought.

1232. At "**Besides, it happens**" [14] he gives the third condition. He says that sometimes a man takes so much time in deliberating that perhaps the opportunity for action occasionally slips by. Likewise, another man may deliberate too hastily. Hence genuine *eubulia* consists not in this but in that rectitude which aims at what is useful for the proper end, manner and time.

1233. At "**Again, one person**" [15] he introduces the fourth condition, saying that one man may deliberate well, without qualification, about the whole end of life. Also it is possible that another may rightly deliberate about some particular end. Hence unqualified *eubulia* will be that which directs deliberation in relation to the common end of human life. But eubulia of a particular kind will direct deliberation in relation to some special end. Because to deliberate well is characteristic of prudent people, unqualified eubulia must be rectitude of deliberation in respect to that end which so-called absolute prudence truly evaluates. This is the common end of the whole of life, as was noted above (1163).

1234. Therefore, it can be seen from all our discussions that eubulia is rectitude of deliberation in relation to an absolutely good end, by suitable methods and at an opportune time.

LECTURE IX
Synesis (Habit of Right Judgment in Practical Individual Cases)

TEXT OF ARISTOTLE (*1142b34–1143a17*) Chapter 10

1. *Nor is synesis, and asynesia, according to which we are called sensible and foolish, entirely the same as science or opinion, for if this were so all men would be sensible.*
1142b34–1143a2; 1235

2. *Nor is it any of the particular sciences, for example, medicine which deals with health, or geometry which deals with magnitudes. Nor is synesis concerned with eternal and unchangeable substances, nor with anything made. But it treats those matters about which men may doubt and seek counsel.*
1143a2–6; 1236

3. *For this reason synesis is concerned with the same things that prudence is.* **1143a6–7; 1237**

4. *But synesis is not the same as prudence, for prudence gives orders inasmuch as its end is to lay down what is to be done or not to be done. Synesis, however, merely forms judgments. In fact judgment (synesis) and good judgment, like people of judgment and people of good judgment, are looked upon as identical.*
1143a7–11; 1238–1240

5. *Likewise synesis is not the same as having or acquiring prudence. But just as learning is called syniene when it uses knowledge, so also when it uses practical evaluation to judge things about which prudence treats, or (as someone else says) to judge well, for eu has the meaning of "well." Hence the name synesis, in accord with which some are called eusyneti (men of good judgment) is derived from the word used in connection with learning. Indeed we often use "learning" in the sense of "understanding."*
1143a11–18; 1241–1242

Chapter 11

6. *The virtue called gnome according to which we say men are lenient and have just evaluation, is nothing more than a correct judgment of what is equitable. A proof of this is that we say the man of equity in a special way is inclined to leniency and that what is equitable has a measure of pardon in certain matters. Gnome itself judges what is equitable and the judgment is right when it corresponds to the truth.*
1143a19–24; 1243–1244

7. *All the preceding habits, it is reasonable to affirm, tend to the same thing. We use the names gnome, synesis, prudence, and understanding in such a way as to imply that the same persons possess gnome and understanding, and on that account are both prudent and sensible. In fact all these habits deal with singulars and particular ultimates,* **1143a25–29; 1245**

8. *inasmuch as man of good sense, or someone pronouncing favorable judgment, or passing a lenient sentence judges the actions which the prudent man commands. Indeed every equitable thing has a relation to all human goods in this, that it refers to another. All these have to do with singulars and particular ultimates, which are practicable things. Because of this the prudent person should know them; likewise synesis and gnome are concerned with things to be done, and these are particular ultimates.* **1143a29–35; 1246**

9. *Understanding in both kinds of knowledge is concerned with ultimates because understanding and not reasoning deals with first principles and ultimates. One kind is about unchangeable and first principles in demonstrations, but the other is about a singular and contingent ultimate in practical matters and about a proposition of a different nature. This latter concerns principles of purposeful activity, for the universal is drawn from singulars. Hence it is necessary that man experience these singulars by sense, and this perception is understanding.* **1143a35–1143b5; 1247–1249**

10. *Therefore the preceding habits seem to be natural. While a man is not naturally wise, he does have good sense, judgment and understanding by nature. This is indicated by the fact that*

we think such aptitudes follow man's years. In fact a particular age of life has understanding and good sense just as if nature caused them.   **1143b6–9; 1250–1252**

11. On this account understanding is both a principle and an end, for demonstrations proceed from them and are given for their sake.   **1143b9–11; 1253**

12. So we must heed the indemonstrable statements and opinions of experienced, old and prudent men no less than demonstrations themselves, since the elderly understand principles by their experience. We have thus far considered the nature of prudence and wisdom, what material each virtue treats and in what part of the soul each exists.   **1143b11–17; 1254–1256**

COMMENTARY OF ST. THOMAS

1235. After the Philosopher has explained *eubulia*, he now explains *synesis*. On this subject he does two things. First [1], he compares *synesis* with science and opinion. Then [3], at "For this reason synesis etc.," he compares *synesis* with prudence. On the first point he does two things. First [1] he shows that not all science or opinion is *synesis*. Next [2], at "Nor is it etc.," he shows that no one science is *synesis*. He says first that *synesis* (by reason of which we call some men *synetos*, i.e., sensible) and its contrary, viz., *asynesis*—by reason of which we call other men *asynetos* (asinine) or foolish—are not entirely the same as science or opinion. Surely there is no one who does not have some science or opinion. If then all science or opinion was *synesis* it would follow that all men would be sensible—something obviously false.

1236. Then [2], at "**Nor is it,**" he shows that no one science is *synesis*, saying that *synesis* is not any of the particular sciences. The reason is that if it was medicine it would deal with health and sickness; and if it was geometry it would deal with magnitudes. Certainly *synesis* is not said to be concerned with other particular sciences like the divine sciences, which treat eternal and unchangeable substances; nor is it said to treat the things done by nature or by man which the natural sciences and the arts consider. But it

has to do with matters about which a man can doubt and deliberate. So it is evident that *synesis* is not a particular science.

1237. Next [3], at "**For this reason synesis,**" he compares *synesis* with prudence. First he infers an agreement between them from our discussion. Since *synesis* is concerned with matters worthy of deliberation which prudence also considers, as was noted above (1164), it follows that *synesis* is concerned with the things treated by prudence.

1238. Second [4], at "**But synesis is not,**" he shows the difference between them. First [4] he shows that *synesis* is not prudence, then [5] at "Likewise synesis etc.," that it is not the source of prudence. He says first that although *synesis* and prudence have to do with the same things, nevertheless they are not identical.

1239. For proof of this we must consider that in speculative matters, in which no transient action exists, there is a twofold operation of reason, viz., first to find out by inquiry, and then to judge the information. These two works belong to the practical reason whose inquiry is deliberation pertaining to eubulia, but whose judgment about matters deliberated pertains to synesis. People who can judge well about things to be done are called sensible. However, practical reason does not stop here but proceeds further to do something. Hence there is required a third work, as it were final and perfecting, viz., to command that the thing be done. This properly belongs to prudence.

1240. Consequently, he says that prudence is preceptive inasmuch as the work of the end is to determine what must be done. But *synesis* merely makes a judgment. And *synesis* and *eusynesia* are taken for the same thing, viz., sound sense, just as *syneti* and *eusyneti*, i.e., people of sense and people of good sense—the work of both is to judge well—are considered to be alike. So it is clear that prudence is more excellent than *synesis*, just as *synesis* is more excellent than *eubulia*, for inquiry is ordered to judgment as to an end, and judgment to command.

1241. Then [5], at "**Likewise synesis**," he shows that *synesis* is not the source of prudence. He says that as *synesis* is not the same as prudence so it is not the same as having prudence, or as assuming or acquiring it. But just as learning, which is the use of knowledge, is called *syniene* in Greek, so also the practical evaluation used by someone to judge things about which prudence treats is called *syniene*. This can even be called judging well, by another, for *eu* in Greek means the same as "well." Hence the name *synesis*, in accord with which some are called *eusyneti* (as it were men of good judgment or of good sense), is derived from this word *syniene* which is used in connection with learning. Indeed we often call learning *syniene*.

1242. The sense then is that *syniene* in Greek means a use of some intellectual habit, which use is not only learning but also judging. But *synesis* is so called from *syniene* by reason of that use which is judging, not by reason of that use which is learning. Hence *synesis* is not the same as having or learning prudence, as some have thought.

1243. At "**The virtue called gnome**" [6] he describes a third virtue called *gnome*. To understand this virtue we must draw from a previous discussion (1070–1090) on the distinction between equity and legal justice. What is legally just is determined according to what happens in the majority of cases. But what is equitable is directive of the legally just thing because the law necessarily is deficient in the minority of cases. As *synesis* signifies a right judgment about the things that happen in the majority of cases, so gnome signifies a right judgment about the direction of what is legally just. Therefore, he says that that virtue called *gnome*—according to which we say some men are *eugnomonas*, i.e., pronounce fair judgments and have correct evaluation or arrive at just decisions—is nothing more than a correct judgment of that which is the object of equity.

1244. A proof of this is that we say the equitable man is especially (*syngnomonicum*) inclined to kindness, as it were tempering judgment with a certain clemency. And what is equitable is especially said to have *syngnome*, i.e., a certain equal measure of pardon. The virtue *syngnome* rightly judges what is equitable, and is correct when it judges what is true.

1245. Next [7], at "**All the preceding habits**," he compares these virtues with one another and with prudence. On this point he does three things. First he mentions the agreement among these habits. Then [8], at "inasmuch as a man etc.," he verifies this. Last [11], at "On this account understanding etc.," he makes an inference from what has been said. He affirms first that all these habits aim at the same thing. And this is reasonable. That they aim at the same thing is evident because they are attributed to the same persons. We use the words *gnome*, *synesis*, prudence, and understanding, referring to the same persons whom we call prudent and sensible as having *gnome* and understanding. That this reference is reasonable is clear from the fact that all the foregoing—called powers because they are principles of action—deal with singulars, which, in the practical order, are particular ultimates, as was stated in the discussion on prudence (1191–1194).

1246. Then [8], at "**inasmuch as**," he verifies what he said: first by reason, and next [10], at "Therefore the preceding etc.," by an indication. On the first point he does two things. First [8] he shows that *synesis* and *gnome* deal with particular ultimates and singulars, just as prudence does. Second [9], at "Understanding in both kinds etc.," he shows the same thing about understanding. He says first that obviously *synesis* and *gnome* deal with singular ultimates inasmuch as the kindly-disposed man of good sense, i.e., one pronouncing favorable sentences, or the compassionate man, i.e., the one passing sentence with clemency, judges those actions that the prudent man commands. But equitable things, about which *gnome* treats, in general can be compared to all human goods inasmuch as each of them has a reference to another—a thing pertaining to the nature of justice. Indeed, it has been said above (1078) that what is equitable is a kind of just thing. So then it has been correctly stated that *gnome* is concerned with the things treated by prudence. However, it is evident that all these have to do with singulars and particular ultimates by reason of the fact that practicable things are singular

and particular ultimates. But prudence, *synesis*, and *gnome* deal with practicable things and so, obviously, with particular ultimates.

1247. Second [9], at "**Understanding in both kinds**," he shows that understanding is concerned with ultimates. He says that understanding in both speculative and practical knowledge has to do with ultimates because understanding and not reasoning deals with first principles and ultimates (from which reasoning starts). But there are two kinds of understanding. One of these is about unchangeable and first principles in demonstrations, for they proceed from the unchangeable and first—that is, indemonstrable—principles which are the first things known and immutable because the knowledge of them cannot be removed from man. But that understanding of practical matters deals with another kind of ultimate: the singular and contingent, and with a different proposition, i.e., not the universal—which is as it were a major—but the particular which is the minor of a syllogism in the practical field.

1248. Why understanding is predicated of an ultimate of this kind is evident from the fact that understanding treats of principles. But the singulars, about which we say understanding is concerned, are principles of what is done for an end, i.e., principles after the manner of a final cause.

1249. It is obvious that singulars have the nature of principles because the universal is drawn from singulars. From the fact that this herb cured this man, we gather that this kind of herb has power to cure. Because singulars are properly known by the senses, it is necessary that man should have experience of these singulars (which we say are principles and ultimates) not just by exterior but by interior sense as well; he said before (1214–1215) that prudence belongs to the sensory power of judging called particular reason. Hence this sense is called understanding whose object is the sensible and singular. In the third book *De Anima* (Ch. 5, 430a25; St. Th. Lect. X, 745) the Philosopher refers to this as the "passive intellect" which is perishable.

1250. Next [10], at "**Therefore the preceding**," he verifies what he said. Since the foregoing habits concern singulars, they must in some way be in contact with the sensitive faculties which operate by means of bodily organs. Consequently these habits seem to be natural, not as from nature entirely but in the sense that some are inclined to them by a natural physical disposition so as to be perfected in them with a little experience. This does not happen with the intellectual habits, like geometry and metaphysics, which deal with things in nature.

1251. And he adds this: no one is called a philosopher (i.e., a metaphysician) or a geometrician by nature. Some indeed are naturally more apt for these roles than others but this is due to a remote and not an immediate bent of mind, as some men are said naturally to have good sense and excellent judgment, and that understanding which we speak of regarding singulars.

1252. An indication of such aptitudes is the opinion we have that they accompany age as physical nature is changed. Indeed there is a particular time of life, old age which, by the cessation of bodily and animal changes, has understanding and good sense as if nature was the cause of them.

1253. Then [11], at "**On this account understanding**," he infers two corollaries from the discussion. The first of

these [11] is that understanding, which discriminates well among singulars in practical matters, not only has to do with principles as in the speculative order but is a quasi-end. In speculative matters demonstrations proceed from principles (considered by understanding), but there are no demonstrations for the principles. On the other hand in practical matters demonstrations proceed from principles, viz., singulars and there are demonstrations for these principles. In practical argumentation, according to which reason moves to action, a singular must be the minor and also the conclusion inferring the practicable thing itself which is a singular.

1254. At "**So we must heed**" [12] he sets down a second corollary. It has just been said (1252) that understanding, dealing with practicable principles, follows from experience and age, and is perfected by prudence. Hence we must pay attention to the thoughts and decisions of experienced, old, and prudent men on what is to be done. Although such opinions and resolutions do not lead to demonstrations, they are nonetheless heeded even more than if they were demonstrations themselves. Such men understand practical principles because they have an experienced eye, i.e., right judgment in practical matters. And principles are more certain than the conclusions of demonstrations.

1255. Regarding the statements just made (1254) we must consider that, as in universals unconditioned judgment about first principles belongs to understanding (and deduction from principles to conclusions, to reasoning) so in particulars unconditioned judgment about singulars belongs to the sensory power of judgment called understanding. We say that prudence, *syne-*

sis, and *gnome* pertain to understanding. However, this is called particular reason, inasmuch as it concludes from one to another; to it belongs eubulia which the Philosopher did not enumerate among the others. Therefore he said it (particular reason) deals with particular ultimates.

1256. Finally he sums up saying that we have discussed the nature of prudence (the principal virtue in practical matters) and wisdom (the principal virtue in speculative matters) and the affairs each of these is concerned with, and that they are not in the same part of the rational soul.

LECTURE X
Doubts About the Usefulness of Wisdom and Prudence

TEXT OF ARISTOTLE (*1143b17–1144b1*) Chapter 12

1. *Someone may raise a doubt about the utility of these virtues.* **1143b18; 1257**

2. *Wisdom, to be sure, explores none of the ways in which man is made happy, for it does not consider any operation.* **1143b19–20; 1258**

3. *Although prudence considers this very thing, why does man need it? Prudence is the virtue concerned with things that are just and honorable and useful to man—the performance of which belongs to the good of man. But we are not more inclined to do things from knowing them (since virtues are operative habits) than we are inclined to fulfill the requirements of health and good condition from knowing them, but from the fact that they are habits. Surely we are not more inclined to activity because we know medicine and gymnastics.* **1143b20–28; 1259–1260**

4. *to be prudent not for the sake of these (virtuous works) but to become virtuous, prudence will not be at all useful for men who are virtuous.* **1143b28–30; 1261–1262**

5. *Nor will it be necessary for those not having virtue because, in order to be virtuous, it makes no difference whether men themselves have prudence or are induced to it by others who have it. It is enough that we make use of prudence; in regard to health, we do not learn medicine even though we want to be healthy.]* **1143b30–33; 1263**

6. *Again, it seems unreasonable that prudence, which is less perfect, should have predominance over wisdom. Prudence indeed has power over singulars and gives orders in regard to them. But we must discuss the questions proposed; up to the present we have merely raised doubts about them.* **1143b33–36; 1264–1265**

7. *We answer first that wisdom and prudence necessarily are objects of choice in themselves; even if neither of them performs any operation, they are virtues perfecting both parts of the soul.* **1144a1–3; 1266**

8. *Wisdom and prudence do, in fact, perform some operation but not as the medical art produces health; as health brings about healthful activities so does wisdom bring happiness. Since wisdom is a part of virtue as a whole, he who has it acts according to it and becomes happy.* **1144a3–6; 1267**

9. *Moreover, a work of virtue is perfected in accord with prudence and moral virtue: moral virtue rectifies the end, and prudence the means to the end. But there is no such virtue in the fourth part of the soul, viz., the power of growth, because this does not have the option of operating or not operating.* **1144a6–11; 1268–1269**

10. *Concerning the objection that, by reason of prudence, men will not the more readily perform good and just deeds, we must begin a little further back, resuming the following heading. We do not call certain men just who do just works, for example, those who do the things decreed by the law, either unwillingly or because of ignorance or some other cause, and not because of the works themselves. We do not call such men just, although they do what they ought to do and even what a good man ought to do. So, as it seems, one ought to do particular things in such a manner to be virtuous, for example, he should do them from choice and for the sake of the virtuous works themselves. Virtue indeed makes the right choice, but whatever things are designed by nature to be done do not pertain to virtue but to some other principle.* **1144a11–22; 1270–1271**

11. *But something more must be said in order to understand these matters better. There is a particular quality called shrewdness, which is of such a nature that it enables a man to do the things ordained to a determined end and to attain the end by means of these things. When the*

*ntention is good, shrewdness is praiseworthy, but when the intention is evil it is called
raftiness. For this reason we call both prudent and crafty people clever.   **1144a22–28; 1272**

12. *Prudence is not this quality but cannot exist without it; the habit in the soul is joined to
his insight by moral virtue, as has been pointed out. This is evident because argumentation in
he practical order has a principle that such an end is the supreme good, whatever that end may
*e, in fact anything may be used as an example. What is the supreme good is not apparent
*xcept to a virtuous man, for evil corrupts and causes deception in practical principles.
Obviously then it is impossible for a man to be prudent who is not virtuous.

1144a28–1144b1; 1273–1274

COMMENTARY OF ST. THOMAS

1257. After the Philosopher has considered the intellectual virtues, he raises some doubts about their utility. On this point he does two things. First [1] he proposes some doubts. Then [7], at "We answer first," he solves them. On the first point he does two things. First [1] he raises a doubt about the usefulness of wisdom and prudence, to which the other virtues are referred as to the principal ones. Second [6], at "Again, it seems etc.," he raises a doubt about the comparison of these two with one another. On the first point he does two things. First [1] he proposes the doubt saying that a man may be uncertain why or how wisdom and prudence are useful.

1258. Second [2], at "**Wisdom, to be sure,**" he pursues the doubt: first in regard to wisdom that seems to be useless. Whatever is useful in human affairs contributes something to happiness, the ultimate end of human life, to which wisdom seems to contribute nothing. Wisdom does not appear to explore any of the ways by which man is made happy because this takes place by means of virtuous operation, as was explained in the first book (224–230). But wisdom does not consider any production, i.e., operation, since it treats the first principles of being. So then it seems that wisdom is not useful to man.

1259. Then [3], at "**Although prudence considers,**" he pursues his doubt about prudence. First he brings forward the argument that prudence is not necessary for man. Next [4], at "If we must assume etc.," he rules out a particular answer. He says first that it is the role of prudence to consider the operations of man by which he may become happy. But on this account it does not seem that man needs it. Prudence is concerned with things just in relation to others and with things noble (or honorable) and good, i.e., useful to man in relation to himself—the performance of which belongs to the good man. But a person does not seem to perform actions that are in accord with some habit from the fact that he knows them but from the fact that he has the habit in relation to them.

1260. Thus it is clear in regard to the body that someone is not more inclined to put into practice the things pertaining to a healthy or well-conditioned man—provided they are not merely activities—because he has a knowledge of medicine or gymnastics, but because he has an inner habit. It happens sometimes that, from a knowledge of his art, a man performs certain healthful activities, but does them incidentally and not according as they come from a habit of health, which is why a healthy man does them. So this does not proceed from man because he knows medicine but only because he is healthy. Therefore, since virtues are habits, a man is not induced to do the works of the virtues as they proceed from the habits and lead to happiness simply because prudence gives him a knowledge of them. And in this manner prudence is not operative of the good.

1261. Then [4], at "**If we must assume,**" he rules out a particular answer. Someone could say: a man in being virtuous is not more ready to perform virtuous acts from the fact that he knows them according to prudence, but he does need prudence to become virtuous, just as a healthy man does not need the art of medicine to perform healthful works but in order that he be made healthy. So we must say that a man ought to be prudent not for the sake of these, viz., virtuous works, but for the sake of becoming virtuous. He excludes this answer for two reasons.

1262. The first reason is that prudence would not be at all useful when men are already good, i.e., virtuous. This seems quite unreasonable.

1263. He gives the second reason at "**Nor will it**" [5]. According to the previous answer it seems that prudence would not be necessary even for those who do not have virtue. In order that men become virtuous it does not seem to make any difference whether they themselves have prudence, or are induced to it by those who have prudence, since in the latter case man is sufficiently disposed to become virtuous, as is clear in regard to health. When we want to regain health, we do not, because of this, take the trouble to learn medicine, but it is enough to follow the advice of doctors. Hence, for a similar reason, it is not necessary to have prudence in order to become virtuous but it is sufficient to be instructed by prudent men.

1264. Next [6] at "**Again, it seems,**" he raises a doubt about the comparison between prudence and wisdom. It was explained before (1186–1189) that prudence is inferior to wisdom in excellence. At least wisdom seems to be prior, i.e., more pre-eminent than prudence, which operates with and gives orders regarding singulars. Even political science is contained under prudence, for it has been explained in the introduction to this work (2631) that political science gives orders as to what sciences ought to be pursued in a state which sciences each man ought to learn, and for what period. So it seems that prudence has authority over wisdom, since to give orders is the function of a judge. But it seems unreasonable that the less perfect should exercise authority over the more excellent.

1265. Continuing with what follows he adds a note, saying that he must discuss the proposed questions, which have been treated under the aspect of doubt up to the present.

1266. Then [7], at "**We answer first,**" he resolves the foregoing doubts. First he solves the doubt about the utility of wisdom and prudence. Next [Lect. XI 1290], at "Nevertheless, neither" (1145a7), he solves the doubt about the comparison between the two. On the first point he does two things. First he solves the doubt in regard to wisdom and prudence in general, then [9] at "Moreover, a work etc." in regard to prudence in particular. In reference to the first he puts forward two explanations. The first of these shows that the arguments presented do not prove conclusively. It does not follow that wisdom and prudence are useless because by them nothing is gained in happiness. Even if neither of them had any operation, they would neverthe-ess be objects of choice in themselves ince they are virtues perfecting both parts of the rational soul, as is evident rom previous discussions (1255). Anything is an object of choice by reason of its perfection.

1267. The second explanation, given at "**Wisdom and prudence**" [8], destroys the arguments. He says that wisdom and prudence in fact do something for happiness. But the example that he had been using was not suitable. Wisdom or prudence is not compared to happiness in the same way as the medical art to health, but rather as health to healthful activities. The medical art brings about health as a particular external work produced, but health brings about healthful activities by use of the habit of health. However, happiness is not a work externally produced but an operation proceeding from the habit of virtue. Hence, since wisdom is a certain species of virtue as a whole it follows that, from the very fact that a man has wisdom and operates according to it, he is happy. The same reason holds in the case of prudence. But he mentioned wisdom particularly because happiness consists more in its operation, as will be explained later in the tenth book (2111–2125).

1268. Next [9], at "**Moreover, a work,**" he solves the objections pertaining particularly to prudence: first, [9] in reference to the doubt that prudence does nothing for virtuous works; then [10], at "Concerning the objection," in reference to the doubt that prudence is not necessary in order that a man be virtuous. He says first—this time as regards prudence in particular—that the objection of prudence not enabling us to perform virtuous works breaks down. This can be false because we perfect the work of virtue

according to both, viz., prudence and moral virtue.

1269. Two things are needed in a work of virtue. One is that a man have a right intention for the end, which moral virtue provides in inclining the appetitive faculty to a proper end. The other is to be well disposed towards the means. This is done by prudence, which gives good advice, judges, and orders the means to the end. In this way, both prudence and moral virtue concur in a virtuous operation: prudence perfecting the part rational by essence, and moral virtue perfecting the appetitive part, rational by participation. But in the other, i.e., nutritive part of the soul—which is altogether devoid of reason—there is no such virtue concurring in human operation. The evident reason for this is that the power of growth does not have the option of operating or not operating. But this characteristic is required for the operation of human virtue, as is evident from previous discussions (305, 308, 382, 496, 502, 503).

1270. At "**Concerning the objection**" [10] he solves the difficulty which pretended to show that a man could be and could become virtuous without prudence. On this point he does two things. First, he shows that prudence cannot exist without moral virtue. Then [Lect. XI, n. 1275], at "We must again etc." (1144b1), he shows that moral virtue cannot exist without prudence. On the first point he does three things. First he shows that for a man to be virtuous, not only moral virtue but also another operative principle is required. Second [11], at "But something more etc.," he shows what it is. Last [12], at "Prudence is not etc.," he shows that prudence makes an addition of a moral virtue to that principle. He says first that to answer the assertion (1262–

1263) that by reason of prudence a man will not perform good and just actions in order to become virtuous, we must begin a little further back, resuming certain things already discussed (1035–1049).

1271. We will begin from this point that, as has been said (1035–1049), some people perform just deeds, and we nevertheless do not call them just, as when they do deeds decreed by law, either unwillingly or because of ignorance or for some other reason like gain, and not out of love for the very works of justice. Men of this sort, I say, are not called just though they perform the actions they should perform and even actions that a good man should perform. So also in particular virtues a man ought to work in some measure in order that he be good or virtuous, just as he works from choice and because the virtuous works themselves are pleasing. It has just been said (1269) that moral virtue makes the right choice in regard to the intention of the end. But the things designed by nature to be done for the end do not pertain to moral virtue but to some other power, i.e., to a certain other operative principle that discovers ways leading to ends. So a principle of this kind is necessary in order that a man be virtuous.

1272. Then [11], at "**But something more**," he shows what that principle is. He states that something further must be said about the things discussed above, so that they may be more clearly understood. There is, therefore, a particular power, i.e., an operative principle called shrewdness, as it were a certain ingenuity or skillfulness. This is of such a nature that, by means of it, man can do the things ordered to an end—either good or bad—that he has presupposed, and by means of the things he does he can share or attain the end. When the intention is good, ingenuity of this sort deserves praise, but when the intention is bad, it is called craftiness, which implies evil as prudence implies good. But, because shrewdness is common to each, it follows that we call both prudent and crafty people shrewd, i.e., ingenious or skillful. So then it seems that wisdom is not useful to man.

1273. At "**Prudence is not**" [12] he shows that prudence adds something to this principle, saying that prudence is not identical with this trait of shrewdness, although prudence cannot be without it. But the habit of prudence in the soul is not joined to this insight, i.e., this perceptive principle of shrewdness, without moral virtue which always refers to good, as has been pointed out (712). The reason for this is clear. As argumentation has principles in the speculative field so it has in the practical field, for instance the principle that such an end is the good and the supreme good, whatever that end be for which a man operates (and anything may be used as an example). Thus for the self-controlled man the supreme good and a quasi-principle is the attainment of moderation in the desires of touch. But the supreme good is not apparent except to the good or virtuous man who has the proper evaluation of the end, since moral virtue rectifies the conception of the end.

1274. That what is really the supreme good does not appear in evil things is evident from the fact that vice the opposite of virtue, perverts the judgment of the reason and causes deception in practical principles, for example, to follow his desires seems the supreme good to the licentious man. It is not possible to reason correctly if we are in error about principles. Since then it pertains to the prudent man to rea-on correctly in practical matters, obviously it is impossible for one to be prudent who is not virtuous, just as a man who errs about the principles of demonstration cannot acquire science.

LECTURE XI
Moral Virtue and Prudence

TEXT OF ARISTOTLE (1144b1–1145a11) Chapter 13

1. *We must again turn our attention to virtue. Virtue has a relation to a similar quality—as prudence to shrewdness, not that they are identical but that they have some likeness. In this way natural virtue is related to the principal virtue, for it seems to everyone that each kind of moral practice exists by nature to some extent. Indeed immediately from birth we are just, temperate, and brave and have other qualities. However, we are looking for something different, a good as a principle, so that virtues of this kind may be in us according to another manner of existence. It is a fact that children and dumb animals have natural habits, but these seem detrimental without the direction of reason. Certainly this much seems clear that, as a powerful body moved without the guidance of vision goes astray more powerfully because it lacks that guidance, so in this matter. But if a principle similar (to prudence) operates, then virtue in the proper sense will be present. Hence, as in the discursive faculty there are two kinds of principles, viz., shrewdness and prudence, so in the moral faculty there are two kinds of principles, viz., natural virtue and the principal virtue. The latter cannot be without prudence.*
1144b1–17; 1275–1280

2. *Therefore, it is said that all virtues are kinds of prudence.* 1144b17–18; 1281

3. *In this, Socrates investigation was correct in one respect and wrong in another. He erroneously held that all virtues are species of prudence, but correctly stated that virtue cannot be without prudence.* 1144b18–21; 1282

4. *An indication of this is that at the present time all men, in defining virtue, place it in the genus of habit and state to what matters it extends and that it is according to right reason. But right reason is that which is according to prudence. Therefore they all seem to guess in some manner that virtue is the kind of habit that is in accord with prudence.* 1144b21–25; 1283

5. *But we must go a little further, for virtue is not only in conformity with reason, but a habit accompanied by reason. But right reason in such matters is prudence. Socrates then was of the opinion that virtues are kinds of reason because he thought they were species of knowledge. But we maintain they are accompanied by reason. Therefore it is obvious from the discussion how it is not possible for a man to be good in the strict sense without prudence, nor to be prudent without moral virtue.* 1144b25–32; 1284–1285

6. *In this way we can refute the argument that some use to prove that virtues are separated one from another. We see that the same man is not equally well inclined by nature to all virtues. Wherefore he will be said to acquire the virtue he has known but not any other.*
1144b32–35; 1286

7. *This does happen in regard to the natural virtues but not in regard to those virtues according to which a man is called absolutely good. The reason is that all the virtues are present simultaneously with prudence, a single virtue.* 1144b35–1145a2; 1287–1288

8. *Evidently man would need prudence (even though it were not practical) because it is a virtue perfecting a part of the soul; he would need it because there will be no right choice without either prudence or virtue, for the latter disposes the end and the former directs the means to the end.* 1145a2–6; 1289

9. *Nevertheless, neither prudence rules over wisdom nor (an inferior thing) over what is more excellent, just as medicine does not rule health. This is so because medicine does not use health but sees how it may be produced; it gives orders for the sake of health but not to it. Again, it would be like saying that political science rules the gods because it gives orders about everything in the state.* 1145a6–11; 1290–1291

COMMENTARY OF ST. THOMAS

1275. After the Philosopher has shown that prudence cannot exist without moral virtue, he now shows that moral virtue cannot exist without prudence. On this point he does three things First [1], he explains his proposition. Second [6], at "In this way we can etc.," he solves a particular incidental doubt. Third [8], at "Evidently man etc.," he brings his principal proposition to a conclusion. On the first point he does two things. First [1] he proves his proposition initially by reason and then by the observations of others at "Therefore, it is etc." [2]. He says first that, since it has been shown (1273) that prudence cannot be without moral virtue, we must again turn our attention to moral virtue, inquiring whether it can be without prudence. It is the same with moral virtue, as has been said about prudence and shrewdness 1272–1274), that although they are not identical nevertheless they have some likeness one to the other, inasmuch as each discovers means suitable for the proposed end. This seems to be the case with natural and principal virtue, i.e., moral which is the perfect kind.

1276. That there is a natural virtue, presupposed to moral, is obvious from the fact that individual virtuous or vicious practices seem to exist in some people naturally; immediately from birth certain men seem to be just or temperate or brave because of a natural disposition by which they are inclined to virtuous works. This natural disposition can be considered from three viewpoints.

1277. It can be considered first on the part of the reason, since the first principles of human conduct are implanted by nature, for instance, that no one should be injured, and the like; next, on the part of the will, which of itself is naturally moved by the good apprehended as its proper object; last, on the part of the sensitive appetite according as, by natural temperament, some men are inclined to anger, others to concupiscence or passions of a different kind either too much or too little, or with moderation in which moral virtue consists. The first two are common to all men.

1278. Hence, according to this, the Philosopher says that some men are brave and just by nature, although those who are so naturally need something good as a principle, so that these virtues may exist in a more perfect manner; the foregoing natural habits or inclinations exist in children and dumb animals, for example, the lion is brave and noble by nature. Nevertheless natural habits of this kind may be harmful unless the discrimination of reason is present.

1279. Moreover, it seems that, as in physical movement when a body is moved by force without the guidance of vision it happens that the moved object is struck and damaged by the force, so also in this matter. If a man has a strong inclination to the work of some moral virtue and does not use discretion with regard to that work of the moral virtue, grave harm will occur either to his own body (as in one who is inclined to abstinence without discretion) or to external things (in one who is inclined to liberality). The same is true in other virtues. But if such an inclination jointly accepts reason in its operation so that it operates with discretion, then there will be a great difference in the excellence of goodness. Likewise the habit, which will be similar to the operation of this kind done with discretion, will be a virtue in the proper and perfect sense, i.e., a moral virtue.

1280. As then in the discursive part of the soul there are two kinds of principles of operation, viz., shrewdness and prudence, so also in the appetitive part pertaining to moral matters there are two kinds of principles, viz., natural virtue and moral, the principal virtue. The latter cannot come into being without prudence, as has been indicated (1275).

1281. Then [2], at "**Therefore, it is,**" he confirms his proposition by the observations of others. He does this first [3] by a statement of Socrates, and next [4], at "An indication etc.," by a statement of Aristotle's contemporaries. On the first point he does two things. First he gives the statement of Socrates, who held that all moral virtues are species of prudence by reason of the previously mentioned relationship between moral virtue and prudence.

1282. Second [3], at "**In this, Socrates'**," Aristotle shows how they (the virtues) fall short, saying that in this statement Socrates' investigation was correct in one respect but wrong in another. Socrates erroneously held that all moral virtues are kinds of prudence, since moral virtue and prudence are in different parts of the soul but he was correct in saying that moral virtue cannot be without prudence.

1283. Next [4], at "**An indication,**" he confirms this by the words of his contemporaries. First he gives their statement. Then [1144b25], at "But we must etc.," he shows how they may be wrong. He says first that an indication that moral virtue is not without prudence is that all of them in defining virtue and placing it in the genus of habit state the scope of virtue and say that this is guidance by right reason.

But it is clear from previous discussion (1111) that right reason in things to be done is right reason under the aegis of prudence. Therefore, when they all define virtue in this way, even though they do not decide it expressly, they seem in some manner to divine or conjecture that virtue is the kind of habit which is according to prudence.

1284. At "**But we must**" [1144b25] he shows how they may be wrong when they talk this way, by saying that their statement needs extension. Not only does it pertain to moral virtue to be in accord with right reason—otherwise someone could be morally virtuous without the need of prudence simply by the fact that he had been instructed by another's mind—but we must add that moral virtue is a habit accompanied by right reason, which of course is prudence. Evidently, therefore, Socrates said too much in expressing the opinion that all moral virtues are forms of reason and not things accompanied by reason, and that they were species of knowledge or prudence.

1285. Others said too little holding that virtue is only in accord with reason. But Aristotle maintains a middle position by stating that moral virtue is according to reason and accompanied by reason. Obviously then, from the discussions (1275–1283), it is not possible for a man to be good in the principal sense, i.e., according to moral virtue without prudence, nor even to be prudent without moral virtue.

1286. Then [6], at "**In this way we can,**" from the previous discussion he solves a particular incidental doubt. First [6] he raises the doubt. Second [7], at "This does happen etc.," he solves the doubt. He says first that from the premises it is possible to refute the argument that certain philosophers have

sed contending that virtues are sepa-
ated from one another, so one virtue
an be had without another. We see
hat the same person is not inclined to
ll the virtues, but one to liberality,
another to temperance, and so on. It is
asy for a man to be led to that to which
e is naturally inclined, but it is diffi-
ult to acquire a thing contrary to a
atural impulse. It follows then that a
han, who is naturally disposed to one
irtue and not to another, has known,
.e., has acquired the one virtue to
vhich he was naturally disposed (he is
aking the position of Socrates who
eld that virtues are kinds of knowl-
dge). But he will never acquire the
ther virtue to which he is not disposed
y nature.

1287. Next [7], at "**This does hap-
•en,**" his statement is verified in re-
ard to the natural virtues but not in
egard to the moral virtues according
o which a man is called good without
ualification. This is true because none
f them can exist without prudence,
or prudence without them, as has
een explained (1275–1283). So when
here is prudence, which is a single
irtue, all the virtues will be simultane-
•us with it, and none of them will be
•resent if prudence is not there.

1288. He expressly says "**a single
irtue**"—if different species of pru-
lence were concerned with the matter
•f different moral virtues (as is the case
vith the different objects in the genus
•f art), one moral virtue would not be
\indered from existing without an-
•ther, each of them having a prudence
orresponding to it. But this is impos-
ible because the same principles of
•rudence apply to the totality of moral
natter so that everything is subjected
o the rule of reason. Therefore, all
noral virtues are connected one with
he other by prudence. However, it can

happen that a man, having other moral
virtues, may be said to be without one
virtue because of the lack of matter, for
example, someone good but poor lacks
magnificence because he does not have
the means to make great expenditures.
Nevertheless, by reason of prudence
which he does possess, he is so disposed that he may become munificent
when he has matter for the virtue.

1289. Then [8], at "**Evidently man,**"
he brings his principal proposition to a
conclusion by a summation of the discussions. He says that it is now evident
from previous discussions (1266) that,
even if prudence were not operative,
man would need it because it is a virtue
which perfects a particular part of the
soul. Again, it is evident that prudence
is operative because right choice, necessary for the operation of virtue, does
not exist without prudence and moral
virtue. The reason is that moral virtue
makes the disposition in regard to the
end, while prudence directs the means
to the end.

1290. Last [9], at "**Nevertheless, neither prudence,**" he solves the doubt
raised about the comparison between
prudence and wisdom, saying that
prudence does not have power over
wisdom, nor does that which is inferior
have power over what is more excellent. He introduces two examples by
way of illustration. The first is that the
art of medicine indeed commands
what ought to be done to obtain health,
but it does not have power over health
because it does not use health itself—
something proper to the art or science
of one governing—as a man uses a
thing over which he has power by commanding it. But the art of medicine
commands how health may be
brought about, in such a way as to give
orders for the sake of health but not to
it. Likewise prudence, or even political

science, does not use wisdom by commanding the manner in which it ought to judge about divine things but it does give orders by reason of it, i.e., ordains how men can arrive at wisdom. Hence, as health is more powerful than the art of medicine—since health is the end of medicine—so wisdom is more excellent than prudence.

1291. The second example is this. Since political science gives orders about all things done in the state, it follows that it should give orders about the things pertaining to divine worship just as it commands what belongs to the study of wisdom. This, therefore, is like the argument that prudence or political science is preferred to wisdom in the sense that one should prefer wisdom to God—a thing obviously unreasonable. Thus he concludes the teaching of the sixth book.

BOOK SEVEN
CONTINENCE AND INCONTINENCE
LECTURE I
Censurable Moral Dispositions and Their Opposites

TEXT OF ARISTOTLE (1145a15–1145b20) Chapter 1

1. Now, making a new start, we must indicate that there are three kinds of dispositions in *oral practice to be avoided, viz., vice, incontinence and brutishness.* **1145a15–17;1292–1296**

2. And the contraries of two of them are obvious, for the one we call virtue and the other *ntinence.* **1145a17–18; 1297**

3. The contrary of brutishness very properly is said to be above us and is called a heroic and *vine virtue.* **1145a18–20; 1298–1299**

4. In this manner Homer presents Priam as boasting that his son Hector was so exceedingly *rtuous that he did not seem to be an offspring of mortal man but of God. If then, as it is said, en become divine it will be because of the excellence of virtue of this kind, viz., a habit opposed brutishness.* **1145a20–25; 1300**

5. In fact neither vice nor virtue is attributed to either dumb animals or God. But the one *ivine virtue) is more honorable than virtue while the other (brutishness) is a kind of vice.* **1145a25–27; 1301**

6. Just as it is rare for men to be godlike—when the Spartans greatly admired someone, they *sed to exclaim: "This man is divine"—so also is it rare for men to be brutish; it is especially mong the barbarians that brutishness is found. Men become brutish both on account of ickness and loss of loved ones, and on account of the prevalence of vice among them (for this ɔason they receive a bad name).* **1145a27–33; 1302–1303**

7. But later we will have to review this habit—vice in general was discussed previously. * low we must investigate incontinence together with effeminacy and voluptuousness. Likewise will be necessary to treat continence and perseverance, for these habits must not be nderstood as identical with virtue and vice, nor as different in kind.* **1145a33–1145b2; 1304**

8. Here, however, we must proceed as in other subjects, stating what appears probable and *'1en presenting the difficulties. In this way we will show everything that is most probable about 'lese movements of the soul—well, if not everything, at least many of the principal things. ndeed a sufficient exposition will be given when the difficulties are solved and the probabilities ɔmain.* **1145b2–7; 1305**

9. It surely seems that continence and perseverance are good and laudable; that incontinence *nd effeminacy are evil and censurable. The continent man seems to be identified with one who bides by reason; but the incontinent man, with one who disregards reason. Knowing that ɔrtain of his actions are evil, the incontinent man nevertheless does them because of passion. ɔn the other hand, the continent man, knowing that his desires are evil, refuses to follow them ɔcause of the judgment of reason.* **1145b8–11; 1306**

10. Likewise the temperate man seems to be continent and persevering and, according to *ɔme philosophers, every continent man is temperate, but according to others he is not. Some ven maintain that all intemperate men are incontinent and all incontinent men intemperate, ɔithout distinction; others distinguish them. Sometimes they say that the prudent man cannot e incontinent; sometimes that certain prudent and godlike men are incontinent.* **1145b11–19; 1307–1308**

11. Besides, men are said to be incontinent in regard to anger, honor, and gain. Such then *re the statements made about these subjects.* **1145b19–20; 1309**

COMMENTARY OF ST. THOMAS

1292. After the Philosopher has defined the moral and intellectual virtues, he now begins to consider certain things that follow from them. First [Lect. I] he treats continence, which is something imperfect in the genus of virtue. Next [Bk. VIII, Lect. I], at "After the previous discussions etc." (1155), he treats friendship, which is a particular effect of virtue. Finally [Bk. X, Lect. I], at "After these matters etc." (1172a18), he treats the end of virtue. On the first point he does two things. First [1] he discusses continence and its contrary. Then [Lect. XI], at "The investigation of pleasure etc." (1152b), he discusses pleasure and pain, which are their matter. He treats the first point from two aspects. First [1] he distinguishes continence from other things belonging to the same genus. Second [9], at "It surely seems etc.," he investigates them. On the first point he does two things. First [1] he distinguishes continence and its contrary from other things belonging to the same genus. Second [7], at "But later we will have etc.," he shows which of these have been discussed and which remain to be discussed. He handles the first point in a twofold manner. First [1] he enumerates the censurable habits or dispositions in moral matters. Then [2], at "And the contraries etc.," he gives their contraries.

1293. He says first that, after the treatment of the moral and intellectual virtues (245–1291)—so that nothing in moral may be passed over—we must make another start, stating that there are three kinds of states to be avoided in moral practice: vice, incontinence, and brutishness.

1294. So it is necessary to understand the difference between these things. As a good action is not withou practical reason and right desire—w pointed this out in the sixth boo (1269)—a perversion of these two fac ulties can bring about an act to b avoided in moral matters. If then per versity occurs on the part of the appe titive faculty so that the practica reason remains right, there will be in continence—a condition that is presen when a man has correct evaluation o what he ought to do or avoid but draw away to the contrary by reason of th passion of desire. But if the perversit of the appetitive faculty becomes s strong that it dominates reason, reaso follows that to which the perverted de sire inclines, as a kind of principle, con sidering it to be the ultimate end Hence a man will perform evil action by choice and for this reason he i called bad, as was noted in the fift book (1058). Therefore a disposition o this kind is given the name of vice.

1295. But we must consider that th perversion of a thing happens from th fact that the natural disposition of tha thing is destroyed. Thus physical sick ness occurs in man because the propor tion of humors belonging to this ma is destroyed. In a similar way perver sion of the appetite, which sometime perverts the reason, consists in the de struction of the commensuration o man's desires. But a destruction of thi kind does not consist in a thing tha cannot be added to or taken from an other, but it has a certain latitude, as i evident in the natural disposition o humors in the human body, for huma nature can be kept in good health wit more or less warmth. Likewise, a cor rect relation in human living is pre served by various degrees of desire.

1296. In one way an upset in har

nony of this kind can arise without exceeding the limits of a human mode of living. Then it will simply be called ncontinence or human vice, like sickness of the human body in which human nature is preserved. In another way the correct relation in human desires can be so corrupted that it exceeds the limits of a human mode of living ike the inclinations of a dumb animal, a lion, or a pig. This is what is called brutishness. It is just as if the temperament of a man's body had been changed into the temperament of a lion or a pig.

1297. Next [2], at "**And the contraries,**" he gives the dispositions contrary to the qualities just mentioned. First [1] he points out two dispositions about which there is no question, noting that the contraries of two of these are obvious, since to vice virtue is opposed and to incontinence, continence.

1298. Second [3], at "**The contrary,**" he shows what is opposed to the third, viz., brutishness. First, he sets forth his proposition. Then [4], at "In this manner etc.," he explains it. He says first that a virtue, which exceeds the usual human mode and can be called heroic or divine, is appropriately said to be opposed to brutishness. Indeed the pagans gave the name hero to the souls of their illustrious dead who, to their way of thinking, were even deified.

1299. To understand this we must remember that the human soul is the middle substance between the higher or divine substances, with which it shares intelligence, and dumb animals with which it shares sensitive powers. Consequently: (1) the affections of the sensitive part are sometimes perverted in man almost like dumb animals (and this is called brutishness, exceeding human vice and incontinence); (2) the rational part in man is perfected and

formed beyond the usual mode of human perfection after a likeness to separated substances (and this is called a divine virtue exceeding ordinary human virtue). Indeed the order of things is so arranged that the mean between different parts touches the two extremes. Likewise, then, in human nature there is something that comes into contact with what is above and something that comes into contact with what is below; yes, and something that occupies the middle.

1300. Then [4], at "**In this manner,**" he clarifies his statement. First he explains that in man there is a kind of heroic or divine virtue. Next [5], at "In fact neither vice etc.," he shows that this virtue is the opposite of brutishness. He illustrates his first point with two examples. The first example is taken from Homer who presents Priam as claiming his son Hector was so exceedingly virtuous that he seemed rather a child of God than of man—beyond the ordinary ways of man something divine appeared in him. His second example illustrates the same point by a pagan proverb believing in the deification of heroes. This is not to be understood, Aristotle says, in the sense that human nature is changed into divine nature but in the sense that the excellence of virtue exceeds the usual human mode. Obviously, then, there is in some men a kind of divine virtue, and he draws the conclusion that this virtue is the opposite of brutishness.

1301. Next [5], at "**In fact neither vice,**" he proves his proposition by two arguments. The first [5] is that vice and virtue are said to be proper to man. Hence, neither vice is attributed to a dumb animal who is inferior to man, nor virtue to God who is superior to man. But divine virtue is more noble than human virtue, which for us is called virtue in the fullest sense. On the other hand, brutish perversity is a kind of vice different from human vice, which is vice in the unqualified sense.

1302. He gives his second argument, at "**Just as it is rare**" [6], by asserting that people rarely have such great virtue, and those who do seem to be divine. Hence, when the Spartans—citizens of a particular section of Greece—marvelled at the virtue of someone, they exclaimed: "This man is divine." Likewise in regard to the vice, brutishness is rarely found among men.

1303. He presents three ways by which men become brutish. The first from a pagan manner of life, e.g., some of the barbarians, who are not accustomed to reasonable laws, fall into the vice of brutishness because of general vicious habits; the second way, from sickness and privations, i.e., loss of loved ones, which makes them lose their minds and become animals; the third way, from an excessive growth in vice, which shamefully stigmatizes them with the name of beast. Since this is true, as divine virtue is rarely found among the good, so brutishness is rarely found among the vicious, it seems that the two things correspond by opposition to one another.

1304. Then [7], at "**But later we will have**," he shows what kind of matters has been discussed and what yet remains. First he connects the preceding with what follows. Next [8], at "Here, however, we must etc.," he explains his method of procedure. He says first that, later in this book (1401–1403), he will review this habit of brutishness. Previously in the treatment of the moral virtues (528–1108) he discussed vice, the opposite of virtue. But now (1306–1468) he must investigate incon-

tinence, which is censured when concerned with pleasures, and effeminacy and voluptuousness, which are censured when concerned with pain. Likewise he must investigate continence which is commendable when concerned with pleasure, and perseverance, which is commendable when concerned with pain, in such a way however, that we do not consider these to be habits—either identified with virtue and vice, or different in kind.

1305. At "**Here, however, we must**" [8] he explains his method of procedure. Here we must proceed in the usual way, i.e., after stating what seems probable in the preceding discussions, the difficulties should be presented. In this way everything that is most probable in the matters discussed will be explained; or if not everything—no human mind is capable of this—at least many of the principal things. The reason is that when difficulties are resolved in any question and probabilities appear as true, a sufficient study has been made.

1306. Next [9], at "**It surely seems**," he investigates continence and incontinence, perseverance, and effeminacy. According to his plan, [Chapter 2] he first proposes what is probable. Then [Lect. II], at "Someone can raise a doubt" (1145b21), he brings forward the difficulties. Last [Lect. III], at "First then we must try," he solves the difficulties (1146b8). On the initial point he does three things. First [9] he proposes what is probable concerning continence and incontinence themselves. Second [10], at "Likewise the temperate man etc.," he proposes what is probable from a comparison of them with other dispositions. Finally, [11], at "Besides, men are etc.," he proposes what is probable about this matter. On the first point he makes three probable statements. The first pertains to the goodness and the badness of these dispositions. He says it is probable that continence and perseverance are good and laudable while incontinence and effeminacy are evil and censurable. The second statement pertains to the definitions of the things themselves. He says that the continent man seems to be identical with the reasonable person who judges what ought to be done reasonably; but the incontinent man seems to depart from reasonable judgment. The third pertains to the operations of these dispositions; he says that the incontinent man knows these particular actions are evil, and nevertheless does them out of passion. On the other hand, the continent man experiences desires that he knows are evil, and does not pursue them because of the judgment of reason. These two remarks are to be extended also to perseverance and effeminacy in connection with pains.

1307. Then [10], at "**Likewise the temperate etc.,**" he makes two probable statements from a comparison of these with other dispositions. The first is taken from a comparison of continence with temperance. He says that the temperate man seems to be continent and persevering. Some philosophers even hold that every continent and persevering man is temperate, but others hold that he is not. Regarding the opposites of these, some were of the opinion that all intemperate men are incontinent, conversely, in a confused way, i.e., without any distinction; but others, that these differ one from another.

1308. The second statement is taken from a comparison with prudence. He says that sometimes it is maintained that the prudent man cannot be incontinent; sometimes, that certain prudent and godlike, i.e., gifted, men are incontinent.

1309. Last [11], at "**Besides, men,**" he states what is probable about their matter, remarking that at times some are called incontinent not only for their concupiscence but also in connection with anger, honor, and gain. These then are the six statements that are usually made about continence and incontinence, perseverance, and effeminacy.

LECTURE II
Doubts Concerning Continence

TEXT OF ARISTOTLE (1145b21–1146b8) Chapter 2

1. *Someone can raise a doubt on how a man who judges correctly is incontinent.*
                                                                1145b21–22; 1310–1312

2. *Certain philosophers, therefore, say this is not possible for a man with knowledge. It is strange, as Socrates thought, that something else should control and enslave a man's knowledge. Indeed Socrates completely defended this line of reasoning, so that for him incontinence did not exist, for he maintained that no one rightly judging does anything but the best, except out of ignorance.*   **1145b22–27; 1313**

3. *This teaching of Socrates casts doubt on much that is clearly evident. So it will be best to examine passion; and, if man sins only through ignorance, the kind of ignorance operating here. Obviously, before the onslaught of passion, an incontinent man knows he ought not to do what he actually does.*   **1145b27–31; 1314**

4. *Some accept one saying of Socrates and reject another. They admit that nothing is more powerful than knowledge but they do not admit that man can do nothing other than what he thinks is better. For this reason they say that the incontinent man, who is overcome by lust, does not have knowledge but only opinion.*   **1145b31–35; 1315**

5. *But if it is opinion and not knowledge nor a strong supposition tending to the contrary but an ineffective belief held by people who are uncertain, it deserves tolerance because a man does not adhere to weak opinions in the fact of vigorous concupiscence. However, tolerance is not extended either to vice or to any other of the censurable dispositions.*   **1145b361146a4; 1316**

6. *Therefore (the incontinent man has) prudence contending against desire, and prudence is the strongest of opinions.*   **1146a4–5; 1317**

7. *This, however, is unreasonable, for a man will be prudent and incontinent at the same time. But no one will maintain that it pertains to a prudent man willingly to perform the basest acts.*   **1146a5–7; 1318**

8. *In this connection it was explained previously that a prudent man not only is concerned with ultimates, but also has the other virtues.*   **1146a7–9; 1319**

9. *Besides, if the continent man is so called from the fact that he has vehement evil desires, the temperate man will not be continent, nor the continent man temperate; for one who is completely temperate does not have evil desires. However, it is necessary for the continent man to have evil desires, for if his desires are good, the habit forbidding him to follow them is evil. Therefore, not every kind of continence is desirable. But if the desires are weak and not evil, then to be continent is not something worthy of respect; if they are weak and evil (to resist them) will not be remarkable either.*   **1146a9–16; 1320**

10. *Moreover, if continence makes a man hold all opinions, then a kind of continence can be evil—in case the opinions are also false.*   **1146a16–18; 1321**

11. *Likewise, if incontinence disposes a man to abandon any and every opinion, it will follow that a kind of incontinence is desirable. Neoptolemus in Sophocles' Philoctetes is an example of this. For he is to be praised for not retaining the opinion of which he had been persuaded by Ulysses, because lying saddened him.*   **1146a18–21; 1322**

12. *Further, the sophistic argument is a cause of doubt. Some men want to argue to indubitable conclusions so that they may appear wise when they attain them; and the syllogism they devise gives rise to doubt. As a result the mind (of the hearer) remains in suspense, since it does not want to admit the conclusion because it is not acceptable, but neither can it rest in the opposite conclusion because it is not able to solve the argument.*   **1146a21–27; 1323**

13. It would appear from this then that imprudence joined with incontinence is a virtue. That a man performs actions contrary to what he judges is due to incontinence. But he judges that good actions are bad and ought not to be done. Therefore, he will be doing good and not bad actions. **1146a27–31; 1324**

14. Furthermore, the man who from persuasion and personal choice pursues pleasures will appear better than one who acts from incontinence rather than reasoning. The persuaded man is more corrigible because he can be dissuaded. On the other hand, to the incontinent man is applicable the proverb: "When water chokes, what can we drink?" If a person performs evil actions because of conviction, he will cease from them when dissuaded; but the incontinent person will do them notwithstanding. **1146a31–1146b2; 1325**

15. In addition, if continence and incontinence are concerned with all dispositions, who will be continent without qualification? No one really has all the species of incontinence, but we do say that some are absolutely incontinent. **1146b2–5; 1326**

Chapter 3

16. Such then are the doubts occurring in this matter; some of them should be solved and some allowed to remain, for the solution of a doubt is found in the truth. **1146b6–8; 1327**

COMMENTARY OF ST. THOMAS

1310. After the Philosopher has stated the conclusions that seem probable concerning continence and incontinence, he now brings up doubts about all that he has said, not, however, in the same order in which he has presented them. In fact, he proposed the doubts in that order in which they first fall under consideration. But on any subject a man first considers the general aspect, for example, whether it is good or bad. Next, he considers the peculiar nature of the thing; third, its operation. Fourth, he compares it to other things with which it agrees; fifth, to those things from which it differs. Finally he considers its external surroundings.

1311. But in presenting the doubts he first submits what is more doubtful [1]. So, then, contrary to these six considerations [2], he places six doubts. The first doubt concerns the third probable statement about the act of the continent and the incontinent man. Next [6], at "Therefore . . . prudence," he places the second doubt concerned with the fifth probable statement, which referred to a comparison with

prudence. The third doubt [9], given at "Besides, if the continent etc.," deals with the fourth probable statement, which relates to a comparison with temperance. The fourth doubt [10], given at "Moreover, if continence etc.," concerns the second probable statement, which had to do with the definition of continence and incontinence. The fifth doubt [14], given at "Furthermore, he who does etc.," is concerned with the first probable statement which treated the goodness and badness of continence and incontinence. The sixth doubt [15], given at "In addition, if continence etc.," regards the sixth probable statement dealing with the matter of continence and incontinence.

1312. In regard to the initial point he first proposes the doubt [1]. On this he remarks that someone can doubt how a man who judges correctly is incontinent in doing the contrary.

1313. Then [2], at "**Certain philosophers,**" he pursues the doubt. First he objects to one part [2]. Next [3], at "This teaching etc.," he objects to the other part. Last [4], at "Some accept etc.," he rejects the solution of certain philosophers. He says first that some hold that it is impossible for a man to be incontinent when he judges correctly as a result of knowledge, because the stronger is not overcome by the weaker. Since then knowledge is a very powerful principle in man, it seems that, with knowledge present, something other would command knowledge and drag it along as a slave, although reason—of which knowledge is a perfection—should rather be in control and command the sensitive part as a slave (so the objection runs). This was the argument of Socrates. So rigidly did Socrates follow his own argument that incontinence might seem impossible. Indeed, he thought that no one who judges correctly does anything except what is best; but that all sin occurs through ignorance.

1314. Next [3], at **"This teaching,"** he objects on the contrary that Socrates' doctrine on this point calls into question matters that are evident. Obviously some people do what they know is wrong. If they really sin through ignorance, which happens while they are under passion's influence, whether concupiscence or anger, an investigation of the kind of ignorance involved is highly desirable. Obviously, before passion supervenes, the incontinent man does not judge he should do what he later actually does in the heat of passion.

1315. At **"Some accept"** [4] he rejects the solution of certain philosophers. First [4] he proposes their solution— that some accept one saying of Socrates, that "Knowledge is not influenced; but reject another, that "the only cause of sin is ignorance." They admit nothing can conquer knowledge, as being better and more powerful. However, they do not admit that man can do

nothing other than what he thinks is better. Consequently, their position is that the incontinent person overcome by sensual pleasures does not have knowledge but opinion.

1316. Then [5], at **"But if it is opinion,"** he rejects this solution by saying that such an incontinent person has either a firm or a weak opinion. If firm then the same argument seems valid for it and for knowledge, because we do not adhere to one less than to the other—more on this later (1137). On the other hand, if the opinion against concupiscence is not firm but irresolute, i.e., remiss and weak, happening to people who are dubious, it seems this should not be imputed a fault but rather deserves tolerance. The reason is that in the face of vigorous concupiscence a man does not cling to opinions feebly held. However, tolerance is not extended to vice or to any of the other censurable dispositions. Incontinence is one of these but fault is not entirely imputed to it.

1317. Next [6], at **"Therefore,"** he raises a doubt about the comparison of continence with prudence, which was the fifth probable statement. First [6] he objects to one part, concluding from the premises that a man can be incontinent although he has prudence directing him to virtue. If the incontinent man has an opinion contending against evil desires—and the opinion is not weak, since in this way they would not be charged as a fault—it remains then that he has a strong opinion maintaining the contrary. But prudence is the strongest of opinions. Therefore, the incontinent person in a special way has prudence contending contrary to desire.

1318. Second [7], at **"This, however,"** he shows that this argument is not tenable for two reasons. First [7], according to these lines of thought it will follow that a man may be prudent and incontinent at the same time. This seems impossible, for no one holds that to perform the basest actions willingly is an act of prudence. It was noted previously in the sixth book (1173) that a person who voluntarily sins in the matter of prudence is more blameworthy.

1319. He presents the second reason [8] at "**In this connection.**" It was explained previously (1208–1212) that the prudent man is not only cognizant that a particular is an ultimate, i.e., has a correct evaluation of individual practicables which he called ultimates in the sixth book (1214)—but also has the other virtues, namely, the moral, as was likewise indicated in the sixth book (1172). Consequently it does not seem possible for any prudent person to act contrary to the virtues.

1320. After this, at "**Besides, if the continent man**" [9], he gives advice on the comparison between continence and temperance, which was the fourth probable statement. To make this clear, he must discuss three other observations he has made. The first is that a man is called continent from the fact that he has vehement evil desires and, notwithstanding these, is not led astray contrary to reason. If this is true, the temperate man will not be continent, nor the continent man temperate, for the man who is completely temperate does not have evil desires in any vehemence. So, to have vehement evil desires is inconsistent with being temperate. However, once the preceding supposition be made, it would be necessary that the temperate man have evil desires if he were continent. The second of the three is that the continent man may have not evil desires but good ones. This being the case, it would follow that whatever habit for-

bids the pursuit of these is evil. But such a habit is continence. Therefore, not every kind of continence is desirable. The third of the three is that the desires the continent man has might not be vehement but weak and feeble. Then, if the desires are evil, to be continent will be worthy neither of respect nor praise; if they are evil and nevertheless weak, it will not be remarkable to resist them. Yet continence is looked upon as something great and worthy of respect. Therefore something unreasonable seems to follow, whatever one of the three positions be maintained.

1321. Then [10], at "**Moreover, if continence,**" he raises a doubt about the very definition of continence, which was the second probable statement. First [10] he presents a difficulty about the nature of continence as stated above (1306): that the continent person is also the man who lives by reason. He says that if continence makes a man embrace every opinion, i.e., persuades him to abide by every opinion and not depart from any, it will follow that some kind of continence is evil; for an opinion can be false. And it is good to reject such a view. Hence it is evil to be governed by it, although continence should be praised as something good.

1322. Next [11], at "**Likewise, if,**" he makes three objections to the notion of incontinence he has already given (1306), namely, that the incontinent man is inclined to abandon reason. The first [11] is that if incontinence abandons every opinion or reason, it will follow that some kind of incontinence is good; nevertheless incontinence should always be censured as an evil thing. This is so because a conjectural reason may prompt the doing of an evil action which it is good to avoid. He gives an illustration. The poet Sophocles narrates that Neoptolemus, who fought in the Trojan war, was persuaded by Ulysses to lie to Philoctetes for a reason that seemed honorable. Afterwards, however, he did not retain the opinion, of which he had been persuaded, because lying was grievous and painful to him; and in this there is something praiseworthy.

1323. He presents the second objection [12], at "**Further, the sophistic,**" stating that the sophistic argument, because misleading, i.e., concluding falsely, is itself a doubt or rather a cause of doubt. The explanation is that the sophists, in order to appear wise, want to infer indubitable conclusions. But when they succeed by argument, the syllogism they devise causes doubt; for the mind of the hearer remains in suspense, since on the one hand the mind does not wish to abide by what reason infers, because the conclusion is not acceptable, and on the other hand, it cannot proceed to the opposite because it does not have the solution of the argument within its power. Nevertheless, the mind is not to be blamed because it did not abide by the reasoning which it did not know how to resolve. Therefore, it does not seem there is incontinence in abandoning any reason whatsoever.

1324. He gives the third objection at "**It would appear**" [13]. If to abandon any reason whatever is incontinent, it follows from this argument that imprudence joined to incontinence is a virtue. Thus virtue will be composed of two vices, which is impossible; and it seems that what was said will follow, that incontinence is the reason why someone performs actions contrary to his judgment. But the judgment he makes that good actions are bad and that he ought not to do them, is the fruit of imprudence. Hence it will follow

that he performs good and not evil actions, which seems to belong to virtue.

1325. Then [14], at "**Furthermore, he who does evil,**" he raises a doubt about the goodness and badness of continence and incontinence. It seems that one who performs evil actions because he is persuaded they are good and consequently pursues and chooses pleasures as good in themselves (as the intemperate man does) is better than another who performs evil actions, not because of reasoning by which he is deceived, but because of incontinence. The man who has been persuaded seems to be more corrigible because he can easily be dissuaded from his present view. But the incontinent man does not seem to be helped by any good advice. Nay rather he seems to be indicated in the proverb that if water, whose drinking refreshes the thirsty, chokes the drinker, what can he drink? In a similar way, if a man performs evil actions as a result of conviction or deception, he will cease to do them when dissuaded, i.e., when the persuasion is withdrawn, as thirst ceases when a drink of water is taken. But in the present case the counselled incontinent man even believes some actions are right, and notwithstanding does different things. Hence the good water of advice does not help but chokes him.

1326. At "**In addition, if incontinence**" [15], he raises a doubt about the matter of continence and incontinence, which was the sixth probable statement. He affirms that if continence and incontinence concern not only concupiscence but anger, wealth, and everything of this kind, he will be unable to determine who is incontinent without qualification. Indeed, no one can be found who will have all the varieties of incontinence. But we do say that some are absolutely incontinent. Therefore, the assertion previously made (1225), that continence and incontinence concern everything does not seem to be true.

1327. Last [16], at "**Such then,**" he sums up in conclusion by indicating that such are the doubts occurring in the matter under discussion. We must solve some of these doubts by showing that they tend to falsehood; others we can leave inasmuch as they are quasi conclusions. When we find the truth about a doubtful point, then we have a genuine solution to a doubt.

LECTURE III
The Solution of Doubts

TEXT OF ARISTOTLE (*1146b8–1147b19*) Chapter 3

1. *First then we must try to find out whether or not some people can be knowingly incontinent; if so, in what way. Next we must determine in what kind of matter a man is continent or incontinent: whether in every form of pleasure and pain or only in some specific forms; whether the continent man and the persevering man are identical or different. Likewise, we must give our attention to whatever matters are related to this investigation.*

1146b8–14; 1328–1329

2. *In the beginning of our inquiry we ask whether the continent and the incontinent differ specifically, by reason of the matter with which they are concerned, or in the manner of dealing with the matter. We ask whether a man may be called incontinent only because he is concerned with particular matter (or also because concerned with any sort of matter); whether only from one or the other, or from both (i.e., limited manner and limited matter) Again, we ask whether or not incontinence and continence deal with all kinds of matter.*   **1146b14–19; 1330–1334**

3. *Incontinence in the unqualified sense is not predicated of a man in all matters but only in that limited matter in which he may be intemperate.*   **1146b19–20; 1335**

4. *Neither is a man said to be continent or incontinent only in this (for then continence would be the same as intemperance), but in conducting himself in a certain way. One (the intemperate man) is led as a result of choice, judging that he must always pursue the present pleasure. But the other (the incontinent man) does not so judge, but pursues the pleasure notwithstanding.*   **1146b20–24; 1336**

5. *It makes no difference in the present argument to say that it is real opinion and not objectively verified knowledge against which people act incontinently or there are some who have only opinion yet are not in doubt, for they think they know with certitude. If then it is said that men with opinion rather than objectively verified knowledge act contrary to conviction because they cling feebly to their views, we answer that this knowledge does not differ from opinion in this matter. There are some people who assent no less firmly to matters of opinion than others to matters of objectively verified knowledge. Heraclitus is an example of this.*

1146b24–31; 1337

6. *Since we say that a man knows in two ways (for he is said to know both when he uses his knowledge and when he has the habit of knowledge without using it), it makes a great deal of difference in doing what he should not:whether a man has the habit of knowledge, but is not using it; or has the habit, and is using it. His situation seems difficult in the latter case, but not if actual consideration is lacking.*   **1146b31–35; 1338**

7. *Yet, since we must use two modes of propositions, there is nothing to hinder a man who knows both from operating against the knowledge he uses about the universal but not against the knowledge he has about the particular. This is so because operations concern particulars. But the universal is understood differently: in one way as it is in itself and in another as it is in a particular case. Thus "Dry foods are good for all men," and "I am a man," or "Such and such a food is dry." But it is possible that a man may not know such a universal either habitually or in a particular case. There is so much difference in the modes of knowing that it should not seem unreasonable for one who acts incontinently to know in one manner, yet it would be astonishing for him to know in another.*   **1146b35–1147a10; 1339–1341**

8. *In addition, a mode of knowing different from those already discussed is found in man, for we see a difference in one knowing by way of habit and in a particular situation. Hence a man seems in some way to have and not to have knowledge, as is evident in one who is asleep or*

drunk. It is in this manner that those under the influence of the passions react. Indeed, anger, sexual desires, and certain passions of this kind clearly change the body; some even lead men to madness. Obviously then we must say that the incontinent are disposed in a similar way.

1147a10–18; 1342

9. *The use of learned terms by the incontinent is not a sign that they operate by a habit of knowledge. In fact men under the influence of these passions mouth demonstrations and declaim the sayings of Empedocles; and youths beginning to learn prate doctrine but do not really know what they are talking about, for doctrine must become connatural to be known and this takes time. So then we must conclude that the incontinent in speaking this way are, as it were, pretending.*

1147a18–24; 1343–1344

10. *Furthermore, someone may want to consider the reason in terms of man's nature. There is one judgment that is universal; and another concerned with particulars that are properly the objects of sense. However, since one formal reason is present in such judgments, the mind necessarily comes to a conclusion, while in the practical order it must immediately be directed to operation. Thus, if a man must taste everything sweet, and this thing is sweet, such as wine or something of the sort, he will at the same time have to taste it when he is able, unless he be prevented from doing so.*

1147a24–31; 1345–1346

11. *Now one universal judgment may say "You must not taste," and another that "Every sweet is pleasant." At the same time a particular judgment may say "This is sweet." In such a case the sweet can be taken when appetite is present. Reason indeed declares that the particular thing is to be avoided but the appetite leads to it because the appetite can move any part of the soul. Hence it happens that a man may act incontinently contrary to reason and judgment.*

1147a31–1147b1; 1347–1348

12. *But this contrariety is not on the part of the reason itself but is incidental. It is appetite and not judgment which is in opposition to right reason. Because of this, dumb animals are not said to be incontinent since they do not have universal judgment but only imagination and memory of particulars.*

1147b1–5; 1349–1350

13, *How this ignorance is dissipated and an incontinent man recovers correct knowledge is the same problem in the case of one inebriated or asleep. This, however, is not properly our problem but ought to be solved by physiologists.*

1147b6–9; 1351

14. *But the ultimate proposition is a judgment according to sensible knowledge, and is directive of our actions; and the man who is under the influence of passion does not have this judgment at all, or has it in such a way that he cannot know actually, but speaks in these matters the way a drunken man repeats the words of Empedocles. Since the ultimate term is neither a universal nor—what amounts to the same thing—an object of scientific knowledge in the manner of a universal (in the practical order), what Socrates was looking for seems to follow. Indeed passion is not present with knowledge taken in the proper sense; and it is not this knowledge but that of the sensible which is dragged along by passion. We have discussed whether a person when he acts incontinently has knowledge or not, and how it is possible for him to have knowledge.*

1147b9–19; 1352–1353

COMMENTARY OF ST. THOMAS

1328. After the Philosopher has stated certain probable propositions and raised doubts about each, he now comes to the solutions. We should note he does not present the solutions in the same order in which he previously either stated the propositions or introduced the doubts, but according as the plan of the discussion requires, i.e., as the solution of one doubt depends on another. First [1] he states his intention; and then [2I], at "In the beginning etc.," he carries out his intention. He says first that, in order to solve these doubts, we must consider at the outset whether or not some people can be incontinent knowingly; and if so, in what way they know. This doubt is solved first because its solution belongs to the question whether or not there is incontinence. We stated previously (1315) that Socrates' contention seemed to be that there was no incontinence. But first we must consider whether each (continence and incontinence) exists.

1329. Then we must consider in what kinds of matter we ought to say a man is continent or incontinent; whether in every form of pleasure and pain or only in some specific forms. This doubt is solved in the second place, although it was proposed in the sixth place (1325), because the beginning of an investigation of the nature of any habit is the consideration of its matter, as is obvious in the manner of procedure followed by Aristotle in the preceding discussions. Since the continent man and the persevering man differ materially, we must ask at the same time whether they differ conceptually. Likewise, we must give our attention to all other matters having a connection and agreement with this consideration.

1330. Next [2], at "In the beginning," he begins to solve the doubts previously raised. First [2] he settles the question on the existence of continence and incontinence by solving the first doubt that was raised about the third probable statement. Second [Lect. IV], he determines the matter of continence and incontinence by solving the sixth doubt that was raised about the sixth probable statement.

Then, because temperance and continence agree in matter, at the same time he here explains the difference between temperance and continence in solving the third doubt that was raised about the fourth probable statement. Likewise he shows whether the intemperate or the incontinent man is worse, in solving the fifth doubt that was raised about the first probable statement. This second part begins at "Now, we must consider etc." (1147b20).

1331. Third [Lect. IX] he explains the nature of continence and incontinence in solving the fourth doubt that was raised against the second probable statement. Likewise, with this he answers the second question that was asked about the fifth probable statement, showing that a prudent man cannot be incontinent. This third part begins at "Can a man be called etc." (1151a29). On the first point he does three things. First [2] he presents in advance certain notions which are necessary for a solution. Then [5], at "It makes no difference etc.," he rejects a false solution. Third [6], at "Since we say etc.," he gives the true solution. In regard to the initial point he does two things. First [2] he states his intention, and then [4] at "Neither is a man etc.," he carries it out.

1332. He says first [2] that to determine these questions our primary effort must be directed towards the knowledge of two points. The first point is whether the continent and the incontinent differ specifically in their subject, i.e., in having limited matter with which they are concerned, as mildness differs specifically from the fact that it has to do with anger; or also in the manner, i.e., in the way of dealing with any matter, as prudence deals with all moral matter but not in the same way as (other) moral virtues.

1333. In explanation of his inquiry, he adds that we must consider whether a man may be called incontinent only because he is concerned with a particular matter, or even only because he is concerned about the whole of some matter without distinction; or whether a man may be called continent or incontinent not only from the one or the other but also from both, i.e., from a limited manner and a limited matter.

1334. Another thing that we ought to consider beforehand is whether or not continence and incontinence deal with all kinds of matter or with a limited matter.

1335. Then [3], at "**Incontinence in the unqualified sense,**" he determines his statements: first [3] the second statement, saying that continent and incontinent in the unqualified sense are not applied to anyone in all matters but in that limited matter in which he is temperate or intemperate, viz., in concupiscence and pleasures of touch.

1336. Second [4], at "**Neither is a man,**" he determines the first statement, saying that someone is said to be continent or incontinent not alone in this, i.e., in respect of some limited matter (for thus he would be identified with the temperate or intemperate man since they deal with the same matter), but a person is said to be incontinent in conducting himself in such a manner, i.e., from the fact that he is concerned with limited matter in a certain way. The reason is that this man, viz., the intemperate, is led to commit sin by choice, in a manner judging that a pleasurable object presented to him always is to be pursued or accepted. But the incontinent man does not engage in this reasoning process; nevertheless, he pursues the pleasurable object when it is present to him.

1337. Next [5], at "**It makes no dif-**

ference," he rejects a false solution that he has already treated (1316). He states that it does not make any difference in the present argument to say that the cognition, contrary to which some act incontinently, is real opinion but not knowledge. The fact is clear that some who act incontinently do not have a weak conviction, like people hesitating, but judge themselves to know certainly that against which they act. If then someone means that they are men with opinion rather than knowledge acting contrary to their convictions because their adherence to their judgments is ineffectual and feeble, our observation is that in the present instance knowledge does not differ from opinion. Some people are not less tenacious of even false opinions than others are of true knowledge. This can be seen in Heraclitus, who was so firmly convinced that everything is in perpetual motion and that no truth remains long in things, that at the end of his life, he was unwilling to talk lest truth should be changed in the meantime, but only wagged his finger to indicate something as is related in the fourth book of the Metaphysics (Ch. 5, 1010 a 12–13; St. Th. Lect. XII, 683–684).

1338. At "**Since we say**" [6] he gives the true solution. First [6] he solves the doubt by some distinctions, then [10], at "Furthermore etc.," by the nature of practical science. In regard to the first point he makes two distinctions. The first [6] is that we say a man knows in two ways: (1) by having a habit he does not use, e.g., the geometrician not studying questions of geometry; (2) by using his knowledge in actually considering its truths. It makes a big difference whether someone doing what he ought not has the habit but does not use it, or has the habit and does use it in thinking. It certainly seems hard for a man to act contrary to what he is actually considering. But it doesn't seem hard for someone to act contrary to what he knows in an habitual way but is not actually considering.

1339. Next [7], at "**Yet, since,**" he makes his second distinction. He says, since practical reason uses two modes of propositions, viz., the universal and the particular, there is no apparent obstacle in a man knowing both propositions in an habitual way but actually considering only the universal and not the particular, and operating contrary to the knowledge. This is so because operations are concerned with particulars. Hence, if a man does not consider the particular it is not astonishing that he acts contrary to it.

1340. We should note, however, that the universal can be taken in two ways. In one way as it is in itself, as in the example "Dry things are good for every man"; in another way as it is in a particular object, for instance, "This is a man," or "That food is dry." Therefore it is possible that a man knows, both habitually and actually, the universal considered in itself but either he does not grasp the universal considered in this particular object, i.e., the universal is not known in an habitual way, or he does not bestir himself, i.e., the universal is not actually known.

1341. Therefore what appeared impossible to Socrates according to these various modes of knowing differs so much that it does not seem unreasonable for a man, who acts incontinently, to have one kind of knowledge, viz., universal alone or even particular—if it is habitual but not actual. But it would seem unreasonable for the man who acts incontinently to have another kind of knowledge, i.e., actual, concerned with the particular.

1342. Then [8], at "**In addition,**" he

makes a third distinction. First [8] he sets forth a difference. Next [9], at "The use of learned terms etc.," he refutes an objection. First he speaks of another mode of knowing in man, over and above the modes discussed. That someone should know by way of habit and not by way of act seems to be understood differently. Sometimes a habit is so responsive that it can go into act immediately when a man wishes. But other times the habit is so bound that it cannot go into act. Hence in one sense a man seems to have a habit and in another sense not to have it, as is evident in one sleeping, a maniac, or a drunkard. Men are disposed in this way when under the influence of the passions. We see anger, sexual desires, and certain passions of this kind obviously change the body externally, for example, in causing body heat. Sometimes such passions generate so much heat that they lead people to insanity. So, obviously, the incontinent are disposed somewhat like those asleep, maniacs, and drunkards, who have the habit of practical science impeded in regard to particulars.

1343. At "**The use of learned terms**" [9] he refutes an objection. Someone could object against the statement made that the incontinent sometimes use terms dealing with knowledge and with the particular. So it seems they do not have a habit that is held in check. But Aristotle refutes this objection, saying that their use of scientific terminology is not a sign that they have an active habit; and he illustrates this by two examples.

1344. The first is that even men who are under the influence of the passions just mentioned, e.g., inebriated and demented, mouth demonstrations in geometry, for instance, and declaim Empedocles' sayings, which are difficult to understand because he wrote his philosophy in meter. The second example is of children who, when they begin to learn, put together words that they utter without any real understanding of what they say. To understand, it is necessary that those things that a man hears become, as it were, connatural to him in order that they may be impressed perfectly on his mind. For this a man needs time in which his intellect may be confirmed in what it has received, by much meditation. This is true also of the incontinent man, for even if he says: it is not good for me now to pursue such a pleasure, nevertheless, in his heart he does not think this way. So then we must judge the incontinent in saying these words are pretending, as it were, because they think one thing in their hearts and reveal another by their words.

1345. Next [10], at "**Furthermore,**" he solves the proposed doubt by the natural process of practical science in applying the preceding distinctions to what he proposed. First [10] he determines the true sense of the question. Second [14], at "But the ultimate," he answers Socrates' objection. Regarding the initial point he does two things. First [10] he sets forth the natural process of practical science in action. Second [11], at "Now one universal," he shows the obstacle which faces the incontinent man. He says first that if we wish to consider why the incontinent man can act contrary to his knowledge by the natural process of practical science, we must take into consideration the two judgments in this process. One is universal, for example, "Every dishonorable act must be avoided"; the other, singular, is concerned with objects which properly are known by sense, for instance, "This act is dishonorable." But, since there is one formal-

ity underlying these judgments, a conclusion necessarily follows.

1346. However, in speculative matters the mind merely draws the conclusion, while in practical matters it goes into operation immediately. Thus, if the universal judgment is that we must taste every sweet thing but the particular judgment that this (some particular object presented) is sweet, the man able to taste immediately tastes if nothing prevents. So runs the syllogism of the temperate man who does not permit concupiscence to have mastery over reason pointing out every dishonorable act must be avoided. The same goes for the syllogism of the intemperate man. His reason does not resist the proposal of concupiscence which inclines to this: that every pleasure is to be seized.

1347. Then [11], at "**Now one universal,**" he explains how fault occurs in the incontinent man. First [11] he shows that there is a restraining factor in this man. Next [12], at "But this contrariety," he explains the reason. Last [13], at "How this ignorance etc.," he explains how this restraint ceases. On the first point the proper consideration is this—reason in the incontinent man is not so completely overcome that he is without genuine knowledge of the universal. Put it this way. The reason proposes a universal judgment forbidding an inordinate tasting of something sweet, e.g., it says that nothing sweet should be tasted outside a certain time. But the appetite proposes that every sweet thing is pleasant, something in itself desired by concupiscence. And, since in a particular case concupiscence may bind reason, the proposal is not accepted under universal reason so as to say also that this is outside the time; but it is taken under the universal aspect of concupiscence so as to say this is sweet. So the conclusion of the operation follows. In this syllogism of the incontinent man there are four propositions, as already indicated (1346).

1348. That the process of practical reason sometimes occurs in this way is evident from the fact that when concupiscence waxes strong, reason declares by a universal judgment that a particular desirable thing is to be avoided, as we just mentioned (1347). But concupiscence inclines to the appetible object by freely proposing and accepting it without the prohibition of reason, now rendered impotent. Concupiscence can be so vehement it can sway any part of the soul, even reason itself if reason does not make a strong effort to resist. Thus the term of the operation takes place, viz., a man may act incontinently contrary to reason and universal judgment.

1349. At "But this contrariety" [12] he explains the reason for this opposition. He states that the present contrariety does not happen from reason itself, as in uncertain people, but only incidentally so far as concupiscence is opposed to correct universal reason. In fact there is no judgment in itself opposed to right reason, as some philosophers have maintained.

1350. From this he infers a corollary, that dumb animals are not called continent or incontinent, for they do not make a universal judgment which is the foundation of rational action, to which concupiscence is opposed; for brutes are moved only by imagination and memory of particulars.

1351. Next [13], at "How this ignorance," he explains how this opposition ceases. He says that the problem of dissipating an incontinent man's ignorance about the particular and of his recovery of correct knowledge is the same as in the case of one inebriated or asleep. Their passions are dispelled when some bodily change occurs. Likewise, since the body is changed by the soul's passions, like concupiscence and anger, this physical change must cease for a man to return to a sound mind. Hence this problem is not proper to our investigation but rather we ought to hear it discussed by physiologists, i.e., physicians (*naturalibus*).

1352. Then [14], at "But the ultimate," in accord with the premises he refutes the argument of Socrates, saying that the proposition and the ultimate, i.e., the particular, judgment is made according to sensible knowledge and is directive of actions concerned with particulars. But a man under the influence of passion either does not have this judgment or premise at all as a habit, or has a restrained habit so that he cannot know actually but speaks in these matters in the way that an inebriate repeats the verses of Empedocles. Since, then, these things are true, and since the universal, which is known by science, is not the ultimate term of practical operations, what Socrates held seems to follow. It is evident from previous statements that passion is not present with the principal knowledge that deals with the universal, since it is found only in the particular. It is not the knowledge of the universal but only the evaluation of the sensible, which is not so excellent, that is dragged along by passion.

1353. Finally, he summarizes the questions discussed: whether a person when he acts incontinently has knowledge or not, and how it is possible for him to have knowledge.

LECTURE IV
The Generic Matter of Continence and Incontinence

TEXT OF ARISTOTLE (*1147b20–1148b14*) Chapter 4

1. Now we must consider further whether anyone is totally incontinent, or whether everyone is said to be incontinent in a particular way. If totally so, then in what kind of matter is a man thus incontinent. **1147b20–21; 1354**

2. It is obvious that the continent and the persevering, the incontinent and the effeminate are concerned with pleasure and pain. **1147b21–23; 1355**

3. But of the objects that give men pleasure some are necessary; others are desirable in themselves, although capable of excess. I call necessary certain material things concerned with food, sex, and other physical goods that we previously established as the matter of temperance and intemperance. I mention as unnecessary, but desirable in themselves, things like victory, honor, riches, and other pleasurable goods of this kind. **1147b23–31; 1356–1357**

4. Therefore, people who go to excess in these things contrary to right reason in them, are not called incontinent simply but with the added note that they are incontinent in matters of money, gain, honor, or anger; as if there were others absolutely incontinent and the former are called incontinent by way of resemblance. Thus when we speak of "man" who was the victor in the Olympics, the common notion of man differed little from the notion of this individual man but it was different. In confirmation of our contention, incontinence is censured not merely as a sin but as a kind of vice either in the full sense or the partial sense. But none of those previously discussed are viciously incontinent. **1147b31–1148a4; 1358–1359**

5. But men who behave badly in physical pleasures, with which the temperate and the intemperate are concerned, and freely pursue excessive pleasures while avoiding discomforts, like hunger and thirst, heat and cold, and so forth pertaining to touch and taste, but contrary to right choice and right reason, are called incontinent not in any limited way, as the incontinent in the matter of anger, but absolutely speaking. Confirmation of this is found in the fact that people are called effeminate in reference to these discomforts but not in reference to others. **1148a4–13; 1360**

6. For this reason we place the incontinent and intemperate, the continent and temperate in the same classification; not that one is the other but because they are concerned with pleasures and pain in some measure, yet not in the same way. Some act from deliberate choice, others without it. **1148a13–17; 1361**

7. Consequently, we say the intemperate person is more blamable than another who sins from violent passion, because the intemperate man pursues excesses and avoids discomforts without passion, or at least only with mild passion. **1148a17–22; 1362**

8. Some kinds of desires and pleasures are in the category of the noble and good. (Some pleasures are by nature desirable; others, just the reverse; and still others are in between, according to the previous division, as in the case of money, profit, victory, and honor.) But in all the intermediate kinds, people are not blamed because they are affected by a desire and love for these things but rather because their desire is excessive in some way. **1148a22–28; 1363–1364**

9. Hence, those who in an unreasonable manner possess or pursue any of the things that are noble and good by nature, for example, people having more zeal than they should about the acquisition of honor, or the care of their children or parents (are not blamed as evil). Certainly these operations are good, and people solicitous about them are praised. However, a kind of vicious excess can exist in these matters, for example, if someone should rebel against the gods as Niobe did, or should act towards his parents as did Satyrus called "father-lover," who seemed to have behaved rather foolishly in this matter. **1148a28–1148b2; 1365**

10. *So then there is no vice in these pleasures because, as was said, each of them is naturally desirable in itself; only their excesses are evil and to be avoided. Likewise there is no incontinence in them, for incontinence not only is a thing to be avoided but is something censurable.*   **1148b2–6; 1366**

11. *But people speak according as there a resemblance to passion, putting limits on incontinence about each thing, for example, a bad doctor or a poor actor whom they would (not) term a bad person without qualification. The same goes for the things called bad in this way, because badness is predicated of any of them only in an analogous sense. So in regard to continence we must judge that only to be incontinence and continence (unqualifiedly) which concerns the same matters as temperance and intemperance. But we predicate incontinence of anger because of a resemblance, and for this reason we qualify, adding that a man is incontinent in anger as we say he is incontinent in honor and gain.*   **1148b6–14; 1367**

COMMENTARY OF ST. THOMAS

1354. After the Philosopher has shown that a man can perform evil actions contrary to the knowledge he possesses (by this we can know whether continence and incontinence exist), he here determines the matter of continence and incontinence. First he shows the matter of each; then [Lect. VII], at "Continence and incontinence etc." (1150a9), he compares them with other habits dealing with the same matter. To clarify the first point he employs a twofold procedure. First [1] he declares his proposition. Second [2], at "It is obvious etc.," he carries out his proposition. The reasoning employed is this: in proposing the sixth doubt, it was already stated that if continence and incontinence were concerned with all matters, no one would be incontinent in an unqualified sense. So, in an effort to solve this doubt, he presents two questions for consideration. The first is: can anyone be incontinent without qualification or is everyone said to be incontinent in a particular way? The second question is, if a man is totally incontinent, in what kind of matter is he so incontinent?

1355. Then [2], at "It is obvious," he carries out his proposition. First [2] he presents the general matter, saying it is evident that the continent and the in-

continent and the persevering and the effeminate are said to be concerned with pleasure and pain.

1356. Next [3], at "But of the objects," he investigates the specific matter of these states. First [3] he shows how continence may be used in different ways about different pleasures. Second [Lect. VI], at "Now we will consider," he compares the kinds of incontinence in different pleasures with one another (1149a24). On the initial point he does two things. First [3] he shows how a man may be called continent or incontinent in different ways according to the difference in human pleasures among themselves; then according to the difference of human pleasures with regard to what is bestial [Lect. V] at "Of natural pleasures etc." (1148b15). In support of the first statement he uses a double process. First [3] he explains his proposition. Second [8], at "Some kinds etc.," he clarifies some statements he had made. The first point demands three clarifications. First [3] he distinguishes human pleasures. Next [4], at "Therefore, people etc.," he shows how in these pleasures a man is called continent or incontinent in different ways. Last [6], at "For this reason," he infers certain corollaries from the premises.

1357. He says first of all that, of those objects giving us pleasure, some are necessary for human life; others are unnecessary but, considered in themselves, desirable for men, however much they are capable of excess and defect. He designates as necessary certain bodily requirements such as those pertaining to food, drink, sex, and material things of this kind, which we previously established as the matter of temperance and intemperance (267, 595, 599, 603). But things desirable in themselves, which he mentions as unnecessary, are victory, honor, riches, and other goods and pleasures of the same kind.

1358. At "**Therefore, people**" [4], he shows in what way a man may be called continent or incontinent in regard to these things: first [4] concerning the unnecessary, and second [5], at "But men who etc.," concerning the necessary. His first remark is that people who go to excess in their pursuit of those unnecessary things in them that are contrary to right reason are not called simply incontinent but with a limitation, for example, incontinent in the matter of money, gain, honor, or anger, as if there were others absolutely incontinent. The former are called incontinent by way of likeness that the addition indicates; thus, when we say "man" the victor in the Olympics, the common notion of man differs little from the proper notion which this addition signifies, although it is different in some way.

1359. As an indication that a man may not be called incontinent without qualification in these matters, he remarks that incontinence is censured not only as a sin that someone can commit even in pursuing what is good though in an inordinate manner; but incontinence is censured as a kind of vice by which we tend to some evil. There is vice either in the complete sense, e.g., when the reason and the appetitive faculty aim at evil (this is the real vice that is contrary to virtue) or in an incomplete sense, e.g., when the appetitive faculty, but not the reason, tends to evil, which occurs in incontinence (proper). But none of the incontinent previously mentioned are censured as wicked but only as sinners because they strive for good, but beyond what is proper. Hence none of them is incontinent without qualification.

1360. Then [5], at "**But men who,**" he shows how someone is called incontinent in regard to necessary things. He observes that men who behave badly in the matter of physical pleasures, with which temperance and intemperance deal, not in such a way that by deliberate choice they pursue excessive pleasures and avoid discomforts, e.g., hunger and thirst and suchlike pertaining to taste and touch—but so that they pursue these things contrary to the right reason in themselves; men of this kind, I say, are called incontinent not with some limitation like the incontinent in regard to anger but without qualification. He also offers confirmation of this by the fact that people are called effeminate—closely related to the incontinent—in reference to such discomforts, for instance, because they cannot undergo hunger or thirst or anything of this type, but not in reference to other things, for example, because they cannot bear poverty and suchlike.

1361. Next [6], at "**For this reason,**" he infers certain corollaries from the premises. The first [6] is that incontinent and intemperate, continent and temperate are placed in the same classification, not in the sense that one of them is the other, but because in some measure they deal with the same things, viz., bodily pleasures and pains, yet not in the same way, for the temperate and intemperate act with deliberate choice while the continent and incontinent act without it.

1362. The second [7], which follows from the first, he sets forth at "**Consequently.**" He says that, from the discussions, obviously the intemperate man is the greater sinner and to be censured because he sins more in pursuing superfluous pleasures and avoiding slight discomforts when he does not feel passion at all or feels it only gently, i.e., mildly. For this reason he is worse than a man like the incontinent fellow, who sins in these matters from violent passion. What would a man do who sins without passion, if he were to experience the vehement desires of youth and the serious discomforts arising from the lack of necessities?

1363. At "**Some kinds**" [8] he clarifies what he had said, assigning reasons why there is no incontinence without qualification in the case of unnecessary things. First [8] he shows why such must be the case. Then [11], at "But people speak etc.," he shows why only limited incontinence is predicated of such people. On the initial point he makes three observations. First [8] he points out what kinds of unnecessary pleasures there are. Next [9], at "Hence, those who etc.," he infers what kind of desire is aroused for these pleasures. Third [10], at "So then there is etc.," he further infers that there is neither vice nor total incontinence in regard to them. He shows first that some species of desires and pleasures concern things that are good and praiseworthy in themselves.

1364. There are three kinds of pleas-ures. Some, to which nature inclines, are desirable by nature. Others are just the reverse, for example, those contrary to the natural inclination. Still others are midway between, witness the case of money and gain, victory and honor. Hence, in those of the middle kind, people are not blamed because they are affected by a desire and love for these things but because they desire them in an excessive manner.

1365. Next [9], at "**Hence, those who,**" he infers from the premises what kind of desire people have for these last types of pleasures. He remarks that those who, contrary to reason, possess or pursue any of the things that are noble and good by nature are not blamed as evil, for instance, people who are more zealous than they should be about honor or about the care of their children or parents. Certainly these operations are good, and men who are properly diligent about them are praised; nevertheless a kind of vicious excess can exist in such matters. Thus if a woman should rebel against God because of excessive love of her children, for example, in the event of their death, as we read of a woman named Niobe; or if a man should do something foolish out of immoderate love of a parent, as a certain Satyrus called philopater or "father-lover" seemed to act very foolishly because of the love he had for his father.

1366. Then [10], at "**So then there is,**" he infers that there is no vice in these pleasures because each of them considered in itself is naturally desirable while only excesses in them are evil and to be avoided. Likewise there is no complete incontinence in these pleasures, because incontinence not only is a thing to be avoided as a sin but is something censurable as being disgraceful. Therefore it is with bodily pleasures, which are disgraceful and servile as was said in book the third (612), that continence is properly concerned. Nor are pleasures of this kind to be desired by men except on account of necessity.

1367. At "**But people speak**" [11] he shows why partial incontinence should be predicated of unnecessary pleasures. He say this happens because of some likeness in passion: as someone has an immoderate passion for bodily pleasures, so too for money and other objects previously mentioned. There is a parallel case when we say a man is a bad doctor or a poor mimic, i.e., actor, who nevertheless is not called simply bad. So then in the things that are called bad in this way, we do not predicate badness of any of them in an unqualified sense but according to a proportionate likeness, because as a bad doctor is compared to what a doctor ought to be so a bad man is compared to what a man ought to be. Likewise in the genus of continence we call that continence and incontinence without qualification which is concerned with the same matters as temperance and intemperance. But with respect to anger we predicate incontinence by similitude, and hence say a man is incontinent in the matter of anger, as we say he is incontinent in the matter of honor or gain.

LECTURE V
Kinds of Pleasure

TEXT OF ARISTOTLE (*1148b15–1149a24*) Chapter 5

1. *Of natural pleasures, some are delightful to every taste, others to different classes of men and animals of the pleasures that are not natural, some become delightful because of sickness or privations, others because of customs or vicious natures. And to each of these pleasures there will be a corresponding habit.*   **1148b15–19; 1368–1371**

2. *I call bestial the pleasure of the man who is said to have slit pregnant women so he could devour the fetuses; of anyone who delights in the brutish practices ascribed to certain savages near the Black Sea: some of whom eat raw meat, others human flesh, and still others, one another's children at their feasts; or Phalaris, according to what is related of him. Men delighting in such pleasures are like beasts.*   **1148b19–24; 1372**

3. *But some people become bestial because of particular ailments, for example, insanity. Laboring under this affliction one man sacrificed his mother and ate her, another murdered his fellow slave and ate his liver. These persons are pathological.*   **1148b25–27; 1373**

4. *Others become bestial because of habit, for instance, certain men who take pleasure in plucking out their hair, biting their nails, eating coal and earth, and having sexual intercourse with males. People act in these ways from the condition of their bodily temperament, or from usage to which they have become accustomed since childhood.*   **1148b27–31; 1374**

5. *No one would accuse of (unqualified) incontinence those in whom nature is the cause of these pleasures, as is the case with women who do not govern their emotions but are governed by them. The same, too, may be said of people who are morbid because of bad habits.*
1148b31–34; 1375–1376

6. *To experience desires for these pleasures exceeds the limits of human vice, as brutishness was said to do.*   **1148b34–1149a1; 1377**

7. *If anyone has the desires and overcomes them or is overcome by them, he is not called continent or incontinent simply but in virtue of a resemblance. It was in this way that we spoke about one having the passion of anger, viz., that he must be called incontinent in part.*
1149a1–4; 1378

8. *Every excess of vice, for example, folly, timidity, intemperance, and harshness is either brutish or caused by sickness.*   **1149a4–7; 1379**

9. *Someone who is so inclined by nature that he fears everything, even the squeak of a mouse, has the timidity of a dumb beast; and the individual who was afraid of a ferret had a pathological condition.*   **1149a7–9; 1380**

10. *Certain silly people are irrational by nature and, living according to the senses, become brutish like the barbarous tribes of distant regions. Others are irrational because of sickness like epilepsy or insanity, and are silly by reason of disease.*   **1149a9–12; 1381**

11. *Sometimes a man may experience these passions but not be overcome, for instance, if Phalaris had kept a boy, desiring to use him for food or unseemly sexual pleasure. At other times a man may not only experience the passions but be overcome by them.*   **1149a12–16; 1382**

12. *As vice which is according to the human mode is called vice without qualification but that which is described as brutish or pathological is termed vice only in the qualified sense, so in the same way we may speak of incontinence, either brutish or pathological, in the limited sense or incontinence according to the human mode only in the unqualified sense. It is obvious then that only (complete) continence and incontinence treat the matters dealt with by temperance and intemperance, and that a different kind of incontinence in a transferred and not the absolute sense is concerned with other matters.*   **1149a16–24; 1383–1384**

COMMENTARY OF ST. THOMAS

1368. After the Philosopher has explained that a man is called continent and incontinent in different ways according to the different human passions and pleasures, he here [1] explains that a man is said to be continent or incontinent in different senses according as his passions and pleasures are human or brutish. On this point he does two things. First [1] he shows among the different kinds of passion and pleasure which are human and which, brutish. Next [5], at "No one would etc.," he shows how continence and incontinence are attributed in a different sense to these (passions and pleasures). The initial point he develops in two stages. First [1] he distinguishes pleasures. Then [2], at "I call bestial etc.," he clarifies his statement by examples. He says first that some pleasures are according to nature, others are not according to nature; and each group is subdivided.

1369. Of the pleasures that are natural, some are delightful to every creature with senses, for example, sweet is naturally pleasing to all who have the sense of taste. Others are naturally delightful to certain classes of animals and men. Some foods are by their nature pleasant to carnivorous animals, others to herbivorous animals. Likewise, among men, cold foods that moderate the temperament are delightful to the choleric, but warm foods are agreeable to the phlegmatic.

1370. Of the unnatural pleasures, some become delightful because of privation, i.e., on account of some supervenient sickness of the body or sadness of soul by which the nature is changed into a different condition. Others become delightful because of evil habit which brings about a quasi-nature. Still others become delightful because of vicious natures, as happens when people have corrupt and perverse bodily temperaments; and, accordingly both the perceptions of their imagination and the affections of their sensitive appetite are most perverse. Likewise, since these powers are acts of bodily organs, they are necessarily proportionate to the temperament of the body.

1371. Because habits are diversified by a complete distinction of objects, corresponding habits will answer to these individual pleasures under discussion; thus some habits will be natural and others unnatural.

1372. Next [2], at "**I call bestial the pleasure etc.**," he exemplifies individually the different kinds of unnatural pleasures; and first [2] those which are delightful because of the malignant nature of men who are, so to speak, bestial since they are like beasts by reason of a corrupt temperament. There is a story about one man who slit the wombs of pregnant women so he could devour the fetuses. Equally horrible are those who delight in practices of the kind reported of certain savages living in the forest near the Black Sea. Some eat raw meat, others human flesh; still others offer one another their children to be food for their feasts. Similar things are narrated about one Phalaris, a most cruel tyrant, who took pleasure in torturing men. Therefore, people who delight in deeds of this kind are, as it were, like beasts.

1373. Second [3], at "**But some people,**" he exemplifies things that become delightful and are contrary to nature because of particular ailments, for example, insanity or madness or something of this sort. There is a story about one man who on becoming insane sacrificed his mother and ate her; still another who murdered his fellow slave and ate his liver.

1374. Last [4], at "**Others become,**" he offers examples of things contrary to nature that become delightful by reason of habit. Some enjoy unnatural pleasures because of mental unbalance or habitual perversion. For example, certain men out of habit take pleasure in pulling out their hair, biting their nails, eating coal and earth, and having sexual intercourse with males. All the preceding can be reduced to two classes. Some people do them because of the tendency of bodily temperament that they had from the beginning; others because of habit, becoming accustomed to things of this kind from childhood. Such people are like individuals who fall into this condition by reason of physical sickness, for evil habit is a kind of psychological sickness.

1375. Then [5], at "**No one would,**" he shows that these unnatural pleasures do not dispose to incontinence simply but only in a qualified sense. He does this in two ways; first [5] by a reason taken from the disposition of those who enjoy the pleasures; second [6] by a reason taken from the nature of the pleasures, at "To experience etc." He says first that no one will accuse of unqualified incontinence men whose bestial nature is the reason for such pleasures. We have already said (1350) that dumb animals are not referred to as continent or incontinent since they exercise no universal judgment but only imagination and memory of particulars. But these men who, by reason of a malignant nature, are like wild beasts indeed do have some, although very little, universal perception, reason in them being weighed down by bad temperament, as is obviously the case

with those physically sick. But what is very little seems to be as nothing. Nor is it likely that the force of a weak argument should repel strong desires. Consequently, these individuals are not called incontinent or continent simply but only in a restricted sense, insofar as some judgment of reason remains with them.

1376. He offers the example of women in whom, for the most part, reason flourishes very little because of the imperfect nature of their body. Because of this they do not govern their emotions in the majority of cases by reason but rather are governed by their emotions. Hence wise and brave women are rarely found, and so women cannot be called continent and incontinent without qualification. The same argument seems valid for those who are ill, i.e., have a diseased temperament because of bad habits, which oppresses the judgment of reason after the manner of a perverse nature.

1377. Next [6], at "**To experience,**" he shows from the very nature of unnatural pleasures that there is no incontinence in the unqualified sense but only in a limited sense. He states his proposition [6], then [8], at "Every excess of vice etc.," he explains it. First [6] he proposes two things. The first is that to experience desires for these pleasures exceeds the limits of human vice, as was previously said also about brutishness (1296, 1299).

1378. The second [7] he proposes at "**If anyone,**" saying that if anyone should have these desires and overcome them, he will be called continent not simply but by reason of some resemblance to virtuous restraint. Or if he should be overcome by them, he will be called incontinent not simply but by way of a resemblance to complete incontinence. In this fashion we poke before on incontinence in regard o anger (1367).

1379. At "**Every excess of vice**" [8] he explains his statement. First [8] he does so in regard to vice; then [11], at "Sometimes a man etc.," in regard to ontinence and incontinence. On the first point we must consider [8] that such an excess of vice can concern vices opposed to all virtues, for example, folly opposed to prudence, timidity opposed to fortitude, intemperance opposed to temperance, and harshness opposed to gentleness; and it can concern each one of the vices, for some of them are brutish habits arising from a malignant nature, others are diseased habits arising from physical or psychological sickness, i.e., a bad habit. Since he has already given examples of intemperance and harshness, he now first exemplifies timidity.

1380. He does this at "**Someone**" [9], saying that temperament may be so timid as to make some afraid of anything, even the squeak of a mouse. This is the timidity of a dumb animal. One man became so fearful from a pathological condition that he was afraid of a ferret.

1381. Then [10], at "**Certain silly people**," he gives examples of folly of some individuals irrational by nature, not because they have no reason but in fact very little, and this much concerned with particulars perceived by sense, so they live only according to the senses. Such individuals are—so to speak—brutish by nature. This happens especially to barbarians living at the ends of the earth, where from unhealthiness of the climate the bodies of the natives are likewise unhealthy, impeding the use of reason. Other people

become irrational because of some sickness like epilepsy or insanity; and these are stupid because of disease.

1382. Next [11], at "**Sometimes a man**," he explains his statement in regard to incontinence. First [11] in what way continence and incontinence resemble the preceding vices. He remarks that a man may at times experience something of these unnatural passions and not be overcome by them, and this looks like continence. This would be the case if the tyrant Phalaris should keep a boy, wanting to use him either for food or unnatural pleasure, but nevertheless actually would not use him. At other times a man may not only experience desires of this kind but also be overcome by them; and this resembles incontinence.

1383. Then [12], at "**As vice**," he shows that in matters of this sort there is no complete continence or incontinence. He says that as vice according to the human mode is called unqualified vice but that which is humanly unnatural is called brutish or pathological vice, and not in the unqualified sense; so in the same way incontinence that is unnatural is predicated with some limitation, like bestial or pathological, but only incontinence according to human mode is called unqualified incontinence.

1384. Finally, in summary, he concludes it is evident from our discussion that only unqualified continence and incontinence treat those matters dealt with by temperance and intemperance, while some kind of incontinence predicated in a transferred rather than in the absolute way is concerned with other matters.

LECTURE VI
Comparison of Different Kinds of Incontinence

TEXT OF ARISTOTLE (*1149a24–1150a8*) Chapter 6

1. Now we will consider that incontinence in the matter of anger is less disgraceful than incontinence in pleasure.   **1149a24–25; 1385**

2. Anger seems to listen to reason to some extent but to hear badly, like hasty servants who hurry off before understanding instructions and then make mistakes in performing them, and again like dogs barking at the first knock before knowing if a friend is coming. Anger listens in this way but, because of the heat and impulsiveness of its nature, moves to inflict punishment without heeding the injunction of reason. When reason or imagination shows a man that he has suffered injury or contempt, he concludes he ought to attack the one who injured him, and immediately becomes angry. But desire, as soon as reason or sense declares a thing delightful, proceeds to enjoy the pleasure. In this respect anger follows reason in some measure, but not so desire, which is thus more disgraceful. Indeed the man incontinent in anger is prevailed upon to a degree by reason but this is not so of one incontinent in sensual desire.   **1149a25–1149b3; 1386–1389**

3. Moreover, a man apparently deserves more pardon for sins about naturally desirable things, because tolerance is more readily extended towards such desires common to all, precisely because they are common. But anger is more natural and more difficult to resist than the desires for excessive and unnecessary pleasures, as is evident in the following examples. A certain man reprimanded for striking his father answered that the father had struck his own father who in turn had struck his father; then pointing to his son he said: "This boy will strike me when he becomes a man, for it is a family trait." Another man, when dragged along by his son, bade the son stop at the doorway, as he himself had dragged his own father only that far.   **1149b4–13; 1390–1392**

4. Again, double dealing sinners are more unjust. Now the angry man does not act deceitfully but openly, nor does anger flare up secretly. On the other hand desire acts like Venus who is called the deceitful daughter of Cyprus and is said to wear a multicolored girdle; of her Homer relates that she craftily steals the wits of the wisest man. Therefore, incontinence of this kind is more unjust and disgraceful than incontinence of anger; it is incontinence in the unqualified sense and is to some extent a vice.   **1149b13–20; 1393–1395**

5. In addition, no one feels sad doing an injury. But what anyone does in anger he does with a feeling of sadness, while the one doing injury acts with pleasure. If then the more unjust things are those against which we are justly very angry, it follows that incontinence arising from sensual desire is more unjust, because no injury is involved in the anger. Therefore it is evident that incontinence concerning sensual desires is more disgraceful than that which concerns anger, and that continence and incontinence in the unqualified sense deal with sensual desires and bodily pleasures.   **1149b20–26; 1396–1397**

6. But we must take up again their differences. As we said in the beginning, some are human and natural both in kind and amount, and others are brutish either as a result of inordinate passion or a pathological condition.   **1149b26–30; 1398**

7. Yet with only the first of these do temperance and intemperance deal. For this reason we do not call dumb animals temperate or intemperate in the proper sense; we do say, in comparing one animal with another, that one species differs from another in uncleanness, in stupidity, or in voraciousness, but this is a figurative way of speaking, for none of them have choice or reason; they are creatures separated from reason as insane men are.   **1149b30–1150a1; 1399–1400**

8. *However, brutishness has less the nature of vice (but is more frightful) for what is best has not been corrupted as in an evil man—it is not present to be corrupt. Therefore, making a comparison to find out which is worse is like comparing an inanimate thing with a living one. The viciousness of that which does not have an intrinsic principle of action is always less blamable, while the intellect is such a principle. So then it is like the comparison between injustice as such and the unjust man. The fact is that each is worse in some sense; certainly the evil man can do ten thousand times more evil than a dumb animal.*   **1150a1–8; 1401–1403**

COMMENTARY OF ST. THOMAS

1385. After the Philosopher has shown how incontinence has to do with different pleasures in different ways, he now compares different kinds of incontinence with each other. First [1] he compares incontinence in the pleasures of touch, which is complete incontinence, with incontinence in the matter of anger, which is incontinence only partially. Then [6], at "But we must take up etc.," he compares human incontinence with brutish or pathological incontinence. He treats the first point in a twofold manner. First [1] he states his proposition, that we must consider that incontinence in the matter of anger is less disgraceful than incontinence in pleasures of touch, with which both temperance and intemperance deal.

1386. Next [2], at "**Anger seems,**" he proves his proposition by four arguments. In the first [2] he says that anger listens somewhat to reason, inasmuch as the angry man reasons in some measure that he ought to inflict punishment for injury done to him. But he hears poorly, i.e., he listens imperfectly to reason because he is not careful to heed the judgment of reason about the amount and the mode of punishment. Among animals, who lack reason, we find anger—as also other activities similar to reason—according to natural instinct.

1387. In clarification of his proposition he introduces two examples. The first is of servants who, because they

are very precipitate, hasten to act before they hear all their instructions, and consequently make mistakes in executing the command which they did not fully understand. The other example is of dogs barking at the first sound of someone knocking at the door before they are aware whether the one knocking is family or friend. So in anger a man listens somewhat to reason but, because of the natural heat and swiftness of the bile inducing to anger, he proceeds to administer punishment before he hears the entire injunction of reason.

1388. Aristotle then, in addition, explains how this may happen. That a man has suffered injury or contempt is made known to him sometimes as a result of reason, as when this actually occurred, and other times as a result of imagination, as when the matter seems so to him, although it is not true. Then the man in anger apparently concludes he ought to attack the one who injured him and, taking an improper mode of vengeance, immediately bestirs himself in anger to inflict punishment before reason decides for him the mode of punishment. On the other hand sensual desire, as soon as something is declared delightful to it by reason or sense, moves to enjoy that pleasure without any reasoning.

1389. The reason for this difference is that the pleasing object has the nature of an end desirable in itself and is like a principle in reference to the conclusion. But damage to be inflicted on another is not desirable in itself as an end having the nature of a principle but as something useful to the end, and has the nature of a conclusion in things to be done. For this reason sensual desire does not move by reasoning but anger does. Consequently, anger follows reason in some measure but not sensual desire, which follows its own impetuosity. In this way something shameful, which is contrary to reason, results in human affairs. So then, obviously, the man incontinent in sensual desire is more disgraceful than the man incontinent in anger. The reason is that the man incontinent in anger is prevailed upon by reason to a degree, but not the sensually incontinent man.

1390. At "**Moreover, a man**" [3] he gives the second argument, saying that if a man sins in things which he naturally desires he is rather deserving of pardon. An indication of this is that tolerance is more readily extended toward the common appetites, for example, of food and drink—since they are natural—if they are taken precisely as common. The desire for food but not for delicate food is natural and common. But anger is more natural and more difficult to resist than desires (not the common ones which are necessary and natural, and less frequently the matter of sin) but those desires that seek superfluous and unnecessary things—those which temperance and intemperance treat, as he has said in the third book (619–624).

1391. To be a peaceful animal is natural to man from the common nature of the species inasmuch as he is a social animal (for every gregarious animal is naturally of this kind); but sometimes a strong tendency to anger results from an individual's nature, which consists in the composition of the body, because of the heat and dryness of easily enkindled humors. The desire for superfluous objects, for example, dainty food, follows rather the imagination and is a conscious passion of the soul rather than a natural temperament.

1392. Hence the tendency to anger is easily propagated from father to son, following as a result of the natural temperament, as is evident in the examples he adds. A certain man reprimanded for striking his father answered that he himself had also struck his own father who had in turn struck his father. Then the man pointing to his son said, "This boy will strike me when he becomes a man; it is a family trait." He gives another example of a man who, when he was dragged out of his home by his son, asked the son to stop when they got to the doorway because he himself had dragged his own father only that far. So then a person incontinent of anger is less disgraceful because anger is more natural.

1393. At "**Again, double dealing**" [4] he gives the third argument, saying that those who sin deceitfully are more unjust because, together with the fact that they cause injury, they also deceive. However, the angry man does not act deceitfully but obviously wants to take vengeance, for he would not be satisfied unless the one punished should know besides that he is being punished because he had given offense to the avenger. Nor does anger flare up secretly or cunningly but impulsively. But the desire for pleasures arises in secret and insidiously, so to speak. Since the pleasurable object is designed by nature to move the appetite immediately on perception, it draws the appetite to itself unless reason takes pains to hinder this.

1394. Hence people speak of the deeitful Cyprian maid, meaning Venus, or she was queen of Cyprus, and so was called a Cyprian as if born in Cyprus. They attribute to her something of the artful woman, saying her girdle is multicolored, by which we understand sensual desire binding reason; varicolored because it directs one's course to something apparently good inasmuch as it is pleasurable but really evil. Likewise, Homer writes that the cunning Venus craftily steals the wits of the very wise man, because she binds the judgment of the reason in particular practical matters.

1395. Therefore, this incontinence concerning sensual desires is more unjust and disgraceful than incontinence concerning anger. If this is true, the incontinence dealing with sensual desires is incontinence in the unqualified sense, as was pointed out previously (1384); and it is a vice in some measure inasmuch as it is deceitful, not that it acts by calculation but that it enters by stealth.

1396. At "**In addition, no one**" [5] he gives his fourth argument: no one inflicting an injury acts with sadness. It has been explained previously in the fifth book (1035–1036) that a man who acts involuntarily does not do something unjust absolutely speaking, but only incidentally, inasmuch as what he does happens to be unjust. But what we do with sadness we seem to do involuntarily. Now anyone who acts immediately from anger is sad, not that he grieves about the punishment he inflicted—he is rather glad about this—but he is sad and moved to anger by the injury he has received. So his act is not simply involuntary because (if it were) what he does would not be imputed to him in any way; but it has a mixture of the voluntary and the involuntary. Therefore, what he does is less

imputed to him inasmuch as he acts under provocation. But the man who does something apparently unjust in itself, when inflicting an injury, operates voluntarily and with pleasure. If then those things seem to be more unjust against which we are justly very angry, it follows that incontinence arising from sensual desire is more unjust because we are more justly aroused against it, as against an evil agent acting with complete voluntariness and with pleasure. But injury is not primarily in the anger but rather in him who has given provocation for the anger. Therefore, we are less justly angry against the angry person who under provocation sins with sadness, and for this reason is less unjust.

1397. Hence he summarizes in conclusion that, obviously, incontinence which concerns sensual desires is more disgraceful than that which concerns anger; that incontinence and continence in the unqualified sense deal with sensual desires and pleasures.

1398. Then [6], at "**But we must take up**," he compares human incontinence with brutish incontinence. He treats this point in a threefold manner. First [6] he takes up again different kinds of sensual desires and pleasures. Next [7], at "Yet with only etc.," he shows with which of these temperance and intemperance, and consequently continence and incontinence, are concerned. Last [8], at "However, brutishness etc.," he compares human with brutish vice or incontinence. He says first that, since continence and incontinence have to do with bodily pleasures we must take up their differences. Some of them, as we indicated previously (1368–1371), are human and natural, i.e., in keeping with human nature both in regard to the genus which is considered according to the things sought, and in regard to the amount which is considered according to the mode, intense or feeble, of seeking. Others are not natural but brutish because of a vicious nature, or they come about by reason of privations and sickness—among these are evil habits.

1399. Next [7], at "Yet only with the first," he shows with which of these temperance is concerned. He states temperance and intemperance have to do only with sensual desires which are human and natural. Hence, properly speaking, we do not call dumb animals either temperate or intemperate. But, figuratively speaking of one animal compared to another, we do say that one kind of animal differs from another (1) in defilement—one is more filthy in living a more vile and unclean life, for example, the pig than the sheep; (2) in sinamoria i.e., stupidity in general—one is more stupid than another, for instance, the ass than the horse; (3) in voraciousness—the wolf is most rapacious.

1400. Hence, by a comparison with these animals which are excessive in this way, other kinds of animals are called temperate or prudent by a kind of similitude but not in the proper sense because none of them has deliberate choice or can reason but is separated from rational nature. All insane persons who have lost the use of reason are like this. But we have said before (1361) that a temperate and an intemperate man act with deliberate choice; and so temperance and intemperance are not found in dumb animals nor in brutish men, nor are they concerned with brutish desires.

1401. At "However, brutishness" [8] he compares brutish with human vice or incontinence, saying that brutishness has less of evil in it considering the condition of a beast (or of a bestial person). But brutishness is more frightening because it does worse things. He proves that brutishness is less evil by the fact that the highest part, i.e., the intellect, is not corrupt and depraved in the animal, as in an evil man, but entirely lacking.

1402. Therefore, to compare a beast with a bad man to discover which is worse, is like comparing a non-living creature with a living one. Non-living creatures, like fire that burns or rock that crushes, do more damage but are farther from the notion of fault. Badness in a thing without an inner principle of its actions is always less blamable since less fault can be attributed to it—badness in man is imputable because he has a principle making him master of his own actions. This principle is the intellect that the brutes lack. Therefore a beast is compared to a man as injustice to an unjust man.

1403. For the habit of injustice by its very nature has an inclination to evil, but the unjust man retains the power to be good or bad. Each is worse in a measure, i.e., the unjust man is worse than injustice and the evil man worse than a brute because an evil man can do ten thousand times more harm than a beast by his reason which he can use to devise very diverse evils. Therefore, as a dumb animal is less guilty than an evil man but is more to be dreaded, so also brutish vice or even incontinence is more to be dreaded but is less culpable and more blameless than human incontinence or vice. Consequently people who are insane or naturally bestial are less severely punished.

LECTURE VII
Continence and Perseverance

TEXT OF ARISTOTLE (*1150a9–1150b28*) Chapter 7

1. *Continence and incontinence deal with pleasures and pains, with desires and aversions—things pertaining to touch and taste about which temperance and intemperance are concerned, as determined previously. In regard to these passions some people act in such a way that they are overcome by the passions that most men master; others overcome the passions against which most men are rather weak.* **1150a9–13; 1404–1405**

2. *Of those who contend with pleasures one is incontinent, and another is continent; of those who contend with sorrows one is called effeminate and another persevering. In between are the habits of most men who, however, are more inclined to the worse habits.* **1150a13–16; 1406–1407**

3. *But some pleasures are necessary, others not necessary; some are necessary up to a point, while excesses and defects are not at all necessary. So it is in the matter of desires and pains. Hence a man is called intemperate who pursues excesses in pleasures by desiring them beyond measure or by deliberately choosing them for their own sake and not for the sake of something else. Since such a one is not sorry for his actions he cannot be cured. But the man who is deficient in things of this nature is the very opposite (i.e., insensible). And he who follows a middle course is temperate. Similarly, someone may shun bodily pains not because he is overcome but because he deliberately chooses. Of those who yield but not from deliberate choice, one is drawn by the force of pleasure and another by aversion from the pain of unsatisfied desire. Therefore these persons differ one from the other.* **1150a16–27; 1408–1411**

4. *Generally speaking, someone doing a shameful act without any passion at all, or with only mild passion, is worse than another who sins with violent passion. Likewise he who strikes another in cold blood is worse than one acting in anger. What would a man who sins without passion do under the influence of passion? For this reason the intemperate is worse than the incontinent person. In the latter there is rather a kind of effeminacy, while the intemperate man is opposed to the temperate.* **1150a27–32; 1412**

5. *The continent man is set opposite the incontinent, and the persevering man is opposite the effeminate. In fact, one is said to be persevering in this that he holds fast, while continence consists in conquering. But holding fast differs from conquering, as not being conquered differs from conquering. For this reason continence is more desirable than perseverance.*
1150a32–1150b1; 1413

6. *The man, however, who fails in resisting those pleasures which most people successfully resist is called effeminate and delicate. Indeed delicacy is a kind of effeminacy. Such is the man who trails his clothing to avoid the wearisome trouble of lifting it and imitates an invalid, not considering himself wretched in resembling a person who is. Likewise this applies to continence and incontinence, for it is not surprising for somebody to be overcome by the more intense and more extreme pleasures or pains; rather his action is excusable if he resists as Philoctetes did, in the play of Theodectus, when bitten by a snake, and Carcinus' Cercyon in the Alope. The same can be said of those who try to keep from laughing but suddenly burst out like Xenophantus did. But a person is called incontinent and effeminate if he succumbs to those pleasures and pains which most people overcome, being unable to resist not because of a disposition of his nature but because of a sickness of soul) as for instance, effeminacy among the Scythian kings. The same goes for women who in this differ from the masculine sex.* **1150b1–16; 1414–1416**

7. *Although it might seem that one fond of amusement is intemperate, he is really effeminate because play is relaxation and rest, which the lover of amusement seeks excessively.*
1150b16–19; 1417

8. *One kind of incontinence is impetuosity and the other, weakness.*   **1150b19; 141**

9. *Some incontinent persons after taking counsel do not abide by the advice they received, because of passion. Others do not take counsel and as a result succumb to passion. Still others are like people who excite themselves but are not stirred up by others. This is the way with those who, experiencing the movement of passion beforehand and arousing themselves and their reasoning powers in advance, are not overwhelmed either by the passion of pleasure or of pain.*

1150b19–25; 1419–142

10. *It is especially the choleric and the depressed who are victims of unbridled incontinence. Neither of these awaits reason's decision but follows the imagination, the former by the quickness of their reaction and the latter by the vehemence of their passions.*   **1150b25–28; 142**

COMMENTARY OF ST. THOMAS

1404. After the Philosopher has shown the nature of the matter about which continence and incontinence in the unqualified sense are concerned, he now compares them to other habits that share the same matter. He discusses this point in a twofold manner. First [1] he shows how the continent and incontinent man differ from the persevering and effeminate man, from the temperate and the intemperate man. Here he solves the third difficulty that was raised against the fourth probable statement (1321–1324). Next [Lect. VIII], at "But the intemperate man etc." (1150b29), he shows who is worse, the incontinent or the intemperate man, and by this he solves the fifth difficulty which was raised against the first probable statement. He treats the initial point under two aspects. First [1] he shows how incontinence differs from other habits. Then [8], at "One kind of incontinence etc.," he distinguishes the different species of incontinence. He considers the first point in two ways. First [1] he distinguishes continence and incontinence from temperance and intemperance, from perseverance and effeminacy. Next [4], at "Generally speaking," he compares these according to goodness and badness. He handles the first point in a twofold fashion. First [1] he distinguishes continence and incontinence from perseverance

and effeminacy. Second [3], at "But some pleasures," he distinguishes both (incontinence and continence) from temperance and intemperance. He discusses the first point from a double aspect. First [1] he shows the agreement; and then, at "Of these who etc." [2] he shows the difference. On the first he notes two points of agreement.

1405. The first is according to the matter which continence and incontinence share with temperance. These deal with pleasures and pains, with desires and aversions—things pertaining to touch and taste about which temperance and intemperance are also concerned, as determined previously in the third book (339, 342, 616, 618, 651). The second point of agreement touches the manner of conducting oneself in regard to the passions. Some people act in such a way that they are overcome by passions in which most men are better disciplined or strong, that is to say, which they overcome still others conquer those passions in which most men are less disciplined or weaker, that is to say, by which the majority are conquered.

1406. Next [2], at "Of those who," he explains the difference. Men win and lose, he says, in contending with these pleasures and pains; and he who is overcome by those pleasures of touch where most people are victorious is alled incontinent, but he who overcomes the pleasures of touch in which most people are overcome is called continent. In connection with the opposite pains, one overwhelmed by those which the majority endure is called effeminate, while another who triumphs over those to which many men succumb is called persevering.

1407. Because there are different degrees of pleasures and pains, and so of men who control and are controlled by them, it is evident that these habits can be for the most part "in-between." However, those habits signifying evil incline more easily to the lower pleasures, for people are said to be more incontinent and effeminate who are overcome by minor pleasures or pains; just as good habits incline more to the higher pleasures, for they are called more continent and persevering who master the greater pleasures and pains. Likewise it can be understood that men may be inclined toward the worse habits, viz., incontinence and effeminacy.

1408. Then [3], at "**But some,**" he shows how these habits differ from temperance. He says some pleasures of taste and touch, for example, of food and drink, are necessary; other pleasures like different seasonings are unnecessary. Those necessary are so up to a certain point, for there is a quantity of food and drink necessary for man. But excesses (of pleasures) are unnecessary and so are deficiencies. The same is true for desires and pains.

1409. Therefore, someone who intentionally pursues excesses immoderately, i.e., in desiring them above measure, or even seeks them by deliberate choice for their own sake and not for the sake of something else, considering them as an end, is called intemperate. Because a man cleaves immovably to that which he intentionally seeks for

itself, the intemperate man is necessarily not sorry about pleasures he has sought. Consequently his vice is incurable, for no one is cured except by being displeased since virtue and vice are in the will. As the intemperate man abounds in his quest for pleasures, so the insensible man—his counterpart—is deficient in the same affairs, as noted in the third book (630–631). But one following a middle course in these matters is temperate. And as the intemperate person seeks bodily pleasures by deliberate choice, so he shuns bodily pain, not by being overcome by them but out of deliberate choice.

1410. Still, of those who do not sin from deliberate choice, one, viz., the incontinent is drawn by the pleasure's power, another—the "soft"—is conquered by dread of pain following the desire, i.e., the deprivation of the thing desired. Hence it is clear that the incontinent, the effeminate, and the intemperate man are each different.

1411. We should note here that previously (1361–1362), in determining the matter of continence and incontinence—lest error creep in—the Philosopher incidentally touched on the difference between the intemperate and the incontinent man—a matter he now makes his prime concern.

1412. At "**Generally speaking**" [4] he compares these habits according to goodness and evil. First [4] he compares the incontinent and the effeminate man with the intemperate. Next [5], at "The continent man etc.," he compares the incontinent man with the effeminate. He says first that, generally speaking, one who does something shameful without any passion at all, or under the influence of what is only ineffectual or mild passion, is worse than one doing something shameful with violent passion. Likewise striking another in cold blood is worse than striking in anger. What might a man sinning without passion do if he was passionate? Consequently the intemperate man, not overcome by passion but sinning by deliberate choice, is worse than the incontinent man who is mastered by passion. Likewise one of these two conditions, being mastered by passion in running away from pain belongs rather to a kind of effeminacy, while the other, sinning by deliberate choice belongs to intemperance. Hence the intemperate person is worse than the "softy."

1413. Next [5], at "**The continent man**," he compares the "soft" man to the incontinent, and the persevering man to the continent. He considers these points in three ways. First [5] he shows which is better. Then [6], at "The man, however, etc.," he explains a likeness previously mentioned. Last [7], at "Although it might seem etc.," he refutes an error. He says first that the continent man is contrasted with the incontinent, and the persevering man is contrasted with the effeminate. One is called persevering in this that he maintains his ground when another urges him to the contrary. But continence is designated from this that it conquers, for what we contain (*continemus*) we have in our power. It is necessary that we should stand firm against pain because pleasure must be bridled or kept in check. Hence the persevering man is compared to the continent man as the unconquered is compared to the conqueror who is obviously more perfect. Consequently continence is more perfect than perseverance. Effeminacy, however, seems worse than incontinence: each consists in defeat but the incontinent person is beaten by a stronger passion.

1414. Then [6], at "**The man, how-**

ever," he makes clear a likeness mentioned previously (1413), between the effeminate and the incontinent person both are beaten by passions that many other people master. He says that the man failing in these pleasures against which even the majority fight to resist and can overcome is called effeminate and delicate. The effeminate and the delicate belong in the same class, for delicacy is a kind of effeminacy. Effeminacy inordinately shuns all weariness but delicacy in the strict sense shuns the weariness of toil. An individual, who trails his clothing after him on the ground to avoid the labor of carrying it—which pertains to delicacy, is overcome by that weariness which he thinks is at hand from tucking up his clothes. Although he acts like an invalid in dragging his clothes, and in this he seems not to be wretched; nevertheless he resembles a wretched person inasmuch as he shuns fatigue only to meet it.

1415. What was said about effeminacy holds true for continence and incontinence. It is not surprising if a person is overcome by the more intense and more extreme pleasures and pains, so that he ought (not) to be called incontinent or effeminate for this reason. Rather he should be pardoned if he attempts to resist and does not yield at once. Aristotle gives the example of Philoctetes who, Theodectus the poet narrates, when bitten by a snake and suffering great pain tried to contain his anguish but could not. Something like this is told about a woman named Melopes who was struck by a man called Carcinus. So also it happens to those who try to keep from laughing yet are not successful and suddenly burst out, as did Xenophantus.

1416. But a man is then called incontinent and effeminate when he succumbs to such pains and pleasures as most people can overcome. Yet his inability to resist passions of this sort does not arise from his type of nature—by reason of which a thing serious for him would be slight for others—but from a debility of mind caused by evil habit. Thus effeminacy from an innate tendency is found in the kings of Scythia who cannot bear labors and pains because of their delicate rearing. The same thing is true of women in comparison with men by the weakness of their nature.

1417. At **"Although it might seem"** [7] he refutes an error. It seems possible that the playful type, i.e., one too much in love with amusement is intemperate because there is a kind of pleasure in amusement, but the Philosopher says that such a person more properly is effeminate. Amusement is a quieting and relaxation of the mind, which the lover of amusement seeks to an excessive degree. Hence he comes in the classification of effeminate, whose characteristic is to shun difficulties and labors.

1418. Next [8], at **"One kind of incontinence,"** he distinguishes the species of incontinence. He treats this point under three headings. First [8] he gives the division, saying that incontinence has a twofold division: impetuosity and weakness.

1419. Then [9], at **"Some incontinent,"** he explains the members of the division. He says that some incontinent people do deliberate when passion arises, but they do not abide by the results of deliberation because of the passion which overcomes them. Incontinence of this kind is called weakness. Other incontinent persons are led by passion because they do not deliberate but when passion arises they follow it

immediately. This incontinence is called impetuosity because of its quickness which forestalls deliberation. However, if they had deliberated they would not have been led astray by passion.

1420. Still others excite themselves in advance and afterwards are not moved when excited by others. This is the way also with those who, feeling the movement of passion beforehand and having previous knowledge of that to which passion inclines, arouse themselves in advance, i.e., provoke themselves and their powers of deduction to resist sensual desire, and consequently they are not changed either by the passion of pleasure that overwhelms the incontinent man, or by the pain that overwhelms the effeminate man.

1421. Last [10], at **"It is especially,"** he shows to whom the second kind of incontinence called impetuosity is attributable. He says that the highly sensitive or the choleric and the depressed are especially incontinent according to the incontinence which is not restrained by counsel, and which is called impetuosity. Neither of these awaits the advice of reason but they follow the first sensual image: the choleric on account of the quickness of their wrath but the depressed on account of the vehemence of their intensified melancholy whose impulse no man can easily endure, for a dry object when kindled burns furiously. On the contrary we are to understand that men with sanguine and phlegmatic temperaments experience the incontinence of weakness on account of the humidity of their temperament which is not strong enough to resist an impression.

LECTURE VIII
The Intemperate Are Worse than the Incontinent

TEXT OF ARISTOTLE (*1150b29–1151a28*) Chapter 8

1. But the intemperate man, as was pointed out before, is not inclined to be penitent, for he is tenacious of his choice. On the other hand, every incontinent man is given to repentance. For this reason, we are not here dealing with our original problem. Consequently, one (the intemperate) is incurable and the other (the incontinent) is curable.   **1150a29–32; 1422–1423**

2. Now vice resembles diseases like dropsy and tuberculosis, while incontinence is like epilepsy. Vice is chronic while incontinence is a kind of intermittent badness. **1150a32–35; 1424**

3. Generally speaking, incontinence and vice are different in kind, for vice is unconscious of itself but incontinence is not.   **1150a35–36; 1425**

4. Among the incontinent the impulsive sort are not as bad as those who, having the advice of reason, do not abide by it. These people give in to a milder passion and do not, like the impulsive, lack deliberation. In fact, incontinent people (i.e., the weak) are like those who become quickly intoxicated by a little wine or by less than most men.   **1151a1–5; 1426–1427**

5. Although incontinence is not vice in the strict sense it is obviously so in a qualified way, for incontinence sins without deliberate choice but vice with deliberate choice.   **1151a5–7; 1428**

6. Besides, there is a similarity in action, as illustrated by what Demodochus said to the Milesians: "You are not foolish but you do the things foolish men do." So too the incontinent are really not unjust but they do unjust deeds.   **1151a7–10; 1429**

7. One man (the incontinent) pursues bodily pleasures excessively and contrary to right reason, and not because he is convinced that they are to be followed. But another (the intemperate) is convinced, because of his inclination, that these pleasures are to be followed. Hence the first is easily persuaded to change but not the second. The reason is that virtue and vice look to a principle that is destroyed by vice and preserved by virtue. Now the principle in actions is the end on account of which we operate, like axioms in mathematics; and just as reasoning does not teach principles in mathematics, so neither does reasoning teach the end in the sphere of action. But the right evaluation regarding the principle of things to be done is derived from a habit of virtue either natural or acquired. Therefore, the man who makes this evaluation is temperate, but he who makes the opposite evaluation is intemperate.   **1151a11–20; 1430–1432**

8. Take the incontinent person exceeding the limits of right reason because of passion that so overcomes him that he does not act according to right reason; still he is not convinced that he should abandon himself to such pleasures without restriction. In this he is better than the libertine, and not absolutely bad, for he retains the highest principle. Nevertheless there is still another person, the very opposite, who keeps to right reason and does not go to excess in passion. From this, it is clear that continence is a good habit but incontinence an evil habit.   **1151a20–28; 1433–1434**

COMMENTARY OF ST. THOMAS

1422. After the Philosopher has shown the difference between the incontinent and the intemperate man, he now shows which is worse. Thus he solves the difficulty raised in the fifth place (1325) about the first probable statement. Aristotle had considered this matter before but rather briefly and only incidentally. Now he gives it formal consideration by two operations. First [1] he explains his intention. Then [7], at "One man etc.," he clarifies a matter formerly assumed. In the first part of the discussion he makes two points. First [1] he shows that the intemperate is worse than the incontinent man. Then [5], at "Although incontinence etc.," he shows what is common to them. On the initial point, first [1] he compares the incontinent with the intemperate man. Then [4], at "Among the incontinent etc.," he compares the two kinds of incontinence. First of all there are three arguments to show that the intemperate is worse than the incontinent man.

1423. In the first reason he says, as was pointed out before (1409), that the intemperate man is not inclined to be penitent since he sins by a deliberate choice in which he persists, having chosen bodily pleasures as an end. But an incontinent man readily repents when the passion to which he gave in passes away. Therefore, it is evident, as previously indicated (1409), that the intemperate man is as incurable as the incontinent is curable. So from the quality of excess Aristotle solves the difficulty mentioned before (1409), which proceeds from this, that incontinence is more incurable than intemperance. Since the intemperate man is indeed more incurable, it is possible to conclude he is worse, just as an incurable disease is worse.

1424. He states his second reason [2] at "Now vice resembles," saying that vice (intemperance) can be compared to long sicknesses such as dropsy and tuberculosis. But incontinence resembles those sicknesses like epilepsy which occur at intervals. This is so because intemperance—and every real vice—is without interruption, being a lasting habit which chooses evils. But

incontinence is not continual because the incontinent man is moved to sin only by reason of passion which quickly passes. Thus incontinence is—so to speak—a kind of transitory vice. But a continuing evil is worse than a passing one. Therefore intemperance is worse than incontinence.

1425. At "Generally speaking" [3] he gives his third reason: the genus of incontinence is different from that of vice under which intemperance is contained. Real vice is hidden from the one having it and his deception consists in thinking that what he does is good. But incontinence is not concealed, for such a person in his right mind knows that the object to which he is drawn by passion is evil. But hidden evil is more dangerous than overt evil. Therefore intemperance is worse than incontinence.

1426. Then [4], at "Among the incontinent," he compares the kinds of incontinence. He says that among the incontinent, impulsive or impetuous people are better or at least not as bad as the weak who still have reason's counsel, although they do not follow it. The weak are worse in two ways. First they are conquered by a milder passion, while the impulsive are overcome by an excessive passion either by surprise or vehemence. He has just proved (1423) by this argument that the intemperate man is worse than the incontinent. This can be considered a fourth argument connected with the preceding three. The second reason is that the weak are not without counsel like the impetuous. The same argument was used before (1419–1420) in the case of the incontinent and the intemperate man, as if the incontinent man deliberated beforehand but not the intemperate. This is not true, for the intemperate man has reflected in advance, sinning by deliberate choice. Therefore, he apparently introduces this point to show that it is really out of place there.

1427. He gives an example, comparing the incontinent person in his weakness with people who quickly or easily become intoxicated by a little wine or by less than most men. Such persons have a poor constitution; in the same way weak people giving in to a milder passion have a poor soul.

1428. Next [5], at "**Although incontinence**," he shows an agreement between the incontinent and the intemperate man in two matters. First [5] in regard to the fact that, although incontinence is not unqualified badness it is still vice in some sense, as previously stated (1379); it is then a quasi–vice, being but transitory. It is obviously not unqualified vice because incontinence sins without deliberate choice but real vice with deliberate choice.

1429. The second point of agreement is given at "**Besides, there is**" [6]. He says incontinence and vice have a similar action, illustrated by one Demodochus, an ancient of the people, who chided the Milesians thus: "Milesians, you are not foolish but you do things like the works of foolish people." So the incontinent are not really bad (i.e., unjust or intemperate) but they do unjust and evil things.

1430. Then [7], at "**One man,**" he gives his reason [7] for his previous statement, that the intemperate person is, in contrast to the incontinent, unrepentant. Next [8], at "Take the incontinent person," Aristotle tells us why the incontinent man repents, saying in the first place that one man pursues bodily pleasures excessively and against the order of right reason not because he is convinced these pleasures are good.

Such a one is incontinent. Another, i.e., intemperate man on the contrary is convinced that these pleasures are to be chosen as good in themselves, because of an inclination he has by habit. Thus the incontinent person who is habitually unconvinced of the goodness of evil pleasures, though actually and in passion so convinced from his false evaluation on the spot, quickly changes when passion fades. In contrast the intemperate person judging physical pleasures are to be chosen in every instance does not depart from his judgment so easily.

1431. After this he gives his argument: virtue and vice concern in the sphere of action a principle that vice destroys and virtue preserves. Now this principle of action is the end for the sake of which we act; in things to be done it takes the place that axioms or first principles have in mathematical demonstrations. Just as principles in mathematics are not taught by reasoning, so neither is the end in the sphere of action taught by reasoning. But man acquires right evaluation regarding the principle of things to be done, i.e, the end, by the habit of virtue either natural or learned by custom.

1432. Then the one making a right evaluation on the objective of physical pleasures, appraising the mean to be a good and an end in these matters, and excesses, an evil, is temperate. In contrast the one making the opposite evaluation from a habit of vice is intemperate. It is clear that anyone making a mistake in principles cannot be easily recalled from error because reasoning does not teach the principles. From this point of view he is not amenable or penitent until the habit causing the error is destroyed by a contrary practice of long standing.

1433. At "**Take the incontinent per-**

son" [8] he shows that the incontinent are amenable and inclined to be penitent. He says that these people exceed the limits of right reason because of passion overcoming them to this extent that they do not act according to right reason, but still not to the extent of convincing them that they should pursue bodily pleasures as good in themselves without restriction. For this reason such people continue in a right evaluation of the end after the cessation of passion which passes quickly. Such is the incontinent person who in this respect is better than the intemperate person and not absolutely evil because he does preserve the highest principle, which is the correct evaluation of the end. But in a sense this man is evil in considering that something contrary to reason is to be done in a particular case. Another person, viz., the continent, the direct opposite of the incontinent person, stays by right reason and in no way departs from it because of passion even in his actions.

1434. From this it is clear that continence is a good habit because it abides by reason. But incontinence is an evil habit because it recedes from right reason in its operation. This was the first probable statement, which he now concludes after the solution of the fifth difficulty raised concerning it.

LECTURE IX
The Continent and the Obstinate Man

TEXT OF ARISTOTLE (1151a29–1152a6) Chapter 9

1. Can a man be called continent who abides by any principle whatsoever and by any choice whatsoever? Or can he only be called continent who abides by right principle and choice? Can a man be called incontinent who does not abide by any principle or choice whatsoever? Can he be called incontinent who does not abide by a principle that is false and by a choice that is wrong—a point that was previously discussed?   1151a29–33; 1435–1436

2. A man who abides or does not abide by any principle at all is called continent or incontinent only incidentally; but a man who abides or does not abide by a true principle and a correct choice is said to be absolutely continent or incontinent. Certainly if someone chooses and pursues this for the sake of that, he essentially chooses and pursues the latter but incidentally the former. But what is essential we predicate in an absolute sense. Therefore, he who adheres to any opinion whatsoever is continent or incontinent in some way; but he who adheres or does not adhere to a true opinion is called continent or incontinent in the complete sense.
          1151a33–1151b4; 1437–1439

3. Some people, however, are tenacious in their opinions; they are called obstinate because they are difficult to convince, and, once convinced, do not easily change.   1151b4–6; 1440

4. They resemble the continent as the spendthrift resembles the generous man, and the rash the courageous man.   1151b6–8; 1441

5. But they differ in many respects; for the continent man is not changed by the passion of sensual desire, because he is easily convinced by a reason offered and remains continent. On the contrary, the obstinate man is not changed by reason, because such people follow passion and are often led from reason by pleasures.   1151b8–12; 1442–1443

6. The word obstinacy refers to the headstrong, since these people are both undisciplined and rude. Opinionated by pleasure and pain, they are glad to win an argument and to remain convinced in their opinion. But they grieve if their judgments seem weak and only opinions. Therefore they bear more resemblance to the incontinent than the continent man.
          1151b12–17; 1444

7. There are others who do not stand by the things that seem good but not because of incontinence. Thus in Sophocles' Philoctetes, Neoptolemus did not abide by what seemed good although he did this by reason of a pleasure that was good, for telling the truth was pleasing to him. He had been persuaded by Odysseus to lie. Surely not everyone who does something for pleasure is intemperate or evil or incontinent but only he who acts for shameful pleasure.
          1151b17–22; 1445

8. Sometimes a man is disposed to enjoy bodily pleasures less than he ought, not abiding by the judgment of reason. Hence, between such a person and the incontinent man there is a mean, viz., the continent man. The idea here is that the incontinent man forsakes reason by enjoying physical pleasures too much but the other by enjoying them too little. But the continent man adheres to reason and is not diverted by either extreme.   1151b23–28; 1446–1447

9. Since, indeed, continence is something good, the two contrary habits are evil, as is obvious.   1151b28–30; 1448

10. Because one extreme rarely happens and is not so evident, it seems that just as temperance is opposed only to intemperance, so in the same way continence is opposed to incontinence.   1151b30–32; 1449–1450

11. Since language is often used in a metaphorical sense, we have come to speak metaphorically of the continence of the temperate man.   1151b32–34; 1451

12. *Indeed the continent man has the ability to do nothing against principle for the sake of carnal pleasures. And the temperate man has the same ability.* **1151b34–1152a1; 1452**

13. *But the first has evil desires while the other, the temperate man, does not; and the second is so disposed that he does not take pleasure contrary to reason. But the continent man is disposed to take pleasure but is not seduced by passion.* **1152a1–3; 1453**

14. *Although the incontinent and the intemperate man do resemble one another, they nevertheless are different. Both seek bodily pleasures; but the intemperate man thinks he should pursue them, while the incontinent man does not.* **1152a4–6; 1454**

COMMENTARY OF ST. THOMAS

1435. After the Philosopher has settled the question of the existence of continence and incontinence, and has explained their objects, he now settles the question of the precise species of continence. Here are his two operations: first [1] he discusses in what sense the continent man abides by every principle and the incontinent man forsakes every principle. Thus the fourth difficulty (1321) against his second probable argument is solved. Next [Lect. X], at "Nor can the same man etc." (1152a7), he raises the question of a prudent person being incontinent. By this he solves the second difficulty raised against the fifth probable statement. On the first point he does two things. First [1] he shows how continence is related to the right principle which is understood as abiding by reason. Then [8], at "Sometimes a man etc.," he shows how continence is related to the general nature of virtue which consists in following a middle course. He develops the first point in a threefold manner. First [1] he shows to what principle the continent man laudably adheres and from what principle the incontinent man blamably departs. Next [3], at "Some people, however etc.," he shows how some men wrongly hold to a principle. Third [7], at "There are others etc.," he shows how others commendably forsake a principle. There are two considerations of the first point.

1436. First [1] he raises the question whether a man, who abides by any principle whatsoever, either true or false, or by any choice whatsoever, either good or bad, may be called continent. Or whether only he who abides by the right principle and choice is called continent. There is a similar question: whether a man who does not abide by any principle or choice at all, or who only does not abide by a right principle or choice may be called incontinent. Or the question can be framed in this way: can a man who does not abide by a wrong principle or choice be called incontinent, as was stated in the preceding difficulties (1322)?

1437. Next [2], at "**A man who abides,**" he solves the question raised, saying that a man who abides or does not abide by any principle at all is said to be continent or incontinent incidentally (secundum accidens), but a man who does or does not abide by a true principle and a correct choice essentially (per se) speaking is said to be continent or incontinent. He explains it in this way. If someone chooses or pursues, i.e., acquires this for the sake of or instead of that, for example, if he chooses gall in place of honey because he thinks it is honey from the resemblance in color, it is obvious that speaking formally he really chooses and seeks a different thing, namely, honey. But incidentally he chooses what is harmful, that which he chooses instead, viz., gall.

1438. The supporting argument runs this way: in desirable things, that to which the intention of the agent is referred is essentially desired. Good, insofar as it is known, is the proper object of the appetitive faculty. But that which is beside the intention is only incidentally desired. Hence the man who means to choose honey and chooses gall instead, essentially (per se) is choosing honey but only incidentally gall. Therefore, there may be people considering a false argument as true, e.g., someone believing as true this statement: "It is good to commit fornication." If then he sticks by this false conclusion, really believing it to be true, he is essentially standing by a true reason but incidentally by a false reason. He intended to abide by a true reason. This same argument holds for the continent man who departs from a false reason which he considers to be true.

1439. So it is evident that a man is essentially continent (or incontinent) who adheres (or does not adhere) to a true reason but incidentally to a false reason. Now what is essential is predicated absolutely but what is incidental we predicate in a limited way. Consequently he, who adheres to any opinion whatsoever, even a false one, is called continent or incontinent in some measure; but he who adheres or does not adhere to a true reason or opinion is called continent or incontinent in the absolute sense.

1440. Then [3], at "**Some people, however,**" he shows how some men wrongly hold to a principle. First [3] he identifies them. Next [4], at "They resemble etc.," he shows how such people compare with the continent man. Third [5], at "But they differ etc.," he

shows the difference. Finally [6], a "The word obstinacy etc.," he shows how they compare with the incontinent man. He says first that there are some who unreasonably stand by their own opinion. These are the people called *ischyrognomones*, i.e., opinionated or obstinate, because it is hard to persuade them of anything. And if they have been convinced of something they are not easily changed from that opinion. This seems to happen especially to the melancholic who admit a thing reluctantly but hold to what they do accept, with great firmness.

1441. At "**They resemble**" [4] he compares these obstinate persons to the continent man. He says that they apparently have some likeness to the continent because they have in excess what the continent have, just as the spendthrift resembles a generous soul, and the rash are like the self-reliant or brave. Such people maintain their opinion more than they should, but the continent man as he should.

1442. Then [5], at "**But they differ,**" he points out the many differences of the obstinate from the continent. For evidence of this we must consider that a person's opinion can be changed in two ways. In one way on the part of reason itself, for example, if a better reason follows. In the other way, on the part of passion perverting the judgment of the reason, particularly in an individual practical case.

1443. This then is the difference, that the continent man is not changed from his principle by the passion of sensual desire, but nevertheless, when it is expedient, he will be rightly convinced when presented with another and better reason. Consequently, he is to be praised because he is not overcome by sensual desire but by reason. But the other, the obstinate, is not changed rom opinion by a new reason but rather follows passion. And many obstinate persons are seduced by pleasures outside reason. They then are censurable in this way because they are overcome by passion rather than prevailed upon by reason.

1444. Next [6], at "**The word,**" he shows what relation the obstinate have to the incontinent man. Those called obstinate, he says, are also known as *diognomones*, i.e., self-opinionated, headstrong men. They are undisciplined because unwilling to be taught by anyone, they are rude in this way—always wanting to follow their own view, they cannot adjust to others. So they are opinionated in their excessive quest of pleasure and avoidance of pain. They are glad when they triumph in conversation with others, i.e., if they are not changed from their opinion by some argument. They are grieved if their judgments or opinions seem so weak that it is necessary to abandon them. Now it is proper to the incontinent and effeminate man to desire pleasures and to avoid pains excessively. Obviously then the obstinate are more like the incontinent than the continent man.

1445. At "**There are others**" [7] he shows in what way some commendably forsake a principle. He says that there are still others who do not abide by the things that seem good to them, not from incontinence but from a love of virtue. Thus, in Sophocles' drama on Philoctetes, Neoptolemus did not adhere to the things seeming good to him, not from incontinence because he had done what he did for pleasure that was not really bad but rather good. He was seeking a good in a sense, in speaking the truth and this was pleasing to him. But he had been persuaded by Ulysses to tell a lie for the good of his country;

he did not keep his resolution out of love for the truth. This did not make him guilty of incontinence. For not everyone who acts for pleasure is intemperate and evil or incontinent, but only those who yield to shameful pleasure.

1146. Then [8], at "**Sometimes a man,**" he shows how continence is related to the notion of virtue, to which it pertains to follow the mean. On this point he does two things. First [8], he shows that continence like temperance consists in a mean. Next [11], at "Since language is etc.," he shows that continence, because of its similarity, is sometimes called temperance. He discusses this initial point under three aspects. First [8] he shows in what things continence is a mean, saying that occasionally someone enjoys physical pleasures less than he should not for a virtuous purpose but out of disgust. This state is not in accord with a correct and reasonable judgment which indicates some necessity for these pleasures. The incontinent man quite otherwise, we know (1444), is not reasonable in enjoying such pleasures more than he should.

1447. So the mean between these two extremes is represented by the continent man. For the incontinent man forsakes reason because of excess and the insensible man because of deficiency. The reason is that the first wants to enjoy pleasures more than he ought and the other less than he ought. But the continent man perseveres in reason and is not diverted from it by either extreme, i.e., too much or too little.

1448. Next [9], at "**Since indeed,**" he shows how (excess and defect of continence) are related to good and evil. It is evident from our discussions (1433–1434) that continence is something good. So it necessarily follows that the two habits opposed to it (by excess and defect) are bad, as is obvious from the very fact that they do not adhere to reason but take either too much or too little.

1449. At "**But because**" [10] he responds to a foreseen question: why is incontinence alone apparently opposed to continence, which should have two contrary habits? This happens because one extreme—departure from reason by defect—is rare, and consequently not so evident as the opposite extreme. Indeed the departure from right reason by excess is quite frequent in bodily pleasure. By the same reason temperance seems to be opposed only to intemperance, since insensibility is not conspicuous because it happens in few cases.

1450. Here we should consider that extremes are opposed to continence in two different respects. First from the point of view of reason to which continence adheres, and under this aspect the analogy has already been presented (1441–1443): what prodigality is to generosity, obstinacy is to continence. The opposite extreme relating to the defect is the vice of instability. Second from the point of view of restraining desire there are extremes. And under this aspect continence is a medium between these extremes—our present problem.

1451. Next [11], at "**Since language is,**" he shows that continence is at times called temperance for its similarity. First [11] in this similarity he compares continence with temperance. Next [14], at "Although the incontinent etc.," he compares incontinence with intemperance. He discusses the first point under three subheadings. First [11] he states his intention: continence is sometimes called temperance metaphorically, since similar things permit metaphor.

1452. Then [12], at "**Indeed the continent,**" he points up the resemblance. The continent person has the ability to do nothing against principle for the sake of carnal pleasures, and the temperate person has the same ability.

1453. Finally [13], at "**But the first,**" he shows several differences. The temperate man does not have the evil desires of the continent because his sensual desire is well ordered by his habit of temperance. The second difference, stated at "and the second etc.," [13], is that the temperate man by his habit of temperance is not delighted contrary to reason, while the continent man is disposed to take unreasonable pleasure though he is not seduced by his passion.

1454. Then [14], at "**Although the incontinent,**" he compares incontinence with intemperance: though the incontinent and the intemperate man seem alike, they do differ. Hence—by resemblance—incontinence is called intemperance. The resemblance is that both pursue carnal delights, but they differ because the intemperate man thinks he should follow such pleasures by perverse judgment on his goal. Quite otherwise the incontinent man has no such idea because his judgment remains unimpaired, as stated previously (1312, 1426, 1428–1430).

LECTURE X
The Prudent and the Incontinent Man

TEXT OF ARISTOTLE (1152a6–)1152a36) Chapter 10

1. Nor can the same man be at once prudent and incontinent,   1152a6–7; 1455
2. for we have shown that a man is simultaneously prudent and virtuous in action.
                                                                   1152a7–8; 1456
3. Again, one is prudent not simply by knowing what is right but especially by doing it; and the incontinent man does not do the right.   1152a8–9; 1457
4. However, nothing hinders a shrewd person from being incontinent. This is why people sometimes seem to be prudent and still incontinent because shrewdness differs from prudence in the way indicated in our previous discussion.   1152a10–13; 1458
5. They are similar because both reason correctly; they differ because the prudent man follows deliberate choice but the incontinent man does not.   1152a13–14; 1459
6. This is not to say that the incontinent man resembles one knowing and actually considering; rather he is like a person asleep or drunk.   1152a14–15; 1460
7. So he acts voluntarily, knowing in some way both what he does and why. But he is not evil for his choice is in a way good.   1152a15–17; 1461
8. Therefore, the incontinent man is partly evil and not absolutely unjust, for he is not a deliberate schemer.

However, some incontinent people do deliberate but do not abide by the deliberation; while the impetuous do not deliberate at all.   1152a17–19; 1462–1463
9. The incontinent man is like a city that reckons everything that is logically necessary and has good laws but keeps none of them; as Anaxandrides sarcastically remarked, a certain city wanted laws but cared nothing about observing them. The evil man, however, is like a city that observes its laws but has only bad ones.   1152a19–24; 1464
10. Continence and incontinence are concerned with matter that goes beyond the habit of the majority, for the continent abide by reason more and the incontinent less than most men can.
                                                                   1152a25–27; 1465
11. Among the kinds of incontinence, that by which the melancholic incontinently operate is more easily cured than the incontinence of those who take counsel but do not abide by it.
                                                                   1152a27–30; 1466
12. Then, too, the habitually incontinent are more easily cured than the naturally incontinent, for it is easier to change a habit than a nature. A habit is difficult to change for the very reason that it is similar to nature; as Evenus would have it: "I say that constant application evolves harmoniously, and it must become men's nature in the end." We have now discussed the notion of continence and incontinence, of perseverance and effeminacy; and we have shown in what way these habits are related to one another.   1152a30–36; 1467–1468

COMMENTARY OF ST. THOMAS

1455. Now that the Philosopher has shown how the continent stand by— and the incontinent depart from—reason, he goes on to raise the question: "Can prudence (the right reason of things to be done) co-exist with incontinence?" And his answer resolves his second hesitation which he was advancing on the fifth probability (1317–1319). In this business there are two steps. First [1] this conclusion that prudence and incontinence are incompatible; second [5], at "They are similar etc.," the relationship of the incontinent to prudence. He discusses the initial step in a threefold manner. First [1] he plots his course, saying that it is impossible for the same man to be prudent and incontinent at the same time.

1456. Then [2], at **"for we have,"** he proves this statement with two arguments. The first [2], already explained in the sixth book (1172, 1273, 1275, 1285, 1287), is this: prudence accompanies moral virtue, so that a prudent person is likewise morally good. But in the present problem of the incontinent there is no moral virtue insofar as the passions are seductive. Therefore it is impossible to be prudent and still incontinent.

1457. At **"Again, one"** he gives his second argument [3]. Prudence involves not just knowledge but practice. According to previous discussions in the sixth book (1216, 1239, 1240, 1269, 1289) prudence not merely counsels and judges what is to be done; it commands. The incontinent man fails in practice, i.e., he does not operate according to right reason. Therefore, the prudent man cannot be incontinent.

1458. Third [4], at **"However, nothing,"** he offers a reason for the phenomenon of prudent people being incontinent. There is no reason why a shrewd character, ingenious and skillful, cannot be incontinent. So it seems at times that prudent people are incontinent precisely because the shrewd have a reputation for prudence. Now the reason (for the mistaken idea) is the difference between prudence and shrewdness, which is (in the way already described in the sixth book— 1275, 1279, 1280) that prudence as it were adds a further connotation to shrewdness.

1459. Then [5], at **"They are similar,"** he compares the incontinent to the prudent man. He treats this point in a twofold manner. First [5] he compares the incontinent to the prudent man. Next [11], at "Among the kinds etc.," he compares the species of incontinence. He develops the first point in two ways. First [5] he makes the comparison. Then [9], at "The incontinent man etc.," he uses a comparison. He handles the initial point in a twofold fashion. First [5] he makes his comparison. Then [8], at "Therefore etc.," he infers a corollary from that. There are three considerations on the first point. First [5] he says what he is going to do. He states that the incontinent is like the prudent man in a limited way—according to reason—for both reason correctly. But they differ according to deliberate choice, the prudent man following it and the incontinent man not.

1460. Here, in the second place [6], at **"This is not,"** he shows in what sense prudence and incontinence approach reason, by denying that the incontinent person—as it were—habitually knows and actually speculates (i.e., considers) particular things to be chosen. Rather he acts like a dreamer or a drunkard and in whom the habit of reason is suspended (cf. previous explanation 1351–1352).

1461. Third [7], at **"So he acts,"** he clarifies his statement about the difference in deliberate choice. The incontinent person sins willingly enough, for he knows in a way (i.e., in general) what he does and why and the other circumstances. Therefore his act is voluntary. Still he is not bad because he does not act by choice; when he is not in the throes of passion, his choice is the good or equitable. But when passion sweeps over him, his choice crumbles and he wills evil. So the incontinent man differs from the prudent man according to deliberate choice because the choice of the prudent man is not corrupted but that of the incontinent man is.

1462. Next [8], at "**Therefore,**" he draws a corollary. Since the incontinent man did make a good choice before passion but wills evil through passion, he is consequently partly bad (he wills evil) but not absolutely unjust or evil (not a schemer doing evil—as it were—deliberately and by choice). However, one class of the incontinent, the weak, deliberate but do not stand by their resolution; another class, the melancholic and the highly sensitive— previously called impetuous (1421)— do not deliberate at all. So it is clear that neither do evil deliberately and by choice.

1463. From these discussions (1455–1462) we can gather what the subject of continence and incontinence is. We cannot say that the subject of each is sensual desire since the continent and incontinent are alike, both having evil desires; nor is the subject of each the reason since both have right reason. It remains then that the subject of each is the will because the incontinent man voluntarily sins, as was just pointed out (1461); the continent man voluntarily keeps to reason.

1464. Then [9], at "**The incontinent man,**" he uses a comparison with which he does two things. First [9] he presents his comparison: the incontinent man resembles a city that plans intelligently, arranges everything logically necessary, has good laws, but keeps none of them. Thus Anaxandrides sarcastically said that a certain city wanted laws but cared nothing about observing them. Likewise, the incontinent man does not use the right reason he has. But the bad or the intemperate man in using perverse reason is like a city observing bad laws.

1465. Next [10], at "**Continence and**

incontinence,**"** he explains the last statement (how the incontinent man is like a city that does not observe good laws). In fact, not every excess of right reason makes a man incontinent, but continence and incontinence are so named as being beyond the inclination or habit of the majority. The continent man adheres to right reason more than most people can, for he is the master of sensual desires which are the master of most people. But the incontinent man abides by reason less than most men, because he is overcome by sensual desires which most men overcome, as indicated before (237, 439, 1406, 1410).

1466. At "**Among the kinds**" [11] he compares the species of the incontinent according to two differences. First [11] he says that among the kinds of incontinence, that by which the melancholic—who do not deliberate— incontinently operate is more easily cured than the incontinence of those who deliberate but do not abide by the deliberation. The reason is that the melancholic, it seems, can be cured when counsel has been taken, but not the others (1442–1443).

1467. Then [12], at "**Then too,**" he compares the incontinent according to another difference. He says that those who are incontinent by habit are more easily cured than the incontinent by nature, i.e., bodily temperament inclining to it, because a habit can be changed more easily than a nature. That, for the sake of which a thing exists, is itself greater. But a habit is difficult to change because of this, that it is like nature. Evenus the poet expresses it this way: "I declare that daily meditation (constant application) develops agreeably, smoothly and harmoniously. This, I say, in the end (when perfected) is nature for all."

1468. Finally he ends with an epilogue that we have discussed the notion of continence and incontinence, of perseverance and effeminacy; and we have shown in what way these habits are related to one another.

LECTURE XI
Pleasure and Pain

TEXT OF ARISTOTLE (1152b1–24) Chapter 11

1. The investigation of pleasure and pain pertains to the philosopher of political science;
1152b1–2; 1469

2. for it is to pleasure and pain as an architectonic end that we refer everything in calling this good and that bad in the absolute sense.   1152b2–3; 1470

3. Besides, it is necessary for the moralist to study these passions, since we have already shown that virtue and vice are concerned with pains and pleasures.   1152b4–6; 1471

4. Moreover, many people maintain that happiness is connected with pleasure. For this reason they call the happy man by a name derived from a verb meaning "to enjoy."
1152b6–8; 1472

5. Some philosophers held that pleasure could be called good neither intrinsically nor incidentally, for goodness and pleasure are not identical. Others were of the opinion that some pleasures are good, but most are evil. Still others maintain that even if all pleasures are good, nevertheless no pleasure can be the highest good.   1152b8–12; 1473

6. According to them, then, pleasure is not a good at all, because it is a sensate process to a natural term; and no process belongs to the classification of ends, for example, the act of building is never a house.   1152b12–15; 1474

7. Moreover, the temperate man shuns pleasure.   1152b15; 1475

8. Again, the prudent man seeks not pleasure but freedom from pain.   1152b15–16; 1476

9. Besides, pleasure hinders a man from being prudent; and the more so as it is more delectable, for example, sexual pleasure. In fact while it is being experienced no one is capable of turning his mind to anything.   1152b16–18; 1477

10. Then too, there is no art of pleasure, although every good is the product of some art.
1152b18–19; 1478

11. Finally, children and dumb animals seek pleasure.   1152b19–20; 1479

12. But not all pleasures of this kind are good, because some are shameful and dishonorable; while others are harmful, causing sickness.   1152b20–22; 1480

13. Furthermore, no pleasure can be the highest good because pleasure is not an end but a kind of generative process. These then are the things usually discussed about pleasure.
1152b22–24; 1481–1482

COMMENTARY OF ST. THOMAS

1469. After the Philosopher has finished his investigation of continence and incontinence, showing that they are concerned with pleasures and pains, now he intends to investigate pleasures and pains themselves. First [1] he states that this consideration fits in with his present intention. Then [5], at "Some philosophers etc.," he proceeds with his intention. He discusses the first point from three aspects. First [1] he states his objective, saying that a

consideration of pleasure and pain pertains to the philosopher who applies himself to political science to which the whole of moral doctrine is reducible as to a principal science, as was pointed out in the beginning (26–30).

1470. Second [2], at "for it is etc.," he demonstrates his proposition by three arguments: first [2], as the end of a master art is the measure to which all affairs of the art are referred, so is pleasure in the matter of moral study. Relevant to pleasure, one thing is called bad, and another, in like fashion, good. A good man is said to be one who is pleased by good things. A bad man, one delighted by evil things. The same judgment is passed on actions inasmuch as something proceeding from wicked pleasure is judged wicked; on the other hand, good, as proceeding from good pleasure. In any science the principal consideration is that which is taken as a rule. Therefore the moral philosopher in a very special way concerns himself with pleasure.

1471. At "**Besides, it is etc.**" [3] his second argument proceeds: it is not only proper but necessary for the moral philosopher to investigate pleasure because his duty is to study virtues and vices. As explained in the second book (266–267, 268, 269–272), moral virtue and vice are concerned with pleasures and pains. Therefore, it is necessary for the moralist to consider pleasure and pain.

1472. Then the third argument [4], at "**Moreover, many people etc.**": the moral philosopher must consider happiness as the ultimate end. But the majority, including Aristotle himself, maintain that happiness is connected with pleasure. Hence, among the Greeks the term "happy" is derived from the verb "to rejoice exceedingly." Therefore, it is the business of the moral philosopher to investigate pleasure.

1473. Then [5], at "**Some philosophers**," he investigates pleasure and pain themselves: first [5] in general; then [Lect. XIV] at "In the matter of etc." (1154a8), in particular he treats physical pleasures with which, as he has already said, continence and incontinence are concerned. He discusses his first point from a double point of view.

First [5] he takes up the opinions of philosophers opposing pleasure. Then [Lect. XIII], at "But it is obvious etc." (1153 b), he determines that the truth is the opposite. On this first point he has three operations: first [5] he gives opinions opposed to pleasure; second [6], at "According to them etc.," he presents supporting arguments; finally [Lect. XII], at "From what follows etc.," he refutes them. First then, three opinions. Some philosophers held that no pleasure could be good either intrinsically or incidentally; and that if a pleasurable thing is good, pleasure and good will not be identical. Others were of the opinion that some pleasures are good but most are evil. Still others maintained that even if all pleasures are good, nevertheless no pleasure can be the highest good.

1474. At "**According to them**" [6] he presents the arguments in favor of these opinions. At the outset he gives the arguments [6] for the first opinion. Then [12], at "But not all etc.," he gives the argument for the second opinion. Last [13], at "Furthermore, no pleasure etc.," he argues for the third opinion. Relative to the first point he offers six reasons. The first [6] is taken from the definition of pleasure given by those who say that pleasure is a kind of process of the senses to a natural term. When something, as it were connatural to us, is consciously produced in our nature, we delight in it, e.g., eating and drinking. Now no such process belongs to the class of ends (building something is not the thing built) but is rather a means to the end. But good has the nature (ratio) of end. Therefore no process, and consequently no pleasure, is good.

1475. The second reason [7], at "**Moreover, the temperate,**" is this. No one is praised as virtuous for avoiding good; yet a temperate man is praised for avoiding pleasures. Therefore, pleasure is not something good.

1476. He gives the third reason at "**Again, the prudent**" [8]. It is this: as the prudent man seeks freedom from pain so he seeks freedom from pleasure. But pain is not good and by the same token neither is pleasure.

1477. The fourth reason [9], at "**Besides, pleasure**," follows. Prudence is not impeded by any good. But prudence is impeded by pleasure, and all the more as the pleasures are greater. From this it seems that of themselves and not merely incidentally they are obstacles. Thus, sexual pleasure obviously very intense, impedes the mind to such an extent that no one is capable of exercising the act of understanding at the time of the act of pleasure, for the whole attention of the mind is drawn to it. Consequently, pleasure is not something good.

1478. The fifth reason [10], at "**Then too**," is the following. Every human good seems to be the work of some art, because man's good comes from reason. But pleasure is not the product of any art, since no art is merely for pleasure. Therefore, pleasure is not something good.

1479. He gives the sixth reason at "**Finally, children**" [11], and it is this. What is childish and animal in man is blamable. But children and dumb animals pursue pleasures. Therefore, pleasure is not something good.

1480. Next [12], at "**But not all**," he shows that not all pleasures are good. He says that this is proved by the fact that some pleasures are shameful, i.e., dishonorable, opprobrious, notoriously evil, etc.; and over and above this, other pleasures are evidently harmful because some cause sickness. So it is clear that not all pleasures are good.

1481. Then [13], at "**Furthermore,**" he proves that no pleasure is the highest good, even if all pleasures are good, for the end is what is best. But pleasure is not an end but rather a kind of process. Consequently, pleasure is not the highest good.

1482. He concludes by way of summary: for all practical purposes, these approximate the points raised against pleasure.

LECTURE XII
Refutation of Previous Arguments

TEXT OF ARISTOTLE (*1152b25–1153a35*) Chapter 12

1. *From what follows it will be clear that these previous arguments do not prove that pleasure is not a good nor that it is not the highest good.* **1152b25–26; 148:**

2. *First of all, good can be distinguished into the absolute and relative good. This distinction is verified of nature and habits, and consequently of movements and processes. Some of these (processes) seem depraved, indeed some are absolutely wicked. However to a particular person they may not seem so, but instead desirable. And again some such processes, ordinarily undesirable, at times—even though the times be few—appear desirable. Some of these are not pleasures at all, but merely appear to be; those for instance that are painful yet taken by the sick as medicine.* **1152b26–33; 1484–148£**

3. *Besides, one good is an activity and another is a habit. Now those actions producing a natural habit are pleasurable only incidentally. But a pleasurable activity in the appetites indicates an undeveloped and imperfect state, and proceeds from some dispositional or natural principle. For there are pleasures without pain and desire, e.g., that which has to do with contemplative activity, and in these nature is not deficient. An indication of this is that delight is not taken in the same pleasurable objects when nature is normal and when it is surfeited. But a normal nature finds pleasure in things essentially enjoyable while a surfeited nature enjoys pleasures opposed to those which are naturally enjoyable, for example, pungent and bitter foods, none of which are pleasant either by nature or without some qualification. Therefore the pleasures they produce are not—simply speaking—pleasant; for, as pleasant things are compared, so the pleasures they cause.* **1152b33–1153a7; 1486–148£**

4. *There is no need for some other thing to be better than pleasure because of the opinion of some that the result is better than the process. Indeed, not all pleasures are processes nor even involve them; in fact some are activities, and consequently, ends. Neither do such pleasures come from something achieved but from use. Not all pleasures have an end extrinsic to themselves but only pleasures connected with things leading to the perfection of our nature. Likewise, for this reason it is not correct to define pleasure as an experienced process; rather it should be called an activity of a natural habit. In place of "experienced" we should put "unimpeded." But pleasure seemed to some a process because concerned with what is principally good (an activity), that they consider a process, although it is really something consequent to it.* **1153a7–17; 1490–1493**

5. *But to prove that pleasures are evil because some pleasurable things cause sickness is about the same as to argue that remedies are bad because expensive. Such pleasure and sickness are of course bad, but not for this reason, since even contemplation may occasionally injure health.* **1153a17–20; 1494**

6. *However, neither prudence nor any other habit is hindered by its own pleasure, although every habit is impeded by alien pleasures. On the other hand, the pleasures connected with investigation and learning make a man investigate and learn more.* **1153a20–23; 1495**

7. *No pleasure—it seems reasonable to say—is the product of art because art does not have the power to bring about any activity but only capacity to act. However, the arts of perfumery and of cookery do seem ordered to pleasure.* **1153a23–27; 1496**

8. *The arguments that the temperate man avoids pleasures, that the prudent man seeks a life free from pain and that children and brutes seek pleasures—all have the same solution; for we*

have shown how some pleasures are good in the absolute sense and how not all pleasures are of this nature. These non-absolute pleasures are pursued by children and animals and cause the grief that the prudent man avoids. The reference is to physical pleasures accompanied by both desire and pain. These are the kind just mentioned (non-absolute goods); and excesses in them make a man intemperate. The temperate man avoids these pleasures, for he has other pleasures distinctively his own. 1153a27–35; 1497

COMMENTARY OF ST. THOMAS

1483. Now that Aristotle has stated the arguments for these previous opinions, he begins their refutation. First of all [1] he outlines his discussion which will show that the arguments advanced do not really prove that pleasure is not good, nor that it is not the very best thing. He begins with the second opinion, "Not all pleasures are good," because in a way this is true. The other two (i.e., the first and the third) he deals with together, because their arguments are so much alike that they can be answered simultaneously.

1484. Then [2], at "**First of all**," he makes the actual rebuttal. First [2] he introduces distinctions to be made, by which we can know how pleasure is good or bad. Next [4], at "There is no need," he refutes arguments already presented. On the first point he makes two distinctions, both taken according to the distinct good which is the object of pleasure. First [2], something is good in two ways: first, absolutely; then, relative to some individual. Because all things tend to good, so do both natures and habits that are ordered either to good absolutely or to the good of an individual. And because movements and generations proceed from particular natures and habits, they too must be consequently related to these things in the same way: some are good absolutely and others for a particular individual. Hence on the supposition that pleasures are

movements and processes, as our opponent contends, four kinds of pleasure must be distinguished.

1485. Some of these are good absolutely, as pleasures in virtuous works. On the contrary, others seem absolutely bad, although in a way desirable to a particular person by reason of some necessity, for example, medicine to a sick man. A third class are not consistently chosen by anyone but only at times and for a short period, e.g., the taking of food in the case of extreme necessity. A fourth class of pleasures comprise counterfeit pleasures because of the perverse disposition of the one who delights in them: such are pleasures accompanied by sadness or pain, and taken to relieve that pain. This is evident of diversions resorted to by the feverish or the weak, for sometimes it seems a relief to a sick man to twist and turn in bed and take bitter foods and so forth.

1486. At "**Besides, one**" [3] he makes the other distinction, that good is twofold. One is an activity, for instance, contemplation; the other is a habit, for example, science. But of these, activity seems to be the perfect good because it is an additional perfection, while habit seems to be the imperfect good because it is an initial perfection. Consequently, genuine and perfect pleasure is found in the good that consists in an activity. Nevertheless those actions or movements produce a natural habit in man, i.e., which are formative natural habits, are indeed pleasurable but only incidentally. They do not yet have the nature of good because they precede even the habit itself, which is the initial perfection. But by reason of a relation to this good they have the nature of goodness and pleasure.

1487. Obviously a pleasurable activity accompanied by desire is not the activity of a perfect habit, since there is nothing left to desire that belongs to the habit when it is perfect. Therefore an activity of this kind must proceed from some dispositional or natural principle, which is accompanied by pain; it is not without pain that a man covets a natural perfection that he does not yet possess.

1488. However, it is evident that not all pleasurable activities are of this kind, because some pleasures are without pain and desire, as obviously is the pleasure that has to do with contemplative activity. Such pleasure is not associated with any need in nature but rather proceeds from its perfection, i.e., from reason perfected by the habit of science. So then the pleasures connected with activities proceeding from habits, i.e., natures and forms already existing, are pleasures in the true and perfect sense. But those producing habits and natures are not pleasures in the true and perfect sense but only in an imperfect manner.

1489. An indication of this is that if pleasures of this kind were really and completely enjoyable, they would be so under any condition. This is patently false because a gorged nature (present when a man has eaten too much) and a temperate or well regulated nature do not enjoy the same pleasure. Nature properly controlled finds delight in things essentially en-

joyable and in keeping with human nature. But a gorged nature enjoys pleasures just the opposite of those that are unconditionally enjoyable. In fact well-fed people enjoy pungent and bitter foods as a help to digestion, although nothing in them is naturally pleasant, not being akin to human nature, but excessive. From this it follows that the pleasures produced by them are not pleasures in the unqualified sense. The reason is that, as enjoyable things are compared, so are the pleasures they cause.

1490. Next [4], at "There is no need," he refutes these arguments (1473–1481): first [4] the refutation of the argument for opinion number three; then [5], at "But to prove etc.," the dismissal of the argument for opinion number two; finally [6], at "However, neither etc.," the refutation of the argument behind the first opinion. He says first there is no need to exclude pleasure entirely as the highest good so that something else must be better than pleasure. Some hold this for the reason that the result is more excellent than the process. But they consider pleasure a kind of process.

1491. Certainly there is a false supposition here, because not all pleasures are kinds of process nor are they accompanied by some process, as is evident from the premises (1487–1489). Only those pleasures that create habits with pain and desire are so. But some pleasures are activities, and have the nature of end because an activity is the second perfection, as has been pointed out (1486). Such pleasures do not come from production, i.e., from things that are being formed but from use. What Aristotle means is: these pleasures do not consist in the formation of habits but in the exercise of already existing habits. Obviously then it is not necessary that the purpose of all pleasures be something other than the pleasures themselves; this is verified only in pleasures following operations that lead to the perfection of a nature and accompany desire.

1492. Likewise, by reason of this we must reject the definition of pleasure introduced with the first argument for the first opinion (1474). It is not right to define pleasure as an experienced process—this is proper to imperfect pleasures—rather we must make the definition that harmonizes with perfect pleasures: pleasure is the connatural activity of a habit already existing.

1493. In place of the word "**experienced**" they used, let us substitute "unimpeded," so that accordingly the definition of pleasure will be: an unimpeded activity of a habit that is natural, harmonizing with the nature of the one having it. Now the impediment to the operation causes difficulty in operating, and this prevents pleasure. For this reason it seemed to some that pleasure is a kind of process because pleasure is concerned with what is principally good, namely, an activity that they consider to be the same as generation, although it is not the same but something consequent to it. In fact generation is a process toward a nature, but activity is the use of a natural form or habit.

1494. Then [5], at "**But to prove,**" he disproves the reason for the second opinion. He says that to conclude that some pleasures are evil because some pleasurable objects lead to sickness is the same as to infer that some remedies are evil because they are expensive. We must say then that both, pleasurable and healthful things, are evil from one angle, inasmuch as pleasurable objects are injurious to health and remedies cost money but they are not evil in this,

that they are curative or delightful. Such logic leads to a conclusion that contemplation is bad because at times it injures health.

1495. At "**However, neither prudence**" [6] he refutes the arguments supporting the first opinion—the first argument has already been resolved (1490–1494). Hence, first [6] he answers the fourth argument. Next [7], at "No pleasure etc.," he replies to the fifth argument. Last [8], at "The arguments that etc.," he disproves the second, third, and sixth arguments together. He says first that neither prudence nor any other habit is impeded by its own pleasure arising from the habit itself but by pleasure alien to it. Nay rather, proper pleasures are a help to every habit. Thus the pleasure which a man takes in investigating and learning causes him to investigate and learn more. So it does not follow that pleasure must be an evil to everyone.

1496. Next [7], at "**No pleasure,**" he replies to the fifth argument, saying that it is reasonable to maintain that no pleasure is a product of art. The reason is that what is truly and properly pleasure follows activity and not process. But art has the power to bring about some process because it is the right plan of things to be made, as was explained in the sixth book (1153, 1160, 1166); however, it does not have the power to bring about activity but only the capacity from which activity springs. Still a rebuttal could be offered: the arts of perfumery and cookery seem ordered to pleasures. Just the same these arts cannot give pleasure; they more precisely manufacture things which may give pleasure.

1497. Then [8], at "**The arguments that,**" he disproves the second, third, and sixth arguments. He says that the fact that the temperate man avoids pleasures (the second reason), that the prudent man seeks a life free from pain (the third reason), and that children and dumb animals seek pleasures (the sixth reason)—all have the same solution. We have shown (1485) how some pleasures are good in the absolute sense, and how not all pleasures are of this kind. Such pleasures (the non-absolute kind) children and brutes seek, and it is the pain in these that the pru-

dent man avoids. The question here concerns physical pleasures accompanied by desire and pain. These pleasures are not good in an unqualified way. And from their excesses a man becomes intemperate. Consequently these same pleasures a temperate man avoids. But still others are characteristic of the temperate man precisely as he enjoys his own activity; and these he does not avoid but rather seeks.

LECTURE XIII
One Pleasure Is the Highest Good

TEXT OF ARISTOTLE (*1153b1–1154a7*) Chapter 13

1. But it is obvious that pain is evil and to be avoided. Now one kind is evil simply, and another in a limited sense, in that it hinders good. But the contrary of what is to be avoided—to the extent it is evil and to be avoided—is good. Therefore pleasure is necessarily a good.
1153b1–4; 1498–1499

2. To answer with Speusippus (that pleasure is opposed to pain and to good) as the greater to the less and to the equal is not a valid solution, for he would not hold that pleasure is something really evil.
1153b4–7; 1500–1503

3. However, there is nothing to prevent some pleasure from being the highest good, even if some pleasures are evil; just as a particular science is the highest even if some sciences are bad.
1153b7–9; 1504

4. Perhaps it is even necessary that, inasmuch as there are unimpeded activities of every habit, and happiness arises from the unimpeded activity of all these habits or of one of them, that activity should be the object most worthy of our choice. And this activity is pleasure. Therefore some pleasure will be the highest good even though many pleasures are absolutely evil.
1153b9–14; 1505

5. For this reason everyone thinks that a happy life is a pleasant one; and understandably they associate pleasure with happiness, for no perfect activity is impeded. But happiness is a perfect good.
1153b14–17; 1506

6. Therefore the happy man needs goods of the body and external goods of fortune so that he may not be impeded in his activity. People who say that a virtuous man is happy even when tossed about and overcome by great misfortune talk nonsense either willingly or unwillingly.
1153b17–21; 1507

7. Because of this need it seemed to some philosophers that good fortune is identical with happiness. But this is not true, because too much good fortune is itself an obstacle. Moreover, it is perhaps not right to call superabundance good fortune, for its limit is fixed by reference to happiness.
1153b21–25; 1508

8. The fact that all things including brutes and men seek pleasure is some indication that it is the highest good; for a belief prevalent among most people never dies completely.
1153b25–28; 1509

9. However, since neither the same nature nor the same habit is the best for all either really or apparently, all do not seek the same pleasure although they all do seek pleasure.
1153b29–31; 1510

10. Perhaps they do not think nor would they acknowledge that they pursue the same pleasure but in fact they do, for all things naturally have in themselves something divine.
1153b31–32; 1511

11. Bodily pleasures have usurped the right to the name because most people are inclined to them and all share them. Moreover, because these pleasures alone are familiar, they are thought to be the only pleasures.
1153b33–1154a1; 1512

12. Obviously if pleasure and pleasurable activity are not something good, the happy man will not live a pleasant life. For what reason would a happy life need pleasure if it were not good?
1154a1–3; 1513

13. But it would be possible to live a happy life in pain, for if pleasure is neither good nor evil, the same would hold for pain. Why then avoid it?
1154a3–5; 1514

14. *Nor would the life of a virtuous man be pleasurable if his activities were not pleasurable.*
1154a5–7; 151

COMMENTARY OF ST. THOMAS

1498. After the Philosopher has treated the opinions and answered the arguments of those attacking pleasure, he now shows the opposite truth. He supports his statement first [1] by direct proofs; then [12], at "Obviously if etc.," by concluding to the inconsistent. On the first point he does two things. First [1] he shows that pleasure is a good; next [3], at "However, there is etc.," that one pleasure is the highest good. He discuses the first point from two aspects. First [1] he gives his argument. Then [2]. at "To answer etc.," he rules out one answer. He remarks first that everyone admits that pain in itself is something bad and to be avoided; and this is twofold. For one kind of pain is evil simply, e.g., sadness about good; the other kind is evil in a limited way, as a hindrance to good, since even sadness about evil hinders the soul from doing the good readily and quickly.

1499. Obviously there are two contraries of what is evil and inadmissible: one is evil and to be avoided, the other is good. Thus to cowardice, an evil, are opposed fortitude as a good and rashness as an evil. But to pain is opposed pleasure as a good; hence he concludes pleasure is necessarily a good.

1500. Then [2], at "**To answer,**" he excludes an answer to this argument. The reason offered doesn't seem valid because it concludes from one disjunctive element to its other part: if some good, or a thing to be avoided, is contrary to what is to be avoided it seems that pleasure which is contrary to pain—something to be shunned—is a good.

1501. For this reason Speusippus, a nephew and successor of Plato in the Academy, answered that, as the greater is opposed to the less and the equal, so is pain opposed to pleasure not as to an equal but as the greater to the less and conversely. Not as an extreme evil to a medium good but as one extreme evil to another, for example what is deficient to what is excessive or the reverse.

1502. But Aristotle says that this answer is not plausible because it would follow that pleasure is really evil according to its own nature, like excess and defect. But no one maintains this.

1503. The Platonists, who were of the opinion that pleasure is not a good did not hold that pleasure is evil simply and in itself, but they denied that it is a good inasmuch as it is something imperfect or an obstacle to virtue, as is evident from the procedure of the previous argument.

1504. Next [3], at "**However, there is,**" he shows that one pleasure is the highest good. First [3] he explains his proposition. Then [11], at "Bodily pleasures," he assigns the reason for an error. He shows the first point [3] by two arguments; the second argument [8] begins at "The fact that etc." On the first point he does two things. First [3] he gives his argument (the first). Next [5], at "For this reason etc.," he clarifies his statement by some indications, inferring some corollaries from the discussions. He treats the first point in a twofold manner. First [3] he refutes a contrary argument. Some pleasures seem to be evil; from this a person can conclude that pleasure is not the best thing. But Aristotle says that this does not prevent pleasure from being the ighest good. Likewise we see that a articular science is the highest, viz., isdom, as was pointed out in the xth book (1184); nevertheless some ciences are bad, not precisely as sciences, but on account of a defect they ave either on the part of their principles—because they proceed from false rinciples—or on the part of the matter, as appears in the practical sciences whose use leads to evil.

1505. Second [4], at **"Perhaps it is,"** e gives the argument for his statement. He says there are some unimpeded activities of every habit. But appiness is an unimpeded activity ither of all good habits or of one of nem, as is evident from the discussions in the first book (118, 130). Hence is necessary that unimpeded activities of this kind are desirable in themselves. But pleasure is an unimpeded ctivity as we have just indicated (492–1493). Consequently there is a ighest pleasure, that in which happiness consists, although many pleasures are unqualifiedly evil.

1506. At **"For this reason"** [5] he larifies his statement by indications, nferring some corollaries. The first [5] s that because happiness is an unimpeded activity—and it also causes pleasure—everyone thinks that the appy life is pleasurable; and they understandably connect pleasure with appiness because no perfect activity s impeded. But happiness is a perfect ood, as was explained in the first book 111, 112, 117, 118, 201, 222). Therefore t is an unimpeded activity inasmuch s it causes pleasure.

1507. From this he further concludes, at **"Therefore the happy"** [6], hat because happiness is an unimpeded activity, the happy man needs he goods of the body, such as general wealth and an uninjured state, then ex-

ternal goods—called goods of fortune—so that he may not be impeded in his activity by a lack of them. People who say that a virtuous man is happy even when tossed about and overcome by great misfortune talk nonsense, whether they say this willingly (as it were assenting to the statement by intuition) or unwillingly (as it were forced by reason contrary to the available evidence). The reference of course is to the Stoic opinion.

1508. He infers a third corollary at **"Because of this need"** [7]: since happiness needs good fortune, it seemed to some philosophers that happiness and good fortune are identical. But this is not so, because too much of the good things is an obstacle to happiness since some people are hindered by wealth from the work of virtue in which happiness consists. Then it is not right that a superabundance of this kind should be called good fortune, since the limit, i.e., the end, or the norm of good fortune is established in comparison with happiness.

1509. Then [8], at **"The fact that,"** he gives his second argument (by inference) to prove that happiness is the highest good. Hence, he first states his argument [8]: the fact that everyone pursues pleasure is some indication that pleasure is the highest good; for a thing on which many, at least, agree cannot be entirely false. Thus, it is proverbial that a saying generally expressed among the people never dies completely. The reason is that nature does not fail in all or in most cases but only in a few. Therefore what is found among all or most men seems to arise from a disposition of nature which inclines neither to evil nor falsehood. So it seems that pleasure in which the desire of all men concur is the highest good.

1510. Next [9], at "**However, since,**" he excludes a possible objection, "Not all desire the same pleasure," by returning that his main contention is not so damaged. This for two reasons: first [9] because the same nature and the same habit are not best for everyone either really or apparently; for the best tendency in a man is one thing and in a horse another. Likewise the best tendency in a young man is different from that in an old man. And because what is agreeable to each one is delightful to him, it follows that not all desire the same pleasure although all do desire pleasure. This is the reason why pleasure, but not the same pleasure, is the highest good for all; just as the same tendency of nature is not the best for all.

1511. He gives the second reason at "**Perhaps they**" [10], stating that it can be said that all men seek the same pleasure according to natural desire but not according to their own judgment. Indeed not all think in their heart or say with their lips that the same pleasure is the best. Nevertheless everyone is inclined by nature to the same pleasure as the highest, namely, the contemplation of rational truth inasmuch as all men naturally desire to know. This happens because all things have in themselves something divine, i.e., an inclination of nature—which is derived from the first principle—or even their (substantial) form itself which is the basis of the inclination.

1512. At "**Bodily pleasures**" [11] he assigns the reason why some philosophers were of the opinion that pleasure is not a good or the highest good. H says the reason is that bodily pleasure have usurped the name pleasure for themselves as an inherited possession because we are more often inclined to them as being connected with the necessary things of life, and because everyone shares in them as being sensibl perceptible and known to all. Moreover, they alone are commonly acknowledged because people consider them the only pleasures. Since pleasures of this kind are not the highest some think pleasure is not the highest good.

1513. Then [12], at "**Obviously if,**" he explains his proposition by concluding to three inconsistencies. The first [12] is that if pleasure and pleasur able activity are not something good it follows that the happy man may not live a pleasant life; for happiness not being a good in itself, the life of a happy man should not require pleasure if pleasure were not something good.

1514. Next [13], at "**But it would,**" he says that if pleasure is not a good it is possible that living in pain is not an evil; for if pleasure is neither good no evil the same would hold for pain which is the opposite. Thus pain would not be something to be avoided.

1515. Last [14], at "**Nor would,**" he concludes to the third inconsistency. I follows that the life of the virtuous man is not pleasurable, if his activities are not pleasurable—which would be the case if pleasure were not a good. But i is obvious that virtue is productive of good.

LECTURE XIV
Physical Pleasures

TEXT OF ARISTOTLE (*1154a8–1154b34*) Chapter 14

1. *In the matter of physical pleasures there are those who maintain that good ones are specially worthy of choice but the others, in which a man becomes intemperate, are not so.*
1154a8–10; 1516

2. *Why then are the opposite pains evil? For good is contrary to evil.*   **1154a10–11; 1517**

3. *Either they are good inasmuch as they are necessary, because what is not evil is good;*
1154a11–13; 1518

4. *or they are good up to a certain point. The reason would seem to be that if in such habits and activities there is not an excess of what is good, neither is such pleasure excessive. But if this excess is present in the habits or activities it will also be present in the pleasure. Now a superabundance of what is good can exist in bodily goods. Moreover, a man is described as evil or pursuing not necessary goods but an excess of them. Indeed everybody enjoys food, wine, and sex, but not always as they should. However, it is the opposite in regard to pain, for everybody shuns not merely its excess but absolutely all of it. In fact pain is not opposed to the excess of physical pleasures, except to the man who pursues this excess.* **1154a13–21; 1519–1521**

5. *Not only must the truth be explained, but the cause of error must also be exposed. This strengthens conviction; for, when it is carefully shown why the untruth seems to be true, the truth becomes more acceptable. Therefore we must show why bodily pleasures seem more desirable.* **1154a22–26; 1522**

6. *The first reason is: they drive away pain; and since pleasure is a remedy against the excesses of pain, men seek abundant pleasures and in general bodily pleasures. These seem vehement inasmuch as they are remedies and for this reason are avidly sought because they appear better when placed alongside their contrary.* **1154a26–31; 1523–1524**

7. *Likewise it seems that pleasure is not something good for these two reasons, as has been said. First, some pleasures are naturally evil and follow from evil actions; these are desirable to certain beings either from birth—for example, dumb animals—or from habituation, like the pleasures of evil men. Second, other bodily pleasures are remedies for some defect. Now it is better to be perfect than in the process of becoming perfect. But pleasures of this kind are taken by those who are being perfected. Therefore they are good only incidentally.*
1154a31–1154b2; 1525–1527

8. *Moreover, because bodily pleasures are vehement they are sought by those incapable of enjoying others. Consequently such men stimulate for themselves a thirst for these pleasures. Since people of this sort do not have other pleasures for recreation, it is not blameworthy for them to enjoy those that are not harmful; but it is wrong if the pleasures are harmful.*
1154b2–6; 1528

9. *Certainly men encounter pain in most matters on account of nature. In fact sensitive nature continually is afflicted, as statements of natural scientists indicate. Some even hold that hearing and seeing cause pain, and they further say we have gotten used to it.*
1154b6–9; 1529–1530

10. *In like manner, on account of their growth young men are in a state similar to that of intoxicated people, and youth is exhilarating.*   **1154b9–11; 1531**

11. *But the melancholic have a continual need of a restorative because of their nature, for their body incessantly undergoes a kind of corrosion due to their temperament. For this reason they are always urged by strong desire; for pleasure drives out both the opposite pain and any*

other when the pleasure is intense. As a result the melancholic frequently become intemperate
and depraved.   **1154b11–15; 153?**

12. *On the other hand pleasures which are without an opposite pain do not have an excess,*
for they are concerned with things which are pleasurable naturally and not incidentally. And I
call those things incidentally pleasurable that are curative. The reason is that when a cure is
wrought by the action of the part that remains healthy, the activity then seems pleasurable. But
those things naturally pleasurable produce an activity proper to this nature. **1154b15–20; 1533**

13. *However, the same object is not always pleasurable to man because our nature is not*
simple but comprises more than one element with the result that we are perishable beings.
Therefore if one element is active, this may be unnatural to the other. But when a balance is
struck the activity seems neither distressing nor pleasurable.   **1154b20–24; 1534**

14. *Wherefore, if the nature of a pleasing thing is simple the action itself will always be most*
delightful. Hence God always rejoices in one simple pleasure; for activity exists not only in
motion but also in immobility, and pleasure is found more in rest than in movement.
                                                                               1154b24–28; 1535

15. *But change is the most delightful of all things, as the poet says. (Yet this happens)*
because of some defect. Just as a man readily changes because he is evil, so does nature for it is
neither simple nor completely good. We have discussed continence and incontinence, pleasure
and pain, the nature of each, and how some of these may be good and others bad. We must now
go on to the discussion of friendship.   **1154b28–34; 1536–1537**

COMMENTARY OF ST. THOMAS

1516. After this general consideration of pleasure and pain the Philosopher now treats in particular those
pleasures with which continence and
incontinence are concerned. He discusses this point in a threefold manner.
First [1] he makes a statement of his
intention. Next [2], at "Why then etc.,"
he manifests some hesitancy. Last [13],
at "However, the same etc.," he gives
his reason for some general observations on pleasures. He says first that,
after our discussions on pleasure in
general (1473–1515), we must turn our
attention also to bodily pleasures to
say that some pleasures are especially
worthy of choice, those which are naturally good. But bodily pleasures, by
reason of which a man becomes intemperate, are not of this kind.

1517. Then [2], at "**Why then,**" he
raises a doubt about previous statements: first [2], stating the doubt; then
[3], at "Either they are etc.," resolving
it. Finally [5], at "Not only etc.," he

gives the argument for his position. On
the first point we should consider that,
in order to prove that pleasure is a
good the Philosopher previously
(1498–1499) argued from the evil of
pain. Now, because he has said that
bodily pleasures are not good, he uses
the same argument as an objection; for,
if good is contrary to evil, a doubt remains—from the fact that bodily pleasures are said not to be good—why the
opposite pains are evil.

1518. Next [3], at "**Either they are,**"
he gives a twofold solution to the objection. First [3] he says that bodily
pleasures are good in some manner
inasmuch as they are necessary to
drive away the opposing pains. The
reason is that at least in this way anything that is not evil by its nature can
be called good.

1519. He gives the second solution
at "**or they are**" [4], saying that bodily
pleasures certainly are good, not absolutely but up to a certain point. His

eason for this is that every pleasure ollows some habit and movement or ctivity. Hence it is necessary that if in he habits and movements or activities here cannot be a superabundance of he better, i.e., an excess above the ,ood, neither can there be an excess in he pleasure that follows. Thus there annot be an excess of the good in that ctivity, which is contemplation of the ruth, because the more a man contem-lates the truth the better he is. There-ore the pleasure that follows is good bsolutely, and not only to a degree. 3ut if there is an excess of what is good n the habits or activities, so too will here be in the pleasure that follows. Now it is evident that there can be too much of a good thing in the physical irea.

1520. Some indication of the fact is n this: a man is said to be bad because he wants these goods excessively hough he may injure nobody. How-ver, he is not evil by his desire and lelight in bodily goods, for everyone njoys food, wine, and sex to some de-ree; on the contrary, some people are lamed for not enjoying pleasures as hey should. From this it is obvious hat bodily pleasure is good up to a ertain point, but its excess is bad.

1521. Pain works out in the opposite way, for the man of virtue flees not just ts excess, but absolutely all pain. Pain hen is not the contrary to excessive physical pleasure; if it were, no one vould be grieved except for the maxi-num departure from excessive pleas-ire. If this were the case, pain would not be so much something to be shunned as to be somewhat tolerated. 3ut the real situation is this: pain is connected with those pursuing exces-sive pleasure. And this happens pre-cisely because by the least lack of pleasures such people are grieved. So

it is that, as excessive physical pleas-ures are bad, so also is pain.

1522. At **"Not only"** [5] he presents his argument for the preceding state-ments. First [5] he states his position. Then [6], at "The first reason etc.," he gives the actual argument. First he says that not only must the solution to the difficulty be given, but the reason for the error in the objection must be found. This is a great help in estab-lishing the credibility of the truth; for, when the reason why the untruth seems to be true is exposed, the student more readily accepts the truth. This is the reason we must discuss why bodily pleasures seem to the majority more desirable than other pleasures, when nevertheless these other pleasures are absolutely good while bodily pleas-ures are so only to a certain degree.

1523. Then [6], at **"The first reason,"** he gives the actual argument. First [6] he tells us just why bodily pleasures seem more desirable. Next [12], at "On the other hand," he presents an argu-ment to show that other pleasures are in reality more desirable. For the first point he offers two arguments: (the first at [6]) while the second [8] is pre-sented at "Moreover, because etc." On the first argument he performs two op-erations. First [6] he gives the reason why bodily pleasures seem more desir-able. Then [7], at "Likewise it seems etc.," he assigns the reason why bodily pleasures do not seem universally good. He says at the outset that the first reason why physical pleasures seem to be more desirable is that they drive out pain; and by their very intensity are a remedy for pain. Indeed pain is not eliminated by every kind of pleasure but by vehement pleasure. For this rea-son men seek abundant bodily pleas-ure to which pain is opposed. But there is no pain opposed to intellectual pleasure—like that found in contemplation—because it is not in an imperfect but a perfect state.

1524. From the very fact that bodily pleasures are remedies for pain they seem to be vehement, measured as they are not only by their nature but even by the contrary which they banish. Consequently they are avidly sought because they look better when placed beside their contrary, for drinking seems much more important to the thirsty. This is why people who want the pleasure of drinking stimulate their thirst by eating salty foods, thus getting more pleasure in the drink.

1525. Next [7], at "**Likewise it seems**," he points out why these pleasures may not seem universally good. He says that, on account of bodily pleasure—as was previously noted (1512)—it "seemed to some people" that pleasure was not a good. The explanation is that there are two kinds of bodily pleasures. Some are naturally evil, resulting from evil activities, and are desirable to certain beings as soon as they are born (for example, dumb animals and brutish men) but to others from habituation, like the pleasures of depraved men. Other bodily pleasures, however, are remedies for some defect.

1526. An indication of this is that they belong only to someone in need. A man does not enjoy food when he is not hungry. Clearly then the pleasure of food is a remedy for the distress of hunger. Obviously it is better for someone to be already perfect than to be in the process of becoming perfect. But pleasures of this kind, which we call medicinal, are taken by those who are being perfected but not by those who are already perfect. They are indulged in because a need of nature is satisfied through what is taken. So then it is

clear that they are not good intrinsically but incidentally inasmuch as they are necessary for something.

1527. He has already touched on these two arguments in two previous solutions (1510–1511). Surely those pleasures that are involved in evil actions exceed the proper measure. Since then physical pleasures are not in themselves good, however more desirable they seem, some thought pleasures are universally not good.

1528. At "**Moreover, because**" [8] he gives the second reason. On this point he does two things. First [8] he presents the reason. Then [9], at "Certainly men etc.," he explains something which he had taken for granted. He says first that, since bodily pleasures are vehement, they are sought by those who cannot enjoy other pleasures, i.e., by those who, since they know nothing of intellectual delights, incline only to physical pleasures. Consequently people artificially arouse in themselves a thirst for such pleasures, on their own volition stimulating themselves to their desires. Remember (1524) those who eat salty foods to induce thirst for drink. Therefore since such people do not have other pleasures for recreation, for them to enjoy such pleasures is not too bad, providing they do not hurt themselves or others. But if the pleasures are harmful they will be wrong and reprehensible; obviously so in adultery and poisonous food.

1529. Next [9], at "**Certainly men**," he assigns the reason for something he had taken for granted, that all men need some pleasure for recreation. First [9] he gives the kind of reason that applies to all in general; then [10], at "In like manner etc.," a reason applicable to young men; finally [11], at "But the melancholic etc.," a reason applicable to the melancholic. He says first that if s not to be considered a fault for some people to enjoy bodily pleasures, when they do not have others, because they need pleasures as a remedy for pain. Men encounter pain in many matters on account of natural movements and activities. In fact sensitive nature is always under tension while at work, and work is wearisome as the statements of the natural scientists attest.

1530. Some say that continual seeing and hearing cause pain inasmuch as they cause strain; because of this an animal needs the relaxation of sleep as is explained in *De Somno et Vigilia* (Ch. , 454a26–33; St. Th. Lect. II). But we are unaware of this sort of hurt because we are accustomed to endure it continually. However, even though seeing and hearing naturally fatigue and strain the bodily organs, nevertheless they give physical pleasure by reason of sense knowledge.

1531. Then [10], at "**In like manner,**" he tells why young men especially need pleasure: because of their growth young men have many disturbances of spirits and humors, such as occur in intoxicated persons. So, on account of activity of this sort young men especially seek pleasure.

1532. At "**But the melancholic**" [11] he assigns the reason on the part of the depressed. He says that the melancholic, by reason of their natural disposition, have a continual need of a remedy for pain because their body undergoes a kind of corrosion due to dryness of temperament. Hence they have a vehement desire for pleasure as a means of dispelling this pain, for pleasure drives out not only the opposite pain—the pleasure of food banishes the pain of hunger—but, if the pleasure is intense, it sometimes drives out other pain. The reason is that it is contrary to all pain according to genus

but not according to species. And because the melancholic vehemently desire pleasures, as a result they frequently become intemperate and depraved.

1533. Next [12], at "**On the other hand,**" he gives the reason why intellectual pleasures are really better, stating that such pleasures lack an opposite pain, which they drive out; they have consequently no excess to render them vicious. These pleasures deal with things which are pleasurable naturally and not incidentally. Here he explains two things: first, the nature of what is incidentally pleasurable. He asserts that those things are pleasurable incidentally that give pleasure inasmuch as they are curative. The reason is that when a man obtains a cure it happens that a healthy condition is brought about and the activity seems pleasurable. Hence when pleasures of this kind are sought outside the need for a remedy they are immoderate. Subsequently he explains that those things are naturally pleasurable that produce an activity of this nature; for the activity proper to a nature, since it is its perfection, is pleasurable to every nature. For this reason the activity of the intellect is pleasurable to man.

1534. Then [13], at "**However, the same,**" he assigns the reason for two observations on human pleasures. The first observation [13] is that the same object is not always pleasurable to man. He says that the reason is that our nature is not simple but composite, and is changeable from one thing to another inasmuch as it is subject to deterioration. For this reason if man performs an action pleasurable to him according to one element, this pleasure is unnatural to him according to a different element. Thus contemplation is natural to man by reason of his intellect but beyond the natural scope of the powers of imagination which try to take an active part in the work of contemplation. Therefore contemplation is not always delightful to man. It is the same with the taking of food, which is natural to man who needs it but not natural to a body already surfeited. But when a man approaches the opposite condition, then what was pleasurable in his previous condition seems to be neither distressing, because the opposite condition has not yet been reached, nor still pleasurable because the other condition has now almost been passed.

1535. From this he concludes, at "**Wherefore, if**" [14], that if the nature of any being that is capable of delight were simple and unchangeable the same action would be most delightful for it. Thus if man were only intellect, he would always take pleasure in contemplating. Hence, since God is simple and unchangeable he rejoices always in one simple pleasure that he takes in the contemplation of himself; for the activity that produces pleasure consists not in motion alone but even in immobility, as is evident in the activity of the intellect. That pleasure which is without motion is greater than pleas-

ure with motion, because what is in motion is on the way to being but what is at rest has complete being, as is obvious from previous discussions (1523).

1536. At "**But change**" [15] he gives the reason for the second observation on pleasure, that change is most delightful to men according to the saying of a certain poet. Aristotle adds that this happens because of some evil, or defect of nature, which is not capable of remaining in the same condition. Just as it is with an evil man who is easily changed and does not have his mind fixed on one thing, so with nature that needs change because it is neither simple nor completely good; for motion is the act of what is imperfect, as is stated in the third book of the *Physics* (Ch. 2, 201b27–202a2; St. Th. Lect. III, 296).

1537. He concludes in summary: in the seventh book he has discussed continence and incontinence, pleasure and pain, the nature of each of these subjects, and how they may be good or bad. Therefore he must now go on to a discussion of friendship. Thus he completes the teaching of the seventh book

BOOK EIGHT
THE NATURE OF FRIENDSHIP
LECTURE I
Friendship, a Subject of Moral Philosophy

TEXT OF ARISTOTLE (*1155a3–1155b16*) Chapter 1

1. *After the previous discussions we must pass on to a consideration of friendship, for it is a kind of virtue or at least accompanies virtue.*   **1155a3–4; 1538**

2. *Besides, friendship is especially necessary for living, to the extent that no one, even though he had all other goods, would choose to live without friends. Indeed the rich, the rulers and the powerful seem to need friends most of all. What purpose do goods of fortune serve if not for the beneficence which is especially and most laudably exercised towards friends? Or how will goods of fortune be preserved and retained without friends? For the greater they are the less secure they become. In poverty and other misfortunes people consider friends their only refuge. Likewise friendship helps young men to guard against wrong-doing; it helps old men to support their deficiencies and faltering movements arising from weakness. Friendship is even useful to people in their prime for the performance of good actions, since two persons working together either in intellectual endeavor or external activity are more effective.*   **1155a4–17; 1539–1540**

3. *By nature the parent feels friendship for its offspring not only among men but also among birds and many other animals. There is also friendship among people who are of the same race with one another, and notably among men in general. Hence we have praise for lovers of their fellow men. Even when traveling abroad we see that every man is a familiar and a friend of every other man.*   **1155a17–22; 1541**

4. *States, it seems, are maintained by friendship; and legislators are more zealous about it than about justice. This is evident from the similarity between friendship and concord; but legislators most of all wish to encourage concord and to expel discord as an enemy of the state.*   **1155a22–26; 1542**

5. *If people are friends there is no need of justice, but just men do need friendship. Likewise what is just seems to be especially favorable to friendship.*   **1155a26–28; 1543**

6. *Friendship is not only necessary but also noble. We praise those who love their friends; and a multiplicity of friendships seem to be a good thing. People even identify good men and friends.*   **1155a28–31; 1544**

7. *On this subject not a few things are uncertain. Some philosophers contend that friendship is a kind of likeness, and that friends are like one another. Hence the saying: "Like seeks like," "Birds of a feather flock together," and other proverbs of this sort. Others, on the contrary, hold that all similar individuals are mutually opposed.*   **1155a32–1155a1; 1545**

8. *Likewise some seek less superficial reasons, those more rooted in nature. Euripides, for instance, maintained that the parched earth longs for rain and when majestic heaven is filled with rain, it longs to fall on the earth. Heraclitus held that contrary contributes to contrary, that the most excellent harmony results from opposites, and that all things have their origin from strife. But others were of a contrary opinion, especially Empedocles who contended that like desires like.*   **1155b1–8; 1546–1547**

9. *Certainly questions belonging to cosmology should be passed over as not pertinent to our present purpose. But we must give our attention to whatever subjects are human and refer to man's morals and passions. Thus, whether all men are capable of friendship or whether evil men can be friends, and whether friendship is of one kind or many kinds.*   **1155b8–13; 1548**

10. *In fact some philosophers thought that there was only one kind of friendship because it is*

susceptible of more and less; they did not accept the sufficient indication that things which differ in species admit of more and less. But we have treated these matters before.

1155b13–16; 1549–1550

COMMENTARY OF ST. THOMAS

1538. After the Philosopher has determined the moral and intellectual virtues and continence, which is something imperfect in the genus of virtue, he now turns his attention to friendship which is founded upon virtue as an effect of it. First he explains by way of introduction what he intends to do. Then [Lect. II], at "Perhaps these questions etc." (1155b17), he begins to treat friendship. He develops the first point in two ways. First [1] he shows that it pertains to ethics to treat friendship. Next [7], at "On this subject etc.," he shows what matters are to be treated in the question of friendship. In regard to the first item he offers six reasons to explain what we must consider about friendship. He states first what has to be treated, after the previous discussions, in examining the subject of friendship, viz., we must consider the things pertaining to the study of moral philosophy, omitting what belongs to the field of the cosmologist. The first reason [1] why we must investigate friendship is that the consideration of virtue is the concern of moral philosophy. Friendship is a kind of virtue inasmuch as it is a habit of free choice—this will be explained later (1559, 1602–1604, 1645, 1831). Also it is reduced to the genus of justice as offering something proportional (a point that will also be discussed later), or at least it accompanies virtue insofar as virtue is the cause of true friendship.

1539. He gives the second reason [2] at "**Besides, friendship.**" Moral philosophy considers all things that are required for human living; and among these friendship is especially neces-sary, to such an extent that no one in his right mind would choose to live in the possession of great external goods without friends. Indeed friends seem most necessary for the wealthy, the rulers, and the powerful, who have abundant external goods. First, for the enjoyment of these goods; there is no advantage to be derived from goods of fortune if no one can be benefited by them, but a benefit is especially and most laudably done for friends. Second, for the preservation of such goods that cannot be retained without friends. The greater the goods of fortune, the less secure they are because many people secretly covet them. Nor are friends useful only in good fortune but also in adversity.

1540. Therefore, in poverty people look upon friends as the one refuge. So then in any situation friends are needed. Likewise friendship is necessary for young men that the help of friends may restrain them from sin, for they themselves are inclined to desires for pleasures, as has been already remarked in the seventh book (1531). On the other hand, friends are useful to the old for assistance in their bodily infirmities; because they are faltering in their movements from weakness, friends are needed to assist them. But even to those who are at their peak, in the very prime of life, friends are useful for the performance of good actions. When two work together, they are more effective. This is true both in rational investigation where one sees what the other cannot see, and external activity in which one is especially a help to the other. Thus it is evident that we must investigate friendship as a state necessary for all.

1541. He presents his third reason [3] at "**By nature the parent.**" By nature a parent feels friendship for its child. This is true not only of mankind but even of birds who obviously spend a long time training their young. And the same goes for other animals. There is also a natural friendship between people of the same race who have common customs and social life. There is above all that natural friendship of all men for one another by reason of their likeness in specific nature. For this reason we praise philanthropists or friends of mankind as fulfilling what is natural to man. This is evident when a man loses his way; for everyone stops even an unknown stranger from taking the wrong road, as if every man is naturally a familiar and a friend of every other man. But those things which are naturally good must be treated by the moralist. Therefore he ought to treat friendship.

1542. At "**States, it seems**" [4] he offers the fourth reason, pointing out that states seem to be preserved by friendship. Hence legislators have greater zeal for maintaining friendship among citizens than even justice itself which is sometimes omitted, for example, in the infliction of punishment, lest dissension be stirred up. This is clear from the fact that concord and friendship are similar. Certainly lawmakers especially want this harmony and eliminate from the citizenry as much as possible contention inimical to the security of the state. Because the whole of ethics seems to be ordered to the good of the state, as was said at the beginning (25), it pertains to ethics to treat friendship.

1543. He states the fifth reason [5] at "**If people,**" saying that if men are

friends there should be no need of justice in the strict sense because they should have all things in common; a friend is another self and there is no justice to oneself. But if men are just they nevertheless need friendship for one another. Likewise perfect justice seems to preserve and restore friendship. Therefore it pertains to ethics to treat friendship much more than justice.

1544. He gives the sixth reason [6] at "**But friendship,**" explaining that we must treat friendship not only because it is something necessary for human living but also because it is something good, i.e., laudable and honorable. We praise *philophiloi*, i.e., those who love their friends; and *poliphilia* (a multiplicity of friendships) seems to be so good that people identify good men and friends.

1545. Then [7], at "**On this subject,**" he shows what should be considered on friendship. First [7] he presents an obvious doubt about friendship. Next [9], at "Certainly questions etc.," he shows the kind of doubts to be resolved about friendship. Last [10], at "In fact some etc.," he rejects an error of certain philosophers. He considers the first point in a twofold manner. First [7] he states conflicting opinions of some thinkers on friendship in human affairs; second [8], at "Likewise some etc.," on friendship in things of nature. He says first that not a few things regarding friendship are uncertain. This is obvious, primarily from the diversity of opinions. Some contend that friendship is a kind of likeness and that like people are friends of one another. In favor of this they quote proverbs: "Like seeks like," "Birds of a feather flock together." Certain birds like starlings do flock together. There are other proverbs of this type. But others, on the contrary, hold that all potters are enemies of each other, since one hinders another's gain. But the truth of the matter is that, essentially speaking, like is lovable; it is, however, hateful incidentally, precisely as an impediment to one's own good.

1546. At "**Likewise some**" [8] he states conflicting opinions about the same subject in things of nature. He says that on this very question some seek loftier, i.e., deeper reasons, more in the manner of cosmologists. Thus Euripides maintained that the parched earth desires rain as if loving its contrary; and that when heaven, worthy of honor on account of its excellence, is filled with rain its longs to fall on the earth, i.e., to send down rain to earth, which is the contrary of its loftiness and fullness. Likewise Heraclitus held that contrary contributes to contrary, as cold things to a man suffering from excessive heat, insofar as the most excellent harmony or equilibrium is produced from different and contrary things. But he said that the contrary does this inasmuch as all things had their origin from strife by means of which the elements, mingled in the beginning, are separated. But others like Empedocles were of an opposite opinion: that like desires like.

1547. Our difficulty is answered: essentially speaking, like is desirable naturally; but incidentally like desires the contrary, inasmuch as it is helpful and medicinal. Cf. his previous discussion on bodily pleasures (1525–1527).

1548. Next [9], at "**Certainly questions**," he shows the kinds of doubts to be resolved about friendship, saying that cosmological questions must be omitted as irrelevant to our present purpose. Attention should be directed to human affairs as connected with morals and man's passions; for instance, whether all men are capable of friendship, or whether evil men are incapable of it, and whether there is one kind or many kinds of friendship.

1549. Then [10], at "**In fact some**," he rejects an error of some philosophers who thought there was only one kind of friendship because all species of friendship are to be compared according to more and less. Thus we say that honorable friendship is greater than useful friendship. But Aristotle says that they have not accepted the adequate explanation that even those things that differ specifically receive more and less inasmuch as they agree generically. For example, we may say that white has more color than black, or by analogy that act is more excellent than potency, and substance than accident.

1550. In conclusion he says that the things just treated pertaining to human activities in regard to friendship were discussed previously in a general way.

LECTURE II
Good, the Object of Friendship

TEXT OF ARISTOTLE (1155b17–1156a5) Chapter 2

1. *Perhaps these questions will be clarified by some knowledge about what is lovable, for it seems that man does not love everything but only what is lovable; and this is either a good in itself or a good that is pleasurable or useful. But the useful good seems to be a means of attaining the good in itself or the pleasurable good. Therefore, the good in itself and the pleasurable will be things lovable as ends.* **1155b17–21; 1551–1552**

2. *Do men then love the good simply or what is good for them? These two things sometimes differ. Likewise the same doubt exists about the pleasurable good itself.* **1155b21–23; 1553**

3. *It seems though that everyone loves what is good for him; and, as the good in itself is lovable, so what is good for each man is lovable for him.* **1155b23–25; 1554**

4. *However, everyone loves not what is good for him but what appears good.* **1155b25–26; 1555**

5. *But this makes no difference, for what is lovable will be what appears good.* **1155b26–27; 1556**

6. *While there are three motives prompting love, certainly the love of inanimate objects is not called friendship. In it there is neither a mutual return nor a will for the good of the objects. Indeed it would be absurd to wish good to wine, although a man does want it to remain unspoiled so he can have it. On the other hand, we say that the good of a friend must be wished for his sake.* **1155b27–31; 1557–1558**

7. *But those wishing good to someone in this way are said to have goodwill when the wish is not reciprocal, for friendship is goodwill with reciprocation.* **1155b31–34; 1559**

8. *Likewise we must add that goodwill may not lie hidden. Many men in fact are of goodwill towards those they have never seen inasmuch as they think such people virtuous or useful. It is possible too that one of these persons might feel the same way. Consequently men of this kind seem to be benevolent towards one another but they cannot be called friends when unaware of one another's feelings.* **1155b34–1156a3; 1560**

9. *Therefore, it is necessary for friendship that men wish good to one another, that this fact be recognized by each, and that it be for the sake of one of the reasons previously mentioned.* **1156a3–5; 1561**

COMMENTARY OF ST. THOMAS

1551. After the Philosopher has shown in the introduction that it is necessary to clarify friendship and what things are to be determined about it, now he begins to treat friendship. First he explains what friendship is. Then [Lect. III], at "Since these objects etc." (1156a5), he distinguishes its kinds. Last [Lect. I, Bk. IX], at "In all friendships etc." (1163b32), he states the properties belonging to the different kinds of friendship. He treats the first point from two aspects. First [1] he in-

vestigates the four parts of the definition of friendship. Next [9], at "Therefore it is necessary etc.," he concludes with the definition of friendship. First [1] he investigates the portion dealing with the object. In regard to this he does three things. First [1] he determines the object of friendship. Second [2], at "Do men then love etc.," he raises a doubt. Third [3], at "It seems though etc.," he gives the answer. He says first that these questions will perhaps be somewhat clarified if we understand the nature of the thing that is lovable, the object of love from which friendship (or love) receives its name.

1552. Not everything is loved indiscriminately because evil as such is not loved, but man loves what is lovable, and this is either good in itself, i.e., honorable, or it is a pleasurable or useful good. The last or useful good seems to be a means of attaining the honorable and pleasurable goods which are lovable on account of themselves as ends. On the other hand, useful good is lovable on account of another, as a means to an end. But the good and the pleasurable taken in general are not distinguished from one another in substance but only in concept. Something is described as good precisely insofar as it is intrinsically perfect and desirable; and pleasurable inasmuch as the appetite rests in it. However, that is not the meaning here: the question here is of man's genuine good, which belongs to reason; and the pleasurable is taken here as that which appeals to the senses.

1553. Then [2], at "**Do men then love**," he raises a doubt on this point: do men love what is the absolute good, or what is good relative to themselves? These sometimes do differ from each other. For instance, to philosophize in itself is good but not in the case of the pauper. The same doubt presents itself in the case of the pleasurable good itself; for an object pleasurable in itself (e.g., a sweet) is not pleasant to one with a sour taste.

1554. At "**It seems though**" [3] he answers the foregoing question. First [3] he states his solution, saying everyone seems to love what is good for him because every faculty tends to the object proportionate to itself. Thus everyone's vision sees what is visible to it. As the totally lovable is the totally good,

so the lovable for each man is that which is good for him.

1555. Second [4], at "**However, everyone**," he argues for the contrary, saying that every man loves not what is really good for him but what seems good for him; for desire tends to an object only as apprehended. Consequently it seems false that what is lovable is what is good for him.

1556. Third [5], at "**But this makes**," he gives the answer that this makes no difference to our proposition; for, when some apparent good is loved it is loved as a good for oneself. Hence it can also be said that what is lovable is what appears good.

1557. The second portion which he gives at "**While there are**" [6], relates to the quality of love. He says that while there are three reasons why men love, viz., the good, the pleasurable, and the useful, friendship does not consist in that love which a man is said to have for inanimate things, like wine or gold. He shows this in two ways. First, because in a love of this kind there cannot be the mutual return that is necessary for friendship, for wine does not love man as man loves wine. Second, because we do not love inanimate things in such a way that we will their good. It would be absurd to say that we willed good to wine; but the good which is wine a man wills for himself. Therefore, in loving wine man obviously does not have benevolence towards the wine but towards himself.

1558. If someone says that a man wishes good to the wine because he wishes that it be preserved, we should consider that a man wants the wine to remain unspoiled so he can have it. In this way he does not desire the preservation of the wine for the good of the wine but for his own good. And this is contrary to the notion of friendship, for we say that the good of a friend must be willed for his sake and not for the sake of the one loving.

1559. The third portion [7], which he presents at "**But those wishing,**" refers to change in the one loved. He explains that when people wish good to someone for his sake we call them benevolent but not friends if the wish is not reciprocated so that the loved one wishes good to, and for the sake of, the one loving. The reason is that we say friendship is benevolence with corresponding requital inasmuch as the one loving is loved in return, for friendship has a kind of exchange of love after the manner of commutative justice.

1560. The fourth portion [8] is taken from the condition for mutual love; and it is stated at "**Likewise we must.**" He says that to complete the notion of friendship we must add that it is a mutual benevolence which is recognized. Many men are benevolent towards those they have never seen, for, from reports, they judge these people are just, i.e., virtuous, or useful to themselves. Likewise it is possible that one of them should have the same feeling towards him who is benevolent in this way. Consequently men of this kind seem to be benevolent towards one another but cannot be friends while they are unaware of one another's feelings.

1561. Then [9], at "**Therefore it is necessary,**" he concludes with the definition of friendship derived from the premises. He says that it is necessary to the notion of friendship that men wish good to one another, that this fact be recognized by them, and that it be for the sake of one of the things previously mentioned, namely, the good, the pleasurable, or the useful.

LECTURE III
Kinds of Friendship

TEXT OF ARISTOTLE (*1156a6–1156b35*) Chapter 3

1. *Since these objects of love differ from each other in kind, the corresponding love and friendship will also differ in kind. There are then three kinds of friendship corresponding to the objects of love. In each of these a recognized return of love is possible, and those loving can mutually will good according to their love.*   **1156a6–10; 1562–1564**

2. *Therefore, of those who love one another for utility, one does not love the other for the other's sake but for the good they mutually gain. The same is true of those who love each other for pleasure, for friends like these do not love witty people because of their character but because they are pleasant companions. Both those who love for utility love for the good they get and those who love for the sake of pleasantness love for the pleasure they enjoy. These do not love a friend because he is a friend but because he is useful or pleasant. Therefore, these friendships are incidental, for a man is loved not for what he is but for some advantage or pleasure.*
        1156a10–19; 1565–1566

3. *Since men do not always remain the same, friendships of this kind are easily dissolved; when those who are loved cease to be pleasant or useful, their friends stop loving them. But the useful is not permanent but is one thing now and then another. Consequently if the reason for friendship no longer exists, the friendship itself is dissolved.*   **1156a19–24; 1567**

4. *This friendship seems to exist especially among old men who do not seek pleasure but utility.*   **1156a24–26; 1568**

5. *It is also suitable for adolescents and youths who seek what is to their advantage. Friends of this kind do not associate much with each other, for sometimes they are not even agreeable to each other. So they do not need such companionship unless it is useful, since they are pleasing to one another only insofar as they hope for some good.*   **1156a26–30; 1569**

6. *To the same classification some assign the friendship of fellow travelers.* **1156a30–31; 1570**

7. *Young men seem to foster friendship mostly for pleasure because they live according to the passions and follow what is pleasing to them at the moment.*   **1156a31–33; 1571**

8. *As they grow older, however, their pleasures undergo change. They quickly make and quickly forsake friends because with the change of pleasure comes at the same time a change of friendship; and youthful pleasure is swift to change.*   **1156a33–1156b1; 1572**

9. *Moreover, young people are amorous; they love on account of passion and pleasure, and this is conducive to intense love. For this reason such persons quickly cease to love; oftentimes they fall in and out of love the same day. But they want to remain together all day and live with one another. This is the way their friendship works.*   **1156b1–6; 1573**

10. *Perfect friendship, however, is friendship between men who are good and resemble on another according to virtue,*   **1156b7–8; 1574**

11. *for those who are alike in virtue wish one another good inasmuch as they are virtuous, and they are virtuous in themselves.*   **1156b8–9; 1575**

12. *But people who wish good to friends for their sake are the truest friends; they do this for the friends themselves and not for something incidental.*   **1156b911; 1576**

13. *Therefore, friendship between such men remains as long as they are virtuous; and virtue is a permanent habit.*   **1156b11–12; 1577**

14. *Likewise each friend is not only good in himself but also to his friend, for the virtuous are good without qualification, and useful and entirely pleasing to one another. This is so because each man's own actions and the actions of a like nature are pleasing to him. But actions of virtuous men are of this or a similar kind.*   **1156b12–17; 1578**

15. *It is reasonable for such friendship to be long lasting, because absolutely all the qualities necessary for friends are joined together in it. Every friendship is for the sake of good or pleasure, either absolutely or to the one loving and according to a kind of likeness. But all the preceding qualities are found in this friendship essentially; and those who are alike according to this friendship have the remaining goods too, because what is without qualification good is also unreservedly pleasurable.* 1156b17–23; 1579

16. *These things then are most lovable. Hence love of them should be most intense, and such friendship the noblest.* 1156b23–24; 1580

17. *Very likely friendships of this kind are rare, since virtuous men are scarce.* 1156b24–25 1581

18. *Besides, time and familiarity are needed. This is so because, according to the proverb, people do not know one another until they eat salt together. But men ought neither to take others as friends nor become friends until each appears to the other worthy of love and is trusted by the other.* 1156b25–29; 1582

19. *However, those who at once offer the services of friendship show that they wish to be friends but in fact are not unless they are lovable to each other and know it. So then the wish for friendship is quickly made but not friendship itself.* 1156b29–32; 1583

Chapter 4

20. *A friendship of this kind is perfect both in regard to duration and the remaining conditions; and in all respects each receives from each the same benefit—as is proper between friends.* 1156b33–35; 1584

COMMENTARY OF ST. THOMAS

1562. After the Philosopher has shown the nature of friendship, he now distinguishes the kinds of friendship. On this point he does two things. First he makes his distinction. Then [Lect. XIII], at "There are three etc." (1162a34), he shows which kinds of friendship give rise to complaints or grumblings. He treats his first point from two aspects. First he distinguishes the kinds of friendship which exist between persons of equal rank. Next [Lect. VII], at "There is another etc." (1158b11), he distinguishes the kinds of friendship that exist between persons of unequal rank. On the first point he does two things. First he distinguishes the kinds of friendship. Second [Lect. VI], at "Consequently, the friendships etc." (1158 b), he shows that these consist in equality. He discusses the first point from three aspects. First [1] he distinguishes the kinds of friendship. Then [Lect. V], at

"Just as in the case etc." (1157b5), he treats them in relation to their acts. Last [Lect. VI], at "But friendship etc." (1158a3), he treats them in relation to their subjects. On the first point [1] he gives the distinction of the kinds. Next [2], at "Therefore of those etc.," he treats the particular kinds.

1563. He says first that there are three kinds of lovable objects, as indicated (1552, 1557), namely, the good as such, the pleasurable, and the useful; these do not differ in kind as three equal species of a genus but are classified by priority and posteriority. Since acts are diversified according to the difference of objects, the types of love will differ in kind according to these three: thus there is one type of love by which a thing is loved for the good, another for the pleasurable, and a third for the useful. Likewise, because love is an act of friendship, there will be three kinds of friendship equal to the three objects of love. One is friendship for the honorable good or the good as such, another for the pleasurable, and a third for the useful.

1564. In each of these the definition of friendship just given is fulfilled, because in each of the three a recognized return of love by someone is possible. Likewise in these three, people can will good to one another according to their love. For example, if men love for the sake of virtue, they wish one another the virtuous good; but if for a good based on utility, they wish one another useful goods; if for a good based on pleasure they wish pleasurable goods.

1565. Next [2], at "**Therefore of those**," he treats the kinds of friendship just mentioned which are contained under friendship not according to equality but according to priority and posteriority. So he does three things. First [2] he treats friendship based on utility and that based on pleasure which share the nature of friendship by posteriority. Then [10], at "Perfect friendship, however etc.," he treats friendship based on the honorable, i.e., good by itself to which the notion of friendship primarily and essentially pertains. Last [Lect. IV], at "But that etc." (1157), he compares the other kinds of friendship with this kind. He discusses the first point from two aspects. First [2] he shows just what the different kinds of imperfect friendship are; then [4], at "This friendship," to whom they belong. On the first point he does two things. First [2] he shows that useful and pleasurable friendships are friendships in an incidental sense. Second [3], at "Since men etc.," he shows that they are easily dissolved.

1566. He says first that of those who love one another for the sake of utility, one does not love the other for the sake of the other but inasmuch as he re-

ceives from the other some good for himself. The same is true of those who love each other on account of pleasantness, for the one does not love the other precisely as witty or virtuous in merriment but merely as pleasant to himself. So it is obvious that those who love for the sake of utility love for the good they get, and those who love for the sake of pleasantness love for the pleasure they enjoy. Thus they do not love their friend for what he is in himself but for what is incidental to him, his utility or pleasantness. Therefore, friendships of this sort plainly are not friendships essentially but incidentally, because a person is not loved for what he is but for utility or pleasure.

1567. Then [3], at "**Since men,**" he shows that friendships of this kind are easily dissolved. They are for the sake of something that is incidental to the persons loved and in this men do not always remain the same. The same man, for instance, is not always pleasant or useful. Therefore, when those who are loved cease to be pleasant or useful, their friends stop loving them. This is very obvious in friendship based on utility, for the same thing is not always useful to a man. It is one thing now, and then another in different times and places. So a doctor is useful for sickness, a sailor for navigation and so on. Since then friendship was cultivated not for the man himself but for the utility he afforded, when the cause of the friendship vanishes the friendship too is consequently dissolved.

1568. At "**This friendship**" [4] he shows to whom these friendships may be attributed. First [4] he shows to whom useful friendships belong; then [7], at "Young men seem etc.," to whom pleasurable friendship. He notes three classes of men who avail themselves of useful friendship. First [4] he says that his friendship seems to exist especially among old men who are not looking for what is pleasurable for the delight of body and sensitive nature, but rather what is useful for help needed for their natural deficiency.

1569. Second [5], at "**It is also,**" he says that is the kind of friendship pursued by adolescents and youths who seek what is useful. They seem quite incapable of possessing mutual love or even of remaining constant companions because sometimes they are not agreeable to one another; neither does one need the companionship of another except for utility. Their association with one another is pleasurable to them inasmuch as it holds some hope of good for which this association is useful.

1570. Third [6], at "**To the same,**" he says that to friendships based on utility some reduce even the friendship of fellow travelers who seem to love one another for the advantage that one derives from another on his journey.

1571. Next [7], at "**Young men seem,**" he shows to whom pleasurable friendship may be attributed. On this point he does two things. First [7] he explains to whom this friendship may be assigned, saying that friendship based on pleasure belongs most of all to youths. This is so because they live according to the impulses of passion since they have not been strengthened in rational judgment by which the passions are regulated. Because all passions terminate at pleasure and pain, as we stated in the second book (296, 441), youths principally seek what is pleasurable at the present moment. The passions belong to the sensitive part of man which is chiefly concerned with the present. But to love a present thing because it is productive of future pleas-

ure coincides with the notion of the useful.

1572. Then [8], at "**As they grow older,**" he shows that these friendships readily change in two ways: first [8], on the part of the pleasurable objects, because other things become pleasing to them with the passing of time. It is not in the same thing that children, adolescents, and youths alike find pleasure; and so they easily make friends and easily forsake them because with the change of pleasure comes a change of friendship. But youthful pleasure is characteristically swift to change since the nature of youth consists wholly in a state of change.

1573. At "**Moreover, young people**" [9] he shows the same thing on the part of those who love. He says that young people are volatile, i.e., quick and vehement in their love because they love not from rational choice but from passion and inasmuch as they are very desirous of pleasure. Therefore they love passionately and intensely. Since passion vanishes as quickly as it appears, such persons as easily fall in love as they cease to love; many times they even fall in and out of love the same day. But as long as the friendship endures these people want to remain together all day long and live in the other's presence inasmuch as they enjoy the company of each other. This is the way their friendship works.

1574. Next [10], at "**Perfect friendship, however,**" he treats the principal kind of friendship which is for the good of virtue. First [10] he points out that this friendship is perfect. He says that the friendship between good men and those alike in virtue is perfect friendship.

1575. Then [11], at "**for those who,**" he proves his statement by explaining the qualities of this friendship. First

[11] he shows that this is friendship essentially and not incidentally. Second [14], at "Likewise each," he shows that it lacks nothing. Third [17], at "Very likely etc.," he shows that it is rare. He handles the first point in a threefold manner. First [11] he shows that the friendship just referred to is friendship essentially and not incidentally. Those who are alike in virtue wish one another good inasmuch as they are virtuous. But they are good in themselves, for virtue is a kind of perfection making man good and his work good. It is clear then that such men wish good to one another in themselves. Therefore they have friendship essentially.

1576. Second [12], at "**But people who**," he concludes from this that friendship of this type is the best friendship; that which is essential is always better than that which is incidental. Since this is friendship essentially and the others incidentally, the virtuous who wish good to friends for their sake and not for the sake of something that may come from them are the highest type of friends.

1577. Third [13], at "**Therefore friendship**," he infers further: from the fact that men of this kind love one another by reason of their goodness, their friendship consequently remains as long as they are good in virtue. But virtue is a permanent habit and does not change easily, as is clear from discussions in the second book (305). Therefore this friendship is lasting.

1578. At "**Likewise each**" [14] he shows that this friendship lacks nothing that belongs to the notion of what is perfect, as is evident in the third book of the Physics (Ch. 6, 207a10; St. Th. Lect. XI, 385). On the first point he does three things. First [14] he shows that this friendship comprehends those things that are found in other kinds of friendship. He explains that each friend is good not only simply or in himself but also in relation to his friend, because those who are virtuous are also good without qualification and useful to one another and completely pleasing. This is so because each man takes pleasure in his own actions and in actions similar to his own. Likewise the actions of virtuous men are those belonging to one man as proper to him and to another as similar to these; for operations that are according to virtue are not contrary to each other but all are according to right reason. So then it is obvious that the friendship of virtuous men comprehends not only good in an unqualified sense but also pleasure and utility.

1579. Then [15], at "**It is reasonable**," he concludes further that it is reasonable for such friendship to be long lasting and not readily transient, because it contains absolutely everything necessary for friends. Every friendship is for the sake of good or pleasure: either in itself (for example, when what is loved is in itself good and pleasurable) or in relation to the one loving which is to be good and pleasurable not in itself and properly but according to a kind of likeness to what is really and properly good and pleasurable. In fact all the preceding things are found in this friendship not incidentally but essentially; and those who are alike according to this friendship have the remaining goods too, because what is simply good is also pleasing. Since this friendship has all the requisites of friendship, it is not easily broken up, for a defective thing is usually set aside.

1580. His third conclusion [16], at "**These things then**," observes that this friendship is the noblest kind because he state in which all the reasons for oving are united is most lovable. Objects of this kind are honorable goods because they are good without qualification and at the same time pleasurable and useful. Hence love in these cases should be most complete, and such friendship the noblest.

1581. Next [17], at **"Very likely,"** he shows that this friendship is rare—an indication of its perfection, for perfection in any class is rather unusual. On this point he does three things. First [17] he explains his intention. Then [19], at "However, those who etc.," he excludes an objection. Last [20], at "A friendship of this kind then etc.," he gives a summary. He explains his intention by two reasons. The first [17] is that this friendship exists between virtuous men. But such men are scarce because of the difficulty of attaining the mean, as was pointed out in the second book (370). Consequently it is very likely that such friendships are rare.

1582. Then [18], at **"Besides, time,"** he gives the second reason. Friendship between men of this kind requires a long time and mutual association so that they can decide among themselves who are virtuous and their friends.

This is so because, according to the proverb, people do not come to know one another before they eat a peck of salt together. But one man ought not to take another as his friend until he appears to the other worthy of being loved and is believed to be so. This rarely occurs. Consequently such friendships are uncommon.

1583. Next [19], at "**However, those who,**" he excludes an objection concerning those who seem to become friends at once. He says that people who quickly offer the services of friendship show that they want to be friends; nevertheless they are not yet friends until they know that they are lovable to one another. Thus it is clear that a man quickly acquires a wish for friendship but not friendship itself.

1584. Last [20], at "**A friendship of this kind,**" he concludes with a summary that this friendship is perfect both in regard to duration because it is lasting, and in regard to the other conditions. It contains everything found in the other kinds of friendship; and friends perform like services for each other—a thing that is necessary for friendship because friends are alike in virtue.

LECTURE IV
Useful and Pleasurable Friendships Compared

TEXT OF ARISTOTLE (*1156b35–1157b5*) Chapter 4

1. *But the friendship for pleasure has a likeness to this friendship, for virtuous men are pleasing to one another. The same can be said about utilitarian friendship since virtuous men are also useful to one another.* **1156b35–1157a3; 158!**

2. *But here again friendships are to a great extent lasting when an equal return, of pleasure for instance, is made by each friend; and not only by a return of pleasure, but also by a return of the same pleasurable object, as happens among the witty. This does not occur between a lover and his beloved, however, for they do not take pleasure in the same things: one in seeing the beloved, the other in receiving the attention of the lover. But when beauty fades, the friendship sometimes breaks up, because the lover is no longer attracted by the beloved and the other no longer receives the adulation of the lover.* **1157a3–10; 1586–1587**

3. *Again, many persons remain friends when they become accustomed to each other's natural dispositions, these being similar.* **1157a10–12; 1588**

4. *Where people do not exchange pleasure but profit in matters of love, their friendship is less intense and also less enduring.* **1157a12–14; 1589**

5. *Likewise, people who are friends by reason of utility break up their friendship when utility ends because they were not lovers of one another but only of profit.* **1157a14–16; 1590**

6. *Therefore, for the sake of pleasure and utility bad people may be friends to one another, or good men may be friends to bad men; and those who are neither good nor bad may be friends with any sort of person. But it is plain that only virtuous men love each other because of themselves, for vicious men do not find pleasure in one another unless some advantage is forthcoming.* **1157a16–20; 1591**

7. *Only the friendship between virtuous men is unchangeable. For it is not easy to believe some evil about a person who often has been proved and never found acting unjustly, and in whom we have discovered whatever is considered worthy of true friendship. But in other types of friendship there is nothing to prevent all such kinds of suspicions from occurring. Indeed men designate as friends both those who love for utility, like alliances between states which seem to be contracted with a view to advantage, and those who love for pleasure, like children. Consequently we too should call men of this sort friends.* **1157a20–30; 1592–1593**

8. *There are then many kinds of friendship. First and principally is the friendship between good men qua good. The remaining types are called friendship by analogy, for some men are friends in virtue of something good or something akin to good; even what is pleasurable seems to be good to those who are fond of pleasures. But these friendships do not combine very well nor do the same persons become friends from motives of utility.*

Things that are incidental are not bound together in all respects. But friendship is divided into these species: evil men can be friends for pleasure or utility, this being their point of resemblance. On the other hand, good men are friends for one another's sake, i.e., in virtue of their goodness. The good then are friends in an absolute sense, but the others only incidentally and because of their resemblance to the good. **1157a30–1157b5; 1594–1595**

COMMENTARY OF ST. THOMAS

1585. After the Philosopher has treated the three kinds of friendship, he now compares them. On this point he does three things. First [1] he shows in what respect the other kinds of friendship are like perfect friendship. Then [6], at "Therefore, for the sake etc.," he shows how they differ. Last [8], at

"There are then etc.," he summarizes what has been discussed. He treats the first point in a twofold manner. First [1] he shows the likeness of the other kinds of friendship with perfect friendship in regard to the reason for loving. He explains that friendship for pleasure has a likeness to perfect friendship to the extent that virtuous men are pleasing to one another. Similarly, utilitarian friendship is like perfect friendship in this that virtuous men are useful to one another.

1586. Second [2], at "**But here again,**" he shows the likeness in regard to the duration of friendship. On this point he does two things. First [2] he shows how useful and pleasurable friendships endure. Next [5], at "Likewise, people who etc.," he shows which of these is more enduring. He discusses the first point from a double aspect. First [2] he proposes two reasons why these two kinds of friendship are lasting; and in this they resemble perfect friendship. Then [4], at "Where people etc.," he states the reasons why they lack permanency. Initially [2] he says that friendships even among those who are friends for utility and pleasure endure for the most part, since such persons make the same and an equal return to one another, for example, pleasure for pleasure. Because there is a variety of pleasures differing in kind and number according to the variety of pleasurable objects, the durability of friendship requires not only a return of pleasure but a return by the same kind of pleasurable object; this occurs among the witty, when one delights in the banter of the other. But this does not necessarily happen among persons who love one another sexually, since sometimes they do not take pleasure in the same things.

1587. But the lover takes pleasure in seeing the beauty of the beloved; and the beloved in receiving favors from the lover. On the termination of these circumstances, pleasurable friendship sometimes breaks up when the attractiveness of the one and the favor of the other cease.

1588. At "**Again, many persons etc.,**" [3] he gives the second reason for durability. He explains that even in friendship based on utility and pleasure many remain friends when one loves the ways of the other, like one lustful person loves the ways of another, or one miser loves the ways of another; not that such ways are attractive of themselves but by reason of habit inasmuch as both persons have like habits. But likeness is essentially a cause of friendship unless it incidentally hinders the good of the individual, as we stated previously (1566). Since evil habits acquired from custom are enduring, such a friendship is lasting.

1589. Then [4], at "**Where people,**" he states the reason why friendship is deficient in durability. He says that people who do not make a return of one pleasurable object for another but of a useful object for a pleasurable one are less friends because of slighter likeness to one another. Hence their friendship is less enduring.

1590. Next [5], at "**Likewise, people who,**" he compares the durability of the two kinds of friendship. He says that men who are friends by reason of utility break up their friendship when utility ceases, because they were friends, not of one another, but of the utility they seek. But pleasure comes more from the beloved in himself, than does utility which sometimes is in an external object.

1591. At "**Therefore, for the sake**" [6] he states two differences by which the two kinds of friendship deviate from perfect friendship. First [6] he infers from the discussions that for the sake of pleasure and utility any type of men can become friends with one another, for example, the good with the good, the bad with the bad, and even those who are neither virtuous nor vicious with both (i.e., the good and the bad), and with each other. But only good men make friends in that perfect friendship by which men are loved for their own sakes; evil men do not provide anything except utility by reason of which they can love one another or find mutual pleasure.

1592. He gives the second difference at "Only the friendship" [7], saying that only friendship between virtuous men, which is the perfect kind, is of itself unchangeable. Friendship is destroyed especially when one friend finds in the other something opposed to their friendship. But this is impossible in friendship between the virtuous. A man does not readily believe some evil about one whom he has often proved and never found doing any wrong and in whom he has discovered whatever is considered worthy of true friendship. Consequently, such a friendship does not break up because it is friendship essentially and not incidentally, and because it is perfect containing in itself everything requisite for friendship—the reasons have been given before (1578–1582); and also because it does not admit as an obstacle to friendship what is now offered as a reason.

1593. But in other kinds of friendship nothing hinders one from believing evil of another and acting unjustly to another. Therefore, some would not be termed friends according to these types of friendship. But people have usually designated as friends of this kind both those who love for the sake of utility (friendship is said to exist among states because of the advantage of mutually fighting against their common enemies) and those who love one another for the sake of pleasure, as is evident among children. So we should follow the customary way of speaking and call such men friends.

1594. Last [8], at "There are then," he summarizes what has been said about the kinds of friendship, stating that there are many kinds of friendship. That between good men, as good, being friendship in the primary and proper sense, while the remaining kinds are called friendship from a likeness to this. Some men are called friends according to these types of friendship to the extent that there is present a likeness to true friendship. It is clear that what is pleasurable seems to be a kind of good to those who love pleasures. So this friendship has a likeness to that which is an unqualified good; and the same argument prevails in the case of useful friendship.

1595. However, these two kinds of friendship are not so combined that friends for utility and friends for pleasure are identical, for things that are incidental are not united in all cases, for instance, what is musical and white. The kinds of friendship just treated are friendships incidentally, as we have pointed out (1566), hence they are not always combined. If then, according to the division of friendship into the foregoing species, the evil can be friends among themselves, to that extent they are like one another in one or other of these aspects. But only the good are friends essentially; others are friends by way of resemblance, to the extent that they resemble the good.

LECTURE V
The Act and Habit of Friendship

TEXT OF ARISTOTLE (*1157b5–1158a1*) Chapter 5

1. *Just as in the case of the virtues, some men are called good by reason of habit and others by reason of performance; so in friendship, some actually live together pleasantly and do good for one another, others who are asleep or separated by place do not actually perform the works of friendship although they have its habit. Distance indeed, does not sever friendship itself but only prevents the acts of friendship.*   1157b5–11; 1596

2. *However, if the absence is prolonged, it apparently makes people forget friendship. So goes the proverb: "Out of sight, out of mind."*   1157b11–13; 1597

3. *Neither old men nor morose men seem inclined to friendship because there is very little that is pleasant in them. No one can continually live with a gloomy person or with one who is unpleasant, for nature avoids the painful and seeks the pleasant.*   1157b13–17; 1598

4. *But those who get along with one another and yet do not live together are more like well-wishers than friends.*   1157b17–19; 1599

5. *Nothing is so characteristic of friends as living together; the needy desire assistance but even the happy (who especially do not like to be alone) wish to spend their time with their friends. Men, however, cannot associate with one another unless they are pleasant and rejoice in the same things; this is found in the friendship of those who are comrades.*   1157b19–24; 1600

6. *Friendship, then, between the virtuous is friendship in the best sense, as we have noted many times. The reason is that what is wholly good and pleasurable seems to be lovable and worthy of choice; and a thing of this nature is lovable and worthy of choice by everyone. But it is for these two reasons that one virtuous man is good in the eyes of another virtuous man.*
                    1157b25–28; 1601

7. *Affection resembles an emotion but friendship itself is similar to a habit.*1157b28–29; 1602

8. *Affection, however, may be bestowed even on lifeless objects. But a return of love for love is accompanied by deliberate choice, and what is done by choice is from habit.* 1157b29–31; 1603

9. *Men wish good to friends for their sake, not from passion but from habit.*
                    1157b31–32; 1604

10. *Likewise, those who love a friend love their own good; for when a good man becomes a friend he also becomes a good to his friend. So each loves what is good for himself and repays equally both in goodwill and in pleasantness. The reason is that friendship is a kind of equality. What has been said applies especially to the friendship which exists between virtuous men.*
                    1157b33–1158a1; 1605–1606

COMMENTARY OF ST. THOMAS

1596. After the Philosopher has distinguished the kinds of friendship, he now treats them in relation to the proper act of friendship. On this point he does two things. First [1] he distinguishes friendship by reason of habit and act. Second [7], at "Affection resembles etc.," he proves what he had assumed. He discusses the first point from three aspects. First [1] he distin-guishes the kinds of friendship by way of habit and act. Then [2], at "However, if etc.," he shows that some lose friend-ship by lack of friendly acts. Last [6], at "Friendship then etc.," he shows that friendship especially between virtuous men arises from the nature of the very act of friendship. He says first that, as in other virtues some men are called good or virtuous by reason of habit (for example, the brave or the generous) even when they are not performing the act of virtue, but others are called virtuous for actually performing a virtuous action; so too in friendship some are friends actually inasmuch as they live together pleasantly and do good for one another—two things that seem to belong to the act of friendship. But others are not actually performing the works of friendship, although they are so disposed by habit that they are inclined to perform such works—this is obvious of friends who are asleep or locally separated from one another. Indeed, separation does not sever friendship itself but only friendship's activity. Thus it is evident that the habit of friendship remains even when its expression ceases.

1597. Then [2], at "However, if the absence," he shows how in some cases friendship ceases from a lack of friendly acts. First [2] he explains his proposition. Second [5], at "Nothing is so etc.," he proves what he had assumed. He explains his proposition in regard to three classes of men. First [2], about those who are separated from one another for a long time. He says that if the absence of friends from one another is prolonged, it seems to cause forgetfulness of a previous friendship. In this way other habits are also weakened and finally disappear from lack of use. As habits are acquired by practice, they must be preserved by practice, for everything is preserved by its cause. For that reason it has become proverbial that many friendships are destroyed through a man's neglect to call upon his friend, to converse and associate with him.

1598. Second [3], at "Neither old men," he shows the same thing about the old and the morose. He says that neither the old nor the morose, i.e.,

people severe in word and social intercourse, seem to be friendly or disposed for friendship because they are not inclined to the activity of friendship, namely, association. Very little that is pleasant is found in them. For this reason they are not easy to live with, for no one can spend his days (i.e., a long time) with a man who is gloomy or with one who is unpleasant. Men and other animals find it natural to avoid pain and seek pleasure which appears to be simply repose of the appetite in a desired good.

1599. Third [4], at "But those who," he shows the same thing about a third class of men, viz., those who are acceptable to one another in this, that one approves the ways and conduct of the other although for some reason the two never live together. Such persons, he says, are more like well-wishers than friends because friendship requires living together for some time.

1600. Next [5], at "Nothing is so," he proves what he had assumed, namely, that living together is required for friendship as its proper act. He says nothing is so characteristic of friends as living together. Previously (1595) he stated that two works belong to the act of friendship: living together and bestowing favors on one another—this is to bring a friend some benefit, a thing that not all but only the needy seek from friends. Even happy people, i.e., those with abundance (who do not like to be alone) desire to spend their days (i.e., a long time) with friends. Nor can men associate with one another if they are not mutually pleasant and do not rejoice in the same things—two qualities found in the friendship of those who are brought up together. So then it is evident that the principal act of friendship is to live with one's friends.

1601. At "Friendship then" [6] he

concludes from the premises that friendship between virtuous men is friendship in the best sense, as we have frequently noted (1574–1579, 1592). That seems to be lovable and absolutely worthy of choice in itself which is wholly good and pleasurable. But something of this nature, i.e., good or pleasurable in itself is lovable and worthy of choice for everyone. But one virtuous man is lovable to another and worthy of choice for these two reasons: each is good and pleasant without qualification, and each is good and pleasant to the other. Consequently, virtuous men especially can live pleasantly with one another.

1602. Then [7], at "**Affection resembles,**" he proves what he had previously assumed: that friendship may be predicated not only according to act but also according to habit. On this point he does three things. First [7] he states his proposal, saying that affection seems to indicate passion. But friendship seems to indicate habit and to be like other habits.

1603. Second [8], at "**Affection, however,**" he proves his proposition by two reasons. The first [8] is that one-sided love can be bestowed even on lifeless objects, as we are said to love wine or gold. But mutual love—which belongs to the notion of friendship, as we have indicated (1557)—is accompanied by deliberate choice, for this is found only among rational beings. But what is done by choice is not done from passion but rather from habit. Therefore friendship is a habit.

1604. He gives the second reason at "**Men wish**" [9], saying that by friendship men wish good to friends for their friends' sake. If men wished good for their own sake they would love themselves rather than others. But to love others for their sake is not from passion because passion, since it belongs to the sensitive appetite, does not go beyond the particular good of the one loving. Consequently, it remains that this is from habit; and so friendship is a habit.

1605. Third [10], at "**Likewise, those who love,**" he answers an implied objection. It has just been said (1601) that what is good to anyone is lovable to him. It seems contrary to this, that a man loves his friend for the friend's sake. But he answers that those who love a friend love what is good to themselves. When a person, who is a good in himself, becomes a friend to someone, he also becomes a good to his friend. So each, in loving his friend, loves what is good for himself; and each makes an equal return to his friend both in the fact of willing—as he wishes good to his friend—and in the kind of willing. He wishes good to his friend not for his own but for the friend's sake. The reason is that friendship is a kind of equality precisely as it requires mutual love. This seems to be an addition above the mode of virtue, for in any virtue the act of the virtuous man is enough. But in friendship the act of one is not sufficient but the acts of two mutually loving one another must concur. For that reason the Philosopher did not state absolutely that it is a virtue but added "or at least accompanies virtue," because it seems to add something above the notion of virtue.

1606. The observations that have been made about friendship seem to be especially applicable to friendship between virtuous men.

LECTURE VI
Friendship in Relation to Its Subject

TEXT OF ARISTOTLE (*1158a1–1158b11*) Chapter 6

1. *But friendship among morose and elderly people occurs less frequently inasmuch as they are more peevish and have little taste for conversations that especially seem to be the marks and cause of friendship. For this reason youths make friends quickly but not old people, for they cannot become friends of those whose company they do not enjoy. The same reason holds for austere persons who, nevertheless, entertain kindly feelings toward one another; for they wish each other well and assist one another in their needs. However, they do not really become friends because they do not live together nor take pleasure in one another's company—activities that are especially characteristic of friendship.* 1158a1–10; 1607–1608

2. *It is not possible to be a friend of many people by perfect friendship, as neither is it possible to be in love with many persons at the same time. Perfect friendship has a likeness to excess, but it is designed by nature for one object only.* 1158a10–13; 1609

3. *Then too it is difficult for many to be exceedingly pleasing at the same time to the same person. But perhaps this would not be expedient.* 1158a13–14; 1610

4. *Besides, friendship implies familiarity and experience which are very difficult.* 1158a14–15; 1611

5. *In friendships for the sake of utility and pleasure many may be pleasing to one. The reason is that many can be useful and pleasant, and their services can be rendered in a short time.* 1158a16–18; 1612

6. *Friendship between such persons, however, seems rather to be for the sake of pleasure since the same activities may be performed by both: they may find delight in one another and in the same things. The friendships of the young are like this.* 1158a18–20; 1613

7. *Their friendship seems more generous than friendship for utility, which is for gain.* 1158a20–21; 1614

8. *But fortunate people have no need of useful friends, although they do need pleasant friends for they must live with others. People can bear unpleasantness for a time but no one can continuously endure something unpleasant—not even good itself if it were displeasing.* 1158a22–25; 1615

9. *For this reason people look for pleasant friends; even those who are friends for virtue's sake must also be pleasant and good to one another. Thus they will have all the requisites for friendship.* 1158a25–27; 1616

10. *Men in power seem to have different classes of friends, some of whom are useful and others pleasant to them; for the same persons are not likely to be friends in both ways.* 1158a27–30; 1617

11. *Nor do the powerful seek pleasant friends who are also virtuous nor friends useful for honorable projects. But to provide amusement they desire some who are witty, and others who are industrious in doing whatever they are commanded. Such qualities, however, are rarely found in the same person.* 1158a30–33; 1618

12. *It has been said, though, that a man can be a pleasant and useful friend at the same time, as in the case of the virtuous person. But a virtuous man does not become a friend of one who is eminent unless the latter is surpassed by the former in virtue. If this does not happen, there is no proportionate equality. But such people (who excel the good man in virtue) are not easy to find.* 1158a33–36; 1619–1620

13. *Consequently, the friendships discussed consist in equality, for friends both do and wish*

he same things for one another; or they exchange one thing for another, for instance, pleasure or utility.   **1158b1–3; 1621**

14. We have explained that these are less perfect and also less enduring friendships. Indeed according to their similarity or dissimilarity to the same thing they seem to be or not to be friendships. Inasmuch as they have a likeness to friendship based on virtue they seem to be friendships; for one kind has pleasure and the other utility. But perfect friendship has both. They differ, however, for perfect friendship is unchanging and permanent while the others quickly change; on account of this dissimilarity the latter do not seem to be genuine friendships.

1158b4–11; 1622–1623

COMMENTARY OF ST. THOMAS

1607. After the Philosopher has distinguished the different kinds of friendship, he now discusses these friendships in relation to their subject, that is, to friends themselves. This aspect he treats from three angles. First [1] he treats the aptitude and ineptitude of some persons for friendship; then [2], at "It is not possible etc.," the number of friends; last [10], at "Men in power etc.," the differentiation of friends. He says first that the more peevish they are, the fewer friendships morose and elderly people form because, presuming on themselves, they follow their own way. For that reason they cannot agree with others: they have little taste for conversation with others both because they are intent on themselves and because they are suspicious of others. But concord and conversation with friends seem especially to be the works of friendship and its cause.

1608. Consequently youths, who find much pleasure in conversation and readily agree with others, quickly make friends. This does not happen with old people, for they cannot become friends of those whose company and conversation they do not enjoy. The same reason holds for morose persons who are quarrelsome and critical of what others do. But such people, i.e., the elderly and the severe, can be benevolent inasmuch as they affectively wish good to others and even effectively assist them in their needs. However they do not really become friends because they do not live with nor take pleasure in the company of their friends—activities that seem to be the special works of friendship.

1609. Then [2], at "**It is not possible**," he treats the number of friends. He explains this point in a threefold manner. First [2] he shows that it is not possible to be a friend to many people by the perfect friendship that exists between virtuous persons. Second [5], at "In friendships etc.," he shows that this happens in two other kinds of friendship: those for utility and pleasure. Third [6], at "Friendship between etc.," he compares the two kinds of friends with one another. He shows first, by three reasons, that it is not possible for a person to be a friend of many people by perfect friendship built on the good of virtue. The first [2] is that, since this friendship is perfect and best, it has a likeness to excess in loving—if the extent of love be considered. But if we consider the notion of loving there cannot be an excess. It is not possible for virtue and a virtuous person to be loved excessively by another virtuous person who regulates his affections by reason. Superabundant love is not designed by nature for many but for one only. This is evident in sexual love according to which one man cannot at the same time love many women in an excessive manner. Therefore, the perfect friendship of the virtuous cannot extend to many persons.

1610. He gives the second reason [3] at "**Then too it is difficult.**" It is this. In perfect friendship friends are exceedingly pleasing to one another. But it is not easy for many to be exceedingly pleasing at the same time to the same individual, because few are to be found who do not have something displeasing to a person affected in some way by man's many defects and conflicting dispositions. Thus it happens that, while one is very pleasing, another may not be. Perhaps it is fortunate and desirable that many cannot be exceedingly pleasing to one man who, while associating with many, would not be able to care for himself. Therefore, one cannot be a friend to many by perfect friendship.

1611. He gives the third reason [4] at "**Besides, friendship etc.**" It is this. In perfect friendship we must become acquainted with a friend by habitual association. But this is very hard and cannot happen with many people. Therefore, one does not have many friends by perfect friendship.

1612. Next [5], at "**In friendships,**" he shows that in the other two kinds of friendship, which are based on utility and pleasure, it is possible for a man to have many friends who are pleasing to him; and this for two reasons. First, because many can be useful and pleasant. Second, because a long period of trial is not required, it suffices that for a short time people provide one another with pleasure, for example, or even some utility.

1613. Then [6], at "**Friendship between such,**" he compares the two kinds of friends. First [6] he states his proposition: with those just mentioned, among whom one can have many friends, friendship for pleasure's sake seems to be more like true friendship; on condition, though that the same thing is done by both, namely, each affords pleasure to the other, for in this way they rejoice in the same things—a characteristic of friendship. In fact, this is an indication that there is one pleasure for those who delight in the same things. But the case is different when pleasure is occasioned on the part of one and utility on the part of the other. However, such are the friendships among youths that on either side they love each other for the sake of pleasure.

1614. Second [7], at "**Their friendship,**" he proves his proposition by two reasons. The first [7] is that in pleasurable friendship friends love one another more generously than in useful friendship in which a profitable return is sought—this friendship seems to be a kind of business affair. Hence friendship for the sake of pleasure is more powerful, as more resembling perfect friendship, which is most generous inasmuch as by it friends are loved for their own sakes.

1615. He gives the second reason [8] at "**But fortunate people.**" It is this. Fortunate men, i.e., the rich, have no need of useful friends since they are sufficient unto themselves, but they do have need of pleasant friends, for they must live with others; and this is impossible without pleasantness. People can bear unpleasantness for a time. But no man can continuously endure something unpleasant; he could not even stand good itself if it were displeasing. Consequently men who do not find pleasure in virtuous activities cannot persevere in them, So then it is evident that pleasurable friendship is more effectual than useful friendship, s being necessary to a great number nd to more generous people.

1616. Third [9], at **"For this reason,"** e infers a corollary from the discussions. Since even an honorable good ould be intolerable if it were distasteul, it follows that friends for virtue's ake must be pleasant to one another. hey must be not only good in themelves, but also good to one another. hus they will have the requisites for iendship.

1617. Next [10], at **"Men in power,"** e treats the distinction of friends. On is point he does three things. First 0] he states his proposition, that men ituated in positions of power are acustomed to different kinds of friends 1 such a way that some are useful to em and others pleasant. It is not sual for the same men to be their iends in both ways.

1618. Second [11], at **"Nor do the** owerful," he proves his proposition om the fact that these powerful men o not seek the pleasures of virtue— is type of pleasure has utility connected with it. Nor do they seek friends seful in the attainment of honorable ood—this utility has a pleasure atched to it. For amusement they seek itty or entertaining people, like coedians. But for utility they desire ther friends (dinos) i.e., shrewd in xecuting whatever is commanded, ither good or bad. These two qualities, iz., shrewdness and jocularity, are not ound in the same person because skillul people are not given to jesting but serious matters. Hence it is evident hat the powerful have different kinds f friends.

1619. Third [12], at **"It has been said,** hough," he answers an objection. omeone can object that friends of the owerful are at the same time pleasant nd useful because, as was explained

previously (1585), a good or virtuous person is at the same time pleasant and useful. But Aristotle answers that the virtuous man does not become a friend of one eminent in power or riches unless the virtuous person is surpassed in virtue by the powerful. If this is not the case, the more powerful one who is surpassed in virtue does not make himself proportionately equal, i.e., does not give proportionate compensation to the virtuous man; that is to say, as the virtuous person defers to him as the more powerful so he should defer to the virtuous man as the better.

1620. Usually, to the extent that men excel in power and riches they think themselves better; and we are not accustomed to find men in power who also excel in virtue or defer to the virtuous as the better.

1621. Then [13], at **"Consequently, the friendships,"** he shows that the kinds of friendship discussed consist in equality. He treats this point in a twofold manner. First [13] he explains his proposition, concluding from the premises that the kinds of friendship just treated consist in equality. Since this is obvious about friendship for the sake of virtue, he proves the proposition in regard to friendship based on utility and pleasure: either men wish and do the same things for one another, i.e., return pleasure for pleasure or utility for utility, or they exchange one for the other, i.e., utility for pleasure or vice versa.

1622. Next [14], at **"We have explained,"** he shows how the two kinds compare with the definition of friendship. He says that from the discussions obviously the kinds of friendship which are less proper are less lasting than the perfect friendship of the virtuous, according to whose likeness or unlikeness friendships seem to be or not to be denominated. Inasmuch as they resemble perfect friendship they seem to be friendship according as one of them has pleasure and another utility. Perfect friendship has both.

1623. But in respect to other qualities they are dissimilar according as perfect friendship is unchanging and lasting.

The remaining kinds, however quickly change; they also differ in many other particulars, as is evident from the previous discussions (1594-1595). On account of this dissimilarity they do not seem to be species of true friendship.

LECTURE VII
Friendship Between Unequals

TEXT OF ARISTOTLE (*1158b11–1159a12*) Chapter 7

1. There is another kind of friendship that consists in an inequality, as the friendship of a ther with a son, or—in general—of an older with a younger person, of a husband with a wife, id of a ruler with his subject. **1158a11–14; 1624–1625**

2. These friendships, though, differ from one another because the friendship of parents for ildren is not the same as the friendship of ruler for subjects; nor is the friendship of a father for son the same as that of a son for a father; nor of a husband for a wife, as of a wife for a husband. **1158a14–17; 1626**

3. Indeed the virtue and function of these persons is different. **1158a17–18; 1627**

4. Different, too, are their motives for loving. Therefore their affections and friendships differ. **1158a18–19; 1628**

5. Certainly the same benefits are not received by each from the other, nor should they be ught. When children give to their parents what is due the authors of their being and when irents give to children what is due their offspring, there will exist between them a lasting and rtuous friendship. **1158a20–23; 1629**

6. In all friendships according to inequality love must be given proportionately. Thus the perior party is loved more than he loves; the same is true of the person who is more useful or ore excellent in any way at all. When love is bestowed according to excellence a kind of quality will arise that seems to belong to friendship. **1158a23–28; 1630**

7. Equality, however, does not seem to be applicable to justice and friendship in the same ay. Equality in justice is accounted first according to excellence and then according to uantity. But in friendship quantitative equality must be considered first and then what is in nformity with excellence. **1158a29–33; 1631–1632**

8. This is clearly the case if there is a great difference in virtue or vice or anything else, for en do not then remain friends; nor do they even expect to be friends. **1158a33–36; 1633**

9. This is evident in the case of the gods because they greatly exceed men in good things; it is ear too of kings, for people in humbler walks of life are not likely to have royal friends; it is true so of the best and wisest men with whom individuals of no distinction do not become friends. **1158136–1159a3; 1634**

10. In such matters then it is not possible to determine exactly at what point men can be iends, for, when many qualities are absent friendship still remains. But if the persons are far moved from one another, like men from God, the friendship ceases. **1159a3–5; 1635**

11. From this a doubt arises that men do not perhaps wish their friends the greatest goods, r example, that they become gods; for then the friends will not benefit them. **1159a5–8; 1636**

12. If it was correctly stated that a man wishes good things to a friend for his sake, we must uppose that the friend remains much the same person as he is. One wishes the most excellent oods to his friend as he is a man; **1159a8–11; 1637**

13. but perhaps not all goods, for everyone wishes good to himself most of all. **1159a11–12; 1638**

COMMENTARY OF ST. THOMAS

1624. After the Philosopher has distinguished the kinds of friendship that consist in equality, he now distinguishes the kinds of friendship that exist between unequal persons. He treats two aspects of this subject. First he determines the things pertaining in general to the distinction of such friendships. Then [Lect. IX], at "As we noted at the outset etc." (1159b25), he treats the distinction of these friendships according to their particular natures. On the first point he does two things. First [1] he discusses the friendships of a superior for a subordinate, as father for son, husband for wife. Second [Lect. VIII], at "Between opposites, however etc." (1159b12), he discusses friendships existing between opposites, like a poor man and a rich man, and so on. He treats the first point in a threefold manner. First [1] he distinguishes the classification of this friendship from the previous kinds of friendships. Then [2], at "These friendships, though etc.," he distinguishes friendships of this type from one another. Last [5], at "Certainly the same benefits etc.," he shows how these friendships are preserved.

1625. He says first that besides the foregoing friendships, which we said (1562–1595) consist in equality from the fact that they belong to persons having likeness in virtue or utility or pleasure, there is another kind of friendship that consists in inequality (inasmuch as one person excels another), as the friendship of a father with a son, or—in general—of an older with a younger person, or of a husband with a wife, or for the most part of a superior with a subordinate.

1626. Then [2], at "**These friendships, though,**" he differentiates these friendships from one another. First [2] he states his proposal, saying that friendships of this type differ in kind. He assigns two differences, one according to various relations of inequality: the friendship of a father for a son is one kind, and of a ruler for his subject is another. Another difference is ac-

cording to the contrasting relation of the superior and subordinate; for the friendship of a father for a son is not the same as the friendship of a son for father, nor is the friendship of a husband for a wife the same as the friendship of a wife for a husband.

1627. Second [3], at "**Indeed the virtue,**" he explains his proposal by two reasons. The first [3] is that, since friendship may be predicated according to habit and act, every friend necessarily should have an habitual disposition to do the things pertaining to friendship as well as the function itself of friendship. But it is clear in the case of the persons just mentioned that the function is not the same, for example of a father toward a son and of husband toward a wife or even of a son toward a father; and consequently there is not the same virtue. Therefore they are also different kinds of friendship.

1628. He gives the second reason [4], at "**Different, too, are.**" It is this. In these friendships there are different motives why people love. It is for different reason that a father loves a son and a son loves a father, and husband loves a wife. But according to the different reasons for loving there are different kinds of love and so different kinds of friendship.

1629. Next [5], at "**Certainly the same benefits,**" he shows how these friendships are preserved. First [5] he explains that they are preserved by the parties mutually offering what they should in regard to loving and being loved. Then [Lect. VIII], at "Because of a desire for honor etc." (1159a13), he explains how loving and being loved are related to friendship. He discusses the first point in a threefold manner. First [5] he shows how these friendships are preserved because the parties

ɪutually offer what is proper. Next [6],
t "In all friendships etc.," he shows
ɪat these reciprocations are consid-
ɪed according to proportionality. Last
ʔ], at "Equality, however etc.," he ex-
ɪains how this applies to justice and
ʔiendship in a different manner. He
ɪays first that in these friendships the
ɪame benefits are not bestowed by each
ʔiend, and it is unnecessary to expect
ɪ return the same benefits that one
ɪestows. For example, a son ought not
ɪ ask of his father the reverence that
ɪe son shows the father, as in the pre-
ɪous friendships pleasure was offered
ɪr pleasure and utility for utility. But
ɪhen children show their parents what
ɪ due those who have generated them,
ɪnd when parents show their children
ɪhat is due their offspring, there will
ɪxist between them a lasting and just or
ɪrtuous friendship.

1630. Next [6], at "**In all friend-
hips,**" he shows how what is proper
ɪ offered in these friendships. He says
ɪat in all friendships involving in-
ɪquality of one person to the other,
ɪve is given proportionately, so that
ɪe superior party is loved more than
ɪe loves; the same is true concerning
ɪe person who is more useful, more
ɪleasant, or more excellent in any way
ɪhatsoever. For when each person is
ɪved by reason of the worth he mani-
ɪsts, an equality of proportion that ap-
ɪarently pertains to friendship will
ɪnsue.

1631. Then [7], at "**Equality, how-
ver,**" he shows how this is applicable
ɪ justice and friendship in a different
ɪanner. First [7] he gives the differ-
ɪnce. Second [8], at "This is clearly
ɪtc.," he makes it clear by an indication.
ɪast [11], at "From this a doubt etc., he
ɪolves a doubt. He says first that equal-
ɪy and proportion, which are consid-
ɪred in the light of one's excellence, are

not found in the same way in justice
and friendship. For, as we have noted
in the fifth book (935) concerning justice, excellence first must be accounted
or judged according to proportion, and
then an exchange will be made according to equality. But in friendship, on
the contrary, an equality between the
persons loving one another first must
be taken into consideration and then
what is in conformity with excellence
must be offered to each.

1632. The reason for this difference
is that friendship is a kind of union or
association of friends that cannot exist
between widely separated persons; but
they must approach equality. Hence it
pertains to friendship to use an equality already uniformly established, but
it pertains to justice to reduce unequal
things to an equality. When equality
exists the work of justice is done. For
that reason equality is the goal of justice and the starting point of friendship.

1633. At "**This is clearly**" [8] he
clarifies his statement by an indication.
He discusses this point in a threefold
way. First [8] he states the indication.
He says that the declaration (1631–
1632) of the prime necessity of equality
in friendship is obvious from the fact
that, if there is a great difference in
virtue or vice or any other thing, men
do not remain friends; nor is it considered suitable for people to maintain
friendship with those who differ considerably from themselves.

1634. Second [9], at "**This is evident,**" he gives three examples. First, of
beings who greatly surpass men in all
good things. Hence they do not maintain friendship with men so as to converse and live with them. These
separated substances Aristotle calls
gods, according to pagan custom. The
second example is of kings whose

friendship people in humbler walks of life are not likely to have. He takes the third example from the best and wisest of men, with whom individuals of little worth do not become friends.

1635. Third [10], at "In such matters," he answers an implied question. Someone might ask what barriers can friendship overcome and what barriers can it not overcome. Aristotle answers that in such matters an exact determination is not possible. But it suffices to know in general that many qualities can be absent from one that are present in the other and the friendship still remains. If the persons are far apart, like men from God, then the friendship we are discussing does not survive.

1636. Then [11], at "From this a doubt," he solves an incidental doubt. First [11] he raises it. He says that from the discussions a doubt arises whether men can wish their friends the greatest goods, for example, that they be gods or kings or most virtuous. It seems not,

because then they will no longer have their friends, and in this way the themselves will lose great benefits viz., their friends.

1637. Next [12], at "If it was," he solves this doubt in two ways. First [12], when it was explained before (1604) that a man wishes good thing to a friend for his sake, we must suppose that the friend himself remain much the same, whatever that may be after the possession of these goods. A person wishes the most excellen goods to a friend as he is a man, not a he is changed into a god.

1638. He gives the second solution at [13] "but perhaps." He asserts that man wishes good to his friend, but no more than to all others, because every one wishes good to himself most of al. Hence it is not reasonable that a man should wish a friend those goods by which he will lose that friend who is a great good.

LECTURE VIII
Loving and Being Loved as Related to Friendship

TEXT OF ARISTOTLE (*1159a12–1159b24*) Chapter 8

1. *Because of a desire for honor most people seem to wish to be loved rather than to love.*
1159a12–14; 1639

2. *For this reason most men are fond of flattery. Now the flatterer is a friend of humbler status or pretends to be of a humbler status and to love more than he is loved.* 1159a14–16; 1640

3. *Being loved seems to be closely connected with being honored, which is something that most men desire.* 1159a16–17; 1641

4. *And yet men do not seem to desire honor for its own sake but only incidentally. The common run of men delight to be honored by the powerful because they hope to obtain something they need; they rejoice in the honor as an omen of good to be received. Others want to be honored by virtuous and wise men, desiring to confirm their own opinion about themselves. They delight, therefore, in a sense of their own goodness, having confidence in the judgment so expressed.* 1159a17–24; 1642–1643

5. *People however take pleasure in being loved for the sake of love.* 1159a25; 1644

6. *Therefore, being loved seems to be better than being honored; and friendship is in itself worthy of choice.* 1159a25–27; 1645

7. *Friendship, however, seems to consist rather in loving than in being loved. An indication of this is that mothers take more pleasure in loving than in being loved by their offspring. Some mothers give to others the rearing of their children; and while knowing them to be their children they love them, but do not seek a return of love if it is impossible both to love and be loved. They seem satisfied to know that their little ones are doing well; they love them even if the children in their ignorance cannot offer what is due a mother.* 1159a27–33; 1646–1647

8. *Since friendship consists rather in and friends are praised for it, the excellence of a friend seems to be found in loving. For this reason persons who love their friends in proportion to their worth remain friends and their friendship is lasting. In this way, more than any other, those who are unequal will become friends because they will thus be made equal. But then friendship is a kind of equality and likeness.* 1159a33–1159b3; 1648–1649

9. *This likeness is found especially among virtuous men, for they remain stable both in themselves and in friendship with one another. They neither ask others to do wrong nor do wrong themselves; and we may say that they even prevent evil. It is characteristic of virtuous men that they neither sin themselves nor suffer their friends to commit sins.* 1159a3–7; 1650

10. *Evil men, however, have no steadfastness, for they do not long remain the same. They are friends for the short time they rejoice together in evil.* 1159a7–10; 1651

11. *But friends for utility and pleasure remain longer in their friendships, for these last as long as pleasure and utility are provided by each party.* 1159a10–12; 1652

12. *Between opposites, however, friendship seems to be formed most of all for utility—thus between a poor man and a rich man, an uneducated man and a learned man—inasmuch as one friend seeks what he needs from the other who gives something in return.* 1159a12–15; 1653

13. *To this type of friendship may be assigned the lover and the beloved, the beautiful and the ugly.* 1159a15–16; 1654

14. *For this reason lovers seem ridiculous at times when they expect as much love as they give—a proper thing if the parties are equally worthy of love. But if they do not have this qualification they appear absurd.* 1159a16–19; 1655

15. *Perhaps one opposite does not seek another in itself but only incidentally, for what is really sought is the mean. This indeed is good for the dry, not that it become wet but reach a*

middle state. The same is true of the hot. Because these matters are foreign to our study, we ma dismiss them. 1159a19–24; 16!

COMMENTARY OF ST. THOMAS

1639. After the Philosopher has determined that friendship between unequal persons is maintained by a proportionality of loving and being loved, he now shows how loving and being loved pertain to friendship. On this point he does two things. First [1] he shows that loving is more characteristic of friendship than being loved. Then [8], at "Since friendship etc.," he shows that friendship is preserved by loving according to excellence or proportionately. He treats the first point from three aspects. First [1] he shows why some people wish rather to be loved than to love. Second [4], at "And yet men etc.," he compares being loved with being honored. Third [7], at "Friendship, however etc.," he shows that loving is more proper to friendship than being loved. He discusses the first point in a threefold manner. First [1] he states his proposition saying that the majority seem to wish rather to be loved than to love; and this because they are lovers of honor. It befits the more worthy, to whom honor is due, rather to be loved than to love.

1640. Next [2], at "**For this reason,**" he confirms his statement. From the fact that many people wish to be loved rather than to love, it follows that they are fond of flattery; they take pleasure in someone fawning upon them. The flatterer is either really a friend of humbler status, since it is characteristic of the lowly to indulge in flattery; or by flattering pretends to be a friend and to love more than he is loved.

1641. Third [3], at "**Being loved,**" he explains his statement (1639) that it is because of honor that men wish rather

to be loved than to love. He states th. being loved seems to be closely co nected with being honored whic many desire. Honor indeed is a ma of goodness in him who is honore and anything that is good or appa ently good is loved.

1642. Then [4], at "**And yet men,**" I compares being loved with being ho ored. On this point he does thre things. First [4] he shows why peop wish to be honored, saying that me apparently desire honor not for itse but incidentally. They seek to be hon ored especially by men of two classe

1643. Many are glad to be honore by the powerful, not for the honor itse but by reason of the hope they deriu from it. They expect to obtain som thing they need from those who hon them. So they delight in the honor as mark of the good disposition or kind affection of the persons honorin them. But there are others who want i be honored by just men, that is, by th virtuous and wise because in this wa they seek to confirm a personal opir ion about their own goodness. Thu they really rejoice in the fact that the are virtuous, as it were, accepting th for the judgment of good men who b the very act of honoring them seem i say they are good.

1644. Second [5], at "**People how ever,**" he teaches that men delight i the fact itself of being loved, since th very possession of friends seems to b the principal external sign of honor.

1645. Third [6], at "**Therefore, bein loved,**" he draws a conclusion. Sinc what is essential is more excellent tha what is incidental, it follows from th remises (1642–1644) that being loved is better than being honored inasmuch as friendship is in itself desirable.

1646. At **"Friendship, however"** [7] he shows in what the excellence of friendship consists: in loving or being loved. He says it consists rather in loving, for friendship is predicated by way of habit, as has been explained (1596, 1602, 1627). But a habit terminates at activity; and loving is certainly an activity, while being loved is rather passivity. Hence loving is more proper to friendship than being loved.

1647. He makes this clear by an example. Mothers who have a strong affection for their children take more pleasure in loving them than in being loved by them. Some mothers give their children to others to rear; knowing the children to be theirs they love them, nevertheless they do not strive much for a return of love, since this is not possible. But it seems enough for the mothers to see that their children do well and are in good health. Thus they love their little ones although the little ones cannot make a suitable return of love because of ignorance, since the children do not know them to be their mothers.

1648. Next [8], at **"Since friendship,"** he shows how friendship is maintained by loving according to excellence or proportionately. First [8] he shows how friendship is lasting because of the proportion that love achieves. Then [9], at "This likeness is found etc.," he compares the different kinds of friendship relative to what has been said before. He says first that, since friendship consists rather in loving than in being loved, friends are praised because they love and not because they are loved; in fact this is the compliment we pay lovers.

1649. Because everyone is praised for his own virtue, the virtue of a lover should be judged according to his love. For this reason persons who love their friends in proportion to their worth remain friends and their friendship is lasting. Thus, when people love one another according to their worth, even those who are of unequal condition can be friends because they are made equal in this way—provided that the one who is more lacking in goodness or some other excellence loves that much more. In this way the abundance of love makes up for the inadequacy of condition. So by a kind of equality and likeness, which properly belong to friendship, people become and remain friends.

1650. Then [9], at **"This likeness,"** he compares the different kinds of friendship in reference to his previous statements. First [9] he shows which friendship is most enduring. He says that the likeness, which causes and preserves friendship, seems to be found especially among virtuous men; for they remain like-minded both in themselves—they do not easily change from one thing to another—and in friendship with one another. This is so because the one has no need for the other to do anything evil for him, which would be contrary to the virtue of the agent. In this way neither of them serves the other in any evil. But if any evil may possibly occur among the virtuous, one rather prevents the other from doing wrong; for it is characteristic of virtuous men that they neither sin themselves nor allow their friends to commit sins.

1651. Second [10], at **"Evil men, however,"** he shows which friendship is least enduring, stating that evil men do not have any steadfastness or stability about them. The reason is that wickedness, to which they adhere, is in itself hateful and so their affection varies when they find nothing in which the will can repose; in this way they do not long remain like-minded. But they desire things contrary to what they previously wanted. Thus they are friends for a short time, as long as they enjoy the evil in which they agree.

1652. Third [11], at "**But friends for utility,**" he shows which friendships hold a middle place in this matter. He says that friends for utility and pleasure remain longer together in friendship than do friends in evil. Utility and pleasure are such that they may be loved. Hence friendships of this kind last as long as pleasure and utility are mutually provided. But it is otherwise with those who are friends for the sake of evil which has no lovableness in itself.

1653. Next [12], at "**Between opposites, however,**" he discusses friendship between persons of disparate condition. First [12] he shows under what species of friendship we may place friendship between opposites. Then [15], at "Perhaps one opposite etc.," he explains how contrary may seek contrary. On the first point he does three things. First [12] he shows that this friendship between persons of disparate condition seems to be for the sake of utility, inasmuch as one friend seeks from the other what he himself needs, and gives something in return to the other. Thus a poor man desires to obtain money from the rich man in return for service.

1654. Next [13], at "**To this type,**" he

shows how this may be characteristi also of pleasurable friendship. H states that to this type of friendship w may reduce sexual love by which th lover loves the beloved; for sometime there is the disparity of beauty anc ugliness. On the other hand, in friend ship based on virtue, there is no dispa rate condition because the greates likeness is found in it, as was notec previously (1580).

1655. Third [14], at "**For this rea son,**" he infers a corollary from th discussion. He says that since some times a contrary condition exists in th lover and the beloved, for example ugliness and beauty, it follows tha sometimes lovers are derided wh think they are worthy of being loved a much as they love. This is fitting wher they are equally worthy of love. But ii they have nothing of such a nature tha they are worthy to be so loved it i ridiculous for them to ask it.

1656. At "**Perhaps one opposite**" [15] he shows how contrary seeks its contrary. He says that this is not true from the nature of the thing (*secundum se*) but incidentally, for what is essentially (*per se*) sought is the mean which is the good of the subject induced to excess by one of contraries. For example, if a man's body is comfortably dry, perspiration is not good and desirable absolutely (*per se*) speaking, but as a means to a middle state attained by the moisture. The same reason holds for what is hot and contraries of this kind. Because these matters belong more to the study of physics, he says they will be passed over.

LECTURE IX
Friendships and Civic Association

TEXT OF ARISTOTLE (*1159b25–1160a30*) Chapter 9

1. *As we noted at the outset, friendship and justice evidently deal with the same topics and persons, for in every association there seem to be some kind of justice and also friendship.*
1159a25–27; 1657–1658

2. *Consequently, fellow voyagers and fellow soldiers are greeted as friends. So too are those who engage in other common ventures; for, to the extent that people share with one another, friendship—and justice too—exists among them.*
1159a27–31; 1659

3. *Correctly then the proverb says that friends' goods are common goods. Indeed friendship consists in mutual sharing.*
1159a31–32; 1660

4. *Brothers and comrades have all things in common. But other associates have certain definite things in common; some have more in common, others less. In accordance with this some friendships likewise differ in degree.*
1159a32–35; 1661

5. *Similarly the notions of justice differ. The same kind of right does not exist between parents and children as between brother and brother; nor are relations between companions the same as between fellow citizens. This is likewise the case in other types of friendship. Therefore, different acts of injustice are found among the persons just mentioned.*
1159a35–1160a3; 1662

6. *Moreover, acts of injustice are aggravated by being done to close friends. For example, it is more shameful to steal money from a comrade than a fellow citizen; to refuse help to a brother than a stranger; to strike one's father than someone else. Friendship and justice naturally increase at the same time as they exist between the same persons and are equally extensive.*
1160a3–8; 1663–1664

7. *All associations are like parts of civic association, for men come together for some advantage and acquire something necessary for life. But civic association seems to be formed and to endure for the sake of advantage, so that the citizens might seek and obtain some benefit accruing. Indeed legislators aim at this, and men call that just which contributes to the common good.*
1160a8–14; 1665–1666

8. *Other associations then seek some private gain. Thus sailors aim at a successful voyage in the hope of making money or something of the sort; fellow soldiers agree on the objective of war whether it be wealth, or victory, or the capture of a city; members of tribes and townships act in a similar way.*
1160a14–18; 1667

9. *Still other associations seem to be formed for the sake of pleasure, for example, religious choirs or minstrels; for they were established respectively to perform at the sacrifices and feasts.*
1160a19–20; 1668

10. *But all these were usually placed under civic association that aims not at present gain but at what is profitable all during life. And the people offer sacrifice and arrange gatherings to render honor to the gods and to acquire rest and pleasure for themselves. For the ancient sacrifices and gatherings took place after the harvest as an offering of first fruits, for at this period men had most leisure.*
1160a21–28; 1669–1670

11. *All these associations seem to be divisions of civic association. Consequently, the various kinds of friendships that we discussed will correspond to these associations.*
1160a28–30; 1671

COMMENTARY OF ST. THOMAS

1657. After the Philosopher has treated the different kinds of friend-

ships existing between unequal persons, he now distinguishes them according to their proper formalities. He handles this in two ways. First he shows that these kinds of friendships are distinguished in much the same way as civic associations. Then [Lect. X], at "There are three kinds etc." (1160a30), he distinguishes the kinds of friendships according to the distinctions of civic units. Concerning the first point he gives this argument. [1] Every friendship consists in association. [7] Every association is reduced to civic association. Therefore all friendships must be understood according to civic associations (*communicationes*). He treats this argument under three aspects. First he proves the first statement [1]; second, at "All associations are etc.," he proves the second statement [7]; third, at "all these associations etc.," he draws a conclusion [11]. He does two things in regard to the first point. First [1] he shows that every friendship consists in association. Next [4], at "Brothers and comrades etc.," he shows that friendship is differentiated according to the diversity of association.

1658. First [1], by the following argument. As was previously explained (1632) justice and friendship deal with the same things. But justice consists in association, for every kind of justice has a relation to another, as we stated in the fifth book (885, 886, 906, 909, 934). Therefore friendship too consists in association.

1659. Second [2], at "**Consequently, fellow voyagers**," he shows the same thing by customary speech. Men are accustomed to call friends those who share in any common undertaking: for example, fellow voyagers who take part in seafaring; fellow soldiers who share in military service. The same is true in other kinds of association, because friendship seems to exist among

people to the extent that they share with one another; and because, in accordance with this, justice also exists among them.

1660. Third [3], at "**Correctly then,**" he proves his contention by a current proverb. It is generally said that friends' goods are common goods. Therefore friendship consists in sharing in common (*communicatio*).

1661. At "**Brothers and comrades**" [4] he shows that friendships differ according to different modes of association. He discusses this point under three aspects. First [4] he explains the diversity of friendships according to the diversity of association. We see that brothers and similar relatives have all things in common, like home, table, and so on. But other friends have particular things as their own; some have more, some less. In accordance with this some friendships are greater, for example, among those who have many things in common; and others are less, as among those who have few things in common. From this it is very evident that if there were no communication there could be no friendship.

1662. Second [5], at "**Similarly the notions,**" he shows that justice is differentiated according to different types of association. The same kind of right is not found in every association, but a different kind. Thus it is obvious that the same right does not exist between father and sons, as between brother and brother. Likewise there is a different justice between etairos, i.e., people of the same age and rearing than between citizens, because they bestow different things on one another as mutually due. The same pattern holds in other kinds of friendship. So it is clear that different types of justice exist between the individuals just mentioned.

1663. Third [6], at "**Moreover, acts**"

of injustice," he shows how justice is differentiated according to the diversity of friendship. He says justice and injustice increase in proportion as they are done to closer friends. The reason is that it is just in a greater degree to do good to a closer friend, and unjust in a greater degree to injure him. So it is more offensive and unjust to rob or steal money from a familiar acquaintance or a comrade than from a fellow citizen; likewise, to withhold help from a brother than a stranger; to strike one's father than to strike someone else.

1664. That justice and friendship are extended at the same time arises from this, that they exist in the same persons and both pertain equally to some communication. This is confirmation of what was stated previously (1661).

1665. Then [7], at "**All associations,**" he shows that all associations are reduced to civic association. He treats this point in a twofold manner. First [7] he shows that all association has a likeness to civic association. Second [8], at "Other associations then etc.," he shows that all other associations are contained under civic association. He says first that every association has some likeness to the parts of civic association. We see that all associations agree in something useful, in the fact that they acquire something necessary for living. And civic association also appears to have this because fellow citizens seem both to have come together in the beginning and to have remained together for their common interest. This is evident for two reasons.

1666. First, because legislators seem to aim at this most of all, to obtain the general welfare. Second, because men call that just in a state which benefits the citizens generally.

1667. Next [8], at "**Other associa-**

tions," he shows that other associations are contained under civic association. On this point he does three things. First [8] he shows how some of the other associations are directed to a particular interest. He says that associations other than the civic intend some private gain. For example, fellow voyagers intend to acquire money or something of the sort if they are merchants. If they are soldiers they agree in the objective of the war, whether this be riches, victory alone, or capture of a city. In this way, too, those who belong to one tribe or one people agree on some private gain.

1668. Second [9], at "**Still other associations,**" he shows that even associations that are apparently formed for pleasure are really for some utility. He says still other associations seemingly exist for pleasure, e.g., choruses or those who sing together in a choir or a dance, and bands or those who play brass instruments like trumpets and cymbals. Associations of this kind were accustomed to be established for the sake of the religious cult so that men may be more pleasantly detained there, and on account of a wedding or nuptials that the groom and bride may have greater pleasure since they share in such great rejoicing.

1669. Third [10], at "**But all these,**" he shows from the premises that all the other previous associations are contained under civic association. He says that all were usually placed under civic association inasmuch as customarily all are directed by it. He gives the explanation because, as previously observed (1667), other associations are ordered to some private advantage. Civic association, however, does not aim at a private and present gain but at what is useful all during life. He shows this especially in regard to associations of persons providing entertainment; and most of all in sacrifices where it seems less evident.

1670. Aristotle says that people who offer sacrifice in gatherings of this kind intend to render honor to God and to acquire for themselves repose and a little pleasure, which is ordered to the good of living. Wherefore the ancients, also, gathered together after the harvest in the autumn to offer sacrifices, that is, to pay first-fruits. This was a suitable time for men to have leisure both that they might rest from their recent labors and because abundant food was available. So obviously all these things are subjected to the ordering of the state as they pertain to the benefit of living.

1671. At "**All these associations**" [11] he leads up to the conclusion intended, viz., that all associations are contained under civic association, as parts of it; to this extent others are directed to particular interests but civic association to the common welfare. Now since friendships are formed in relation to associations of this kind, it follows that the distinction of friendships should be observed according to the distinction of civic association.

LECTURE X
Distinction of the Kinds of States

TEXT OF ARISTOTLE (1160a31–1161a16) Chapter 10

1. There are three kinds of polity and just as many perversions or corruptions of it. These forms are kingdom, aristocracy, and a third aptly named timocracy from (timos) rewards. This last is usually called by most people simply polity.   **1160a31–35; 1672–1673**

2. Of these, however, the best is kingdom and the worst timocracy.   **1160a35–36; 1674**

3. The perversion of kingdom is called tyranny. Both are forms of monarchy but they differ very much, for a tyrant aims at his own selfish interest while a king strives for the good of his subjects. No man is truly a king who is not adequate of himself to rule and does not abound in all good things. Such a one is in need of nothing and therefore will not work for himself but for his subjects. Then too a king not independent of his subjects will resemble a ruler chosen by lot. But the very opposite of a king is a tyrant because he seeks his own profit. Obviously, this corruption is the worst, for the worst is contrary to the best. But a ruler deviates from a monarchy into tyranny, for the perversion of a monarchy is tyranny, and a wicked king becomes a tyrant.   **1160a36–1160b12; 1675–1677**

4. But aristocracy degenerates into an oligarchy through the wickedness of rulers who do not distribute the goods of the state according to merit but usurp all or most of them for themselves; and who always keep the same people in office, aiming at riches for the most part. As a result a few men, and those evil, gain control in place of the very virtuous.   **1160b12–16; 1678**

5. And timocracy deteriorates into democracy with which it is coterminous, for timocracy is also the rule of the masses, and all who own property are equal. Nevertheless, democracy has a minimum of perversion, as it departs very little from the character of the polity. Consequently, these are the ways in which polities are most easily transferred, being the least in degree and easiest to make.   **1160b16–22; 1679–1680**

6. Likenesses of these very forms of government can be exemplified in domestic affairs.
1160b22–24; 1681

7. Certainly the association of a father with his sons has the form of a monarchy, for he takes care of their interests. Hence Homer calls Jove "father" because paternal rule is the ideal of a monarchy.   **1160b24–27; 1682**

8. With the Persians the authority of a father is tyrannical; they use their sons as slaves. But the authority of a master over slaves is tyrannical, for he uses them to his own advantage. This procedure appears to be right while that of the Persians is wrong, because different kinds of authority are suitable for different kinds of persons.   **1160b27–32; 1683**

9. But the authority of husband and wife seems to be aristocratic, because the husband has dominion over the affairs pertaining to him according to his dignity and he hands over to the wife whatever pertains to her.   **1160b32–35; 1684**

10. On the other hand, when the husband is in charge of everything the rule is changed into an oligarchy, for then he acts unfairly and not according to his greater dignity. And when wives have dominion by reason of being heiresses, authority is not in virtue of excellence but according to riches and power, as is the case in oligarchy.   **1160b35–1161a3; 1685**

11. Among brothers authority seems to be timocratic, for they are equal aside from the difference in age; wherefore if their ages differ much the friendship will not then be called fraternal.   **1161a3–6; 1686**

12. Democracy, however, exists in those groups living together without a master (all being on an equal footing); in them the director has weak authority and everyone follows his fancy.
1161a6–9; 1687

COMMENTARY OF ST. THOMAS

1672. After the Philosopher has explained that the species of friendship are reducible to civic or political association, he now distinguishes them according to the divisions of political association. On this point he does two things. First he distinguishes the species of friendship according to the divisions of political association or states. Then [Lect. XII], at "All friendship then etc." (1161b11), he subdivides these kinds of friendship. He treats the first point in a twofold manner. First [1] he distinguishes the kinds of states one from another; second [Lect. XI], at "Each form of etc." (1161a10), according to these he distinguishes the kinds of friendship. He discusses the first point under two aspects. First [1] he distinguishes the kinds of states; second [6], at "Likenesses of these etc.," he points out the kinds of domestic association that resembles them. He handles the first point in a threefold manner. First [1] he indicates the forms of government; second [2], at "Of these, however etc.," he compares them; third [3], at "The perversion of kingdom etc.," he shows how they are corrupted.

1673. He says first that there are three forms of polity and just as many corruptions or violations. The three good forms are kingdom or the rule of one; aristocracy or the government by the best, in this that a society is governed by virtuous men. It seems fitting that there be another kind too, although some authors do not recognize it, as is evident in the fourth book of the *Politics* (Ch. 8, 1293b22–1294a29; St. Th. Lect. VII, 604–613). This is aptly called timocracy from *timos*—timos means reward—because under this form of government rewards are bestowed on the poor when they serve in a judicial capacity and penalties are imposed on the rich when they do not, as is clear from the fourth book of the *Politics* (Ch. 9, 1294a30–1294b41; St. Th. Lect. VIII, 614–620). Some are accustomed to call it by the common name polity from the fact that it is common to rich and poor, as appears in the fourth book of the *Politics* (Ch. 3–4, 1289b27–1290b20; St. Th. Lect. II, 544–556).

1674. Then [2], at "**Of these, however**," he compares these forms of government. He says that the best among these is kingdom in which the best qualified man rules. The worst, i.e., the least good, is timocracy in which many mediocre men govern. In the middle is aristocracy in which a few very good men rule; however, their power of doing good is not so great as in the best form where one ruler has the fullness of power.

1675. At "**The perversion of kingdom**" [3] he treats of the corruptions or perversions of these political systems. First [3] about the corruptions of kingdom; second [4], at "But aristocracy degenerates etc.," about the corruption of aristocracy; third [5], at "And timocracy deteriorates etc.," about the corruption of timocracy. He explains the first point under two headings. First he states his intent, saying that perversion or corruption of kingdom is called tyranny. He makes this clear first by the fact that they agree in kind, for both are forms of monarchy, i.e., rule by one. Just as one man governs in a kingdom so also in a tyranny.

1676. Then he indicates the difference between them, saying that they are vastly different. It seems that they are contraries since contraries are things that differ greatly and are in the same genus. He manifests this difference by saying that a tyrant in his government aims at what is useful to himself, but a king strives for what is beneficial to his subjects.

1677. He proves this by the fact that a ruler cannot truly be called a king who is not of himself adequate to rule, that is, excelling in all goods both of soul and body and external things, so he is worthy and able to govern. But when he is so endowed he needs nothing, so will not work for his own interest, which the poor characteristically do, but rather for the benefit of his subjects—as the affluent do. A man not excelling in all goods can better be called *clerotos*, as if chosen by lot to rule, than king. But a tyrant is the very contrary of a king because he seeks his own profit. So obviously this corruption is the worst, for the worst is contrary to the best. But a ruler deviates from a kingship that is best, as we have noted (1676), to a tyranny that is nothing else than a perversion of monarchy or one-man rule; and when a king becomes wicked he is called a tyrant. Hence it is evident that tyranny is the worst perversion.

1678. Next [4], at "**But aristocracy,**" he treats of the perversion of aristocracy, saying that an aristocracy degenerates into an oligarchy which is the government of a few. This happens by the wickedness of the rulers not distributing the goods of the state according to merit but usurping all or the greater part of them for themselves; and always keeping the same people in office, aiming especially at enriching themselves and their friends. By reason of this a few evil men come into power in place of very good men who rule in an aristocracy.

1679. At "**And timocracy deteriorates**" [5] he treats of the perversion of timocracy, saying it deteriorates into democracy, which is rule of the populace. In fact these two are coterminous or bordering upon one another, for they are alike in two ways. First, because timocracy or government of rewards is likewise the rule of the masses, just as democracy is. Second, in both forms of government all who occupy places of honor are equal. On the other hand they differ because in a timocracy the common good of the rich and the poor is intended, but in a democracy the good of the poor alone is aimed at. Hence the perversion inherent in democracy is the least, for it departs very little from timocracy which is a kind of good government.

1680. He concludes then that these forms of government change very much from one to another, and so are easily perverted, as has been pointed out (1675–1679).

1681. Then [6], at "**Likenesses of these very forms,**" he distinguishes between states and households according to resemblances to these forms (of rule). First [6] he shows what among them corresponds to a kingdom and a tyranny; second [9], at "But the authority etc.," what corresponds to aristocracy and oligarchy; third [11], at "Among brothers etc.," what corresponds to timocracy and democracy. He discusses the first point under three aspects. First [6] he states his intent, saying that a model and example of these forms of government can be found in domestic affairs.

1682. Next [7], at "**Certainly the association etc.,**" he shows which domestic relation corresponds to a kingdom. He states that association between a father and his sons resembles a kingship because a father has care of his sons, as a king of his subjects. Hence Homer calls Jove "father" because of his royal power. Indeed the rule of a father in his home is a kind of kingship.

1683. Third [8], at "**With the Persians,**" he shows what corresponds to household tyranny. He distinguishes two kinds. The first is the way Persian fathers look upon sons; for they treat their sons as slaves. The second is the way masters manage slaves; masters intend their own profit in the use of slaves. However, these two procedures differ, for the one in which masters employ slaves for their usefulness seems to be right. But the other in which fathers use their sons as slaves seems to be wrong. The reason is that completely different persons should be governed in different ways. Consequently, it is wrong for a man to govern children and slaves in the same manner.

1684. At "**But the authority**" [9] he shows what in households corresponds to aristocracy and its opposite. He treats his point in a twofold manner. First [9] he shows what corresponds to aristocracy. He says that the authority by which a husband and a wife govern a household is aristocratic because the husband has dominion and charge over the affairs that pertain to him according to his dignity and he hands over to the wife those matters that pertain to her.

1685. Second [10], at "**On the other hand,**" he states two procedures corresponding to oligarchy. One occurs when the husband wants to arrange everything and leaves the wife in charge of nothing. This does not accord with his dignity nor with what is best. The other procedure exists when wives have complete authority because they are heiresses, and then their authority does not arise from their excellence but from their riches and power, as in an oligarchy.

1686. Third [11], at "**Among brothers,**" he shows what corresponds to timocracy and its opposite. First [11], what corresponds to timocracy. He says that the authority wielded by brothers in a household seems to be timocratic because brothers are equal except for difference in their ages; if their ages are far apart, their friendship seems to be in a way paternal and not fraternal.

1687. Then [12], at "**Democracy, however,**" he shows what corresponds to democracy. He states that a resemblance to democracy exists in groups living together who have no director—companions staying at an inn, for instance. There all are on the same footing; if anyone has authority it is weak, for example, the one in charge of paying expenses. Each member has power in the dwelling, as in a democracy each individual has quasi-equal power and the directors can do little.

LECTURE XI
Friendships Conform to Kinds of States

TEXT OF ARISTOTLE (*1161a10–1161b10*) Chapter 11

1. *Each form of government seems to involve a kind of friendship inasmuch as justice is present.* **1161a10–11; 1688**

2. *The friendship of a king and his subjects is one of superiority in beneficence, for he confers benefactions on them if he is a good ruler, taking care that his subjects act virtuously; he is regarded as a shepherd of his flock. Hence Homer called Agamemnon the shepherd of his people.* **1161a11–15; 1689**

3. *Such too is the friendship of a father.* **1161a15; 1690**

4. *These friendships, though, differ in the greatness of benefits. A father is the cause of his son's existence (considered the greatest good in this life), rearing, and instruction—benefits that are attributed also to a man's ancestors.* **1161a16–18; 1691**

5. *Likewise, by nature a father rules his sons, an ancestor his descendants, and a king his subjects.* **1161a18–20; 1692**

6. *Friendships of this type imply a kind of excellence in the ruler. For this reason parents are honored; and so justice is not the same for both parties but must be proportioned to their worth. This is true also of friendship.* **1161a20–22; 1693**

7. *But the friendship between husband and wife resembles that found in an aristocracy. For it is in accordance with virtue, and more good is attributed to the better qualified although what is due each one is assigned to him. In this way justice is preserved.* **1161a22–25; 1694**

8. *Friendship between brothers is similar to that among comrades, for they are equal and around the same age; and persons like this have much the same training and habits. There is a likeness to this in the friendship found in a timocracy, for the citizens aim at equality and virtue; they share power equally and in turn. So their friendship too will be one of equality.* **1161a25–30; 1695**

9. *On the other hand, as in corrupt forms of rule there is little justice, so there is little friendship.* **1161a30–31; 1696**

10. *It is minimal in the worst system, for in a tyranny no friendship, or very little, is found.* **1161a31–32; 1697**

11. *In those regimes where nothing is shared by the ruler and the subjects no friendship exists, nor is there any justice; for the subject is like a tool to an artisan, the body to the soul, a slave to a master. These objects are benefitted by the things that use them. But lifeless instruments are not subjects for friendship (or justice); nor are horses or cattle; neither is a master a friend to a slave qua slave, for they have nothing in common. In fact a slave is a living tool, and a tool a lifeless slave.* **1161a32–1161b5; 1698–1699**

12. *Consequently, there can be no friendship with a slave qua slave but only qua man. Indeed a man can have a kind of justice toward anyone who can share something according to law or agreement. The same too holds for friendship with a man inasmuch as he is a man. There is then little room for friendship or justice under tyrannies.* **1161b5–9; 1700**

13. *In democracies, however, friendship is most fully realized, for where all are equal there is much sharing.* **1161b9–10; 1701**

COMMENTARY OF ST. THOMAS

1688. After the Philosopher has distinguished the kinds of political and domestic association, he now distinguishes the corresponding kinds of friendships. He discusses this point in a twofold manner. First [1] he states his intent. He says each form of government and political order apparently involves a kind of friendship from the fact that in every polity a kind of justice is found. But friendship and justice are in some way concerned with the same matters, as we have indicated (1658, 1664).

1689. Second [2], at "**The friendship**," he explains his statement: first [2] in regard to good forms of government; next [9], at "On the other hand etc.," in regard to evil systems. He treats the first point under three headings. First [2] he shows how friendship can exist on the basis of kingdom; then [7], at "But the friendship etc.," on the basis of aristocracy; last [8], at "Friendship between brothers etc.," on the basis of timocracy. On the first point he does two things. First [2] he shows how friendship may exist between a king and his subjects. Second [3], at "Such too is etc.," he compares a father's friendship with a king's. He says first that by reason of benefit a superabundant friendship exists between a king and his subjects, as between a benefactor and a beneficiary. It is proper to a king to confer benefits on his subjects, for if he is a good ruler he takes care that they perform good deeds, and strives to make his subjects virtuous. Hence, inasmuch as he leads his subjects as a shepherd his flock, he is even given the title. Thus Homer called King Agamemnon shepherd of his people.

1690. Then [3], at "**Such too is**," he compares paternal with regal friendship. He considers four aspects of this point. First [3] he compares a father's friendship with a king's, saying that the friendship of a father is like that of a king.

1691. Second [4], at "**These friend-**

ships, though,**" he shows the difference between the two friendships, noting that they differ in greatness of benefits. Although the benefaction of a king absolutely speaking is greatest insofar as it extends to all the people, nevertheless the benefaction of a father is greater in relation to one person. A father is the cause of the son's three greatest goods. First, by generation he is the cause of the son's existence (considered the greatest good); second, by upbringing, of his rearing; third, of his instruction. These three goods are attributed not only to fathers in regard to their sons but also to the ancestors, viz., the grandfathers and the great-grandfathers in regard to their grandsons and great-grandsons.

1692. Third [5], at "**Likewise, by nature**," he proves his statement that the friendship of a father is like a king's. By nature a father is the ruler of his son and an ancestor of his descendants, just as a king is a ruler of his subjects. Consequently, sons are under the dominion of their father,—and grandsons, of their grandfather, just as subjects are under the dominion of their king.

1693. Fourth [6], at "**Friendships of this type**," he shows the basis of agreement for all such friendships. He states two common features: one, that they all consist in a kind of excellence of one person over the other. Since this is obvious in the case of a king and his subjects, he manifests it concerning fathers and sons. Because the father greatly excels, parents are honored by their sons; for honor is due to one who excels—as we pointed out in the first book (214)—and the same must be said of ancestors. The other feature is that in friendships of this nature the same thing is not just on the part of each. The king, therefore, must not do the same for his subject as the subject must do for his king, nor the father the same for his son as the son for his father. But what is just must be judged for both parties according to worth so that each does for the other what is proper, because in this way friendship between them entails one loving the other in a fitting manner.

1694. Next [7], at "**But the friendship**," he shows that there is a friendship corresponding to aristocracy. He says that friendship between husband and wife is similar to that found in an aristocracy in which a few are entrusted with authority by reason of excellence, on account of which they are loved. Since those in authority are better qualified, more good is attributed to them inasmuch as they are esteemed above others; and nevertheless what is proper to each is assigned to him. Indeed virtuous men constituted in power do not take from their subjects the good that belongs to them. By this procedure justice is preserved in accordance with aristocracy; and the same is true in a friendship between a husband and wife. The husband, being more worthy, is placed over the wife; however, the husband does not direct the affairs belonging to the wife.

1695. At "**Friendship between brothers**" [8] he shows how friendship is understood in accordance with timocracy. He states that friendship between brothers is similar to *etairiciae*, i.e., friendship between persons of the same age, for brothers are equal and alike in age. Persons of this kind have the same training and habits for the most part because habits follow the way of living, as was indicated in the second book (248, 315). From this there appears an obvious likeness between such a friendship and friendship corresponding to timocracy in which citizens, who are in control, are equal and

fair or virtuous. Hence it is just that they rule in turn so that one does not have all the power but a part of it, which makes them equal in power. So too is the friendship among them. This is also clearly observed in friendship among those who are brothers and of a like age or upbringing.

1696. Then [9], at "**On the other hand**," he shows how there is friendship corresponding to corrupt forms of government. He discusses this point under three aspects. First [9] he shows that in such systems there is very little friendship; second [10], at "It is minimal etc.," he shows in which of these the least friendship exists; third [13], at "In democracies, however etc.," he shows in which of these most friendship exists. He says first that, as there is little justice in perversions, i.e., corrupt forms of rule, so also there is little friendship, for this in some way concerns the same thing as justice.

1697. Next [10], at "**It is minimal**," he shows in which corrupt political system friendship is minimal. On this point he does three things. First [10] he states his proposition; second [11], at "In those regimes etc.," he proves it; third [12], at "Consequently, there can be etc.," he shows how the statement should be understood. He says first that, since there is little friendship in corrupt regimes, it follows that there is the least friendship in the worst regimes, viz., in tyrannies in which no friendship or very little exists.

1698. Second [11], at "**In those regimes**," he proves his proposition. Friendship consists in sharing in common, as we have explained (1655–1660, 1661). Obviously then if nothing is shared between ruler and ruled—as when the ruler aims at his own good—no friendship can exist between them; nor can there be any justice between them inasmuch as the ruler usurps for himself all the good due to the subject. But this happens under tyranny because the tyrant does not strive for the common good but for his own. Thus he acts with his subjects like a workman with a tool, a soul with the body, or a master with a slave, for the tyrant uses his subjects as slaves.

1699. These three objects just mentioned are benefitted by the persons who use them, to the extent that the objects are moved, i.e., the slave by the master, the body by the soul, the tool by the workman. However, those who use things do not have friendship toward them. Even if they somehow benefit the things, they intend by this the good of the things only as it is related to their own good. This is particularly obvious of an artisan in relation to lifeless instruments which are not objects of friendship or justice because they do not share in the activity of human life. Indeed horses and cattle are not objects of friendship though they do have life. So, too, a master does not have friendship with a slave because they share nothing, but all the good of the slave is the master's as all the good of a tool is the artisan's. In fact a slave is, as it were, a living tool and conversely a tool is, as it were, a lifeless slave.

1700. Third [12], at "**Consequently, there can be,**" he shows how his statement (1699) is to be taken. He says that according to the premises there is no friendship of a master for a slave qua slave, although there is friendship for him precisely as man. A friendship can exist between any two men inasmuch as they can share something according to law or arrangement, i.e., agreement or promise. In this way a master can have friendship with a slave as a human being. Thus it is obvious that under tyranny, in which rulers use subjects as slaves, there is little friendship or justice.

1701. Then [13], at "**In democracies, however,**" he shows in which corrupt political system friendship is most fully realized. He says that this occurs in democracy. In this system the rulers strive in many ways for the general welfare inasmuch as they want the common man to be equal to the talented man, and they aim principally at the good of the people. On the other hand an oligarchy takes a middle course since it neither works for the good of the many like a democracy nor for the benefit of one like a tyranny but for the good of a few.

LECTURE XII
Subdivisions of Friendship

TEXT OF ARISTOTLE (*1161b11–1162a32*) Chapter 12

1. *All friendship then involves common participation (communicatio), as has been pointed out.*   **1161b11–12; 1702**

2. *One may, however, set apart from other friendships those between blood relatives and comrades.*   **1161b12–13; 1703**

3. *But civic friendships—existing between fellow tribesmen, and fellow voyagers—and others of this kind have more evident signs of association; this seems an acknowledged fact. Among these also will be placed friendship between fellow travelers.*   **1161b13–16; 1704**

4. *Friendships between relatives, however, seem to be of various kinds and to depend on paternal friendship.*   **1161b16–17; 1705**

5. *Parents indeed love their children as part of themselves. But children love their parents as the authors of their existence.*   **1161b18–19; 1706**

6. *Now parents know the identity of their children better than children know the identity of their parents.*   **1161b19–21; 1707**

7. *Moreover, the procreator is nearer to the offspring than the offspring to the procreator, for the product belongs to the producer, e.g., a tooth or a hair or the like to its owner; but the producer does not belong to the product at all, or belongs to it only in a minor way.*
                                                                                       1161b21–24; 1708

8. *But length of time produces the same result. Parents love their children from birth but children love their parents only after a lapse of time and the acquisition of reason or understanding.*   **1161b24–26; 1709**

9. *From these observations it is obvious that mothers love their children more (than fathers do).*   **1161b26–27; 1710**

10. *Undoubtedly parents love their children as themselves, for their offspring are, as it were, the parents themselves existing separately. But children love their parents because begotten by them.*   **1161b27–30; 1711**

11. *Brothers, though, love one another—being generated by the same parents, for identity of origin with them makes the brothers identical with one another. For this reason brothers are said to be of the same blood, of the same stock, and so on. They are then the same, existing as different individuals.*   **1161b30–33; 1712**

12. *Similarity in upbringing and age is a great aid to friendship, for "men of a year like to draw near," and people living the same way are comrades. Hence fraternal friendship resembles that of comrades.*   **1161b33–1162a1; 1713**

13. *Nephews, however, and other kindred are linked together by derivation from brothers who are the sons of the same parents. They are more closely or distantly related as they are nearer or farther removed from their common ancestor.*   **1162a1–4; 1714**

14. *Children have friendship for their parents—and men for their gods—as for something transcendently good. The reason is that parents are in a special way the causes of their children's existence, upbringing and training.*   **1162a4–7; 1715**

15. *Such friendship contains more pleasure and utility than an outsider's friendship inasmuch as parents and children live more in common.*   **1162a7–9; 1716**

16. *Friendship among brothers has all the features of friendship among comrades; and it has them more perfectly when the brothers are virtuous and alike in general inasmuch as they are closer to one another. For (a) they love each other from birth; (b) they have the same parents,*

rearing, and education and so are alike in character; (c) their friendship has been fully and
convincingly tested by time.						1162a9–15; 171?

17. In the case of other relatives a proportionate communication of friendship is found.
						1162a15–16; 171€

18. Between man and wife a natural friendship seems to exist, for they are more inclined by
nature to conjugal than political society. This is so because the home is older and more
necessary than the state, and because generation is common to all animals.
						1162a16–19; 1719–172(

19. Only to this extent do other animals come together. Men, however, cohabit not only to
procreate children but also to have whatever is needed for life. Indeed, from the beginning,
family duties are distinct; some are proper to the husband, others to the wife. Thus mutual
needs are provided for, when each contributes his own services to the common good.
						1162a19–24; 1721–172?

20. Therefore, this friendship seems to possess both utility and pleasure. But it can exist for
the sake of virtue if the husband and wife are virtuous, for each has his proper virtue and they
can delight in it.						1162a24–27; 172?

21. Children seem to be a bond of union. Hence sterile couples separate more readily, for
children are a common good of both parties; and what is common maintains friendship.
						1162a27–29; 1724

22. To ask how man and wife—and friends in general—ought to live together is the same as
to ask how they ought to be just. And justice does not seem to be observed in the same towards a
friend, a stranger, a comrade, and a fellow student.			1162a29–33; 172?

COMMENTARY OF ST. THOMAS

1702. After the Philosopher has distinguished the kinds of friendship according to the species of political and domestic association, he now subdivides the kinds of friendships. On this point he does two things. First [1] he states a general principle for dividing and subdividing friendships. Then [4], at "Friendships between relatives, however etc.," he gives special treatment to some particular kinds of friendships. He discusses the first point under three aspects. First [1] he proposes a general principle for distinguishing the kinds of friendship, concluding from the premises that all friendship consists in common participation (*communicatio*), as has been pointed out (1698).

1703. Second [2], at "One may," he distinguishes, by reason of common participation, the kinds of friendship that seem to have less in common. He

says that, according to the diversity of common participation, friendship can be distinguished in itself and from others into consanguineous (or that between blood relatives) and companionate (or that between comrades). Blood relatives have a common origin, and comrades a common upbringing.

1704. Third [3], at "But civic friendships," according to this he distinguishes friendships that seem to have more in common. He states that civic friendships (i.e., those among fellow tribesmen, fellow voyagers or men sailing together) and all others of this kind (for example, between fellow soldiers or fellow students) have more evident signs of association than the friendships of blood relatives or comrades; for in the former we must clearly acknowledge that association is the cause of friendship. (Friendship beween fellow travelers can be placed in his category.) But the friendship of blood relatives or comrades does not have any present and permanent mode of communicating, and so is less obvious.

1705. Then [4], at **"Friendships between relatives, however,"** he treats in particular some kinds of friendship: first [4], friendship between relatives; second [18], at "Between man and wife etc.," friendship existing between husband and wife. On the first point he does two things. First [1] he distinguishes the kinds of friendship between blood relatives. Next [14], at "Children have friendship etc.," he points out the characteristics of each division. He discusses the first point under three headings. First [4] he treats a father's friendship for his son; second [11], at "Brothers, though etc.," the friendship of brothers for one another; third [13], at "Nephews, however etc.," the friendship of other blood relations. He handles the first point in a threefold manner. First [4] he proposes in what way paternal friendship is related to other friendships between blood relatives. He says that friendship between blood relatives seems to have great variety, i.e., to be divided into many species by reason of the different grades of consanguinity; nevertheless, all such friendships depend on paternal friendship as a starting point. This will be clear from what follows.

1706. Second [5], at **"Parents indeed,"** he gives the reason for this friendship. He says that parents love their children as part of themselves; they are generated from the seed of their parents. Hence the son is a separated part of the father, so to speak. Consequently this friendship is nearest to the love of a man for himself, from which all friendship is derived, as will

be indicated in the ninth book (1797). With reason then paternal friendship is considered to be the starting point. But children love their parents as the source of their existence, much like a separated part would love the whole from which it is separated.

1707. Third [6], at **"Now parents are,"** he compares a father's friendship with a son's. He discusses this point in a three-fold fashion. First [6] he ranks paternal friendship above filial; next [9], at "From these observations etc.," maternal above paternal; last [10], at "Undoubtedly parents etc.," he clarifies his statement. He gives three reasons for the initial assertion. The first is this [6]. The more a man knows the causes for love, the more reasonable it is that he love more. It has been noted (1076) that parents love their children as part of themselves. But children love their parents as the authors of their existence. Now fathers can know their offspring better than their children can know they are their children, for the parents know the generative action (which produced the child) but the children do not since they were not yet born. Hence it is reasonable for parents to love their children more than children their parents.

1708. He assigns the second reason [7] at **"Moreover, the procreator."** It is this. The basis for love in every friendship of blood relatives is the relationship of one person to another. But the principal or begetter is nearer to the begotten than the thing made to the maker or the begotten to the begetter. The offspring is—as it were—a separated part of the procreator, as we have indicated (1706, 1707). Hence it seems to be compared to the procreator as a separable part to the whole, for example, a tooth or a hair or the like. But such parts, which are separated from the whole, have an affinity to the whole because the whole includes them in itself, and not the opposite. For that reason the whole seems not to belong to the parts at all or to belong to them less than if the converse were the case; for even if a part pertains to the whole, nevertheless it is not identical with the whole itself, as all the parts are included in it. Consequently, it is reasonable that parents love their children more than children their parents.

1709. He gives the third reason [8] at "**But length of time etc.**" Obviously friendship is strengthened with the passage of time. But it is evident that parents love their children for a greater length of time than do children their parents. Indeed parents love their children as soon as they are born. But children love their parents only after some time has elapsed and they attain intelligence or the use of reason, or at least the capacity to distinguish their parents from others. For, in the beginning, children call all men fathers and all women mothers, as mentioned in the first book of the *Physics* (Ch. 1, 184b12; St. Th. Lect. I, 11). It is reasonable then for parents to love their children more than children love their parents.

1710. Then [9], at "**From these observations,**" he compares a mother's love with a father's. He says that it can be clearly shown from the previous considerations why mothers love their children more than fathers do. The first reason he gives does not need proof because mothers know better than fathers who their children are. Likewise in regard to time, for mothers before fathers conceive the affection of love for their children because they are more constantly in their company. But the second reason is applicable in one part but not in the other. For the father disposes the son's principal part, the

form; and the mother disposes the matter, as is noted in the treatise *De Generatione Animalium* (Bk. II, Ch. 1, 731b13 sq.).

1711. Next [10], at "**Undoubtedly parents love,**" he clarifies what he stated in the second reason, that children are closer to their parents than the converse. This is so because parents love their children as themselves. Children generated by their parents are as it were the parents themselves, differing from them only in the fact of their distinct existence. On the other hand, children love their parents not as though they were part of their parents but as begotten by them.

1712. At "**Brothers, though**" [11] he explains fraternal friendship. First [11] he gives the basis of this friendship. Then [12], at "Similarity in upbringing etc.," he shows the means of strengthening this friendship. He remarks first that brothers love one another because they are begotten by the same parents. Things that are identical with one and the same thing are identical in some fashion with one another. Since then children are identical in some way with their parents, as has been observed (1711), the children's identity with the parents makes the children identical in some way. Consequently we say that brothers are the same by blood, by stock, and so on. Although the parents' blood (the common origin) is entirely the same, this identity also endures in some measure even in the children who are separated from their parents and from one another.

1713. Then [12], at "**Similarity in upbringing,**" he explains how this friendship is strengthened. He observes that fraternal friendship is fostered greatly by the fact that brothers are reared together and are nearly the same age, since it is natural for people alike in years to love one another. Likewise, companions or persons of common upbringing usually have an identical manner of life which is a cause of mutual love. Consequently, fraternal friendship resembles friendship between comrades or persons brought up together.

1714. At "**Nephews, however**" [13] he defines the friendship of other blood relatives. He states that nephews and other kindred are connected with one another by relationship of generation and friendship to the extent that they derive their origin from brothers, sons of the same parents. In fact they are called blood relatives because they are descended from these very persons. Such people are said to be more or less related inasmuch as they are nearer or farther removed from their procreator, i.e., original ancestor, for the first must be the measure of all.

1715. Next [14], at "**Children have friendship,**" he indicates the characteristics of these friendships: first [14], of paternal friendship; second [16], at "Friendship among brothers etc.," of fraternal friendship; third [17], at "In the case etc.," of friendship between other blood relatives. To the first friendship he assigns two characteristics. The first [14] is that children have friendship for their parents as to a kind of superior good. The reason is that parents are special benefactors—the cause of their children's existence, upbringing, and training. Man's friendship for God is also of this nature.

1716. Then [15], at "**Such friendships,**" he states the second characteristic. Friendship between children and parents has pleasure and utility in a greater degree than outside friendship in proportion as they live a life more in common. Because of this they become especially useful and pleasant to one another.

1717. At "**Friendship among brothers**" [16] he gives the characteristic of fraternal friendship. He observes that the same features are found in friendship of brothers as in the friendship of comrades or persons living together. And if brothers are just or virtuous and entirely alike in their habits, then friendship is greater from this common upbringing inasmuch as they are closer to one another. This is due to three considerations. First, to length of time, since they love each other almost as soon as they are born. Second, to a more perfect likeness. Brothers born of the same parents seem more alike in their ways and hence appear to have the same natural disposition; they have been reared together and trained in a similar fashion by their parents. Third, this is due to the proof of friendship since they have put each other to the test; and for that reason their friendship is highest and firmest.

1718. Next [17], at "**In the case,**" he assigns the third characteristic of friendship between other kinsmen. He says that matters pertaining to friendship between other kindred should be understood in proportion to fraternal friendship since other blood relatives are descended from brothers, as indicated above (1714).

1719. Then [18], at "**Between man and wife,**" he treats friendship between husband and wife. He discusses this point under three headings. First [18] he assigns the reason for this friendship. Second [21], at "Children seem to be etc.," he points out the means that can strengthen this friendship. Third [22], at "To ask how man and wife etc.," he answers a question. On the first point he does two things. First [18] he offers the proper reason for this friendship. Then [20], at "Therefore, this etc.," he shows how this friendship shares the general reasons for friendship. He treats the first point from two aspects. First [18] he assigns the particular reason for the friendship that is common both to man and other animals. Next [19], at "Only to this extent etc.," he gives another reason restricted to men. He remarks first that a natural friendship seems to exist between man and wife. He proves this by recourse to a higher principle; for man is by nature a political animal, and it is more natural for him to be a "conjugal" (*conjugale*) animal. Aristotle presents two arguments.

1720. The first is that antecedent and necessary things seem to belong to nature more completely. But domestic society, to which the union of man and wife pertains, is antecedent to civil society; for the part is antecedent to the whole. Domestic society is also more necessary because it is ordered to acts necessary for life, viz., generation and nourishment. Obviously then man is inclined by nature more to conjugal than political society. The second reason is that generation of offspring, to which the union of man and wife is ordered, is common to other animals and therefore follows the nature of the genus. So it is clear that man is by nature more a conjugal than a political animal.

1721. Then [19], at "**Only to this extent,**" he indicates the proper reason for conjugal friendship which belongs to man alone. He concludes from the premises that pairing of male and female among other animals exists exclusively for generation of offspring, as has been noted (1720). But union of male and female among men occurs not only for the procreation of children but also for the functions needed in

human living. These functions—it is immediately apparent—are so divided between man and woman that some are proper to the husband, like external works; and others to the wife, like sewing and other domestic occupations. Thus mutual needs are provided for, when each contributes his own services for the common good.

1722. Obviously then conjugal friendship among men not only is natural as among other animals—where it is directed to the work of nature, viz., generation—but also domestic as directed to a sufficiency for family life.

1723. At "**Therefore, this**" [20] he shows how this friendship shares the common reasons for friendship. He observes that from previous statements conjugal friendship obviously has utility inasmuch as it furnishes a sufficiency for family life. Likewise it provides pleasure in the generative act, as is the case with other animals. But when the husband and wife are virtuous, their friendship can be based on virtue. In fact there is a virtue proper to both husband and wife that renders their friendship delightful to each other. Clearly then friendship of this kind can be based on virtue, utility, and pleasure.

1724. Next [21], at "**Children seem,**" he indicates a means of making this friendship strong. He remarks that children seem to be a cause of a stable and lasting union. Hence, sterile couples who fail to have children are separated more readily. In fact, divorce was granted in former times because of sterility. And the reason for this is that children are a common good of both husband and wife whose union exists for the sake of children. But what is common continues and preserves friendship which also consists in sharing (communicatio), as has been pointed out (1702).

1725. At "**To ask how man and wife**" [22] he answers an inquiry, viz., how a man and wife ought to live together. He himself replies that to ask this is the same as to inquire how justice exists between man and wife; for they ought to live together in such a way that each fulfills what is just to the other. This will be different for different persons, for the same justice must not be observed toward friend, stranger, comrade and disciple. Therefore, a study of this kind belongs to domestic ethics or political science.

LECTURE XIII
Quarrels and Complaints in Friendship

TEXT OF ARISTOTLE (*1162a34–1163a23*) Chapter 13

1.*There are three kinds of friendship, as was noted at the outset. In each of them some men are friends on a basis of equality and others on a basis of superiority. (Virtuous people become friends, and a more virtuous person becomes a friend of a less virtuous person; people having the same and different usefulness become friends for pleasure or utility.) Equal friends must be equated in affection and in the other aspects of friendship, but unequal friends must bestow something proportionate to superior merits.*   **1162a34–1162b4; 1726–1727**

2. *It is to be expected that complaints and quarrels take place solely or especially in friendships for utility.*   **1162b5–6; 1728**

3. *But friends by reason of virtue are prompt to help one another, for this is the peculiar characteristic of virtue and friendship. And when each person is intent on serving his friend complaints and contentions do not occur. Indeed no one is going to inflict pain on a person who loves him and acts well towards him, but a grateful recipient does a favor in return. Even the greater benefactor receiving what he desires will not complain of his friend, for each seeks what is good.*   **1162b6–13; 1729–1730**

4. *Nor do complaints often occur in friendships for pleasure, for friends have simultaneously what they desire in the enjoyment of each other's company. And a person will appear ridiculous to complain of another's unpleasantness since he can terminate the relationship when he wishes.*   **1162b13–16; 1731**

5. *Disputes, however, are frequent in friendships for utility. For people using one another for advantage always are looking for something, and think they have less than their due. They complain of not receiving as much as they need when they are so deserving. On the other hand their benefactors say they have not sufficient to give as much as the beneficiaries want.*   **1162b16–21; 1732**

6. *As justice is of two kinds: one unwritten, and the other legal; so utility in friendship is of two kinds: one moral and the other legal. And, when exchanges are not made according to the same kind of utility quarrels arise and friendships are broken up.*   **1162b21–25; 1733–1734**

7. *Now legal utility is expressed in agreements. This is either of a commercial type, in hand to hand dealings; or of a liberal type in allowing a period of delay, though the quid pro quo is determined. In the latter case the debt is clear and unambiguous, yet the postponement indicated a friendly attitude. For this reason some states do not permit judicial action over such agreements but assume that people dealing in good faith should honor it.*   **1162b25–31; 1735**

8. *Moral utility, however, is not expressed in definite words, but the gift is made to any other as to a friend. But the giver expects something equal or better in return, as if he were not making a gift but a loan; and when the exchange and repayment do not take place he will complain. This happens because all or most men approve what is noble but choose what serves their interests. Now it is noble to confer a benefit without expecting another in return but it is profitable to receive a benefit.*   **1162b31–1163a1; 1736–1737**

9. *But when a person can, he should make a return worthy of what he has received, doing this of his own accord. For a man must not make someone a friend against his will; he makes a mistake in the beginning by accepting a gift from a person from whom he should not have taken it. Indeed the gift is not from a real friend nor from someone acting for the sake of a real friend. In this case the recipient must arrange payment as is done on fixed terms, and actually repay if he can; if he cannot, he is not expected to do so even by the giver. Therefore when possible he*

should repay; but he should consider at the outset the person from whom he is going to receive a benefit and the kind of benefit offered, so that he may accept or decline the benefit.

1163a1–9; 1738–1739

10. It is uncertain, though, whether repayment should be measured by the utility to the recipient, and made according to it, or by the kindness of the giver. 1163a9–12; 1740

11. For people who receive benefits belittle them; they say they receive such as are insignificant to their benefactors and obtainable from others. Conversely, benefactors maintain that they give the best they have—things not to be had from others—and that they give them in times of danger and great need. 1163a12–16; 1741

12. Therefore, in useful friendship the measure is the utility to the receiver. For he needs the help and it is given to him on the assumption of an equal return. Now the help of the benefactor will be only as much as the recipient gets from it, and he must repay what he received, or even more for that would be more generous. In friendships of virtue, however, complaints do not arise. Here the intention of the giver has a likeness to a measure, for intention is the essential element in virtue and moral practice. 1163a16–23; 1742–1743

COMMENTARY OF ST. THOMAS

1726. After the Philosopher has distinguished the kinds of friendships, he now shows how complaints or grumblings arise in friendships. He does this under three headings. First [1] he indicates what must be done to avoid quarrels in friendships. Second [2], at "It is to be expected etc.," he points out the friendships in which quarrels occur. Third [6], at "As justice is of two kinds etc.," he explains the cause of quarreling. He says first there are three kinds of friendship: for virtue, for pleasure, and for utility; and in any one of these, men can be friends on terms of equality or of merit. He takes up each kind on this very point.

1727. A friendship for virtue may exist between equally virtuous men or between a more virtuous and a less virtuous man; a friendship for pleasure, between equally pleasant men or between a more pleasant and a less pleasant man; a friendship for utility may provide advantages in equal measure or in a greater and less measure. If then friends would be equal in any kind of friendship, they must be equated both in respect to loving—so that each loves the other equally—and

in respect to the other requirements such as the courtesies of friends. But if they were unequal each must bestow something in proportion to his superiority or inferiority.

1728. Then [2], at "It is to be expected," he points out the friendships in which quarrels occur. First [2] he proposes his intention. Next [3], at "But friends by reason of etc.," he explains it. He observes first that it is reasonable for complaints and quarrels—according as one friend accuses another or complains about him—to take place either solely or especially in friendship for utility.

1729. At "But friends by reason of" [3] he explains his intention. First [3] he shows that complaint or quarreling does not occur in friendship for virtue. Then [4], at "Nor do complaints etc.," he points out too that it does not happen often in friendship for pleasure. Last [5], at "Disputes, however etc.," he shows that complaining and quarreling take place frequently in utilitarian friendship. He remarks first that virtuous friends are prompt to help one another, because doing good for a friend is the proper function of virtue and friendship. And when each strives to serve his friend, complaints and contentions cannot possibly arise.

1730. Indeed no one wants to cause sorrow to a person who loves him and acts well towards him; but if the recipient of a benefit is grateful he will be anxious to give another benefit in return. Although the person who is supposedly more excellent may not receive as much as he gave, nevertheless—if allotted what he desires—he will not complain of this friend. What both desire is the good, i.e., the proper and honorable, and this will be the thing that does not exceed the friend's means.

1731. Next [4], at "**Nor do complaints,**" he explains how it is with friendship for pleasure. He says that complaints and quarrels, though possible at times, do not arise very often in friendships based on pleasure; for if friends enjoy one another's company each has what he desires, viz., pleasure. For that reason there is no place for a quarrel. But if one person does not find another pleasant it is ridiculous to complain of him not being pleasant, since the one has it in his power not to stay in the other's company.

1732. At "**Disputes, however**" [5] he indicates the case of friendship for utility, observing that this friendship suffers especially from complaints and quarrels. For those who use one another for advantage always want more than is given them and think they receive less than their due. Consequently, they complain of not receiving as much as they need, especially when they are deserving of so much. But, on the other hand, their benefactors say they haven't enough to give what the beneficiaries want.

1733. Then [6], at "**As justice is of two kinds,**" he gives the reason for

quarreling in friendship for utility: first [6] in respect to equals; next [Lect. XIV], at "Disagreements happen etc.," in respect to unequals (1163a24). He handles the first point in a twofold manner. First [6] he assigns the cause. Then [10], at "It is uncertain, though etc.," he brings out a difficulty. He discusses the first point from two aspects. First [6] he proposes the cause of quarrels in friendship based on utility. Second [9], at "But when a person etc.," he tells how to avoid such quarrels. He treats the first point under two headings. First [6] he states the cause. Then [7], at "Now legal utility etc.," he explains his statement. He affirms first that justice is of two kinds. One is unwritten but implanted in reason and is called natural justice by him on a previous occasion (1081). The other is written in the law and is called legal justice in the fifth book (1081).

1734. Likewise, utility properly acquired in friendships is of two kinds. One is moral, according as a person provides another with help (utilitatem) in conformity with moral practice. The other is legal utility, according as a person provides another with help in conformity with a statute of law. Now complaints arise in useful friendships especially when an exchange of utility is not made according to the same standard. One bestows help according to the requirements of law, but the other demands it according to moral practice. And in this way friendship is broken up.

1735. Next [7], at "**Now legal utility,**" he clarifies his statement: first [7] in regard to legal utility; then [8], at "Moral utility, however etc.," in regard to moral utility. He notes first that legal utility is expressed in definite words or pacts entered into by agreement of both parties. This is twofold. One is entirely formal—after the manner of buying and selling done from hand to hand—e.g., when someone immediately takes what is promised him for service rendered. The other is more liberal allowing a period of delay, although the quid pro quo must necessarily be determined. Thus the debt is clear and unambiguous, but the postponement of it is a kind of friendly gesture. For this reason some do not require a judicial exercise of justice but honor their word in business dealings; and it is thought they should be loved for this.

1736. At "**Moral utility, however**" [8] he explains what moral utility is. He says it is not expressed in definite words or compacts made by agreement, but without any contract externally declared a person gives to someone else what is usually given gratis to a friend. However, the man who makes a worthy gift intends and expects in return something equal or even better, as if he were not making a gift but a loan. But when an exchange does not take place in such a way that the recipient restores and pays equal or more, the giver will accuse the recipient and complain of him.

1737. After that he assigns the cause of these actions. He remarks that what he just said, viz., the person who gives gratis seeks a return, happens because all, or most people, wish or approve what is noble but actually choose what serves their interests. But that a man confer a benefit on another without intending a benefit in return is noble. Consequently, men want to appear to confer benefits in this way in order to be acceptable to others. But it is profitable to receive benefits. Therefore, whatever else they may pretend, men choose what is profitable.

1738. Then [9], at "**But when a per-**son,**" he shows how quarreling of this kind is to be avoided. He says the recipient of a benefit, when he can, should make a return worthy of the gifts he has received; and he should do this of his own accord because a man should not make someone a friend against his will, in the sense of being willing to accept gratis from a person who is unwilling to give gratis. But the man who accepts a benefit made a mistake in this at the outset in accepting a favor of a person from whom he should not have taken it. For he does not receive a benefit from a real friend nor from one who bestowed it for the sake of him to whom it was given but for an expected advantage. Hence the recipient of a benefit ought to repay the giver on fixed terms or compacts made by agreement. And if he can return to the giver the equal of what he received, he ought to insist on making complete repayment. But if he is unable to repay, neither he who bestowed nor he who accepted the benefit thinks it proper to demand this.

1739. We should remark then that, when possible the recipient ought to make repayment to the kind of benefactor who is intent on repayment. But when a man accepts a benefit he ought to consider at the beginning the person from whom he is receiving it, whether from a friend freely giving or from one who seeks repayment. Likewise he ought to consider under what conditions he is accepting the benefit, whether he could make a return or not, so that he may accept or decline the benefit.

1740. Next [10], at "**It is uncertain, though,**" he raises a difficulty on the matters discussed. First [10] he proposes the difficulty, stating it is doubtful whether the recommended repayment ought to be measured by the utility conferred on the recipient of the benefit or by the action of the bestower of the benefit.

1741. Second [11], at "**For people who receive etc.,**" he gives the reason for the difficulty. Recipients of benefits in attempting to belittle the favors obtained say they received what was only a trifle for their benefactors, such as they themselves were able to get from others. On the contrary, though, benefactors wanting to extol their benefits maintain that they gave the best they had, which were such as could not be gotten from others, and that they gave these in times of danger and great need.

1742. Third [12], at "**Therefore, in useful friendship etc.,**" he solves the difficulty by saying that repayment ought to be measured by the utility accruing to the recipient's benefit. He is the one who needed the benefit and it is sufficient for him to attempt an equal return. Indeed the help of the benefactor was only as much as the receiver obtains from it; and if it effects more it is better. In friendships of virtue, however, complaints do not arise, as has been indicated (1729–1730).

1743. Nevertheless a return must be made in them; and here the intention or will in the giver of the benefit has a likeness to a measure, because a measure in any genus is the principal element in that genus. But the excellence of virtue and moral practice lies in intention. For that reason, in friendship based on virtue a return ought to be made according to the will of the person who bestowed the benefit even if someone obtained little or no help from it.

LECTURE XIV
Complaints in Friendships Between Unequals

TEXT OF ARISTOTLE (*1163a24–1163b28*) Chapter 14

1. *Disagreements happen too in friendships between unequals. Here each thinks he deserves ore, and when he does not get it the friendship is broken up.*   **1163a24–26; 1744**

2. *For the better person thinks that more is coming to him, since greater benefit is due to a ⸱tter person. The more useful friend is of a similar mind, arguing that the useless man should ⸱t receive an equal share, for we would have a kind of public benefaction and not friendship if ⸱e advantages of friendship were not allotted according to the value of the benefits bestowed. In ⸱is view friendship ought to be considered a business partnership: those who invest more ⸱ould get bigger returns.*   **1163a26–32; 1745–1746**

3. *But the needy and the less worthy say the opposite, maintaining it is the part of a good ⸱iend to assist those in need. What would be the use, they say, of having a good or powerful ⸱iend if nothing is to be gained from him?*   **1163a32–35; 1747**

4. *Both seem to estimate correctly what is just. And each ought to get from the friendship ⸱mething more, not of the same thing though, but the superior should receive greater honor ⸱d the inferior greater gain.*   **1163b1–3; 1748**

5. *Honor certainly is compensation for acts of virtue and kindness while gain provides ⸱sistance against need.*   **1163b3–5; 1749**

6. *It seems to happen this way in civil affairs, for the man who does not contribute any good ⸱ the community is not honored. But he who benefits the community receives a common ⸱od—honor is just that. A person cannot expect to be honored by the community and ⸱multaneously made rich. Indeed no one could bear to have the smaller share in everything. But ⸱e person losing in wealth receives honor, and another expecting gifts receives riches; thus ⸱ch is equated in proportion to merit, and friendship is preserved—as has been explained. ⸱herefore, our friendship with unequals should be so conducted that the friend, who benefits us ⸱ money or virtue, is recompensed in the way that is possible, namely, in honor.*
1163b5–14; 1750–1751

7. *Friendship indeed asks what is possible, not what is equal in value, for not all benefits can ⸱ repaid in honor as is evident in honors due to God and parents. No one can ever repay them ⸱hat they deserve, although the man who serves them to the best of his ability appears to be ⸱irtuous.*   **1163b15–18; 1752**

8. *Therefore, a son is not at liberty to disown his father, though a father may disown his son.*
1163b18–19; 1753

9. *For a debt ought to be paid. But in discharging it the son can give nothing equal to the ⸱essings bestowed. Therefore he will always be in debt. Now creditors have the power to ⸱ismiss their debtors; and a father, his son.*   **1163b2022; 1754**

10. *At the same time no one ever seems to disown his son unless he is extremely wicked, for ⸱en aside from natural friendship it is human not to refuse help. But if a son is bad he will ⸱void supplying his father's needs, or at least will not be in a hurry to do so. For the majority ⸱e willing to accept benefits but avoid conferring them as something unprofitable This is the ⸱xtent of our discussion of these questions.*   **1163b22–28; 1755–1756**

COMMENTARY OF ST. THOMAS

1744. After the Philosopher has shown the manner in which com-

plaints arise in useful friendship between equals, he now shows how complaints occur in friendships between unequals. He discusses this point under three headings. First [1] he states the disagreement usually happening in these friendships. Next [2], for "For the better person etc.," he gives the reason for disagreement. Last [4], at "Both seem etc.," he defines the truth. He remarks first that some difference and discord among friends exist also in friendships between unequals when each, the superior and the inferior, thinks it right that he should have more. If he does not get it the friendship is broken up for this reason.

1745. Next [2], at "**For the better person**," he offers the reason for this disagreement. First [2] he states the reason motivating the superior parties; then [3], at "But the needy etc.," the reason influencing the inferior parties. He observes first that in friendship for virtue the better person thinks it reasonable for him to receive the greater benefit; for if good is due to the good man then more good is due to the better one. Likewise, in friendship for utility the more useful person thinks he should receive the greater benefit.

1746. It is not fitting, they contend, that he who is less useful should receive the equal of the more useful partner; for this would be a kind of public benefaction or service and not friendship, if the advantages arising from friendship were not distributed according to the value of works so that the man who does better work would have more. In fact they think that, as in business enterprises, the bigger investors receive larger returns from the general fund, so also in friendship the person who contributes more to friendship should receive more.

1747. Then [3], at "**But the needy**," he gives the reasons influencing the inferior parties. The needy in useful

friendship and the less worthy in vi tuous friendship argue to the contrar they maintain that it is the role of friend excelling in good to provid adequately for friends in need. In fa there would not seem to be any advar tage for an inferior person to have virtuous or powerful friend if nothin ought to be received from him.

1748. At "**Both seem**" [4] he define the truth. First [4] he proposes th truth; then [5], at "Honor certainl etc.," he explains it; last [8], at "Ther fore, a son etc.," he deduces a corollar from the discussion. He says first tha each, the superior and inferior, seem to estimate correctly what is just, be cause something more—not of th same thing though—ought to be give to each: to the superior, greater hono but to the needy, greater gain.

1749. Next [5], at "**Honor certainly,** he clarifies his statement (1748): first [by argument; and second [6], at " seems to happen etc.," by illustratior third [7], at "Friendship indeed etc., he proves an assertion previousl made. He notes first that more hono ought to be given to the superior pe son because honor is a suitable com pensation for acts of virtue an kindness—in which worthy people ex cel. On the other hand, gain provide assistance against need which inferio persons feel.

1750. At "**It seems to happen**" [6] h manifests the same point by an exam ple. We see it happen this way in civi affairs, for the man who does not con tribute any good to the community i not honored. But he who bestows som benefit on the community is given common good, honor. It is not easil possible for someone to get riches an honors from the community simulta neously. Indeed no one could bear t have the smaller share of everything onor and riches alike. But the person who loses money by the expenses incurred in serving the community is given honor by the state, and the person who expects gifts for his service is given riches.

1751. It was pointed out previously (693) that the observance and recognition of excellence creates a proportionate equality among friends, and thus preserves friendship. As states confer honors on some and wealth on others according to their excellence, so we must handle unequal friends. We should render honor to one who performs a useful service by bestowing riches or who does virtuous acts; we should do this in such a way that compensation is made—perhaps not in the equivalent but in that service which is possible.

1752. Then [7], at "**Friendship indeed**," he proves that it is sufficient to return what is feasible. The reason is that friendship asks of a friend what is possible but not always what is equal in value, since this would be absolutely impossible at times. Surely not all benefits can be repaid in adequate honor, as is obvious in honors rendered to God and parents who can never be worthily recompensed. However, if a man serves God and parents according to his ability, he seems to be just or virtuous.

1753. At "**Therefore, a son**" [8] he deduces a corollary from the discussion. First [8] he concludes that it is not lawful for a son to disown his father but it is lawful sometimes for a father to disown his son.

1754. Second [9], at "**For a debt etc.,**" he clarifies his conclusion by two reasons. The first is [9] that the son being indebted to the father for the benefits received ought to repay. But he is unable to make a repayment that the benefits deserve. Therefore he will always remain in debt. For this reason he is not at liberty to disown his father. But creditors have the power to dismiss their debtors, so a father has the power of dismissing his son.

1755. He states the second reason at "**At the same time no one**" [10], observing that no son seems to forsake his father and disown him except out of excessive wickedness. Because of the natural friendship between father and son, it is human that no one should thrust out a person who has supported him. Thus it would be most wicked for a son to expel his father. But if a son is bad the father ought to put him out, or at least not work hard to provide adequately for him, since the son would thereby increase in wickedness. For the majority are willing to accept benefits but avoid assisting others as something unprofitable.

1756. He concludes by way of summary that he has discussed those questions pertaining only to the kinds of friendship. Thus he finishes the teaching of the eighth book.

BOOK NINE
PROPERTIES OF FRIENDSHIP
LECTURE I
Proportionate Properties in Friendship

TEXT OF ARISTOTLE (*1163b32–1164b21*) Chapter 1

1. In all friendships of dissimilar persons proportion equates the parties and preserves ʃndship, as has been indicated. Thus in justice between citizens a return according to value is ɪde to the shoemaker for the shoes he gives. A similar thing is done to the weaver and to other ʈisans.   **1163b32–35; 1757–1758**

2. For that reason people invented money to serve as a common measure, and all salable ɔds were referred to it and measured by it.   **1164a1–2; 1759**

3. In friendship, however, the lover sometimes complains because his lavish love is not ʈurned—but perhaps he has nothing deserving of love. On the other hand, the beloved very ɛn complains that the lover had promised everything before, but now fulfills nothing.
                                                                       1164a2–6; 1760

4. These accusations are made when the lover seeks pleasure and the beloved, utility; and ither has the qualities the other seeks. Consequently, the friendship is broken off since the very ɪsons why it was formed no longer remain. The parties did not love one another for ɛmselves but for advantages to be gained, and these were not enduring; hence neither were the ʃendships enduring. But friendship based on virtue remains, as we have indicated, because ːh friend is loved for himself.   **1164a6–13; 1761**

5. Friends quarrel when given favors different from what they desire, for failure to get what ɯan wants is like getting nothing. This recalls the lyre-player who was promised that the ʈter he sang the more he would be paid, but next morning when he demanded fulfillment of ɛ pledge the man who promised replied that he had already given pleasure (i.e., of expectation) ʳ pleasure. Certainly if each had wished this it would have been satisfactory. But if one wanted ɪusement and got it while the other wanted gain and did not get it, an unfair exchange was ɪde; for a man is intent on acquiring what he needs and will give what he possesses to get it.
                                                                  1164a13–22; 1762–1763

6. But who is to fix the amount due to each, the person giving or the person receiving the ɯefit? The giver evidently seems to leave this to the recipient as, they say, Protagoras used to ɂ. For when he taught he told the student to estimate the value of the knowledge imparted; and ɔtagoras accepted no more. But in such matters some are satisfied to "let a man have his fixed ɂ."   **1164a22–27; 1764–1765**

7. Those who first accept money and then carry out nothing they promised—their promises ɪng extravagant—are proper targets for complaints; they are not doing what they undertook ɂ do. The Sophists were forced to this course, for nothing would have been given for their ɪching. Such persons then are justly accused for not doing what they are paid to do.
                                                                       1164a27–33; 1766

8. Where the gift is not made with a promise of service, people who give for the sake of others ɪnnot be complained of—as we have noted. This is in accord with the nature of friendship for ʳtue; and a return is made in view of the giver's intention which has a special relevancy in a ʲend and virtue. A similar course should be followed with those imparting philosophy, for their ɂlue cannot be measured in terms of money nor can they be given an equivalent return. ːʳhaps it suffices that we repay them what is possible, as is done with the gods and our parents.
                                                                  1164a33–1164b6; 1767–1768

9. *If the gift is not of this nature but was made in view of a recompense, a return which seems fair to both parties must be arranged. When this is not possible, appraisal of compensation by the beneficiary will seem not only necessary but just.*   1164b6–10; 17⟨

10. *A person will have what is just when he is repaid according to the help and pleasure afforded the recipient; and this is what happens in buying.*   1164b10–13; 17⟨

11. *In some places the law prescribes that no legal action is possible in voluntary contracts, taking the position that a person who trusts another should be repaid according to the terms of the original agreement. It supposes that the person receiving the benefit makes a more just arrangement. In general those who have things and those who want them do not make equal valuations; each group puts a big price on what it owns and has for sale. But a return is made according to the appraisal of the recipient.*   1164b13–20; 17⟨

12. *However, a man ought to appraise a benefit not at the value it seems to have after he get. it but at the value it had before he received it.*   1164b20–21; 17⟨

COMMENTARY OF ST. THOMAS

1757. After the Philosopher has shown the nature of friendship and defined the kinds of friendship, he now discusses the properties of friendship in the ninth book. First he gives the properties. Then [Lect. VIII], at "Likewise the question etc." (1168a28), he raises doubts on questions already settled. He treats the first point from two aspects. First he considers matters pertaining to the preservation and the breaking up of friendship. Next [Lect. IV], at "Kindly acts etc." (1166 a), he investigates the effects of friendship. He discusses the first point in a twofold manner. First he treats matters pertaining to the preservation of friendship. Second [Lect. III], at "A question comes up etc." (1165a37), he considers questions concerned with its destruction. He handles the first point under three headings. First [1] he proposes a means of preserving friendship. Then [2], at "For that reason etc.," he shows how friendship is disturbed by the absence of this means. Third [6], at "But who is etc.," he recommends remedies against disturbance of this sort.

1758. Obviously, friendship between equals is preserved by a fair return. Hence he first explains how it is possible to preserve friendship exis ing between persons unlike one a other—a thing that seems rathe doubtful. He observes that in all suc friendships between dissimilar pe sons, like father and son, king and sul ject and so on, friendship is equate and preserved by something which analogous or proportionate to each. F makes this clear by an example foun in political justice; accordingly, we sai in the fifth book (975–976) that a retur in conformity with proportiona value is made to the shoemaker for th shoes he gives. The same thing appli to the weaver and other artisans.

1759. Then [2], at "For that reason he shows how friendship is disturbe by lack of a proportion. He treats th point in a twofold manner. First [2] h states the reason why disturbance o this sort cannot happen in an exchang based on justice. He observes that i exchanges between citizens there found a common measure, currenc to which all articles of exchange a referred as to a criterion; and the price is measured by means of cu rency. Consequently what is to b charged for them can be determine But the relations, which are exchange friendship, for example, affections, and services of friends, cannot be computed in money. Therefore,

1760. Second [3], at "**In friendship, however,**" he explains how friendship is disturbed by lack of a proportionate measure. He shows this first [3] from the fact that one friend does not repay the other; then [5], at "Friends quarrel etc.," from the fact that repayment is not what was deserved. He discusses the first point under two headings. First [3] he proposes the cause of the disturbance in friendship. Next [4], at "These accusations are made etc.," he shows in which friendships this occurs. Concerning the first point we must note that repayment in friendship is judged according to two phases. First in relation to the interior act of love. On this aspect he says that in friendship the lover sometimes complains that, while he lavishes love on the beloved, the beloved does not return the love; and at times his complaint is unjustified, for instance, if he does not have anything making him deserving of love. Second, repayment of friendship is made in external gifts or services. Regarding this aspect he remarks that the beloved very often complains because the lover had promised him everything in the beginning but delivered nothing in the end.

1761. Next [4], at "**These accusations are made,**" he shows in which friendships this occurs. He remarks that these mutual complaints between lover and beloved take place when the lover seeks pleasure and the beloved wants utility. But sometimes these qualities are not present because the beloved neither provides pleasure for the lover, nor the lover utility for the beloved. Consequently, the friendship is broken off, since the very reasons for

its existence no longer remain. The persons did not love one another for themselves but for the conditions mentioned, viz., utility and pleasure; and these are not enduring, so neither are friendships of this kind. But friendship for the sake of virtue is permanent—as we have indicated (1622–1623)—because friends love each other for themselves according to virtue.

1762. At "**Friends quarrel**" [5] he shows how friendship is disturbed because repayment is not made in the service sought but in something else. He observes that very often friends contend among themselves when they have been given favors different from those they desire; for failure to get what a man wants is like getting nothing at all.

1763. He gives an example of a lyre-player who was promised that the better he sang the more he would be paid. But the morning after playing, when he asked fulfillment of the pledge, the man who promised replied that he had already returned pleasure for pleasure, because conversely he had given the musician pleasure. If the lyre-player was looking for pleasure, the repayment made him was sufficient. But if the one who promised wanted amusement and the player gain, an unfair exchange was made since one party has what he wanted but the other does not. The man who offers a service is intent on getting what he needs and he gives what he possesses to get it.

1764. Then [6], at "**But who,**" he recommends remedies against these disturbances in friendship. He discusses this point from two aspects. First [6] he suggests the means to be used to preserve peace in friendship. Next [Lect. II], at "On the other hand etc." (1164b22), he resolves a difficulty. He treats the first point under two headings. First [6] he explains who should determine a proper repayment in friendship. Then [8], at "Where the gift etc.," he shows how this repayment is made. He handles the first point in a twofold manner. First [6] he shows that the estimate of a fair repayment should be made by the person who first receives the benefit. Second [7], at "Those who first etc.," he shows how complaint in friendship follows from this person's negligence.

1765. He notes first that the arrangement of the amount of repayment pertains to both: the man who bestowed and the man who received the benefit. However, he who bestowed it seems to leave the estimate of the repayment to him who received it. Thus it is said that when Protagoras the philosopher taught students, he told each to reward him with presents that seem to the student fair for the instruction received from the teaching; and Protagoras accepted only that much. In such services of friendship some are satisfied to be recompensed according to the recipients' judgment of the benefits. In this way they seem to receive an adequate fee, because it is given for the man doing the favor and not for the favor done. This is why it seems satisfactory that the fee suffice for the man even if it is not equal to the benefit.

1766. Next [7], at "**Those who first,**" he shows how friendship is disturbed by negligence on the part of those who first receive. He remarks that those who first accept money before they render any service, and then do none of the things they promised—perhaps because their promises were extravagant—naturally meet with complaints since they do not perform what they promised. This is what the Sophists are driven to do, because nothing would be given them for everything they know if the decision was left to their students, for all their learning consist in shallow and trifling doctrines. So then these men are accused when they do not perform the duties for which they accept a fee.

1767. At "**Where the gift**" [8] he shows how repayment ought to be made in friendship: first [8], in friendships based on virtue; then [9], at "I the gifts etc.," in other kinds of friendships. He observes first that where the gift is not made with an agreement o: promise of a certain service, as was done in the friendships already treated, men sometimes bestow benefits for the sake of the person receiving them and not in view of a return. It is evident from discussion in the eighth book (1743) that such people are not to be complained of, for this is characteristic of friendship according to virtue in which a return must be made by considering the intention or will of the doer. Indeed, intention has a special relevancy to friendship and virtue, as has been noted (1538).

1768. Our view regarding friendship which consists in the sharing (*communicatione*) of virtue is the view we should take of sharing of philosophy, for instance, between master and student. The value of philosophy to someone learning is not measurable in terms of money; neither can a student make an equivalent return to his teacher, but perhaps that return, which suffices for God and parents, is to be made.

1769. Then [9], at "**If the gift,**" he shows the way a return is made in the other kinds of friendship. He discusses this point from three aspects. First [9] he proposes his intention. Second [10], at "A person will have etc.," he proves is proposal. Third [12], at "However, man etc.," he answers an implied question. He says first that, if the benefit is of such a nature that the person does not give for the friend's sake but wishes repayment, there must be a return that seems fair to both the giver and the recipient. If this is not possible, then he who was benefited ought to determine a compensation that is reasonable; such a procedure is not only necessary but just.

1770. At "**A person will have**" [10] he proves his proposal: first [10] by argument; then [11], at "In some places etc.," by the authority of law. He notes first that a fair repayment will be determined according to the help a person receives from a friend's benefit in useful friendship and from pleasure acquired in pleasurable friendship. Buying, too, seems to be done in this fashion, that a man's appraisal of a thing will be the price he pays for it. But the amount of help or pleasure derived from a benefit can best be known by the person receiving the help or pleasure. Consequently, it is necessary and just to make repayment according to his judgment.

1771. Next [11], at "**In some places,**"

he proves the same point by the authority of law. He observes that in some states the law prescribes that no redress is possible in voluntary agreements for one of the parties who afterwards pleads deception. If a person voluntarily trusts someone with a benefit or service, payment must be made according to the judgment of the person trusted in conformity with the conditions of the original exchange. For legislators are of the opinion that the person who was given the benefit at the outset ought to arrange the repayment more justly than he who granted it. They think this way because there are many things which are not valued at the same price by those who have them and by those who want to have them. Indeed, individuals apparently think that the goods they offer are worth a big price. But a return ought to be made according to the appraisal of the recipients.

1772. At "**However, a man**" [12] he answers an implied question. He says that a man ought to estimate a benefit not at the price that he considers fair after he receives it but at the value he gave it before he received it.

LECTURE II
Doubts on the Duties of Friendship

TEXT OF ARISTOTLE (1164b22–1165a35) Chapter 2

1. *On the other hand these questions are raised: whether a man ought to give preference to his father in all matters and obey him; or ought he when ill to obey his doctor; or ought he when a soldier to obey his general. Likewise, must someone aid a friend in preference to a virtuous man? Must a person return a favor to a benefactor or oblige a friend, if unable to satisfy both?*
1164b22–27; 1773

2. *Certainly it is not easy to come to a decision in all such contingencies; for they vary greatly in degree, merit, and necessity. However, it is clear that all the deferences are not to be rendered to the same person.*
1164b27–31; 1774

3. *As a rule a man ought to recompense a benefactor rather than present gifts to friends, just as he ought to repay a loan rather than make one to a friend.*
1164b31–33; 1775

4. *Perhaps this course is not always to be followed, for instance, in a case of ransom from robbers. Ought a man to ransom a person—whoever he may be—who has freed him from prison? Or ought he to repay the benefactor, who is not captive, but asks repayment? Or ought he ransom his father even before himself?*
1164b33–1165a2; 1776

5. *It is then a general rule that a debt should be paid, as we have stated. But if a gift has a special goodness or urgency it ought to be given. For sometimes previous benefits must not be returned equally, for example, when the benefit is bestowed on a person known to be virtuous but compensation is paid to the other who is considered wicked. Indeed a loan is not always to be made to a man who has given a loan; for the lender looks for profit from a good man, but the good man lends with no hope of gain from a bad man. Therefore, if all this is true, no equality is present; if it is not really true, but only thought to be then the action will not seem unreasonable.*
1165a2–12; 1777–1778

6. *As we have indicated many times, discussions about our passions and actions have that definiteness belonging to their subject matter.*
1165a12–14; 1779

7. *It is obvious that the same honors are not to be paid everyone. Hence all homage is not given to a father, just as all sacrifices were not offered to Jove. Since different obligations are due parents, brothers, friends, and benefactors, what is proper and becoming ought to be rendered to each group. And such is apparently the custom. For people send wedding invitations to relatives belonging to the family and interested in its activities. For this reason they think that kindred particularly should meet at funerals.*
1165a14–21; 1780–1781

8. *It seems that children should especially provide enough food for their parents; they are indebted to their parents for life itself, and should aid them rather than themselves in a spirit of honor similar to that given to the gods. However, a man should not render every honor to his parents nor the same honor to his father and mother, nor again to a philosopher and a general. To his father he ought to give the honor proper to a father, and to a mother honor belonging to a mother. Similarly, to all elderly persons he should show honor appropriate to age by rising for them, giving them seats, and so on. To friends and brothers he should offer confidence and community of goods. Moreover, to kinsmen, fellow tribesmen, fellow citizens, and others of this standing, a person must always try to allot appropriate honor, and to accord each his due in conformity with propinquity and virtue or usefulness.*
1165a21–33; 1782–1783

9. *Judgment in these matters is easy when people are of the same class, but difficult when they are of different classes. Nevertheless, we should not avoid the decision but make it as best we can.*
1165a33–35; 1784

COMMENTARY OF ST. THOMAS

1773. After the Philosopher has investigated the preservation of friendship by proportionate repayment, he now raises doubts concerning benefits and repayments to friends. First [1] he raises the doubts; then [2], at "Certainly it is not etc.," he solves them. In treating the initial point he presents three doubts. The first is whether a man must assist his father in all matters and obey him rather than anyone else, or whether he must obey other persons in some matters. For example, must a feverish or sick patient obey the doctor before his father; ought a soldier follow the general's orders rather than his father's? The second doubt: whether someone is bound to help his friend in preference to a virtuous person. The third doubt: whether a man ought to make a return to a benefactor for a favor before he makes a present to a friend, if unable to satisfy both.

1774. Next [2], at "**Certainly it is not**," he solves these questions: first [2] by a general answer; second [3], at "As a rule a man ought etc.," by specific answers. He remarks first that it is not easy to decide all these questions with certitude, because their many variations can be considered in all sorts of ways—for instance, the greater or less degree that someone is a good man or friend or benefactor. Likewise, there is a difference sometimes in goodness or necessity. Thus it seems to be better to help a virtuous person or a friend but more necessary to help a benefactor. However, in these matters all the deference is not to be given to the same person, but one kind to some and another kind to others.

1775. At "**As a rule**" [3] he solves previous questions by specific an-

swers. First [3] he solves the third doubt. Then [7], at "It is obvious etc.," he solves the first doubt, and this is understood to include the solution to the second doubt. He treats the first point under three aspects. First [3] he teaches what must be observed generally. He notes that a man should make a return to a benefactor before making a present to a friend, if it is not possible to do both. The reason is that a person is bound in honor to return benefits in the same way he is bound to repay a loan in legal justice.

1776. Second [4], at "**Perhaps this course etc.**," he offers a case where this statement does not hold. He says that what has been affirmed is not always to be observed, for instance, in the event that someone can be freed from robbers. It can be uncertain which of three choices should be made. First, ought a man to liberate from robbers a person—whoever he may be—who ransomed him from prison at one time? Or, second, ought a man repay this benefactor who has not been captured but asks a return in some other form? Or, third, ought a man to ransom his father from robbers? The third choice must be made in preference to the others, because it seems that a man is bound to ransom his father even before himself.

1777. Third [5], at "**It is then etc.**," he shows how we must observe what was said previously. First [5] he explains his intention. Next [6], at "As we have indicated etc.," he deduces a corollary from the discussion. He remarks first that his preceding directive, that we must pay a debt rather than give presents, is to be generally observed. But if a gratuitous gift has a special goodness (say a very virtuous man needs assistance) or urgency (for example, someone is in a position to ransom his father) it ought to be given preference. For the return, which a person makes for previous benefits, sometimes cannot be equalized by a gratuitous gift; for example, when on the one hand the benefit is bestowed on a man known to be virtuous, and on the other a return is made to him who is considered to be wicked.

1778. Nor is it surprising that a benefactor must not be repaid sometimes, for a person is not always bound to accommodate someone who has accommodated him. Sometimes a bad man does a favor for a good man, thinking to make a profit out of it. But the good man does not expect gain from a loan to a bad man. If then the man is really bad, obviously there is no equality between what should be returned to him and to the virtuous person. If, however, the benefactor is not really bad but the recipient thinks so, it does not seem unreasonable to make a gift to the good man instead.

1779. Then [6], at "**As we have indicated,**" he deduces a corollary from the discussion. Obvious from our present study (1774–1778) is the truth we have affirmed many times that discussions about human actions and passions cannot settle anything with certitude; likewise they cannot settle the matters treated by human actions and passions.

1780. Next [7], at "**It is obvious,**" he solves the first doubt. First [7] he explains that not all honors are to be shown to a father. Second [8], at "It seems that etc.," he decides what honors are to be given to certain persons. He notes first that evidently not the same honors are to be paid everyone. Hence all homage is not to be offered

to a father, just as all sacrifices among the pagans were not offered to Jove but some were given to the other gods. Different obligations are due to parents, brothers, friends, benefactors; hence those which are proper and belong to each group are to be attributed to them. Likewise, the same notion is applicable to virtuous persons.

1781. In fact, people seem to act in this way; they send wedding invitations to all those who belong to the family, since, as a result of weddings, the family is increased. They also invite their kindred to activities connected with weddings. For the same reason men think that relatives should meet in kedea or council to discuss matrimonial matches.

1782. At "**It seems that**" [8] he shows what honors are to be given to certain persons. First [8] he explains his intention. Then [9], at "Judgment in these matters etc.," he shows in what cases judgment is easy and in which difficult. He says that in the matter of food, it seems that children ought to provide enough for their parents before all others. They are indebted in this way to their parents as the authors of their existence by generation. Consequently, in matters belonging to the conduct of life itself, they should aid their parents rather than themselves. Likewise, men owe honor to their parents, the authors of their existence, as to the gods.

1783. However, man is not bound to render every honor to his parents, since he neither owes the same honor to father and mother, nor does he owe his father the honor due a philosopher or a general. But a son ought to give his father the honor proper to a father, and to his mother the honor that belongs to a mother. Similarly, one should show honor to an elderly citizen on account of his age by rising and bowing to him and so on. Besides he ought to trust and share what he has with friends and brothers, and also with kinsmen, fellow tribesmen, fellow citizens and others of this standing. A person must always try to allot to everyone what is appropriate and to accord each his due in conformity with the dignity of age or virtue like wisdom, and with the exercise of an office like military commander.

1784. Then [9], he shows where this is easy and where difficult. He remarks that judgment in such matters is easy when people belong to one class. For example, of two relatives we must help rather the closer; of two wise men, the wiser. But it is more difficult to make judgment if people are of different classes, for instance, whether we ought to help a wiser person in preference to a near relative. Although this matter is hard to decide, nevertheless we should not shirk its consideration but settle the problem as best we can.

LECTURE III
Minor Doubts on the Dissolution of Friendship

TEXT OF ARISTOTLE (*1165a37–1165b36*) Chapter 3

1. A question comes up—should or should not friendship be dissolved when people no longer remain the same? **1165a36–1165b1; 1785**

2. It is not surprising that friendship is broken off between people who are friends for utility or pleasure when these advantages no longer exist. Since the friendship was based on utility and pleasure that have ceased, it is reasonable for the friendship to cease. **1165b1–4; 1786**

3. But someone will justly complain of a friend who loves for gain or pleasure but pretends to love for virtue. As we remarked in the beginning, many differences arise when people are not friends in the way they think they are. If then a person deceives himself in thinking he is being loved for virtue—the other doing nothing of the sort—he has only himself to blame. But if he is deceived by the pretense of the other he can blame the deceiver even more justly than he could blame counterfeiters, because the wrongdoing is against a more precious good. **1165b4–12; 1787–1788**

4. If, however, a person is accepted as good but later becomes bad, and this is apparent, should he still be loved? **1165b13–14; 1789**

5. It is quite impossible, for not everything should be loved but only good. Neither is it reasonable to be a lover of evil nor to become like an evil man; and we have indicated that like makes friends with like. **1165b14–17; 1790**

6. Should the friendship then be broken off immediately? **1165b17–18; 1791**

7. Not always, but only when friends are confirmed in evil. If they will accept guidance, we are even more bound to help them morally than we should be to assist them financially; for this is more noble and more proper to friendship. But when a man breaks off such a friendship he does nothing unreasonable; he was not a friend to such a person and consequently withdraws from the friendship of one who has changed and cannot be regenerated. **1165b118–22; 1792**

8. If, however, one friend remains the same but the other becomes better so that a greater difference in virtue exists between them, should the more advanced cultivate the other? **1165b23–24; 1793**

9. No. He cannot. This becomes evident especially among friends of the remote past, for instance, in friendships begun in childhood. For, if one remains a child mentally and the other becomes very talented, they will have no way of being friends since they do not find satisfaction or delight or pain in the same things; they do not even share them with one another. And without this sharing, friendship is impossible. But we have already treated these questions. **1165b24–31; 1794**

10. Is a person then to behave toward him no differently than if he had not been a friend? **1165b31–32; 1795**

11. He should remember the former intimacy; and as we think a man ought to act more kindly toward friends than strangers, so he should make some concessions to former friends by reason of past friendship, provided that the separation was not due to extreme wickedness. **1165b32–36; 1796**

COMMENTARY OF ST. THOMAS

1785. After the Philosopher has investigated the questions pertaining to the preservation of friendship, he now treats the questions dealing with its dissolution. He discusses this point under two headings. First [1] he inquires when a friendship should be dissolved. Then [10], at "Is a person then etc.," he shows how a person should behave towards a friend after the dissolution of friendship. He treats the first point from two aspects. First [1] he examines the dissolution of friendship for those who have changed from their former status. Next [8], at "If, however, one etc.," he examines the dissolution of friendship for those who remain in the same status. He handles the first point in a threefold manner. First [1] he proposes the doubt. Second [2], at "It is not surprising etc.," he offers a solution for friendship based on utility and pleasure; and third [4], at "If, however, a person etc.," for friendship based on virtue. He says first that a question comes up—should or should not friendship be dissolved for those who do not remain in the same state in which they were friends?

1786. Then [2], at "**It is not surprising,**" he solves the doubt so far as it concerns useful or pleasurable friendship. First [2] he shows in what manner these friendships are destroyed. Next [3], at "But someone will etc.," he explains how just complaints may arise in them. He observes first that it is not surprising for friendship to be broken up between people who are friends for utility or pleasure when the advantages no longer exist. The reason is that in these friendships men love pleasure and utility, and not the persons for themselves. Hence, when utility or pleasure ceases it is understandable that friendship should cease.

1787. At "**But someone will**" [3] he shows how complaints may justly arise in these friendships. He remarks that someone will fairly complain of a friend who loves for gain or pleasure but pretends to love for virtue. We stated in the beginning of this treatise

that there are several varieties of friendship. Hence it is possible that some are not friends in the way they think they are, i.e., according to the same kind of friendship. For instance, if they are friends for utility and think they are friends for the sake of virtue. In this case, if a man believes he is loved for virtue and deceives himself—the one who loves him contributing nothing to the deception—he ought to blame himself.

1788. But when a person is deceived by the pretense of the other, he can accuse the deceiver even more justly than he could counterfeiters, for the malice of a person pretending virtue consists in an act against a more precious good. Certainly virtue is more precious than money. So people counterfeiting virtue are more wicked than those who forge money.

1789. Next [4], at "**If, however, a person,**" he answers the question as it concerns friendship based on virtue. First [4] he shows that this friendship should be broken off between those who do not remain virtuous; then [6], at "Should the friendship etc.," how it is to be broken off. He treats the first point from two aspects. First [4] he repeats the question. If we should admit a person to our friendship as a good man, and he later becomes so bad that his wickedness is obvious: should we still love him?

1790. Then [5], at "**It is quite,**" he answers the question again making two comments. One, it is impossible for the evildoer, whose wickedness is evident, to be loved by a virtuous man who cannot love everything but only the honorable good. Second, it is unreasonable to love a man who has become evil; it is neither useful nor fitting, since a person should not love evil nor become like a perverse man.

This might follow if friendship were preserved with an evil man. We have indicated (1654) that like makes friends with like; thus it is impossible to maintain friendship with an evil person without becoming somewhat like him in evil.

1791. At "**Should the friendship**" [6] he shows how this friendship should be broken off. First [6] he asks the question: should a person immediately dissolve a friendship with a man who has become bad?

1792. Second [7], at "**Not always,**" he answers the question, replying that we should not immediately break off this friendship with all persons but only with those who are incurable owing to their excessive wickedness (i.e., cannot be returned readily to the path of virtue). But if some would accept guidance so they could come back to a virtuous status, they ought to be given more assistance to regain good morals than lost possessions; for virtue is more noble and more proper to friendship than money. And when someone breaks off friendship with one who has become bad he does not seem to do anything unreasonable, because he was not a friend to a vicious but a virtuous person. Consequently, a friend reasonably withdraws from the friendship with a man who has changed from his previous condition and cannot be regenerated.

1793. Next [8], at "**If, however, one,**" he treats the dissolution of friendship. First [8] he raises the question. One friend may remain in his former condition but the other becomes more virtuous; and thus a great difference in virtue may exist between the two. Hence the question arises whether the person who has advanced

in virtue ought to treat as a friend the other who has made no advance.

1794. Second [9], at "**No. He cannot,**" he solves the question, observing that it is impossible for the one who is advancing in virtue to continue friendship with him who is standing still. This is especially apparent among friends of the remote past, e.g., in friendships begun in childhood. For, if one remains a child mentally while the other becomes very talented they cannot go on being friends, since they do not have the same tastes, nor are they delighted and pained by the same things. And without this it is impossible to preserve friendship which requires most of all that friends live together. But they cannot live with one another unless they are pleased, delighted, and distressed by the same objects. These questions have been discussed already (1607–1623).

1795. Then [10], at "**Is a person then,**" he investigates how someone ought to behave towards a friend after the dissolution of the friendship. First [10] he asks the question whether, after severing the friendship, a person should no longer behave on rather friendly terms, just as if he had not been a friend in the past.

1796. Next [11], at "**He should,**" he answers the question in this way. A man should remember a former intimacy, as we think he should act more kindly towards friends than strangers. So too because of a past friendship a man ought to act more kindly towards persons who were once his friends, except in the one case where separation from the friend was due to his excessive wickedness. For then a man should show no marks of friendliness to another whose friendship he has terminated.

LECTURE IV
The Acts or Effects of Friendship

TEXT OF ARISTOTLE (*1166a1–166b29*) Chapter 4

1. Kindly acts done for friends, and the determining factors in friendship, seem to be derived from a man's attitude towards himself. 1166a1–2; 1797

2. A friend is defined: (a) as one who wills and does what is good (or apparently good) for the sake of his friend. 1166a2–3; 1798

3. (b) Likewise as one who wills that his friend exist and live for the friend's sake—mothers feel this toward their children, and former friends toward one another after a quarrel.
1166a4–6; 1799

4. (c) As one who lives with another and (d) has the same tastes, or (e) shares the same sorrows and joys with his friend. (This, too, happens especially with mothers.) Now friendship will be defined by some one of these characteristics. 1166a6–10; 1800–1801

5. Each of these is the standard of the virtuous man in relation to himself, and of other men in relation to themselves inasmuch as they consider themselves virtuous. 1166a10–11; 1802

6. As we have pointed out, virtue and the virtuous man seem to be a standard for everyone.
1166a12–13; 1803

7. For he is consistent with himself, always desiring the same things with his whole soul; he wishes for himself both genuine and apparent goods, and produces them. Indeed it is the mark of a good man to take pains to achieve the good, and he does this for himself, i.e., for the sake of the intellectual part which seems to be a man's real self. 1166a13–17; 1804–1805

8. Likewise, he desires his own life and preservation and especially that of his thinking faculty. For existence is a good to a virtuous man and everyone wishes what is good for him. No one would choose to have everything which exists at the price of becoming someone else. (God even now possesses the good, but he always is what he is at any time.) And it seems that the thinking part of man is the man himself or at least the most important part.
1166a17–23; 1806–1807

9. Such a man wishes to converse with himself. He does this with pleasure, for memory of past triumphs is sweet, and hope for the future is encouraging. Besides, his mind is filled with topics for contemplation. 1166a23–27; 1808

10. He keenly feels his own sorrows and joys, for the same thing is painful or pleasant to his whole being, and not one thing to one part and another to another. To tell the truth, he has few regrets. Therefore, each of these characteristics is attributable to the virtuous man himself.
1166a27–30; 1809–1810

11. However, he feels toward his friend as toward himself, for a friend is another self. Consequently, friendship seems to consist in any of these characteristics, and people who have them are friends. 1166a30–33; 1811

12. But whether a person has friendship for himself is a question that must be dismissed for the present. Friendship seems to exist inasmuch as there are two or more having the characteristics mentioned; and if the friendship excels it is similar to the love of a man for himself. 1166a33–1166b2; 1812

13. The attributes discussed seem to belong to the greater part of mankind who, though wicked, apparently have a share of them insofar as they are satisfied with themselves and think themselves virtuous. But none of the thoroughly perverse or wicked either actually have these attributes or appear to have them; even the lesser evildoers hardly have them. 1166b2–7; 1813

14. They differ, though, from one another in desiring one pleasure and wishing for another; they are like the incontinent who choose harmful pleasures instead of those that they really think are good for them. Again, others from faintheartedness or laziness avoid doing what they are convinced is in their best interests. **1166b7–11; 1814**

15. *But those who commit many cruel deeds and are hated for their wickedness seek to avoid living, and take their own life.* **1166b11–13; 1815**

16. *Wicked people therefore seek association with their own kind; they cannot stand themselves, being mindful of many unpleasant deeds in the past and believing, if alone, they will do the same in the future. But when in the company of others they are disposed to forget. Thus they do not experience friendship for themselves, having nothing in them worth loving.* **1166b13–18; 1816**

17. *People of this sort neither rejoice nor grieve with themselves, for their soul is at the same time delighted and distressed when abstaining from certain pleasures. Thus it is drawn this way and that as if by conflicting forces.* **1166b18–22; 1817**

18. *If it is impossible to grieve and rejoice at the same time, it is still true that a person can regret after a little while that he indulged in pleasures and wish that he had not acquired a taste for them. In fact a bad man is filled with remorse. It seems then that the evil person is not amicably inclined even towards himself, for he has nothing lovable about him.* **1166b22–26; 1818**

19. *If to be in such a state is wretched, a man ought to shun evil with great ardor and make every effort to be virtuous. In this way he will acquire friendship for himself and will become a friend of another.* **1166b26–29; 1819**

COMMENTARY OF ST. THOMAS

1797. After the Philosopher has defined the preservation and dissolution of friendship, he now treats its effects. First [1] he indicates the effects of friendship. Then [Lect. V], at "Goodwill resembles etc." (1166b30), he describes them. He discusses the first point in a threefold manner. First [1] he lists the effects of friendship. Second [5], at "Each of these etc.," he shows how good men are disposed towards them; third [13], how bad men are disposed towards them, at "The attributes discussed etc." He treats the first point under two aspects. First [1] he describes the origin of the effects or acts of friendship. Next [2], at "A friend is defined etc.," he lists these effects or acts. He says first that the kindnesses and friendly acts that are done by a man for a friend and are the determining factors in friendship seem to have their origin in his attitudes towards himself. Thus it seems that one person is a friend of another if he acts the same

way for a friend as he might for himself.

1798. Next [2], at "A friend is defined," he lists the works of friendship, which are three. One consists in the voluntary offering of benefits [2]. He observes that people consider someone a friend who wills and does what is good or apparently good for the sake of his friend. He says "wills and does" because one without the other is not enough for friendship. In fact the good deed does not seem to be friendly if a person unwillingly benefits another or neglects to do his will by action. He says "what is good or apparently good" because now and then someone for friendship gives another presents he thinks good for the other, though they are not. He says "for the sake of his friend" because if a man were voluntarily to give benefits to another not—as it were—intending the other's good but his own (e.g., when an owner feeds a horse because he derives profit or himself), he does not seem to be a friend of that person but of himself.

1799. The second work, which he describes at "**Likewise as one who wills etc.,**" is proper to goodwill [3]. He remarks that a friend wills his friend to be and to live for his friend's sake and not for his own, as would be the case were he to seek only personal gain from him. Mothers feel this way towards their children, i.e., will their existence and life. Friends, too, have a similar feeling toward one another when a misunderstanding occurs in their friendship. Even though they do not want to live together on friendly terms because of the misunderstanding, at least they wish their friends to exist and live.

1800. The third work is described at "**As one who lives etc.,**" and is proper to concord [4]. This can be considered in reference to three characteristics. The first refers to exterior association; the second to discrimination; the third to the emotional states which always end in joy or sorrow. Hence he observes that people call someone a friend who has close contact with another (the first characteristic), has the same tastes (the second), and shares sorrows and joys (the third). These are also noticed in mothers with respect to their children.

1801. He adds, by way of summary, so to speak, that friendship is defined by some one of these characteristics; for people think there is friendship in men having any one of these qualities.

1802. Then [5], at "**Each of these,**" he shows how good men are constituted in this matter. First [5] he shows how a virtuous person refers these effects to himself; next [11], at "However, he feels etc.," how he refers them to someone else. Last [12] at "But whether a person etc.," he raises a question. He considers the first point under three aspects. First [5] he proposes his intention. Second [6], at "As we have pointed out etc.," he gives his reason for his previous remark. Third [7], at "For he is consistent etc.," he clarifies his principal proposition. He says first that all these characteristics belong to a virtuous man in relation to himself, and they belong to other men who are not virtuous in relation to themselves at least inasmuch as they think they are virtuous.

1803. At "**As we have pointed out**" [6] he gives his reason for what is referred to under the second heading. Every man in fact does friendly acts for himself insofar as he considers himself virtuous, since virtue and the good man seem to be a standard for everyone. For what is the perfect being in any order of reality must be considered a measure in that order, because all other things are judged more or less perfect according as they approach or recede from what is most perfect. Consequently, since virtue is the proper perfection of man and the virtuous man is perfect in the human species, this should be taken as the measure in all man's affairs.

1804. Next [7], at "**For he is consistent,**" he clarifies his principal proposition. First [7] he shows that the virtuous man himself suitably has what is proper to beneficence; second [8], what is proper to goodwill, at "Likewise, he desires etc."; third [9], what is proper to concord, at "Such a man etc." He says first that the virtuous man desires for himself both genuine and apparent goods, for these latter are identical with genuine goods for him; the reason is that he wishes the goods of virtue, the real good of man. Nor is this desire ineffective in him, but he produces these goods for himself because it is a mark of a good man to labor for the achievement of good.

1805. We said in the second book that virtue makes its possessor good and his work good (222, 307, 309). And the virtuous person wants this and acts for himself, i.e., for the sake of the intellectual element which is foremost in man. Indeed everything seems to be especially what is foremost in it. But the virtuous man strives always to do what is reasonable. It is evident then that he always wishes for himself the absolute good.

1806. Then [8], at "**Likewise, he desires**," he shows that the virtuous man himself suitably has what belongs to goodwill. The Philosopher remarks that the virtuous man especially wishes himself life and conservation in being chiefly for that part of the soul where wisdom resides. If a man is virtuous he must want what is good for him because everyone desires good things for himself. But the good of a virtuous man is that he be virtuous.

1807. However, if a man were to become something else—e.g., if he were transformed into a stone or an ass as the fables relate—he would not trouble himself about whether he had all good things in his transformed state. For that reason everyone wishes himself to exist so that his identity is preserved. But the being that remains identical in his existence is God; he does not wish himself some good he does not now possess but possesses perfect good in himself. He always is what he is at any time, since he is unchangeable. Now we are like God most of all by our intellect which is incorruptible and unchangeable. Therefore every man's existence is thought of in terms of his intellect. Hence, a virtuous man who lives entirely according to his

intellect and reason especially wishes himself to exist and to live. He also wishes himself to exist and live according to what is permanent in him. On the other hand a person who wishes himself to exist and live chiefly in terms of his body, which is subject to change, does not really wish to be and to live.

1808. At "**Such a man etc.**" [9] he shows how a virtuous man appropriately has in himself what is proper to concord. First [9] in regard to companionship; he remarks that the virtuous man wishes most of all to converse with himself by turning to his soul and meditating alone. He does this with pleasure: first regarding the memory of past events since the recollection of former triumphs is sweet to him; second regarding hope for the future, for he anticipates success and this is pleasant to him; third regarding present knowledge, for his mind is filled with reflections, i.e., true and useful deliberations.

1809. Second [10], at "**He keenly etc.**," Aristotle shows that the virtuous man is at peace with his own passions. He keenly feels his own sorrows and joys since the same thing is painful or pleasant to his whole being (i.e., both the sensitive and intellectual part) and not one thing to one part and another to another. The reason is that his sensitive power is subject to reason to such an extent that it obeys reason's prompting, or at least does not resist for the virtuous man is not led by the passions of the sensitive part so that when passion subsides he must repent of having acted against reason. But he always acts according to reason and does not readily have regrets. Thus he is at peace with himself.

1810. He concludes by way of epi-gue that the characteristics discussed re appropriate to a virtuous man in elation to himself.

1811. Next [11], at "**However, he eels,**" he shows how a virtuous man hould adapt these characteristics to is friend. Aristotle notes that a virtu-us man is disposed to his friend as to imself because a friend is—so to peak—another self by affection, that , a person feels for a friend what he eels for himself. Consequently, it eems that friendship consists in any of hese characteristics that people expe-ience toward themselves; and that hose are real friends who have these haracteristics.

1812. Then [12], at "**But whether a erson,**" he raises a question—does a nan have friendship toward himself? Ie observes that this question must be ostponed since it is a semantic prob-em rather than a real one. Friendship eems to exist among any persons who ossess two or three of the charac-eristics mentioned. And when the riendship for others excels, it is similar o the love a man has for himself. Con-equently, someone wishing to prove is friendship for another is accus-omed to say "I love you as myself." Ience it doesn't really make any dif-erence whether the word friendship is pplied to self, because the reality of riendship abundantly belongs to a nan in regard to himself.

1813. At "**The attributes discussed**" 13] he shows how bad men are dis-osed toward these works of friend-hip. First [13] he shows that these vorks cannot belong to evil men. Sec-nd [19], at "If to be in such etc.," he educes a corollary from the discus-ion. He treats the first point from two spects. First [13] he proposes his in-ention. Then [14], at "They differ,

though etc.," he explains his proposi-tion. He says first that these works of friendship seem to belong to many in respect to themselves in spite of the fact that they are evil men. However, we must understand that the more they share in these works of friendship for themselves the more they are satis-fied with themselves and think they are virtuous. But those who are com-pletely perverse or wicked neither re-sort to these works nor seem to live together; and scarcely any evil man finds such behavior agreeable to him. Indeed there are few evil men who think they are virtuous or who are un-aware of their wickedness.

1814. Next [14], at "**They differ, though,**" he explains his proposition. First [14] he shows that bad men are not suitable to have the work of friend-ship belonging to beneficence; second, nor that belonging to goodwill, at "But those who etc." [15]; third, nor that belonging to concord, at "Wicked peo-ple, therefore etc." [16]. He remarks first that bad men are at odds with themselves because they desire some pleasures agreeing with their sensitive appetite at the same time that they wish others agreeing with their reason. Such is obviously the case with the incontinent who want harmful pleas-ures instead of those they reasonably judge good. Others from fainthearted-ness and laziness neglect to do what they know is good. Thus they are dou-bly lacking in beneficence towards themselves: in one way, so far as they do what is harmful; in the other, so far as they shun what is beneficial.

1815. Then [15], at "**But those who,**" he shows that they are not suitable to have the work that belongs to good-will. He observes that criminals who have perpetrated many frightful deeds—so that their very personalities are hated by men—do not want to exist or live. But life becomes a burden for them because they know that they are offensive. And they actually so flee from life that they sometimes do away with themselves.

1816. At "**Wicked people, therefore**" [16] he shows that evil men are not suitable to have the work that belongs to concord. First [16] regarding companionship. Evil men cannot converse with themselves by turning to their soul but they seek to associate with others by speaking and co-operating with them in external words and works. They act in this way because when thinking alone about themselves they remember many distressing evils they committed in the past and they are convinced they will do the same in the future—this is painful to them. But when they are in company they forget their wrongdoings in the distraction of external activities. So, since they have nothing in themselves worth loving, they feel no love for themselves.

1817. Second [17], at "**People of this sort,**" he explains that they can not find internal peace with their passions. He observes that people of this sort are not conscious of their own joys and sorrows. In fact their soul struggles against itself, for the sensitive part resists the reason. On the one hand it grieves, when withdrawing from pleasures, because of evil that dominates it and causes distress in the sensitive part; and on the other hand it rejoices according to reason that

judges evil pleasures are to be avoided. In this way one part of the soul draw an evil man one way, but the other par draws him the opposite way; just as i his soul were rent into conflicting drives and fought with itself.

1818. Third [18], at "**If it is impossi ble**" he eliminates a doubt. Someone might contend that it is impossible for an evil person to grieve and rejoice a the same time about the same matter and it is true so far as the two experi ences are concerned, although each can be caused at the same time in dif ferent parts of the soul. He maintains then that if a wicked man cannot be pained and pleased at the same time nevertheless shortly after the gratifica tion he is saddened that he was de lighted a moment ago, and wishes he had not indulged in such pleasures Indeed evil men are filled with re morse because, after the impulse of evil or passion that caused the wicked ness subsides, their reason tells then they did wrong and they are remorse ful. It is obvious then that evil men are not inclined to friendship for them selves, for they have nothing in then worthy of friendship.

1819. At "**If to be in such**" [19] he concludes from the premises that, if is so extremely wretched to live with out friendship for oneself, we ought to shun evil with increased ardor, and make every effort to become virtuous For in this way a person will have friendship for himself and be capable of becoming a friend to others.

LECTURE V
Goodwill

TEXT OF ARISTOTLE (1166b30–1167a21) Chapter 5

1. Goodwill resembles but is not really friendship.   1166b30; 1820

2. For goodwill may be felt towards people who are unknown to us or who are unaware of it, but not friendship—questions we have discussed already.   1166b31–32; 1821

3. Nor is it love, for it does not include intensity or desire; and these effects follow love.   1166b32–34; 1822

4. Moreover, love is accompanied by familiarity while goodwill may arise suddenly, as it does toward athletes in contests; spectators become well disposed and sympathetic to the contestants but will take no active part, for they feel goodwill suddenly and love only superficially.   1166b34–1167a3; 1823

5. Goodwill certainly seems to be the beginning of friendship, as pleasure derived from seeing is the beginning of love. For no one loves who has not been first delighted by what he has seen. However, a man who delights in the form of another does not therefore love him; but there is love if he desires the beloved when he is absent and longs for his presence. In a similar way people cannot become friends unless they first have goodwill. But they are not therefore friends, since the benevolent only wish good to others but are neither active in their behalf nor distressed by their misfortunes. Therefore, by extension of meaning, goodwill can be called an ineffective friendship, though it does develop into friendship from continual and habitual goodwill.   1167a3–12; 1824–1825

6. But it is not friendship based on utility nor that based on pleasure.   1167a12–13; 1826

7. For there is no place for goodwill in these friendships. In that for utility the recipient is merely acting justly when he returns goodwill for benefits received; and the person who wishes another to prosper in the hope of getting rich by means of him does not seem to have goodwill to the other but to himself. Likewise, a man is not a friend who is anxious about someone in order to make some use of him.   1167a13–18; 1827–1828

8. As a general rule goodwill is created by reason of virtue and equity when a person seems to another to be good or brave or the like in the way competing athletes do, as we have pointed out.   1167a18–21; 1829

COMMENTARY OF ST. THOMAS

1820. After the Philosopher has shown what the works of friendship are and who does them, he now treats the works individually. These works of friendship can be reduced to three: beneficence, goodwill, and concord—as we have indicated (1789–1801). So he now delineates the three of them. First [1], concerning goodwill that consists in an interior affection for a person. Second [Lect. VI], at "Likewise, concord etc." (1167a21), concerning concord which consists also in affection but based on personal considerations.

Third [Lect. VII], at "Benefactors seem etc." (1167b16), concerning beneficence that consists in exterior proof of friendship. He considers two aspects of the first point. First [1] he shows that goodwill is not friendship; then [5], at "Goodwill certainly etc.," that it is the beginning of friendship. He discusses the first point in a twofold manner. First [1] he shows that goodwill is not friendship in its habitual character; next [3], at "Nor is it etc.," nor is it love in terms here of passion, as noted in the eighth book (1602). He treats the first point under two headings. First [3] he states his intention, observing that goodwill seems to resemble friendship inasmuch as all friends must be of goodwill.

1821. Second [2], at "**For goodwill may be**," he proves his statement by two arguments. The first is that goodwill can be felt for strangers whose acquaintance one does not have from familiar association. But this is impossible in friendship. The second argument is that goodwill can be unknown to the person who has our goodwill—this cannot be said of friendship. These questions were discussed in the beginning of the eighth book (1560).

1822. Then [3], at "**Nor is it love,**" he shows that goodwill is not love for two reasons. The first [3] is that goodwill does not include intensity of soul or desire, i.e., passion of the sensitive appetite which by its impulse extends the soul with a kind of violence towards an enticing object. This occurs in the passions of love but not in goodwill, which consists in a simple movement of the will.

1823. He assigns the second reason at "**Moreover, love**" [4]. He remarks that love is accompanied by familiarity, for it indicates a vehement impulse of the soul, as was just stated. But the soul is not accustomed to be moved instantly and with vehemence towards an object, but is led gradually to what is greater. Therefore, love increases by means of familiarity. But, since goodwill implies a simple movement of the will, it can arise suddenly, for instance, when people watch athletic contests. The spectators become kindly disposed to one of the two contestants and would be pleased if this particular athlete won. However, they would do nothing to bring this about, because men are instantly benevolent and love

superficially, i.e., according to a mere feeble movement of the will that does not break forth into action.

1824. Next [5], at "**Goodwill certainly,**" he shows that goodwill is the beginning of friendship. He handles this point in a twofold manner. First [5] he proves that goodwill is the beginning of friendship. Second [6], at "But it is not etc.," he shows which friendship has goodwill as its beginning. He observes that goodwill is called the beginning of friendship, as pleasure at the sight of a woman is the beginning of love for her. For no one begins to love a woman unless he has been first delighted by her beauty. However, when a man is pleased at the sight of a woman's form he does not immediately love her. But it is sign of complete love that he desires her, as if he feels her absence keenly and longs for her presence when she is absent. The same is true of friendship and goodwill, for it is impossible for people to be friends unless they have goodwill first.

1825. Nevertheless, they cannot be called friends from the fact that they have goodwill, because people of goodwill merely wish good to the objects of their benevolence; but not to the extent of doing good deeds for them nor of being distressed by their misfortunes. Consequently, it can be said, changing our way of speaking, that goodwill is a kind of lazy friendship because it is not joined with any friendly activity. But when a person continues a long time in goodwill and becomes used to wishing well to anyone, his soul is strengthened in willing good, so that his will is not idle but active. In this way friendship arises.

1826. At "**But it is not**" [6] he shows which friendship has goodwill as its beginning. First [6] which friendship does not have goodwill as its beginning; then [8], at "As a general rule," which does. He discusses the first point in a twofold manner. First [6] he states his intention. He notes that goodwill is not raised by length of time and habit to the genuine kind of friendship that is based on utility or pleasure.

1827. Second [7], at "**For there is no place,**" he proves his statement. Goodwill does not develop into that friendship which has no room for it. But goodwill has no place in the friendships just mentioned. This is obvious in pleasurable friendship where each friend desires from the other his own enjoyment—a thing that is sometimes accompanied by harm to the other, thus destroying goodwill. However, goodwill is possible in useful friendship, so far as concerns the recipient of benefits; for he returns goodwill at least for the benefits he has received, if he acts justly.

1828. If one wishes another to be healthy and prosperous because he hopes to have an abundance of possessions through the other, he does not seem to have goodwill toward that other, from whom he hopes to become rich, but towards himself. Likewise a person does not seem to be a friend of someone who is anxious about that person's good for his own advantage, i.e., in order to make some use of him.

1829. Then [8], at "**As a general rule,**" he shows which friendship has goodwill as its beginning. Aristotle remarks that in general goodwill seems to exist for a person because of his virtue and equity; it seems to someone that the person, towards whom he is benevolent, is good or brave or the like—qualities which people are accustomed to praise. He notes this reaction we have manifested toward athletes for whom we have goodwill on account of the courage or similar virtue they seem to possess.

LECTURE VI
Concord

TEXT OF ARISTOTLE (1167a22–1167b16) Chapter 6

1. *Likewise, concord seems to belong to friendship, and for this reason it is not identity of opinion that can exist among people unknown to one another.*   **1167a22–24; 1830**

2. *Nor do we say that people are in concord who agree on any subject whatsoever, for example, the heavenly bodies. For common agreement on these questions does not pertain to the notion of friendship.*   **1167a24–26; 1831**

3. *But we do say that citizens of a state are in concord when they agree on what is useful and vote for the same measures, and work together to achieve them. Therefore they have concord about things to be done,*   **1167a26–29; 1832**

4. *which concern important matters capable of achievement by both or all parties. Thus the citizens are in concord when they all think that public officials should be elected, or that they should become allies of the Spartans, or that Pittacus should be their ruler (when he is also willing to rule). But when two rivals want power, like the rivals in the Phoenissae, they introduce discord. For there is no concord when each of the parties wants something for himself, but only when they want it for the same person, as the common people and the upper classes wish the best men to rule. In this case everyone gets what he strives after.*   **1167a29–1167b2; 1833–1835**

5. *Concord then seems to be friendship among citizens, as is commonly held. For it deals with affairs that advance their interests and concern their lives.*   **1167b2–4; 1836**

6. *Now this kind of concord is found among virtuous men, for they are in accord with themselves and with one another, being, so to speak, of one mind. Their wills remain constant and do not ebb and flow, like Euripos. They desire what is just and useful, and work together for these goals.*   **1167b4–9; 1837–1838**

7. *But it is impossible for vicious men to agree—except in a trifling way—just as it is impossible for them to be friends; for they desire a full share of the advantages but shirk their portion of labor and service. And while each man is intent on gaining these profits he watches his neighbor to prevent him from obtaining them (the public good is destroyed by lack of vigilance!). Consequently, contention arises when they force each other to give way but are unwilling to render justice themselves.*   **1167b9–16; 1839**

COMMENTARY OF ST. THOMAS

1830. After the Philosopher has defined goodwill, he now considers concord. First [1] he explains its nature; then [5], at "Concord then etc.," how it is related to friendship among citizens. He discusses the first point under two aspects. First [1] he investigates the category of concord; second [2], at "Nor do we say etc.," its subject matter. He says first that concord seems to belong to the category of friendship. We have already pointed out (1800) that friends characteristically make the

same choices, and the formal reason of concord consists in this. Obviously then concord is not homodoxia, meaning identity of opinion. It can happen that people who do not know one another hold the same opinion, although there is no concord among them, as there is no friendship.

1831. Then [2], at "**Nor do we say,**" he examines the subject matter of concord. First [2] he shows what matters it does not concern. He observes that men are not said to be in concord who agree on any subject whatsoever, like people who hold the same opinion about speculative questions, the heavenly bodies for instance. Common agreement on these truths does not pertain to the concept of friendship, because friendship arises from preference; but judgment in speculative problems is not derived from compulsory preference. Consequently, nothing prevents some friends from holding different views and others the same views on these questions. It is evident then that concord, which pertains to the notion of friendship, does not deal with matters of this kind.

1832. Second [3], at "**But we do,**" he shows the matters within concord's competence. First [3] he explains in general that it is concerned with things to be done. He remarks that citizens of a state are said to have concord among themselves when they agree on what is useful, so that they vote for the same measures and work together on projects they consider for their interests. Thus it is evident that concord deals with things to be done.

1833. Then [4], at "**which concern,**" he explains in particular with what practicable matters concord is concerned. He indicates two kinds. One, that it refers to affairs having some importance; for people do not disrupt concord because of disagreement over minor points. The other, that matters of concord are of such a nature that they can belong to both agreeing parties, or even to all men or citizens of a state. If someone agrees with another that he may have what no one can possibly have, it is not of much concern to concord.

1834. He offers as an illustration states that are said to have concord, for example, when all the citizens hold the same opinion, that rulers should be determined by election and not by lot or succession; when the Athenians think they should form a military alliance with the Spartans to fight together against common enemies; when all the citizens agree that a particular man, Pindar, let us say, should be ruler (if however he be willing to rule). At such times people who have these wishes are said to be in concord.

1835. But when each wishes to rule they begin to quarrel, like the characters in the play Phoenissae. Indeed concord does not consist in the fact that both should wish good for themselves, however much there may seem to be a similarity to an equitable will, since everyone wishes good to himself. On the contrary it is a cause of discord. But in order to have concord, men must agree on the same numerical thing. For example, the common people and the upper classes are in agreement that the best men should rule. In this way, when everyone concurs in the same objective, all get what they are striving for.

1836. Next [5], at "**Concord then,**" he shows how concord is related to friendship among citizens. He notes that political friendship, either between citizens of the same state or between different states, seems to be identical with concord. And people usually speak of it in this way: that states or citizens of one mind have friendship for one another.

1837. At "**Now this kind**" [6] he indicates the possessor of concord. First [6] he shows that it is found among virtuous men; then [7], at "But it is impossible etc.," that it is not found among bad men. He observes first that concord of the sort we have defined is found among those who are virtuous. These men behave in such a way that they are in accord with themselves and one another inasmuch as they do not change their mind either regarding choices or works. The reason is that good men seemingly are not given to regrets; we have already noted this (1592). He adds "so to speak" because it is impossible for men to have absolute immutability in this life.

1838. To explain the statement, he subjoins that they are of the same mind because the wills of these men remain fixed in good and do not change from one object to another, like Euripos, a strait along the coast of Greece where the water ebbs and flows. Such virtuous men wish what is just and useful, and they work together for these goals.

1839. Then [7], at "**But it is impossible**," he shows that concord is not found among vicious men. He remarks that bad men cannot agree, except perhaps in a trifling way, any more than they can be friends. Consequently,

they cannot be of one mind because they want more than their share of all the advantages but are unwilling to bear the labors—performed by the community and incumbent on them—and administrations, i.e., expenses or services of any kind. And while each one wishes this: to have more of the benefits and less of the burdens, he inquires about his neighbor and prevents him from obtaining what he himself covets. Thus while the common good of justice is not preserved, the common possession of concord among them is destroyed. In this way contention arises when a person forces another to observe justice towards him while he himself is not willing to render justice to the other but wants more advantages and less disadvantages—a condition that is against the equality of justice.

LECTURE VII
Beneficence

TEXT OF ARISTOTLE (1167b16–1168a27) Chapter 7

1. Benefactors seem to love those they have benefited, more than those who are well treated *love* their benefactors. **1167b17–18; 1840**

2. This seems unreasonable and we look for an explanation. **1167b18–19; 1841**

3. Many people think the reason is that beneficiaries are debtors while benefactors are *creditors. Just as in the case of loans, borrowers wish that the lenders did not exist, but the latter worry about the welfare of their debtors; so the bestowers of benefits wish the recipients to live in order to receive their thanks, but the recipients care little about giving thanks. Epicharmus would perhaps say that people who are of this opinion look at things in a bad light. But it does have the appearance of being very human, for most men are forgetful and more desirous of getting benefits than giving them.* **1167b19–28; 1842–1843**

4. But perhaps the reason is more in the nature of things and there is no parallel in the case *of lenders. For they do not love their debtors but wish them to be preserved for the sake of gain. On the other hand benefactors love and feel friendship for those who receive their benefactions even when the recipients are of no use now and may never be.* **1167b28–33; 1844**

5. This happens with craftsmen, for each one loves his product more than he would be loved by it were the product alive. Likewise, it occurs especially with poets who love their own poems doting on them as their children. A similar situation exists with benefactors, for the person benefited is the result of their efforts and they love him more than he loves them. The reason for this is that for all men their existence is a thing to be chosen and cherished. But our existence consists in an actuality, i.e., in living and operating, and the operation is in a way the agent in action. For this reason craftsmen love their products because they love their existence; and this is natural, for the product manifests in actuality what the agent is in potentiality.
1167b33–1168a9; 1845–1847

6. Then, too, for the benefactor his action is morally good, therefore he finds joy in its object. But to the recipient there is nothing noble in his relation to the giver. If any good exists, it is utilitarian and has less of pleasure and friendship. **1168a9–12; 1848**

7. However, there is pleasure about the present in activity, about the future in hope, and about the past in memory. But the most delightful of these is activity, and it is more lovable too. For the benefactor then his activity remains since good is enduring; but for the recipient the utility passes away. **1168a13–17; 1849**

8. Likewise, the memory of noble things is pleasant but that of useful things is either not at all or, at best, to a less degree pleasant. On the other hand, the opposite seems to be true with expectation. **1168a17–19; 1850–1851**

9. Moreover, loving resembles activity, but being loved resembles passivity. Assuredly then those who excel in activity love and have the concomitants of love. **1169a19–21; 1852**

10. Besides, people have greater love for things they get as a result of labor. Thus, those who earn wealth value it more than those who inherit it. Now there is nothing burdensome about receiving a benefit but bestowing one involves much labor. For this reason mothers are fonder than fathers of their children; they suffer more pains in giving them birth; and they know better than fathers who their children are. And this, too, seems to be applicable to benefactors.
1168a21–27; 1853–1854

COMMENTARY OF ST. THOMAS

1840. After the Philosopher has defined goodwill and concord, he now considers beneficence. First [1] he states an incident connected with it, observing that benefactors seem to love those they benefit, more than those who are well treated love their benefactors.

1841. Second [2], at "**This seems**," he raises a question on this point, remarking that the statement is puzzling because it seems contrary to reason. For beneficiaries are bound because of debt to love their benefactors but not conversely.

1842. Third [3], at "**Many people**," he answers the question, assigning the reason for this phenomenon. First [3] he gives an apparent reason; then [4], at "But perhaps etc.," he gives the real reasons. He says many think the reason is that beneficiaries are in debt to their benefactors. But a debt is owed to benefactors as to lenders. Now we see in the case of loans that borrowers wish their lenders did not exist, so as to be free of debt. On the other hand, lenders, who have payments coming, take care of the welfare of their debtors for fear of losing what is owed to them. So too benefactors wish existence and life to those they have benefited for the sake of receiving thanks from them. But beneficiaries are not solicitous about returning thanks but wish to be excused from this duty. For that reason they love their benefactors very little.

1843. The philosopher-poet Epicharmus in approving this reason might say that people who accept it consider men's bad qualities; but it seems a common practice. In fact most people forget benefits and want to get more than they give.

1844. Then [4], at "**But perhaps**," he assigns four real arguments. He makes two observations on the first argument. First [4] he prefers this argument to that given earlier (1842–1843). He says that the reason for the statement just made seems to be the more natural one that is now offered, because it is taken from the nature of a benefit—unlike the reason assigned previously which is taken on the part of the lender. Lenders do not indeed love the people they oblige, but wish them preservation not for love but for profit. Benefactors, however, feel love and real affection for those who receive their benefactions even when the recipients are not at all useful now and without promise of usefulness later.

1845. Next [5], at "**This happens**," he offers the first argument, observing that benefactors feel toward their beneficiaries the same way as artists feel towards their creations. Every craftsman loves his own product more than he would be loved by it were the product living by any chance. Apparently this is especially true of poets doting on their poems as parents on their children. Indeed, poems partake of reason—by which man is man—to a greater degree than other mechanical works. There is a similarity here to what occurs when benefactors love those they have benefited; for a person who is well treated by another is in a way his product. For this reason benefactors love their product, i.e., the beneficiaries, more than the reverse.

1846. After giving the illustrations, he adds a general argument. The reason behind these statements is that existence is something chosen and cherished by everyone—to the extent

1at a thing exists it is good, and good
; worthy of choice and lovable. But
1is existence consists in an actuality,
)r to exist is to live and consequently
) operate. There can be no life without
ital action of some kind. Hence the
erformance of vital actions is desir-
ble to everyone. But the producer ac-
ually producing is in some way the
vork produced, for the action of the
1over and cause is in the thing moved
1d caused. For that reason craftsmen,
•oets, and benefactors love their pro-
luctions because they love their own
xistence; and it is natural that every-
hing should love its own being.

1847. He clarifies his argument for
his deduction that men love their crea-
ions, when he adds "the product
manifests in actuality what the agent is
1 potentiality." For a man exists inasmuch as he has a rational soul; the soul
; the first act of a physical body having
ife potentially, i.e., being in potential-
ty to vital operations. So then man's
irst esse consists in the fact that he has
he capacity for vital actions. And the
1andiwork that a man produces in the
ctual exercise of vital activity indi-
ates the reduction of this potentiality
o actuality.

1848. He presents his second argument [6] at "**Then, too, for the benefac-
or,**" and treats it from two aspects.
'irst [6] he gives the argument, stating
hat everyone loves his own good. But
he benefactor's good consists in his
·ery act of bestowing benefits. For this
eason the benefactor takes joy in his
)eneficiary, as the person in whom his
;ood it attained. But the recipient, who
ccepts the benefit, finds nothing noble
n the giver or benefactor; for it is not a
·irtuous act to receive benefits from
nother. But if he sees any good it is
Itilitarian, and this is less pleasing and

lovable than a noble good. Thus, obviously, the benefactor is less worthy of
love in the eyes of the beneficiary than
conversely.

1849. Second [7], at "**However,
there is etc.,**" he proves in two ways
what he has subjoined. First [7], in general. What is pleasurable about the present is activity itself or operation;
about the future, hope; about the past,
memory. The most pleasurable of
these is activity that is also more lovable than hope or memory. But for the
benefactor the honorableness of his
own activity remains, because an honorable good does not pass away
quickly but is enduring. In this way he
delights in the person he benefits as in
a present good. But the utility that the
recipient gets passes away easily. Thus
the beneficiary delights in his benefactor as a memory of the past. Consequently, the honorable good that the
benefactor finds in the beneficiary is
more delightful and lovable than the
useful good that the beneficiary sees in
his benefactor.

1850. Next [8], at "**Likewise, the
memory,**" he proves the same point
again; he observes that the memory of
virtuous or honorable deeds, which a
person performed in the past, is pleasant. But the memory of useful goods,
which a person possessed at one time,
is either not pleasant at all (as when he
grieves over their loss) or is pleasant
(as when he retains some) to a degree
less than the memory of honorable
goods. However, the contrary seems to
be true about the expectation of future
goods; it is more pleasant to look forward to useful than honorable goods.

1851. The reason for this diversity is
that only a known good gives pleasure,
not an unknown one. But no one
knows an honorable good except the

person who has it. Consequently, honorable goods are known if they are in the past but not if they are merely in the future. On the other hand, useful goods both past and future are known, but help from past goods has vanished. However, help from them in the future gives pleasure as a remedy against tomorrow's needs. Hence a man is more delighted with the hope of useful goods than with their memory or even the hope of honorable goods. But he takes more pleasure in the memory of honorable goods than useful goods. Now a benefactor remembers an honorable good but a beneficiary a useful one. Therefore, the beneficiary is more pleasing and lovable to the benefactor than the other way round.

1852. He presents the third argument at "**Moreover, loving**" [9], remarking that loving is like activity; for it is characteristic of a lover to wish and to do good for the beloved. On the other hand, being loved is more like passivity. But the agent excels the patient. Consequently, it is reasonable that those excelling in activity—such as benefactors, artists and poets—should love and have the consequent acts of love.

1853. He assigns the fourth argument at "**Besides, people have**" [10]. Everyone prefers the results of his own work. So, those who by their own zeal and labor earn riches value them more highly than people who receive them as an inheritance from their parents or a donation from a benefactor—hence those receiving them in this manner are more generous, as we have pointed out in the fourth book (674). Now, for a person to receive a benefit requires no labor on his part. But for a person to confer a benefit is a laborious task demanding work and toil. It is reasonable then that benefactors love their beneficiaries more than the reverse.

1854. He strengthens his argument by giving the example of mothers who love their children more than fathers do: both because mothers bear heavier burdens than fathers in the generation of children by carrying and giving them birth and because mothers can know better than fathers who their children are. Likewise, it seems to be characteristic of benefactors to love their beneficiaries inasmuch as they labor for them.

LECTURE VIII
Doubt Concerning Love of Self

TEXT OF ARISTOTLE (*1168a28–1168b28*) Chapter 8

1. Likewise the question arises whether a person should love himself most or someone else.
1168a28–29; 1855

2. For men criticize those who love themselves most, and call them self-lovers, as if this were term of disgrace.
1168a29–30; 1856

3. The bad man apparently does everything for himself, and the more he acts this way, the orse he is. Therefore people complain that he does nothing unrelated to himself. On the other nd the virtuous man does what is honorable. And the better he is the more he works for the od and for his friend's sake, even overlooking his own interests.
1168a30–35; 1857

4. But the facts are not in agreement with the arguments presented, and this is hardly rprising. It is commonly held that we ought to love best the person who is our best friend. But at man who most wishes good to another for his sake is his best friend, even if no one will now about it. Certainly a man, in his attitude toward himself, best fulfills these conditions,
1168a35–1168b4; 1858

5. and indeed all other conditions which enter into the definition of a friend.for, as has been ointed out, all the attributes of friendship are derived from this relationship, and are extended other men.
1168b4–6; 1859

6. Likewise, all the proverbs are in accord with this position. For example, "Friends are of ne mind and heart"; "Friends share alike"; "Friendship is equality"; and "Friends are near as nee and shin." Now all these sayings are verified especially of a person in relation to himself, r he is his own best friend, and therefore ought to love himself best.
1168b6–10; 1860

7. It is questionable then which opinion we ought to follow, since both seem plausible.
1168b10–12; 1861

8. Perhaps in such discussions we must distinguish and determine both to what extent and what way each side is expressing the truth. If we understand how each uses the expression lover of self," the truth may then be evident.
1168b12–15; 1862

9. People using it as a term of reproach call those self-loving who assign to themselves more an their share of money, honors, and physical pleasures. For these goods are desired and ealously sought as being best by most men, and as a result become a source of contention. ence those who are plentifully supplied with such things gratify their desires and passions in eneral and the irrational part of their soul. But most men are like this, and so the epithet has en taken from the generally existing type that is evil. Men then, who are lovers of self in this nse, are justly condemned.
1168b15–23; 1863–1864

10. Obviously, it is the people who amass these goods for themselves who are usually called elf-loving; for if a person were zealous above all else to do works of justice, or temperance, or ny other virtue, devoting himself entirely to the acquisition of good, no one would censure such man as a lover of self.
1168b23–28; 1865

COMMENTARY OF ST. THOMAS

1855. After the Philosopher has reated the preservation and dissolu- ion of friendship along with the works f friendship, he now raises some dif- iculties concerning it. First [1], on the part of the one who loves; then [Lect. XII], at "Should a man then etc." (1170b20), on the part of those who are loved. He discusses the first point from two aspects. First he solves the doubt concerning the love a person has for himself. Next [Lect. X], at "Some doubt whether etc." (1169b3), concerning the love a person has for others. He considers the first point in a threefold manner. First [1] he states the doubt. Second [2], at "For men criticize etc.," he shows its plausibility. Third [8], at "Perhaps in such etc.," he offers the solution. He remarks first that a doubt exists whether a person should love himself most, or someone else more than himself.

1856. Then [2], at "For men criticize," he shows that the doubt is plausible. First [2] the objects on one side; next [4], at "But the facts etc.," on the other side. Last [7], at "It is questionable then etc.," he finishes doubting on the question. He treats the first point under two headings. First [2] he introduces the fact that men criticize those who love themselves most; and it is accounted as evil that some people are self-lovers.

1857. Second [3], at "The bad man" he observes that the evil person does everything for gain; and the more he follows this, the worse he is. And the more consistently he does this, the more severely people blame him as one who does nothing unrelated to himself, i.e., nothing for the good of others but only for his own. However, virtuous men do not act for themselves alone; rather they do what is honorable both for themselves and their friends. For this reason they frequently overlook their own advantages.

1858. At "But the facts" [4] he objects on the opposite side. He states that the facts are not in agreement with the reasons just presented, according to which men are shown to love themselves most. And this is not in a way unlikely. First [4] because, according to the general opinion, we must love best

the person who is our best friend. But that man who most wishes good to another for his sake is his best friend even if no one else might know it. Certainly these conditions exist especially in a man's attitude towards himself, for everyone especially wishes good to himself. Evidently then a man ought to love himself most of all.

1859. Second [5], at "and indeed," he introduces in favor of this view the point he has just made (1858). He observes that all the other conditions determining and defining the nature of friendship are found in a man's attitude toward himself, as he noted there. The reason is that all the attributes of friendship, which are considered in reference to others, are derived from the amicable relation a person bears towards himself.

1860. Third [6], at "Likewise, all," he offers several proverbs to the same purpose. He notes that all current proverbs are in accord with this position, that a man should love himself most of all. For example, "Friends are of one mind and heart"; "Friends share alike"; "Friendship is equality"; and "Friends are akin as knee and shin" (which are very close). All these sayings show us that friendship consists in a kind of oneness that especially belongs to a man in relation to himself. Thus all the quoted proverbs are verified particularly of a person toward himself. And this because a man is his own best friend, and so a person ought to love himself most of all.

1861. Next [7], at "It is questionable," he finishes doubting on the question. He remarks that there is a reasonable doubt which of these arguments we ought to accept, since both appear to have some plausibility.

1862. At "Perhaps in such" [8] he solves the doubt he has discussed. First

.] he determines the method of solu-
on; then [9], at "People using etc.," he
ves the solution. He observes that in
ıch discussions which marshal prob-
ble reasons for each side, we must
istinguish and define to what extent
nd in what way each is expressing the
ruth. In this way, if we understand
ow a love of self is used in both parts
f the objections, the truth we seek will
ppear.

1863. Then [9], at "**People using,**" he
olves this doubt by making a distinc-
ion. First [9] he shows how a man may
e called a lover of self in the blame-
vorthy sense; next [Lect. IX], at "But
uch a man" (1168b29), in the praise-
vorthy sense. He considers the first
ooint in a twofold manner. First [9] he
explains his intention. Second [10], at
'Obviously, it is the people etc," he
proves his statement. He says first that
people, who consider "lover of self" a
term of reproach, call those self-loving
who assign themselves more than their
share of material goods, like money,
honors, and physical pleasures (of
food and sex, for instance), for the majority desire goods of this nature, and
men give their attention to them as
though they were best.

1864. Because most people try to acquire an excessive amount of them,
which everyone is unable to have,
strife and contention arise over these
goods. Besides, those who are more
plentifully supplied with them utilize
this abundance to satisfy their desires
and all passions in general, and accordingly the irrational part of the soul to
which the passions belong. Thus men
who seek goods of this sort love themselves according to the irrational or
sensitive part of their soul. Most men
are such that they follow sense rather
than reason. Therefore, the epithet
"lover of self" has been taken from
what is evil—this is appropriate to
many people. Thus, philautos, i.e.,
lover of self in this sense can be frequently found among men, and is
rightly condemned.

1865. At "**Obviously, it is the people**" [10] he proves his statement. He
notes that, obviously, most people
usually call philautoi or lovers of self
those who amass for themselves these
goods pertaining to the irrational side
of man. For, if a person should wish to
abound in goods of reason, i.e, virtuous actions—for example, if he wishes
among other things to do especially
the works of justice or temperance or
any other virtue—so that he always
wants to acquire honorable good for
himself, no one from the crowd will
call him philautos or lover of self. Or if
some wise man should call him self-
loving, he will not say this in censure.

LECTURE IX
A Virtuous Man's Love of Self

TEXT OF ARISTOTLE (1168b28–1169b2) Chapter 8

1. But such a man rather than his vicious counterpart seems to be a lover of self,

1168b28–29; 186•

2. for he assigns to himself the noblest and best goods.   1168b29–30; 186•

3. He yields to the leading principle in him and makes everything obey it.   1168b30–31; 186•

4. As a state, or any other society, seems to be identical with the most dominant element in it, so too does a man. Consequently, a person who loves and yields to this part will be a lover of self in a marked degree.   1168b31–34; 186•

5. Furthermore, a person is called continent or incontinent inasmuch as this element is in control or not, which supposes that it is man himself.   1168b34–35; 187•

6. And the actions that men do according to reason seem to be their own in the most proper sense, and to be voluntary.   1168b35–1169a1; 187•

7. It is evident then that everyone is, or chiefly is, this part; that the just man loves it exceedingly. He is therefore singularly a lover of self   1169a2–4; 187•

8. in a sense other than that of the man who is censured. The difference is between living according to reason and according to passion, between desiring what is good and desiring what seems advantageous.   1169a4–6; 1873•

9. But those who busy themselves with good works in an exceptional manner receive the approval and praise of all.   1169a6–8; 1874

10. And if everyone strives for what is good and aims at doing what is best, the whole community will satisfy its needs and each member will possess the best of goods, since virtue is the best good.   1169a8–11; 1875

11. Therefore, it is reasonable for the virtuous man to love himself, because in doing good he will help both himself and others. But it is unfortunate for the bad man, because he injures both himself and his neighbors by following his passions.   1169a11–15; 1876

12. As a result, what the evil man ought to do is in conflict with what he does, for the reason always chooses good for itself. But the good man obeys his reason.   1169a15–18; 1877

13. It is true of the virtuous man that he does many actions for the sake of his friends—and country—and if necessary dies for them. He will sacrifice money, honor, and all the goods men strive for, gaining for himself an honorable good.   1169a18–22; 1878

14. For he will prefer a short period of intense delight to a long period of quiet existence, an illustrious life of a year to an ordinary life of many years, a single notable good deed to many insignificant ones. Certainly those who die for others seem to obtain this result; thus, they choose a great good for themselves.   1169a22–26; 1879–1880

15. Likewise, they throw away money so that their friends may gain more. This way a friend gets the money but the virtuous man acquires an honorable good and thus assigns to himself what is better.   1169a26–29; 1881

16. He acts in the same manner toward honors and position. For the good man readily sacrifices all preferments for a friend, since this action seems a laudable good. It is reasonable then to consider him virtuous when he prefers what is honorable to all other goods.

1169a29–32; 1882

17. He may even defer to his friend in performing actions; for it is better to be the cause of a friend's acting than to act himself. In all praiseworthy activity, the good man assigns to himself the larger share of virtue.   1169a32–1169b1; 1883

18. *A person then ought to be a lover of self in this sense, as we said before, but not in the* *nse that most are lovers of self.*   1169b1–2; 1884

COMMENTARY OF ST. THOMAS

1866. After the Philosopher has ▮hown how a man may be called a ▮over of self in the blameworthy sense, ▮e now shows how a man may be ▮alled a lover of self in the praisewor- hy sense. He discusses this point from ▮wo aspects. First [1] he shows that ▮here exists a way, different from the ▮receding, in which someone is a lover ▮f self. Then [9], at "But those who ▮tc.," he shows that to be a lover of self ▮n this sense is praiseworthy. He con- ▮siders the first point under three head- ▮ngs. First [1] he shows that man is ▮self-loving who takes for himself an ▮abundant share of the goods of reason. Next [7], at "It is evident then etc.," he ▮shows that the virtuous person is of this nature. Finally [8], at "in a sense other than etc.," he shows that this manner of loving oneself differs from that previously discussed. He treats the first point in a threefold fashion. First [1] he proposes his intention. He says that this man, who is anxious to excel in the works of virtue, seems to be *philautos* or a lover of self, rather than the man who assigns to himself an excessive amount of physical goods.

1867. Second [2], at "**for he assigns,**" he proves his proposition by two argu- ments. The first [2] is that a person loves himself more, to the extent that he assigns to himself greater goods. But he, who makes it his business to excel in virtuous works, assumes for himself the goods that are noblest and best, i.e., the honorable kind. There- fore, such a one especially loves him- self.

1868. He offers the second reason at "**He yields**" [3]. A person of this type bestows good things on the principal element in him, namely, the intellect; and he induces all parts of the soul to obey the intellect. But the more some- one loves an object, the more he loves what is more principal in it. It is evi- dent then that the man who wishes to be eminent in good works loves him- self in a high degree.

1869. Third [4], at "**As a state,**" he proves what he had taken for granted: that the person who loves the most dominant element in him, the intellect or reason, particularly loves himself. He proves this by three arguments. The first [4] is: in the state it is the most authoritative part that especially seems to be the state. Hence what the rulers of a state do is said to be done by the whole state; and the same reason holds for any other composite of sev- eral parts. Consequently, in man it is his reason or intellect, his principal ele- ment, that especially seems to be man. Therefore, he who loves his intellect or reason, and treats it well seems to be philautos or a lover of self most of all.

1870. He presents the second argu- ment [5] at "**Furthermore.**" Someone is said to be continent because he con- trols himself and incontinent because he does not. It is to the extent that a man observes reason by following its judgment, rather than repudiates rea- son on account of incontinence that he is this element, i.e., his intellect. So it seems that such a man truly loves him- self who loves his intellect.

1871. He states the third argument [6] at "**And the actions.**" He observes that men's reasoned actions seem to be theirs in the most proper sense and to be done voluntarily. What a man does because of concupiscence or anger he does not seem to do by his own will but under the direction of an external impulse. It is evident then that man is in a particular fashion what conforms to his intellect and reason. Hence he especially loves himself when he loves his intellect and reason.

1872. Next [7], at "**It is evident then**," he shows who is properly a lover of self in this sense. He remarks that it is obvious from the discussion (1869, 1870, 1871) that everyone is his intellect or reason, or rather (since several other ingredients concur in the essence of man) it can be said that man is especially this part, i.e., intellect or reason because it is the formal and perfective element of the human species. Obviously, the virtuous person loves his intellect or reason exceedingly, because he perfectly preserves and universally obeys it. Hence it is clear that the virtuous person is philautos or a lover of self.

1873. Then [8], at "**in a sense other than**" he explains that this manner of loving oneself differs in kind from that previously discussed. He notes that the virtuous person is a lover of self according to a kind of self-love that differs from the brand censured before (1863–1865). He gives two differences: one, on the part of the activity, for the good man loves himself inasmuch as he lives according to reason. For the man who is blamed lives according to passion, following the irrational desires of his soul, as has been pointed out (1864). The other difference exists on the part of the motive. For the good man loves himself inasmuch as he seeks for himself what is the absolute good. But the man who is blamed loves himself inasmuch as he seeks what seems a useful good but is really harmful.

1874. At "**But those who**" [9] he

shows that to love oneself in the second way is praiseworthy. First [9] he presents his proposition. Then [13], at "It is true etc.," he excludes from the person who loves himself in the second way that for which the lover of self is blamed. He discusses the first point under three headings. First [9] he shows that the man who loves himself according to reason is worthy of praise. For this man is anxious to excel in good works, as we have indicated (1867). But it is evident that everyone approves and praises those who busy themselves with virtuous activity in a manner different from other men, i.e., in a more extensive manner. It is obvious, therefore, that the person who loves himself according to virtue is to be praised.

1875. Second [10], at "**And if everyone**," Aristotle shows that this person is also helpful both to himself and others. We just said that he who loves himself according to virtue is eager to perform exceptionally good actions. But if all strove for what is good so that everyone aimed to excel his neighbor in virtue by doing his best the whole community would have its needs satisfied. The reason is that one would come to the assistance of another and the goods that are best, viz., virtues, would become the property of each.

1876. Third [11], at "**Therefore, it is reasonable**," Aristotle deduces two corollaries from the discussion. The first [11] is that it is best for the good man to love himself because in doing good he helps both himself and others. But it is unfortunate that the bad man loves himself because in following his evil desires he will injure both himself and his neighbors by depriving himself of virtue and them of physical goods.

1877. He states the second corollary

t "**As a result**" [12], noting that what ʜe evil man does is opposed to what ɛe ought to do; he is acting against his ɪntellect or reason. But the intellect alⅯays chooses what is best for itself. Ⱨhus the bad man does not do what he ɦould do. On the other hand it is characteristic of the virtuous man to obey ɪis reason always.

1878. Then [13], at "**It is true,**" he ⅹcludes from the person who loves ɪimself according to virtue the comⅼaint previously lodged (1855–1865) ɡainst a lover of self, that he does othing for anyone else. He treats this oint in a threefold manner. First [13] ɛe states his intention. Next [14], at For he will prefer etc.," he explains his ɪntention. Finally [18], at "A person ɦen ought etc.," he sums up the truth f the question in an epilogue. He ⅼotes first the truth of the statement ɓout the good man, that he, far beond all other men, will do many acts ɔr the sake of his friends and country. ⅼven if it is necessary to die for a friend ɭe will not forsake him. He will, as it ⅾere, cast aside and disdain wealth, ⅼonor, and all other external goods for ⱱhich men strive, for the sake of a ⅽiend; by means of all this he procures ɔr himself an honorable good that is ɦore excellent. Hence even in this way ɭe shows more love for himself and ⱅrocures his greater good.

1879. Next [14], at "**For he will,**" he ⅹplains his statement. First [14], conⅽerning death that a good man will ɪndergo for his friend. Then [15], at Likewise, they throw away etc.," conⱱerning the fact that he contemns exterⱅal goods for his friend. Finally [17], at ˈHe may even etc.," concerning virtuⱅus actions which a good man someⅼimes entrusts to his friends. He ⅇmarks first that the good man dying ɔr his friend procures good for him-

self, because he chooses to delight for a short time in a brilliant work of virtue rather than for a long time in a quiet existence, i.e., indifferently in mediocre works of virtue.

1880. He prefers an illustrious life of a year to an ordinary life of many years. Similarly, he prefers a single notable good deed to many insignificant ones. Although those who die for virtue may live more briefly, nevertheless by endangering themselves for a friend they do a greater good in this one action than in many other actions. Thus, in acting virtuously by exposing their lives for a friend they choose a great good for themselves. From this it is clear that they love themselves very much.

1881. At "**Likewise, they throw away**" [15] he explains this point concerning contempt for external goods. First [15] in respect to money. He says that virtuous people throw away, i.e., despise or disperse, money for the sake of friends so that their friends gain more with the money. This way also they really love themselves more; for when a person gives money to a friend and acquires an honorable good for himself, obviously he assigns the greater good to himself, and under these circumstances loves himself more.

1882. Second [16], at "**He acts,**" he explains the same point in respect to honors and dignities, noting that the good man behaves in the same way towards honors and position. For he readily gives up all these preferments for a friend, since this very action is a virtuous and laudable work. Clearly then the virtuous person acts in a reasonable manner when he chooses the great good of virtue instead of all external goods; and so he loves himself most.

1883. Then [17], at **"He may even,"** he shows the same point about virtuous actions themselves. He observes that the virtuous man sometimes even defers to his friend in doing good actions. For instance, if a virtuous work is to be done by him or another person, he lets his friend do it to derive profit and praise in this way. However, even here the virtuous person takes what is better for himself; for it is better and more virtuous to cause his friend to do these actions than to do them himself.

This is particularly true when the opportunity remains for him to do the same or greater deeds at another time. Thus it is evident that the good man assigns to himself the larger share of virtue in praiseworthy activity, and so has much love for himself.

1884. He concludes by way of summary [18] that a person ought to be a lover of self as we said the good man is, but not as most men, who are not virtuous, are lovers of themselves.

LECTURE X
A Doubt on a Happy Man's Need of Friends

TEXT OF ARISTOTLE (1169b3–1170a13) Chapter 9

1. Some doubt whether or not a happy man needs friends.   1169b3–4; 1885

2. It is said that because happy people are self-sufficient they do not need friends; since they have all good things, being self-sufficing, they need nothing else. Now a friend is looked upon as another self who provides what a man himself cannot.   1169b4–7; 1886

3. Hence the saying: "If fortune favors us, what need of friends?"   1169b7–8; 1887

4. There seems to be an inconsistency in attributing to a happy man all goods but not friends since a friend seems to be the greatest of external goods.   1169b8–10; 1888

5. If it is more characteristic of a friend to give than to receive a benefit, more proper to virtue and a virtuous man to do good for others, and better to be kind to friends than strangers, then the virtuous person will need friends whom he can benefit.   1169b10–13; 1889

6. This is why the related question arises: does a man need friends more in prosperity or in adversity? Undoubtedly, the unfortunate man needs them to help him, and the fortunate man needs friends he can help.   1169b13–16; 1890

7. It seems strange indeed to make the happy man a solitary. For no one would choose to have the whole world if he had to live alone, since man is naturally a social animal and fitted by nature to live with others. Therefore, the happy man lives in this way because he has what is naturally good. But obviously it is better to live with friends and virtuous men than with strangers and chance acquaintances. Therefore the happy man needs friends. 1169b16–22; 1891

8. What then are the followers of the first opinion holding, and to what extent is their opinion true? Do they, like the majority, look upon friends as useful people? Certainly the happy man will not need such friends for he has useful goods already; nor will he need those whom one chooses for their pleasantness, except to a slight extent. Indeed the happy man does not require pleasure from the outside, for his life is pleasant in itself. Since then he does not stand in need of friends of this sort, he seems not to need friends at all. 1169b22–28; 1892–1893

9. Certainly this is not true. For we said in the beginning that happiness is an activity; and activity obviously is a coming into being and is not like something in one's possession. But happiness consists in living and doing, and the activity of the good man is virtuous and pleasurable in itself, as we noted earlier. Of all pleasures, happiness is proper to a virtuous man. Now we can study our neighbors better than ourselves and their actions better than our own. Evidently then virtuous persons find pleasure in the actions of friends who are good men, since they have both qualities that are naturally pleasurable. The happy man, therefore, will need such friends inasmuch as he wants to study actions that are good and his own, and the actions of the virtuous man who is his friend are of this nature.   1169b28–1170a4; 1894–1896

10. Besides, people think that a happy man should live pleasantly. Now the man who lives alone does have a hard life, since it is not easy to keep up a continuous activity by oneself. But with others and in relation to others it is less difficult. Therefore, his activity will be more continuous and delightful in itself, as it ought to be for the happy man. Indeed the good man, as such, rejoices in virtuous actions but is distressed by those which arise from wickedness; he is like a musician pleased by good music but irritated by bad.   1170a4–11; 1897–1898

11. Then too a companionship in virtue results from living with good men, as Theognis remarks.   1170a11–13; 1899

COMMENTARY OF ST. THOMAS

1885. After the Philosopher has investigated and solved the question that was raised about a person loving himself, he now solves the question that was raised of a person loving another. First [1] he proposes the doubt. Then [2], at "It is said etc.," he shows that the doubt is reasonable. Finally [8], at "What then are etc.," he solves it. He notes first that there is a doubt whether or not the happy man needs friends.

1886. Then [2], at "It is said," he shows that the doubt is reasonable by raising difficulties for both sides. First [2] he objects for the negative; next [4], at "There seems to etc.," for the affirmative. He objects in a twofold manner for the initial position. First [2] by an argument. Some say that happy people are self-sufficing and do not need friends; they have all good things, and so, being complete in themselves, they seem to need nothing else. But a friend, inasmuch as he is another self, seems to be necessary to provide what a man cannot obtain by himself. So, apparently, a happy person does not need friends.

1887. Second [3], at "Hence the saying," he offers a pagan proverb in favor of the same view: "When the spirit is benign there is no need of friends." The pagans, especially the Platonists, believed the order of providence was such that human affairs were governed by divine dispensation through intermediary spirits. Some of the spirits, they held, were favorable; others malevolent. Therefore, the proverb says that when a man enjoys the favor of divine providence, as happy people seem to do, he has no need of friends.

1888. At "There seems to be" [4] he objects for the opposite side by three arguments. (He offers the first [4].) It seems unreasonable to assign all external goods to a happy man, and not assign him friends, since a friend is the greatest of external goods.

1889. He treats the second argument at "If it is more characteristic" [5], handling it in a twofold manner. First [5] he presents the argument. We have pointed out already that it is more characteristic of a friend to give than to receive a benefit. But it is proper to virtue to impart benefits; and happiness consists in virtuous action, as indicated in the first book (127–128). The happy man then is necessarily virtuous and beneficent. But it is better for a man to be good to friends than strangers, other things being equal, because he does this with more pleasure and alacrity. Consequently, since a happy person is virtuous he needs friends whom he can benefit.

1890. Second [6], at "This is why," he deduces a doubt from the premises: whether a man has need of friends more in adversity than in prosperity. He seems to need friends in both circumstances, for the unfortunate man needs friends to help him, and the fortunate man needs friends he can help. But this doubt will be pursued later (1925–1943).

1891. He presents the third argument at "It seems strange indeed" [7], saying that it appears unreasonable for the happy man to be a solitary; for this is contrary to everyone's choice. No one would choose to live alone all the time, even after he had all other goods, because man is naturally a social animal and fitted by nature to live with others. Since, therefore, the happy person has what is naturally good for man, he should have people to live with. Obviously it is better for him to live with friends and virtuous men than strangers and others. Thus, it is clear that the happy man needs friends.

1892. Next [8], at "**What then are**," he solves the preceding doubt. First [8] he shows how those, who deny that a happy man needs friends, may be saying what is true; then [9], at "Certainly this is not etc.," how they may be saying what is false. He says first that since we have just proved that the happy man does need friends we must consider what the followers of the first opinion are holding, when they deny the happy man's need of friends, and to what extent their opinion may be true.

1893. On this question we should note that most men consider as friends those useful to them in the bestowal of external goods—and these alone are appreciated by the common run of men. Therefore, the happy man does not need friends like this, for the goods he has are enough. Likewise, he does not need friends for pleasantness, except in that minor way—that we need jests for relaxation. Cf. the fourth book (844–845). Indeed, the happy man does not require external pleasure for which such friends are absolutely necessary, for his life is pleasant in itself, as we have indicated in the first book (145). Since then he does not stand in need of these useful and pleasant friends, it seems that he has no need of friends.

1894. Then [9], at "**Certainly this is not**," he shows that their statement is not entirely true. First [9] he proves this by moral arguments; next [Lect. XI], at "Looking more profoundly etc." (1170a13), by a more intrinsic reason. He offers three reasons for the initial point. First [9] it is not true that, if the happy man does not need useful and pleasant friends, he does not therefore need any friends at all, as affirmed previously (1892–1893). For there are virtuous friends whom he does need. The primary reason for this is that happiness is an operation (144, 145, 180, 1267).

1895. It is evident that operation consists in doing; it is not an entity existing in the manner of permanent things, as if it were a possession that, once obtained, a man would be happy without the necessity of doing anything. But happiness consists in continual living and doing. Now the operation of the virtuous man must be good and pleasurable in itself because it is essentially good, as indicated in the first book (156). But among pleasures good operation is the pleasure proper to the virtuous man, for the person who would not delight in virtuous operation would not be virtuous, as we stated in the first book (158).

1896. We can have pleasure only in what we know. But we can examine our neighbors better than ourselves and their actions better than our own because every man is a bad judge of his own case on account of the private affection he has for himself. Evidently then virtuous persons find pleasure in the actions of those who are both virtuous men and friends of theirs; in them are found both qualities pleasurable by nature, namely, the good and the lovable. In this way, therefore, the happy man will need these virtuous friends inasmuch as he seeks to study the virtuous actions of the good man who is his friend. Since a man's friend is another self, so to speak, the friend's actions will be his own in a sense.

1897. He presents the second argument at "**Besides, people think**" [10]. It is generally thought, he says, that the happy man should live pleasantly; for pleasure is one of the conditions for happiness—we have noted this in the first book (158). But he who lives by himself experiences a hard and burdensome life; pleasure that he enjoys following upon activity must be interrupted, for it is not easy for a man to be continuously active by himself, i.e., when living alone. But it is easy if he lives with another, since a kind of interchange of activities takes place while they perform good actions for one another. In this way pleasure is continued.

1898. If then a man lives with friends, his virtuous activity delightful in itself will be more continuous. And this ought to be true for the happy man so that he may have uninterrupted

pleasure in works of virtue. For the good man as such rejoices in virtuous actions performed either by himself or others. Moreover, he is grieved by contrary actions arising from another's wickedness, like a musician who is pleased by good music but irritated by bad.

1899. He presents the third argument at "**Then too**" [11]. Here he observes that because the virtuous person lives on friendly terms with good men there results ascesis or a companionship in virtue, as the poet Theognis has remarked. Such an association is advantageous for anyone disposed to virtue, just as other human activities also are more satisfactorily accomplished in partnership.

LECTURE XI
Why a Happy Man Needs Friends

TEXT OF ARISTOTLE (*1170a13–1170b19*) Chapter 9

1. *Looking more profoundly into the matter it seems that a virtuous friend is naturally desirable to a virtuous man.*   1170a13–14; 1900

2. *For, as has been noted, what is naturally good is in itself good and desirable to the virtuous person.*   1170a14–16; 1901

3. *Now life in animals is defined by capacity for perception, in men by capacity for perception and thought. But capacity is reduced to operation, and what is principal consists in operation. Life, therefore, seems to be principally an act of perception or thought.*
                                                          1170a16–19; 1902

4. *Likewise, life is numbered among the things that are good and pleasant in themselves; for it is a determinate entity, and what is determinate pertains to the nature of the good. Now what is good naturally is good to the virtuous person. This is the reason why life seems delightful to all men.*   1170a19–22; 1903–1905

5. *However, we must not argue from an evil and corrupt life, or one passed in pain, because such life is indeterminate as are the attributes connected with it. This will be made clearer in the following discussion on pain.*   1170a22–25; 1906

6. *If life itself is good and pleasant (and this is apparent from the fact that all men desire it) then it will be especially so to virtuous and happy people. For life is most desirable to such men and their existence happy in the highest degree.*   1170a25–29; 1907

7. *When a man sees, he is aware that he is seeing; when he hears, he is aware that he hears; when he walks, he is aware that he walks. Similarly in all other activities there is a faculty in us that is aware that we are active; we perceive that we perceive, we understand that we understand, and in this we perceive and understand that we exist. For existence was defined as perception or thought. But perceiving that one is alive is numbered among the goods that are delightful in themselves because life is by its nature a good, and to perceive the good existing in oneself is pleasurable. Now life is desirable especially for the virtuous because for them it is good and pleasant at the same time; and when they perceive what is good in itself they rejoice.*
                                                          1170a29–1170b5; 1908

8. *But the good man feels toward his friend as toward himself, since his friend is another self. Therefore, just as his own existence is desirable to everyone, so, or nearly so, is his friend's existence. Now a virtuous person's existence is desirable because he perceives that it is good, and the perception is desirable in itself. Consequently, he ought to be conscious of his friend's existence too; this takes place in associating with one another and sharing conversation and thoughts. In this way we understand living together as applied to men; we do not understand it in the sense of feeding together as applied to cattle. If then a happy man's existence is desirable in itself, inasmuch as it is naturally good and pleasant, and his friend's existence is much the same, then a friend will be one of the desirable goods.*   1170b5–17; 1909–1911

9. *But what is desirable for the happy man he must have, or else he will be in want. To be happy, therefore, a man needs virtuous friends.*   1170b17–19; 1912

COMMENTARY OF ST. THOMAS

1900. After the Philosopher has given the moral reasons indicating that the happy man needs friends, he now shows the same point by a more fundamental reason. First [1] he shows that it is desirable for a happy man to have a friend. Then [9], at "But what is etc.," he concludes in addition that the happy man needs friends. He treats the first point from two aspects. First [1] he proposes his intention. He observes that if someone wishes to judge by a more fundamental reason it will be very evident that for a good and happy man a virtuous friend is naturally even more desirable than other external goods.

1901. Second [2], at "**For, as has been noted etc.,**" he proves his proposition. First [2] he shows what is naturally desirable and pleasant to the virtuous person respecting himself. Then [8], at "But the good man etc.," he shows what is desirable and pleasant respecting his friend. He discusses the first point under two headings. First [2] he shows that existence and life are naturally desirable to the good man. Next [7], at "When a man sees etc.," he shows that it is delightful and desirable to feel this. For the first statement he offers this reason [2]. Whatever is naturally good is in itself good and desirable to the good man, as is clear from the discussion in the seventh book (1533). But existence and life are naturally good and desirable to living creatures. Therefore, existence and life are good and desirable to the virtuous person.

1902. The major is self-evident in the text. He states the minor at "**Now life etc.**" [3], and makes three observations on it. First [3] he shows the nature of life, remarking that in all animals life is defined in general by the capacity for sensation. But in man it is defined by the capacity for perception relative to what he has in common with other animals or by capacity for thought relative to what he has proper to himself. Now every capacity is reduced to

operation as to its proper perfection. Consequently, what is principal is operation and not mere capacity, for act is more excellent than potency, as is proved in the ninth book of the *Metaphysics* (Ch. 8, 1049b4–1050b6; St. Th. Lect. VII–VIII, 1844–1866). From this it is evident that for animal or man life in the full sense is an act of sensation or thought. Indeed a slumbering individual—since he does not actually feel or think—does not live completely but has a half a life, as was stated in the first book (234–235).

1903. Second [4], at "**Likewise, life,**" he shows that life is naturally good and pleasant. He notes that life itself is numbered among the things which are good and pleasant in themselves. He proves this from the fact that life is something determinate; and what is determinate pertains to the nature of the good.

1904. To understand this we should bear in mind that potentiality, considered in itself, is indeterminate because it can be many things; but it becomes determinate by means of act, as is obvious with matter and form. Potentiality, however, without act is potentiality with privation which constitutes the nature of evil; just as perfection achieved by activity constitutes the nature of good. For that reason, as a thing is evil to the extent that it is indeterminate, so it is good to the extent that it is determinate.

1905. But life is something determinate especially as it principally consists in an operation, as we just pointed out (1902). So it is evident that life is naturally good. Now what is naturally good is also good to the virtuous person, since the good man is the norm in human kind, as we have indicated (1898). Consequently, since life is naturally good, we see that it is pleasant to all men.

1906. Third [5], at "**However, we,**" he removes a doubt. He points out that in stating life is naturally good and pleasant (1901, 1903–1905) we must not include evil, i.e., vicious and corrupt, life that departs from the right order, nor life lived in pain. Such life is not naturally good because it is indeterminate, i.e., lacking in proper perfection, just as the attributes connected with it are indeterminate. Everything is made determinate by what exists in it; hence, if this is indeterminate, then the thing itself will be indeterminate. For example, if sickness is indeterminate, the sick body will be indeterminate and ill, as also will be moral evil and corruption or pain. This will be made clearer in the pertinent questions following, where pain will be discussed (2048–2049).

1907. Then [6], at "**If life,**" he deduces a conclusion from this argument. He remarks that if life itself is naturally good and pleasant (this is apparent not only from the foregoing argument but also because all men desire it) then life will be good and pleasing to virtuous and happy people most of all. Since their existence is fullest and happiest, it must be most desirable to them.

1908. Next [7], at "**When a man,**" he shows that perception of being alive is desirable and pleasant to the virtuous person. For a man who knows that he sees is conscious of his seeing, and the same is true with someone who knows that he hears. Likewise in other cases a person is conscious that he is active. In this reflective act in which we perceive that we perceive and understand that we understand, we perceive and understand that we exist. We have said

before (1902) that man's existence and life are in the fullest sense perception or thought. But that someone should be conscious he is alive is numbered among the goods which are delightful in themselves, because life is by its nature good, as we have already proved (1903–1905); and the consciousness that he possesses good is delightful. Since life is desirable especially to the virtuous, for whom existence is good and pleasurable, evidently then the realization that they perceive and understand is delightful to them. The reason is that simultaneously in the very act (by which they are aware that they perceive and understand) they recognize what is good in itself, viz., existence and life; and they are delighted by this.

1909. At "**But the good man**" [8] he shows from the premises what is desirable and pleasant to the virtuous and happy person with regard to his friend. He observes that the good man feels for his friend as if he were himself, since his friend is in a way another self. Therefore, just as his own existence is desirable and delightful to every virtuous man, so is his friend's existence desirable and delightful to him—if not equally, at least very nearly so. For the natural unity a man has with himself is greater than the unity of affection he has with his friend. We have just noted (1907, 1908) that the good man's existence and life are desirable to him because he perceives that they are good. But this perception, by which someone perceives good existing in him, is delightful in itself. Consequently, as a person rejoices in the perception of his own existence and life, so it is simply necessary for him to perceive them in his friend in order to rejoice in him.

1910. This takes place through constant association and the exchange of ideas and reflection. In this way men are said to dwell with one another in an appropriate manner, not as cattle feeding together, but as human beings living a life that is proper to them.

1911. Thus he concludes from the premises what he had set out to do. He declares that a happy man's own existence is desirable in itself inasmuch as it is naturally good and pleasant; since the existence and life of a friend are close to the life of a virtuous and happy man by affection, the friend too will be desirable to him.

1912. Then [9], at "**But what is,**" he shows in addition that friends are necessary for the happy man. What is desirable for the happy man he must have, or else a deficiency will remain; and this is contrary to the notion of happiness which calls for a sufficiency. Therefore it is necessary that the man, who is in a state of happiness, should have virtuous friends. Here he is discussing the kind of happiness that is possible in this life, as we have indicated in the first book (113).

LECTURE XII
Limitation of the Number of Friends

TEXT OF ARISTOTLE (*1170b20–1171a20*) Chapter 10

1. *Should a man then make as many friends as possible? or, just as it has been wisely said about traveling: "May I be called neither a great traveler nor a homebody," perhaps it will be fitting in friendship that a man should be neither without friends nor with an excessive number.*
                                                                    1170b20–23; 1913

2. *This statement seems to be quite applicable to those who make friends for utility. For it is burdensome to repay the services of many people and a man's life is not long enough for the task. Therefore, more friends than are sufficient for our own life distract and prevent us from noble living, and there is no need for them.*   **1170b23–28; 1914–1915**

3. *Likewise, a few friends for pleasantness are enough, as a little seasoning is enough in food.*
                                                                    1170b28–29; 1916

4. *But a question arises concerning virtuous friends, whether we should have as many as possible, or is there a limit to the number of one's friends as there is to the population of a city? Ten men do not make a city and with one hundred thousand men it is no longer a city. Perhaps, the exact size is not a particular number, it might well be any mean between definite limits.*
                                                                    1170b29–33; 1917

5. *The number of one's friends too should be limited; they may be as numerous as the people with whom a man can associate and divide himself, for this attribute seems to belong in a special way to friendship. That one cannot live and share himself with great numbers is all too evident.*
                                                                    1170b33–1171a4; 1918

6. *Besides, one's friends must be friends of one another, if they are all to spend their time together. But with a large number this is hard to achieve.*   **1171a4–6; 1919**

7. *It is difficult also to share intimately in the joys and sorrows of a great number of people. Indeed a man may very likely be called upon to rejoice with one and grieve with another at the same time.*   **1171a6–8; 1920**

8. *Perhaps then it is not well to seek as many friends as possible but as many as are sufficient for living together. It does not seem possible to have a great many friends for the reason that one cannot love several persons. Indeed love is a kind of excess of friendship, and this is possible with one person only, or with a very few.*   **1171a8–13; 1921**

9. *We see that this is so in practice, for people do not have many friendships of the comradely type—comrades are said to sing in pairs. Those who have a host of friends and are on familiar terms with everybody seem to be real friends of no one; they are, though, friends in the way proper to fellow citizens, and are generally called obsequious.*   **1171a13–17; 1922–1923**

10. *One may have friendship with many as fellow citizens and not be obsequious but really virtuous. But it is not possible to be friends to a large number for their own and for virtue's sakes. A man should be satisfied to find a few such friends.*   **1171a17–20; 1924**

COMMENTARY OF ST. THOMAS

1913. After the Philosopher has discussed doubts concerning friendship on the part of those who love, he now discusses doubts on the part of those who are loved. He states three doubts concerning the initial point. The first

[1] concerns the number of friends; the second doubt [Lect. XIII], at "Are friends more etc.," concerns the need of friends (1171a21); the third [Lect. XIV], at "May we say then etc.," concerns the companionship of friends

(1171b29). He treats the first point in a twofold manner. First [1] he proposes the doubt, whether or not a man ought to make as many friends as possible. A sound point seems to have been made about traveling in someone's proverb: "May I be called neither a gadabout nor a stay-at-home," that is, let it not be said of me that I wander aimlessly through many countries nor that I never leave home for the purpose of traveling. The same is appropriately applied to friendship, thus that a man should be neither without friends nor with an excessive number.

1914. Second [2], at "**This statement,**" he solves the question. First [2] as it concerns useful friendship. He remarks that the statement about avoiding a superfluous number of friendships seems to be quite applicable to those who are friends for convenience or utility, because if a man has many such friends from whom he receives favors, conversely he must bestow many favors. This is excessively burdensome so that those who wish to act in such a way do not have enough time.

1915. Therefore, if a man's useful friends are more numerous than necessary for his own life, they distract and hinder him from the blessings of a life which consists in virtuous activity. The reason is that while a person gives extra attention to the business of others, he cannot properly care for himself. Evidently then a man has no need of many useful friends.

1916. Second [3], at "**Likewise, a few,**" he observes that a few friends are enough also for pleasantness. External pleasantness which is provided by friends of this kind is sought in human living, like seasoning in food which suffices even when very little is used. Hence even a few pleasant friends are

sufficient for a man that he may relax with them for a short time.

1917. Third [4], at "**But a question,**" he solves a question regarding virtuous friends. First [4] he proves his proposition by a reason; then [9], at "We see etc.," from experience. He discusses the first point in a threefold manner. First [4] he repeats the question. He says that it remains to be considered whether someone ought to make as many virtuous friends as possible so that the more he has the better he is. Or should he set some limit to the number of friends, as is evident concerning the number in a city, which is not composed of only ten men, neither on the other hand is it composed of ten myriads (a myriad equals ten thousand), for such a number of citizens forms not a city but a country. But how great a multitude is required for a city has not been determined according to a particular number, because a city can be large or small. However, there can be two extremes, and whatever is a mean between these can be determined as a suitable population for a city.

1918. Second [5], at "**The number of,**" he solves the question, saying there should not be an immense number of friends but the number ought to be limited. He proves this by three arguments. The first [5] is that friends can be as numerous as the people with whom a man can closely associate, for this attribute seems to belong to friendship more than others, i.e., seems suitable to virtuous friendship. Obviously it is not possible for a person to associate with a vast multitude and share himself among many people. Clearly then one cannot have a great number of virtuous friends.

1919. He offers the second argument at "**Besides, one's friends**" [6]. It is vident that friends ought to live with ne another. So, if a man has many iends, it is likewise necessary that all nese should be mutual friends. Othervise they cannot pass their time in ach other's company, nor consequently live on friendly terms. But it is ifficult to arrange this among a great nany so that they may be friends of ne another. Thus it is apparently impossible for one man to have a multiide of friends.

1920. He presents the third arguient at "**It is difficult also**" [7]. We aid above (1894–1898) that a friend ejoices with a friend. But it is difficult or anyone to share intimately in the oys and sorrows of a great number of eople. It may very likely happen that person must at the same time rejoice rith one and grieve with another, rhich is impossible. Therefore, it is out f the question for a man to have a vast umber of friends.

1921. Third [8], at "**Perhaps then,**" e concludes what he proposed for disussion, that it is well for a man not to eek as many friends as possible but as nany as are enough for living toether, because it does not seem possile for a man to be very friendly to reat numbers. So, likewise, one man annot love many women by an inense sexual love because perfect riendship consists in a kind of excess f love which can be felt for only one r a very few persons. For what is suerlative always belongs to the few, nce achievement of the highest perction cannot take place in most cases ue to a multiplicity of defects and indrances.

1922. Then [9], at "**We see,**" he roves his proposition from experince. We see in practice that a person as friendship for a few, for one does

not have many friends according to the friendship of comrades, i.e., companions or partners. This is shown by a proverb according to which comrades are said to sing in pairs.

1923. It is a widespread custom for young people to stroll two by two singing in good fellowship. But *polyphiloi*, i.e., those who have a host of friends or are on familiar terms with everybody seem to be real friends of no one, for they do not associate long with any particular person but are friendly with everyone in passing. However, such persons are said to be friends in a civil way as is usual among citizens who judge friendship according to compliments and familiarities of this sort. Those who are friendly with a great number of people in this fashion are generally called obsequious, which means an excess of external pleasantness, as was explained in the fourth book (816, 828).

1924. Finally [10], at "**One may,**" he shows the kind of friendship people have who are said to be friends with many. He observes that this is possible according to political friendship not only in the sense that an obsequious person is a friend of many but also in the sense proper to a virtuous person. It has been indicated above (1836) that friendship between citizens seems to be identified with concord. But the good man is of one mind with many in affairs pertaining to civic life. However, it is not possible for a virtuous man to have friendship for a great number so that he loves them for themselves and not only for utility or pleasure. But rather it ought to be pleasing and dear to a man if he can have a few such friends for the sake of virtue and themselves.

LECTURE XIII
Friends Needed in Both Prosperity and Adversity

TEXT OF ARISTOTLE (1171a20–1171b28) Chapter 11

1. *Are friends more necessary in good fortune or bad? They are sought in both situations; for the unfortunate need help, and the fortunate need friends to live with and benefit, since they want to do good to others.*   **1171a20–23; 192!**

2. *Friendship then is more necessary in adversity because we need useful friends to help us. But it is more honorable in prosperity; hence we seek virtuous friends, as it is preferable to benefit and live with men of this character.*   **1171a23–27; 192(**

3. *Indeed, the very presence of friends is pleasant in both good and bad fortune;*

1171a27–29; 192"

4. *and sorrow is assuaged by the presence of sympathetic friends.*   **1171a29–30; 192!**

5. *Therefore, someone may question whether friends actually assume the burden of grief as it were, or—this not being the case—the pain is diminished by their comforting presence and the consciousness of their sympathy. Whether sorrows are alleviated for these or some other reasons need not be discussed; at any rate what we have described seems to take place.*

1171a30–34; 1929–193!

6. *But the presence of sympathetic friends seem to have a mixed effect. The very sight of them is a comfort, especially when we are in distress, and a help in assuaging sorrow; for a friend, if he is sympathetic, is a consolation both by his countenance and his words, as he knows our feelings and what grieves and comforts us. On the other hand, it is painful to be aware that misfortunes cause the friend sorrow, since everyone avoids causing pain to his friends.*

1171a34–1171b6; 193!

7. *Hence persons of a manly bent naturally fear lest their friends be saddened on their account. And, unless a man is excessively insensitive to pain, he can hardly bear the sorrow that his sorrow causes his friends; nor is he willing to have others weep with him, for he is not given to lamenting. However, men of a womanish disposition are pleased to have fellow-mourners, and love as friends those who sympathize with them. But in all things we ought to imitate the man of noble character.*   **1171b6–12; 1934–193.**

8. *However, in prosperity the presence of friends provides both pleasant conversation and the consciousness that our friends are pleased with our benefactions.*   **1171b12–14; 193(**

9. *For this reason a man ought to press his friends to share his good fortune (for a noble man should be generous) but be reluctant to ask them to share his misfortune (for he should impart to them as little as possible of his troubles). Hence the saying: "No more than I need burdened be." A man should ask his friends especially when they can furnish him great assistance with little inconvenience to themselves.*   **1171b15–19; 1937–193!**

10. *Conversely, a man even uninvited should go promptly to friends in distress. For it is the part of a friend to be of service especially to those who are in need and do not think it becoming to ask. This is more honorable and pleasing to both. On the other hand, a man should readily join with his friends in prosperity, for even here friends are necessary. But he ought to approach them tardily to receive their kindness, for it is not becoming to show eagerness in accepting the help of friends. However, he should at all costs beware of a reputation for repudiating their advances—a thing that happens at times. Consequently, the presence of friends seems desirable in all circumstances.*   **1171b20–28; 1940–194!**

COMMENTARY OF ST. THOMAS

1925. Now that the Philosopher has solved the doubt on the number of friends, he here proposes a doubt about the need for friends. He discusses this point under three headings. First [1] he presents the doubt. Then [2], at "Friendship then etc.," he solves it. Finally [3], at "Indeed, the very presence etc.," he proves an assumption. He says first it can be questioned whether a man needs friends more in prosperity or adversity, for obviously friends are necessary in both situations. In adversity a man needs friends to help him overcome misfortunes. But in prosperity men need friends to live with and to benefit, for they want to do good to others.

1926. Then [2], at "**Friendship then**," he offers the solution to the question. He concludes from the premises that friends are necessary for a man in those reverses where he needs the help which friends supply, as was just noted (1925). Consequently, in this condition a man needs useful friends to help him. But in prosperity it is better and more honorable to have friends. So in these circumstances men seek virtuous friends, because it is more desirable to benefit and associate with persons of this character.

1927. At "**Indeed, the very presence**" [3] he proves an assumption, viz., that friends are needed in both circumstances. First [3] he proposes his intention, saying that the very presence of friends is pleasant in both good and bad fortune.

1928. Next [4], at "**and sorrow is,**" he proves his proposition. First [4] as it concerns adversity; second [8], at "However, in prosperity etc.," as it concerns prosperity; third [9], at "For this reason etc.," he deduces a corollary from the discussions. He treats the first point in a threefold manner. First [4] he explains his proposition, observing that people in sorrow feel consolation from the presence of sympathetic friends.

1929. Second [5], at "**Therefore, someone,**" he seeks the reason for this observation (1928). He offers two reasons, hesitating to decide which is stronger. The first is taken from the example of people who carry a heavy weight; one of these is relieved by another who joins in lifting that load with him. In a similar way it seems that one person may more easily bear the burden of sorrow if another bears the same burden with him.

1930. But this similarity does not seem to apply to sorrow itself, for the other does not take on himself a part of the same numerical sorrow which someone feels, so that his sorrow may be lightened. However, it can apply to the cause of the sorrow. For example, if a man grieves because of damage that he suffered while a friend undergoes part of the damage, the injury of the other—and consequently the sorrow—is diminished.

1931. The second reason is better and belongs to the sorrow itself. It is evident that every extraneous pleasure lightens sorrow. But the presence of a sympathetic friend brings gladness in two ways. In one way, because the very presence of a friend is delightful. In the other way because, perceiving that his friend sympathizes with him, he delights in his friendship; and thus his sorrow is lessened.

1932. Since it is outside his principal intention, he adds that we must dismiss for the present the question whether, because of these observations (1929–1931) or some other reason, our griefs are assuaged by the presence of sympathetic friends. Nevertheless, what we have described certainly happens (1931).

1933. Third [6], at "**But the presence,**" he shows that the presence of a sympathetic friend has an admixture of sorrow. First [6] he explains his proposition. Next [7], at "Hence persons etc.," he deduces a corollary from the discussions. He remarks first that the presence of sympathetic friends seems to have an admixture of pleasure and pain. The very sight of a friend is comforting for the other general reason, and especially to an unfortunate person whose sorrow is assuaged by the friend; to this extent a man consoles his friend both by his countenance and his word if he is epidexios, i.e., apt at offering sympathy. For one friend knows the feeling of another, and what comforts and distresses his friend; thus he can apply a fitting remedy for sorrow. In this way then the presence of a sympathetic friend is pleasing. But on the other hand it is distressing inasmuch as a man feels that his friend is saddened in his misfortunes. Indeed every rightly disposed person avoids, as much as he can, being the cause of pain to his friend.

1934. Then [7], at "**Hence persons,**" he concludes from the premises that people, who have a manly soul, naturally fear and take care lest their friends be saddened on account of themselves. It is of the nature of friendship that a person should wish to benefit a friend and not be the cause of some evil to him. Manly people do not allow

their friends to be saddened for them in any way unless the help, which i provided by their friends to overcom their sorrow, should far outweigh th distress of the friends. For they perm their suffering to be alleviated by modicum of suffering on the part c their friends. In all cases manly nature are unwilling to have others weep wit them, for they themselves are nc given to lamenting.

1935. However, there are some me of a womanish disposition who ar pleased to have others sorrowing wit them at the same time, and love a friends those who mourn with then But among the different types of ind viduals we ought to imitate in every thing men of nobler or more manl character.

1936. Next [8], at "**However, i prosperity,**" he explains the secon part of his proposition, viz., that th presence of friends in prosperity i praiseworthy. He remarks that th presence of friends in prosperity a fords two pleasures. First, convers tion with friends, because it is pleasar to converse with one's friends. Secon the fact that he now sees that hi friends are pleased by his benefaction For everyone seeks to be a cause c delight to his friends.

1937. At "**For this reason**" [9] h deduces a corollary from the discus sion, which contains some moral doc trines. First [9] in reference to thos who call their friends together. The [10], at "Conversely," in reference t those who of their own accord ap proach their friends. He presents thre moral principles touching on the firs point. First Aristotle concludes fror the premises that, since it is pleasin, for a man to see his friends find pleas ure in his own opulence, he ough promptly to invite his friends to share his prosperity. For a good man should benefit his friends.

1938. The second principle is that a man should tardily and reluctantly summon his friend to share his misfortunes. For he ought to transfer to his friend as little as possible of his troubles. As proof he offers the proverb of one who said: "None other than I need burdened be." As if to say: "It is enough that I suffer misfortune; my friends need not bear them."

1939. The third principle is that friends should be asked to participate in misfortunes when they can, with little trouble, furnish great assistance and the like to a person.

1940. Then [10], at **"Conversely,"** he offers three principles on the part of people going of their own accord to friends. The first is that sometimes a man, even uninvited, ought to go readily to friends who are suffering misfortunes. For a friend appropriately confers benefits especially on those who are in need and are ashamed, or think it unbecoming to ask this of a friend. In this way, when assistance is given to a person not requesting it, the action is performed in a better or more honorable way both for the donor and the petitioner. The reason is that the giver seems to bestow more spontaneously and the beneficiary to act more virtuously in being reluctant to burden a friend. This is also more satisfying to both, since the recipient does not feel the embarrassment that a man suffers in making a request of a friend; and the giver is more pleased that unasked he does a good turn as of his own accord.

1941. The second principle is that a man should readily offer to join with his friends in prosperity (and this is necessary) for a person needs friends to co-operate with him.

1942. The third principle is: if someone wishes to be kindly received by a well-to-do friend, he ought to approach the friend modestly, i.e., reluctantly and not readily. For it is not proper to show oneself eager to accept help from a friend. But a man ought to fear and beware of a reputation for (un)pleasantness, i.e., lest he get the name of being displeasing to his friend because he is troublesome or makes himself a nuisance. This obviously happens sometimes; for, when people occupy themselves too much in accepting favors, they become burdensome and displeasing to their friends. Or, according to another reading, a man should fear, i.e., beware of, the reputation for pleasure in lingering: so that his friend gets the impression that he likes to stay on with him for the sake of benefits.

1943. Finally, he concludes from the premises that the presence of friends is desirable in all circumstances.

LECTURE XIV
Friends' Pleasure in Living Together

TEXT OF ARISTOTLE (*1171b29–1172a15*) Chapter 12

1. May we say then that, as lovers delight especially in seeing the persons they love and prefer this sense to all others because love begins and is preserved by this sense, so friends desire companionship of each other most of all?   **1171b29–32; 1944–1945**

2. Friendship is in fact a partnership.   **1171b32–33; 1946**

3. And as a man is to himself so is he to his friend. But the consciousness of his own existence is desirable; and so, of his friend's existence. Now the activity of this consciousness takes place in living together—a thing, therefore, they naturally desire.   **1171b33–1172a1; 1947**

4. Every man wishes to share with his friends whatever constitutes his existence or whatever makes his life worth living. Hence some drink or play at dice together, others join in athletic sports or in the study of philosophy; each class taking part in the activity they love best in life. Since they want to live with their friends, they engage in those occupations whose sharing gives them a sense of living together.   **1172a1–8; 1948–1949**

5. Thus friendship of evil men is bad; for, being unstable, they associate in wickedness and are made evil by becoming like each other.   **1172a8–10; 1950**

6. But the friendship of virtuous men is good and is increased by their conversation. Indeed they seem to become better by working and living together, for they see in each other what is at the same time pleasing to them. Hence the saying: "Noble deeds from noble men." So much then for our treatment of friendship; next we will begin to treat pleasure.   **1172a10–15; 1951–1952**

COMMENTARY OF ST. THOMAS

1944. Now that he has completed the treatise on the number and need of friends, he here inquires about their living together. He discusses this question in a threefold manner. First [1] he proposes the question. Then [2], at "Friendship is etc.," he indicates the truth. Finally [5], at "Thus friendship etc.," he deduces a corollary from the discussion. He says that living together is based on a likeness of friendship to sensual love, in which we observe that lovers desire most of all to see the persons they love. They prefer this sense, sight, to the other external senses because the passion of love begins especially by seeing—as has been noted (1822–1823)—and is preserved by this sense. In fact, this love is stimulated in a particular way by beauty that is perceived by sight.

1945. The question then is, what in friendship is analogous to seeing? Is it

companionship itself? thus that, as lovers delight most in seeing one another, so friends in living with one another. In a different text this point is presented not as a question but as a conclusion. The text reads: "Accordingly then as lovers etc." This can be concluded from what has already been proved (1936, 1943), that the presence of friends is pleasing in all circumstances.

1946. Then [2], at "**Friendship is,**" he indicates the truth in this question or conclusion by three reasons. The first [2] is that friendship consists in a partnership (*communicatione*), as is clear from our discussion in the eighth book (1698, 1702, 1724). But people share themselves with one another especially by living together. Hence living together seems to be most proper and pleasing to friendship.

1947. He offers the second reason at

"**And as a man**" [3]. As a man is to himself so is he to his friend—this is obvious from previous statements (1797). But in reference to himself a man is so constituted that the consciousness of his own existence is desirable and delightful to him. Therefore it is also delightful to him to be conscious of his friend's existence. But this is present in living together, since they are conscious of one another by reason of the mutual activity they perceive. Consequently, friends naturally desire to live together.

1948. He presents the third reason at "**Every man wishes**" [4], taken from experience. We see that men wish to share with their friends the activity they most enjoy, which they consider their existence and choose to live for— as it were ordering their whole life to it.

1949. Consequently, some wish to drink with their friends; others, to play together at dice; still others, to take exercise with them in tournaments, wrestling and so on; or even to hunt or study philosophy together. In this way each class wishes to remain with his friends in that activity which they love best among all the pursuits of this life. As they want to live with their friends, they mutually engage in occupations of this kind which they greatly enjoy, and which they think constitute their whole life. They take part in these activities whose sharing gives them the sense of living together. Thus it is clear that living together is most desirable in friendship.

1950. Next [5], at "**Thus friendship**," he draws a conclusion from the premises about the friendship of good and evil men. First [5] concerning evil men, that their friendship is bad; for they find pleasure in evil deeds most of all, and take part in them with one another. Being unstable, they always go from bad to worse since one becomes evil by imitating the other.

1951. Second [6], at "**But the friendship**," he draws a conclusion concerning the good, that friendship between virtuous men is good and is always increased in goodness by exemplary conversation. Friends become better by working together and loving each other. For one receives from the other an example of virtuous work which is at the same time pleasing to him. Hence it is proverbial that man adopts noble deeds from noble men.

1952. Finally, he concludes with the epilogue that such is our treatment of friendship and that next we must discuss pleasure (1953–2064). Thus he terminates the teaching of the ninth book.

BOOK TEN
PLEASURE. HAPPINESS.

LECTURE I
Pleasure

TEXT OF ARISTOTLE (*1172a19–1172b8*) Chapter 1

1. *After these matters we ought perhaps next to discuss pleasure.* **1172a19; 1953–1954**

2. *For it seems to be adapted especially to humankind. This is why masters of households teach children by means of pleasure and pain.* **1172a19–21; 1955**

3. *Likewise, it seems that a man's rejoicing in the things he ought and hating the things he ought has great importance for moral virtue; they extend throughout the whole of life, having influence and power for virtue and a happy life, since men choose pleasure and shun pain—motives that should not, it seems, determine our choice.* **1172a21–26; 1956–1957**

4. *Moreover, they (pleasure and pain) particularly admit of much uncertainty. Some people say that pleasure is a good, while others, on the contrary, maintain it is something very evil—some of them because they are convinced, and others because they think it better for human living to declare pleasure an evil, though it is not—for most men are disposed to it and are in fact slaves of pleasure. Therefore they are to be induced to the opposite, since in this way they will attain the mean.* **1172a27–33; 1958–1959**

5. *But perhaps this is not a wise attitude, for in questions concerning the passions and actions, arguments are less convincing than facts. Therefore, when arguments are at variance with facts they are spurned and their truth destroyed. If a man who censures pleasure is seen in his own way to desire it, his inclination to it seems to indicate that all pleasure is desirable. For the majority of people do not draw nice distinctions. Consequently, true arguments are most useful not only for science but also for living, for when they are in accord with the facts they are accepted, and so move those who understand their truth to live by them.*

These matters have been discussed sufficiently. Let us pass on to the treatment of pleasure. **1172a33–1172b8; 1960–1963**

COMMENTARY OF ST. THOMAS

1953. After the Philosopher has finished the consideration of the moral and intellectual virtues—and of continence and friendship which have a relation to virtue—in the tenth book he intends to consider the end of virtue. First, concerning the end of virtue that perfects man in himself; then [Lect. XIV], at "Have we sufficiently etc." (1179a33), concerning the end of virtue in relation to the common good, the good of the whole state. He discusses the first point from two aspects. First he defines pleasure which is designated by some as the end of virtue. Next [Lect. IX], at "After the discussion etc." (1176a30), he defines happiness, which in the opinion of everyone is the end of virtue. He treats the first point in a twofold manner. First [1] by way of introduction he shows we must consider pleasure. Second [Lect. II], after the introduction, at "Eudoxus thought etc." (1172b9), he pursues his proposition. He considers the first point under two headings. First [1] he proposes his intention.

1954. He remarks that after the previous treatise (245–1952), it is logical for pleasure to be treated in passing, i.e., briefly. To be sure he had already treated pleasure in the seventh book (1354–1367), inasmuch as it is the object of continence. Hence there his study dwelt chiefly on sensible and bodily pleasures. But here he intends to consider pleasure as an adjunct to happiness. Therefore, he gives special attention to intellectual and spiritual pleasure.

1955. Then [2], at "**For it seems,**" he proves by three reasons why we must treat pleasure. The first [2] is taken from the relation of pleasure to us. For pleasure seems in a marked degree to be naturally adapted to humankind. For this reason *orakizontes*, i.e., rulers of households, teach children especially by means of pleasure and pain. People who wish to induce children to good or restrain them from evil try to please the well-behaved, e.g., with small presents, and to punish those who misbehave, e.g., by whipping. Since moral philosophy considers human affairs, it is the business of moral science to treat pleasure.

1956. At "**Likewise, it seems**" he presents the second reason [3], which is taken from a comparison with virtue. He says that it seems to be a particular concern of moral virtue that a man enjoy the things he ought and hate the things he ought and grieve over them. For moral virtue consists principally in the regulation of the appetite; and this is judged by the regulation of pleasure and pain which all the movements of the appetitive part follow, as has been pointed out in the second book (296). And he adds: they, viz., pleasure and pain extend to all phases of human life, exerting great influence on man to be virtuous and live happily. This cannot happen unless his pleasures and pain are properly ordered.

1957. Men frequently choose even harmful pleasures and avoid even salutary afflictions. But it seems that the man who wishes to be virtuous and happy ought not to choose pleasure

and reject pain as such, that is, commit evil deeds or omit virtuous actions on this account. And, conversely, it can be said that he must not choose to do evil or avoid good for the sake of these, i.e., to obtain pleasure and shun pain. Obviously then it is the function of moral philosophy to treat pleasure, just as it treats moral virtue and happiness.

1958. He offers a third reason [4] at "**Moreover, they.**" It is taken from the uncertainty prevalent concerning pleasure. He discusses this point from two aspects. First [4] he enumerates the different opinions about pleasure, from which the uncertainty arises. Then [5], at "But perhaps this etc.," he rejects a statement contained in the opinions. He says first that we must treat pleasure and pain for another reason: because they admit of much uncertainty. This is obvious from the different views of thinkers who discuss these subjects.

1959. Some say pleasure is a kind of good. Others, on the contrary, maintain that it is something very bad—and this in different ways. For some hold the opinion because they are convinced that it is so and believe they are speaking the truth. But others, though they may not believe that pleasure is an evil, nevertheless judge it better for human living to declare that pleasure is an evil—although it is not—to withdraw men from pleasure to which the majority are inclined (for people are in fact slaves to pleasure). For this reason men must be induced to the opposite, i.e., to have an aversion to pleasures by declaring them evil. In this way we attain the mean, that is, men use pleasures with moderation.

1960. Then [5], at "**But perhaps this,**" he rejects the last statement. It hardly seems correct for people to say what they do not believe—that pleas-res are evil just to withdraw us from hem, because in questions of human ctions and passions we give less credence to words than to actions. For if a man does what he says is evil, he incites by his example more than he restrains by his word.

1961. The reason for this is that everyone seems to choose what appears to him good in a particular case, the object of human actions and passions. When, therefore, a man's arguments are at variance with his clearly manifest actions, such arguments are spurned; and consequently the truth enunciated by them is destroyed. Thus it will happen in our proposition.

1962. If someone censuring all pleasure is seen to give way to a pleasure he might give the impression that all pleasure ought to be chosen. The common people cannot determine by distinguishing this as good and that as evil, but without discrimination they accept as good what appears good in one instance. In this way, then, sound arguments seem to be useful not only for science but also for good living, for they are convincing to the extent they are in accord with actions. For this reason such arguments move those who understand their truth to live by them.

1963. Finally, he concludes in an epilogue that these matters have been discussed sufficiently. Now we must pass on to the observations made by others about pleasure.

LECTURE II
Opinions on Pleasure as a Good

TEXT OF ARISTOTLE (1172b9–1173a13) Chapter 2

1. Eudoxus thought that pleasure is an absolute good because he saw all creatures, both rational and irrational, seeking it. But in every case what is desirable is good, and what is most desirable is the greatest good. Hence the fact that all things are drawn to the same object shows that it is a most excellent good for all, since everything finds its own good just as it finds its own food. Now what is good for all and what all desire is an absolute good.

1172b9–15; 1964–1965

2. But his arguments were accepted because of his excellent character rather than for their merit. For he appeared to be a man moderate in the different pleasures; and consequently did not seem to defend his opinion as a lover of pleasure but because it was really true.

1172b15–18; 1966

3. He also thought that his view was otherwise substantiated by pleasure's contrary. Since pain in itself is an object to be avoided by all, so its opposite is likewise an object to be chosen.

1172b18–20; 1967

4. Moreover, that is most worthy of choice which we choose not because or for the sake of another. Now, it is admitted that pleasure is such an object. For no one asks to what end a man is pleased, so that pleasure in itself is desirable.   **1172b20–23; 1968**

5. Further, pleasure added to any good makes it more desirable. Thus the addition of pleasure to just or temperate action enhances its goodness.   **1172b23–25; 1969**

6. But this argument seems to prove only that pleasure is a good and not a greater good than any other. For every good joined to another is more desirable than by itself.   **1172b26–28; 1970**

7. It is by an argument of this kind that Plato attempts to nullify the previous view, by showing that pleasure is not an absolute good. He argued that the life of pleasure is more desirable with prudence than without it. But if the combination is better, pleasure is not an absolute good; for a good of this type does not become more desirable by any addition.

1172b28–32; 1971–1972

8. Obviously nothing else either will be an absolute good if it is made more desirable by the addition of any of the things that are good in themselves. What then is there of this nature that we can share? This is what we are looking for.   **1172b32–35; 1973**

9. Those who deny that what all beings desire is good are talking nonsense. For that which all men believe to be true, we say is really so; and the man who rejects this belief expresses beliefs hardly more acceptable. If only creatures without understanding desire pleasures, some weight might be conceded in the contention; but if intelligent beings do so too, it does not seem to make sense. Perhaps even in evil men there is some natural good better than themselves which seeks their own proper good.   **1172b35–1173a5; 1974–1977**

10. Nor does the argument seem to be correct about the contrary. They say that if pain is evil it does not follow that pleasure is good, for evil is also opposed to evil. And both good and evil are opposed to what is neither the one nor the other. In this they were correct but their statement does not apply to the present question. For, if both were evil, both ought to be avoided; but if neither was evil, neither should be an object of aversion, or both should be equally so. However, as it is, man seems to avoid the one as evil and to seek the other as good. In this way then they are in opposition.   **1173a5–13; 1978–1979**

COMMENTARY OF ST. THOMAS

1964. After the Philosopher has shown that we must treat pleasure, he now begins to treat it. First he continues with the opinions of others. Then Lect. V], at "The nature and quality etc." (1174a13), he defines the truth. He discusses the first point under two headings. First [1] he proceeds with the opinion of those who set pleasure in the category of good; next [7], at "It is by an argument etc.," with the contrary opinion. He considers his first point from two aspects. First [1] he presents the arguments Eudoxus used to prove that pleasure is in the category of good. Second [4], at "Moreover, that is etc.," he offers the arguments Eudoxus used to prove that it is the greatest good. He handles the first point in a twofold manner. First [1] he shows how Eudoxus proved that pleasure is in the genus of good on the part of pleasure itself; then [3], at "He also thought etc.," how Eudoxus proved this on the part of the contrary. He treats the first point in two ways. First [1] he proposes the opinion and argument of Eudoxus. Next [2], at "But his arguments etc.," he shows why the opinion and argument were accepted.

1965. He says first that Eudoxus was of the opinion that pleasure comes under the category of good because he saw that all creatures, both rational and irrational, i.e., men and brutes, seek pleasure. But what all choose seems to be proper and good and has great influence in goodness because it can attract every appetite to itself. And so, the fact that all are moved toward the same object, viz., pleasure, indicates that pleasure is not only a good but a most excellent good. For it is obvious that everything seeks to find what is good. Thus food is good to all animals who commonly desire it. Therefore it is evident that pleasure sought by all is a good.

1966. Then [2], at "But his arguments," he shows why Eudoxus was especially given credence. He observes that Eudoxus' arguments were accepted because of the moral virtue of the speaker rather than their cogency. He was indeed a man moderate in the different pleasures, being more exemplary than others. For this reason, when he praised pleasure, he did not seem to be speaking as a lover of pleasure but because it was really true.

1967. Next [3], at "He also thought," he presents Eudoxus' argument that was taken on the part of the contrary. He remarks that Eudoxus thought it no less clear from the contrary (i.e., on the part of pain rather than on the part of pleasure itself) that pleasure belongs to the category of good. For it is obvious that pain in itself ought to be avoided by everyone. Hence the contrary, pleasure, apparently ought to be chosen by everyone.

1968. At "Moreover, that is" [4] he presents two arguments of Eudoxus to show that pleasure is the greatest good. The first is this [4]. That seems most worthy of choice, and consequently the greatest good, which is chosen not because of another incidental to it, or for the sake of something as an end. But all men plainly acknowledge this about pleasure. For no one asks another why he desires pleasure, which would indicate that pleasure is desirable in itself. Therefore pleasure is good in the highest degree.

1969. He offers the second argument [5] at "**Further, pleasure,**" explaining it in a twofold manner. First [5] he presents the argument itself. It is evident that pleasure added to any good makes it more desirable. Thus the addition of pleasure to just action and temperate conduct increases their goodness, for a man is better who takes pleasure in a work of justice or temperance. From this he (Eudoxus) wished to conclude that pleasure was best, as enhancing the goodness in all actions.

1970. Next [6], at "**But this argument,**" he shows the flaw in this argument. He remarks that the reason just given proves that pleasure comes under the category of good, but not that it is a greater good than any other. For it is also true of any good that, when joined to another, it constitutes a greater good than it was by itself.

1971. Then [7], at "**It is by an argument,**" he pursues the opinion of those who maintain that pleasure is not a good. First [7] he explains how they meet the preceding arguments. Second [Lect. III], at "However, it does not follow etc." (1173a14), he gives the arguments they allege to the contrary. He discusses the first point from two aspects. First [7] he shows how they used in the opposite way the argument previously advanced to show that pleasure is the highest good. Next [9], at "Those who deny etc.," he shows how they met the other arguments. He treats the first point in a twofold manner. First [7] he explains how Plato used this argument to prove the opposite. Then [8], at "Obviously nothing else etc.," he rejects Plato's process of reasoning. He observes first that, by the reason just given, Plato, who held the contrary opinion, attempted to nullify what has been asserted (1965–1970), by showing that pleasure is not

a good in itself nor in the absolute sense. It is evident that pleasure is more worthy of choice when accompanied by prudence. Since then pleasure combined with something else is better, he concluded that pleasure is not a good in itself. That which is a good in itself does not become more desirable by an addition of something else.

1972. On this point we must understand that Plato named as a good in itself that which is the essence of goodness; for example, man in himself (*per se*) is the essence of man. But to this essence of goodness nothing can be added that is good in a way other than by participating in the essence of goodness. So, whatever goodness is an addition is derived from the very essence of goodness. Thus the good in itself does not become better by any addition.

1973. At "**Obviously nothing else**" [8] Aristotle rejects Plato's process of reasoning. According to this argument obviously nothing in human affairs will be good in itself, since every human good added to any good in itself is rendered more desirable. For nothing can be found associated with human life that is of such a nature that it does not become better by the addition of another good. But we are seeking something of this kind associated with human life. People who hold that pleasure is a good mean a human good and not the divine good itself, which is the essence of goodness.

1974. Next [9], at "**Those who deny,**" he shows how the Platonists met Eudoxus' arguments proving that pleasure is a good. First [9], how they met the argument taken on the part of pleasure itself; then [10], at "Nor does the argument etc.," the argument taken on the part of the contrary. They answered the first argument by deny-g this: that which all desire is good. ut Aristotle rejects this, observing at those who oppose the argument of udoxus by maintaining that what all esire is not necessarily good seem to lk nonsense.

1975. That which all believe to be ue, we say, is really so. And we hold is as a principle, because it is impos- ble for natural judgment to fail in all ses. But, since the appetite tends only that which seems good, what is de- red by all seems good to all. So, pleas- re that all desire is good.

1976. The man who rejects what is ccepted by everyone expresses views at are hardly more acceptable. That osition might be defended if only ose creatures who are without un- erstanding, like dumb animals and vil men, desired pleasures. The rea- on is that the senses judge good only its immediacy; and in this way it ould not be necessary that pleasure e a good simply but only that it be a ood here and now. But since even telligent creatures desire some pleas- re, it does not seem to make any nse.

1977. However, if even all creatures hich act without understanding de- red pleasure, it might still be prob- ble that pleasure was a good, because ven in wicked men there is some atural good that tends to the desire of suitable good; and this natural good better than evil men as such. As vir- ue is a perfection of nature—and for is reason moral virtue is better than atural virtue (we noted this in the ixth book, 1275–1280)—so, since vice a corruption of nature, the natural

good is better: the integral thing is bet- ter than the corrupt. But it is clear that evil men are diversified by their con- nection with vice, for vices are contrary to one another. Therefore, the object on which evil men agree, viz., the desire of pleasure, seems to belong rather to nature than vice.

1978. Then [10], at "**Nor does the argument,**" he shows how they an- swered the argument taken on the part of pain. They held that, even if pain is an evil, it does not follow that pleasure is good; since we know that evil is op- posed not only to good but also to evil, for example, rashness is opposed not only to fortitude but also cowardice. And both good and evil are opposed to that which is neither good nor evil, as the extremes are opposed to the mean, for there is such an act considered ac- cording to its species, for instance, to pick up a straw from the ground, or the like.

1979. However, Aristotle in refuta- tion of this process of reasoning re- marks that they are correct in reference to this opposition of evil to evil, but their statement does not apply to the present question. For pain is not op- posed to pleasure, as evil to evil. If both were evil, both would have to be avoided; just as good as such is to be sought, so evil as such is to be avoided. But if neither of them was evil, neither should be an object of aversion, or they should be viewed in the same light. However, as it is, all men seem to avoid pain as evil and seek pleasure as good. Thus then they are opposed to each other as good and evil.

LECTURE III
Pleasure Is Not a Good According to Plato

TEXT OF ARISTOTLE (1173a13–1173b20) Chapter 3

1. However it does not follow that if pleasure is not a quality, therefore it is not a good; for neither virtuous activities nor happiness are qualities either.   **1173a13–15; 1980–198**

2. But they maintain that good is determinate, and that pleasure is indeterminate, because it admits of more and less.   **1173a15–17; 198**

3. Now if they judge in this way about partaking of pleasure, then the same applies to justice and other virtues according to which some are clearly said to be more or less virtuous. For people are in fact just and brave in a greater or less degree, and can act more or less justly and temperately. However if their judgment is based on the nature of the pleasures themselves, perhaps they are not stating the real cause since some pleasures are pure (or unmixed) and others mixed. Why may not pleasure be like health which is determinate and still admits of degrees? Health is not constituted by the same proportion of humors in all men, nor by one proportion always in the same person; but, even when diminished, it remains up to a certain point, and so differs in degree.   **1173a17–28; 1983–198**

4. Again, they postulate that the good in itself (per se) is perfect, while movements and processes of generation are imperfect; and then they try to show that pleasure is a motion or process.   **1173a29–31; 198**

5. But they do not seem to be correct. In fact pleasure is not a motion, for swiftness and slowness are proper to all movement, if not absolutely like the motion of the earth, then relative to another moving body. But neither of these is true of pleasure. A man can become pleased quickly just as he can get angry quickly; but he cannot be pleased quickly, not even in relation to somebody else, as he can walk, grow, and so on quickly. Therefore someone can change into a pleasurable state quickly or slowly, but he cannot function or be pleased in that state quickly.   **1173a31–1173b4; 1990–199**

6. And how can it be a process of generation? It does not seem that any chance thing can be generated from any other chance thing, but everything is dissolved into that from which it came; and pain would be the destruction of that which pleasure generates. Further, they affirm that pain is a deficiency of the natural state and pleasure a replenishment. But these experiences are bodily passions. If then pleasure is a replenishment of the natural state, the part replenished will feel the pleasure. Consequently the body can feel pleasure. However, this does not seem to be the case. Therefore, pleasure is not replenishment; but after replenishment takes place, a man will feel pleasure just as after a surgical operation he will feel pain.   **1173b4–13; 1993–199**

7. This opinion seems to arise from pains and pleasures associated with food. Certainly people who are distressed beforehand by lack of food receive pleasure by replenishment. However, this is not the case with all pleasures. For pleasures of (mathematical) knowledge are not preceded by pain, nor are the pleasures of sense—for example, smell—and sounds and sights; and the same is true of memories and hopes. If these are the result of generation, by what are they generated? No lack of anything has occurred to be replenished. **1173b13–20; 1995–199**

COMMENTARY OF ST. THOMAS

1980. After the Philosopher has dismissed the Platonists' opposition to the arguments of Eudoxus, he now presents their arguments against Eudoxus' position. He treats this point in a twofold manner. First [1] he proposes the arguments designed to show that pleasure does not belong to th tegory of good. Then [Lect. IV], at he distinction between etc." 173b33), he offers the arguments to ow that pleasure is not an absolute d universal good. Since the first set arguments conclude falsely, there- re Aristotle presents and disproves em at the same time. He gives four guments on the first point. The first] is this. Good seems to come under e genus of quality; for, to a person king what the quality of a thing is we swer that it is good. But pleasure is t a quality. Therefore it is not a good.

1981. But Aristotle rejects this, ob- rving that even if pleasure does not me under the genus of quality, it es not follow that pleasure is not a od. For good is predicated not only quality but also of every genus, as as indicated in the first book (81).

1982. He presents the second argu- ent [2] at **"But they maintain."** First] he offers the reason of the Platonists emselves. They hold that good is de- rminate, as is evident from the dis- ssion in the ninth book (1887). Now easure is indeterminate according to em—a statement they proved from e fact that it admits of degrees. Thus ey concluded that pleasure did not me under the genus of good.

1983. Next [3], at **"Now if they etc.,"** rejects such an argument. On this int we must remember that a thing mits of degrees in two ways: one, in e concrete; the other, in the abstract. mething is called more and less by ason of nearness to an object or re- oteness from it. When, therefore, a ing that exists in a subject has one- ss and simplicity, it does not admit more and less in itself. Hence it is not id to admit of degrees in the abstract. t it can be predicated according to ore and less in the concrete because e subject partakes more and less of

such a form, as is evident in the case of light which is an undivided and simple form. Consequently, light itself is not predicated according to more and less. However, a body is termed more or less luminous from this that it partakes of light more or less perfectly.

1984. On the other hand, when there exists a form that in its nature indicates a proportion between many individu- als referred to one principle, that form admits of degrees even according to its own nature. This is evident of health and beauty: each implies a proportion appropriate to the nature of an object designated as beautiful or healthy. And since a proportion of this kind can be more or less appropriate, conse- quently beauty and health considered in themselves are predicated accord- ing to more and less. It is obvious from this that unity, by which something is determinate, is the reason why a thing may not admit of degrees. Since then pleasure does admit of degrees, it seemed not to be something determi- nate and consequently not to belong to the genus of good.

1985. Therefore, Aristotle in oppos- ing this observes that, if the Platonists hold that pleasure is something inde- terminate because it admits of degrees in the concrete—by reason of the fact that someone can be pleased more and less—they will have to admit the same about justice and other virtues accord- ing to which people are designated such more and less. Certainly some men are just and brave in a greater or less degree. The same is true concern- ing actions, for someone can act more and less justly and temperately. Thus, either virtues will not belong to the genus of good, or the reason offered does not remove pleasure from the ge- nus of good.

1986. However, if they maintain

that pleasure admits of degrees on the part of the pleasures themselves, we must consider that perhaps their argument may not apply to all pleasures; but they are indicating the reason why some pleasures are pure and unmixed, for example, the pleasure following the contemplation of truth, and other pleasures are mixed like those following a pleasing combination of some kinds of sensibles, for instance, pleasures resulting from musical harmony or the blending of tastes or colors. Obviously, pure pleasure of itself does not admit of degrees but only mixed pleasure, inasmuch as a pleasing combination of sensibles causing pleasure can be more or less agreeable to the nature of the person enjoying it.

1987. Nevertheless, neither is it necessary that pleasures, which in themselves admit of degrees by reason of their admixture, are not determinate or good. Nothing prevents pleasure, which allows of more or less, from being determinate—as health is in fact. Qualities of this kind may be called determinate inasmuch as they reach in some way that to which they are ordered although they might come closer. Thus a mixture of humors contains the reason for health from the fact that it attains a harmony in human nature; and by reason of this it is called determinate attaining its proper end, so to speak.

1988. But a temperament that in no way attains this is not determinate but is far from the notion of health. For that reason health of itself admits of more and less because the same proportion of humors is not found in all men, nor is it always the same in one and the same person. But, even when diminished, health remains up to a certain point. Hence health differs according

to degrees; and the same is true of pleasure.

1989. At "**Again, they postulate**" he offers the third argument [4] and discusses it in a twofold manner. First [he proposes the argument. The Platonists held that what is good in itself (per se) is something perfect. But motion and processes of generation are imperfect, for motion is an act of an imperfect thing, as stated in the third book of the Physics (Ch. 2, 201b27–202a2; St. Th. Lect. III, 296). Consequently they maintain that no motion or process of generation belongs to the genus of good. And they try to establish that pleasure is a motion or a process of generation. Hence they conclude that pleasure is not a good in itself (per se).

1990. Then [5], at "**But they do not seem,**" he rejects this argument under two aspects. First [5], as to their assertion that pleasure is a motion. He states that they are apparently not correct when they maintain that pleasure is motion, for every motion seems to be swift or slow. But swiftness and slowness are not proper to motion considered absolutely and in itself but in relation to something else. For example, the motion of the earth, i.e., the daily motion, in which the whole heavens revolve, is called swift in comparison with other motions.

1991. The reason for this—as is pointed out in the sixth book of the Physics (Ch. 2, 232a25–232b20; St. Th. Lect. III, 766–773)—is that a thing called "swift" which moves a great distance in a short time and "slow" a little distance in a long time. Now "great" and "little" are predicated relatively as indicated in the Categories (Ch. 6, 5b15–30). But neither swiftness nor slowness are attributable to pleasure. To be sure a man can become pleased quickly, just as he can become angry quickly. But we do not say that a man can be pleased quickly or slowly, not even in comparison with someone else, as we do say that a man can walk quickly or slowly, can grow quickly or slowly, and so on. So then obviously someone can be changed into a state of pleasure, i.e., can arrive at it quickly or slowly.

1992. This is so because we can attain pleasure by a kind of motion. But we cannot function quickly in the state of pleasure so that we are quickly pleased. The reason is that the act of being pleased consists in something done (*in facto*) rather than in something taking place (*in fieri*).

1993. Next [6], at "**And how can it be**," he rejects the Platonists' argument to uphold their opinion that pleasure is a process of generation. He discusses this point in a twofold manner. First [6] he shows that pleasure is not a process of generation. Then [7], at "This opinion seems etc.," he shows the origin of this opinion. He remarks first that pleasure does not appear to be a process of generation, for it does not seem that any chance thing is generated from any other chance thing. But everything is dissolved into that from which it is generated. If pleasure is a generation, pain must be the destruction of the same thing which pleasure generates. This is affirmed by the Platonists who hold that pain is a deficiency in what is according to nature, for we see that pain follows a person's privation of those things to which he is naturally united. Likewise they maintain that pleasure is a replenishment because pleasure follows when something naturally belonging to a man is added to him.

1994. But Aristotle rejects this argument because privation and replenishment are bodily passions. If then pleasure is a replenishment of what is according to nature, the part replenished will feel pleasure. Consequently the body can feel pleasure. But this does not seem to be the case because pleasure is a passion of the soul. Therefore it is clear that pleasure is not a replenishment or a process of generation but a consequence of it. A man feels pleasure after replenishment just as he feels pain and distress after a surgical operation.

1995. Then [7], at "**This opinion seems,**" he shows its origin. He observes that the view that sees pleasure as a replenishment and pain as a privation seems to arise from pains and pleasures concerned with food. People who beforehand are distressed by the lack of food, afterwards are pleased by replenishment. But this does not occur in connection with all pleasures where replenishment of a deficiency does not take place. For pleasures resulting from mathematical studies do not have an opposite pain, which they say consists in a deficiency. Thus pleasures of this sort do not exist for a replenishment of a need. It is evidently the same with some pleasures of sense such as smell, sound and the sight of physical objects.

1996. Besides, many delightful hopes and memories exist; and no cause can be assigned whose generations are pleasures of this sort, because there are no preceding defects which are replenished by means of these pleasures. But it was pointed out (1993) that if pleasure is the generation of a thing, pain is its destruction. Therefore, if any pleasure is found without the defect of pain, it follows that a pain is not the correlative of every pleasure.

LECTURE IV
A Fourth Argument that Pleasure Is Not a Good

TEXT OF ARISTOTLE (*1173b20–1174a12*) Chapter 3

1. *In answer to those who bring forward very disgraceful pleasures it can be said that these are not pleasant; for even if they are pleasing to the ill-disposed, we must not assume that they are really pleasant—except to such people—any more than what is wholesome or sweet or bitter to the sick is so in fact, or any more than objects which seem white to persons with diseased eyes are actually white.*   1173b20–25; 1997–19

2. *Or we may concede that pleasures are desirable but not from these sources. Thus wealth desirable but not as the price of betrayal, so too is health but not as a result of eating things indifferently.*   1173b25–28; 19

3. *Again, we may say that pleasures differ in kind: some are derived from honorable sources and others from base sources. Now it is impossible to enjoy the pleasure proper to the just man without being just, to enjoy the pleasure proper to a musician without being musical. And this applies to other pleasures.*   1173b28–31; 20

4. *The distinction between a friend and a flatterer seems to show that pleasure is not a good or that pleasures differ in kind. For a friend is thought to intend good in his association but the flatterer, pleasure; the latter is blamed with reproach but the former praised, for no other reason than the ends they pursue.*   1173b31–1174a1; 20

5. *And certainly no one would choose to retain the mind of a child throughout life in order have the pleasures that children are thought especially to enjoy. Nor would anyone choose to find pleasure in doing an extremely shameful act even though he might never have to suffer pain as a result.*   1174a1–4; 20

6. *Likewise, there are many things we should be eager about even though they do not produce pleasure, for example, sight, memory, knowledge, possession of virtues. It makes no difference whether pleasures necessarily follow these activities, for we would choose them if no pleasure resulted. It is obvious, therefore, that pleasure is not a good in itself (per se), that not every pleasure is desirable, and that some pleasures are desirable in themselves, being different from the others in kind or in their sources. We have now treated sufficiently the opinions about pleasure and pain.*   1174a4–12; 2003–20

COMMENTARY OF ST. THOMAS

1997. After the Philosopher has disproved the three arguments of the Platonists concluding that pleasure does not belong to the category of good, he now [1] refutes a fourth argument that they draw from the vileness of some pleasures. The Platonists adduce certain disgraceful pleasures, like adultery and drunkenness, to show that pleasures do not come under the category of good. But Aristotle answers this argument in a threefold manner.

1998. First [1], as someone might observe, disgraceful pleasures are not

pleasant in the absolute sense. If some pleasures are delightful to the ill-disposed, it does not follow that they a pleasing in themselves but only to persons prone to vice. Just as the things that seem healthful to the sick are not in themselves healthful, so the things that seem sweet or bitter to people with perverted taste are not in themselves sweet or bitter; nor are objects that seem white to persons with diseased eyes really white. This solution proceeds on the assumption that unqualified pleasure for man is what

•leasant according to reason—a circumstance not possible with physical pleasures of this kind, although they are pleasing to the senses.

1999. He presents the second refutation [2] at "**Or we may concede.**" It can be admitted that all pleasures are desirable but not in relation to all persons. For example, it is good to be enriched, but it is not good for a traitor to his country to be enriched because in this way he can do more harm. Likewise health is good but not for one who has eaten something harmful. Thus eating a snake sometimes cures a leper although it may destroy health. Similarly bestial pleasures are certainly desirable for animals but not for men.

2000. At "**Again, we may say**" [3] he offers the third refutation, observing that pleasures differ in kind. Pleasures resulting from virtuous actions differ in kind from those resulting from shameful actions, for passions differ according to their objects. The unjust man cannot enjoy the pleasure proper to the just man, just as an unmusical person cannot enjoy a musician's delight. And the same applies to other pleasures.

2001. Then [4], at "**The distinction between,**" he proves that pleasure is not a good in itself (*per se*) and in a universal sense, for three reasons. Concerning the first reason [4] he remarks: the difference between a friend and a flatterer shows that pleasure is not a good or that there are different kinds of pleasure, some honorable and others base. A friend converses with a friend to some good purpose, but the flatterer to please. Hence a flatterer is blamed with reproach but a friend is praised, and so it is clear that they converse out of different motives. There-

fore pleasure is one thing and good another.

2002. He presents the second reason [5] at "**And certainly no one.**" No man, he says, would choose to retain a childish mind all his life so that he might always have the so-called pleasures of childhood. Nor would anyone choose to take pleasure in doing extremely shameful actions throughout his life even if he might never have to suffer pain. This statement is made against the Epicureans who maintain that shameful pleasures are to be shunned only because they bring about greater suffering. Thus it is clear that pleasure is not a good in itself (*per se*), because it would have to be chosen under every circumstance.

2003. He states the third reason [6] at "**Likewise, there are.**" Obviously there are many things a man should be eager about even though no pleasure results from them, for example, sight, memory, knowledge, the possession of virtue. It makes no difference in the case whether pleasures follow from these activities, because he would choose them even if they brought about no pleasure. But that which is good in itself (*per se*) is of such a nature that without it nothing is desirable, as is evident concerning happiness. Therefore pleasure is not a good in itself (*per se*).

2004. Finally, he summarizes in conclusion that it seems obvious from the premises that pleasure is not a good in itself (*per se*), and that not every pleasure is desirable; and that some pleasures are desirable even in themselves, being different from evil pleasures either in their kind or in their sources. We have now discussed sufficiently the opinions of others on pleasure and pain.

LECTURE V
Pleasure Is Neither a Motion Nor a Process of Change

TEXT OF ARISTOTLE (1174a13–1174b14) Chapter 4

1. *The nature and quality of pleasure will become clearer if we take up the question again from the beginning.*   **1174a13–14; 200**

2. *Now, seeing seems perfect at any moment whatsoever, for it does not require anything coming later to complete its form. But pleasure appears to be a thing of this nature: it is a whole, and at no time can anyone find a pleasure whose form will be completed if it lasts longer.*
1174a14–19; 2006–200

3. *Therefore, pleasure is not a form of motion.*   **1174a19; 2008–200**

4. *For every motion involves duration and is a means to an end, e.g., the process of building that is perfect when it effects what it aims at—a thing achieved either over the whole time or at the final moment. All the movements are imperfect during the portions of that time and are different in kind from the completed process and from one another. Thus in building a temple the fitting of the stones is different from the fluting of a column, and both are different from the construction of the whole edifice. And while the building of the temple is a perfect process requiring nothing more to achieve the end, laying the foundation and constructing the triglyph are imperfect processes (each produces only a part). Therefore they differ in kind, and it is not possible to find motion specifically perfect at any one moment but, if at all, only in the whole space of time.*   **1174a19–29; 2010–201**

5. *The same is true of walking and other movements. For, if locomotion is motion from one point in space to another, it also has differences in kind—flying, walking, leaping, and so on. And not only this, but there are differences in walking itself; for the starting and finishing points of the whole racecourse are not the same as those of a part of the course, nor are those of one part the same as those of another; nor is the motion of traversing this line and that line the same, since a runner not only travels along a line but along a line existing in place and this line is in a different place from that. We have adequately discussed motion in another work, and it seems that motion is not complete at any moment but there are many incomplete motions differing in kind, since the starting and finishing points specify the motion. On the other hand pleasure is specifically complete at any and every moment. It is obvious then that motions are different from one another and that pleasure belongs to the things which are whole and complete.*
1174a29–1174b7; 2013–201

6. *Likewise, this is thought to be the case because motion necessarily occupies a space of time, but pleasure does not because that which occurs in a moment is a whole.*   **1174b7–9; 2018–201**

7. *From these considerations it is obviously a mistake to speak of pleasure as motion or a process of generation. For these attributes cannot be predicated of all things but only of such as are divisible and not wholes. Thus there is no process of generation in the act of seeing, in a point or in unity, nor is there any motion in them. Consequently there is no motion or process in pleasure either, for it is a whole.*   **1174b9–14; 2020–202**

COMMENTARY OF ST. THOMAS

2005. After the Philosopher has outlined other opinions about pleasures, he now gives the real definition. First he shows that pleasure does not come under the category of motion or process of generation, as the Platonists held. Then [Lect. VI], at "Again, every sense etc." (1174b14), he defines its nature and characteristic quality. He treats the first point from two aspects

First [1] he proposes his intention and method of procedure, remarking that the nature of pleasure (according to its genus) and its quality (whether it is good or bad) will be made clearer from the following discussion if we take up this question again from the beginning.

2006. Next [2], at "**Now, seeing seems**," he carries out his proposition. He does this in a threefold manner. First [2] he introduces a principle necessary for an explanation of the proposition. Then [3], at "Therefore, etc.," he proves the proposition. Third [7], at "From these considerations etc.," he concludes what he principally intended. He says first that the operation of the sense of sight called seeing is complete at any moment whatsoever. It does not require anything coming later to perfect its form. This is so because seeing is completed in the first instant of time. Now if time were needed for its completion, no time whatsoever would suffice but a certain duration would be necessary, as is the case with other activities occurring in time whose generation requires a particular measure of time. But seeing is perfected in a moment. The same is true of pleasure.

2007. Pleasure is a whole, i.e., something completed in the first instant of its inception. Thus a space of time cannot be assigned in which pleasure may take place, in the sense that more time is needed to complete its form, as in those activities whose generation requires an interval of time. The moment of human generation can be indicated because more time is necessary to perfect the human form.

2008. At "**Therefore**" [3] he proves the proposition by two arguments. The first [3]: every movement or process of generation is perfected after a lapse of time and the motion is not yet completed in a part of that time. This is not true of pleasure. Therefore pleasure is neither a movement nor a process of generation.

2009. In connection with this argument he first [a, i] states a conclusion, deducing from the preceding principle—in which virtually the whole reason is contained—that pleasure is not a motion.

2010. Next [4], at "**For every motion**," he presents the major of the previous argument: every motion involves duration; and every motion is a means to an end, i.e., has an end to which it is ordered and which it attains with the lapse of time. He shows this first [4] concerning the process of generation. For the art of building perfects its operation when it completes what it intends, namely, a house. It does this in some whole interval of time; and all the processes are imperfect during the portions of that time and are different in kind—and even among themselves—from the complete process. The reason for this is that generation receives its species from the form which is the end of the process.

2011. But the form of the whole operation is one thing and the forms of the individual parts are another. Hence the processes also differ from one another in kind. For if a temple is constructed in a certain period of time, one portion of that time is occupied in fitting the stones for the building of the wall, another portion in fluting (virgantur) the columns, i.e., sculpturing them in the manner of rods (virgarum) But during the whole time the temple itself is constructed. And these three operations differ in kind: the fitting of the stones, the fluting of the columns, and the construction of the temple.

2012. On this point we should note

that, as the form of the whole temple is perfect but the forms of the parts are imperfect, so also the building of the temple itself is a perfect process—it requires nothing else to complete the plan of the builder—but laying the foundation is an imperfect process, as is also constructing the triglyph or the sculptured columns arranged in three rows above the foundation. And both of these are the making of a part having the nature of what is imperfect. It is evident then that the preceding constructions of the whole and of the parts differ specifically; and that we are not to understand that motion is specifically perfect at any part of the time but is completed in the whole period of time.

2013. Then [5], at "**The same is true,**" he shows the same thing concerning locomotion. He observes that what is said about the process of generation seems also to be true about walking and all other movements, for it is obvious that all locomotion or local movement is motion from one point in space to another, i.e., from one term to another. Thus motion must be differentiated in kind according to a difference of terms. There are different kinds of locomotion among the animals: flying (suitable to birds), walking (suitable to gressorial creatures), leaping (suitable to grasshoppers) and other movements of this kind. These differ according to the different kinds of moving principles, for the souls of different animals do not belong to the same classification.

2014. The kinds of locomotion differ not only in the foregoing manner but also in one of these species, for instance, walking which is of different kinds. For traveling the whole racecourse and traveling a part of it do not have the same starting point and fin-

ishing line, i.e., the same terms a que and ad quem. And the case is simila to traveling this or that part of the course because the boundaries are no the same. The motion of traversing thi line and that line is not the same spe cifically, although all lines as such be long to the same species.

2015. As motions are constituted in a determined position or location, they are understood as differing specifically according to the difference of places which is taken according to a differen disposition in regard to the first en compassing space. Now a runner no only travels along a line but along a line existing in place because this line is in a different place from that. Clearly then the whole locomotion differs spe cifically from each of its parts accord ing to the difference of boundaries, in such a way however that the whole motion is perfect specifically but the parts imperfectly so.

2016. Because complete knowledge of the nature of motion might be re quired for a clarification of these points, he adds that a precise, i.e., ade quate and complete, account of motion has been given in another work, the *Physics* (Bk. III, Ch. 1–3, 200b12-202b29; St. Th. Lect. I–V, 275–325). Bu it is enough to say here that motion is not perfect at every moment, but there are many imperfect motions differing in the different parts of time from the fact that the starting points and the finishing lines, i.e., the terms of the motion, specify the motion.

2017. Having thus explained the major of the proposition he then adds the minor, that the form of pleasure is complete at any and every moment—this has been shown from previous dis cussions (2007). He concludes then tha pleasure and generation or change ob viously differ from one another, and that pleasure is numbered among things that are whole and complete because pleasure has the completion of its form in every part.

2018. He proposes the second argument [6] at "**Likewise, this is thought.**" It is that motion is impossible except in a space of time, as proved in the sixth book of the *Physics* (Ch. 3, 234a24–234b9; St. Th. Lect. V, 794–795), but pleasure is possible without an interval of time. It has been pointed out that a feeling of pleasure is a whole for the reason that this feeling occurs in a moment and is completed immediately. Therefore pleasure is not a motion.

2019. We should note that the difference from which this argument proceeds is the cause of the difference from which the first argument proceeded. Therefore the form of pleasure is complete at every moment but not so motion, because pleasure is instantaneous while all motion occupies an interval of time. And the Philosopher's way of speaking shows this when he says "Likewise, this is thought to be the case etc."

2020. Then [7], at "**From these considerations,**" he concludes from the premises what he principally intended. He remarks it is clear from the premises (2006–2019) that philosophers are mistaken in speaking of pleasure as a motion or process of generation. The concept of motion and generation cannot be predicated of everything but only of divisible things that are not whole and are not completed immediately.

2021. Neither is it possible to speak of seeing as a process of generation in such a way that seeing attains completion successively. Nor can we speak of a point or unity in a similar fashion. For these are not generated but accompany certain things. Likewise motion cannot be attributed to them, and consequently not to pleasure, which is also a whole, i.e., has its perfection in being indivisible.

LECTURE VI
The Nature and Properties of Pleasure

TEXT OF ARISTOTLE (*1174b14–1175a21*) Chapter 4

1. *Again, every sense functions in relation to its object, and functions perfectly when it is in good condition and directed to the finest object falling under it. This seems to be the best description of perfect activity.*   **1174b14–17; 2022–2023**

2. *It does not seem to make any difference whether the sense itself acts or man in whom the sense resides; in either case the most perfect activity proceeds from the best-conditioned agent in relation to the most excellent of the objects falling within its competence.*   **1174b17–19; 2024**

3. *And this activity is most perfect and most pleasant, for there is a pleasure corresponding to each sense, and also to thought and contemplation. Now, that activity is most pleasant that is most perfect, and the most perfect activity belongs to the best-conditioned faculty in relation to the most excellent object falling within its competence.*   **1174b19–23; 2025–2026**

4. *However, pleasure does not perfect the activity in the same way as the sensible object and the sense—both of which are good—perfect it, just as health and a doctor are not in the same way the cause of being healthy.*   **1174b23–26; 2027**

5. *That there is a pleasure corresponding to each sense is obvious, for we speak of sights and sounds as pleasant.*   **1174b26–28; 2028**

6. *It is also obvious that pleasure is greatest when the sense is keenest and active in relation to its corresponding object. So long, then, as the sensible object and the perceiving subject remain in this condition, the pleasure will continue since the agent and the recipient are both at hand.*   **1174b28–31; 2029**

7. *But pleasure perfects activity not as an inherent habit but as a kind of supervenient end like the bloom of health perfects youth.*   **1174b31–33; 2030–2031**

8. *So long then as the sensible or intelligible object and the discerning or contemplative subject are as they should be, there will be pleasure in the activity. For while the active and passive elements are unchanged in themselves and in their relation to one another the same result is produced.*   **1174b33–1175a3; 2032**

9. *How is it then that no one can feel pleasure continuously? Is it from fatigue? Certainly no creature with a body is capable of uninterrupted activity. Therefore pleasure also is not continuous, for it accompanies activity.*   **1175a3–6; 2033**

10. *Some things give us pleasure when new but later do not, because at first the mind is stimulated and is intensely active about them. This is so in the case of sight when we look at something intently; later however our reaction is not of this nature but becomes relaxed. For this reason pleasure too slackens.*   **1175a6–10; 2034–2035**

11. *It might be thought that all men seek pleasure because they all desire life. Now life is a form of activity, and everyone is concerned with the things he loves most and devotes himself to their activities. For example, a musician pays close attention to good music, a student of philosophy is intent on intellectual problems, and so on. Since then pleasure perfects these activities, it also perfects life, which all desire. Consequently it is reasonable that men seek pleasure, for it perfects life which is desirable to everyone.*   **1175a10–17; 2036**

12. *The question whether we choose life for the sake of pleasure or pleasure for the sake of life can be dismissed for the present. Indeed they seem to be united and not to admit of separation, since there is no pleasure without activity.*   **1175a18–21; 2037–2038**

COMMENTARY OF ST. THOMAS

2022. After the Philosopher has   shown that pleasure is not in the category of motion, as some thinkers maintained, he now explains the nature and properties of pleasure. First he shows what pleasure is. Then [Lect. VII], at "Consequently pleasures etc." (1175a22), he treats the variations among pleasures. The first point is discussed in a twofold fashion. First [1] he shows what pleasure is. Next [8], at "So long then etc.," from this he defines the properties of pleasure. He considers the first point under two headings. First [1] he shows that pleasure is a perfection of activity. Second [5], at "That there is a pleasure etc.," he clarifies what he has said. He handles the first point in a threefold manner. First [1] he explains what is the perfect activity. Then [3], at "And this activity etc.," he shows that pleasure is the perfection of activity. Third [4], at "However, pleasure etc.," he shows how pleasure can perfect activity. He discusses the first point from two aspects. First [1] he explains his proposition.

2023. He observes that the activity of each sense is the functioning of an agent in respect to a sensible thing that is the sense's object. Hence in the activity of sense two elements are considered: the sense itself that is the active principle, and the sensible thing that is the object of the activity. Consequently, the best condition on the part of both sense and object is required for the perfect activity of sense. For this reason he adds that sense functions perfectly when the activity of sense is well-conditioned in relation to the finest or fittest of the objects falling under the sense. This activity seems to be especially perfect which proceeds from sense in relation to an object of this kind.

2024. Next [2], at "**It does not seem**," he mentions a doubt. Since he has just said that sense is active (2023) and—in

the first book of the *De Anima* (Ch. 4, 408b11–18; St. Th. Lect. X, 151–162)— that the soul does not act but man acts by means of the soul, consequently he adds that it makes no difference to our purpose whether it is the sense itself that acts or man (or animal) in whom the sense resides. The reason is: no matter which is affirmed, obviously it is true concerning each that the most perfect activity proceeds from the best-conditioned agent with respect to the most excellent object falling within the competence of such an agent. For the perfection of the activity seems to depend especially on these two: the active principle and the object.

2025. Then [3], at "**And this activity,**" he shows that pleasure is a perfection of activity. We shall see that the same activity which we said is most perfect is also most pleasant; wherever a perfect activity is found in any percipient, there also a pleasant activity is found, for a pleasure corresponds not only to touch and taste but also to every sense—not only to sense but also to contemplation inasmuch as the intellect contemplates some truth with certitude.

2026. Among these activities of sense and intellect, that is most pleasant which is most perfect. But the most perfect is that belonging to sense or intellect well-conditioned in relation to the best of the objects that fall under sense or intellect. If then perfect activity is pleasant, and most perfect activity most pleasant, it follows that activity is pleasant to the extent that it is perfect. Therefore pleasure is the perfection of activity.

2027. At "**However, pleasure**" [4] he shows how pleasure can perfect activity. He observes that pleasure does not perfect activity (of sense, for example) in the same way as the object (which is the sensible) and the active principle (which is the sense)—all of which are good elements contributing excellence to the activity—perfect it. Thus health and a doctor are not in the same manner the cause of being healthy, but health is a cause by way of form and a doctor by way of agent. Likewise pleasure, the perfection of activity, perfects activity by way of form; a well-conditioned sense, a mover that is moved, by way of agent; but a suitable sensible object perfects activity, as a mover that is unmoved. The same reasoning is also valid concerning the intellect.

2028. Next [5], at "**That there is,**" he clarifies what he has said. First [5] it is clear, he states, that there is a pleasure corresponding to each sense—as was just pointed out (2025)—from the fact that we say and perceive that there are pleasant sights like beautiful forms and sounds like melodious songs.

2029. Second [6], at "**It is also,**" he clarifies another premise by remarking that it is clear from experience that seeing, hearing, and every activity of sense are exceedingly pleasant when the sense is keenest or strongest and acts in relation to its corresponding best object. So long as the sensible object itself and the animal possessing the sense remain in this condition, the pleasure remains, as is apparent also in other activities. And so long as the condition of the agent and recipient are the same, the effect is necessarily the same.

2030. Finally [7], at "**But pleasure perfects,**" he clarifies a previous statement (2027) about the manner in which pleasure perfects activity. For it was stated that pleasure perfects activity not efficiently but formally. Now, formal perfection is twofold. One is intrinsic constituting a thing's essence,

but the other is added to a thing already constituted in its species.

2031. He says first that pleasure perfects activity not as a habit that is inherent, i.e., not as a form intrinsic to the essence of the thing, but as a kind of end or supervenient perfection, like the bloom of health comes to young people not as being of the essence of youth but as following from a favorable condition of the causes of youth. Likewise pleasure follows from a favorable condition of the causes of activity.

2032. Then [8], at "**So long then,**" he defines the reasons for certain properties of pleasure from what has been defined about its nature. First [8] he considers the duration of pleasure; next [11], at "It might be thought etc.," its desirability. He discussed the first point from three aspects. First [8] he shows how long pleasure should last. He observes that there will be pleasure in activity so long as, on the one hand, the object (sensible or intelligible) and, on the other, the agent itself (which perceives by sense or contemplates by intellect) are well-conditioned. The reason for this is that as long as the condition of the active and passive elements remains the same and the relation between them remains the same, so long will the effect remain the same. Hence if the good condition of the knowing faculty and of the object is the cause of pleasure, as long as this lasts pleasure necessarily lasts.

2033. Next [9], at "**How is it then,**" he assigns the reason why pleasure cannot be continuous. No one, he says, continuously feels pleasure since he grows weary from activity that pleasure accompanies, and in this way activity is not pleasant. This is so because all creatures with bodies capable of suffering are unable to be continuously active, for their bodies are changed in their condition by motion connected with activity. The body itself is subservient in some manner to every activity of the being whose body it is: either immediately to sensitive activity, which is produced by a bodily organ, or mediately to intellectual activity, which uses the activities of the sensitive powers generated by bodily organs. Therefore activity cannot be continuous on the part of its productive principle; and so pleasure also cannot be continuous, for it accompanies activity (155, 1486, 1496).

2034. Third [10], at "**Some things,**" he gives the reason why new things are more pleasing. He remarks that things when new are more delightful but later are not equally so. The reason for this is that at first the mind is eagerly inclined toward such things on account of desire and curiosity and so is intensely or vehemently active about them.

2035. Vehement pleasure accompanies this, as is evident in people who, from curiosity, look hard at something they have not seen previously. Later though, when they become accustomed to the sight, their reaction is not of such a nature that they look so intently or do anything else as before. But they act in a relaxed manner and for this reason the pleasure also fades, i.e., is felt less keenly.

2036. The [11], at "**It might be thought,**" he presents the reason why pleasure is desired by everyone. He treats this point in a twofold manner. First [11] he explains his proposition, observing that a man can judge with reason that all men naturally seek pleasure because they all naturally desire life. But life according to its ulti-

mate perfection consists in a form of activity, as pointed out in the ninth book (1846). Therefore everyone is especially active about those things which he loves most of all and devotes himself to their activities. Thus a musician listens most attentively to good music; a lover of wisdom applies himself especially to the contemplation of intellectual problems or studies. Since then pleasure perfects activity—as was indicated (2036)—consequently it perfects life itself which all desire. Thus it is reasonable that everyone should seek pleasure from the fact that it perfects life which is desirable to everybody.

2037. Next [12], at "**The question whether,**" he raises a doubt by reason of the discussion. We have stated that all desire pleasure and likewise all desire life which is perfected in activity. But objects of desire, as well as objects of knowledge, have an order among themselves. Therefore a doubt can arise whether men seek life for the sake of pleasure or, conversely, pleasure for the sake of life.

2038. He says that the doubt must be dismissed at present because these two questions are so joined that they do not admit of any separation. For there is no pleasure without activity, and on the other hand there can be no perfect activity without pleasure, as has been noted (2025, 2026). However activity, rather than pleasure, seems to be principal. For pleasure is a repose of the appetite in a pleasing object which a person enjoys by means of activity. But a person desires repose in a thing only inasmuch as he judges it agreeable to him. Consequently the activity itself that gives pleasure as a pleasing object seems to be desirable prior to pleasure.

LECTURE VII
Pleasures Differ in Kind

TEXT OF ARISTOTLE (*1175a21–1175b24*) Chapter 5

1. *Consequently pleasures seem to differ in kind. For we judge that different kinds of things are perfected by different perfections. This is thought to be true both of natural organisms and of productions of art, for instance, animals, trees, paintings, statues, a house, and a receptacle. Likewise, activities differing in kind are perfected by things differing in kind. Moreover, activities of intellect differ from those of the senses; and the latter differ from one another, and so then do the pleasures that perfect them.*   1175a21–28; 2039–2041

2. *This will also be evident from the fact that each pleasure is akin to the activity it perfects, for an activity is stimulated by a pleasure proper to it. People who work pleasurably judge each thing better and investigate them more accurately. For example, those who find pleasure in the study of geometry become geometricians and grasp each problem more clearly. Similarly, those who love music, architecture, and other arts make progress in their own field when they enjoy their work. But pleasure intensifies activity and what intensifies a thing is proper to it. Therefore properties of things differing in kind must themselves differ in kind.*
1175a29–1175b1; 2042–2043

3. *A still clearer indication of this is given by the fact that activities are hindered by pleasures arising from other activities. For people who love the flute are incapable of paying attention to a discussion when they hear someone playing the flute because they enjoy the music more than their present activity. Therefore, the pleasure connected with flute-playing destroys that activity which is concerned with discussion. A similar thing happens in other cases where a person tries to do two things at the same time; the more pleasant activity drives out the other, and if it is much more pleasant it does so more effectively so that the other ceases altogether. For this reason when we take intense pleasure in something we can scarcely do anything else; and when we take relaxed pleasure in some things we can be engaged in others. For example, people who eat sweets at stage-plays do so especially when the actors are poor. Since then pleasure proper to activities strengthens, prolongs and improves them, and since other pleasures injure these activities, it is clear that pleasures differ greatly.*   1175b1–16; 2044–2047

4. *Indeed alien pleasures produce nearly the same effect as proper pains, for activities are destroyed by their proper pains. For instance, if writing or doing sums proves to be an unpleasant and painful task, a person neither writes nor does sums because the activity is painful. Activities then are affected in a different manner by their proper pleasures and pains—these arise from the nature of the activities. But alien pleasures are said to have an effect resembling pain, for they both destroy activity although not to the same degree.*
1175b16–24; 2048–2049

COMMENTARY OF ST. THOMAS

2039. After the Philosopher has explained the nature and properties of pleasure, he now explains the difference among pleasures. He discusses this point from two aspects. First [1] he explains the difference of pleasures taken on the part of the activities; then [Lect. VIII], at "It is thought etc." (1176a3), the difference taken on the part of the subject. He treats the first point in a twofold manner. First [1] he shows how pleasures may differ in kind according to the difference among activities; next [Lect. VIII], at "Since activities differ etc." (1175b25), how they differ in goodness and badness. He handles the first point in two ways. First [1] he shows by reason that pleasures differ in kind on the basis of differing activities; then [2], at "This will also etc.," he manifests the same proposition by indications. He observes first: since pleasure is the perfection of activity, it follows that just as activities differ in kind so pleasures too seem to differ. Thus we commonly judge as intrinsically evident (*per se notum*) that those things that differ in kind are perfected by specifically different perfections. Certainly this is obvious concerning essential perfections which constitute a species. And it is necessarily the same with other consequent perfections, provided they are proper, because they follow the essential principles of the species. We see this happen in the case both of natural and artistic objects.

2040. In natural objects surely, because the perfection of animals, which consists in keenness of sense, is one thing; and the perfection of trees, which consists in their fruitfulness, is another. And in artistic objects, because the perfection of paintings—that they be characterized by pleasing colors—is one thing, and the perfection of statues—that they aptly represent the individuals, whose images they are—is another. Likewise the perfection of a house—that it be a solid dwelling—is one thing, and the perfection of a receptacle—that it have a large capacity—is another. Consequently activities differing specifically must be perfected by specifically different pleasures.

2041. It is clear that activities of mind or intellect differ in kind from activities of the senses; similarly the activities of the senses differ from one another. The reason is that they are differentiated according to objects and according to the faculties which are principles of activities. Consequently pleasures that perfect activities differ specifically.

2042. Then [2], at "**This will also,**" he manifests the same proposition by indications. First [2] by the fact that activity is stimulated by its own pleasure. He observes first that this difference among pleasures corresponding to activities is evident from the fact that each pleasure is ascribed by a kind of affinity to the activity it perfects, because each activity is intensified by its own pleasure, as everything is naturally intensified by what is similar and agreeable.

2043. We notice that people who do any intellectual work with pleasure can judge each point better and investigate accurately the questions which pleasantly engage their attention. For example, geometricians who take pleasure in the study of geometry can grasp more clearly each problem of this science because their mind is detained longer by that which is pleasant. And the same reason holds for all others (similarly occupied), for instance, those who love music and delight in it, those who love architecture, and so on—that because they find pleasure in such work they make great progress in their art. Evidently then pleasures intensify activities. But it is clear that what intensifies an action is proper to it. Consequently things that are different are intensified by different things. Therefore if activities, which are intensified by pleasure, differ in kind—as we have shown (2039–2041)—the intensifying pleasures themselves should be specifically different.

2044. At "**A still clearer**" [3] he presents another indication taken from the hindrance to the activities derived from other activities. First [3] from this he shows the difference among pleasures. Next [3], at "Indeed alien pleasures etc.," he compares alien pleasures with pains belonging to the activities. He says first that the remarks (2042–2043) about the difference among pleasures corresponding to the activities are more apparent from the fact that the activities are hindered by the pleasures arising from other occupations. From this then our contention is more evidently sustained because the fact that pleasures intensify activities might be ascribed to the general nature of pleasure but not to the particular nature of this pleasure according to which pleasures differ from one another.

2045. But it is very clear that pleasures differ in kind when we discover that activity is promoted by its own pleasure but impeded by extraneous pleasure. For we see that flute-favorers simply cannot hear people talking to them when listening to flute-playing because they take more pleasure in the music of the flute than in their present activity, i.e., hearing talk intended for them. Evidently then pleasure arising from flute-playing impedes the mind's reflective activities. The same thing apparently happens in other situations when someone is doing two things at once.

2046. For it is obvious that the more pleasant activity drives out the other, to the extent that if there is a great difference in the amount of pleasure, a person entirely neglects the activity less pleasurable to him. Consequently when we take vehement pleasure in something we are incapable of doing anything else. But when something pleases us quietly, i.e., mildly or hardly at all, we can be doing other things too, as is evident of people at a show. Those who find little amusement in what

they see there can be busy eating sweets—a diversion only moderately pleasant. People do this especially when watching athletes fighting poorly in public games, so that viewing such a contest is not pleasing to them.

2047. A proper pleasure then (a) strengthens the activities from which it proceeds, so that a person exerts himself more vigorously in them; (b) it prolongs the activities, so that a person stays longer at them; (c) it improves the activities so they attain their end more perfectly. Likewise other pleasures—those accompanying other activities—obstruct or harm all this; hence these facts clearly demonstrate that pleasures differ much from one another, for what one pleasure helps, another hinders.

2048. Next [4], at "**Indeed alien pleasures**," he compares extraneous pleasures with pains proper (to the activities) so that the difference among pleasures may in this way be more obvious. He observes that extraneous pleasure (which is caused by some other activity) and proper pain (according to which a person suffers from the activity itself) produce nearly the same effect on an activity. For, evidently, pain arising from an activity destroys it. For instance, if it is unpleasant or rather trying for someone to write or tally figures he will neither write nor tally, owing to the painful nature of such activity.

2049. In this way then activities are affected in a different manner by proper pleasures and pains, as it were being caused by these very activities; but extraneous pleasures are caused by other activities. We have just noted (2045–2046) that extraneous pleasures have an effect resembling proper pain. For in either case activity is destroyed "although not in the same manner") but more so by proper pain which is directly and by reason of itself opposed to pleasure. On the other hand the contrariety of extraneous pleasure arises from another source, viz., activity.

LECTURE VIII
The Morality of Pleasures

TEXT OF ARISTOTLE (1175b24–1176a29) Chapter 5

1. *Since activities differ in goodness and badness, and some are to be chosen, others to be avoided, and still others are indifferent, the same is true also of their pleasures; for a proper pleasure corresponds to each activity. Thus the pleasure proper to a virtuous activity is good and that proper to a vicious activity is bad.*   **1175b24–28; 2050**

2. *Just as desires for honorable things are praiseworthy, those for base things are blameworthy. But pleasures accompanying activities are more proper to them than the desires. For the latter are separated in time and distinct in nature from activities, while the former are intimately connected with them and so closely linked as to raise a doubt whether activity is identical with pleasure. However, we are not to understand that pleasure is thought or sensation—this would be unreasonable—although some people have identified them because they are connected. Therefore, just as activities are different, so too are their pleasures.*
1175b28–36; 2051–2055

3. *Now sight differs in purity from touch, and hearing and smell from taste; similarly pleasures of intellect differ from those of the senses, and each class has differences within itself.*
1175b36–1176a3; 2056

4. *It is thought that each creature has its own pleasure just as it has its own activity, for pleasure corresponds to activity. This will be apparent to a person who considers each thing. Certainly a horse, a dog, a man have different pleasures. As Heraclitus says: an ass prefers grass to gold, since food is more pleasant than gold to asses. Therefore creatures differing in species have different kinds of pleasures. On the other hand it is reasonable to hold that things of the same species have similar pleasures.*   **1176a3–9; 2057–2058**

5. *However, pleasures differ considerably among men. For the same things delight some men but sadden others, and things distressing and odious to some are pleasant and attractive to others. This happens in the case of things sweet to the taste, since the same objects do not seem sweet to a sick man and to one in good condition; nor does the same temperature feel warm to an invalid and to a healthy man. The same holds good in other cases too.*   **1176a10–15; 2059–2061**

6. *In all cases, that seems to be really so which appears to the good man. If this is correct, as it seems to be, and if the measure of everything is virtue and the good man as such, then the things that appear to him to be pleasures are really pleasures and the things that he enjoys are really pleasant. Wherefore it is not surprising that things painful to him are evidently pleasant to someone. For men are subject to much perversion and deterioration. But these things are not pleasant (in themselves) but only to these people and others similarly inclined. It is obvious then that pleasures admittedly disreputable are pleasures only to men of perverted taste.*
1176a15–24; 2062–2063

7. *But of the pleasures that seem to be virtuous we must discuss which kind and which particular pleasure are peculiarly human. This will be clear from the activities, for the pleasures result from the activities. Therefore, whether the perfect and happy man has one or many activities, it will be the pleasures perfecting these that will be called human in the principal sense. The other pleasures will be so only in various secondary ways, as are the activities.*
1176a24–29; 2064

COMMENTARY OF ST. THOMAS

2050. After the Philosopher has shown that pleasures differ in kind according to the difference of activities, he now shows that pleasures differ in goodness and evil according to the difference of activities. First [1] in moral goodness; then [3], at "Now sight differs etc.," in physical goodness, which is judged according to purity and impurity. He discusses his first point in a twofold manner. First [1] he states his proposition. Next [2], at "Just as desires etc.," he proves his proposition. He says first that, since activities differ according to goodness and badness, i.e., virtue and vice—in such a way that some activities (the virtuous) are to be chosen, others (the vicious) are to be shunned, and still others are in neither class by their nature but can become either—so also do pleasures. The reason is that each activity is accompanied by a proper pleasure, as was stated previously (2039). Hence the pleasure proper to a virtuous activity is good, and the pleasure proper to a vicious activity is bad.

2051. Next [2], at "**Just as desires**," he proves his proposition by a reason taken on the part of desires. We see that the desires by which we want good or honorable objects are praiseworthy, for example, if a person wants to act justly or bravely. But desires for base objects are blameworthy, for example, if a person desires to steal or fornicate. Obviously the pleasures by which we enjoy these activities are closer and more proper to the activities than are the desires by which we want them.

2052. Desires are separated from activities by time, for we desire to do an act before we do it. They are also distinct by nature because activity is an act of a perfect thing but desire is an act of something imperfect and not yet achieved. But pleasures are closely connected with activities because both belong to something perfect. They are also closely linked by time for, if a person has not yet performed an action he is not enjoying this action because pleasure concerns a present thing, as desire a future one. Pleasure is closely linked to activity to such a degree that it seems to be a matter of doubt whether activity is identical with pleasure.

2053. However, we must not say that this is so. Pleasure indeed can be felt only in the activity of the senses or intellect, for creatures lacking perception cannot experience pleasure.

2054. Nevertheless, pleasure is identical neither with the activity of the intellect nor with the activity of the senses. Pleasure pertains rather to the appetitive part. But it is unreasonable that some should think that pleasure is identical with activity because it is not separated from it.

2055. Thus it is evident that, as activities differ according to virtue and vice, so too do pleasures. From this it is clear that some thinkers have inconsistently proclaimed that pleasures are (not) good and bad.

2056. At "**Now sight differs**" [3] he shows the difference between pleasures based on purity and impurity. Obviously activities of the senses differ according to purity, for the activity of sight is purer than that of touch; similarly, the activity of smell than that of taste. But activity that is more immaterial is called purer. According to this the purest of all sensitive activities is sight because more immaterial, having as it does less admixture of material conditions—both on the part of the object which becomes actually (in actu) visible by light derived from the sun and on the part of the medium which is altered only by a spiritual change. For the same reasons the activity of touch is most material because the qualities of passible matter are its objects and its medium is not separate but contiguous. And the same difference in purity is observed between sensible pleasures among themselves. Likewise activities and pleasures of intellect, as being more immaterial, are purer than those of the senses.

2057. Then [4], at "**It is thought,**" he shows what the difference of pleasures is—relative to the subject. First [4] in regard to animals of different species. Next [5], at "However, pleasures etc.," in regard to men. He says first: since pleasure accompanies activity, it seems that each thing has its own pleasure just as it has its own activity. That each thing has its own activity is apparent from the fact that activities follow the forms of things according to which the things differ in kind. That each thing has its own pleasure is apparent if anyone wishes to consider things individually.

2058. For it is clear that a horse finds pleasure in one thing, a dog in another, and man in a third; as Heraclitus says, an ass prefers grass to gold, since the nourishment afforded him by the grass is more pleasant to him than the gold. Thus it is obvious that things differing in kind have pleasures specifically different. On the other hand it is reasonable that the things that do not differ in

kind have a similar pleasure followin the nature of the species.

2059. At "**However, pleasures**" [5 he explains the difference amon pleasures in men. First [5] he show that men have different pleasure Then [6], at "In all cases etc.," he show that the principal pleasure is found i the virtuous man. Finally [7], at "But c the pleasures etc.," he shows which i the principal pleasure among th pleasures of a virtuous man. He say first: although it seems reasonable tha creatures alike in kind should have common sort of pleasure—this is so i the case of other animals—neverthe less men, who are all of the same spe cies, do have very different pleasure just as they have different activities.

2060. The reason is that activitie and pleasures of other animals follov their natural tendency, which is th same in all animals belonging to th same species. But activities and pleas ures of men spring from reason that i not determined to one behavioral pat tern. Consequently certain things de light some men and sadden others; an things distressing and odious to som are pleasant and attractive to others.

2061. Situations of this kind occu because everyone takes pleasure i what he loves. And this happens be cause some are well or badly dispose according to reason. This is the case i regard to the taste of sweet things sinc the same objects do not seem sweet t a sick man who has a diseased tast and to a well man who has a health taste; the same object does not seer hot to a person with a defective sens of touch and to a person whose touc is normal. This is true also of the othe senses.

2062. Then [6], at "**In all cases,**" h shows that the pleasure of virtuou persons is the principal human pleasure. He observes: in all cases of this kind connected with human passions and activities, that seems to be really so which appears to the good man who has correct judgment about such things, for example, the healthy man about what is sweet. And if this is correct—and it seems to be—that virtue is the measure by which we should judge all human affairs and that a man is good inasmuch as he is virtuous, it follows that real pleasures are those which appear so to the virtuous man, and that genuinely delightful things are those which the virtuous man enjoys.

2063. But it is not surprising that some things which are painful to the virtuous man are delightful to other men. For this happens on account of the many corruptions and various deteriorations of man which pervert his reason and appetite. Thus the things that the virtuous person repudiates are not pleasurable in themselves but only to the evilly inclined. Therefore it is obvious that pleasures which all admit to be disreputable must be declared pleasures only to depraved men.

2064. Finally [7], at "**But of the pleasures,**" he shows that there is one principal pleasure among those of the good man. Aristotle notes that of the virtuous pleasures we must consider which kind and which particular one constitute the chief pleasure of man. This, he says, will be clear from the activities that the pleasures follow. The reason is that, whether the perfect and happy man has one or many proper activities, obviously the pleasures accompanying these activities are the chief pleasures of man. The others are contained under the chief pleasures in various secondary ways, as happens in the case of activities.

LECTURE IX
The Nature of Happiness

TEXT OF ARISTOTLE (*1176a30–1177a11*) Chapter 6

1. *After the discussion of the various kinds of virtue, friendship, and pleasure, it remains for us to treat happiness in a general way, inasmuch as we consider this to be the end of human activity. But our discussion will be more concise if we reassert what has been stated already.*
                                                                    1176a30–33; 2065

2. *We have said that happiness is definitely not a habit. If it were it might be enjoyed by a person passing his whole life in sleep, living the life of a vegetable, or by someone suffering the greatest misfortune. If then this inconsistency is unacceptable, we must place happiness in the class of activity, as was indicated previously.*   **117a33–1176b2; 2066–2067**

3. *But some activities are necessary and desirable for the sake of something else while others are desirable in themselves.*   **1176b2–3; 2068**

4. *Now it is clear that we must place happiness among the things desirable in themselves and not among those desirable for the sake of something else. For happiness lacks nothing and is self-sufficient. But those activities are desirable in themselves that are sought for no other reason than the activity itself.*   **1176b3–7; 2069**

5. *Such actions are thought to be in conformity with virtue, for to do virtuous and honorable deeds is a thing desirable in itself. But agreeable amusements also seem to be desirable in themselves; they are not chosen for the sake of other things, since they are rather harmful than helpful, causing men to neglect their bodies and property.*   **1176b7–11; 2070**

6. *Many apparently happy persons have recourse to such pastimes. This is why the ready-witted in conversation are favorites with tyrants; they show themselves agreeable in furnishing the desired amusement for which the tyrants want them. So these pleasures are thought to constitute happiness because people in high places spend their time in them.*
                                                                    1176b12–17; 2071–2072

7. *But perhaps such persons prove nothing; for virtue and intelligence, the principles of good actions, do not depend on the possession of power. Nor should bodily pleasures be thought more desirable, if these persons without a taste for pure and liberal pleasure resort to physical pleasures. Children too think that objects highly prized by them are best. It is reasonable then that just as different things are valuable to a child and to a man, so also are they to good and bad men. Therefore, as we have often mentioned, those actions are worthy and pleasant that appear so to a good man. Now that activity is most desirable to everyone that is in accordance with his proper habit. But the activity most desirable to a good man is in accord with virtue. Consequently, his happiness does not consist in amusement.*   **1176b17–28; 2073–2075**

8. *Surely it would be strange that amusement should be our end—that we should transact business and undergo hardships all through life in order to amuse ourselves. For we choose nearly all things for the sake of something else, except happiness which is an end itself. Now it seems foolish and utterly childish to exert oneself and to labor for the sake of amusement. On the contrary, to play in order to work better is the correct rule according to Anacharsis. This is because amusement is a kind of relaxation that men need, since they are incapable of working continuously. Certainly relaxation is not an end, for it is taken as a means to further activity.*
                                                                    1176b28–1177a1; 2076–2077

9. *Moreover, a life lived in conformity with virtue is thought to be a happy one; it is accompanied by joy but not by the joy of amusement. Now we say that those things that are done in earnest are better than ludicrous things and things connected with amusement, and we say that the activity of the better part or the better man is more serious. But an activity that*

belongs to a superior faculty is itself superior and more productive of happiness. Surely anyone can enjoy the pleasures of the body, the bestial man no less than the best of men. However, we do not ascribe happiness to the bestial man, if we do not assign him a life properly human. Therefore happiness does not consist in pursuits of this sort but in virtuous activities, as has been stated already. **1177a1–11; 2078–2079**

COMMENTARY OF ST. THOMAS

2065. After the Philosopher has considered pleasure, he now takes up the consideration of happiness. First [1] he connects this with his earlier treatment. Then [2], at "We have said etc.," he carries out his proposal. He makes a threefold division of the first point. First he enumerates the subjects already treated: virtues were discussed from the second book to the eighth (245–1537), friendship in the eighth and ninth books (1538–1952), and pleasure in the first part of the tenth book (1953–2064). Next he mentions what remains to be discussed, viz., happiness, which we must touch upon and briefly treat in a general way or in outline, just as we have previously treated other moral questions (43–230). Moreover, we must discuss happiness because everyone in general considers it the end of all human activities. Now, in order that activities be directed to an end without error it is necessary for the end to be known. Finally, he indicates the method of treating happiness, observing that we must reassert what was said about it initially (43–230). In this way our discussion will be more concise if we treat it from the beginning.

2066. Then [2], at "**We have said,**" he carries out his intention. First [2] he explains the genus of happiness, showing that it is not a habit, but an activity. Next [3], at "But some activities etc.," he shows the nature of virtuous activity. Finally [Lect. X], at "If happiness etc." (1177a12), he investigates to what virtue the activity belongs. He says first—as was indicated in the first book (118–130, 152–153)—that happiness is not a habit. For two incongruities might follow: the first is that, since habits remain in a person asleep, it might follow—if happiness were a habit—that a sleeper might be happy throughout his whole life or a greater part of it. But this is unreasonable because one who is asleep does not perfectly exercise vital activities except those belonging to the vegetative soul found in plants to which happiness cannot be attributed. It is certain that sensation and external movements cease when a man is asleep; and internal images are distorted and imperfect. Likewise, intellectual activity in a sleeping person is imperfect, if indeed there is any. On the other hand, only activities of the nutritive part are perfect (in the sleeping person).

2067. A second incongruity is that virtuous habits remain in persons suffering misfortune, but their virtuous activities are hindered by reason of the misfortune. If then happiness is a habit, it might follow that the unfortunate were really happy. The Stoics, though, did not think this to be an inconsistency since they held that external goods are in no way human goods; and for this reason man's happiness cannot be diminished by misfortunes. However, this is contrary to the common opinion that judges misfortune to be inconsistent with happiness. Therefore, according to those who reject these illogical consequences it must be said that happiness is not a habit but is to be placed among activities, as has been stated in the first book (118–130, 152–153).

2068. At **"But some activities"** [3] he shows that happiness is a virtuous activity. He discusses this point from three aspects. First [3] he shows that happiness is contained under the activities desirable in themselves (*secundum se*). Then [5], at "Such actions etc.," he divides these actions into virtuous and agreeable. Finally [6], at "Many apparently happy etc.," he shows under which classification happiness falls. He treats the first point in a twofold manner. First [3] he proposes a division of activities. He notes that some activities are necessary for something else and to be chosen for the sake of other things, being desirable only for this end; other activities are worthy of choice in themselves (*secundum seipsas*) because, even if no further benefit might come from them they have a characteristic of desirability in themselves.

2069. Second [4], at **"Now it is clear,"** he shows that happiness falls under those activities that are desirable in themselves and not under those which are desirable for the sake of something else. For it is of the nature of happiness to be self-sufficient and in need of nothing further, as is evident from what was said in the first book (118). But those activities are designated as desirable in themselves, from which nothing further than the activity itself is sought, inasmuch as they lack nothing to make them worthy of choice. Thus it is clear that happiness is an activity desirable in itself.

2070. Then [5], at **"Such actions,"** he subdivides activities desirable in themselves. He says first that these seem to be virtuous actions because it is absolutely (*per se*) desirable to man

that he choose those things that are of themselves (*per se*) good and honorable. Consequently some people call an object honorable because it draws us by its virtue and attracts us by its excellence. Second, even agreeable amusements seem to be desirable of themselves. For it does not seem that men choose these pastimes for any utility, since people are more often harmed than helped by such activities. In fact, because of amusements men seem to neglect both their bodies, which are exposed to pains and dangers, and their possessions by reason of the expenses they incur.

2071. Next [6], at **"Many apparently happy,"** he shows under which classification happiness falls. First [6] he explains why some may think that happiness consists in amusement. Then [7], at "But perhaps etc.," he rejects the reason offered for this. Finally [8], at "Surely it would etc.," he resolves the truth. He says first that many who are looked upon as happy have recourse to pastimes of this kind, inasmuch as they want to be amused. Consequently, tyrants highly approve persons of ready wit in conversation for the sharpness of their jests.

2072. He calls people in power tyrants because those who are occupied with amusements do not seem to strive for the common interest but for their own gratification. Moreover, tyrants make favorites of the ready-witted because they show themselves pleasing to tyrants in the very things that are desired, i.e., in pleasant amusements for which the tyrants want such men. Thus then happiness is said to consist in pleasures of this nature because persons in power—whom men consider happy—spend their time in them.

2073. Then [7], at **"But perhaps,"** he rejects the preceding reason. He remarks that rulers of this sort cannot be accepted as sufficient evidence that happiness consists in amusement. For these persons are superior to other men only in worldly power, but from this it does not follow that their actions are virtuous, since moral and intellectual virtues, the principles of good deeds, do not depend on a man being powerful. Consequently it is not necessary that amusements, to which princes devote their leisure, be the most excellent activities.

2074. Likewise it does not necessarily follow that a prince is well-behaved in relation to the appetite that is directed by virtue. And so, if the powerful do not interiorly perceive in active and contemplative virtue the pleasure which is pure (i.e., without the corruption of the one enjoying it), and liberal (i.e., in keeping with reason by which man is free in his actions), and therefore resort to bodily pleasures among which amusements are numbered; for this reason we must not judge that these pleasures or activities are more desirable than others. We see that boys too, lacking understanding and virtue, consider childish pleasures they pursue as precious and best, although these have no great significance and are little valued by grown men. It is reasonable then that just as different things seem valuable to boys and mature men so also are they valued by wicked and virtuous persons.

2075. We have often indicated before (494, 1905) that those actions are really excellent and pleasant that are judged such by a good man who is the norm of human acts. But, as an activity that is agreeable to anyone as it arises from a proper habit seems to him to be most desirable, so a virtuous activity is most desirable and excellent to a good man. Consequently happiness must be placed in this activity and not in amusement.

2076. At **"Surely it would"** [8] he resolves the truth, proving by two arguments that happiness does not consist in amusement. The first argument [8] is taken from the fact that happiness is the end. If it should consist in amusement, this inconsistency would follow, that the purpose of man's whole life would be amusement so that he would engage in trade and undergo all other labors solely to amuse himself. This would follow because we choose nearly all other things, except happiness which is the ultimate end, for the sake of something else. But it seems foolish and thoroughly childish for a man to pursue contemplation and tiresome action for the sake of amusement.

2077. On the contrary, according to the opinion of Anacharsis it seems proper for a person to amuse himself for a time so that later he may work harder. The reason is that relaxation and rest are found in amusement. But, since men cannot work continuously, they need rest. Hence it is clear that amusement or rest is not an end because this rest is for the sake of activity in order that afterwards men may work more earnestly. Obviously then happiness does not consist in amusement.

2078. He presents the second argument [9] at **"Moreover, a life."** Some people place happiness in amusement because of the pleasure found in it. Now happiness does have some pleasure because it is an activity of virtue which is accompanied by joy, but not by the joy of amusement. The reason is that, since happiness is the highest good of man, it must consist in what is best. But we hold virtuous things, that are seriously done, to be better than amusing things that are playfully done. This is evident from the fact that activity which belongs to the better part of the soul and is proper to man is more virtuous. But obviously an activity belonging to a better part is better and consequently more productive of happiness.

2079. Anyone can enjoy the pleasures of the body, even a bestial man no less than the noblest of men. But no one ascribes happiness to a bestial man, or to the animal part of the soul, just as we do not assign to him life which is properly human. Clearly then happiness does not consist in pursuits of this kind, i.e., in physical pleasures—among which amusements are counted—but only in virtuous activities, as has been stated already (2075, 2078).

LECTURE X
Happiness, an Activity According to the Highest Virtue

TEXT OF ARISTOTLE (*1177a12–1177b4*) Chapter 7

1. *If happiness is an activity in accordance with virtue, it is reasonable that it should be in accordance with the highest virtue; and this will be the virtue of the best part in us. Whether this part be the intellect or something else that seems to rule and control us by nature and to understand noble and divine things, whether it be itself divine or the most divine element in us, the activity of this part in accordance with its proper virtue will constitute perfect happiness.*

1177a12–17; 2080–2085

2. *Now we have already said that this activity is contemplative—a conclusion in harmony both with our previous discussion and with the truth.* 1177a17–19; 2086

3. *For contemplation is the highest operation, since the intellect is the best element in us and the objects of the intellect are the best of the things that can be known.* 1177a19–21; 2087

4. *It is also most continuous: we can contemplate truth more continuously than we can carry on any other activity.* 1177a21–22; 2088–2089

5. *Again, we think that pleasure is necessarily mingled with happiness. But the most delightful of all activities in accordance with virtue is admittedly activity in accordance with wisdom. For philosophy or the pursuit of wisdom offers pleasures marvelous both in purity and permanence; and it is reasonable that those who have attained the truth will spend their life more pleasantly than those who are occupied in pursuing the truth.* 1177a22–27; 2090–2092

6. *Then too the quality of self-sufficiency will be found especially in contemplation. For the philosopher indeed needs the necessaries of life no less than the just man and other virtuous men do. However, when the necessities have been provided, the just man still needs people toward whom and with whose aid he may act justly. The same is true of the temperate man and the brave man and so on. But the philosopher can contemplate by himself, and the more so the wiser he is. While it is perhaps better for him to have fellow workers nevertheless he is the most self-sufficient.* 1177a27–1177b1; 2093–2096

7. *Moreover, this activity would seem to be loved for its own sake, for nothing is produced by it apart from the act of contemplation. On the other hand, from practical activities we acquire a greater or less benefit apart from the action itself.* 1177b1–4; 2097

COMMENTARY OF ST. THOMAS

2080. Now that the Philosopher has shown that happiness is an activity in accordance with virtue he begins here to show which virtue this activity follows. First [1] in general; then [2], at "Now we have etc.," in particular. He states first: since happiness is an activity in keeping with virtue—as explained also in the first book (119, 124, 128, 131, 151, 160 and elsewhere)—we reasonably deduce that happiness is an activity in accordance with the highest virtue. For it was shown in the first book (65, 67, 128, 169, 171) that happi-

ness is the best of all human goods as the goal of them all. Likewise, since the better activity flows from the better faculty—as was just stated (2078)—logically the best activity of man will be the activity of the part that is best in him. The truth of the matter is: the best part of man is his intellect.

2081. But, as some have thought differently on this point and there is no place here to discuss such matters, for the present he leaves the question in doubt: is the intellect or something else best in man? However, he does offer some evidence from which we can conclude that the intellect is the best of us.

2082. First, from a comparison with inferior things that the intellect rules and controls by reason of its superiority. Certainly the intellect or reason rules the irascible and concupiscible appetites in presiding over them by a quasi-political power, though they can of course resist reason to some extent. On the other hand the reason controls the physical members which obey its command blindly without contradiction. Therefore the reason or intellect governs the body as a slave by a despotic power, as pointed out in the first book of the *Politics* (Ch. 5, 1254b4; St. Th. Lect. III, 64).

2083. Second, he offers some indications of the intellect's superiority by comparison with higher or divine things to which the intellect is compared in a twofold manner. First, by a special relation to these objects: only the intellect understands things that are essentially noble or divine. In the other way the human intellect is compared to divine things by a natural affinity for them—in a different fashion corresponding to the knowledge of different objects.

2084. Some philosophers held that the intellect is something imperishable and separate; and in their system the intellect would be a divine thing, for we call those beings divine that are imperishable and separate. Others, like Aristotle, considered the intellect a part of the soul; and in this view the intellect is not something divine by itself (simpliciter) but the most divine of all the things in us. This is so because of its greater agreement with the separated substances, inasmuch as its activity exists without a bodily organ.

2085. But whatever way the intellect may be constituted, in keeping with what has been said, happiness is necessarily an activity of this best element in accordance with the virtue proper to it. For the perfect activity required for happiness can come only from a power perfected by a habit that is the power's virtue making the activity good.

2086. Then [2], at "**Now we have**," he shows in particular the activity of what virtue constitutes happiness. He makes two points here. First [2] he shows that perfect happiness consists in the activity of contemplative virtue. Next [Lect. XIII], at "But, being man etc." (1178b33), he connects perfect happiness with external things. He discusses the first point from two aspects. First [2] he shows that perfect happiness consists in the activity of contemplation. Second [Lect. XII], at "But life etc." (1178a9), he prefers this happiness to that which consists in action. He treats the first point in a twofold manner. First [1, a] he shows that happiness consists in contemplative activity. Then [Lect. XI], at "Such a life etc." (1177b26), he shows how happiness is related to man. He handles the first point in two ways. First [a, i] he states his intention. From previous discussion in the sixth book (1190) contemplative activity obviously belongs to the intellect in accordance with its proper virtue, i.e., principally in accord with wisdom, which includes understanding and science. And that happiness consists in such activity seems in harmony with our discussions on happiness in the first book (118–130) and with truth itself.

2087. Next [3], at "**For contemplation**," he proves his statement by six arguments. The first [3]: happiness is the highest activity, as was pointed out before (2080). But the highest of human activities is contemplation of truth; and this is evident from the two reaons by which we judge the excellence of activity. First, on the part of the faculty that is the principle of the activity. Thus this activity is obviously the highest, as the intellect is also the best element in us (explained before in 2080–2085). Second, on the part of the object determining the species of the activity. Here too this activity is the highest because, among the objects that can be known, the suprasensible—especially the divine—are the highest. And so it is in the contemplation of these objects that the perfect happiness of man consists.

2088. He offers the second argument 4] at "**It is also.**" As shown in the first book (129), happiness is especially continuous and lasting. But the most continuous of all human activities is the contemplation of truth. For it is clear that man can persevere in the contemplation of truth more continuously than in any other activity.

2089. The reason for this is that interruption of our activity is necessary, for we are incapable of laboring without a break. Now distress and weariness come about in our labors from the passibility of the body, which is changed and removed from its natural condition. Since the intellect in operating uses the body very little, it follows that its activity is only slightly affected by toil and fatigue. And there would be none of this if the intellect did not need the phantasms existing in the organs of the body. Thus it is clear that happiness is found most of all in the contemplation of truth because of its freedom from labor.

2090. He presents the third argument [5], at "**Again, we think,**" by observing that we commonly suppose that pleasure is associated with happiness—as was indicated in the first book (129). But the most delightful of

all virtuous activities is the contemplation of wisdom—an evident fact conceded by everyone. For, in the contemplation of wisdom philosophy offers pleasures marvelous both in purity and permanence. The purity of these pleasures is perceived in this: they deal with immaterial objects; their permanence, in that their objects are unchangeable.

2091. A person taking pleasure in material objects incurs some impurity of affection from being engrossed with inferior things; and a person taking pleasure in changeable objects cannot have lasting enjoyment since, when the object affording pleasure is changed or destroyed, the pleasure itself ceases and sometimes becomes painful. Now he calls the pleasures of philosophy marvelous because of the infrequency of such pleasures among men who find enjoyment in material things.

2092. Contemplation of truth is twofold: one consists in the investigation of truth, the other in the reflection on the truth already discovered and known. The second is more perfect since it is the term and end of investigation. Consequently greater pleasure is found in the consideration of truth already known than in its investigation. For this reason he declares that people who already know the truth and have their reason perfected by its intellectual virtue spend their life more delightfully. Hence perfect happiness does not consist in contemplation indiscriminately but in that which corresponds to its proper virtue.

2093. He gives the fourth argument [6] at "**Then too the quality.**" We have shown in the first book (107–114) that self-sufficiency, in Greek *autarchia*, is necessary for happiness. But this self-sufficiency is found most of all in contemplation for which man needs only what is commonly required for social living. For the necessaries of life are indeed needed both by the wise or contemplative man and by the just man and others possessing the moral virtues that perfect the active life.

2094. When the necessaries of life are sufficiently provided, the man who is good according to moral virtue needs still more. The just man needs other men for his activity; first, those toward whom he should act justly, since justice refers to another person—as was pointed out in the fifth book (909, 934). Second, he needs others as helpers to do justice, for in this a man frequently requires the assistance of many people. The same argument holds for the temperate or the brave man and for other persons good according to moral virtue.

2095. But this is not the case with the contemplative philosopher who can contemplate truth even if he lives by himself. The reason is that contemplation of the truth is an entirely internal activity not proceeding externally. And the more a person can contemplate the truth when living by himself the more perfect he will be in wisdom. This is so because such a man knows much and has little need of help and instruction from others.

2096. This does not mean that companionship is not a help to contempla-tion, since two together are more effective in intellectual and practical activity, as was pointed out in the eighth book (1540). For this reason he adds that it is better for the philosopher to have fellow workers in the study of truth because sometimes one sees what does not occur to another, who is perhaps wiser. And although the philosopher is helped by others, nevertheless of himself he is more adequate than anyone for his own activity. So it is evident that happiness is found in the activity of wisdom most of all.

2097. He states the fifth reason [7] at "**Moreover, this activity.**" Now happiness is so desirable in itself (*per se*) that it is never sought for the sake of anything else, as explained in the first book (111). But this is evident only in the contemplation of wisdom which is loved for itself and not for something else. In fact the contemplation of truth adds nothing to a man apart from itself, but external activity secures for him a greater or less benefit beyond the action, for example, honor or favor with others; this is not acquired by the philosopher from his contemplation except incidentally, inasmuch as he communicates to others the truth contemplated—something that is now a part of external activity. Therefore it is obvious that happiness consists in contemplation most of all.

LECTURE XI
Happiness and Leisure

TEXT OF ARISTOTLE (1177b4–1178a8) Chapter 7

1. And happiness is thought to depend on leisure, for we are busy in order to have leisure, and we wage war in order to attain peace. Now the exercise of the practical virtues is evident in political and military affairs, but actions concerned with these seem to be without leisure. This is completely the case with warlike activity, for no one chooses to wage war or provoke it merely for the sake of fighting. Indeed a man would be considered a murderous character if he turned his friends into enemies for the sake of causing battles and slaughter. But the activity of the statesman is also without leisure, and aims at—apart from participation in politics—positions of power and honor or even the happiness of himself and fellow citizens as something distinct from political activity (and we are investigating it as something distinct). Even if, among the activities of the moral virtues, political and military actions stand out prominent both in nobility and in greatness, they are without leisure, aim at some other end, and are not desirable for their own sakes. On the other hand the activity of the intellect, being contemplative, is thought to be different by reason of serious application, both in desiring no end beyond itself and in possessing a proper pleasure that increases its activity. So contemplation seems to have self-sufficiency, leisureliness, freedom from labor (as far as humanly possible), and all other activities usually assigned to the happy man. Therefore, man's perfect happiness will consist in this activity of the intellect, if a long span of life be added (as nothing belonging to happiness should be incomplete).   **1177b4–26; 2098–2104**

2. Such a life is higher than the human level; and it is not lived by man according to the human mode but according to something divine in him. And so far as this differs from the composite, to that extent its activity differs from the activity flowing from the other kind of virtue. Therefore, if the intellect is divine in comparison with man, so is its life divine in comparison with human life.   **1177b26–31; 2105–2106**

3. Nor ought we to follow the philosophers who advise man to study human things, and mortals to study mortality, but we ought to strive to attain immortality so far as possible and to exert all our power to live according to the best thing in us. For, though this is a small part of us, it far surpasses all else in power and value; it may seem, even, to be the true self of each, being the principal and better part. Consequently it would be strange if a person were to choose to live not his own life but the life of some other. Moreover, our previous statement is applicable here: what is proper to the nature of each thing is best and most pleasant for it. So then the life of the intellect is best and most pleasant for man since the intellect more than anything else is man. This life, therefore, will be the happiest.   **1177b31–1178a8; 2107–2110**

COMMENTARY OF ST. THOMAS

2098. After Aristotle has presented five reasons to show that happiness consists in the contemplation of truth, he now adds a sixth reason [1], not previously mentioned, arising from a feature of happiness. Now happiness involves a kind of leisure. For a person is said to have leisure when he has nothing further to do—a condition in which he finds himself on arriving at some goal. For this reason the Philosopher adds that we are busy in order to have leisure, that is, we are active in working—this is being busy—in order to rest at the end, and this is having leisure. And he finds an example of this in soldiers who wage war to obtain a desirable peace.

2099. We should note, as the Philosopher stated before (2077), that rest should be taken for the sake of activity. But there he was speaking of rest which, before attaining the end, suspends activity because of the impossibility of uninterrupted labor—this rest being ordered to activity as an end. On the other hand leisure is rest in the end to which activity is ordered. Thus understood, leisure is a special property of happiness, the ultimate end; it is not found in the activities of the practical virtues. Prominent among these are the virtues dealing with political affairs involving the direction of the common or most divine good and with warfare involving the defense of the common good against enemies; nevertheless in such activities leisure has no part.

2100. In the first place this is entirely clear in military operations since no one chooses to wage war or to provoke it solely for the sake of fighting, which would be to have leisure for warfare. The reason is that if someone were to make his end the waging of war he would be a murderous character turning his friends into enemies so that he could fight and kill.

2101. Second, it is obvious that there is no place for leisure in political activities. But a man wants something besides mere participation in politics, like positions of power and honor; and—since these objectives do not constitute the ultimate end, as was pointed out in the first book (60–72)—it is rather fitting that by means of politics a person should wish to obtain happiness for himself and everyone else; happiness of this kind sought in political life is distinct from political life itself, and in fact we do seek it as something distinct. This is contemplative happiness to which the whole of political life seems directed; as long as the arrangement of political life establishes and preserves peace giving men the opportunity of contemplating truth.

2102. Among the activities of the moral virtues political and military actions stand out preeminent both in nobility (they are most honorable) and in greatness (they concern the greatest good, i.e., the common good), and these actions do not themselves possess leisure but are directed to a further end and are not desirable for their own sakes. Hence perfect happiness will not be found in the activities of the moral virtues.

2103. But the activity of the intellect, which is contemplative, seems to differ from the preceding activities by reason of serious application, since man applies himself to it for its own sake so that he seeks no further end. This activity also contains a proper pleasure proceeding from itself and augmenting it. So then such contemplative activity of the intellect clearly provides for man the attributes customarily assigned to the happy person: self-sufficiency, leisureliness, and freedom from labor. And I say this insofar as it is possible for man living a mortal life in which such things cannot exist perfectly.

2104. Therefore man's perfect happiness consists in contemplation of the intellect, if a long span of life be added. This indeed is necessary for the well-being of happiness, as nothing belonging to happiness should be incomplete.

2105. Then [2], at "Such a life," he shows how this contemplative life is associated with man. First [2] he explains his proposition. Second [3], at "Nor ought we etc.," he rejects an error. He says first that the kind of life that has leisure for the contemplation of truth is higher than the human level.

nce man is composed of soul and
ody with a sensitive and intellectual
ature, life commensurate to him is
ought to consist in this, that he di-
cts by reason his sensitive and bodily
fections and activities. But to engage
lely in intellectual activity seems
roper to the superior substances pos-
ssing only an intellectual nature that
ey participate by their intellect.

2106. For this reason in explaining
s statement he adds that man living
this manner, i.e., occupied in con-
mplation, does not live as man, com-
osed of diverse elements, but as
mething divine is present in him,
artaking in a likeness to the divine
tellect. And on that account, as the
tellect considered in its purity differs
om a composite of soul and body so
e contemplative activity differs from
e activity following moral virtue,
hich is properly concerned with hu-
an affairs. Therefore, just as the intel-
ct compared to man is something
ivine, so the contemplative life,
hich is based upon the intellect, is
mpared to the life of moral virtue as
vine to human life.

2107. Next [3], at **"Nor ought we,"**
rejects the error of some philoso-
hers who advised man that he must
rive to know the things of man, and
ortals the things of mortals. This was
e advice of the poet Simonides, as
pears in the beginning of the **Meta-
hysics** (Ch. 2, 982b30–983a4; St. Th.,
, 61–63). But the Philosopher calls it
lse, since we must strive to attain
mortality so far as possible, and ex-
t all our power to live according to
ason—the best of all the elements in
an who is truly divine and immortal.
r, though this best element is a small
art, being incorporeal and most sim-
le, and consequently lacking great-
ess, nevertheless it surpasses

everything human in the extent of its
power and value.

2108. It excels in power by its activities, which are akin to superior beings
and have authority over inferior beings, and so in a way it embraces all
things. Likewise, it excels in value as
regards the excellence of its nature,
since the intellect is immaterial and
simple, incorruptible and incapable of
suffering. Now each human being, i.e.,
the whole man, seems to be the intellect if it is true—nay rather because it
is true—that the intellect is the principal and better part of man.

2109. We have stated in the ninth
book (1868, 1872) that each thing is
thought to be especially that which
constitutes its chief part, since all other
parts are its tools, so to speak. And so
when man lives in accordance with the
activity of the intellect, he lives in accordance with the life most proper to
him; for it would be strange if a person
were to choose to live not his own life
but the life of some other. Hence they
give unwise counsel who say that man
should not engage in intellectual contemplation. And the statement made
in the ninth book (1807, 1847, 1869–
1872) that what accords with reason is
proper to man is applicable also to our
present purpose. For that which is best
in each thing's nature is most proper to
it. But what is best and proper consequently is most delightful because everyone delights in a good that is
pleasing to him. So then, if man is especially his intellect, since this is the
principal element in him, evidently life
according to the intellect is most delightful and proper to him in the highest degree.

2110. Nor is it contrary to our previous assertion (2106) that this is not on
the human level but above man. Indeed it is not on the human level con-

sidering man's composite nature, but it is most properly human considering what is principal in man—a thing found most perfectly in superior substances but imperfectly and by participation, as it were, in man. Nevertheless this small part is greater than all the other parts in man. Thus it is clear that the person who gives himself to the contemplation of truth is the happiest a man can be in this life.

LECTURE XII
Happiness and the Moral Virtues

TEXT OF ARISTOTLE (*1178a8–1178b32*) Chapter 8

1. But life in accordance with the other kind of virtue is happy only in a secondary degree.
1178a8; 2111

2. Its activities are merely human, for we perform works of justice, fortitude, and the other virtues when we observe what is due to everyone in our mutual dealings, our services and various kinds of actions and passions. And all these are human experiences. Besides, some of these matters seem to pertain to the body, and moral virtue is thought to be ascribed especially to the passions. Prudence too is connected with moral virtue, and moral virtue with prudence since the principles of prudence are taken from the moral virtues and the rectitude of the moral virtues from prudence. And both, being connected with the passions, will belong to the nature of the composite. Now the virtues of the composite are human, and so then are life and happiness following these virtues. The intellect, however, is something separate. We have then sufficiently treated this point, and a fuller explanation would be more than our purpose requires.
1178a8–23; 2112–2116

3. But contemplative happiness seems to need little dispensing of external goods or less than the happiness based on moral virtue. Both indeed need the necessities of life and in an equal degree, even if the statesman is more troubled than the philosopher about the requirements of the body and the like. On this point they differ little but in their activities there is a wide difference. For the generous man needs the means to practice liberality and the just man to make a return of services (since mere wishes are not evident and even the unjust pretend that they want to act justly). Likewise the brave man will need strength if he performs any act in accordance with his virtue; and the temperate man will need opportunity. Otherwise, how can he or any other virtuous person be recognized? Further, it may be asked whether choice or action is more important in virtue, which appears to involve both; surely it is evident that perfection consists in both. Now for action many things are required and the more so the greater and nobler the deeds are; but for the activity of the contemplative man nothing of the kind is needed. In fact it can be said that external goods are obstacles to contemplation. But the contemplative person, insofar as he is man and lives with others, chooses to perform virtuous acts. Hence he will need external goods to live a human life.
1178a23–1178b7; 2117–2120

4. That perfect happiness is a form of contemplative activity will be clear from what follows. Now we suppose that the gods are supremely happy and blessed. But what kind of actions should we attribute to them? Just actions? The gods will appear rather ridiculous making contracts, returning deposits and so on. Brave actions—in undergoing terrors and running risks because it is good to do so? Or liberal actions? But to whom will they give? Besides it will be strange for them to have money and the like. If they are called temperate, the praise will be distasteful since they do not have lustful desires. In fact, a thorough review shows all the circumstances of these actions trifling and unworthy of the gods. However, we commonly think of them as living and active, for we must not suppose that they are asleep like Endymion. If then we take away from a living being action, and production besides, what is left except contemplation? Therefore the activity of God, which is transcendent in happiness, is contemplative; and that most akin to it among human activities is the greatest source of happiness.
1178b7–23; 2121–2123

5. This is further indicated by the fact that the other animals do not partake of happiness, for they are completely deprived of this activity. The life of the gods is completely happy; the same is true of man's life insofar as it contains a likeness of contemplative activity. But none of the other

animals possess happiness because they do not share in contemplation. So then contemplation and happiness are coextensive; and the more deeply people contemplate, the happier they are, not by accident but by reason of contemplation which is itself admirable. Consequently happiness consists principally in some form of contemplation.   **1178b24–32; 2124–212**

COMMENTARY OF ST. THOMAS

2111. After he has shown that perfect happiness consists principally and primarily in intellectual contemplation, the Philosopher next introduces a kind of secondary happiness arising from the activity of the moral virtues. First [1] he proposes his intention: although a man who engages in the contemplation of truth is happiest, another is happy in a secondary degree as he lives by the standard of a different virtue, prudence, which directs all the moral virtues. For, just as happiness of contemplative living is attributed to wisdom which, as the preeminent virtue, contains in itself other speculative habits, so too the happiness of active living, which is gauged by the activities of the moral virtues, is attributed to prudence perfecting all the moral virtues, as was pointed out in the sixth book (1275–1284).

2112. Then [2], at "**Its activities,**" he proves his proposition by four reasons. First [2]: because activities conforming to the other active virtues are human activities, since they concern human affairs. In the first place they deal with commonplace external matters in the life of man. For the works of justice, fortitude, and the other virtues, which we do for one another, are manifest in our dealings, as when men mutually exchange their goods in conformity with justice; in our services, as when one man succors another in need; and in all kinds of actions and passions where the moral virtues observe what is due to everyone. And all these are human experiences.

2113. Second, some matters of the virtues seem to pertain to the body and the passions of the soul to which moral virtue is ascribed by a kind of affinity. For many moral virtues deal with the passions, as is apparent from previous discussions (367). So then moral virtue concerns human affairs inasmuch as it deals with external goods, bodily goods, and the passions of the soul.

2114. Prudence, considered as an intellectual virtue, is connected with moral virtue by a kind of affinity; the reverse of this is likewise true, because the principles of prudence are taken from the moral virtues whose ends are the principles of prudence. Moreover, the rectitude of the moral virtues is taken from prudence because prudence makes the right choice of means, as evident from the sixth book (1268–1269). Likewise, moral virtue and prudence are joined at the same time with the passions because the passions are regulated by both. And since the passions belong to the composite they are common to the whole composite of soul and body.

2115. It is obvious then that both moral virtue and prudence are concerned with the composite. Now virtues of the composite, properly speaking, are human inasmuch as man is composed of soul and body. Hence life in accordance with these, namely, prudence and moral virtue, is also human (and is called the active life). Consequently happiness consisting in this kind of life is human. But contemplative life and contemplative happiness, which are proper to the intellect, are separate and divine.

2116. It should suffice for the present to say this much on the matter, for fuller explanation would be more than what belongs to our purpose. The question is treated in the third book *De Anima* (Ch. 5, 430a22; St. Th. Lect. X, 742–743), where it is shown that the intellect is separate. Therefore it is evident that happiness of contemplative living is more excellent than happiness of active living according as something separate and divine is more excellent than that which is composite and human.

2117. He continues with the second reason [3] at "**But contemplative**": life and happiness based on contemplative virtue have little need—or less than those based on moral virtue—for external goods to be dispensed to man. For it is true that both the contemplative and active forms must have the necessaries of life, like food, drink, and so on; although the statesman is more concerned about the body than the philosopher, since external activities are performed by the body. Nevertheless on this point there is little difference, rather each equally needs the necessities. But in the matter of activities the difference between them is considerable because the virtuous man requires much for his activities, as the generous man obviously needs the means to practice liberality, and likewise the just man needs money to pay what he owes.

2118. And if it be argued that even he will to give is an act of liberality and he will to repay is an act of justice—these are possible without money—we should bear in mind that man's will is hidden without external activities. In fact, many unjust persons pretend they want to act justly. But in order to show

whether a man is brave some external act is necessary; and so he ought to perform some work of fortitude externally. Likewise, the temperate man must have the opportunity of enjoying pleasures in order to manifest temperance. Otherwise, if there is no occasion for action, neither the virtuous person (the temperate or brave) nor any other can be recognized.

2119. For this reason it can be asked, which is more important in moral virtue, internal choice or external acts, since both are requirements of virtue? And although choice is more important in moral virtue, as indicated previously (322, 1129), nevertheless not only choice but also external activity is required for the complete perfection of moral virtue. But for external actions a man needs many things, and the more so the greater and nobler the deeds are.

2120. On the other hand the person engaged in contemplation needs none of these things for the exercise of his activity. Rather it can be said that external goods hinder a man from contemplation on account of the anxiety they impose on him, distracting his mind so he cannot give himself completely to contemplation. But if the contemplative person requires external goods, this will be because a man needs the necessities of life, or because he lives with many persons he must help at times; and to this extent he chooses to live in accordance with moral virtue. Therefore he will need these things to live a human life. Thus it is evident that contemplative happiness is more excellent than active happiness, which follows moral virtue.

2121. In presenting the third reason [4], at "**That perfect happiness**," he says that perfect happiness evidently should consist in contemplative activity because the gods (i.e., separated substances) seem supremely happy and blessed. Yet we cannot ascribe to them the acts of the moral virtues. If the activities of justice were attributed to them they would appear ridiculous in the rôle of making contracts, depositing their goods with others, and so on. Nor can bravery be attributed to them in the sense that they undergo terrors and run risks for the sake of the common good; nor does liberality, as a human virtue, befit them.

2122. They should not be described as giving to any mortal the kind of gifts that men freely bestow, because it is unseemly to say that they make presents of money or the like. And if anyone complimented them for temperance, such praise would be more distasteful than pleasing to God. For it is not laudable for God to be without lustful desires since his nature does not have them. So then, in running through all the moral virtues it is apparent that their acts are trifling and unworthy of the gods, i.e., the superior substances.

2123. On the other hand, though, they are thought to live and consequently to be active. We cannot suppose they do nothing but sleep like a philosopher who is said to have slept all his life. If therefore we take away from the life of the gods the action of the moral virtues and prudence, and then further take away production—which is the property of art—there remains in God no other activity excelling in happiness except contem-plation; and he exercises all his activit in the contemplation of wisdom. From this it is clear that of all human activi ties the one most akin to divine con templation is the greatest source o happiness.

2124. He then proceeds with th fourth reason at "**This is further**" [5] an indication that perfect happines consists in the contemplation of wis dom is that irrational animals which do not partake of happiness are com pletely deprived of this activity. The reason is that they are without intellec by which we contemplate truth. To some extent though they share in the activities of the moral virtues: the lior for instance, in the act of fortitude anc liberality, the stork in the act of filia piety. And this they do in a reasonabl way.

2125. The life of the gods (i.e., the intellectual substances) is completel' happy because they have only intellec tual life; and the life of men is happ insofar as some likeness of this con templative activity is found in them But none of the animals possess happi ness because they do not share at all i contemplation. Consequently it is evi dent that the more extensive contem plation is, the more extensiv happiness is; and people who can con template more deeply are happier, no from something incidental but from the contemplation, which is in itsel admirable. It follows then that happi ness consists principally in some form of contemplation.

LECTURE XIII
Happiness and External Goods

TEXT OF ARISTOTLE (*1178b33–1179a32*) Chapter 8

1. But, being man, the happy person will also need external prosperity, for human nature is not of itself (per se) sufficient for the activity of contemplation; the body too must have health and food and other requirements.   **1178b33–35; 2126–2127**

2. Yet, even if man's happiness is not possible without external goods, we must not think that it will require many and great possessions. For self-sufficiency does not depend on a superabundance—neither does judgment nor action—and it is possible to do good deeds without ruling land and sea; one can act virtuously with moderate means. (Experience clearly demonstrates this, for private citizens seem to be not less but more active in good works than the powerful.) It is sufficient then that this much is available, for the life of the man who acts virtuously will be happy.   **1179a1–9; 2128–2129**

3. Solon probably gave a good description of a happy man as one who has a moderate share of external goods, has done (in Solon's opinion) the most virtuous actions, and has lived temperately. For a man can with only moderate means do what he ought.   **1179a9–13; 2130**

4. Anaxagoras also seems to think that a happy man need be neither rich nor powerful; and he is not surprised that this may seem strange to the majority, since they judge by externals, the only things they know.   **1179a13–16; 2131**

5. So the views of the philosophers seem to harmonize with our arguments, and consequently have some credibility. However, in practical matters the truth is tested by a man's conduct and way of living, for these are the dominant factors. We must therefore examine the preceding opinions by judging them from the facts and from the actual life (of the philosopher). If they agree with the facts we should accept them; if they disagree we should consider them mere theories.   **1179a16–22; 2132**

6. But the man who is active intellectually and cultivates his mind seems to be most worthily disposed and most beloved of the gods. Now if the gods have any care of human affairs—it is generally believed they have—it would be reasonable for them both to delight in that which is best in us and most akin to them (this of course is the intellect) and to confer favors on those who love and honor this most—as if the gods themselves are solicitous for their friends who act rightly and honorably. But that all these attributes belong especially to the philosopher is obvious. He is therefore most beloved by the gods; and he will, in all probability, be also most happy. If this be so then the philosopher will be the happiest of men.   **1179a22–32; 2133–2136**

COMMENTARY OF ST. THOMAS

2126. Now that the Philosopher has shown what perfect happiness is, he here shows its relations to external things. First [1] he explains how the happy man is disposed toward inferior creatures; then [6], at "But the man etc.," towards God. He discusses the first point in a twofold manner. First [1] he shows to what extent the happy man needs external and earthly goods. Next [3], at "Solon probably etc.," he confirms this by the authority of the philosophers. He treats the first point from two aspects. First [1] Aristotle proves that the happy person needs external goods; second [2], at "Yet, even if etc.," that he does not need many and great possessions. The Philosopher remarks first that the happy man has need of external prosperity, since human nature is not self-sufficient for the activity of contemplation, due to the condition of the body which requires external goods for its sustenance. On the other hand an intellectual and incorporeal substance is of itself (*per se*) sufficient for contemplative activity.

2127. But man must first of all have a healthy body in order to contemplate, because the sensitive powers he uses in contemplation are weakened by sickness; the mind is also diverted from attention to contemplation. Likewise man must have food and bodily nourishment and other help so that everything necessary for human living be furnished him.

2128. Then [2], at "**Yet, even if,**" he shows that a man does not need many external things for happiness. Aristotle notes that even if it is not possible for a person to enjoy the happiness of this life without the external goods necessary for human living, nevertheless we must not think he needs great wealth. For the self-sufficiency required for happiness does not consist in a superabundance of riches; nature, in fact, needs only a few things. Moreover, superabundance makes people less self-sufficient, since a man must have the help or service of many servants to guard and manage excessive possessions. Besides, rectitude of judgment, by both speculative and practical reason, and external virtuous action are possible without an abundance of riches.

2129. Because this statement regarding the judgment of reason is evident, he therefore explains it in relation to virtuous action which seems to need many things—we noted this before (2112–2116). It is possible, he says, for people to do good deeds without ruling land and sea, without—so to speak—abundant wealth. A moderate portion of riches is sufficient for good

deeds. Experience shows this clearly, for private citizens apparently perform not less but rather more noble deeds than potentates do. Indeed potentates are hindered from many virtuous actions both by too many occupations and cares and by pride and excessive riches. On the other hand, a moderate amount of wealth enabling a man to perform good works is sufficient for happiness; for if someone should act virtuously, his life would be happy, since happiness consists in virtuous activity—as was indicated previously (119, 124, 128 190, 1267, 2085 et passim).

2130. Next [3], at "**Solon probably,**" he confirms his opinion by the sayings of the philosophers. First [3] he proposes their observations; then [5], at "So the views etc.," he shows they are credible in this matter. He makes two references on the first point. First [3] he introduces the opinion of Solon that happy men are well supplied with external goods. For such men especially act virtuously and live temperately, because people with moderate possessions can do what they ought; those with great resources are prevented from this by too much anxiety or by pride, while those without resources must be excessively solicitous about getting food. Besides, these persons lack the opportunity for virtuous activity in most cases.

2131. Second [4], at "**Anaxagoras also,**" he reduces to the same position the opinion of Anaxagoras: "a happy man need be neither rich nor powerful." Nor will he be surprised if this may seem strange to many, since the majority judge by externals, the only things they know. For they are ignorant of intellectual goods, which are the real human goods according to which a man is happy.

2132. At "**So the views**" [5] he shows that we should accept the observations of the philosophers in this matter, concluding from the premises that their views harmonize with his arguments. Hence they have some credibility. However, in practical matters the truth of a man's assertion is tested more by deeds and his way of living than even by argument, because the dominant or principal factor in practical affairs consists in them, i.e., deeds and way of life. For in questions of this kind our principal aim is not knowledge but conduct, as stated in the second book (255–256). This is why we ought to consider what has been said by comparison with the actions and life of the philosophers. Statements in keeping with the conduct of the philosophers should be accepted. For instance, abundant riches are not needed for happiness, and the philosophers do not seek them. But if their actions are not in accord we should suspect that their words lack truth. This is evident concerning the opinion held by the Stoics who maintained that external goods are not human goods; yet, their actions show the contrary, for they desire and seek these as goods.

2133. Then [6], at "**But the man,**" he shows how the happy man is disposed toward superior beings, i.e., towards God: a man happy in contemplative happiness seems to be most worthily disposed—inasmuch as he excels in that which is best in us—and also most pleasing to God, since he exercises his intellect in contemplating the truth, and cultivates intellectual pursuits.

For, supposing—as is really the case—that God exercises solicitude and providence over human affairs, it is reasonable for him to delight in that which is best in men and most akin or similar to himself. This part is the intellect, as is clear from the premises (2109). Consequently it is reasonable that God should confer his greatest favors on those who love and honor their intellect preferring its good to all other goods—as if the gods themselves are solicitous for men who act rightly and honorably.

2134. Now all these attributes clearly belong to the philosopher: he loves and honors his intellect, the most pleasing to God of all human things; he also acts honorably and rightly. It remains then that he is dearest to God. But that man is happiest who is loved most by God, the source of all good. Likewise, since man's happiness is said to consist in the fact that he is loved by God, we conclude that the philosopher is happy in the highest degree.

2135. Arguing in this vein, Aristotle evidently places the ultimate happiness of man in the activity of wisdom—a question decided in the sixth book (1267)—and not in an unbroken series of actions of the active (*agens*) intelligence, as some imagine.

2136. Likewise, we must keep in mind that he does not specify perfect happiness, but such as can be ascribed to human and mortal life. Hence, in the first book (202) he states: "Those we call happy are men etc."

LECTURE XIV
The Need of Virtue

TEXT OF ARISTOTLE (*1179a33–1180a24*) Chapter 9

1. *Have we sufficiently discussed in a general way what should be investigated in these matters about virtues, friendship, and pleasure in order to bring our project to a conclusion?*
1179a33–35; 2137

2. *Indeed, as they say, the end of science in practicable matters is not to investigate and to know individual things but rather to do them. Therefore it is not sufficient to have knowledge of virtue; we must try to possess and practice virtue, or try any other actual way of becoming virtuous.*
1179a35–1179b4; 2138

3. *Were persuasive words sufficient of themselves to make men virtuous, many great rewards would be due according to Theognis; and it would be necessary to give them to those who persuade. At present it seems that persuasive discourse can challenge and move youths of excellent character and can fill the lover of the good with virtue. But it cannot arouse the majority to virtue, for most people are not subject by nature to shame but to fear; nor do they refrain from evil because of disgrace but because of punishment. In fact, since they live by passion, they follow their own pleasures, by which the passions themselves are nourished, and avoid the contrary pains. They do not know what is truly good and pleasant, nor can they taste its delight. What words would reform people of this sort? It is impossible or at least difficult to change by argument what is held by inveterate habit.*
1179b4–18; 2139–2142

4. *It is perhaps a thing worthy to be esteemed if we attain virtue after having everything that seems to make men just. Some philosophers think that men are virtuous by nature; others, that they become virtuous by practice; still others, that they become virtuous by instruction. Certainly what pertains to nature is not in our power but comes from some divine cause to a man who is very fortunate. However, discourse and instruction are not effective with everyone but the soul of the hearer must be prepared by good habits to rejoice in the good and hate the evil, just as the soil must be well tilled to nourish the seed. Indeed the man who lives according to passion will not listen to a discourse on virtue nor will he understand it. How is it possible to persuade such a man? In general, passion does not yield to argument but to violence. Obviously there must pre-exist a natural disposition in some way akin to virtue by which a man loves what is good and hates what is evil.*
1179b18–31; 2143–2147

5. *But it is difficult properly to direct anyone to virtue from his youth unless he is reared under good laws; to live a temperate and hard life is unattractive to most people but particularly the young. For this reason the rearing of children and their activities ought to be regulated by law. Thus good things will not be distasteful after they have become habitual.*
1179b31–1180a1; 2148–2149

6. *It is not enough that the young receive proper rearing and care, but on arriving at manhood they must learn these very things by experience and become accustomed to them. For this we need laws even throughout the whole of man's life, for most men are more attentive to coercion than argument, to what is hurtful than to what is good.*
1180a1–5; 2150

7. *For this reason some think that legislators ought to stimulate men to virtue and exhort them on moral grounds: the obedient who are just should be aroused by means of pre-existing habits, the insubordinate and the degenerate should be visited with pains and punishments but the absolutely incurable should be completely banished. The reason is that the just man living a good life obeys exhortation but the evil man seeking pleasure is punished like a beast of burden. Hence, they say, those pains should be inflicted that are especially opposed to the pleasures men love.*
1180a5–14; 2151–2152

8. *As we have stated, the man who is going to be virtuous must have careful rearing and good habits; then he should live according to a moral code and refrain from evil either by his own will or by coercion. This is possible only to men whose lives are directed by intelligence and right order having coercive force. Certainly this power is not contained in the precept of a father nor does it belong to anyone who is not a ruler or a person in authority. But the law includes coercive force, whereas instruction proceeds from prudence and reason.*   **1180a14–22; 2153**
    9. *Some men hate people who oppose their inclinations, even when the opposition is just. But the law in commanding what is just is not irksome.*   **1180a22–24; 2154**

COMMENTARY OF ST. THOMAS

2137. After the Philosopher has determined virtue's end, which in the virtuous man is pleasure or happiness, now he determines the other end, which is understood in comparison with the common good. He shows that, besides this moral science, it is necessary to have another science, the legislative, whose object is the common good. On this point he does three things. First [1] he shows the necessity of legislation. Next [Lect. XV], at "Only in Sparta etc." (1180a25), he shows the necessity of a man's becoming a legislator. Last [Lect. XVI], at "Then we must etc." (1180b28), he shows how a man can become a legislator. He treats the first point from two aspects. First [1] he asks a question about the adequacy of the general discussion—inasmuch as the matter should be discussed generally and schematically—on the subjects for investigation: happiness, virtues, friendship, and pleasure. Is the choice we made treating the good of man really finished and perfected, or is there some more to be added?

2138. Next [2], at "**Indeed, as they say,**" he settles the question, showing that something more is required. First [2] he shows it is necessary that a man become good. Then [3], at "Were persuasive words etc.," he shows that habituation to virtuous living is required for a man to become good. Last [5], at "But it is difficult etc.," he shows that

to have this habituation legislation is required. He says first that the end of the science concerned with practicable matters is not to know and investigate individual things, as in the speculative sciences, but rather to do them. And since we become virtuous and doers of good works in accordance with virtue, it is not sufficient for the science whose object is man's good that someone have a knowledge of virtue. But he must try to possess it as a habit and practice it. Or if it is thought that a man can become good in another way than by virtue, then he must try to possess that.

2139. Then [3], at "**Were persuasive words,**" he shows that habituation is required in order that a man become good. First [3] he shows that persuasive words alone are not enough; second [4], at "It is perhaps etc.," that habituation is needed. He says first that if persuasive words sufficed to make men virtuous, many great rewards would be due to a man for his skill, i.e., because of the art of persuading to the good; and it would be absolutely necessary to give great rewards to those who persuade. But this is not generally true.

2140. We see that persuasive words can challenge, and move to good, generous youths who are not slaves of vice and passion and who have excellent natural dispositions inasmuch as they are inclined to virtuous operations.

And those who truly love the good can become *catocochimon*, i.e., full of virtue and honor, for such as are well-disposed to virtue by good advice are incited to the perfection of virtue.

2141. But many men cannot be induced to virtue because they are not subject to shame which fears disgrace, but rather are coerced by the dread of punishment. They do not refrain from evil because of disgracefulness but because of the punishments feared. In fact they live according to their passions and not according to reason; thus their own desires increase and they avoid pains opposed to the pleasures sought—pains inflicted on them by punishments. They do not know what is really good and pleasant, nor can they taste its delight. But people like these cannot be changed by any argument.

2142. Something acceptable must be proposed to change a man by argument. Now, one who does not relish an honorable good but is inclined toward passion does not accept any reasoning that leads to virtue. Hence it is impossible, or at least difficult, for anyone to be able to change a man by argument from what he holds by inveterate usage. So also in speculative matters it is not possible to lead back to truth a man who firmly cleaves to the opposite of those principles to which goals are equivalent in practical matters, as indicated previously (223, 474, 1431).

2143. Next [4], at "It is perhaps," he shows that habituation is required for a man to become virtuous. To acquire virtue, Aristotle says, we ought not to be satisfied with mere words. But we ought to consider it a thing of great value if—even after possessing everything that seems to make men virtuous—we attain virtue. There are three views on these matters. Some philoso-

phers maintain that men are virtuous by nature, i.e., by natural temperament together with the influence of the heavenly bodies. Others hold that men become virtuous by practice. Still others say that men become virtuous by instruction. All three opinions are true in some degree.

2144. Certainly the natural temperament is a help to virtue; this agrees with what was said in the sixth book (1276–1280) that some people seem brave or temperate right from birth through a natural inclination. But natural virtue of this kind is imperfect, as we pointed out then; and its completion requires that the perfection of the intellect or reason supervene. For this reason there is need of instruction that would be enough if virtue were located in the intellect or reason alone— the opinion of Socrates who maintained that virtue is knowledge. However, because rectitude of the appetitive faculty is needed there must be habituation inclining this faculty to good.

2145. But what pertains to nature manifestly is not in our power but comes to men from some divine cause: from the influence of the heavenly bodies in regard to man's physical condition, and from God Himself—who alone governs the intellect—in regard to the movement of man's mind to good. In this men are really very fortunate to be inclined to good by a divine cause, as is evident in the chapter **De Bona Fortuna**.

2146. It was explained previously (2139–2142) that discourse and instruction are not effective with everyone. But, that they be effective the soul of the hearer must be prepared by many good customs to rejoice in the good and hate the evil, just as the soil must be well tilled to nourish the seed abundantly. As seed is conditioned in the earth, so admonition in the soul of the hearer. Indeed the man who lives by passion will not eagerly hear words of advice, nor even understand, so that he can judge the advice to be good. Therefore he cannot be persuaded by anyone.

2147. Generally speaking, passion that—when firmly rooted by habituation—masters man does not yield to argument but must be attacked by violence to compel men to good. So, evidently, for exhortation to have an effect on anyone there must necessarily preexist habituation by which man may acquire the proper disposition to virtue so that he can love the honorable good and hate what is dishonorable.

2148. Then [5], at "**But it is difficult**," he shows that legislation is required for virtuous habituation. First [5] he shows that all men become virtuous by means of law. Next [8], at "As we have stated etc.," he shows that this cannot be done properly without law. He discusses the first point in a twofold manner. First [5] he discloses his proposition. Second [7], at "For this reason etc.," he presents evidence for it. On the first point he does two things. First [5] he explains his proposition about the young; then [6], at "It is not enough etc.," about others. He says first that it is difficult for anyone to be guided from his youth to virtue according to good customs unless he is reared under excellent laws by which a kind of necessity impels a man to good.

2149. To live a temperate and a hard life by refraining from pleasures and by not abandoning the good on account of labors and pain is unattractive to many, especially to young men who are prone to pleasures, as we have indicated in the seventh book (1531). For

this reason the rearing of children and their activities must be regulated by good laws; thus they will be forced, as it were, to become accustomed to good things which will not be distasteful but pleasant after the habit has been formed.

2150. At "It is not enough" [6] he shows that others too need legislation. He says that it is not enough for young men to be reared under good laws and to be well taken care of, but, even more, adults must discover honorable ways to act and become accustomed to them. For this reason we need laws not only in the beginning when someone is growing to manhood but generally throughout man's entire life. Many indeed there are who obey by necessity or force instead of persuasion; they pay more attention to deprivation, i.e., the hurt they receive from punishment than to what is honorable.

2151. Next [7], at "**For this reason,**" he presents some evidence for his proposition. He says that, since the restraint induced by law is required for the virtuous life of man, some legislators think that man must be summoned to virtue in this way: the virtuous—who of their own free will comply with what is honorable—should be aroused to good by means of pre-existing customs, by showing the goodness of what is proposed. But the insubordinate and the degenerate are allotted physical punishments like beatings and other chastisements, censure and loss of their possessions. However, the absolutely incurable are exterminated—the bandit, for instance, is hanged.

2152. It is this way because the virtuous man, who adjusts his life to the good, heeds the mere counsel by which good is proposed to him. But the evil man who seeks pleasure ought to be punished by pain or sorrow like a beast of burden—the ass is driven by lashes. Hence, they say, those pains should be inflicted that are directly contrary to cherished pleasures, for example, a drunkard should be forced to drink only water.

2153. Then [8], at "**As we have stated,**" he shows that law is necessary to make men good, for two reasons. The first is [8] that the man who is going to become virtuous must have careful rearing and good customs; and afterwards he should live by a moral code so that he refrains from evil either by his own will or even by coercion contrary to his will. This is possible only when a man's life is directed by some intellect that has both the right order conducive to good and the firmness, i.e., the coercive power, to compel the unwilling. Certainly the coercive power is not contained in the precept of a father, nor does it belong to any other counselor who is not a ruler or a person in authority. But the law includes coercive power inasmuch as it is promulgated by the ruler or prince; likewise it is an instruction issuing from prudence and reason which gives guidance towards the good. Therefore, law is obviously necessary to make men virtuous.

2154. He gives the second reason [9] at "**Some men,**" saying that people willing to oppose the inclinations of others are hated by their opponent, even when the opposition is just; they are considered to act from a malicious zeal. But the law commanding good deeds is not irksome, i.e., burdensome, or odious because it is proposed in a general way. Therefore the conclusion stands that law is necessary to make men virtuous.

LECTURE XV
Man Must Be Capable of Legislating

TEXT OF ARISTOTLE (*1180a24–1180b28*) Chapter 9

1. *Only in Sparta and a few other states does the lawmaker seem to have considered the questions of education and modes of conduct. For matters of this kind are neglected in most states and each man lives as he pleases dealing with wives and children as the Cyclopes do. Therefore it seems best that there be strict public supervision and that we should be able to carry it out. Since men neglect this as a common duty, it seems fitting that each man should do something to help his children and friends become virtuous; or at least select the means for it. Apparently this can best be done, judging by the preceding statements, if a man becomes a legislator.* **1180a24–34; 2155–2156**

2. *Public supervision is obviously done in accordance with law; and good supervision is achieved by good laws. It makes no difference whether the laws are written or not, nor whether they instruct one or many, any more than it does in music, gymnastics, or other skills. In fact public laws and customs have the same place in states as paternal precepts and customs have in families. In the latter case super-vision is even more effective by reason of relationship and benefits conferred, for children first love their parents and readily obey them out of natural affection.* **1180a34–1180b7; 2157–2159**

3. *Furthermore, instruction for general use varies according to each case: in the art of medicine, for instance, fast and rest are usually beneficial to people running a fever but perhaps not for a particular patient. So in athletic contests, an athlete presumably does not use the same plan of battle against every opponent. Thus it would seem that individual attention produces better results in particular cases, for everyone is more likely to get what is suitable. But a thing will be done with the greatest care if a doctor or a trainer or any other working artist knows in a universal way what is common to all men or to a particular class. This is so because the sciences are said to be and actually are concerned with universals. But the unscientific individual may also be successful; for nothing hinders a person from producing a cure even without universal knowledge provided that from experience he can diagnose the symptoms in each case. Thus people seem to be skillful in doctoring themselves but are unable to help others. Nevertheless, if a man wishes to become an artist or a theoretician he must have recourse to the universal and know it in some measure; for the sciences deal with the universal, as we have indicated previously. Likewise the man who wants to make people—either a few or many—better by his supervision must try to become a legislator, if it is true that we are made virtuous by means of laws. The reason is that the ability to dispose any individual adequately is not possessed by everyone but, if anyone can do it, it is the man who knows scientifically. This is evident in the medical art and in other fields where prudence and supervision are employed.* **1180b7–28; 2160–2163**

COMMENTARY OF ST. THOMAS

2155. After the Philosopher has shown that legislation is necessary to make men virtuous, he now shows that a man should be a maker of laws. First [1] he indicates his intention. Then [2], at "Public supervision etc.," he proves his proposal. He says first that, as was just pointed out (2148–2154), legislation is needed for education and the activities of men; nevertheless, only in Sparta and a few other states does the legislator seem to have paid attention to the legal regulation of children's education and to the established modes of conduct. But matters of this kind are neglected in most states where each man lives as he pleases dealing with his children and wife as he wishes, like the Cyclopes—certain barbarous tribes who are not accustomed to laws. Therefore it is best that there be strict supervision by public authority over the education of children and the virtuous activities of the citizens and that man be so instructed to be able to do this properly.

2156. But men commonly neglect this duty because it is plain they show no public concern for it. Hence it seems fitting that each private person do something to help his children and friends to become virtuous; or if he cannot, at least he should select the means to make this possible. Apparently it can best be done, according to the preceding statements, if a man becomes a legislator, i.e., if he acquires the skill to be able to make good laws. So, to be a legislator pertains principally to a public person, secondarily however also to a private person.

2157. Next [2], at "**Public supervision**," he proves his proposal by two arguments. He says first [2] that general supervision, as it is exercised by public officials whose function is to frame laws, obviously is done in accordance with law; thus the supervision is exercised over some people inasmuch as laws are made for them. But good supervision is properly achieved by means of good laws.

2158. It makes no difference for our proposal whether this is done by means of written or unwritten laws, or by laws instructing one or many. As is evident also in music, gymnastics, and other skills, it does not matter in the present connection whether instruction is imparted in writing or not; for writing is used to keep information for the future. Neither does it matter whether instruction in such subjects is offered to one or many. Therefore it seems to come to the same thing that a father of a family should instruct his son or a few domestics by a verbal or written admonition, and that a prince should make a law in writing to govern all the people of the state. In fact public laws and customs introduced by rulers hold the same place in states as do paternal precepts and customs introduced by parents in families.

2159. This is the only difference: a father's precept does not have full coercive power like the royal decree, as was noted previously (2153). Consequently he shows that to some extent this (supervision) is more suitable to a private than a public person by reason of relationship and benefits because of which children love their parents and are readily obedient out of natural affection. So then, although the royal decree is more powerful by way of fear, nevertheless the paternal precept is more powerful by way of love—a way that is more efficacious with people not totally depraved.

2160. At "**Furthermore, instruction**" [3] he gives the second argument. He says that instruction that is generally useful varies for particular cases. Thus it is evident in the art of medicine that fast and rest are usually beneficial to people running a fever so nature will not be burdened with an abundance of food, and heat will not be generated by activity. But perhaps this is not advisable for a particular fever-stricken patient because fast might weaken him too much; and perhaps the patient might need activity to dissolve the gross humors. The same thing is obvious in athletic contests because the athlete does not use the identical plan of battle against every pponent. In this way the operation of each practical art will seem more certain if special attention is paid to each individual; thus everyone will better acquire what is suitable to him.

2161. However, a thing will be done with the greatest care, if a doctor or a trainer or any other artisan (*artifex*) knows in a universal way what is common to all men or what will benefit all men of a particular class, for example, the irascible. This is so because science is said to be, and actually is, concerned with universals. Therefore he who proceeds from universal knowledge can best care for an individual case. Nevertheless this is not the only way a healer can produce a cure; nothing hinders him from curing a particular patient without universal knowledge provided that from experience he can properly diagnose the symptoms of each patient. Thus some people seem to be skillful in doctoring themselves because they know their own symptoms from experience, but they are not qualified to help others.

2162. Although a man can operate well in a particular situation without universal knowledge, nevertheless if he wishes to become an artist he must strive for generalized knowledge that he may know the universal in some measure. This is likewise necessary for one who wishes to be a speculative scientist like the geometrician or the physicist. It was indicated before (1213, 1352) that the sciences deal with this matter, namely, universals. This is the case too with men who exercise supervision to make people virtuous.

2163. It is possible that someone, without art and science by which the universal is known, can make this or that man virtuous because of the experience he has had with himself. However, if someone wants to make people—either a few or many—better by his supervision he ought to try to acquire a universal knowledge of the things that make a man virtuous; in other words, he ought to try to become a legislator so that he knows the art by which good laws are framed since we are made virtuous by means of laws, as was pointed out previously (2153–2154). The reason is that the ability to prepare properly any good disposition in man by introducing it and by removing its opposite, for example, health and sickness, virtue and vice, does not belong to everyone but only to the man who knows scientifically. This is evident in the medical art and in all other fields where supervision and human prudence are employed. In all these a man must not only know particulars but have a knowledge of universals because some things may happen which are included under universal knowledge but not under the knowledge of individual cases.

LECTURE XVI
How to Learn the Science of Lawmaking

TEXT OF ARISTOTLE (*1180b28–1181b23*) Chapter 9

1. Then we must inquire, after these discussions, from whom and how the science of lawmaking may be learned.   **1180b28–29; 2164**

2. Is it not, as in the other areas of knowledge, from those versed in political science? (Legislation) seems to be a part of political science.   **1180b29–31; 2165**

3. Or are we to say that political science is different from the other sciences and arts? Certainly in the other practical sciences persons, like doctors and painters, who teach technique seem to be the very ones who put it into practice. However, in political science the Sophists profess to teach the art and none of them puts it into operation, that being left to those who are engaged in politics.   **1180b31–1181a1; 2166–2167**

4. These seem to perform their public activities more from a kind of habit and experience than from intellectual discernment.   **1181a1–3; 2168**

5. Apparently they do not produce anything either in speeches or in writing about matters of this kind; although it might be more to their credit than the composition of speeches on judicial procedure and the art of persuasion. Furthermore they do not make their own sons or any of their friends statesmen. Nevertheless, they would reasonably have done so, if they could. Surely they could leave nothing better to their countries; nor could they choose anything more acceptable to themselves—nor for that matter to their best friends—than the ability to make others statesmen.   **1181a3–9; 2169–2170**

6. Nevertheless experience does seem to contribute not a little, for merely living in a political environment would not have made statesmen of them. And thus we may conclude that those who would wish a knowledge of politics must have (in addition) practice.   **1181a9–12; 2171**

7. But the Sophists who profess to teach political science seem to be a long way from teaching it. Indeed they appear to misunderstand completely what kind of science it is and what its subject matter is.   **1181a12–14; 2172**

8. Otherwise they would not make political science identical with rhetoric and even lower; nor would they think it easy to make laws simply by collecting approved statutes and then choosing the best of them—as though a choice did not demand the actual employment of intellect, and as though right judgment were not the greatest thing, as is evident in music. In fact people who have experience with particulars make correct judgments about performances and understand by what means and in what way the works are accomplished and what harmonizes with what. But the inexperienced understandably are ignorant whether a work is done well or badly, on the basis of what is in books. Now laws are, as it were, the effects of the art of politics. Therefore, how can a man learn law-making from compilations of laws, or judge what laws are best? Surely men do not seem to become doctors from books although the authors try to describe not only the cures but the means of curing, what remedies must be prescribed for each individual condition. Nevertheless, these things seem to be useful to the experienced but not to the inexperienced.   **1181a14–1181b6; 2173–2177**

9. Perhaps then collections of laws and constitutions will be useful to those who are able to consider and judge which works or laws may be good or bad and which are suitable to the circumstances. But those who review things of this kind without ability cannot properly judge except by chance; although perhaps they will become more capable of understanding them.   **1181b6–12; 2178**

10. Since our predecessors have left the subject of legislation uninvestigated, perhaps it will

be much better for us to attempt to treat this and the forms of government in general. In this way we can complete philosophy with regard to political science as it deals with human affairs.
                                                                1181b12–15; 2179

11. Therefore, first we will attempt in passing to secure whatever fragments of good are to be found in the statements of our predecessors. Next, on the basis of the constitutions we have collected, we will study the things that preserve states and the things that corrupt states; we will consider what influences corrupt particular forms of government, and why some states are governed well and others badly. After these discussions we will begin to inquire what is the ideal state, how it ought to be organized and what laws and customs it should follow. This then will serve as a beginning.
                                                                1181b15–23; 2180

COMMENTARY OF ST. THOMAS

2164. After the Philosopher has shown that a man should be a lawmaker, he now asks how one becomes a lawmaker. First [1] he states his intention. He concludes from the premises that, since it was shown (2157–2163) to be expedient for man to become a legislator, he must inquire after these discussions whence a man may learn the science of lawmaking: by experience or education, and how this may be achieved.

2165. Second [2], at "**Is it not etc.,**" he carries out his intention. First [2] he shows that the means familiar to previous philosophers were not sufficient to teach anyone the science of lawmaking. Next [10], at "Since our predecessors etc.," he concludes that this has to be discussed by itself. He treats the first point from two aspects. First [2] he shows the way someone should learn lawmaking. Then [3], at "Or are we to say etc.," he shows that this does not follow in practice. He says first that it seems reasonable that the origin and manner of becoming a legislator take place as in other practical sciences which are for the sake of political science. Nor is it out of place for me to treat political science while inquiring about legislation. The reason, as stated in the sixth book (1197–1198), is that legislation is a part of political pru-

dence, for legislation is a kind of architectonic political science.

2166. Then [3], at "**Or are we to say,**" he shows this—that it seems reasonable—does not follow in practice because of the difference among those who busy themselves about legislation. First [3] he proposes their diversity. Next [4], at "These seem etc.," he shows their deficiencies. He says first that, although there would reasonably appear to be a resemblance between this and other sciences, nevertheless something different seems to be observed in political science and the other practical arts—others are called sciences inasmuch as they have principles of knowledge, and aptitudes inasmuch as they are principles of operation. Indeed in the other practical arts, the people who impart these arts by teaching them seem to be the very ones who practice them: doctors, for example, teach medicine and practice their art. The same situation prevails for painters and any others who operate by art.

2167. However, it seems to be otherwise in political science. Some, the Sophists, profess to teach legislation, but none of them puts it into practice. But others, viz., the politicians seem to practice it.

2168. Next [4], at "**These seem,**" he

shows the deficiencies of both: first [4] of the politicians, and then [7] at "But the Sophists etc." of the Sophists. On the first point he does three things. First [4] he states what he has in mind about the deficiency of the politicians. Their public activities seem to be performed more from an aptitude or a kind of habit acquired by custom, and from experience than from intellectual discernment, i.e., reason or science.

2169. Second [5], at "**Apparently they etc.**," he verifies his statement by two indications. The first is that those who work scientifically can give the reason, written or oral, for the things they do. But politicians do not seem to produce any work on political science either in speeches or writing. Certainly writing of this kind would be much better than the discourses on judicial procedure—by which people are taught how they ought to judge according to certain fixed canons—and on eloquence by which they are taught to speak publicly according to the rules of rhetoric.

2170. The second indication is that men who work scientifically can form other scientific workers by teaching. But men of the kind who practice politics do not make their sons or any of their friends statesmen. Nevertheless it is reasonable that they would so if they could. Surely they could confer on their countries no greater benefit, which would remain after them, than to be the means of making other good statesmen. Likewise there would be nothing more acceptable to themselves than the ability to make other men statesmen—they could do nothing more useful even for their best friends.

2171. Third [6], at "**Nevertheless experience**," he refutes an error. Someone might judge from the premises that experience in practicing politics

would not be useful. But Aristotle says that, although it is not enough, nevertheless it contributes not a little toward making a man a statesman. Otherwise, some would not become better statesmen by the practice of political life. And experience in political life seems necessary for those who desire to know something about the art of political science.

2172. At "**But the Sophists**" [7] he shows the deficiency that the Sophists suffer. On this point he does three things. First [7] he states his proposition, saying that the Sophists who profess to teach political science seem to be a long way from teaching it. Indeed they appear to misunderstand completely what kind of knowledge political science is as well as its subject matter.

2173. Next [8], at "**Otherwise they,**" he verifies his proposition by indications, first in regard to his statement that they do not know its characteristic nature. If they understood this they would not identify it with rhetoric; for rhetoric can give persuasive arguments in praise or censure of a person both in assemblies and in the courts—and this on a threefold basis: demonstrative, deliberative, and judicial. But according to them political science only teaches a man to form judgments. They think men are good statesmen who know how to make laws for forming a judgment.

2174. He gives the second indication for his statement that they do not know the subject matter of political science. If they knew this they would not think it easy to frame laws—in accordance with legislation which is the principal part of political science—for they declare that it suffices for lawmaking to collect different approved statutes, choose the best, and institute them.

2175. They err in two ways on this point. In one way by maintaining that to become a legislator it is enough to collect laws and choose the best among them. The reason is that for legislation a man must not only judge about the laws in use but also devise new laws, in imitation of the other practical arts; for a doctor not only judges about the known remedies for effecting a cure but can discover new ones. They err in another way—which he touches upon after disposing of the first error. It not easy for a man to choose the best laws because choice does not depend on the intellect alone, and right judgment is an important matter, as is evident in music.

2176. People who have experience with particulars make correct judgment about results and understand by what means and in what manner these results can be produced, and what kinds are suited to what persons or things. But the inexperienced are understandably ignorant whether a work is done well or badly on the basis of what they read in books, for they do not know how to put into practice what is in the books. Now laws to be framed are, as it were, the results of the art of politics; they are framed as rules for activities of the state. Consequently, men who do not know what kind of results are suitable do not know what kind of laws are suitable.

2177. Therefore it is impossible from a collection of laws for a man to learn the science of lawmaking or to judge what kind of laws are best unless he has experience. Likewise it seems impossible for men to become good doctors only from remedies given in books, even though the authors of these remedies try to determine not only the cures but also the means of curing, how remedies must be pre-

scribed according to the individual conditions of men. Nevertheless all these things seem useful only to people with experience and not to those who are ignorant of particulars because of inexperience.

2178. Last [9], at "**Perhaps then,**" he infers from the foregoing remarks that we must reject the error that a collection of written laws is absolutely useless. He says—we have already indicated this—that the same applies to remedies in textbooks as to our problem; to collect laws and constitutions, i.e., ordinances of different states, is useful for those who can consider and judge from practice which works or laws may be good or bad, and what kinds are suitable in the circumstances. But those who have not the habit acquired by practice and want to review written documents of this kind cannot properly judge them except by chance. However, they do become more capable of understanding such things by the fact that they have actually read through the written laws and constitutions.

2179. At "**Since our predecessors**" [10] he points out that he is about to discuss how a man may learn lawmaking. First [10] Aristotle shows that this is incumbent upon him. He says that previous persons, viz., philosophers who preceded him, left a poorly organized treatise on legislation. Hence it is well for us to attempt to treat legislation and, in general, the whole question of government, of which lawmaking is a part. In this way we can extend philosophic teaching to political science, the practical knowledge concerned with human affairs—a subject that seems to have been taught last according to this view.

2180. Then [11], at "**Therefore, first,**" he shows in what order he is going to carry this out. He says that he will first attempt in passing to touch upon what in part was well treated in political science by our predecessors, i.e., by earlier philosophers. This he will do in the second book of the Politics. After that he will consider which of the various forms of government preserve the states (the good forms are the kingdom, aristocracy, and the citizens' government) and which forms corrupt the states (the bad forms are tyranny of one ruler, oligarchy, and democracy). Besides, we must consider what things preserve or corrupt particular forms of government, and the reasons why some states are governed well and others badly. This he will determine in the Politics from the third to the seventh book. Then after the previous discussions he begins to inquire what is the ideal state, how it ought to be organized, and what laws and customs it should follow. But before all these things he sets down in the first book certain principles from which he says we must begin. This will serve as a connecting link with the work on the Politics and as a conclusion to the whole work of the Ethics.

ALPHABETICAL INDEX OF SUBJECTS
(Numbers refer to sections of Commentary)

ᴐod (cont.)
ᴐredicated of many by analogy, 96
ᴅiffers in different acts, 104
ᴅhe end of every activity, 105
ᴅn every art is that for which things are
  done, 105
ᴅmost perfect good is desired for its own
  sake, 109
ᴅerfect good is self-sufficient, 112
ᴅf a thing consists in its operation suited to
  its form, 257
ᴅesults from a united and complete cause,
  320
ᴅs perceived moves the desire, 515
ᴅow a thing may appear, 519
ᴅin the law) achieved in one way, 1080
ᴅroper object of the appetite has the nature
  of end, 1438
ᴅhe object of pleasure, 1484
ᴅbsolute and relative, 1484, 1553
ᴅwofold: activity and habit, 1486
ᴅ thing is good insofar as intrinsically
  desirable, 1552, 1979
ᴅman's genuine good belongs to reason, 1552
ᴅdistinguished from the pleasurable in
  general only in concept, 1552
ᴅonly a known good gives pleasure, 1851
ᴅany good joined to another constitutes a
  greater good, 1970, 1973
ᴅas such is to be sought, 1979
ᴅpredicated of every genus, 1981

ᴐod, final
ᴅof each thing is its ultimate perfection, 12,
  119

ᴐod Action
ᴅnot without practical reason and right
  desire, 1294

ᴐod Fortune
ᴅnorm of good fortune established in
  comparison with happiness, 1508

ᴐod Man (*see also* Virtuous Man)
ᴅsimply, one who has a good will, 451
ᴅpleased by good things, 1470
ᴅdoes not expect gain from a loan to a bad
  man, 1778
ᴅthe norm of human kind, 1898, 1905
ᴅconsiders virtuous activity most desirable,
  2075
ᴅthe norm of human acts, 2075

ᴐoodness
ᴅpresent only when all circumstances are
  rightly ordered, 320

ᴐod, Separated
ᴅnot an operation of man, 98
ᴅa pattern of good produced, 99
ᴅknowledge of not used by arts and sciences,
  100

Goods, External
  moral consideration of, 34
  tools of happiness, 187
  subject to change by their nature, 188
  needed as adornments of happiness, 194
  riches and honors, 343

Goods, Human
  three classes of, 142

Goods of Fortune
  secondary in happiness, 193, 1507
  a help to virtuous operations, 756
  without virtue cannot make man
    magnanimous, 757
  not born gracefully without virtue, 757

Goods of the Soul
  the most important, 142–143
  changeable only indirectly, 188
  some goods of the soul belong to the
    intellect, others to the activity of living,
    188

Goodwill
  makes a man act well, 451
  makes a man good simply, 451
  consists in an interior affection, 1820
  resembles friendship, 1820–1821, 1825
  is not love, 1822–1823
  the beginning of friendship, 1824–1826
  not in friendship of utility or pleasure,
    1827–1828
  seems to exist for a person because of his
    virtue, 1829

Government
  good and bad forms of, 2180

Grammarian
  one who produces a grammatical work in a
    grammatical way, 281

Great and Little
  predicated relatively, 1991

Group
  civil, 4
  domestic, 4

Habit
  plays no part in things according to and
    contrary to nature, 248 a sort of nature,
    265, 549
  formation of habit shown by pleasure or
    sorrow following operation, 266
  disposes to do things making it worse and
    better, 271
  a disposition determining a power, 298
  twofold: good and bad, 298
  distinguished by act and object, 322, 327,
    713, 992, 1151
  of moral virtue defined, 494
  known by its object, 892, 896
  is known from its contrary, 892, 914

Liberal Man (cont.)
characteristically distributes wealth, 660, 682
specially loved, 665
gives in conformity with reason, 666, 672,
677, 679–680
gives cheerfully, 667, 669
does not take from improper sources,
670–671, 680
not eager to accept benefits, 670
seeks wealth as a means for giving, 671
gives more than he retains, 672
differs from the spendthrift, the munificent
man, the miser, 679
saddened by disordered giving, 681
Lie
essentially evil, 837
Life
three prominent types of, 58-60
of nutrition, sense, and reason, 124–126
of reason proper to man, 126
virtuous life is pleasurable, 154, 157–158,
1907
subject to many changes, 177
in full sense is sensation or thought, 1902
in itself is good and pleasant, 1903, 1905,
1908
is something determinate, 1905
perfected in activity, 1905, 1907, 2036, 2037
of pain and evil not naturally good, 1906
naturally desired by all men, 2036
of the intellect is most delightful, 2109
"Like"
how like is lovable; how, hateful, 1545
naturally desirable, 1547
Likeness
essentially a cause of friendship, 1588
Living Together
most proper and pleasing to friendship,
1946, 1949
Loan
defined, 929
Local Motion
definition and kinds of, 2013–2014
the whole of local motion differs specifically
from each o its parts, 2015
Lovable, the
the object of love, 1551
an honorable or pleasurable useful good,
1552
the totally lovable is totally good, 1554
is what appears good, 1556
Lovable Objects
three kinds of, 1563
do not differ as equal species, 1563
Love
implies a connaturality of appetite with
good loved, 293

Love (cont.)
cause of pleasure in the soul, 600
three types of, 1563
an act of friendship, 1563
one-sided love bestowed on lifeless objects,
1603
mutual love belongs to notion of friendship
1603
indicates a vehement impulse of soul, 1823
increases by means of friendship, 1823
of self according to reason is worthy of
praise, 1874–1875
intense sexual love with many women not
possible for a man, 1944
passion of love begins especially by seeing,
1944
Loved
being loved connected with being honored,
1641, 1645
men delight in being loved, 1644
Lover
takes pleasure in beauty of the beloved, 158
not always worthy of being loved as much
as he loves, 1655
wishes and does good for the beloved, 1852
desires most to see the person loved, 1944,
1945
Lover of Self
used as a term of reproach, 1863–1864
in the praiseworthy sense, 1866–1868
true lover of self loves his intellect,
1870–1871
according to virtue is praised, 1874
according to virtue is helpful to others, 1875
Loving
more characteristic of friendship than being
loved, 1639, 1646
is an activity, 1646
is like activity, being loved like passivity,
1825
Lust
a vice strictly ordered to concupiscence, 916
Magnanimity
mean between honor and dishonor, 345
concerned with great honors, 346, 735,
742–744, 791
consists in a certain size, 738
seems to consist in an extreme, 741
has a mean, 741
differs from fortitude, 746
tends to what is great in all virtues, 746, 749
759
cannot exist without virtue, 749, 757
Magnanimous Man
thinks himself worthy of great things,
736–738